The Emergence
of Sociological Theory

The Dorsey Series in Sociology

Advisory Editor
CHARLES M. BONJEAN
The University of Texas at Austin

The Emergence of Sociological Theory

Second Edition

Jonathan H. Turner
University of California at Riverside

Leonard Beeghley
University of Florida

Charles H. Powers
Santa Clara University

The Dorsey Press   Chicago, Illinois 60604

Acquisitions editor: *Paul O'Connell*
Project editor: *Jane Lightell*
Production manager: *Stephen K. Emry*
Cover Designer: *Maureen McCutcheon*
Compositor: *Weimer Typesetting Co., Inc.*
Typeface: *10/12 Palatino*
Printer: *Arcata Graphics/Kingsport*

LIBRARY OF CONGRESS
Library of Congress Cataloging-in-Publication Data

Turner, Jonathan H.
   The emergence of sociological theory / Jonathan H. Turner, Leonard Beeghley, Charles H. Powers.—2nd ed.
      p.   cm.
   Bibliography: p.
   Includes index.
   ISBN 0-256-06208-0: $35.00
   1. Sociology—History. 2. Sociology—United States—History.
I. Beeghley, Leonard. II. Powers, Charles H. III. Title.
HM19.T97 1989
301'.09—dc19   87-36604
                                                                                    CIP

Printed in the United States of America

1 2 3 4 5 6 7 8 9 0 K 6 5 4 3 2 1 0 9

To the memory of TALCOTT PARSONS,
whose *The Structure of Social Action* and later
works demonstrate the importance of
social theory that builds upon the
accomplishments of the early masters.

PREFACE

Much as with its predecessor, this revised edition of *The Emergence of Sociological Theory* seeks to outline in detail the development of sociological theory from 1830 to 1930. Our efforts have been guided by several intellectual commitments which should be outlined at the outset. First, we are primarily concerned with the emergence of sociological theory, and hence, many topics that might be covered in a history of sociology and social thought are not included in these pages. Second, in our concern with theory, we have examined those scholars who contributed the most to the development of abstract concepts, models, and propositions in sociology. Other pioneers in sociology who contributed only to other facets of the discipline, such as the development of research techniques or the formation of professional associations, or those whose ideas have not withstood scrutiny, are omitted from our analysis. Third, because we have emphasized the theoretical content of a scholar's work, our concern is not with the history of social thought, but with the origins and development of theoretical concepts and propositions, although we have added long sections on the personal biographies of scholars and the context of their time in order to place into broader perspective their crucial ideas. Since one of our goals has been to understand the intellectual connections among purely theoretical ideas in sociology, we have ventured back into the eighteenth century, but only to the extent that eighteenth-century social thought directly influenced the emergence of theory between 1830 and 1930.

These intellectual commitments may appear as constraints, but they also have allowed us to analyze the first 100 years of sociological theory in depth and with great intensity. This analysis deals with three related questions. First, what are the intellectual origins of key concepts, models, and propositions of sociology's first great theorists? Second, what is the profile and nature of the basic works of the early theorists? And third, what is the enduring theoretical legacy of the early theorists? Thus for each scholar covered in the pages to follow, our analysis examines the origins of his ideas, the nature of his basic works, and the legacy of abstract models and principles that he has provided modern sociological theory.

This last issue is of great importance, since it is our feeling that the purely theoretical legacy of the early masters has not been fully appreciated or utilized. By presenting their ideas more formally, we hope to demonstrate the power of early theory and to excite others to use their concepts and propositions more self-consciously. Sociology has not, we feel, "stood on the shoulders of giants"; rather, it has stood in their shadow, primarily because sociologists have yet to extract the essence of the giants' theories. It is to this goal that this book is dedicated.

Jonathan H. Turner
Leonard Beeghley
Charles H. Powers

CONTENTS

CHAPTER 11
The Sociology of Émile Durkheim

CHAPTER 16
The Emergence of Modern Theoretical Perspectives 470

LIST OF TABLES AND FIGURES

The Emergence
of Sociological Theory

CHAPTER 1

Auguste Comte and the Emergence of Sociological Theory

New ideas typically emerge in times of change, turmoil, and conflict. Although "social thought" is as old as human existence, scientifically oriented social thought emerged only after great scientific achievements in the sixteenth and seventeenth centuries—achievements that dramatically altered people's conception of the physical universe and how it is to be understood. But sociology is the result of more than the scientific revolution; it emerged from the tumultuous period in which new discoveries about the operation of the physical world were accompanied by dramatic changes in patterns of social organization.[1]

The word *revolution* has perhaps become overused in commentaries. Yet this term captures the dramatic nature of changes in the social, moral, and intellectual fabric of European society in the sixteenth and seventeenth centuries. For the term *revolution* denotes the decisive and radical nature of change, although this change often took many decades to be fully realized. Thus, the economic, political, religious, and intellectual revolutions of post-Renaissance Europe are not so much sudden transformations as evolutionary processes that nevertheless altered decisively the nature of the social world. Even the most cataclysmic event, the French Revolution of 1789, was only the culmination of changes in eighteenth-century France.

---

[1]Robert A. Nisbet in his *The Sociological Tradition* (New York: Basic Books, 1966), chap. 2, has presented this line of argument under "The Two Revolutions." While this discussion owes much to Nisbet's work, there are great differences in emphasis between this discussion and Nisbet's. For other interesting discussions of this period, see Ernst Cassirer, *The Philosophy of the Enlightenment* (Boston: Beacon Press, 1955; originally published in 1932); R. V. Sampson, *Progress and the Age of Reason* (Cambridge, Mass.: Harvard University Press, 1956); J. Salwyn Schapiro, *Condorcet and the Rise of Liberalism* (New York: Octagon Books, 1963), chaps. 1–3; and E. J. Hobsbawm, *The Age of Revolution* (New York: Mentor, 1967). For some more general summaries of pre-nineteenth-century social thought, see Howard Becker and Harry Elmer Barnes, *Social Thought from Lore to Science* (New York: Dover, 1938); and Robert A. Nisbet, *The Social Philosophers: Community and Conflict in Western Thought* (New York: Thomas Y. Crowell, 1973).

1

Sociology thus emerged during a period of change in the nature of the social order and in the context of intellectual discourse. Such discourse was highlighted in France by the advocacy of Auguste Comte for a science of society, which he first termed *social physics* and, later and somewhat reluctantly, changed to *sociology*. Before examining Comte's advocacy, however, we should first pause and examine the revolutionary changes that created an environment receptive to a new science.

SOCIOLOGY AND THE FORCES OF CHANGE

The Economic Revolution

During much of the eighteenth century, the last remnants of the old economic order were crumbling under the impact of the commercial and industrial revolutions. Much of the feudal order had been eliminated by the expansion of trade during the seventeenth century. Yet economic activity in the eighteenth century had become greatly restricted by guilds, which controlled labor's access to skilled occupations, and by chartered corporations, which restrained trade and production.

The eighteenth century saw the growth of free labor and more competitive manufacturing. The cotton industry was the first to break the hold of the guilds and chartered corporations, but with each decade, other industries were subjected to the liberating effects of free labor, free trade, and free production. By the time large-scale industry emerged—first in England, then in France, and later in Germany—the economic reorganization of Europe had been achieved. Large-scale industry and manufacture simply accelerated the transformations in society that had been occurring for decades.

These transformations involved a profound reorganization of society. Labor was liberated from the land; wealth and capital existed independently of the large noble estates; large-scale industry accelerated urbanization of the population; the extension of competitive industry hastened the development of new technologies; increased production encouraged the expansion of markets and world trade for securing raw resources and selling finished goods; religious organizations lost much of their authority in the face of secular economic activities; family structure was altered as people moved from land to urban areas; law became as concerned with regularizing the new economic processes as with preserving the privilege of the nobility; and the old political regimes legitimated by "divine rights" successively became less tenable.

Thus, the emergence of a capitalist economic system inexorably destroyed the last remnants of the feudal order and the transitional mercantile order of restrictive guilds and chartered corporations. Such economic changes greatly altered the way people lived, created new social classes (such as the bourgeoisie and urban proletariat), and led not only to a revolution of ideas but also to a series of political revolutions. These changes were less traumatic in England than in France, where the full brunt of these economic forces clashed with the Old Regime. It was in this volatile mixture of economic changes, coupled with the scientific revolution of the sixteenth and seventeenth centuries, that political and intellectual revolutions were to be spawned. And out of these combined revolutions, sociology was to emerge.

The Political Revolution

The Revolution of 1789 marked a dramatic transformation in French society. The Revolution and the century of political turmoil that followed provided early French sociologists with their basic intellectual problem: how to use the "laws of social organization" to create a new social order. Yet, in many ways, the French Revolution was merely the violent culmination of changes that had been occurring in France and elsewhere in Europe for the entire eighteenth century.

By the time of the French Revolution, the old feudal system was merely a skeleton. Peasants were often landowners, although many engaged in the French equivalent of tenant farming and were subject to excessive taxation. The old landed aristocracy had lost much of its wealth through indolence, incompetence, and unwillingness to pursue lucrative, and yet low-status, occupations. Indeed, many of the nobility lived in genteel poverty behind the walls of their disintegrating estates. And as they fell into severe financial hardship, the affluent bourgeoisie were all too willing to purchase the land. Indeed, by 1789 the bourgeoisie had purchased their way into the ranks of the nobility as the financially pressed monarchy sold titles to upwardly mobile families. Thus, by the time of the Revolution, the traditional aristocracy was in a less-advantageous position, many downtrodden peasants were landholders, the affluent bourgeoisie were buying their way into the halls of power and prestige, and the monarchy was increasingly dependent on the bourgeoisie for financial support.

The structure of the state best reflects these changes in the old feudal order. By the end of the eighteenth century, the French monarchy had become almost functionless. It had, of course, centralized government through the suppression of old centers of feudal power, but its monarchs were now lazy, indolent, and incompetent. The real

power of the monarchy increasingly belonged to the professional administrators in the state bureaucracy, most of whom had been recruited
from the bourgeoisie. The various magistrates were virtually all recruited from the bourgeoisie, and the independent financiers, particularly the Farmers General, had assumed many of the tax-collecting
functions of government. In exchange for a fixed sum of money, the
monarchy had contracted to the financiers the right to collect taxes,
with the result that the financiers collected all that the traffic could
bear and, in the process, generated enormous resentment and hostility
in the population. With their excessive profits, the financiers became
the major bankers of the monarchy, with the king, nobility, church,
guild master, merchant, and monopolistic corporate manufacturer
often coming to them for loans.

Thus, when the violent revolution came, it hit a vulnerable political system that had been in decline for most of the eighteenth century.
The ease with which it crumbled highlighted its vulnerability, while
the political instability that followed revealed the extent to which the
ascendance of the bourgeoisie and large-scale industrialists had been
incomplete. In other societies where sociology was also to emerge, this
transition to industrial capitalism and new political forms was less tumultuous. Particularly in England, the political revolution was more
evolutionary than revolutionary, creating a sociology distinctly different than that in France (see the next chapter).

The political and economic changes of the eighteenth century were
accompanied by intensified intellectual activity. Reacting to economic
and political changes, and the concomitant reorganization of social life,
much of the eighteenth century was consumed by intellectual ferment.
On the one hand, these intellectuals reflected the changes occurring
around them; and yet, on the other hand, their forceful advocacy
helped cause these changes. Whether physiocrats like Adam Smith in
England or philosophers like Voltaire and Rousseau in France, social
thinkers in the eighteenth century began to exert a powerful influence
on public opinion—and in the process, they helped accelerate the very
changes to which their work had initially represented a response. This
influence of ideas and ideology on social events in the eighteenth century makes the social thought of the times a true intellectual
revolution.

The Intellectual Revolution

The intellectual revolution of the eighteenth century is commonly
referred to as the *Enlightenment*. As we will explore in more detail in
the next chapter, the Enlightenment in England and Scotland was dominated by a group of thinkers who argued for a vision of human beings

and society that both reflected and justified the industrial capitalism that first emerged in the British Isles. For scholars such as Adam Smith, individuals are to be free of external constraint and allowed to compete, thereby creating a better society. In France, the Enlightenment is often termed the *Age of Reason* and was dominated by a group of scholars known as the *philosophes*. And it is out of the intellectual ferment generated by the French philosophes that sociology was born.

Although the Enlightenment was fueled by the political, social, and economic changes of the eighteenth century, it derived considerable inspiration from the scientific revolution of the sixteenth and seventeenth centuries. Through a long and often acrimonious route, the scientific revolution reached a symbolic peak, at least in the eye of eighteenth-century thinkers, with Newtonian physics. The post-Newtonian view of science was dramatically different than previous views. The old dualism between reason and the senses had broken down, and, for the first time, it could be confidently asserted that the world of reason and the world of phenomena formed a single unity. Through concepts, speculation, and logic, the facts of the empirical world could be understood; and through the accumulation of facts, reason could be disciplined and kept from fanciful flights of speculation.

The world was thus viewed as orderly, and it was now possible to understand its complexity through the use of reason and the collection of facts. Newton's principle of gravity was hailed as the model for this reconciliation between reason and senses. Physics was to become the vision of how scientific inquiry and theory should be conducted. And the individual and society were increasingly drawn into the orbit of the new view of science. This gradual inclusion of the individual and society into the realm of science represented a startling break with the past, since heretofore these phenomena had been considered the domain of morals, ethics, and religion. Indeed, much of the philosophes' intellectual effort involved the emancipation of thought about humans from religious speculation, and while the philosophes were far from scientific, they performed the essential function of placing speculation about the human condition in the realm of reason. Indeed, as can be seen in their statements on universal human rights, laws, and on the natural order, much of their work consisted of attacks on established authority in both the church and state. From notions of "natural law" it was to be but a short step to consideration of the laws of human organization. And many of the less shrill and polemical philosophes— first Montesquieu, then Turgot and Condorcet—were to actually make this short step and seek to understand the social order in terms of principles they felt were the equivalent in the social realm of Newton's law of gravitation.

The philosophes' view of human beings and society were greatly influenced by the social conditions around them. They were vehemently opposed to the Old Regime in France and highly supportive of the interest of the bourgeoisie in free trade, free commerce, free industry, free labor, and free opinion. And in fact, the large and literate bourgeoisie formed the reading public that bought the books, papers, and pamphlets of the philosophes. Thus, their concern with the "laws of the human condition" was as much, and probably more, influenced by their moral, political, and ideological commitments as by a dispassionate search for scientific laws. Yet, it would be mistaken to ignore the extent to which the philosophes raised the possibility of a science of society molded after the image of science in physics and biology.

The basic thesis of all philosophes, whether Voltaire, Rousseau, Condorcet, Diderot, or others, was that humans have certain "natural rights," which were violated by institutional arrangements. It would be necessary, therefore, to dismantle the existing order and substitute a new order considered more compatible with the essence and basic needs of humankind. The transformation was to occur through enlightened and progressive legislation; ironically, the philosophes were to stand in horror as their names and ideas were used to justify the violent Revolution of 1789.

In almost all of the philosophes' formulations was a vision of human progress. Humanity was seen to be marching in a direction and was considered to be governed by a "law of progress" that was as fundamental as the law of gravitation in the physical world. In particular, those who were to exert the most influence on Auguste Comte—Turgot, Condorcet, and Saint-Simon—built their intellectual schemes around a law of progress. Thus, the philosophes were, on the one hand, decidedly unscientific in their moral advocacy, but they offered at least the rhetoric of post-Newtonian science in their search for the natural laws of human order and in their formulation of the law of progress. It is out of these somewhat contradictory tendencies that sociology emerged in the work of Auguste Comte, who sought to reconcile the seeming contradiction between moral advocacy and detached scientific observation.

The more enlightened of the philosophes, men such as Montesquieu, Turgot, and Condorcet, were to present the broad contours of this reconciliation to Comte: the laws of human organization, particularly the law of progressive development, can be used as tools to create a better society. With this mixture of concerns—moral action, progress, and scientific laws—the Age of Reason ended and the nineteenth century began. From this intellectual milieu, as it was influenced by social, economic, and political conditions, Comte was to pull diverse and often contradictory elements and forge a forceful statement on the nature of a science of society. But before examining the specifics of Comte's thought, we should first examine the scholars from whom Comte took the most important concepts.

THE INTELLECTUAL ORIGINS OF COMTE'S THOUGHT

Auguste Comte's sociology emerged from the economic, political, and social conditions of post-revolutionary France. No social thinker could ignore the oscillating political situation in France during the first half of the nineteenth century or the profound changes in social organization that accompanied the growth of large-scale industry. Yet, despite the influence of these forces, the content of Comte's sociology represents a selective borrowing of ideas from the Enlightenment of the eighteenth century. Comte absorbed, no doubt, the general thrust of the philosophes' advocacy, but he appears to have borrowed and then synthesized concepts from four major figures: (1) Charles Montesquieu, (2) Jacques Turgot, (3) Jean Condorcet, and (4) Henri Saint-Simon. In addition, Comte seems to have been influenced by the liberal tradition of Adam Smith and the physiocrats as well as by the reactionary traditionalism of such scholars as de Maistre and de Bonald.[2] In our review of the origins of Comte's thought, then, we will focus primarily on the influence of Montesquieu, Turgot, Condorcet, and Saint-Simon, with a brief mention of the traditional and liberal elements in Comte's thinking.

Montesquieu and Comte

In Chapter 10, when we examine the culmination of French sociology in the work of Émile Durkheim, Charles Montesquieu's ideas will be explored in more detail. For the present, we will stress those key concepts that Comte borrowed from Montesquieu. Written in the first half of the eighteenth century, Montesquieu's *The Spirit of Laws* can be considered one of the first sociological works in both style and tone.[3] Indeed, if we wanted to push back seventy-five years the founding of sociology, we could view *The Spirit* as the first distinctly sociological work. There are, however, too many problems with

---

[2]Lewis Coser's *Masters of Sociological Thought* (New York: Harcourt Brace Jovanovich, 1978), pp. 25–27, is the first work to bring this line of influence to our attention.

[3]Charles Montesquieu, *The Spirit of Laws*, vols. 1 and 2 (London: Colonial Press, 1900; originally published in 1748).

Montesquieu's great work for it to represent a founding effort. Its significance resides more in the influence it had on scholars of the next century, particularly Comte and Durkheim (see Chapters 10 and 11).

In *The Spirit*, Montesquieu argued that society must be considered a "thing." As a thing, its properties could be discovered by observation and analysis. Thus, for Montesquieu, morals, manners, and customs, as well as social structures, are amenable to investigation in the same way as are things or phenomena in physics and chemistry. Comte's concern with "social facts," and later, Durkheim's proclamation that sociology is the study of social facts, can both be traced to Montesquieu's particular emphasis on society as a thing.

As a thing, Montesquieu argued, society can be understood by discovering the "laws" of human organization. Montesquieu was not, as we emphasize in Chapter 10, completely clear on this point, but the thrust of his argument appears to have been that the laws of society are discoverable in the same way that Newton had, in Montesquieu's mind, uncovered the laws of physical matter. This point was to become extremely important in Comte's sociology. Indeed, Comte was to prefer the label *social physics* to *sociology*. In this way Comte could stress that social science, like the physical sciences, must involve a search for the laws of social structure and change.

Montesquieu also viewed scientific laws as a hierarchy—a notion that, along with Saint-Simon's emphasis, was to intrigue Comte. Sciences low in the hierarchy, such as physics, will reveal deterministic laws, as was the case for Newton's principle of gravitation. Sciences higher in the hierarchy will, Montesquieu argued, be typified by less determinative laws. The laws of society, therefore, will be more probabilistic. In this way, Montesquieu was able to retain a vision of human freedom and initiative within the context of a scientific inquiry. Comte appears to have accepted much of this argument, for he was to stress that the complexity of social phenomena renders strictly determinative laws difficult to discover. For Comte, sociological laws would capture the basic tendencies and directions of social phenomena.

Montesquieu's *The Spirit* also developed a typology of governmental forms. Much of this work is devoted to analyzing the structure and "spirit" (cultural ideas) of three basic governmental forms: republic, monarchy, and despotism. The details of this analysis are less important than the general thrust of Montesquieu's argument. First, there is an implicit developmental sequence in Montesquieu's argument, although not to the degree evident in the next generation of social thinkers, such as Turgot and Condorcet. Second, Montesquieu's abstract typology was constructed to capture the diversity of empirical systems in the world and throughout history. Thus, by developing a typology with an implicit developmental sequence, a better sense for the operation of phenomena was believed to be achieved—a point of emphasis that was to be central to Comte's scheme. And third, Montesquieu's separate analysis of the "spirit of a nation" and its relation to structural variables, especially political structures, was adopted by Comte in his analysis of societal stages that reveal both "spiritual" (ideas) and "temporal" (structural) components.

In sum, then, Montesquieu laid much of the intellectual foundation on which Comte was to build his scheme. The emphasis on society as a thing, the concern for laws, the stress on hierarchies of laws, the implicit developmental view of political structures, the belief that empirical diversity can be simplified through analytical typologies, and the recognition that the social world is composed of interdependent cultural and structural forces were all to find their way into Comtean sociology, as well as the sociology of Comte's intellectual successors, such as Durkheim. But Montesquieu's ideas were transformed in Comte's mind under the influence of other eighteenth-century scholars, particularly Turgot, Condorcet, and Adam Smith.

Turgot and Comte

Jacques Turgot was one of the more influential thinkers of the eighteenth-century Enlightenment. As a scholar, and for a short time as the finance minister of France, Turgot's ideas exerted considerable influence within and outside intellectual circles. Like that of many scholars of his time, Turgot's work was not published in the conventional sense but initially appeared as a series of lectures or discourses that were, no doubt, informally distributed. Only later, in the early nineteenth century, were many of Turgot's works edited and published.[4] Yet Turgot's ideas were well known to his contemporaries as well as his successors, particularly Condorcet, Saint-Simon, and Comte.

In 1750 Turgot presented two discourses at the Sorbonne; and from this date he established himself as a major social thinker. The first discourse was delivered in July and was entitled "The Advantages which the Establishment of Christianity Has Procured for the Human Race."[5] The second discourse was given on December 11, 1750, and

---

[4]Du Pont de Nemours, for example, published a nine-volume edition of Turgot's work between 1808 and 1811, which, while deficient in many respects, brought Turgot's diverse pamphlets, discourses, letters, anonymously published articles, private memoranda, and so on together for the first time. Comte certainly must have read this work, although it is likely he also read many of the original articles and discourses in their unedited form. See also W. Walker Stephens, ed., *The Life and Writings of Turgot* (London: Green, 1895).

[5]See Du Pont de Nemours, *Collected Works of Baron A. R. J. Turgot*, 9 volumes (Paris, 1908–1911).

was entitled "Philosophical Review of the Successive Advances of the Human Mind."[6] While the first discourse is often discounted in sociological circles, it presented a line of reasoning that was to be reflected in Comte's writings. Basically, Turgot argued that religion performed some valuable services for human progress, and while religion is no longer an important ingredient in human development, it made subsequent progress possible. For had Christianity not existed, basic and fundamental events such as the preservation of classical literature, the abolishment of cruel treatment of children, the eradication of extreme and punitive laws, and other necessary conditions for further progress would not have been achieved. Comte took this idea and emphasized that each stage of human evolution, particularly the religious or theological, must reach its zenith, thereby laying the conditions necessary for the next stage of human development.

The second 1750 discourse influenced Comte and other sociologically inclined thinkers more directly. In this discourse, Turgot argued that because humans are basically alike, their perceptions of, and responses to, situations will be similar, and hence they will all evolve along the same evolutionary path. Humanity, he argued, is like an individual in that it grows and develops in a similar way. Thus the human race will be typified by a slow advancement from a less developed to a more developed state. Naturally, many conditions will influence the rate of growth, or progress, for a particular people. Hence progress will be uneven, with some peoples at one stage of growth and others at a more advanced stage. But in the end, all humanity will reach a "stage of perfection." Comte saw much in this line of argument, since it implicitly accounted for variations and diversity among the populations of the world. Populations differ because their societies are at different stages in a single and unified developmental process.

In this second discourse, Turgot also presented a rather sophisticated version of economic determinism. Change occurs as a result of economic forces that inevitably produce alterations in society. For example, the invention of agriculture produces an economic surplus, which, in turn, allows for the expansion of the division of labor. Part of this expansion involves commercial activity, which encourages innovations in shipbuilding, and the extensive use of ships causes advances in navigation, astronomy, and geography. The expansion of trade creates towns and cities, which preserve the arts and sciences, thereby encouraging the advance of technologies. Thus Turgot saw

---

[6]Reprinted in English in Ronald L. Meek, ed. and trans., *Turgot on Progress, Sociology, and Economics* (Cambridge: Cambridge University Press, 1973).

progress in more than a moralistic or metaphorical sense; he recognized that structural changes in one area of a social system, especially in economic activity, create pressures for other changes, with these pressures causing further changes, and so on. This mode of analysis was to anticipate by one hundred years Marx's economic determinism, and it was to influence evolutionary theorizing in France for 150 years.

Turgot's next works made more explicit the themes developed in these two early discourses. *On Universal History*[7] and *On Political Geography*[8] were apparently written near the end of Turgot's stay at the Sorbonne, perhaps around 1755. *On Political Geography* is most noteworthy for its formulation of the three stages of human progress—an idea that was to become a central part of Comte's view of human evolution. Moreover, the notion of universal stages is used not only to explain human development but also to account for the diversity of human societies—an analytical tactic similar to that used by Montesquieu. All societies of the world are, Turgot argued, at one of three stages, whether "hunters, shepherds, or husbandmen." *On Universal History* developed even further the notion of three stages, presenting a number of ideas that were to become central to Comte's sociology. First, Turgot divided evolution into "mental" and "structural" progression so that development involves change in economic and social structures as well as in idea systems. Second, the progress of society is explicitly viewed as the result of internal structural and cultural forces rather than as a result of intervention by a deity. Third, change and progress are thus understandable in terms of abstract laws that depict the nature of stasis and change in social systems. And fourth, Turgot's empirical descriptions of what we would now call hunting, horticultural, and agrarian societies are highly detailed and filled with discussion of how structural and cultural conditions at one point in time create pressures for new structures and ideas at the next point in time.

Later in his career, probably during the 1760s, Turgot turned his analytical attention increasingly to economic matters. Around 1766 Turgot formulated his *Reflections on the Formation and Distribution of Wealth*,[9] which parallels and, to some extent, anticipates the ideas developed by the physiocrats in England. Turgot's advocacy of free trade, his analysis of the ways in which supply and demand influence prices, and his recognition of the importance of entrepreneurs to economic development are extremely sophisticated for his time. And out of this analysis,

---

[7]Ibid.
[8]Du Pont, *Collected Works.*
[9]See Meek, *Turgot on Progress,* for an English translation.

an implicit fourth stage of development is introduced: as capital increasingly becomes concentrated in the hands of entrepreneurs in advanced agricultural societies, a commercial type of society is created. Much of Turgot's description of the transition to, and the arrangements in, this commercial stage were to be restated by Marx, Spencer, and Comte in the nineteenth century, although only Comte would be directly influenced by Turgot's economic analyses. Yet Comte was never to expand on Turgot's great insights into the importance of economic variables on the organization and change of society. Only the emphasis on entrepreneurial activity in industrial societies was to be retained—a fact that, in the end, would make Comte's analysis of structural change superficial in comparison to that of Turgot, Spencer, and Marx.

In sum, then, Turgot dramatically altered the course of social thought in the eighteenth century. Extending Montesquieu's ideas in subtle but nevertheless important ways, he developed a mode of analysis that influenced Comte both directly and indirectly. The idea of three stages of progress, the notion that structures at one stage create the necessary conditions for the next, and the stress on the lawlike nature of progress became integral parts of Comte's sociology. Much of Turgot's influence on Comte, however, may have been indirect, working its way through Condorcet, whose work was greatly affected by Turgot.[10]

Condorcet and Comte

Jean Condorcet was a student, friend, and great admirer of Turgot, and thus it is not surprising that Condorcet's work represents an elaboration of ideas developed by Turgot. Throughout Condorcet's career, which flowered during and then floundered after the French Revolution, he concerned himself with the relation of ideas to social action. In particular he emphasized the importance of science as a means for the "infinite perfectability" of the human race. The culmination of his intellectual career was the short and powerful *Sketch for a Historical Picture of the Progress of the Human Mind*,[11] which was written while Condorcet was in hiding from an unfavorable political climate.

Progress of the Human Mind was written in haste by a man who knew he would soon die, and yet it is by far his best work. In its hur-

---

[10]Indeed, Condorcet wrote *Life of Turgot* in 1786, which Comte, no doubt, read with interest.

[11]Marquis de Condorcet, *Sketch for a Historical Picture of the Progress of the Human Mind* (London: Weidenfeld and Nicolson, 1955; originally published in 1794; translated into English in 1795).

ried passages, he traced ten stages of human development, stressing the progression of ideas from the emergence of language and simple customs to the development and elaboration of science. Condorcet felt that with the development of science and its extension to the understanding of society, humans could now direct their future toward infinite perfectability. Human progress, Condorcet argued, "is subject to the same general laws that can be observed in the development of the faculties of the individual," and once these faculties are fully developed, "the perfectability of man is truly indefinite; and that the progress of this perfectability, from now onwards independent of any power that might wish to halt it, has no other limit than the duration of the glove upon which nature has cast us."[12]

The historical details of Condorcet's account are little better than Turgot's, but several important changes in emphasis were to influence Comte's thinking. First, Condorcet's stress on the movement of ideas was to be retained in Comte's view of progress. Second, the emphasis on science as representing a kind of intellectual takeoff point for human progress was to be reaffirmed by Comte. And third, the almost religious faith in science as the tool for constructing the "good society" was to become central to Comte's advocacy. Thus, Comte's great synthesis was to take elements from both Turgot's and Condorcet's related schemes. Turgot's law of the three stages of progress was to be used instead of Condorcet's ten stages, but Condorcet's emphasis on ideas and on the use of science to realize the laws of progress was to be preserved.

Yet Comte's synthesis was, in some respects, merely an extension of ideas that his master, Saint-Simon, had developed in rough form. And to understand fully the origins of Comte's thought, and hence the emergence of sociology, we must explore the volatile relationship between Saint-Simon and Comte. From their interaction sociology was officially born.

Saint-Simon and Comte

In many ways, Claude-Henri de Saint-Simon represented a bridge between the eighteenth century and the early nineteenth century. Born into an aristocratic family, Saint-Simon initially pursued a nonacademic career. He fought with the French in the American Revolution; traveled the world; proposed a number of engineering projects, including the Panama Canal; was politically active during the French Revolution;

---

[12]Ibid., p. 4.

became a land speculator in the aftermath of the 1789 Revolution; and amassed and then lost a large fortune. Only late in life, at the turn of the century, did Saint-Simon become a dedicated scholar.[13]

The relationship between Saint-Simon's and Comte's ideas has been debated ever since their violent quarrel and separation in 1824. Just what part of Saint-Simon's work is Comte's, and vice versa, will never be completely determined. But it is clear that between 1800 and 1817, Saint-Simon's ideas were not influenced by Comte. For not until 1817 did the young Comte join the aging Saint-Simon as a secretary, student, and collaborator. In the seven years between 1817 and 1824, Comte's and Saint-Simon's ideas were intermingled, but we can see in the pre-1817 works of Saint-Simon many of the ideas that became a part of Comte's sociology.[14] The most reasonable interpretation of their collaboration is that Comte took many of the crude and unsystematic ideas of Saint-Simon, refined and polished them in accordance with his greater grasp of history and science, and extended them in small but critical ways in light of his exposure to Montesquieu, Turgot, Condorcet, Adam Smith, and the traditionalists. To appreciate Saint-Simon's unique contribution to the emergence of sociology, then, we must first examine the period between 1800 and 1817, and then the post-1817 work, with speculation on the contribution by Comte to these later works.

Saint-Simon's Early Work, 1800–1817.   Saint-Simon had read Condorcet carefully and concluded that the scientific revolution had set the stage for a science of social organization.[15] He argued in his first works that the study of humankind and society must be a "positive" science, based on empirical observation. Like many others of this period, Saint-Simon saw the study of society as a branch of physiology, since society is a type of organic phenomenon. Like the growth of any organic body, society is governed by natural laws of development, which are to be

---

[13]See Keith Taylor, *Henri Saint-Simon* (London: Croom Helm, 1975), pp. 13–29, for a concise biographical sketch of Saint-Simon.

[14]The most important of these works are *Letters from an Inhabitant of Geneva* (1803); *Introduction to the Scientific Studies of the Nineteenth Century* (1807–8); *Essays on the Science of Man* (1813); and *The Reorganization of the European Community* (1814). Unfortunately, much of Saint-Simon is unavailable in convenient English translations. For convenient secondary works where portions of the above appear, see F. M. H. Markham, *Henri Comte de Saint-Simon* (New York: Macmillan, 1952), and Taylor, *Henri Saint-Simon*. For interesting commentaries, see G. G. Iggers, *The Political Philosophy of Saint-Simon* (The Hague: Mouton, 1958); F. E. Manuel, *The New World of Henri de Saint-Simon* (Cambridge: Cambridge University Press, 1956); and Alvin Gouldner, *Socialism and Saint-Simon* (Yellow Springs, Ohio: Collier Books, 1962).

[15]Saint-Simon gave Condorcet explicit credit for many of his ideas.

revealed by scientific observation. As an *organism*, then, the study of society would involve investigation of social *organi*zation, with particular emphasis on the nature of growth, order, stability, and abnormal pathologies.[16]

Saint-Simon saw that such a viewpoint argued for a three-part program: (1) "a series of observations on the course of civilization" must be the starting point of the new science; (2) from these observations, the laws of social organization would be revealed; and (3) on the basis of these laws, humans could construct the best form of social organization. From a rather naive and ignorant view of history,[17] Saint-Simon developed a law of history in which ideas move from a polytheistic stage to a Christian theism, and then to a positivistic stage. In Saint-Simon's eye, each set of ideas in human history had been essential to maintaining social order, and with each transition there was a period of crisis. The transition to positivism, therefore, revolved around the collapse of the feudal order, and its religious underpinnings, and the incomplete establishment of an industrial order in European societies, with its positivistic culture of science.

In analyzing this crisis in European society, Saint-Simon noted that scientific observations first penetrated astronomy, then physics and chemistry, and now physiology, including both biological and social organs.[18] With the application of the scientific method to social organization, the decline of the traditional order must give way to a new system of ideas. Transitional attempts to restore order, such as the "legal-metaphysical" ideas of the eighteenth century, must give way to a "terrestrial morality" based on the ideas of positivism—that is, the use of observations to formulate, test, and implement the laws of social organization.[19]

Founded on a terrestrial morality, this new order was to result from a collaboration of scientists and industrialists. In Saint-Simon's early thought, scientists were to be the theoreticians, while industrialists were to be the engineers who performed many of the practical tasks of reconstructing society. Indeed, scientists and industrialists were to be the new priests for the secular religion of positivism.

[16]The French word for *organizations* means both "organization" and "organic structure." Saint-Simon initially used the term to refer to the organic structure of humans and animals and then extended it to apply to the structure of society.

[17]For an interesting commentary, see Walter M. Simon, "Ignorance Is Bliss: Saint-Simon and the Writing of History," *International Review of Philosophy* 14, nos. 3 and 4 (1960), pp. 357–83.

[18]See Peyton V. Lyon, "Saint-Simon and the Origins of Scientism and Historicism," *Canadian Journal of Economics and Political Science* 27, February 1961, pp. 55–63.

[19]These ideas begin to overlap with Saint-Simon's collaboration with Comte.

Saint-Simon's thought on social reorganization, however, was to undergo considerable change between 1814 and 1825, when he fell ill and died. Yet the broad contours of his thought were evident before Comte joined him in 1817. But the increasingly political and religious tone of Saint-Simon's writings were to alienate the young Comte, who saw the more detailed study of history and the movement of ideas as necessary for the formulation of the scientific laws of social organization. Ironically, Comte's own work was, later in his career, to take on the same religious fervor and extremes as Saint-Simon's last efforts.

Comte's early sociological work owed much to Saint-Simon's initial period of intellectual activity. The law of the three stages was to become even more prominent; the recognition of the successive penetration of positivism into astronomy, physics, chemistry, and biology was to be translated into a hierarchy of sciences, with physics at the bottom and sociology at the top; and the belief that sociology could be used to reconstruct industrial society was to be part of Comte's program. Comte was, however, to reject much of Saint-Simon's argument. In particular, he did not accept the study of social organization as a part of physiology; on the contrary, he was to argue that sociology is a distinct science with its own unique principles. In this vein, he also rejected Saint-Simon's belief that one law of all the universe could be discovered; instead, Comte recognized that each science has its own unique subject matter, which can be fully understood only in terms of its own laws and principles. But these objections aside, much of Comte's early work represented the elaboration of ideas developed and then abandoned by Saint-Simon as the aging scholar became increasingly absorbed in the task of reconstructing society.

Saint-Simon's Later Work. After 1814 Saint-Simon turned increasingly to political and economic commentary. He established and edited a series of periodicals to propagate his ideas on the use of scientists and industrialists to reconstruct society.[20] Saint-Simon's terrestrial morality thus became elaborated into a plan for political, economic, and social reform.

---

[20]All of these journals were shortlived, but they eventually gave Saint-Simon some degree of recognition as a publicist. These journals included *The Industry* (1816–18); *The Political* (1819); *The Organizer* (1819–20); *On The Industrial System* (1821–22), actually a series of brochures; *Disasters of Industry* (1823–24); and *Literary, Philosophic, and Industrial Opinions* (1825). From the latter a portion on religion was published separately in book form as *New Christianity,* Saint-Simon's last major statement on science and the social order. Another important work of this last period was *On Social Organization.* In all of these works there is a clear change in tone and mood; Saint-Simon is now the activist rather than the detached scholar.

The emphasis was on *terrestrial* because Saint-Simon had argued that the old supernatural basis for achieving order could no longer prevail in the positivistic age. Yet by his death, Saint-Simon recognized that a "religious sense" and "feeling" are essential to the social order. People must have faith and believe in a common set of ideas—a theme that was to mark all French sociology in the nineteenth century. The goal of terrestrial morality, therefore, is to create the functional equivalent of religion with positivism. Scientists and artists are to be the priests and the "spiritual" leaders,[21] while industrialists are to be the "temporal" leaders and to implement the spiritual program through the application of scientific methods to production and the organization of labor.

For Saint-Simon, terrestrial morality had both spiritual and temporal components. Spiritual leaders give a sense of direction and a new religious sense to societal activity. Temporal leaders assure the organization of industry in ways that destroy hereditary privilege and give people an equal chance to realize their full potential. The key to Saint-Simon's program, then, was to use science as the functional equivalent of religion and to destroy the idle classes so that each person worked to his or her full potential. While Saint-Simon visualized considerable control of economic and social activity by government (in order to prevent exploitation of workers by the "idle"), he also believed that people should be free to realize their potential. Thus Saint-Simon's doctrine is a mixture of free enterprise economics and a tempered but heavy dose of governmental control (a point of emphasis that has often led commentators to place him in the socialist camp).

Saint-Simon's specific political, educational, and social programs were, even for his time, naive and utopian, but they nevertheless set into motion an entire intellectual movement after his death. Auguste Comte, however, was highly critical of Saint-Simon's later writings, and he waged intellectual war with the Saint-Simonians after 1825. While Comte wrote much of Saint-Simon's work between 1817 and 1824, Comte's contribution is recognizable because it is more academic and reasoned than is Saint-Simon's advocacy.[22] Yet as we will come to see, Comte's own work took on the same religious extremes as Saint-Simon's. Thus Comte clearly accepted in delayed and subliminal form much of Saint-Simon's advocacy for the use of science as a functional substitute for religion.

---

[21]Saint-Simon was initially anti-Christian; but with *New Christianity* he changed his position so that the new spiritual heads of society are "true Christians" in that they capture and advocate the implementation of the "Christian spirit."

[22]For example, Comte wrote much of *The Organizer* (1819–20), especially the historical and scientific sections.

St. Simon: Scientists & artists → "spiritual leaders" → sense of direction
    industrialists → "temporal leaders" → organization and implementation

But Comte's real contribution comes not from Saint-Simon's political commentary but from his systematization of Saint-Simon's early historical and scientific work, for out of this effort sociology as a self-conscious discipline first emerged.

Liberal and Conservative Trends in Comte's Thought

We can see that Saint-Simon's work revealed both liberal and conservative elements. He advocated change and individual freedom, and yet he desired that change produce a new social order and that individual freedom be subordinated to the collective interests of society. Comte's work also revealed this mixture of liberal and conservative elements in that the ideas of economic liberals, such as Adam Smith, and conservatives or traditionalists like de Maistre and de Bonald all played a part in Comte's intellectual scheme.

Liberal Elements in Comte's Thought.   In England Adam Smith had the most decisive effect on social thought in his advocacy of an economic system consisting of free and competitive markets. His *Wealth of Nations* (1776), however, is more than a simple model of early capitalism; the fifth book reveals a theory of moral sentiments and raises a question that was to concern Comte and, later, Durkheim: how can society be held together at the same time that the division of labor compartmentalizes individuals? For Smith this dilemma was not insurmountable; whereas for French sociologists who had experienced the disintegrating effects of the Revolution and its aftermath, the splitting of society into diverse occupations posed a real intellectual problem. For French sociologists, the solution to this liberal dilemma involved the creation of a strong state that coordinated activities, preserved individual liberties, and fostered a set of unifying values and beliefs.

Comte also absorbed liberal ideas from the French followers of Adam Smith, particularly Jean-Baptiste Say, who had seen the creative role played by entrepreneurs in the organization of other economic elements (land, labor, capital). Saint-Simon appears to have had a notion of entrepreneurship in mind in his proposal that the details of societal reconstruction be left to "industrialists," but Say's explicit formulation of the creative coordination of labor and capital by those with "industry" was to influence explicitly Comte's vision of how a better society could be created by entrepreneurs.[23]

---

[23]Naturally, Say and Saint-Simon did not explicitly use the concept *entrepreneurs*. But they clearly grasped the essence of this economic function.

Traditional Elements in Comte's Thought.   Saint-Simon had attacked those who, in the turmoil of the Revolution, wanted to return to the Old Regime. Writing outside France, such Catholic scholars as de Maistre and de Bonald argued that the Revolution had destroyed the structural and moral fiber of society.[24] Religious authority had not been replaced by an alternative; the order achieved from the old social hierarchies had not been reestablished; and the cohesiveness provided by local communities and groups had been allowed to disintegrate. Both Saint-Simon and Comte, as well as an entire generation of French thinkers, agreed with the traditionalist's diagnosis of the problem but disagreed with the proposed solution. For the traditionalists, the reinstatement of religion, hierarchy, and traditional local groupings (on the feudal model) was the solution.

Although Comte became an atheist in his early teens, he had been reared as a Catholic; hence he shared with many of the traditionalists a concern about order and spiritual unity. But Comte had also been influenced by the Enlightenment and liberal economic doctrines, and thus he saw that a return to the old order was not possible. Rather it is necessary to create the functional equivalent of religious authority and to reestablish nonascriptive hierarchies and communities that would give people an equal chance to realize their full potential. For Comte, then, the religious element is to be secular and positivistic; hierarchies are to be based on ability and achievement rather than on ascriptive privilege; and community is to be re-created through the solidarity of industrial groups. Comte was thus to give the traditionalist's concerns a liberal slant, although his last works were decidedly authoritarian in tone—perhaps revealing the extent to which the traditionalists' ideas had remained with Comte.

[margin note: need of the religious-like authority to maintain stability & order ↓ but must be secular and positivistic]

In reviewing the massive economic, political, and intellectual changes of the eighteenth century, as well as the specific thinkers who preceded Comte, we can see that the emergence of sociology was probably inevitable. Science had become too widespread to be suppressed by a return to religious orthodoxy, and the economic and political transformations of society under the impact of industrialization and urbanization were in need of explanation. All that was necessary was for one scholar to take that final step and seek to create a science of society. Drawing from the leads provided by his predecessors, Auguste Comte took this final step. And in so doing, he gave the science of society a name and a vision of how it should construct theory.

---

[24]See Robert A. Nisbet, *Tradition and Revolt* (New York: Random House, 1968).

THE SOCIOLOGY OF AUGUSTE COMTE

Auguste Comte's works can be divided into two distinct phases: (1) the early scientific stage between 1820 and 1842 and (2) the moralistic and quasi-religious phase, which began in the later 1830s and culminated between 1851 and 1854. The scientific phase involved the publication of several important articles and then, between 1830 and 1842, the five volumes of *The Course of Positive Philosophy*,[25] where the science of society was formally established. The second period in Comte's life is marked by personal tragedy and frustration; during this period he wrote *System of Positive Polity*,[26] which represented his moralistic view of how society should be reconstructed. Despite the excessive moral preachings of this work, its vision of science as the tool for reconstructing society was to be an important element in sociology's mission as seen by later generations of French sociologists.

In our review of Comte's work, we will focus primarily on his purely sociological works—that is, on those from his scientific phase. We will, of course, not ignore his more moralistic efforts, but as we will come to appreciate, they did not contribute to the emergence of sociological theory. Thus we will examine Comte's most important early essay, "Plan of the Scientific Operations Necessary for Reorganizing Society,"[27] which was written in 1822, just before his break with Saint-Simon. In this essay are the germs of both Comte's scientific and moralistic phases. Then, and for the bulk of our examination of Comte's work, we will explore Comte's greatest treatise, *The Course of Positive Philosophy*, which was written in installments between 1830 and 1842. And finally, we will briefly examine the moralistic thoughts of Comte in his *Course of Positive Philosophy*.

Comte's Early Essays

It is sometimes difficult to separate Comte's early essays from those of Saint-Simon, since the aging master often put his name on

---

[25]We will use and reference Harriet Martineau's condensation of the original manuscript. This condensation received Comte's approval and currently is the most readily available translation. Martineau changed the title and added useful margin notes. Our references will be to the 1896 edition of Martineau's original 1854 edition: Auguste Comte, *The Positive Philosophy of Auguste Comte*, vols. 1, 2, and 3, trans. and cond. H. Martineau (London: George Bell and Sons, 1896; originally published in 1854).

[26]Auguste Comte, *System of Positive Polity*, vols. 1, 2, 3, and 4 (New York: Burt Franklin, 1875; originally published 1851–54).

[27]Auguste Comte, "Plan of the Scientific Operations Necessary for Reorganizing Society," reprinted in Gertrud Lenzer, ed., *Auguste Comte and Positivism: The Essential Writings* (New York: Harper Torchbooks, 1975), pp. 9–69.

works penned by the young Comte. Yet the 1822 essay, "Plan of the Scientific Operations Necessary for Reorganizing Society," is clearly Comte's and represents the culmination of Comte's thinking while working under Saint-Simon. This essay also anticipates, and in fact presents an outline of, the entire Comtean scheme as it was to unfold over the succeeding decades.

In this essay Comte argued that it is necessary to create a "positive science" based on the model of other sciences. This science would ultimately rest on empirical observations; but, like all science, it would seek to formulate the laws governing the organization and movement of society—an idea implicit in Montesquieu's *The Spirit of Laws.* This new science was to be termed social physics. Once the laws of human organization have been discovered and formulated, then they can be used to direct society. Scientists of society are thus to be social prophets, indicating the course and direction of human organization.

Comte felt that one of the most basic laws of human organization is the "law of the three stages," a notion clearly borrowed from Turgot, Condorcet, and Saint-Simon. Such stages can be described as the "theological-military," "metaphysical-judicial," and "scientific-industrial." Each stage is typified by a particular "spirit"—a notion that first appeared with Montesquieu and was elaborated on by Condorcet—and by temporal or structural conditions. Thus the theological-military stage is dominated by ideas that make reference to the supernatural, while being structured around slavery and the military. The metaphysical-judicial stage, which follows from the theological and represents a transition to the scientific, is typified by ideas that refer to the fundamental essences of phenomena and by elaborate political and legal forms. And the scientific-industrial stage is dominated by the "positive philosophy of science" and industrial patterns of social organization.

Several points of emphasis in this law were given greater emphasis in Comte's later work. First, the social world reveals both cultural and structural dimensions, with the nature of culture or idea systems being dominant—an idea probably taken from Condorcet. Second, idea systems, and the corresponding structural arrangements that they produce, must reach their full development before the next stage of human evolution can come into being. Thus one stage of development creates the necessary conditions for the next. Third, there is always a period of crisis and conflict as systems move from one stage to the next, since elements of the previous stage stand in conflict to the new, emerging elements of the next stage. Fourth, movement is always a kind of oscillation, for society "does not, properly speaking, advance in a straight line."

These aspects of the law of three stages led Comte to the conviction that cultural ideas about the world are subject to the dictates of

[Handwritten margin notes: positive science; empirical observ.; laws; direction; ideas are dominant over structure ↓ both must reach full development before next stage ↓ crisis is during transitions]

[Handwritten notes at bottom:]
3 stages
① theological-military → supernatural, slavery, military
② metaphysical-judicial → fundamental essences of phenomena; elaborate political/legal forms
③ scientific-industrial → positive philosophy of science / industrial organization

this law. All ideas about the nature of the universe must move from a theological to a scientific or "positivistic" stage. Yet some ideas about different aspects of the universe move more rapidly through the three stages than others. Indeed, only when all the other sciences—first astronomy, then physics, later chemistry, and finally physiology—have successively reached the positive stage will the conditions necessary for social physics have been met. And with the development of this last great science, it will become possible to reorganize society in terms of scientific principles rather than theological or metaphysical speculations.

Comte thus felt that the age of sociology had arrived. It was to be like Newton's physics, formulating the laws of the social universe. And with the development of these laws, the stage was set for the rational and scientific reorganization of society. There is much of Saint-Simon in this advocacy, but Comte felt Saint-Simon was too impatient in his desire to reorganize society without the proper scientific foundation. The result was Comte's *Course of Positive Philosophy*, which sought to lay the necessary intellectual foundation for the science of society.

Comte's *Course of Positive Philosophy*

Comte's *Course of Positive Philosophy* is more noteworthy for its advocacy of a science of society than its substantive contribution to understanding how patterns of social organization are created, maintained, and changed. *Positive Philosophy* more nearly represents a vision of what sociology can become than a well-focused set of theoretical principles. In reviewing this great work, then, we will devote most of our attention to how Comte defined sociology and on how he thought it should be developed. Accordingly, we will divide our discussion into the following sections: (1) Comte's view of sociological theory, (2) Comte's formulation of sociological methods, (3) Comte's organization of sociology, and (4) Comte's advocacy of sociology.

Comte's View of Sociological Theory.   As a descendant of the French Enlightenment, Comte was impressed, as were many of the philosophes, with the Newtonian revolution. And thus Comte argued for a view of sociological theory that, in modern times, we would call axiomatic. All phenomena are subject to invariable natural laws, and it is the task of sociologists to use their observations to uncover the laws governing the social universe, in much the same way as Newton had formulated the law of gravity. As Comte emphasized in the opening pages of *Positive Philosophy*:

> The first characteristic of Positive Philosophy is that it regards all phenomena as subject to invariable natural *Laws*. Our business is,—seeing how vain is any research into what are called *Causes*, whether first or

final,—to pursue an accurate discovery of these Laws, with a view to reducing them to the smallest possible number. By speculating upon causes, we could solve no difficulty about origin and purpose. Our real business is to analyse accurately the circumstances of phenomena, and to connect them by the natural relations of succession and resemblance. The best illustration of this is in the case of the doctrine of Gravitation.[28]

Several points are of great importance in this view of sociological theory. First, sociological theory is not to be concerned with causes per se, but rather with the laws that describe the basic and fundamental relations of properties in the social world. The original vision of sociological theory, then, was more *axiomatic* than *causal process*. Currently, causal process forms of theory dominate sociology, a trend that would have dismayed Comte. Second, there is an explicit rejection of "final causes"—that is, analysis of the results of a particular phenomena for the social whole. There is a certain irony in this disavowal since Comte's more substantive work was to help found sociological functionalism—a mode of analysis that often examines the functions or final causes of phenomena. Third, there is a clear recognition that the goal of sociological activity is to reduce the number of theoretical principles by seeking only the most abstract and only those that pertain to understanding fundamental properties of the social world—a point of emphasis that, unfortunately, has been lost in modern sociology's concern with introducing multiple and manifold variables into theoretical activity. Comte thus held a vision of sociological theory as based on the model of the natural sciences, particularly the physics of his time. For this reason Comte preferred the term *social physics* to *sociology*.[29]

The laws of social organization and change, Comte felt, will be discovered, refined, and verified through a constant interplay between theory and empirical organization. For, as Comte observed in the opening pages of *Positive Philosophy*, "if it is true that every theory must be based upon observed facts, it is equally true that facts cannot be observed without the guidance of some theory."[30] But Comte in later

---

[28]Comte, *Positive Philosophy*, vol. 1, pp. 5–6 (emphasis in original).

[29]In Comte's time, the term *physics* meant to study the "nature of" phenomena. It was not merely the term for a particular branch of natural science. Hence Comte's use of the label *social physics* had a double meaning: to study the "nature of" social phenomena and to do so along the lines of the natural sciences. Comte abandoned the term *social physics* when he realized that the same term was being used by the Belgian statistician Adolphe Quetelet. Comte was outraged that his original label for sociology had been used in ways that ran decidedly counter to his vision of theory. Ironically, sociology has become more like Quetelet's vision of social physics, with its emphasis on the normal curve and statistical manipulations, than Comte's notion of social physics as the search for the abstract laws of human organization—an unfortunate turn of events.

[30]Comte, *Positive Philosophy*, vol. 1, p. 4.

pages became even more assertive and argued that what we might now term *raw empiricism* runs counter to the goals of science. For Comte saw strict empiricism as an absolute hindrance to the development of sociological theory. In a passage that sounds distinctly modern, while offering some good advice, Comte noted:

> The next great hindrance to the use of observation is the empiricism which is introduced into it by those who, in the name of impartiality, would interdict the use of any theory whatever. No other dogma could be more thoroughly irreconcilable with the spirit of the positive philosophy. . . . No real observation of any kind of phenomena is possible, except in as far as it is first directed, and finally interpreted, by some theory.[31]

And, as he went on to conclude:

> Hence it is clear that, scientifically speaking, all isolated, empirical observation is idle, and even radically uncertain; that science can use only those observations which are connected, at least hypothetically, with some law.[32]

For Comte, then, the goal of sociology is to seek to develop abstract theoretical principles. Observations of the empirical world must be guided by such principles, with an eye to testing abstract principles against the empirical facts. Empirical observations that are conducted without this goal in mind are not useful in science. Theoretical explanation of empirical events thus involves seeing how they are connected to each other in lawlike ways. For social science "endeavors to discover . . . the general relations which connect all social phenomena: and each of them is *explained*, in the scientific sense of the word, when it has been connected with the whole of the existing situation."[33]

Comte held a somewhat ambiguous view of how such an abstract science should be "used" in the practical world of everyday affairs. He clearly intended that sociology must initially establish a firm theoretical foundation before efforts to use the laws of sociology for social engineering. In volume 1 of *Positive Philosophy,* Comte stressed:

> We must distinguish between the two classes of Natural science;—the abstract or general, which have for their object the discovery of the laws which regulate phenomena in all conceivable cases; and the concrete, particular, or descriptive, which are sometimes called Natural sciences in a restricted sense, whose function it is to apply these laws to the actual history of existing beings. The first are fundamental;

---

[31]Ibid., vol. 2, p. 242.
[32]Ibid., p. 243.
[33]Ibid., p. 240 (emphasis in original).

and our business is with them alone; as the second are derived, and however important, they do not rise to the rank of our subjects of con-templation.[34]

In Comte's eye, sociology must not allow its scientific mission to be confounded by empirical descriptions or by an excessive concern with a desire to manipulate events. Yet once sociology is well established as a theoretical science, its laws can be used to "modify" events in the empirical world. Indeed, such was to be the historic mission of social physics. And as Comte's later works were to testify, he took this mission seriously, and at times to extremes. But Comte's early work is filled with more reasoned arguments for using laws of social organization and change as tools for creating a variety of new social arrangements. In fact, Comte stressed that the complexity of social phenomena give them more variation than either physical or biological phenomena, and hence it would be possible to use the laws of social organization and change to modify empirical events in a variety of directions.[35]

In sum, then, Comte believed sociology could be modeled after the natural sciences. It could seek and discover the fundamental properties and relations of the social universe, and, like the other sciences, it could express these in a small number of abstract principles. Observations of empirical events could be used to generate, confirm, and modify sociology's laws. And once a well-developed set of laws had become formulated, they could be used as tools or instruments to modify the social world.

Comte's Formulation of Sociological Methods.   Comte was the first social thinker to take seriously methodological questions—that is, how are facts about the social world to be gathered and used to develop, as well as to test, theoretical principles? Comte advocated the use of four methods in the new science of social physics: (1) observation, (2) experimentation, (3) comparison, and (4) historical analysis.[36] Each of these is discussed below.

Observation.   For Comte, positivism is based on use of the senses to observe *social facts*—a term that the next great French theorist, Émile Durkheim, was to make the center of his sociology (see Chapters 10 and 11). But much of Comte's discussion of observation involves arguments for the "subordination of Observation to the statical and dynamical laws of phenomena"[37] rather than a statement on the procedures

---

[34]Ibid., vol. 1, p. 23.

[35]See, for example, the following passages in *Positive Philosophy*, vol. 2, pp. 217, 266, 234, 235, and 238.

[36]Ibid., pp. 241–57.

[37]Ibid., p. 245.

unguided observation → useless

by which unbiased observations are to be conducted. Comte simply argued that observation of empirical facts, when unguided by theory, will prove useless in the development of science. Yet Comte must be given credit for firmly establishing sociology as a science of social facts, thereby liberating thought from the debilitating realm of morals and metaphysical speculation.

Experimentation. Comte recognized that artificial experimentation with whole societies, and other social phenomena, is impractical and often impossible. But he noted that natural experimentation frequently "takes place whenever the regular course of the phenomenon is interfered with in any determinate manner."[38] In particular, Comte thought that, much as is the case in biology, pathological events allow "the true equivalent of pure experimentation" in that they introduce an artificial condition and allow investigators to see normal processes reasserting themselves in the face of the pathological condition. Much as the biologist can learn about normal bodily functioning from the study of disease, so social physicists can learn about the normal processes of society from the study of pathological cases. This view of sociological experiments was to inspire later thinkers, such as Durkheim; in many ways, it still guides the modern rationale for the study of deviance. Thus while Comte's view of "natural experimentation" was certainly deficient in terms of the logic of the experimental method, it was nonetheless to fascinate subsequent generations of scholars.

study of pathology

Comparison. Just as comparative analysis in biology has proven useful, so the comparison of social forms with those of lower animals, with coexisting states, and with past systems can generate considerable insight into the operation of these social forms. By comparing elements that are present and absent, and similar or dissimilar, knowledge about the fundamental properties of the social world can be achieved.

comparison

Historical Methods. Comte saw this procedure as a potential method, since he originally classified it as a variation of the comparative method (that is, comparing the present with the past). But his "law of the three stages" indicates the importance of a broad historical process. Comte thought that, ultimately, the laws of social dynamics could be developed only with careful observations of the historical movement of societies.

history must be understood

In sum, then, Comte saw four basic methods as appropriate to sociological analysis. His formulation of the methods is, of course, quite deficient by modern standards. We should recognize, however, that prior to Comte little attention had been paid to how social facts were

---

[38]Ibid., p. 246.

to be collected. And thus, while the specifics of Comte's methodological proposals are not always useful, their spirit and intent were most important. Social physics was, in Comte's vision, to be a theoretical science capable of formulating and testing the laws of social organization and change. Comte's formulation of sociology's methods added increased credibility to this claim.

Comte's Organization of Sociology.   Much as Saint-Simon had emphasized, Comte saw sociology as an extension of the study of "organisms" in biology to "social organs." Hence sociology was to be the study of social *organization*. This emphasis forces the recognition that society is an "organic whole" whose components stand in relation to each other. To study these parts in isolation is to violate the essence of social organization, and to compartmentalize inquiry artificially. For, as Comte emphasized, "there can be no scientific study of society, either in its conditions or its movements, if it is separated into portions, and its divisions are studied apart."[39]

Implicit in this emphasis is a mode of analysis that later became known as *functionalism.* As the prestige of biology grew in the nineteenth century, attempts at linking sociological analysis to the respected biological sciences increased. Eventually scholars were to begin asking: What is the function of a structure for the body social? That is, what does a structure "do for" the social whole? Comte implicitly asked such questions and even offered explicit analogies that were to encourage subsequent organismic analogizing. For example, his concern with social pathology revealing the normal operation of society is but one illustration of a biological mode of reasoning. And in his later work, Comte was to argue explicitly in biological terms when he viewed various structures as analogous to "elements, tissues, and organs" of biological organisms.[40] But in his early works, this organismic analogizing is limited to dividing social physics into statical and dynamical analysis.

This division, we suspect, represents a merger of Comte's efforts to build sociology on biology and to retain his heritage from the French Enlightenment. As a scholar who was writing in the tumultuous aftermath of the French Revolution, he was concerned with order and stability. The order of biological organisms, with their interdependent parts and processes of self-maintenance, offered to Comte a vision of how social order should be constructed. Yet the Enlightenment had

---

[39]Ibid., p. 225.

[40]See, in particular, his *System of Positive Polity,* vol. 2, pp. 221–76, on "The Social Organism."

emphasized "progress" and movement of social systems, holding out the vision of better things to come. For this reason Comte was led to emphasize that "ideas of Order and Progress are, in Social Physics, as rigorously inseparable as the ideas of Organization and Life in Biology: from whence indeed they are, in a scientific view, evidently derived."[41] And thus Comte divided sociology into (1) social statics (the study of social order) and (2) social dynamics (the study of social progress and change). These two aspects of Comte's sociology are explored in more detail below.

social statics ↓ study of social order

social dynamics ↓ study of change & progress

1. For Comte, social statics is the study of social structure, its elements, and their relations. He first analyzed "individuals" as elements in the analysis of social structure. Generally, Comte viewed the individual as a series of capacities and needs, some of which are innate, while others are acquired through participation in society.[42] But Comte did not view the individual as a "true social unit"; indeed, he relegated the study of the individual to biology—an unfortunate oversight since it denied the legitimacy of psychology as a distinct social science. The most basic social unit, Comte argued, is "the family." It is the most elementary unit, from which all other social units ultimately evolved:

> As every system must be composed of elements of the same nature with itself, the scientific spirit forbids us to regard society as composed of individuals. The true social unit is certainly the family,— reduced, if necessary, to the elementary couple which forms its basis. This consideration implies more than the physiological truth that families becomes tribes, and tribes become nations: so that the whole human race might be conceived of as the gradual development of a single family. . . . There is a political point of view from which also we must consider this elementary idea, inasmuch as the family presents the true germ of the various characteristics of the social organism.[43]

Comte thus took a strong sociologistic position in that social structures cannot be reduced to the properties of individuals. Rather, social structures are composed of other structures and can only be understood in terms of the properties of, and relations among, these other structures. Comte's analysis of the family then moves to descriptions of its structure—first the sexual division of labor and then the parental relation. The specifics of Comte's analysis are not important since they are flawed and inaccurate. Far

[41]Comte, *Positive Philosophy*, vol. 2, p. 141.
[42]Ibid., pp. 275–81.
[43]Ibid., pp. 280–81.

more important is the view of structure that he implied: social structures are composed of substructures and develop from the elaboration of simpler structures.

After establishing this basic point, Comte moved to the analysis of societal social structures. His opening remarks reveal his debt to biological analysis and the functional orientation it was to inspire:

> The main cause of the superiority of the social to the individual organism is, according to an established law, the more marked is the specialization of the various functions fulfilled by organs more and more distinct, but interconnected; so that unity of aim is more and more combined with diversity of means.[44]

Thus as social systems develop, they become increasingly differentiated, and yet, like all organisms, they maintain their integration. This view of social structure led Comte to the problem that Adam Smith had originally suggested with such force: How is integration among parts maintained in the face of increasing differentiation of functions? This question was to occupy French sociology in the nineteenth century, culminating in Émile Durkheim's theoretical formulations (see Chapters 10 and 11). As Comte emphasized:

> If the separation of social functions develops a useful spirit of detail, on the one hand, it tends on the other, to extinguish or to restrict what we may call the aggregate or general spirit. In the same way, in moral relations, while each is in close dependence on the mass, he is drawn away from it by the expansion of his special activity, constantly recalling him to his private interest, which he but very dimly perceives to be related to the public.[45]

Comte's proposed solution to this problem reveals much about how he viewed the maintenance of social structure. First, the potentially disintegrating impact of social differentiation is countered by the centralization of power in government, which will then maintain fluid coordination among system parts. Second, the actions of government must be more than "material"; they must also be "intellectual and moral."[46] Hence human social organization is maintained by (a) mutual dependence of system parts on each other, (b) centralization of authority to coordinate exchanges of parts, and (c) the development of a common morality or spirit

[44]Ibid., p. 289.
[45]Ibid., p. 293.
[46]Ibid., p. 294.

among members of a population. To the extent that differentiating systems cannot meet these conditions, pathological states are likely to occur.

In presenting this analysis, Comte felt that he had uncovered several laws of social statics since he believed that differentiation, centralization of power, and development of a common morality are fundamentally related to the maintenance of the social order. While Comte did not carry his analysis far, he presented Durkheim with both the basic question and the broad contours of the answer.

2. Comte appeared far more interested in social dynamics than statics, for "the dynamical view is not only the more interesting . . . , but the more marked in its philosophical character, from its being more distinguished from biology by the master-thought of continuous progress, or rather of the gradual development of humanity."[47] Social dynamics studies the "laws of succession" or the patterns of change in social systems over time. In this context Comte formulated the details of his law of the three stages in which idea systems, and their corresponding social structural arrangements, pass through three stages: (a) the theological, (b) the metaphysical, and (c) the positivistic. The basic cultural and structural features of these stages are summarized in Table 1–1.

Table 1–1 ignores many details that have little relevance to theory.[48] But the table communicates, in a rough fashion, Comte's view of the laws of succession. Several points of amplification on the contents of Table 1–1 should be made. First, each stage sets the conditions for the next. For example, without efforts at explanation in terms of references to the supernatural, subsequent efforts at more refined explanations would not have been possible; or without kinship systems, subsequent political, legal, and military development would not have occurred, and the modern division of labor would not have been possible. Second, the course of evolution is additive: new ideas and structural arrangements are added to, and built on, the old. For instance, kinship does not disappear, nor do references to the supernatural. They are first supplemented, and then dominated, by new social and cultural arrangements. Third, during the transition from one stage to the next, elements of the preceding stage, on the one hand, and the emerging stage, on the other, come into conflict, creating a period of anarchy

---

[47]Ibid., p. 227.

[48]Most of *Positive Philosophy,* vol. 3, is devoted to the analysis of the three stages. For a more abbreviated overview, see vol. 2, pp. 304–33.

TABLE 1–1 Comte's "Law of the Three Stages"

System	Stages		
	Theological	Metaphysical	Positivistic
Cultural (moral) system:			
a. Nature of ideas	Ideas focused on non-empirical forces, spirits, and beings in the supernatural realm.	Ideas focused on the essences of phenomena and rejection of appeals to supernatural.	Ideas developed from observation and constrained by the scientific method; rejection of speculation not based on observation of empirical facts.
b. Spiritual leaders	Priests	Philosophers	Scientists
Structural (temporal) system:			
a. Most prominent units	Kinship	State	Industry
b. Basis of integration	Attachment to small groups and religious spirit.	Control by state, military, and law.	Mutual dependence; coordination of functions by state; and general spirit.

and turmoil. Fourth, the metaphysical stage is a transitional stage, operating as a bridge between theological speculation and positivistic philosophy. Fifth, the nature of cultural ideas determines the kinds of social structural (temporal) arrangements, circumscribing what social arrangements are possible. And sixth, with the advent of the positivistic stage, true understanding of how society operates is possible, allowing for the manipulation of society in accordance with the laws of statics and dynamics.

While societies must eventually pass through these three stages, they do so at different rates. Probably the most important of the variable empirical conditions influencing the rate of societal succession is population size and density—an idea taken from Montesquieu and later refined by Durkheim. Thus Comte felt that he had discovered the basic law of social dynamics in his analysis of the three stages; and, coupled with the laws of statics, a positivistic science of society—that is, social physics or sociology—would allow for the reorganization of the tumultuous, transitional, and conflictual world of the early nineteenth century.

Comte's Advocacy of Sociology.   Comte's *Positive Philosophy* can be viewed as a long and elaborate advocacy for a science of society. Most of the five volumes involve a review of the development of other sciences, with an eye toward showing how sociology represents the culmination of positivism. As the title, *Positive Philosophy*, underscores, Comte was laying a philosophical foundation and justification for all science and then using this foundation as a means for supporting sociology as a true science. Comte's advocacy takes two related forms: (1) to view sociology as the inevitable product of the law of the three stages and (2) to view sociology as the "queen science," standing at the top of a hierarchy of sciences. These two interrelated forms of advocacy went a long way toward legitimating sociology in the eyes of a hostile intellectual world and should, therefore, be examined briefly.

Comte saw all idea systems as passing through the theological and metaphysical stages and then moving into the final positivistic stage. Ideas about all phenomena must pass through these stages, with each stage setting the conditions for the next and with considerable intellectual turmoil during the transition from one stage to the next. Ideas about various phenomena, however, do not pass through these stages at the same rate, and in fact, a positivistic stage in thought about one realm of the universe must often be reached before ideas about other realms can progress to the positivistic stage. As the opening pages of *Positive Philosophy* emphasize:

> We must bear in mind that the different kinds of our knowledge have passed through the three stages of progress at different rates, and have not therefore arrived at the same time. The rate of advance depends upon the nature of knowledge in question, so distinctly that, as we shall see hereafter, this consideration constitutes an accessory to the fundamental law of progress. Any kind of knowledge reaches the positive stage in proportion to its generality, simplicity, and independence of other departments.[49]

Thus thought about the physical universe reached the positive stage before conceptions of the organic world, since the inorganic world is simpler and since organic phenomena are built from inorganic phenomena. In Comte's view, then, astronomy was the first science to

---

[49]Ibid., vol. 1, pp. 6–7.

reach the positivistic stage; then came physics, next came chemistry, and after these three had reached the positivistic (scientific) stage, then thought about organic phenomena could become more positivistic. The first organic science to move from the metaphysical to the positivistic stage was biology or physiology. And with biology now a positivistic doctrine, sociology could move away from the metaphysical speculations of the seventeenth and eighteenth centuries (and the residues of earlier theological thought) toward a positivistic mode of thought.

Sociology has been the last to emerge, Comte argued, because it is the most complex and because it has had to wait for the other basic sciences to reach the positivistic stage. For the time, such a line of argument represented a brilliant advocacy for a separate science of society, while at the same time it justified the lack of scientific rigor in social thought when compared to the other sciences. Moreover, while dependent on, and derivative of, evolutionary advances in the other sciences, sociology would study phenomena that distinguish it from the lower inorganic phenomena as well as the higher organic science of biology. Although it is one of the organic sciences, sociology will be independent and study phenomena that "exhibit, in even a higher degree, the complexity, specialization, and personality which distinguish the higher phenomena of the individual life."[50]

In this argument is the notion of a "hierarchy of the sciences," with sociology at the top of the hierarchy.[51] This notion of hierarchy represents yet another way to legitimate sociological inquiry. On the one hand, it offered an explanation for why sociology was not as developed as the other, highly respected, sciences, while on the other hand it placed sociology in a highly favorable place (at the top of a hierarchy) in relation to the other "positive sciences." For if sociology could be viewed as the culmination of a long evolutionary process and as the quiescence of the positive sciences, its legitimacy could not be questioned. Such was Comte's goal, and while he was only marginally successful in his efforts, he was the first to see clearly that sociology could be like the other sciences and that it would be only a matter of time until the old theological and metaphysical residues of earlier social thought would be cast aside in favor of a true science of society. This advocacy, which takes up the majority of pages in *Positive Philosophy*, rightly assures Comte's claim to being the "founder of sociological theory."

---

[50]Ibid., vol. 2, p. 258.

[51]The hierarchy, in descending order, is sociology, biology, chemistry, physics, and astronomy. Comte added mathematics at the bottom, since ultimately all sciences are built from mathematical reasoning.

A Note on Comte's *System of Positive Polity*

Many events converged to change the direction of Comte's thought in his later career. The frustration over not receiving an academic appointment and the death of his first love, Clothilde de Vaux, were probably the most significant forces that took Comte away from the search for the laws of the social universe toward the religion of humanity. The four volumes of *The System of Positive Polity,*[52] published between 1851 and 1854, still contain many of the old appeals to a scientific sociology, but the real intent of the book is to reconstruct society on the basis of a new religious spirit. In much the same way as his early mentor, Saint-Simon, basked in the glory of a quasi-religious movement in his late years, so now Comte proclaimed himself "The Founder of Universal Religion" and as "The Great Priest of Humanity."

Comte's early essays anticipated both the concern for creating a unifying spirit for the maintenance of social order as well as the desire to reconstruct and reorganize society. But the emotional and often irrational extremes of *Positive Polity* mark it as a religious doctrine, more than a piece of science. Comte established himself as the High Priest of the new religion after the publication of *Positive Polity,* and he began an entirely new life:[53] He sent decrees to his disciples; he established churches; he advocated love as the unifying force of humanity; he sought to counsel political leaders in the manner of old theologians; and he preached to all who would listen on the virtues of the new religion. In *Positive Polity* can even be found a calendar of rituals to be performed during the year by members of the Universal Religion of Humanity.

Positive Polity does, nonetheless, contain some sociological insights. Yet we have concentrated on *Positive Philosophy* because these same insights are stated less ambiguously and without moralistic preachings from Comte, the new High Priest of Humanity.

COMTE IN RETROSPECT

For all of his advocacy of a science of society and for his insistence that sociology seek the laws of social organization, Comte himself did not develop any true sociological laws. He thought his law of the three stages was the equivalent of Newton's law of gravitation for the understanding of social dynamics, and he implicitly argued that the pro-

---

[52]Comte, *System of Positive Polity.*

[53]See Coser, *Masters of Sociological Thought,* pp. 29–41, for a more detailed summary of Comte's personal life as it relates to *System of Positive Polity.*

posed relationship between structural differentiation, on the one hand, and integration in terms of interdependence and unifying cultural symbols, on the other, captured the fundamental nature of social statics. Yet Comte's law of the three stages is more of an historical description than a law, and his views on social statics, while promising, are not well developed.

Comte's contribution thus resides not so much in his actual theoretical principles as in the vision of social science that his work represented. Others, such as Spencer in England and later Durkheim in France, were to build on the suggestive leads in Comte's analysis of statics and dynamics. And most important, Comte provided an image of what sociology could be; although Comte's work was rejected in his later years, it resurfaced in the last decades of the nineteenth century and stimulated a burst of sociological activity. For whatever the flaws in Comte's grand scheme, he had the right vision of what a science of society should be. And while it remained for others to execute this vision, Comte understood better than his contemporaries and better than many scholars today that a science of society must seek the fundamental principles by which patterns of social organization are created, maintained, and changed.

For this reason, then, sociological theory first emerged with Auguste Comte. Although humans had thought about their condition for centuries, Comte explicitly recognized the need for, and nature of, sociological theory. It is in this recognition that Comte's great contribution resides. And so it is with Comte that sociological theory explicitly emerges—and it is to the work of those who followed Comte that we dedicate the following pages. More specifically, we will emphasize the works of those theorists after Comte who made a difference in how sociologists develop theory.

Yet despite Comte's eloquence, the new science of sociology did not immediately capture the imagination of scientists and intellectuals, nor did it win converts among academics. Indeed it was often seen as an intrusion into, or a threat to, more established disciplines, such as law, morals, philosophy, economics, and even psychology. The nineteenth century is thus a period in which sociology fought for recognition as a unique science and for admission into academic circles. Some scholars successfully waged the battle and became prominent academics, as was the case for such intellectual giants as Max Weber, Émile Durkheim, and George Herbert Mead. Others, such as Herbert Spencer, achieved immense popularity outside academic circles. Some, like Georg Simmel, experienced considerable discrimination in the academic community. And still others, such as Karl Marx, never saw themselves as sociologists or as scientists and never became a part of established intellectual or scientific circles.

The founding figures of sociology were thus a diverse group, situated in different positions in varying social contexts. But they all had one feature in common: a desire to understand the dynamics of human social organization. In their unique way, each was to ask the fundamental question of all sociological theory: How and why are patterns of social organization created, maintained, and changed? In addressing this question, scholars of the nineteenth and early twentieth centuries made the tentative efforts to realize the goals of all science: to create theory. We now turn to understanding their theories.

CHAPTER 2

The Origin and Context of Herbert Spencer's Thought

BIOGRAPHICAL INFLUENCES ON SPENCERIAN SOCIOLOGY

Herbert Spencer was born in Derby, England, in 1820. Up to the age of thirteen, he was tutored by his father at home. He subsequently moved to his uncle's home in Bath, where his private education continued.[1] Thus, except for a few months of formal education, Spencer never really attended school outside his family, a fact that was to influence the course of his career. And yet he received a very solid education in mathematics and science from his father and uncle; and this technical education, in the end, encouraged Spencer to view himself as a philosopher and to propose a grand project for uniting ethics, natural science, and social science. This great project was termed *Synthetic Philosophy* and indicates that Spencer's work moves way beyond the disciplinary border of sociology. In fact only rather late in his career (between 1873 and 1896) did he turn his attention to sociology. Spencer thus thought big in a time when the intellectual world in general, and academia in particular, was specializing and compartmentalizing.

This breadth and scope of inquiry probably accounts for the popularity of Spencer's work, since it raised questions that intrigued both the lay public and scholars in particular specialties. His popularity is evidenced by the fact that a good many of his works first appeared in serial form as installments in popular science magazines, and only later were they bound together in book volumes. But even after their publication in magazines, Spencer's ideas remained popular; indeed, 100,000 copies of his books were sold before the turn of the century—an astoundingly high figure for that time and place. Even more amazing, however, is that they are not mere popularizations of ideas but rather academic works. They could hardly be considered light reading, but apparently their vision and scope captured the imagination of their

---

[1] Jonathan H. Turner, *Herbert Spencer: A Renewed Appreciation* (Beverly Hills, Calif.: Sage Publications, 1985), chap. 1; *Herbert Spencer, an Autobiography* (London: Watts, 1926).

readers. Anyone who reads Spencer today cannot help but be captured by the power of his ideas and perhaps even their arrogance, for who today would proclaim it possible to unite all of the sciences and questions of ethics under one set of general principles?

If Spencer had received a formal education and advanced degrees from established universities, as his father had, his thinking would likely have been more focused and restrained. By today's standards, elite universities of the last century offered very broad training in letters and science, but even by the yardstick of the last century, Spencer would have been compelled by tradition and established genres to recognize that, after all, one does not undertake to explain the entire universe with a few general principles. Formal education has a tendency to limit horizons and force concentration on narrow topics, but since Spencer avoided the halls of academia in his youth and throughout his career, he was not bound by its rules of scholarship.

In a quiet way, Spencer's work flaunts the rules of academia. Spencer never read very much; instead he picked the brains of distinguished scholars. Instead of burying himself in the library, Spencer frequented London clubs and was friends with the most eminent scientific and literary figures of his time. And from them, no doubt, he learned much by listening carefully and asking probing questions.[2] One suspects that Spencer as a kind of intellectual sponge, absorbing ideas on contact. How else could a man write detailed works on ethics, physics, biology, psychology, sociology, and anthropology, while at the same time maintaining a constant flow of pointed and popular social commentary? Moreover, unlike academics who used students to do much of their leg work, Spencer employed professional academics. His research assistants tended to be Ph.D.s who either needed the money or found the assigned tasks interesting. It seems likely, of course, that an uncredentialed, private scholar employing credentialed academics represented somewhat of an affront to the academic establishment, although Spencer managed to maintain cordial relations with many important academics.

Yet despite Spencer's enormous popularity with the literate lay public, he was an inordinately private individual. Indeed he was rather neurotic and odd. He hardly ever gave public lectures; he spent a good

---

[2]For example, see Hugh Elliot, *Herbert Spencer* (New York: Holt, Rinehart & Winston, 1917); and David Duncan, *Life and Letters of Herbert Spencer* (London: Methuen, 1908). In his *Masters of Sociological Thought* (New York: Harcourt Brace Jovanovich, 1977), Lewis Coser has best summarized Spencer's relationship with his contemporaries when he notes that from informal conversations, Spencer was supplied "with scientific facts he used so greedily as building blocks for his theories. Spencer absorbed his science to a large extent as if through osmosis, through critical discussions and interchanges with his scientific friends and associates" (p. 110).

part of the day in bed, either writing or complaining about real and imagined ailments; he remained a lifetime bachelor who, at best, had only one great love affair (and even here the nature of the relationship is not clear); he lived in rather sparse and puritan circumstances despite his inherited wealth and substantial royalties; and when he got older, his somewhat dour disposition became punctuated with considerable bitterness as his ideas came under increasing attack and then passed into obscurity. Yet many of those who knew him, and even the nurses who cared for him during his last years of failing health, emphasized that he was still a thoughtful and engaging individual.

It is perhaps not so surprising, then, that Spencer is an enigma to us. He was a lone and private scholar in a time when scholarship was becoming an increasingly monopoly of academia; and despite his popularity, he never revealed a public presence and persona. Finally, he was a global thinker in a time of increasing specialization. The result, we can speculate, was that as his scholarly ideas came under criticism by specialized academics and as his political commentary became less fashionable, he had few students and adherents to carry his case; and he was too neurotic to come out in public to defend himself, although he did make a celebrated and trumpeted tour of America in the early years of this century to espouse his moral philosophy (which became an embarrassment to those who recognized the importance of his scholarly ideas). As a consequence, Spencerian philosophy and sociology disappeared very rapidly after Spencer died. There were no students and academic colleagues to carry forward his grand synthesis, with the consequence that one of the first important theoretical works of the modern era opens with the question "Who now reads Spencer?" Today very few academics read Spencer. As we hope to demonstrate in the next chapter, this marks a great intellectual tragedy, for we now have a stereotypical and largely inaccurate view of Spencer, which keeps us from fully appreciating the powerful quality of his ideas. A modern contemporary on Spencer might read as follows:

> Herbert Spencer, the first self-conscious English sociologist, advocated a sociological perspective that supported the dominant political ideology of free trade and enterprise. He naively assumed that "society was like an organism" and developed a sociology that saw each institution as having its "function" in the "body social"—thereby propagating a conservative ideology and legitimating the status quo. What is even worse, Spencer coined the phrase *survival of the fittest* to describe the normal state of relations within and between societies—thus making it seem right that the elite of a society should possess privilege and that some societies should conquer others.

There are elements of truth in a surface portrayal such as this, but there is also a great distortion, as we will come to see in this and the next chapter. Spencer was indeed an ideologue, but no more than many other sociologists of the last century—or today, for that matter. While his ideas were progressive and radical for their time, they are now considered right wing and conservative. But in contrast to many others, such as Marx and Durkheim, Spencer's social and political ideology does not appear very often in his scientific work; rather, it is packaged in separate volumes in ethics. Furthermore, as the above contemporary view emphasizes, Spencer did make analogies to organic forms, but these are far more sophisticated than is typically recognized (especially since Spencer had written a large, two-volume work on biology before embarking in sociology). It is also true that Spencer developed functional analysis, but it is not as naive or simplistic as many contend. In fact Spencerian functionalism is highly sophisticated and avoids many of the pitfalls of contemporary functionalism. And, of course, Spencer did coin the phrase *survival of the fittest*, which, we suspect, was to be his biggest mistake. But we should emphasize that in doing so, he came very close to postulating the principle of natural selection ten years before Darwin published his thesis; and in fact, Darwin acknowledges Spencer in the preface of *On the Origin of Species.*

But we should not be carried away with a defense of the much-maligned and enigmatic Spencer. The power of his ideas will, we believe, speak for themselves. Let's now return to tracing Spencer's biography and its impact on the development of his thought. Then we will be in a better position to appreciate his theoretical ideas.

Since Spencer had not received a formal education, he felt himself unqualified to attend college. Thus, in 1837, he sought to use his mathematical and scientific training as an engineer during the construction of the London and Birmingham Railway. The practical application of his training in mathematics had an enormous impact on Spencer's later thinking, for he was always to be attuned to the consequences of structural stress on the dynamics of the physical and social universe; and he was to express these consequences in the form of equations (although the relationships were usually stated verbally). Yet the impact of these four years as an engineer could not be foreseen in the next turns in his intellectual life.

In 1841, when the railroad was completed, Spencer returned to his birthplace in Derby; over the next few years, he wrote several articles in the radical (for his time) press and numerous letters to the editor of a dissenting newspaper, *The Nonconformist*. In these works he argued for limiting the power of government; and while these ideas are often defined as "conservative" today, they were seen as "liberal" and "radical" in the last century. After several years as a kind of fringe figure in radical politics and journalism, Spencer secured a permanent position as a subeditor for the London *Economist* in 1848. The appointment marked a turning point in Spencer's life, and from this time on, his intellectual career accelerated. In 1851 Spencer published *Social Statics*,[3] a work that has haunted him to this day and has been largely responsible for our present-day view of Spencer as a social Darwinist, a libertarian, and perhaps a right-wing ideologue. In this work Spencer championed the cause of laissez-faire—free trade, open markets, and nonintervention by government. And he asserted that individuals have the right to do as they please, as long as they allow others to do the same. Yet despite its negative impact on our retrospective view of Spencer, the book was well received and opened doors into the broader intellectual community, although it remained a cross to bear as he began to write less ideological and more scholarly works.

In 1853 the uncle who had tutored him in science and mathematics died and left him a substantial inheritance. This inheritance allowed Spencer to quit his job as an editor and assume the life of a private scholar full time. Despite his emotional problems—depression, insomnia, and reclusiveness—Spencer was enormously productive as a private scholar. His collected works span volumes and run into thousands upon thousands of pages. Moreover, with his more ideological tract out of his system, at least until the end of his life, he used the hard-nosed skills of an engineer and scientist to write a series of brilliant works. In 1854 he published *Principles of Psychology*, which was used as a text at Harvard and Cambridge. In 1862 he published *First Principles*, which marked the beginnings of his grand Synthetic Philosophy that sought to unify ethics and science under one set of elementary principles. Clearly the young Spencer, who had felt himself unqualified for college, was gaining confidence. Between 1864 and 1867 he published the several volumes of his *Principles of Biology*, which sought to apply the abstract "first principles" of the universe to the dynamics of organic realm. And in 1873 he began to think about the super-organic—that is, organization of organic forms. In particular he initiated an analysis of how human organization, as the most obvious type of super-organic organization, could illustrate the plausibility of his first principles. He opened this movement into the domain of sociology with a methodological treatise on the problems of humans studying themselves; and in so doing, he emphasized that laws of human organization could be discovered and used in the same way as in the physical and biological sciences. In 1874 the first serialized installments of Spencer's *The Principles of Sociology* appeared, and for the next twenty years, Spencer devoted himself to sociology and to articulating the basic laws of human organization. The last portions of *The Principles of Sociology* were

---

[3]For complete references to this and other works by Spencer, see footnotes later in this chapter and in the next chapter, where these works are discussed.

published in 1896. At the same time he was preparing these last parts of his sociology, Spencer was publishing his *The Principles of Ethics*, which restated the then liberal, but now conservative, social philosophy of laissez-faire. Because this philosophy was published in separate volumes from the now scholarly work in sociology, it intrudes less than might otherwise have been the case.

Thus while Spencer's work in sociology spans only a twenty-year period in a much longer and comprehensive intellectual career, his sociology reflects other scholarly and political concerns. In turn, these other concerns are the product of the general intellectual milieu of nineteenth-century England as well as specific scholars in this milieu. To understand Spencerian sociology, then, we should note some of the other forces influencing his thinking.

THE POLITICAL ECONOMY OF NINETEENTH-CENTURY ENGLAND

In contrast to France, where decades of political turmoil had created an overconcern for collective unity, England remained comparatively tranquil. As the first society to industrialize, England enjoyed considerable prosperity under early capitalism. Open markets and competition appeared to be an avenue for increased productivity and prosperity. It is not surprising, therefore, that social thought in England was dominated by ideological beliefs in the efficiency and moral correctness of free and unbridled competition not only in the marketplace but in other realms as well.[4]

As noted above, Spencer advocated a laissez-faire doctrine in his philosophic works. Individuals should be allowed to pursue their interests and to seek happiness as long as they do not infringe on others' rights to do so. Government should be restrained and should not regulate the pursuits of individuals. And, much like Adam Smith, Spencer assumed a kind of "invisible hand of order" as emerging to maintain a society of self-seeking individuals. Most of Spencer's early essays and his first book, *Social Statics*, represent adaptations of laissez-faire economics. But Spencer's social and economic philosophy was to be supplemented by more scientific analyses in biology.

---

[4]The major legitimating work in this context was the first volume of Adam Smith's *An Inquiry into the Nature and Causes of the Wealth of Nations* (London: Cadell and Davies, 1805).

THE SCIENTIFIC MILIEU OF SPENCER'S ENGLAND

Spencer's early training with his father and uncle was primarily in mathematics and science. More important, his informal contacts as a free-lance intellectual were with such eminent scientists as Huxley, Hooker, Tyndall, and even Darwin. Indeed Spencer read less than he listened, for he clearly acquired an enormous breadth of knowledge by talking with the foremost scientists of his time. Biographers have frequently commented on the lack of books in Spencer's library, especially for a scholar who wrote with such insight in several different disciplines. Yet despite Spencer's reliance on informal contacts with fellow scientists, several key works in biology and physics appear to have had considerable impact on his thought.

Influences from Biology

In 1864 Spencer wrote the first volume of his *Principles of Biology,* which represented one of the most advanced treatises on biological knowledge.[5] Later, as we will see, Spencer sought to apply the laws of biology to "super-organic bodies,"[6] revealing the extent to which biological knowledge influenced Spencer's more purely sociological formulations. Spencer credited three sources for some of the critical insights that he was later to apply to social phenomena: (1) Thomas Malthus, (2) Von Baer, and (3) Charles Darwin.

1. Spencer was profoundly influenced by Thomas Malthus's *Essay on Population.* (Mathus, of course, was not a biologist, but his work had an influence in this sphere and hence is discussed in this section.) In this work Malthus had emphasized that the geometric growth of population would create conditions favorable to conflict, starvation, pestilence, disease, and death. Indeed Malthus argued that populations grow until "checked" by the "four horsemen": war, pestilence, famine, and disease.

---

[5]In *Principles of Biology* (New York: Appleton-Century-Crofts, 1864–67), Spencer formulated some original laws of biology that still stand today. For example, his formulation of the relationship among growth, size, and structure are axiomatic in biology today. Yet few biologists are aware that it was Spencer, the engineer turned scientist, who formulated the law that among regularly shaped bodies, surface area increases as the square of the linear dimensions, while volume increases as the cube of these dimensions—hence requiring new structural arrangements to support and nourish larger bodies.

[6]This was Spencer's phrase for describing patterns of social organization.

Spencer reached a much less pessimistic conclusion than Malthus, for the competition and struggle that ensues from population growth would, Spencer believed, lead to the "survival of the fittest" and hence to the elevation of society and "the races." Such a vision corresponded, of course, to Spencer's laissez-faire bias and allowed him to view free and open competition not just as good economic policy but as a fundamental "law of the organic universe."[7] In addition to these ideological uses of Malthus's ideas, the notion of competition and struggle became central to Spencer's more formal sociology. For he saw evolution of societies as the result of territorial and political conflicts. And in fact, he was one of the first sociologists to understand fully the significance of war and conflict on the internal patterns of social organization in a society.

2. Spencer was also influenced by Harvey's embryological studies as well as by Milne-Edward's work, which had borrowed from social thought the phrase "the physiological division of labor." Indeed, as Spencer so ably emphasized, biologists had often borrowed from social discourse terms that he was merely borrowing back and applying in a more refined manner to the "superorganic realm." Yet the credit for recognizing that biological forms develop from undifferentiated, embryologic forms to highly differentiated structures revealing a physiological division of labor was given by Spencer to Von Baer.

Von Baer's principles allowed Spencer to organize his ideas on biological, psychological, and social evolution. For as Spencer came to emphasize, evolution is a process of development from an incoherent, undifferentiated, and homogeneous mass to a differentiated and coherent pattern in which the functions of structures are well coordinated.[8] Conversely, dissolution involved movement from a coherent and differentiated state to a more homogeneous and incoherent mass. Thus Spencer came to view the major focus of sociology as the study of the conditions under which social differentiation and de-differentiation occur.

3. The relationship between Darwin and Spencer is reciprocal in that Spencer's early ideas about development exerted consider-

---

[7]See, for example, his *Autobiography*; also see the long footnote in *First Principles* (New York: A. L. Burt, 1880; originally published in 1860).

[8]This idea can be found in its early form in one of Spencer's early essays, "Progress: Its Law and Cause," first published in 1857 (*Westminster Review*, April 1857). Also, see Spencer's article, "The Developmental Hypothesis," *The New Leader* (1852).

able influence on Darwin's formulation of the theory of evolution,[9] although Darwin's notion of "natural selection" was apparently formulated independently of Spencer's emphasis on competition and struggle. Only after *On the Origin of Species* was in press did Darwin recognize the affinity between the concepts of *survival of the fittest* and *natural selection*. Conversely, Darwin's explicit formulation of the theory of evolution was to reinforce, and give legitimacy to, Spencer's view of social evolution as the result of competition among populations, with the most organizationally "fit" conquering the less fit and hence increasing the level and complexity of social organization. Moreover, Darwin's ideas encouraged Spencer to view differences among "the races" and societies of the world as the result of "speciation" of isolated populations, each of which adapted to varying environmental conditions. In fact, Spencer's continuous emphasis on environmental conditions—both ecological and societal—as shaping the structure of society is the result, no doubt, of Darwin's formulations.

The theory of evolution also offered Spencer a respected intellectual tool for justifying his laissez-faire political beliefs. For both organic and super-organic bodies, he argued, it is necessary to let competition and struggle operate free of governmental regulation. To protect some segments of a population is to preserve the "less fit" and hence reduce the overall "quality of civilization."[10]

From biology, then, Spencer took three essential elements: (1) the notion that it is from competition among individuals, or collective populations, that many of the critical attributes of both individuals and society emerge; (2) the view that social evolution involves movement from undifferentiated to differentiated structures marked by interrelated functions; and (3) the recognition that differences among both individuals and social systems are the result of having to adapt to varying environmental conditions. These broad insights were supplemented by a number of discoveries in the physical sciences of Spen-

---

[9]Indeed Darwin explicitly acknowledges Spencer's work in the introduction to *On the Origin of Species* (London: Murry, 1890; originally published in 1859). And at one point in his life, Darwin was moved to remark that Spencer was "a dozen times his intellectual superior." For more lines of influence, see *Life and Letters of Charles Darwin* (New York: Appleton-Century-Crofts, 1896).

[10]It is not hard to see how these ideas were to be transformed into what became known as *Social Darwinism* in America. A more accurate term would have been *Social Spencerianism*. See Richard Hofstadter, *Social Darwinism in American Thought* (Boston: Beacon Press, 1955).

cer's time, and together with Spencer's biologically based ideas, the "first principles" of his general Synthetic Philosophy were forged.

Physical Science Influences

From informal education within his family and from contacts with the most eminent scientists of his time, Spencer acquired considerable training in astronomy, geology, physics, and chemistry. In reading Spencer's many works, it is impossible not to be impressed by his knowledge of wide varieties of physical phenomena and their laws of operation. Spencer's Synthetic Philosophy was thus to reflect his debt to the physical sciences, particularly in regard to (1) the general mode of his analysis and (2) the specific principles of his philosophy.

1. All of Spencer's work is indebted to the post-Newtonian view of science—that is, the existence of universal laws that could explain the operation of phenomena in the world. Indeed Spencer was to go beyond Newton and argue that there are laws transcending all phenomena, both physical and organic. In other words, there are laws of the universe or cosmos that can be discovered and used to explain, at least in general terms, physical, organic, and super-organic (social) events. Spencer was to emphasize that each domain of reality—astronomical, geological, physical, chemical, biological, psychological, and sociological—revealed its own unique laws that pertained to the properties and forces of its delimited domain. And yet he also believed that, at the most abstract level, there are a few fundamental or first principles that cut across all domains of reality.

2. In seeking these first principles, Spencer relied heavily on the physics of his time. He incorporated into his Synthetic Philosophy notions of force, the indestructibility of matter, the persistence of motion, and other principles that were emerging in physics. We will discuss these in more detail when examining Spencer's scheme in depth, but we should emphasize that much of the inspiration for Spencer's grand scheme came from the promise of post-Newtonian physics.

Thus Spencer's Synthetic Philosophy emerged out of a synthesis of ideas and principles being developed in physics and biology. Yet the precise way in which these ideas were used by Spencer in his sociological work was greatly influenced by his exposure to Auguste Comte's vision of a positive philosophy (see previous chapter). And hence, before we can fully appreciate Spencer's philosophy, we need to review his somewhat ambivalent and defensive reaction to Comte's work.

SPENCER'S SYNTHETIC PHILOSOPHY AND THE SOCIOLOGY OF AUGUSTE COMTE

Spencer's relation to Auguste Comte is rather unclear. In 1864 Spencer published an article entitled "Reasons for Dissenting from the Philosophy of M. Comte" in which he sought to list the points of agreement and disagreement with the great French thinker.[11] Spencer emphasized that he disagreed with Comte over the following issues: (a) that societies pass through three stages, (b) that causality is less important than relations of affinity in building social theory, (c) that government can use the laws of sociology to reconstruct society, (d) that the sciences have developed in a particular order, and (e) that psychology is merely a subdiscipline of biology.

Spencer also noted a number of points in which he was in agreement with Comte, but he stressed that many other scholars besides Comte had similarly advocated (a) that knowledge comes from experiences or observed facts and (b) that there are invariable laws in the universe. But most revealing are the few passages where Spencer explicitly acknowledged an intellectual debt to Comte. Spencer accepted Comte's term, *sociology,* for the science of super-organic bodies, and, most important, he gave Comte begrudging credit for reintroducing the organismic analogy back into social thought. Spencer stressed, however, that Plato and Hobbes had made similar analogies and that much of his organismic thinking had been influenced by Von Baer.

Yet one gets the impression that Spencer was working too hard at dissociating his ideas from Comte. And the fact that his most intimate intellectual companions, George Elliot and George Lewis, were well versed in Comte's philosophy argues for considerable intellectual influence of Comte's work on Spencer's initial sociological inquiries. True, Spencer would never accept Comte's collectivism, but he was to extend two critical ideas clearly evident in Comte's work: (1) social systems reveal many properties of organization in common with biological organisms, and hence a few principles of social organization can be initially borrowed (and, of course, altered somewhat) from biology, and (2) when viewed as a "body social," a social system can be analyzed in terms of the contribution of its various organs to the maintenance

---

[11]The article is conveniently reprinted in Herbert Spencer, *Reasons for Dissenting from the Philosophy of M. Comte and Other Essays* (Berkeley, Calif.: Glendessary Press, 1968). The article was written in a somewhat defensive manner in an effort to distinguish Spencer's first book, *Social Statics* (New York: Appleton-Century-Crofts, 1888; originally published in 1850), from Comte's use of these terms. Spencer appears to have "protested too much," perhaps seeking to hide some of his debt to the positive philosophy of Comte.

of the social whole. There can be little doubt, then, that Spencer was stimulated by Comte's analogizing and implicit functionalism. But as Spencer incorporated these ideas, they were altered by his absorption of key insights from the physical and biological sciences.

WHY READ SPENCER?

When compared to other scholars, whom we will analyze in later chapters, the intellectual influences on Spencer are less clear. He did not attend a university, and hence his mentors cannot be traced within the walls of academia. Nor did he ever hold an academic position, thereby avoiding compartmentalization in a department or particular school of thought. As a free-lance intellectual, he borrowed at will and was never constrained by the intellectual fads and foibles that sweep through academia. The unrestrained scope of Spencer's scheme makes it fascinating, and perhaps this same feature makes Spencer's work less appealing to present-day scholars, who tend to work within narrow intellectual traditions.

Yet, as we will explore in depth in the next chapter, Spencer offered many important insights into the structure and dynamics of social systems. And while he presented these insights in the vocabulary of the physics and biology of his time, they still have considerable relevance for sociological theorizing. Thus, as we approach the analysis of Spencer's basic works, we should be prepared to appreciate not only the scope of his work but also the profound insights that he achieved into the nature of social systems.

CHAPTER 3

The Sociology of
Herbert Spencer

Herbert Spencer viewed himself as a philosopher, and, as such, he considered it appropriate to write both ethical and scientific treatises. As noted in the last chapter, his overall intellectual scheme, in both its scientific and ethical components, is termed the *Synthetic Philosophy*. Yet it is not difficult to distinguish Spencer's moralistic preachings from his formal scientific work since they tended to be kept separate. In our review of Spencer's basic work, we will try to distinguish the moral and scientific elements of the Synthetic Philosophy, and in this way, we can appreciate Spencer as both a profound sociological theorist and a poor philosopher.[1]

SPENCER'S MORAL PHILOSOPHY

Social Statics and *Principles of Ethics*

In his later years Spencer often complained that his first major work, *Social Statics*,[2] had received too much attention. For he saw this book as an early and flawed attempt to delineate his moral philosophy, and hence it is not representative of his more mature thought. And yet the basic premise of the work is repeated in one of his last works,

---

[1]Spencer's complete works, except for his *Descriptive Sociology* (see later analysis), are conveniently pulled together in the following collection: *The Works of Herbert Spencer*, 21 vols. (Osnabruck: Otto Zeller, 1966). However, our references will employ the separate editions and pagination of each of his individual works. Moreover, many of the dates for the works to be discussed span several years since Spencer sometimes published his works serially in several volumes (frequently after they had appeared in periodicals). Full citation will be given when discussing a particular work.

[2]Herbert Spencer, *Social Statics; or, The Conditions Essential to Human Happiness Specified, and the First of Them Developed* (New York: Appleton-Century-Crofts, 1888). This was originally published in 1851; the edition cited here is an offset print of the original.

Principles of Ethics.[3] Thus despite Spencer's protests, there is considerable continuity in his moral arguments, although we should emphasize again that Spencer's more scientific statements can and should be separated from these ethical arguments.

Since Spencer's moral arguments did not change dramatically, we will concentrate on *Social Statics.* The basic argument of *Social Statics* can be stated as follows: Human happiness can only be achieved when individuals can satisfy their needs and desires without infringing on the rights of others to do the same. As Spencer emphasized:

> Each member of the race . . . must not only be endowed with faculties enabling him to receive the highest enjoyment in the act of living, but must be so constituted that he may obtain full satisfaction for every desire, without diminishing the power of others to obtain like satisfaction: nay, to fulfill the purpose perfectly, must derive pleasure from seeing pleasure in others.[4]

In this early work, as well as in *Principles of Ethics,* Spencer saw this view as the basic law of ethics and morality. He felt this law was an extension of laws in the natural world, and, in fact, much of his search for scientific laws represents an effort to develop a scientific justification for his moral position. Indeed Spencer emphasized that the social universe, like the physical and biological realms, reveals invariant laws. But Spencer turned this insight into an interesting moral dictum: Once these laws are discovered, humans should obey them and cease trying to construct, through political legislation, social forms that violate these laws. In this way Spencer was able to base his laissez-faire political ideas on what he saw as a sound scientific position: The laws of social organization can no more be violated than those of the physical universe, and to seek to do so will simply create, in the long run, more severe problems.[5] In contrast to Comte, then, who saw the discovery of laws as the tools for social engineering, Spencer took the opposite tack and argued that once the laws are ascertained, people should "implicitly obey them!"[6] And for Spencer, the great ethical axiom, "derived" from the laws of nature, is that humans should be as free from external regulation as is possible. Indeed the bulk of *Social Statics* seeks to show how his moral law and the laws of laissez-faire capitalism converge and, implicitly, how they reflect biological laws of unfettered competition and struggle among species. The titles of some of the chapters best communicate Spencer's argument:

---

[3]Herbert Spencer, *Principles of Ethics* (New York: Appleton-Century-Crofts, 1892–98).
[4]Spencer, *Social Statics,* p. 448.
[5]Ibid., pp. 54–57.
[6]Ibid., p. 56.

"The Rights of Life and Personal Liberty," "The Right to the Use of the Earth," "The Right of Property," "The Rights of Exchange," "The Rights of Women,"[7] "The Right to Ignore the State," "The Limit of State-Duty," and so forth.

In seeking to join the laws of ethics, political economy, and biology, Spencer initiated modes of analysis that were to become prominent parts of his sociology. First, he sought to discover invariant laws and principles of social organization. Second, he began to engage in organismic analogizing, drawing comparisons between the structure of individual organisms and societies.

> Thus do we find, not only that the analogy between a society and a living creature is borne out to a degree quite unsuspected by those who commonly draw it, but also, that the same definition of life applies to both. This union of many men into one community—this increasingly mutual dependence of units which were originally independent—this gradual segregation of citizens into separate bodies, with reciprocally subservient functions—this formation of a whole, consisting of numerous essential parts—this growth of an organism, of which one portion cannot be injured without the rest feeling it—may all be generalized under the law of individuation. The development of society, as well as the development of man and the development of life generally, may be described as a tendency to individuate—*to become a thing*. And rightly interpreted, the manifold forms of progress going on around us, are uniformly significant of this tendency.[8]

Spencer's organismic analogizing often goes to extremes in *Social Statics*—extremes that he was to avoid in his later works. For example, he was led at one point to argue that "so completely . . . is a society organized upon the same system as an individual being, that we may almost say that there is something more than an analogy between them."[9]

Third, *Social Statics* also reveals the beginnings of Spencer's functionalism. Societies, like individuals, are viewed by Spencer as having survival needs with specialized organs emerging and persisting to meet these needs. And "social health" is defined in terms of how well these needs are being met by various specialized "social organs."

Fourth, Spencer's later emphasis on war and conflict among societies as a critical force in their development can also be observed. While decrying war as destructive on the one hand, he argued that,

---

[7]Spencer's arguments here are highly modern and, when compared to Marx's, Weber's, or Durkheim's, are quite radical.

[8]Spencer, *Social Statics*, p. 497.

[9]Ibid., p. 490.

on the other hand, it allows the more organized "races" to conquer the "less organized and inferior races"—thereby increasing the level and complexity of social organization. This line of argument was to be dramatically tempered in his later, scientific works, with the result that he was one of the first social thinkers to see the importance of conflict in the evolution of human societies.[10]

In sum, then *Social Statics* and *Principles of Ethics* are greatly flawed works, representing Spencer's moral ramblings. We have examined these works first because they are often used to condemn Spencer's more scholarly efforts. While some of the major scientific points of emphasis can be seen in these moral works, and while Spencer's scientific works are sprinkled with his extreme moral position, there is, nonetheless, a distinct difference in style, tone, and insight between his ethical and scientific efforts. And thus we would conclude that the worth of Spencer's thought is to be found in the more scientific treatises, relegating his ethics to deserved obscurity. We will therefore devote the balance of this chapter to understanding Spencer's sociological perspective.[11]

SPENCER'S *FIRST PRINCIPLES*

The Basic Laws

In the 1860s Spencer began to issue by subscription his general Synthetic Philosophy. The goal of this philosophy is to treat the great divisions of the universe—life, mind, and society—in terms of scientific principles. The first work in this rather encompassing scheme is *First Principles*, published in 1862.[12] In this book Spencer delineated the "cardinal" or "first principles" of the universe. Drawings from the biology and physics of his time, Spencer felt that he had perceived, at the most abstract level, certain common principles that apply to all realms of the universe. Indeed it must have been an exciting vision to feel that one had unlocked the mysteries of the physical, organic, and

---

[10]Ibid., p. 498.

[11]It should be remembered that this perspective was developed between 1873 and 1896. For a more complete and detailed review of Spencer's sociology during this period, see Jonathan H. Turner, *Herbert Spencer: A Renewed Appreciation* (Beverly Hills, Calif.: Sage Publications, 1985).

[12]Herbert Spencer, *First Principles* (New York: A. L. Burt, 1880; originally published in 1862). The contents of this work had been anticipated in earlier essays, the most important of which are "Progress: Its Law and Cause," *Westminster Review* (April 1857), and "The Ultimate Laws of Physiology," *National Review* (October 1857); moreover, hints at these principles are sprinkled throughout the first edition of *Principles of Psychology* (New York: Appleton-Century-Crofts, 1880; originally published in 1855).

super-organic (societal) universe. Basically, Spencer postulated three general principles:

1. The indestructibility of matter.
2. The continuity of motion in a given direction.
3. The persistence of the force behind movement of matter in a given direction.

From these three general principles, several corollaries could be derived:

4. The transferability of force from one type of matter and motion to another.
5. The tendency of motion to pass along the line of least resistance.
6. The rhythmic nature of motion.

In enumerating these six principles, Spencer's initial purpose was to view the universe as a constant process, over time and in space, of "an unceasing redistribution of matter and motion" and a "transference of force." These processes, Spencer felt, are true of celestial bodies, chemical compounds, organic evolution, and social aggregates. Thus the goal of his Synthetic Philosophy is to discover the composite laws that combine these six laws and that allow for understanding of the evolution and dissolution of all phenomena.

The Laws of Evolution and Dissolution

Commentators often fail to recognize that Spencer viewed the universe as in a constant and cyclical process of "structuring" and "de-structuring" or, in his terms, "evolution" and "dissolution." Too often Spencer is viewed by his detractors as a strict evolutionist, when in fact he was interested in the transformations of structures, whether these transformations involve development or dissolution of phenomena.

With regard to evolution—that is, creating more differentiated and complex structures—Spencer saw aggregation of matter, the deflection of the motion contained in this matter, and the redistribution of the force of this motion as the critical variables. For example, when single-cell organisms aggregate, their motion is deflected, with the result that they differentiate into specialized organs. As this deflection occurs, the force of the motion is dissipated as it encounters resistance so that at some point the differentiated cells come into equilibrium. Similarly, when people aggregate, the retained motion that originally brought them together is deflected in various directions, creating pressures for differentiation of individuals and groups. But the force of their motion dissipates over time, with the result that their pattern of differentiation reaches an equilibrium point.

As corollaries to these principles of evolution, Spencer added that when the motion accompanying aggregation is great—that is, it is of great force—then the redistribution of this motion and differentiation of the aggregate will be extensive and the dissipation of force will take considerably longer. Thus if one nation conquers another (a situation of high force and great motion), Spencer would predict considerable deflection of motion and consequent differentiation of the population.

Thus evolution involves the related processes of aggregation of matter and its attendant motion as well as the force accompanying the motion of the elements that are aggregated. Under these conditions the force of the motion pushes different elements in a variety of directions, causing differentiation. But what holds the elements together as they move apart and differentiate? Spencer's answer is that evolution also involves integration of matter and the retained motion—that is, as elements of an aggregate differentiate, they become mutally dependent on each other. Thus as plants or animals develop separate and specialized organs, these organs provide vital substances for each other. Similarly, as people differentiate, they become mutually dependent on each other—that is, they become integrated.

When viewed in this light, much of the rather strange vocabulary in Spencer's definition of evolution can hopefully make more sense. For Spencer, evolution is "a change from a less coherent form to a more coherent form, consequent on the dissipation of motion and integration of matter."[13] But Spencer added that such a change from incoherence to coherence involves a "change from a homogeneous to a heterogeneous state."[14] Whether it be the solar system, a plant, a geological form, an animal, a psychological state of mind, or a society, evolution conforms to this law.

Spencer then sought to explain why evolution involves movement from a homogeneous to a more differentiated state. And in so doing, he introduced several additional principles, which are still useful in understanding many diverse phenomena: (1) the principle of instability of the homogeneous, (2) the principle of multiplication of effects, and (3) the principle of segregation.

1. The principle of instability of the homogeneous argues that when a force strikes a grouping of unlinked homogeneous elements, they are inherently more unstable than when the same force hits differentiated and integrated elements. When a force hits a differentiated and integrated mass, the mutual dependence of

---

[13]Spencer, *First Principles*, p. 243.
[14]Ibid., p. 286.

the elements offers resistance, whereas when the elements are alike and unlinked, they will be scattered in many different directions; over time, they will become different as a result of their retained motion propelling them into diverse environments.

2. The principle of multiplication of effects states that as initially homogeneous parts are effected differently by a force, they become even more differentiated. The reason for this is that the retained motion pushes the parts in different directions, and as the undissipated force allows for their further elaboration and development, their differences become even more accentuated. For example, similar people who migrate (a force and motion) to new and diverse regions can become easily distinguished from each other since their initial differences are multiplied and amplified by their subsequent elaborations of biological (skin color, for example) and cultural (values, beliefs, and so on) traits as they adapt to diverse circumstances.

3. The principle of segregation explains how multiplication of differences can occur. Once elements become isolated from each other and must exist in somewhat varying environments, then they must make adjustments to different circumstances. As these adjustments occur, the elements become even more differentiated. For example, biological speciation occurs as a result of isolation and confinement of members of the same species to different ecological niches; over time, as the members of the original species adapt to their new circumstances, they eventually become distinct species. Spencer felt that the same processes occurred among and within super-organic systems. For as populations become isolated and elaborate (in terms of the principle of multiplicative effects), they must adapt to diverse environmental demands and hence become differentiated from each other.

Thus, for Spencer, evolution occurs because homogeneous masses are inherently unstable, and as forces push elements in different directions, their segregation in diverse environments creates differences among the elements as they adjust to different milieus. Moreover, the retained motion, as it allows segregated elements to elaborate, leads to the multiplication of differences. For Spencer, outside forces are far more disruptive to homogeneous than to heterogeneous aggregates, and once such forces can segregate the elements in an aggregate, they are likely to multiply, over time, their initial difference. Whether these processes are true of all the universe is uncertain, but the principles do seem applicable to many realms of the social universe.

As we have emphasized, Spencer also recognized that evolution and dissolution are related processes. Structures elaborate, and then they often dissolve. And while Spencer saw that the history of

humankind had generally been one of evolution, particular populations and societies have evolved and then dissolved. At the most abstract level, Spencer viewed dissolution as occurring when the retained
motion of matter and its accompanying force are completely dissipated,
creating a situation in which environmental factors that have caused
the dissipation of force (by providing resistance) can begin to act as a
counterforce and disrupt the existing structure. Thus only so long as a
differentiated system can maintain its motion through the production
of forces against the environment can it evolve. For example, should a
population run out of food or cease producing a military advantage,
then it is likely that environmental forces—whether predators, disease,
or other militaristic societies—can begin to impinge on this population, causing its dissolution as a distinct entity.

These principles of evolution and dissolution are, of course, somewhat obscure, and they are rather grand and cosmic in tone. Yet as a
general metaphor for understanding the institutionalization and de-in-
stitutionalization of social structures, there is much to recommend
them. First, structuring and de-structuring are seen to occur in terms
that can be described by invariant laws. Second, explicit variables such
as (a) size and concentration of a population, (b) the strength of forces
that brought this population together, (c) the nature and extent of environmental resistance to such forces, (d) the capacity to maintain
forces that can overcome environmental resistance, and (e) the ability
to maintain interdependence in the face of differential actions, segregation, and multiplication of differences are all variables relevant to
understanding the basic processes of differentiation, integration, malintegration, and de-differentiation in social systems. Whether in the
context of organizational research, small-group experiments, historical
analyses of societal development, or cross-national comparisons of contemporary societies, these variables, first seen by Spencer with great
clarity, are relevant to most sociological explanations.

Yet Spencer was to move considerably beyond this general metaphor of evolution. He was to propose many specific propositions and
guidelines for a science of society. For ultimately, Spencer's contribution to sociological theorizing does not reside in his abstract formulas
on cosmic evolution but rather in his specific analyses of societal social
systems—what he called *super-organic* phenomena. This contribution
can be found in two distinct works, *The Study of Sociology*, which was
published in serial form in popular magazines in 1872, and the more
scholarly *The Principles of Sociology*, which was published in several volumes between 1876 and 1896. The former work is primarily a methodological statement on the problems of sociology, whereas the latter is a
substantive work that seeks to develop abstract principles of evolution
and dissolution and, at the same time, to describe the complex interplay among the institutions of society.

SPENCER'S *THE STUDY OF SOCIOLOGY*

The Study of Sociology[15] was originally published as a series of articles in *Contemporary Review* in England and *Popular Science Monthly* in America. It represents Spencer's effort to popularize sociology and to address "various considerations which seemed needful by way of introduction to the *Principles of Sociology*, presently to be written."[16] Most of the book is a discussion of the methodological problems confronting the science of sociology. At the same time, and in less well-developed form, there are a number of substantive insights that were to form the core of Spencer's *Principles of Sociology*. In our review we will first examine Spencer's methodological discussion, and then his more theoretical analysis, even though this division does not correspond to the order of Spencer's presentation.

The Methodological Problems Confronting Sociology

The opening paragraph of Chapter 4 sets the tone of Spencer's analysis:

> From the intrinsic natures of its facts, from our natures as observers of its facts, and from the peculiar relation in which we stand toward the facts to be observed, there arise impediments in the way of Sociology greater than those of any other science.[17]

Spencer went on to emphasize that the basic sources of bias stem from the inadequacy of measuring instruments in the social sciences and from the nature of scientists who, by virtue of being members of society, observe the data from a particular vantage point. In a series of insightful chapters—far superior to any statement by any other sociologist of the nineteenth century—Spencer outlined in more detail what he termed *objective* and *subjective* difficulties.

Under objective difficulties, Spencer analyzed the problems associated with the "uncertainty of our data." The first problem encountered revolves around the difficulty of measuring the "subjective states" of actors and, correspondingly, of investigators' suspending their own subjective orientation when examining that of others. A second problem concerns allowing public passions, moods, and fads to determine what is investigated by the sociologists, since it is all too easy to let the popular and immediately relevant obscure from vision more fundamental questions. A third methodological problem revolves around the "cherished hypothesis" in which, regardless of its merit or

---

[15]Herbert Spencer, *The Study of Sociology* (Boston: Routledge & Kegan Paul, 1873).
[16]Ibid., p. iv.
[17]Ibid., p. 72.

importance, an investigator can be driven to pursue a particular problem while neglecting more significant problems. A fourth issue concerns the problem of personal and organizational interests influencing what is seen as scientifically important. Large-scale governmental bureaucracies, and individuals in them, will tend to seek and interpret data in ways that support their interests. A fifth problem is related to the second in that investigators often allow the most visible phenomena to occupy their attention, creating a bias in the collection of data toward the most readily accessible (not necessarily the most important) phenomena. A sixth problem stems from the fact that any observer occupies a position in society and hence will tend to see the world in terms of the dictates of that position. And seventh, depending on the point of time in the ongoing social process at which observations are made, varying results can be induced—thereby signaling that "social change cannot be judged of in its general direction by inspecting any small portion of it."[18]

Spencer's discussion is timely even today, and his advice for mitigating these objective difficulties is also relevant: Social science must rely on multiple sources of data, collected at different times in varying places by different investigators. Coupled with efforts by investigators to recognize their bias, their interests, and their position in society as well as their commitment to theoretically important (rather than popular) problems, these difficulties can be further mitigated. Yet many subjective difficulties will persist.

There are, Spencer argued, two classes of subjective difficulty: intellectual and emotional. Under intellectual difficulties, Spencer returned to the first of the objective difficulties: How are investigators to put themselves into the subjective world of those whom they observe? How can we avoid representing another's "thoughts and feelings in terms of our own"?[19] For if investigators cannot suspend their own emotional states in order to understand those of others under investigation, then the data of social science will always be biased. Another subjective intellectual problem concerns the depth of analysis, for the more one investigates a phenomenon in detail, the more complicated are its elements and their causal connections. Thus how far should investigators go before they are to be satisfied with their analysis of a particular phenomenon? At what point are the basic causal connections uncovered? Turning to emotional subjective difficulties, Spencer argued that the emotional state of an investigator can directly influence estimations of probability, importance, and relevance of events.

---

[18]Ibid., p. 105.
[19]Ibid., p. 114.

After reviewing these difficulties, and emphasizing that the distinction between subjective and objective is somewhat arbitrary, Spencer devoted separate chapters to the "educational bias," "bias of patriotism," "class bias," "political bias," and the "theological bias." Thus, more than any other sociologist of the nineteenth century, Spencer had a clear recognition of the many methodological problems confronting the science of society.

Spencer felt the problems of bias could be mitigated not only by attention to one's interests, emotions, station in life, and other subjective and emotional sources of difficulty but also by the development of "mental discipline." He believed that by studying the procedures of the more exact sciences, sociologists could learn to approach their subject matter in a disciplined and objective way. In a series of enlightening passages,[20] he argued that by studying the purely abstract sciences, such as logic and mathematics, one can become sensitized to "the necessity of relation"—that is, to the fact that phenomena are connected and reveal affinities. By examining the "abstract-concrete sciences," such as physics and chemistry, one is alerted to causality and to the complexity of causal connections. And by examining the "concrete sciences," such as geology and astronomy, one becomes alerted to the "products" of causal forces and the operation of lawlike relations. For it is always necessary, Spencer stressed, to view the context within which processes occur. Thus by approaching problems with the proper mental discipline—with a sense of relation, causality, and context—many methodological difficulties can be overcome.

The Theoretical Argument

The opening chapters of *The Study of Sociology* present a forceful argument against those who would maintain that the social realm is not like the physical and biological realms. On the contrary, Spencer argued, all spheres of the universe are subject to laws. And in fact, every time people express political opinions about what legislators should do, they are admitting implicitly that there are regularities, which can be understood, in human behavior and organization.

Given the existence of discoverable laws, Spencer stressed, the goal of sociology must be to uncover the principles of morphology (structure) and physiology (process) of all organic forms, including the super-organic (society). But, Spencer cautioned, we must not devote our energies to analyzing the historically unique, peculiar, or transitory. Rather sociology must look for the universal and enduring

---

[20]Ibid., pp. 314–26.

properties of social organization.[21] Moreover, sociologists should not become overconcerned with prediction of future events, since there will always be unanticipated and unknowable empirical conditions in the future that will influence the weights of variables and hence the outcomes of events. Much more important is the discovery of the basic relations among, and the fundamental causal forces of, phenomena.

In the early and late chapters of *The Study of Sociology*, Spencer sought to delineate, in very sketchy form, some of the principles common to organic bodies. And in so doing, he foreshadowed the more extensive analysis in *Principles of Sociology*. Spencer acknowledged[22] Comte's influence in viewing biology and sociology as parallel sciences of organic forms and in recognizing that understanding of the principles of biology is a prerequisite for discovering the principles of sociology. For as Spencer was to emphasize in all of his sociological works, certain principles of structure and function are common in all organic bodies.

Spencer even hinted at some of these principles, which were to be elaborated on in the volumes of *Principles of Sociology*. One principle is that increases in the size of both biological and social aggregates create pressures for differentiation of functions. Another principle is that such differentiation results in the creation of distinctive regulatory, operative, and distributive processes. That is, as organic systems differentiate it becomes necessary for some units to regulate and control action, for others to produce what is necessary for system maintenance, or for still others to distribute necessary substances among the parts. A third principle is that differentiation initially involves separation of regulative centers from productive centers, and only with the increases in size and further differentiation do distinctive distributing centers emerge.

Such principles are supplemented by one of the first functional orientations in sociology. In numerous places, Spencer stressed that to uncover the principles of social organization, it is necessary to examine the social whole, to determine its needs for survival, and to assess various structures in terms of how they meet these needs.[23] While this functionalism was always to remain somewhat implicit and subordinate to Spencer's search for the principles of organization among

---

[21]Ibid., pp. 58–59.

[22]Ibid., p. 328.

[23]For example, Spencer was led to remark: "While . . . each society . . . presents conditions more or less special, to which the natures of citizens must adapt; there are certain conditions which, in every society, must be fulfilled to a considerable extent before it can hold together, and which must be fulfilled completely before social life can be complete." Ibid., p. 347.

super-organic bodies, it was to influence subsequent thinkers, particularly Durkheim.

In sum, then, *The Study of Sociology* is a preliminary work to Spencer's *Principles of Sociology*. It analyzes in detail the methodological problems confronting sociology; it offers guidelines for eradicating biases and for developing the proper "scientific discipline"; it hints at the utility of functional analysis; and, most important, it begins to sketch out what Spencer thought to be the fundamental principles of social organization. During the next two decades after the publication of *The Study of Sociology*, Spencer sought to utilize the basic principles enunciated in his *First Principles* as axioms for deriving the more specific principles of super-organic bodies.

SPENCER'S *PRINCIPLES OF SOCIOLOGY*

Between 1874 and 1896 Spencer wrote in serial form his *Principles of Sociology*,[24] which is both a theoretical and descriptive work. As such, it is filled with powerful analytical statements and insightful empirical observations. In reviewing this long work, we will first discuss the general classes of variables that Spencer saw as influencing human organization and change; then we will devote most of this section to delineating Spencer's more analytical statements; and finally, we will close with a brief summary of Spencer's more interesting empirical observations on various social institutions.[25]

Critical Variables in Super-Organic Evolution

In a way reminiscent of Comte, Spencer divided scientific inquiry into the study of inorganic, organic, and super-organic phenomena. Super-organic[26] sciences are those concerned with the coordinated relations among individual organisms, with the result that insect

---

[24]Herbert Spencer, *The Principles of Sociology*, 2 vols., 8 parts (New York: Appleton-Century-Crofts, 1885; originally initiated in 1874). This particular edition is the third and is printed in five separate books; subsequent references are all to this third edition. Other editions vary in volume numbering, although part numbers are consistent across various editions.

[25]Domestic institutions are examined in part 3 of volume 1; ceremonial institutions are examined in part 4 of volume 2; political in part 5; ecclesiastical in part 6; professional in part 7; and industrial in part 8.

[26]As Spencer defined it in *Principles of Sociology*, part 1, "Of course no absolute separation exists. If there has been Evolution, that form of it here distinguished as super-organic must have come by insensible steps out of the organic. But we may conveniently mark it off as including all those processes and products which imply the coordinated actions of many individuals."

societies and human communities are both part of the super-organic realm. But Spencer quickly emphasized that human societies, by virtue of their complexity and constant transformation, are the core of the super-organic sciences. And thus a science, termed *sociology*, is to dictate the basic mode of super-organic inquiry.

Such inquiry is to be evolutionary, since there can be little doubt, Spencer felt, that over the long run human patterns of social organization have followed the basic law of evolution, which he had articulated in *First Principles*. Human societies have moved from an unstable, homogeneous mass to more differentiated and coherent structures. The first goal of sociology, then, is to enumerate the general classes of variables influencing the direction, speed, and nature of such evolutionary changes. Spencer termed these variables the "factors of social phenomena," of which there are three general classes: internal conditions, external conditions, and derived conditions. Each of these factors is briefly examined below.

1. Under internal or intrinsic conditions, Spencer listed many variables that are not relevant today in analyzing societal systems—intelligence, physical traits, and emotional states.[27] More important is the general thrust of his analysis: The attributes of actors in a system determine, at least to some extent, the properties of the system. But Spencer was quick to stress that once actors revealing certain initial attributes come together, an emergent reality is created. And once created, the properties of this emergent structure, as much as the nature of the individuals involved, will influence the subsequent course of its development.

2. As a biologically oriented scholar, and as one who came close to articulating the theory of evolution,[28] Spencer was always concerned with the impact of environmental variables on patterns of social organization. Such external factors as climate, surface (fertility of soil, amount of land space, and so forth), configuration of surface (desert, plains, mountains, and so on), and the nature, abundance, and access to flora and fauna are all, in Spencer's vision, critical variables in sociological inquiry. Particularly among

---

[27]By today's standards, many of Spencer's statements are racist, as were those of Tylor, Morgan, Durkheim, Weber, and many others of the nineteenth century. Spencer's great fallacy was the result of not having genetic theory to supplement Darwin's view of evolution; thus he was led to view populations of the world as fundamentally different in terms of intelligence and other basic attributes.

[28]See Darwin's acknowledgments in *On the Origin of Species*.

simple, homogeneous societies, which have not elaborated internal structures, are external environmental variables influential.[29]

3. Derived conditions can be both internal and external, for as societies evolve they create internal conditions that influence their subsequent development, and they become a part of each other's external environment. And with further evolution, derived factors become increasingly more important and take precedence over the attributes of individual actors and the physical environment. Under such derived conditions, Spencer felt that (*a*) the size and density of social aggregates[30] and (*b*) their relations with neighboring societies are the most important. Large and concentrated populations, as well as conflictual relations with other societies, are likely to have considerable impact on the internal structure of a society and its subsequent evolutionary development. Yet Spencer also saw such factors as cultural beliefs and material products as significant derived factors that could shape patterns of social organization.

In sum, then, Spencer opened his formal sociological analysis with a definition of sociology's basic subject matter—the super-organic and its evolution—and an overview of the general classes of variables influencing the structure and change of social systems. The remaining sections of *Principles of Sociology* then seek to analyze the super-organic realm in more detail.

The Super-Organic and the Organismic Analogy

Part 2 of volume 1 of *Principles of Sociology* contains virtually all of the theoretical statements of Spencerian sociology. Employing the organismic analogy—that is, comparing organic (bodily) and super-organic (societal) organization—Spencer developed a perspective for analyzing the structure, function, and transformation of societal phenomena. Too often commentators have criticized Spencer for his use of the organismic analogy; but in fairness to Spencer, we should emphasize that he generally employed the analogy cautiously. The basic point of the analogy is to stress that since both organic and super-organic

---

[29]It should be recalled from *First Principles* that Spencer regarded homogeneous systems as inherently unstable and particularly susceptible to environmental influence.

[30]Émile Durkheim was later to incorporate these variables into his scheme. See Chapters 10 and 11 of this book.

systems reveal organization of component parts, they should reveal certain common principles of organization. As Spencer stressed:

> Between society and anything else, the only conceivable resemblance must be due to *parallelism of principle in the arrangement of components.*[31]

As one who saw in his *First Principles* a unity in evolutionary processes among realms of the entire universe and as one who had enumerated the principles of biology, it is not surprising that Spencer should begin his analysis of the super-organic by trying to show certain parallels between principles of societal and bodily organization. In fact, current general systems theory, living systems theory, and the cybernetic sciences all seek to do exactly what Spencer had proposed.[32] The critical question does not hinge on whether organismic analogizing is good or bad science but on whether or not Spencer's use of the organismic analogy is productive and achieves insight into the creation, maintenance, and change in patterns of social organization. It is on this latter criterion that we should judge Spencer's scheme.

Spencer began his analogizing by discussing the similarities in and differences between organic and super-organic systems.[33] Among important similarities, he delineated the following:

1. Both society and organisms can be distinguished from inorganic matter, for both grow and develop.

2. In both society and organisms, an increase in size means an increase in complexity and differentiation.

3. In both, a progressive differentiation in structure is accompanied by a differentiation in function.

4. In both, parts of the whole are interdependent, with a change in one part affecting other parts.

5. In both, each part of the whole is also a microsociety or organism in and of itself.

6. And in both organisms and societies, the life of the whole can be destroyed, but the parts will live on for a while.[34]

---

[31]Spencer, *Principles of Sociology,* vol. 1, p. 448 (emphasis in original).

[32]Walter Buckley, *Sociology and General Systems Theory* (Englewood Cliffs, N.J.: Prentice-Hall, 1967); C. Bertalanffy, "General Systems Theory," *General Systems Yearbook* 1, 1956, pp. 1–16.

[33]Spencer, *Principles of Sociology,* vol. 1, pp. 449–62.

[34]This particular listing is taken from Jonathan H. Turner, *The Structure of Sociological Theory* (Chicago: Dorsey Press, 1985), p. 43.

Among the critical differences between a society and an organism, Spencer emphasized the following:

1. The degree of connectedness of the parts is vastly different in organic and super-organic bodies. There is close proximity and physical contact of parts in organic bodies, whereas in super-organic systems there is dispersion and only occasional physical contact of elements.

2. The nature of communication among elements is vastly different in organic and super-organic systems. In organic bodies, communication occurs in terms of molecular waves passing through channels of varying degrees of coherence, whereas among humans communication occurs by virtue of the capacity to use language to communicate ideas and feelings.

3. In organic and super-organic systems, there are great differences in the respective consciousness of units. In organic bodies, only some elements in only some species reveal the capacity for conscious deliberations, whereas in human societies all individual units exhibit the capacity for conscious thought.

The Analysis of Super-Organic Dynamics

If all Spencer had ever done was make the above analogies, there would be little reason to examine his work. The analogies represent only a sensitizing framework, but the real heart of Spencerian sociology is in the portrayal of the dynamic properties of super-organic systems. We begin with an examination of Spencer's general model of system growth, differentiation, and integration; and then we will see how he applied this model to societal processes.

System Growth, Differentiation, and Integration. As Spencer had indicated in *First Principles*, evolution involves movement from a homogeneous state to a more differentiated state with the dissipation of motion and integration of matter. Among both organic and super-organic bodies, Spencer stressed, certain common patterns of movement from undifferentiated states can be observed.

First, growth in an organism and in society involves development from initially small units to larger ones.

Second, both individual organisms and societies reveal wide variability in the size and level of differentiation.

Third, growth in both organic and super-organic bodies occurs in terms of compounding and recompounding—that is, smaller units are initially aggregated to form larger units (compounding), and then these larger units join other like units (recompounding) to form an even larger whole. In this way organic and super-organic systems become larger and more structurally differentiated. Hence growth in size is always accompanied by structural differentiation of those units that have been compounded. For example, small clusters of cells in a bodily organism, or a small primitive society, initially join other cells or small societies (thus becoming compounded); then these larger units join other units (thus being recompounded) and form still larger and more differentiated organisms or societies; and so on for both organic and super-organic growth.

Fourth, all evolution must involve a dissipation of motion and integration of matter, which means that growth and structural differentiation must be accompanied by integration. Thus organic and societal bodies must reveal structural integration at each stage of compounding. Without such integration, recompounding is not possible. For instance, if two societies are joined, they must be integrated before they can, as a unit, become compounded with yet another society. In the processes of compounding, growth, differentiation, and integration, Spencer felt he saw parallel mechanisms of integration in organisms and societies. For both organic and super-organic systems, integration is achieved increasingly through the dual processes of centralization and mutual dependence of unlike parts. For example, in organisms, as the nervous system and the functions of the brain become increasingly centralized and differentiated, the organs are ever more interdependent; whereas in super-organic systems, as political processes become more and more centralized and differentiated, institutions are increasingly dependent on each other.

Fifth, in organic and super-organic systems, the dissipation of motion and integration of matter through mutual dependence and centralization of control increase the "coherence" of the system and its adaptive capacity in a given environment. Such increased adaptive capacity often creates conditions favoring further growth, differentiation, and integration, although Spencer emphasized that dissolution often occurs when a system overextends itself by growing beyond its capacity to integrate matter and dissipate motion.

These general considerations, which were initially outlined in Spencer's 1862 book on *First Principles*, offer a model of structuring in social systems. In this model the basic processes are (*a*) forces causing growth in system size (whether by compounding smaller units or internal creation of new units); (*b*) the differentiation of units in terms of the "laws" of segregation and multiplication of effects (the homogeneity to heterogeneity portion of the law of evolution); (*c*) the processes whereby differentiated units become integrated (the integration of matter and dissipation of motion portions); and (*d*) the creation of a "coherent heterogeneity," which increases the level of adaptation to the environment.

Thus, for Spencer, institutionalization is a process of growth in size, differentiation, integration, and adaptation. With integration and increased adaptation, a new system is institutionalized and capable of further growth, provided there is a "force" that can join social systems or otherwise increase the number of units. For example, a society that grows as the result of conquering another will tend to differentiate along conquered and conqueror lines; it will centralize authority; it will create relations of interdependence; and hence it will become more adapted to its environment. The result of this integration and adaptation is an increased capacity to conquer more societies—hence setting into motion another wave of growth, differentiation, integration, and adaptation. Similarly, a nonsocietal social system such as a corporation can begin growth through mergers or expenditures of capital, but it soon must differentiate functions and then integrate them through a combination of mutual dependence of parts and centralization of authority. If such integration is successful, it has increased the adaptive capacity of the system, and it can grow, if some force (such as capital surplus) is available. This vision of institutionalization is diagramed in Figure 3–1.

Figure 3–1 outlines the stages of institutionalization. As is emphasized, the fundamental processes of growth, differentiation, integration, and adaptive upgrading are, to some extent, conditioned by (*a*) external factors, such as the availability of natural resources, (*b*) internal factors, like the nature of the internal units, and (*c*) derived factors, such as the existence of other societies or internal values and beliefs. It is also important to emphasize that, when viewed this way, much of the rather strange terminology in Spencer's definition of evolution is rendered more understandable. Some "force," whether economic capital, a new technology, a need to gather resources, new values and beliefs, and so on, sets into "motion" system growth. This motion, as it acts differently on various units, sends them in different directions and "segregates" them such that their differences are "multiplied" as the retained motion allows for their elaboration in response to their distinctive environments. Yet if the system is not to explode apart, the units or "matter" must be "integrated," thereby dissipating or channeling the motion of the parts in ways that increase the "coherence" of the whole. Such coherence increases the adaptive capacity of the system.

Conversely, to the extent that integration is incomplete and/or the force that drives the system is spent and cannot be replaced, then dissolution of the system is likely. Thus social systems grow, differentiate,

FIGURE 3–1 Spencer's Model of Institutionalization

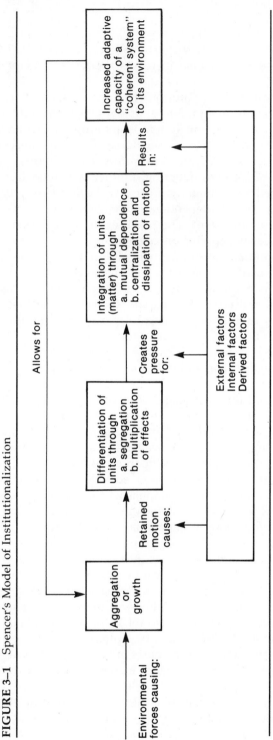

integrate, and achieve some level of adaptation to the environment, but at some point their driving force is spent or units cannot become integrated, setting the system into a phase of dissolution.

Stages of Societal Evolution. Spencer argued that increases in the size of a social aggregate necessitate the elaboration of its structure. Such increases in size are the result of (*a*) internal increases in numbers of members and (*b*) joining with other social aggregates. As we saw in the last section, Spencer visualized much growth as the result of compounding and recompounding—that is, by successive joining together of previously separate social systems through treaties, conquest, expropriation, and other means. Spencer also employed the concept of compounding in another sense: to denote successive stages of internal growth and differentiation of social systems. This second usage is related to the first, since growth forces internal differentiation. For while the joining of societies causes growth, and hence necessitates internal differentiation of the system, Spencer sometimes discussed compounding of the internal system without reference to how increases in size occur. With this latter use of the concept of compounding, we will begin our discussion of structural elaboration as conceptualized by Spencer.

Spencer consistently made reference to primary, secondary, and tertiary compounding.[35] Primary compounding occurs when an initially homogeneous structure undergoes rudimentary structural differentiation among three great classes of functions: (*a*) *regulatory* functions, in which separate structures for stabilizing relations with the external environment and relations among the system's internal components can be observed; (*b*) *operative* or sustaining functioning, where specific structures for meeting the internal needs of the system are evident; and (*c*) *distributive* functions, in which particular structures for carrying vital substances and information among differentiated system parts are observable. Spencer implied that (*a*) and (*b*) are the first and most developed axes of differentiation in simple compound systems, with (*c*) being only incipient. Moreover, Spencer also emphasized that in simple compound societies, all three functional divisions within organic and super-organic systems may not be great. For example, the differentiation of regulative and operative structures may only be observable in the sexual division of labor in kinship units of a "primitive" band, with men performing leadership, hunting, and warfare activities and with women engaging in domestic work.[36]

Secondary compounding occurs, Spencer argued, when the structures involved in regulatory, operative, and distributive functions undergo further differentiation. For example, internal administrative

---

[35]Spencer, *Principles of Sociology,* vol. 1, pp. 479–83.
[36]The accuracy of Spencer's description is not at issue here.

structures may become distinguished from warfare roles in the regulative system; or varieties of domestic activities, with specialized persons or groups involved in these separate activities, may become evident; and distinguishable persons or groups involved in external trade and internal commerce may become differentiated. Tertiary compounding occurs when these secondary structures each undergo further internal differentiation so that one can observe distinct structures involved in varieties of regulatory, operative, and distributive processes.

Figure 3–2 represents these dynamics diagrammatically as a model. This model outlines the "stages" of societal evolution in three respects. First, Spencer saw five basic stages: (1) simple without head (leadership), (2) simple with head (leadership), (3) compound, (4) double compound, and (5) treble compound. Second, Spencer visualized each stage as being denoted by (1) a given degree of differentiation *between* regulatory, operative, and distributive processes and (2) a level of differentiation *within* each process. And third, as differentiation between and within regulatory, operative, and distributive processes occurs, the nature of these processes changes with each stage of compounding (as denoted by the descriptive labels in each box in Figure 3–2; for more detailed descriptions see Table 3–1 later in the chapter).

Contained within Spencer's view of the stages of evolution is a mode of functional analysis on which we should comment. By viewing social structures with reference to regulatory, operative, and distributive processes, Spencer implicitly argued that these three processes represent basic functional needs of all organic and super-organic systems. Thus a particular structure is to be assessed in terms of its contribution to one or more of these three basic needs. But Spencer's functionalism is even more detailed, for he argued in several places that all social structures have their own internal regulatory, operative, or distributive needs, regardless of which of the three functions they fulfill for the larger social whole in which they are located.[37] Furthermore, he noted that these internal needs or requisites can be visualized as four universal functions: (*a*) intake of necessary materials for maintenance of the system, (*b*) operations on these materials so that they can be converted into useful commodities and distributed within the system, (*c*) the regulation of internal activity in relation to external conditions, and (*d*) the carrying away of wastes and potentially harmful materials.[38]

---

[37]Spencer, *Principles of Sociology,* vol. 1, p. 477.

[38]This brief discussion anticipates the four requisites that Talcott Parsons was later to use in his elaborate action theory. See, for example, Talcott Parsons, *Action Theory and the Human Condition* (New York: Free Press, 1978).

FIGURE 3–2   Spencer's Model of Evolution

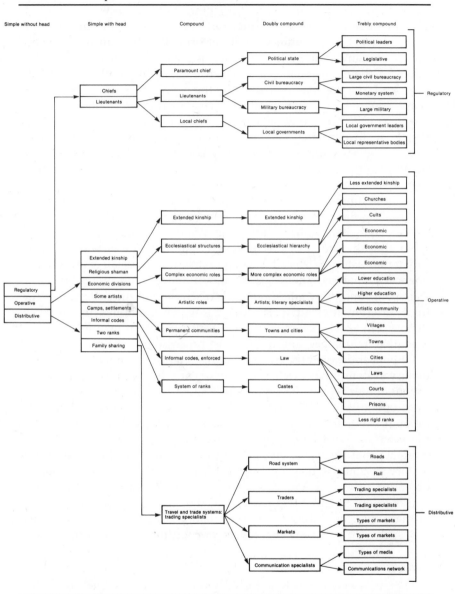

Under *social functions*, Spencer also argued that structural changes are accompanied by changes in their function.[39] As a structure becomes differentiated from other structures, it assumes ever more

---

[39]Spencer, *Principles of Sociology*, vol. 1, pp. 488–90.

specialized functions for the system. The result of this process is for increasingly specialized structures, performing narrow functions, to become dependent on each other for vital materials and information. Since the specialized units cannot perform all of the processes needed for their maintenance, they become increasingly dependent on each other for their continuance and survival. This differentiation of structures and functions, accompanied by the need for coordination of functions, forces social and bodily systems to develop high degrees of integration if they are to survive. And if such integration is achieved, then the capacity of the organism or social structure to survive in its environment is increased.[40] Spencer felt differentiated structures could more readily adjust and adapt to a variety of environmental conditions than could homogeneous systems.[41]

These functional considerations are, in many ways, subordinate to Spencer's primary goal: to document the nature, form, and direction of societal evolution. In so doing, he devoted considerable attention to specifying the properties of differentiation among and within regulatory, operative, and distributive systems. To appreciate the power of Spencer's analysis, then, we should minimize his more functional statements and draw attention to his discussion of the pattern of structural differentiation in social systems, which is implied in his evolutionary model. To do this, we will return to Spencer's discussion of operative, regulatory, and distributive processes.

Spencer devoted the majority of his attention to analyzing the regulatory system.[42] His discussion revolves around delineating those conditions under which the regulatory system (a) becomes differentiated from operative and distributive processes and (b) becomes internally differentiated. To a very great extent, the conditions for (a) and (b) are the same and can be summarized in two general statements: (1) the more a social aggregate engages in external conflict, the more its regulatory system will develop; and (2) the more extensive are the internal operative processes within a system, the more its regulatory system will develop. Spencer also recognized the feedback processes inherent in these two conditions: Once a regulatory system becomes developed in response to either internal needs for coordination or external threat,

[40] Much of Spencer's analysis here is similar to Talcott Parsons' later discussion of the process of "adaptive upgrading" that accompanies his work on evolution. See *Societies: Evolutionary and Comparative Perspectives* (Englewood Cliffs, N.J.: Prentice-Hall, 1966).

[41] Spencer had first made this generalization in *First Principles*, and later he applied it to the organic realm in *Principles of Biology* (New York: Appleton-Century-Crofts, 1866).

[42] Spencer, *Principles of Sociology*, vol. 1, part 2, pp. 519–48.

its development encourages expanded internal and external activities. For example, in a series of enlightening and contemporary passages, Spencer documented how war forces the development of a warlike governmental form; and once this form is created, it seeks out conflict with other societies, even when the original conflict under which it initially emerged has been resolved.

In general the development of the regulatory system reveals a certain pattern. First, as it grows in size, it internally differentiates. Such differentiation is initially between separate military subsystems (which are oriented to the external environment) and internal administrative agencies (which seek to regularize operative and distributive processes). After this initial two-part differentiation, a third subsystem of the overall regulatory system differentiates separate monetary structures that facilitate the movement of persons and commodities both within a system and between different systems. Second, as the regulatory system grows in size and internally differentiates, it becomes increasingly centralized. And third, as the regulatory system becomes large and centralized, the volume of information necessary for regulatory activities increases, and the central decision-making offices become increasingly dependent on subordinate units for necessary information.

As both regulatory and operative processes develop, Spencer argued, pressures for transportation, communication, and exchange among larger and more differentiated units increase. The result of these pressures is for new structures to emerge as part of a general expansion of distributive functions. Spencer devoted considerable attention to the historical events causing increases in transportation, roads, markets, and communication processes, and by themselves, these descriptions make for fascinating reading. At the most general level, he concluded:

> The truth we have to carry with us is that the distributing system in the social organism, as in the individual organism, has its development determined by the necessities of transfer among inter-dependent parts. Lying between the two original systems, which carry on respectively the outer dealings with surrounding existences, and the inner dealings with materials required for sustentation [sic] its structure becomes adapted to the requirements of this carrying function between the two great systems as wholes, and between the sub-divisions of each.[43]

As the regulatory and operative systems expand, thereby causing the elaboration of the distributive system, this third great system differentiates in ways that facilitate increases in (1) the speed with which

---

[43]Spencer, *Principles of Sociology*, vol. 1, p. 518.

material and information circulate and (2) the varieties of materials and information that are distributed. And as the capacities for rapid and varied distribution increase, then regulatory and operative processes can develop further; as the latter expand and differentiate, new pressures for rapid and varied distribution are created. Moreover, in a series of insightful remarks, Spencer noted that this positive feedback cycle involves an increase in the ratio of information to materials distributed in complex, differentiating systems.[44]

In sum, then, Spencer's view of structural elaboration emphasizes the processes of structural growth and differentiation through the joining of separate systems and through internal increases in size. As an evolutionist, Spencer took the long-range view of social development as growth, differentiation, integration, and increased adaptive capacity; then, with this new level as a base, further growth, differentiation, integration, and adaptive capacity would be possible. Spencer's view of structural elaboration is thus highly sophisticated, and while flawed in many ways, it is the equal of any other nineteenth-century social theorist.

System Dialectics and Phases.   Spencer saw war as an important causal force in human societies. In his analysis war forces a society to develop centralized regulatory structures in order to expand and coordinate internal operative and distributive processes. Yet there is an ironical or dialectical effect of war on a society: Once operative and distributive processes become expanded under conditions of external conflict, they increasingly begin to exert pressures for less militaristic activity and for less constrained and authoritarian centralization. For example, a nation at war will initially centralize along authoritarian lines in order to mobilize resources for the war effort; but as such mobilization expands the scope of operative and distributive processes, they develop an autonomy of their own and begin to press for greater freedom from centralized control. In this way Spencer was able to visualize war as an important force in societal development; but, at the same time, he was to see it as an impediment to development after a certain level of growth in internal system processes. And in an enlightening chapter on "social metamorphoses,"[45] Spencer argued that the dynamic force underlying the overall evolution of the super-organic from homogeneous to heterogeneous states is the successive movement of societies in and out of "militant" (politically centralized and author-

---

[44]Of course, the absolute amounts of both increase, but the processing of information—credits, accounts, ideas, purchase orders, and so on—increases as a proportion of things circulated.

[45]Spencer, *Principles of Sociology*, vol. 1, pp. 577–85.

itarian) and "industrial" (less centralized) phases. This cyclical dynamic is presented in Figure 3–3, which views these phases somewhat more abstractly than in Spencer's portrayal.

Figure 3–3 presents what is one of the most interesting (and often ignored) arguments in Spencerian sociology. For Spencer, there is always a dialectical undercurrent during societal evolution (and dissolution) that revolves around the relationship between regulatory and operative processes. On the one hand, each of these initial axes of differentiation encourages the growth and development of the other in a positive feedback cycle, while, on the other hand, there is also a kind of inherent tension and dialectic between the two. For example, war expands regulatory functions; increased regulatory capacity allows for more extensive coordination of operative processes; greater operative capacity encourages expanded war efforts and hence expansion of the

FIGURE 3–3   Phases of Institutionalization

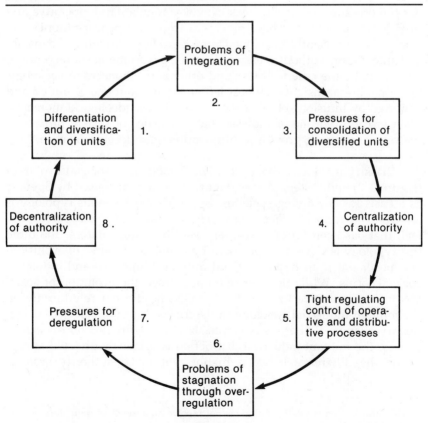

regulatory system. But at some point in this positive feedback cycle, development of internal operative structures primarily for war making becomes counterproductive, limiting the scope and diversity of development in operative processes. Over time, and under growing pressures from the internal sector, the warlike profile of the regulatory system is reduced. Then operative processes expand and differentiate in many different directions (in accordance with the laws of segregation and multiplication of effects); but, over time, they become too divergent, poorly coordinated, and unregulated. A war can provide, Spencer thought, the needed stimulus for greater regulation and coordination of these expanded and diversified operative processes, thus setting into motion the cycle once again.

Such had been the case throughout evolutionary history, Spencer thought. But curiously, Spencer also seemed to argue that modern, industrial capitalism now made the need for war and extensive regulation by a central state obsolete. No longer would it be necessary, in Spencer's capitalistic utopia, for centralized government, operating under the pressures of war, to seek extensive regulation of operative and distributive processes. These processes were, in Spencer's utopian vision, now sufficiently developed and capable of growth, expansion, and integration without massive doses of governmental intervention. As was to be the case for Marx and other early pioneers in sociology, Spencer's initial insights are best left alone, without being diluted and distorted by infusions of ideology. For in his less-ideological moments, Spencer captured one of the essential properties of system processes: the relations among growth, centralization, and decentralization.[46]

Classifying Social Systems. These models of societal evolution (Figure 3–2) and system phases (Figure 3–3) were also used by Spencer as a basis for classifying societies. Spencer's most famous typology is on what he termed *militant* and *industrial* societies—a typology, we feel, that has been grossly misinterpreted by commentators. Too often this typology is viewed as representing a unilinear course of evolutionary movement from traditional and militant to modern and industrial societal forms. While Spencer often addressed the evolution of societies from a primitive to a modern profile, he did not rely heavily on the militant-industrial typology in describing types or stages of evolutionary change. Rather, as is emphasized in Figure 3–3 on dialectical phases, the militant-industrial distinction is primarily directed at capturing the difference between highly centralized authority systems

---

[46]Decentralization is relative and does not involve an absence of regulatory control but rather less direct control when compared to militaristic systems.

where regulatory processes dominate and less centralized systems where operative processes prevail.[47] The term *industrial* does not necessarily mean industry in the sense of modern factories and markets. Instead industrial pertains to the degree of vitality and diversity in operative processes, whether these be those of a primitive or modern society. Thus both the simplest and most modern societies can be militant or industrial. Spencer hoped, of course, that modern industrial capitalism would be industrial rather than militaristic, but as we noted in the last section, Spencer saw societies as cycling in and out of centralized and decentralized phases. And this is the dynamic that the typology is meant to capture. Table 3–1 delineates the features of militant and industrial systems.

The distinction between militant and industrial societies emphasizes that during the course of social growth, differentiation, integration, and adaptive upgrading,[48] societies move in and out of militant (dominance of regulatory) and industrial (operative) phases. Militant phases consolidate the diversified operative structures of industrial phases. The causes of either a militant or industrial profile for a system at any given time are varied, but Spencer saw as critical (a) the degree of external threat from other systems and (b) the need to integrate dissimilar populations and cultures. The more threat from external systems and/or the more diverse the populations of a system (an internal threat), the more likely it is to reveal a militant profile. But once external and internal threats have been mitigated through conquest, treaties, assimilation, and other processes, then pressures for movement to an industrial profile increase. Such is the basic dynamic underlying broad evolutionary trends from a homogeneous to a heterogeneous state of social organization.

Spencer's other typology, which has received considerably less attention than the militant-industrial distinction, addresses the major stages in the evolution of societies. Whereas the militant-industrial typology seeks to capture the cyclical dynamics underlying evolutionary

---

[47]The reason for the misinterpretation of Spencer's intent resides in the fact that the typology is introduced at several points in *Principles of Sociology*. If one reads its usage in his discussion of political and industrial (economic) institutions, it would be easy to see the typology as Spencer's version of the stages of evolution. But if one reads the more analytical statement in the early chapter on social types and constitutions in volume 1, paying particular attention to the fact that this chapter precedes the one on social metamorphoses, then our interpretation is clear. And since Spencer uses another typology for describing the long-run evolutionary trends, it seems unlikely that he would duplicate this effort with yet another typology on militant-industrial societies. See, in particular, *Principles of Sociology*, vol. 1, part 2, pp. 569–80.

[48]We are using Talcott Parsons' terms here because they best connote Spencer's intent. See Parsons, *Societies*.

TABLE 3–1   Spencer's Typology of Militant and Industrial Societies

Basic System Processes	Militant	Industrial
1. Regulatory processes:		
a. Societal goals	Defense and war.	Internal productivity and provision of services.
b. Political organization	Centralized; authoritarian.	Less centralization; less direct authority on system units.
2. Operative processes:		
a. Individuals	High degrees of control by state; high levels of stratification.	Freedom from extensive controls by state; less stratification.
b. Social structures	Coordinated to meet politically established goals of war and defense.	Coordinated to facilitate each structure's expansion and growth.
3. Distributive processes:		
a. Flow of materials	From organizations to state; from state to individuals and other social units.	From organizations to other units and individuals.
b. Flow of information	From state to individuals.	Both individuals to state and state to individuals.

movement, Spencer's also attempts to describe the distinctive stages of long-term societal development, as was modeled earlier in Figure 3–2. This typology revolves around describing the pattern and direction of societal differentiation. As such, it is concerned with the processes of compounding. As was evident in Figure 3–2, Spencer marked distinctive stages of societal growth and differentiation: simple (with and without leadership), compound, double compound, and treble compound.

In Table 3–2 we have taken Spencer's more descriptive narrative and organized it in a somewhat more formal way. But the listing of characteristics for simple (both those with leaders and those without), compound, double compound, and treble compound in terms of regulatory, operative, and distributive and demographic dimensions captures the essence of Spencer's intent. Several points need to be emphasized. First, while certain aspects of Spencer's description are flawed, his summary of the distinctive stages is equal, or superior, to any that have been recently delineated by anthropologists and sociologists.[49] Second, this description is far superior to any developed by other anthropologists and sociologists of Spencer's time, whether the scholar be Tylor, Morgan, Maine, Weber, Marx, Durkheim, or any of many who developed evolutionary typologies.

Spencer sought to communicate with this typology what we can term *structural explanations.* The basic intent of this mode of explanation is to view certain types of structures as tending to coexist. As Spencer concluded:

> The inductions arrived at . . . show that in social phenomena there is a general order of co-existence and sequence; and therefore social phenomena form the subject-matter of a science reducible, in some measure at least, to the deductive form.[50]

Thus, by reading down the columns of Table 3–2, we can see that certain structures are likely to coexist within a system. And by reading across the table, the *patterns* of change in structures with each increment of societal differentiation can be observed. Moreover, as Spencer stressed, such patterns of social evolution conformed to the general law of evolution enunciated in *First Principles:*

> The many facts contemplated unite in proving that social evolution forms a part of evolution at large. Like evolving aggregates in general, societies show *integration,* both by simple increase of mass and by coalescence and re-coalescence of masses. The change from *homogeneity* to *heterogeneity* is multitudinously exemplified; up from the simple tribe, alike in all its parts, to the civilized nation, full of structural and functional unlikenesses. With progressing integration and heterogeneity goes increasing *coherence.* We see the wandering group dispersing, dividing,

---

[49]See, for example, Parsons, *Societies,* and *The System of Modern Societies* (Englewood Cliffs, N.J.: Prentice-Hall, 1971); Gerhard Lenski and Jean Lenski, *Human Societies* (New York: McGraw-Hill, 1978); and Morton H. Fried, *The Evolution of Political Society* (New York: Random House, 1967).

[50]Spencer, *Principles of Sociology,* vol. 1, part 2, p. 597.

TABLE 3–2 Spencer's Stages of Evolution

	Simple Society		Compound Society	Double Compound	Treble Compound (never formally listed)
	Headless	Headed			
Regulatory system	Temporary leaders who emerge in response to particular problems	Permanent chief and various lieutenants	Hierarchy of chiefs, with paramount chief, local chiefs, and varieties of lieutenants	Elaboration of political state; bureaucratized; differentiation between domestic and military administration	Modern political state
Operative system:					
a. Economic structure	Hunting and gathering	Pastoral; simple agriculture	Agricultural; general and local division of labor	Agriculture; extensive division of labor	Industrial capitalism
b. Religious structure	Individualized religious worship	Beginnings of religious specialists: shaman	Established ecclesiastical arrangements	Ecclesiastical hierarchy; rigid rituals and religious observance	Religious diversity in separate church structures

80

c. Family structure	Simple; sexual division of labor	Large, complex; sexual and political division of labor	Large, complex; numerous sexual, age, and political divisions	Large, complex; numerous sexual, age, and political divisions	Small, simple; decrease in sexual division of labor
d. Artistic-literary forms	Little art; no literature	Some art; no literature	Artists	Artists; literary specialists; scholars	Many artistic literary specialists; scholars
e. Law-customs	Informal codes of conduct	Informal codes of conduct	Informal codes; enforced by political elites and community members	Positive law and codes; written	Elaborate legal codes; civil and criminal
f. Community structure	Small bands of wandering families	Small, settled groupings of families	Village; permanent buildings	Large towns; permanent structures	Cities, towns, and hamlets
g. Stratification	None	Chief and followers	Five or six clear ranks	Castes; rigid divisions	Classes; less rigid
Distributive system: a. Materials	Sharing within family and band	Intra- and interfamilial exchange and sharing	Travel and trade between villages	Roads among towns; considerable travel and exchange; traders and other specialists	Roads, rail, and other nonmanual transport; many specialists

TABLE 3–2 Spencer's Stages of Evolution (*concluded*)

	Simple Society		Compound Society	Double Compound	Treble Compound *(never formally listed)*
	Headless	*Headed*			
b. Information	Oral, personal	Oral, personal	Oral, personal; at times, mediated by elites or travelers	Oral; written; edicts; oracles; teachers and other communications specialists	Oral; written; formal media structures for edicts; many communications specialists
Demographic profile:					
a. Size	Small	Larger	Larger; joining of several simple societies	Large	Large
b. Mobility	Mobile within territory	Less mobile; frequently tied to territory	Less mobility; tied to territory; movement among villages of a defined territory	Settled; much travel among towns	Settled; growing urban concentrations; much travel; movement from rural to urban centers

held together by no bonds; the tribe with parts made more coherent by subordination to a dominant man; the cluster of tribes united in a political plexus under a chief with sub-chiefs; and so on up to the civilized nation, consolidated enough to hold together for a thousand years or more. Simultaneously comes increasing *definiteness.* Social organization is at first vague; advance brings settled arrangements which grow slowly more precise; customs pass into laws which, while gaining fixity, also become more specific in their applications to varieties of actions; and all institutions, at first confusedly intermingled, slowly separate, at the same time that each within itself marks off more distinctly its component structures. Thus in all respects is fulfilled the formula of evolution. There is progress towards greater size, coherence, multiformity, and definiteness.[51]

In sum, then, Spencer provided two basic typologies for classifying societal systems. One typology—the militant-industrial distinction—is not primarily developmental or evolutionary in scope, as is too often assumed. Rather it is a typology of cyclical phases of all societies at any particular stage of evolution. The second typology is less well known but probably more important. It delineates the structural features and demographic profile of societies at different stages of evolution. In this typology is a series of statements on what structures tend to cluster together during societal growth and differentiation. This typology is, in many ways, the implicit guide for Spencer's structural and functional analysis of basic societal institutions, which comprises parts 3 through 7 in volumes 1 and 2 of *Principles of Sociology.* We should, therefore, close our review of *Principles of Sociology* by briefly noting some of the more interesting generalizations that emerge from Spencer's description of basic human institutions.

The Analysis of Societal Institutions

Fully two-thirds of *Principles of Sociology* is devoted to an evolutionary description and explanation of basic human institutions.[52] For Spencer, institutions are enduring patterns of social organization that (1) meet fundamental functional needs or requisites of human organization and (2) control the activities of individuals and groups in society. Spencer employed a "social selection" argument in his review of institutional dynamics. The most basic institutions emerge and persist because they provide a population with adaptive advantages in a given

---

[51]Ibid., p. 596.
[52]See Turner, *Herbert Spencer,* for a more detailed review of Spencer's institutional analysis.

environment, both natural and social. That is, those patterns of organization that facilitate the survival of a population in the natural environment and in the milieu of other societies will be retained or "selected"; as a consequence, these patterns will become institutionalized in the structure of a society. Since certain problems of survival always confront the organization of people, it is inevitable that among surviving populations a number of common institutions would be evident for all enduring societies—kinship, ceremony, politics, religion, and economy. Spencer discusses more than these five institutions, but our review will emphasize only these, since they provide some of the more interesting insights in Spencerian sociology.

Domestic Institutions and Kinship.[53]   Spencer argued that kinship emerges to meet the most basic need of all species: reproduction. Because a population must regulate its own reproduction before it can survive for very long, kinship was one of the first human institutions. This regulation of reproduction involves the control of sexual activity, the development of more permanent bonds between males and females, and the provision of a safe context for rearing children.

Spencer's discussion of kinship is extremely sophisticated for his time. After making the above functional arguments, Spencer embarked on an evolutionary analysis of varying types of kinship systems. While flawed in some respects, his approach was nonetheless insightful and anticipated similar arguments by twentieth-century anthropologists. Some of the more interesting generalizations emerging from his analysis include:

1. In the absence of alternative ways of organizing a population, kinship processes will become the principal mechanism of social integration.

2. The greater the size of a population without alternative ways of organizing activity, the more elaborate will be a kinship system and the more it will reveal explicit rules of descent, marriage, endogamy, and exogamy.

3. Those societies that engage in perpetual conflict will tend to create patrilineal descent systems and patriarchical authority; as a consequence, they will reveal less equality between the sexes and will be more likely to define and treat women as property.[54]

---

[53]Spencer, *Principles of Sociology*, vol. 1, part 3, pp. 603–757. See also Leonard Beeghley, "Spencer's Analysis of the Evolution of the Family and the Status of Women: Some Neglected Considerations," *Sociological Perspectives* (formerly *Pacific Sociological Review*) 26, August 1983, pp. 299–313.

[54]See Turner, *Herbert Spencer*, p. 115.

Ceremonial Institutions.[55]   Spencer recognized that human relations are structured in terms of symbols and rituals. Indeed he tended
to argue that other institutions—kinship, government, and religion—
are founded on a "preinstitutional" basis revolving around interpersonal ceremonies, such as the use of (*a*) particular forms of address,
(*b*) titles, (*c*) ritualized exchanges of greetings, (*d*) demeanors, (*e*) patterns of deference, (*f*) badges of honor, (*g*) fashion and dress, and
(*h*) other means for ordering interactions among individuals. Thus as
people interact they "present themselves" through their demeanor,
fashion, forms of talk, badges, titles, and rituals; and in so doing they
expect certain responses from others. Interaction is thereby mediated
by symbols and ceremonies that structure how individuals are to behave toward one another. Without this control of relations through
symbols and ceremonies, more macro institutional structures could not
be sustained.

Spencer was particularly interested in the effects of inequality on
ceremonial processes, especially inequalities created by centralization
of power (as is the case in the militant societies depicted in Table 3–1).
From his more detailed analysis emerges a number of interesting
generalizations:

1. The greater the degree of political centralization in a society, the
   greater will be the level of inequality; and hence the greater will be
   the concern for symbols and ceremonials demarking differences in
   rank among individuals.

2. The greater the concern over differences in rank, (*a*) the more likely
   are people in different ranks to possess distinctive objects and titles
   to mark their respective ranks and (*b*) the more likely are interactions between people in different ranks to be ritualized by standardized forms of address and stereotypical patterns of deference and
   demeanor.

3. And conversely, the less the degree of political centralization and
   level of inequality, the less are people concerned about the symbols
   and ceremonies that demark rank and regulate interaction.[56]

Political Institutions.[57]   In his analysis of political processes in society, Spencer also developed a perspective for examining social class
structures. In Spencer's view, problems of internal conflict resulting
from unbridled self-interest and the existence of hostility with other

---

[55]Spencer, *Principles of Sociology*, vol. 2, part 4, pp. 3–216.
[56]See Turner, *Herbert Spencer*, p. 122.
[57]Spencer, *Principles of Sociology*, vol. 2, part 5, pp. 229–643.

societies have been the prime causal forces behind the emergence and elaboration of government. While governments reveal considerable variability, they all evidence certain common features: (1) paramount leaders, (2) clusters of sub-leaders and administrators, (3) large masses of followers who subordinate some of their interests to the dictates of leaders, and (4) legitimating beliefs and values that give leaders "the right" to regulate others. Spencer argued that once governmental structures exist, they are self-perpetuating and will expand unless they collapse internally for lack of legitimacy or are conquered from without. In particular, war and threats of war centralize government around the use of force to conquer additional territories and internally regulate operative processes, with the result that governmental structures expand. Moreover, the expansion of government and its centralization create or exacerbate class divisions in a society, since those with resources can use them to mobilize power and political decisions that can further enhance their hold on valued resources. Thus Spencer developed a very robust political sociology; and while a listing of only a few generalizations cannot do justice to the sophistication of Spencer's approach, some of his more interesting conclusions include:

1. The larger the number of people and internal transactions among individuals in a society, the greater the size and degree of internal differentiation of government.

2. The greater the actual or potential level of conflict with other societies and within a society, the greater will be the degree of centralization of power in government.

3. The greater the centralization of power, the more visible will be class divisions and the more likely will these divisions create potential or actual internal conflict.

Religious Institutions.[58]   Spencer's analysis emphasized that all religions share certain common elements: (1) beliefs about supernatural beings and forces, (2) organized groupings of individuals who share these beliefs, and (3) ritual activities directed toward those beings and forces presumed to have the capacity to influence worldly affairs. Religions emerge in all societies, Spencer argued, because they increase the survival of a population by (a) reinforcing values and beliefs through the sanctioning power of the supernatural and (b) strengthening existing social structural arrangements, especially those revolving around power and inequality, by making them seem to be extensions of the supernatural will.

---

[58]Ibid., part 6, pp. 3–159. We should note how close this view of religious functions is to that to be developed by Émile Durkheim. See Chapter 11 of this book.

Spencer provided an interesting scenario on the evolution of religion from primitive notions of "ancestor spirits" to the highly bureaucratized monotheistic religions that currently dominate the world. Spencer saw the evolution and structural patterns of religion as intimately connected to political processes, leading him to propose the following generalizations:

1. The greater the level of war and conquest by a society, the greater are problems of consolidating diverse religious beliefs, thereby forcing the expansion of the religious class of priests to reconcile diverse religions and create polytheistic religions.

2. The greater the degree of political centralization and the level of class inequalities in a society, the more likely is the priestly class to create a coherent pantheon of ranked deities.

3. The greater the reliance of government on the priestly class to provide legitimation through a complex system of religious beliefs and symbols, the more this class can extract wealth and privilege from political leaders, thereby consolidating their distinctive class position and creating an elaborate bureaucratic structure for organizing religious activity.

4. The more centralized a government and the more it relies on religious legitimation by a privileged and bureaucratized class of priests, the greater the likelihood of a religious revolt and the creation of a simplified and monotheistic religion.

Economic Institutions.[59]   For Spencer, the long-term evolution of economic institutions revolves around (*a*) increases in technology or knowledge about how to manipulate the natural environment, (*b*) expansion of the production and distribution of goods and services, (*c*) accumulation of capital or the tools of production, and (*d*) changes in the organization of labor. In turn, these related processes are the result of efforts to achieve greater levels of adaptation to the environment and to meet constantly escalating human needs. That is, as one level of economic adaptation is created, people's needs for new products and services escalate and generate pressures for economic reorganization. Thus as new technologies, modes of production, mechanisms of distribution, forms of capital, and means for organizing labor around productive processes are developed, a more effective level of adaptation to the natural environment is achieved; and as increased adaptive capacity is established, people begin to desire more. As a result, economic production becomes less and less tied to problems of survival in the natural environment during societal evolution and ever

---

[59]Ibid., part 8, pp. 327–608.

more the result of escalating wants and desires among the members of a society.

Spencer further argued that war decreased advances in overall economic productivity, since mobilization for war distorts the economy away from domestic production toward the development of military technologies and the organization of production around military products or services. For Spencer, war depletes capital, suppresses wants and needs for consumer goods, encourages only military technologies, and mobilizes labor for wartime production (while killing off much of the productive labor force). Only during times of relative peace, then, will economic growth ensue. Such growth in the domestic economy will be particularly likely to occur when there are increases in population size. In Spencer's view escalating population size under conditions of peace creates pressure for expanded production while, at the same time, escalating needs for new kinds of products and services. These and many other lines of argument in Spencer's analysis of the economy have a highly modern flavor; but unlike his approach to other institutions, he presents few abstract generalizations, and so we will not attempt to conclude with any here.

This brief summary of Spencer's analysis of basic institutions does not do justice to the sophistication of his approach. As much as any scholar of his time, or today, Spencer saw the complex interrelationships among social structures. One reason for this sophistication in Spencer's analysis is his in-depth knowledge of diverse societies, which he acquired through the efforts of researchers hired to construct descriptions of historical and contemporary societies. Throughout Spencer's work, his ideas are illustrated by references to diverse societies. Such familiarity with many historical and contemporary societies came from his efforts to build a "descriptive sociology."

A NOTE ON SPENCER'S *DESCRIPTIVE SOCIOLOGY*

Using his inheritance and royalties, Spencer commissioned a series of volumes that sought to describe the characteristics of different societies.[60] These volumes were, in Spencer's vision, to contain no theory or supposition, but rather they were to constitute the "raw data"

---

[60]The full title of the work reads: *Descriptive Sociology, or Groups of Sociological Facts.* The list of volumes of *Descriptive Sociology* is as follows: vol. 1: *English* (1873); vol. 2: *Ancient Mexicans, Central Americans, Chibchans, Ancient Peruvians* (1874); vol. 3: *Types of Lowest Races, Negritto, and Malayo-Polynesian Races* (1874); vol. 4: *African Races* (1875); vol. 5: *Asiatic Races* (1876); vol. 6: *North and South American Races* (1878); vol. 7: *Hebrews and Phoenicians* (1880); vol. 8: *French* (1881); vol. 9: *Chinese* (1910); vol. 10: *Hellenic Greeks* (1928); vol. 11: *Mesopotamia* (1929); vol. 12: *African Races* (1930); and vol. 13: *Ancient Romans* (1934). A revised edition of volume 3, edited by D. Duncan and H. Tedder,

from which theoretical inductions could be made or by which deductions from abstract theory could be tested. These descriptions became the data source for Spencer's sociological work, particularly his *Principles of Sociology*. As he noted in the "Provisional Preface" of volume 1 of *Descriptive Sociology:*

> In preparation for *The Principles of Sociology,* requiring as bases of induction large accumulations of data, fitly arranged comparison, I . . . commenced by proxy the collection and organization of facts presented by societies of different types, past and present . . . the facts collected and arranged for easy reference and convenient study of their relations, being so presented, apart from hypotheses, as to aid all students of social science in testing such conclusions as they have drawn and in drawing others.[61]

Spencer's intent was to use common categories for classifying "sociological facts" on different types of societies. In this way he hoped that sociology would have a sound data base for developing the laws of super-organic bodies. In light of the data available to Spencer, the volumes of *Descriptive Sociology* are remarkably detailed. What is more, the categories for describing different societies are still useful. While these categories differ slightly from volume to volume, primarily because the complexity of societies varies so much, there is an effort to maintain a consistent series of categories for classifying and arranging sociological facts. Volume 1, *The English,* illustrates Spencer's approach.

First, facts are recorded for general classes of sociological variables. Thus, for *The English,* "facts" are recorded on the following:

1. Inorganic environment.
   a. General features.
   b. Geological features.
   c. Climate.
2. Organic environment.
   a. Vegetable.
   b. Animal.
3. Sociological environment.
   a. Past history.
   b. Past societies from which present system formed.
   c. Present neighbors.

---

was published in 1925; a second edition of volume 6 appeared in 1885; volume 14 is a redoing by Emil Torday of volume 4. In addition to these volumes, which are folio in size, two unnumbered works appeared: Ruben Long, *The Sociology of Islam,* 2 vols. (1931–33); and John Garstang, *The Heritage of Solomon: An Historical Introduction to the Sociology of Ancient Palestine* (1934).

[61]*The English,* classified and arranged by Herbert Spencer, compiled and abstracted by James Collier (New York: Appleton-Century-Crofts, 1873), p. vi.

4. Characteristics of people.
   a. Physical.
   b. Emotional.
   c. Intellectual.

It will be recalled that this initial basis of classification is consistent with Spencer's opening chapters in *Principles of Sociology.* (See his section on "Critical Variables.")

Second, the vast majority of *The English* is devoted to a description of the historical development of British society, from its earliest origins to Spencer's time, with respect to the following topic headings:

Division of labor	Religious ideas and superstitions
Regulation of labor	Knowledge
Domestic laws—marital	Language
Domestic laws—filial	Distribution
Political laws—criminal,	Exchange
civil, and industrial	Production
General government	Arts
Local government	Agriculture, rearing,
Military	and so forth
Ecclesiastical	Land—works
Professional	Habitations
Accessory institutions	Food
Funeral rites	Clothing
Laws of intercourse	Weapons
Habits and customs	Implements
Aesthetic sentiments	Aesthetic products
Moral sentiments	Supplementary materials

Third, for some volumes, like *The English,* more detailed descriptions under the above headings are represented in tabular form. Thus *The English* opens with a series of large and detailed tables, organized under the general headings "regulative" and "operative" as well as "structural" and "functional." The tables begin with the initial formation of the English peoples around A.D. 78 and document through a series of brief statements, organized around basic topics (see above list), up to around 1850. By reading across the tables at any given time period, the reader is given a profile of the English for that period. By reading down the columns of the table, the reader can note the patterns of change of this society.

The large, oversize volumes of *Descriptive Sociology* make fascinating reading. They are, without doubt, among the most comprehensive and detailed descriptions of human societies ever constructed, certainly surpassing that of Weber or any other comparative social scientist of the late nineteenth and early twentieth centuries. While the descriptions are flawed by the sources of data (historical accounts and travelers' published reports), Spencer's methodology is sound; and since he employed professional scholars to compile the data, they are as detailed as could be at the time. Had the volumes of *Descriptive Sociology* not lapsed into obscurity[62] and had they been updated with more accurate accounts, modern social science would, we believe, have a much firmer data base for comparative sociological analysis and for theoretical activity.

THE ENDURING LEGACY

Probably more than any scholar in this book, Spencer's ideas have been lost, at least from sociology's conscious imagination. Yet Spencerian ideas appear everywhere in modern sociology, indicating his legacy has endured in implicit and transmuted form. Some of Spencer's ideas have had to be rediscovered; others come to us through scholars such as Durkheim; and still others have become so much a part of the sociological perspective that we have forgotten their origin.

Ultimately, the mark of great theorists is the number and power of abstract "laws" about the dynamics of human organization that emerge from their texts. There are, we feel, some of sociology's most fundamental laws in Spencer's work, and so in closing we should list them in order to make explicit the enduring legacy:

1. The larger a social system, the greater will be its level of structural differentiation.

2. The greater the rate of growth of a social system, the greater its rate and degree of structural differentiation.

3. The more growth in the numbers of members in a social system is concentrated, the more likely is that growth to be accompanied by high rates of structural differentiation.

4. The more growth and differentiation at one point in time has resulted in structural integration of system units, the more likely is that system to grow and differentiate further at a subsequent point in time.

---

[62]The methodological premise and substance of Spencer's *Descriptive Sociology* was later adopted by the anthropologist George Murdock in his *Human Area Relations Files*, which, it should be emphasized, are not analytically superior to Spencer's efforts. The data for Murdock's files were obviously better than those available to Spencer and his collaborators.

5. The more a social system has initiated the process of structural differentiation, the more likely is the initial axes of differentiation to be between regulatory and operative structures.

6. The more a social system has differentiated separate regulatory and operative structures, and the greater the volume of activity in that system, the more likely are separate mediating structures involved in distributive processes to become differentiated from regulatory and operative structures.

7. The more differentiated the three major axes in a social system, the greater its integrative problems; and hence the more likely are relations of mutual interdependence and centralized authority to develop in that system.

8. The greater the degree of differentiation along the regulatory axes, the more likely is differentiation to occur initially between structures dealing with (a) the external environment and (b) internal activities; and only after the differentiation of (a) and (b) is differentiation of regulatory structures for facilitating the exchange of resources likely to occur.

9. The greater the degree of differentiation along the operative axes, the more likely are diverse activities to become spatially separated and localized.

10. The greater the degree of differentiation along the distributive axes, (a) the greater the *rate* of movement of materials and information in the system, (b) the greater the *variety* and volume of materials and information distributed in the system, and (c) the higher the *ratio* of information to materials distributed in the system.

11. The greater the degree of external environmental threat to a differentiating system, the greater the degree of internal control exercised by the regulatory system.

12. The greater the degree of threat to system stability posed by dissimilar units, the greater the degree of internal control exercised by the regulatory system.

13. The greater the degree of control by the regulatory system, the more growth and differentiation of operative and distributive structures are circumscribed by the narrow goals of the regulatory system.

14. The more operative and distributive structures are circumscribed by centralized regulatory structures, the more likely are they, over time, to resist such control; and the more they resist, the more likely is centralized control to decrease.

15. The less operative and distributive processes are circumscribed by centralized regulatory structures, the greater are problems of internal integration, and the more likely is the regulatory system to increase efforts at centralized control.

16. The greater the degree of structural differentiation in a system, and the greater its level of internal integration, then the greater its adaptive capacity to diverse environments.

CHAPTER 4

The Origin and Context of Karl Marx's Thought

BIOGRAPHICAL INFLUENCES ON MARX'S THOUGHT

Karl Marx, theorist and revolutionary, was born to Heinrich and Henrietta Marx on May 5, 1818, in the city of Trier. Located in the Rhineland in what is now Western Germany, Trier was (and is) the commercial center of the Moselle wine-growing area. Descended from a long line of rabbis on both sides of the family, the young Marx lived in a stable bourgeois (or middle-class) household. His father, a lawyer and lover of ideas, converted to Lutheranism in 1817 in order to protect his position. Although Jewish by heritage, the elder Marx appears to have had little interest in organized religion, being attracted to the deism characteristic of the Enlightenment. The young Marx was apparently close to his father and learned of Voltaire, Rousseau, and other writers on individualism and human progress from him.

As Marx grew up, he was also influenced by an upper-class Prussian, Ludwig von Wesphalen, whose daughter Jenny he eventually married. Despite status differences between the two families, von Wesphalen took a liking to Marx, encouraging him to read and introducing him to the great German writers of the time, Johann Goethe and Johann Shiller, as well as to the classical Greek philosophers.

This intellectual background paved the way for his subsequent study of the philosophy of G. W. F. Hegel and the political economy of Adam Smith, leading eventually to a theoretical critique of the capitalist social order. Just as important, however, these aspects of his background made Marx peculiar among nineteenth-century revolutionaries, for he was neither thwarted nor persecuted as a young man.[1] Thus, while he was arrogant, vain, and vindictive toward enemies, Marx was also positive and self-confident throughout his adult life.

---

[1]Isaiah Berlin, *Karl Marx: His Life and Environment* (New York: Oxford University Press, 1963), p. 33.

Hegel and the Young Hegelians

After graduating from the Trier gymnasium (or high school), the seventeen-year-old Marx enrolled at the University of Bonn in 1835. After a year, however, he left for the more cosmopolitan and sophisticated University of Berlin. Here Marx came into contact with Hegel's idealism. The great philosopher, who had only recently died, dominated intellectual life in Germany at that time. Marx also met youthful academic interpreters of Hegel, who called themselves Young Hegelians. Marx's association with them constituted his first contact with people who did not blindly accept the dominant values and norms of German society.

The Young Hegelians, including such forgotten men as Max Stirner, Bruno Bauer, David Strauss, and Ludwig Feuerbach, saw themselves as radicals. And they were, in fact, irreligious and liberal; they were what we might today call hippies who questioned the established order in Prussia (where Berlin was located). Marx noted their influence on him in a now famous letter to his father. "There are moments in one's life," he wrote, "which are like frontier posts marking the completion of a period but at the same time clearly indicating a new direction." After studying Hegel's idealism, he continued, "I arrived at the point of seeking the idea in reality itself."[2]

The last phrase is important, for Marx was asserting that he now rejected Hegel's idealism in favor of studying "reality itself," as defined by the Young Hegelians. In effect he had begun to question the status quo. He had also begun the long process of transforming philosophy into social science. This transition, however, occurred in a very despotic social context. During most of the nineteenth century, Prussia was perhaps the most repressive nation in Europe, with organized religion supporting the state's activities. Those who questioned the established order, religious or political, were treated as subversive. Hence over time the Young Hegelians saw their writings censored and found themselves dismissed from faculty positions.

Nonetheless, the young Marx prepared himself for a life in academia. In addition to studying philosophy, he wrote hundreds of poems, a novel, a play modeled after a Greek tragedy, and much more. In 1841 Marx received a doctorate based on a thesis titled "The Difference between the Democritean and Epicurean Philosophy of Nature."[3]

---

[2]Karl Marx, "Discovering Hegel" (Marx's letter to his father), in *The Marx-Engels Reader*, ed. Robert C. Tucker (New York: W. W. Norton, 1978), pp. 7–9.

[3]Karl Marx, "The Difference between the Democritean and Epicurean Philosophy of Nature," in *Activity in Marx's Philosophy*, ed. Norman D. Livergood (The Hague: Martinus-Nighoff, 1967), pp. 57–109.

Unfortunately, his academic patrons had been dismissed from their posts and were unable to obtain a position for him. Marx was thus left without career prospects.

Lacking alternatives, Marx tried journalism, becoming a writer for—and eventually editor of—a liberal newspaper, the *Rheinisch Zeitung* (or *Rhineland News*). In this role he battled the Prussian censors constantly, writing articles on the poverty of the Moselle valley winegrowers, the harsh legal treatment received by peasants who stole timber to heat their homes in winter, and the repressiveness of various European governments. Within six months the Prussian authorities suppressed the paper and Marx was out of work, a situation that recurred frequently during his life. In the aftermath he turned again to studying Hegel. The result was "A Contribution to the Critique of Hegel's *Philosophy of Right*."[4] Although unpublished at the time, this essay constitutes Marx's decisive break with Hegel's idealism, particularly its religious and philosophical justification of the political status quo in Germany.

Paris and Brussels

Marx, now married to Jenny von Westphalen, moved to Paris in 1843. He was twenty-five years old. As Paris was the intellectual center of Europe at that time, the years Marx spent there allowed him to meet many radicals and revolutionaries: the Russian Michael Bakunin, the poet Heinrich Heine, and the tailor Wilhelm Weitling, among others. In addition Marx came into contact with the emerging discipline of political economy during this period, reading Adam Smith, David Ricardo, Pierre Proudhon, and many more. Perhaps most important, however, in September 1844 Marx met the man who became his lifelong friend and partner: Friedrich Engels. The son of a wealthy German industrialist, Engels wrote the first great urban ethnography, *The Condition of the Working Class in England in 1844*, along with an essay, "Outlines of a Critique of Political Economy," during this same period.[5] These works helped Marx to see the new urban working class, the proletarians, as real human beings with practical problems made worse by the systematic exploitation characteristic of capitalism at that time.

---

[4]Karl Marx, "A Contribution to the Critique of Hegel's *Philosophy of Right*," in Tucker, ed., *Marx-Engels Reader*, pp. 16–26, 53–66.

[5]Friedrich Engels, *The Condition of the Working Class in England* (Stanford, Calif.: Stanford University Press, 1968). The current translation omits the year 1844 from the title. Friedrich Engels, "Outlines of a Critique of Political Economy," in *The Economic and Philosophic Manuscripts*, ed. Karl Marx (New York: International, 1964), pp. 197–228.

One result was that Marx now rejected the ideas of the Young Hegelians as politically timid. In fact, the first product of his collaboration with Engels, a pompous and nearly unreadable tome titled *The Holy Family,* consisted of a diatribe against the Young Hegelians.[6] As we will discuss later, of all the Young Hegelians, only Feuerbach had a long-term impact on Marx's work. Another, more significant result was that Marx wrote a series of notebooks, the now famous *Economic and Philosophic Manuscripts,* in which he set forth his initial interpretation of capitalism as inherently exploitive and alienating.[7] In 1845 Marx was forced to leave Paris by the French government, and he moved to Brussels.

Shortly after arriving in Brussels, Marx and Engels wrote *The German Ideology,* a more effective work, which they intended as a final settling of accounts with the Young Hegelians. According to Marx and Engels, the German philosophers were less concerned with "reality itself" than with ideas about reality. They had not, in other words, really rejected Hegel. Although we will describe the theoretical implications of *The German Ideology* in the next chapter, Marx and Engels used the opportunity to poke fun at Stirner, Bauer, and the others, as in the following example.

> Once upon a time an honest fellow had the idea that men were drowned in water only because they were possessed with the idea of gravity. If they were to knock this idea out of their heads, say, by stating it to be a superstition, a religious idea, they would be sublimely safe against any danger from water. His whole life long he fought against the illusion of gravity, of whose harmful results all statistics brought him new and manifold evidence. This honest fellow was the prototype of the German revolutionary philosophers of our day.[8]

In contrast to the Young Hegelians, Marx now saw himself as a true revolutionary, dedicated to the overthrow of capitalist society—violently if necessary. Thus he and Engels joined with other European émigrés and radicals in a variety of revolutionary organizations: the League of the Just, the German Workers' Educational Association, the Communist League, and the International Working Man's Association. Both Marx and Engels were dominating personalities, determined to lead working-class people toward a revolutionary reorganization of society. Here is a prophetic description of Marx by Paul Annenkov, a Russian who knew him during these years.

---

[6]Karl Marx and Friedrich Engels, *The Holy Family* (Moscow: Foreign Languages Publishing House, 1956).

[7]Marx, *Economic and Philosophic Manuscripts.*

[8]Karl Marx and Friedrich Engels, *The German Ideology* (New York: International, 1947), p. 3.

He was most remarkable in his appearance. He had a shock of deep black hair and hairy hands and his coat was buttoned wrong; but he looked like a man with the right and the power to demand respect, no matter how he appeared before you and no matter what he did. His movements were clumsy but confident and self-reliant, his ways defied the usual conventions in human relations, but they were dignified and somewhat disdainful; his sharp metallic voice was wonderfully adapted to the radical judgments that he passed on persons and things. He always spoke in imperative words that would brook no contradiction and were made all the sharper by the almost painful impression of the tone which ran through everything he said. This tone expressed the firm conviction of his mission to dominate men's minds and prescribe them their laws. Before me stood the embodiment of a democratic dictator such as one might imagine in a daydream.[9]

In 1847 Marx and Engels decided to compose a statement of revolutionary principles under the aegis of the Communist League. Accordingly, Engels wrote an initial draft in catechism form titled "Principles of Communism" and sent it to Marx.[10] During the early days of 1848, Marx completely rewrote the draft and, while the final version incorporated many of Engels's ideas, the document printed in February of that year was strikingly different and original: *The Communist Manifesto.*[11] Although it had little immediate impact, the publication of the *Manifesto* occurred at a time of great political ferment in Europe. Many observers, not all of them radicals, believed that some form of communist revolution was inevitable in Western European societies. Later that year, revolts broke out all over the continent. In Paris, for example, workers held the city against the onslaught of the French army for six weeks. Ultimately, however, the workers and peasants were defeated throughout Europe, often after bloody battles. In 1849 Marx returned to Paris, still (like many others) believing that a communist insurrection was imminent. Subsequently, under pressure from the French government, he left for London, where he lived the remainder of his life.

The London Years

Now thirty years old, Marx withdrew from public life altogether for about fifteen years, concentrating instead on devising his theoretical analysis of capitalism. Toward this end he studied and wrote copiously, producing notebook after notebook of observations about the

---

[9]Quoted in David McLellen, *Karl Marx: His Life and Thought* (New York: Harper & Row, 1973), p. 452.

[10]Friedrich Engels, "Principles of Communism," in *The Birth of the Communist Manifesto,* ed. Dirk Struik (New York: International, 1971), pp. 169–92.

[11]The edition we are using is reprinted in Struik, ed., *Birth of the Communist Manifesto,* pp. 85–126.

nature of capitalist societies and criticism of economics as then practiced. These materials, almost all unpublished at the time, eventually appeared as *The Grundrisse* (or *Notebooks*), *The Theory of Surplus Value*, and *A Contribution to the Critique of Political Economy*.[12] Finally, Marx's greatest book appeared in 1867, when he was forty-nine years old: *Capital*, volume 1.[13]

Although he intended to produce a multi-volume work, only volume 1 appeared at the time, and it usually stands alone as a theoretical analysis of capitalism. While Engels subsequently edited and published the second and third volumes, he observed that the first "is in a great measure a whole in itself and has for more than twenty years ranked as an independent work."[14] As we will explain in the next chapter, *Capital* is more than a narrow work of economics; it is, rather, a theoretical analysis of capitalist social systems.

This tremendous quantity of work, however, did not bring in much money. Although Marx's income was adequate, neither he nor Jenny could manage money very well, with the result that the family lived in constant financial peril through most of these years. During much of this period, Marx served as European correspondent for the New York *Daily Tribune*, and the income from these articles constituted his main source of financial support. In addition, Engels, who benefited from an inheritance, periodically sent Marx money or ghostwrote articles for the *Tribune*. Apart from their economic circumstances and the death of two children in infancy, however, Marx and his family appear to have enjoyed a settled and happy life during these years. Only after the death of his mother in 1863 and the receipt of a bequest from socialist Wilhelm Wolff did Marx's financial worries decline.

Although aloof from public life during the years in London, Marx, like many radicals, still believed that economic crises would produce some form of workers' revolt. In 1864 the International Working Man's Association was formed in London. Composed of working people from most European nations, the organization proposed to destroy the capitalist system and substitute some form of collective control of the society. Abandoning his long reticence, Marx joined the group and, characteristically, quickly became its dominating force. Apart from ongoing work on *Capital*, all his energies were devoted to the International (as it was called). One side benefit, perhaps intended, was that

---

[12]Karl Marx, *The Grundrisse* (New York: Random House, 1973); *The Theory of Surplus Value* (Moscow: Foreign Languages Publishing House, 1963); *A Contribution to the Critique of Political Economy* (New York: International, 1970). Only the last was published in Marx's lifetime, in 1859.

[13]Karl Marx, *Capital*, vol. 1 (New York: International, 1967).

[14]Friedrich Engels, "Preface to the First English Edition," in Marx, *Capital*, vol. 1, p. 5.

Capital received considerable publicity. Unlike Marx's previous works, which had been generally ignored, *Capital* was widely read and quickly translated into French, Russian, English, and Italian—with Marx supervising these efforts. Aside from this activity, Marx immersed himself in political life, attempting to show how theory and revolution can be combined in practice.

In 1871 the long-awaited workers' revolt occurred in the aftermath of the Franco-Prussian War. As in 1848, however, the proletarians were suppressed, again with much loss of life. At this time Marx produced his last great political pamphlet, *The Civil War in France*, in which he defended the Paris workers protesting the government.[15] Soon afterward the International split apart and ceased to exist. It was to be Marx's last effective political role.

In the years after 1870, Marx finally achieved a really comfortable lifestyle. Engels, very wealthy by this time, gave him a bequest, and he settled into the life of a Victorian gentleman—albeit a radical one. A famous man, revered by socialists and revolutionaries around the world, Marx was sought out for advice by those who would defend the rights of working people. But he wrote far less and without much creativity. It was as if relative prosperity robbed Marx of his anger, the source of his insight.

Jenny's death in 1881 deprived Marx of his lifelong companion. His oldest daughter, also named Jenny, followed in January 1883. On March 14 of that same year, Marx died in his armchair. He was sixty-five years old.

Karl Marx's analysis of capitalism represents one of the most striking and original achievements in the history of social thought. As we will show in Chapter 5, he constructed a theoretical analysis that sought to account for the origins of capitalism, its historical stability, and its eventual demise. In the process he combined social theory and revolutionary action in a way that has never been duplicated. That his work is shortsighted in some respects and misbegotten in others does not detract from its evocativeness. Yet, like all scholars, Marx benefited from the legacy of concepts and ideas that had been advanced by others.

Marx was a voracious reader, and his writings are filled with detailed analyses of the philosophers and political economists of the day. In the remainder of this chapter, we sketch the ways in which Marx was influenced by Hegel, Ludwig Feuerbach, and the Young Hegelians, Adam Smith and the other capitalist political economists, and Friedrich Engels.

---

[15]Karl Marx, "The Civil War in France," in Karl Marx and Friedrich Engels, *Selected Works*, vol. 2 (Moscow: Progress Publishers, 1969), pp. 178–244.

G. W. F. HEGEL AND KARL MARX

The origin of Marx's sociological theory lies in his youthful reaction to the writings of George William Friedrich Hegel. In four main books, *The Phenomenology of Mind* (1807), *The Science of Logic* (1816), *The Encyclopedia of Philosophy* (1817), and *The Philosophy of Right* (1821), Hegel developed one of the most original, complex, and obscure philosophical doctrines ever devised.[16] Marx transformed Hegel's philosophy into an empirically based social science, albeit a peculiar one, in which Hegel's idealism is decisively rejected while his reliance on dialectical analysis is retained and applied to the material world. To appreciate Hegel's influence on Marx, we need to briefly discuss idealist philosophy and Marx's major criticisms of it. Only then will the continuity and discontinuity between the two men's ideas become clear.

Hegel's Idealism

In Hegel's writing, idealism is a complex philosophical doctrine that can only be superficially sketched here. The essence of idealism consists in the denial that things in the finite world—such as trees, houses, people, or any other physical object—are ultimately real. In Hegel's words, idealism "consists in nothing else than in recognizing that the finite has no veritable being."[17] For Hegel, true reality is embodied in that which is discovered through reason. In thus emphasizing the importance of thought, Hegel followed a philosophical tradition that originated with Plato. From this point of view, the objects perceived by the senses are not real: They are merely the phenomenal appearance of a more ultimate reality of ideas. Only "logical objects," or concepts, constitute ultimate reality. As Hegel wrote, "it is *only* in thought that [an] object is truly in and for itself; in intuition or ordinary perception it is only an appearance."[18] Hegel continued by asserting that if only concepts are real, then the ultimate concept is God, and his philosophy is essentially an attempt at proving the existence of God through the application of reason. According to Hegel, previous philosophers had seen only finite things as real and had relegated the infinite (or God) to the "mere 'ideal.'" He argued that his separation is artificial and cannot show how God exists and acts through people, since it involves a logical impossibility: Finite things, which must

---

[16]G. W. F. Hegel, *The Phenomenology of Mind* (New York: Macmillan, 1961); *The Science of Logic* (London: Allen & Unwin, 1969); *The Encyclopedia of Philosophy* (New York: Philosophical Library, 1959); and *The Philosophy of Right* (Oxford: Clarendon Press, 1942).

[17]Hegel, *Science of Logic*, p. 154.

[18]Ibid., p. 585 (emphasis in original).

inevitably perish, remain; while the infinite, which is absolute and cannot perish, is kept separate and placed in an abstract and mentally conceived beyond. If this latter were true, Hegel argued, then God could not have come to earth in the form of Jesus, and the bread and wine of the Last Supper were merely bread and wine.

Hegel argued that there is an inherent dialectical relationship between God (the infinite) and people (the finite). The essence of the dialectic is contradiction: Each concept implies its opposite or, in Hegel's terms, each concept implies its negation. Thus, after proposing that "the finite has no veritable being," Hegel immediately said, "the finite is ideal"—that is, its essence lies in that which contradicts it: the infinite, God. In this way the finite world of flesh and blood is annihilated (at least in thought) and "the infinite can pass over from the beyond to the here and now; that is, become flesh and take on earthly attire," as Jesus did a long time ago.[19] Hence while this phrase states the issue too simply, Hegel believed human history can be considered the autobiography of God, since it only "exists" through its negation by the infinite and the latter's manifestations in this world. Yet, as in Christianity, even as the finite world of things is destroyed, it is saved. In Hegel's words, "the finite has vanished in the infinite and what *is*, is only the *infinite*," or everlasting life.[20] One implication of this analysis is a belief in the reality of transubstantiation. Another implication, which is also characteristic of some forms of Christianity, is a relatively passive acceptance of the political status quo. For example, Hegel said "all that is real is rational; and all that is rational is real."[21] Statements like this were taken by many as a sanctification of the Prussian state, with its despotism, police government, star chamber proceedings, and censorship. Hence the Prussian government glorified Hegel's philosophy for its own purposes and, when he died, gave him a state funeral.

Marx's Rejection of Hegel's Idealism

Marx reacted strongly against Hegel's idealism, criticizing it in a number of ways. First, and most important, he completely rejected Hegel's assertion that finite or empirical phenomena are not ultimately real. All his other criticisms follow from this basic point. Marx believed

---

[19]Lucio Colletti, *Marxism and Hegel* (Atlantic Highlands, N.J.: Humanities Press, 1973), p. 12. This is a good Marxist source. One of the best non-Marxist commentaries is John N. Findlay, *Hegel: A Re-Examination* (London: Allen & Unwin, 1958).

[20]Hegel, *Logic of Science*, p. 138 (emphasis in original).

[21]Quoted in Friedrich Engels, "Ludwig Feuerbach and the End of Classical German Philosophy," in Marx and Engels, *Selected Works*, vol. 3, p. 337.

that when empirical phenomena are only understood as thoughts, then people's more significant practical problems are ignored. Neither material objects nor relationships can be changed by merely thinking about them. The puerile quality of Hegel's point is evident, Marx suggested, in a simple example: If people are alienated such that they have no control over their lives or the material things produced by their labor, they cannot end their alienation by changing their perception of reality (or by praying, for that matter).[22] Rather people must change the social structure in which they live—that is, they must make a revolution in this world rather than wait for the next. Marx believed life in this world posed a variety of very practical problems that people could only solve in hard-headed ways, and human reason is of little use unless it is applied to the problems that exist in the finite world.

Second, according to Marx, Hegel's emphasis on the ultimate reality of thought led him to misperceive some of the essential characteristics of human beings. For example, Marx charged that while Hegel correctly "grasps labor as the essence of man," "the only labor which [he] knows and recognizes is abstractly mental labor."[23] Yet people have physical needs, Marx noted, such as for food, clothing, and shelter, which can only be satisfied by productive activity in the finite world. Hence, for Marx, the most significant labor is productive activity rather than mental activity. Similarly, Marx said that Hegel's belief in the unreality of finite things led him to a position in which people are regarded as nonobjective, spiritual beings. But Marx asserted that people are "natural beings"—that is, they have physical needs that can only be satisfied in this world.

> As a natural, corporeal, sensuous, objective being [a person] is a suffering, conditioned and limited creature, like animals and plants. That is to say, the objects of his instincts exist outside him, as objects independent of him; yet these objects are objects that he needs—essential objects, indispensable to the manifestation and confirmation of his essential powers. To say that man is a corporeal, living, real, sensuous, objective being full of natural vigor is to say that he has real, sensuous, objects as the objects of his being or of his life, or that he can only express his life in real sensuous objects.[24]

Marx's third criticism is also an outgrowth of the first in that he rejected the religious motif that pervades Hegel's work. As noted above, Hegel denied reality to the finite world in order to prove the existence of God, albeit a Christian God. But Marx believed that when

---

[22]Marx, *Economic and Philosophical Manuscripts*, p. 175.
[23]Ibid., p. 177.
[24]Ibid., p. 181.

"reason" is applied to such impractical problems, people are prevented from recognizing that they are exploited and that they have an interest in changing the status quo in this world. For Marx, the next world was a religious fantasy not worth worrying about. Thus he was particularly vitriolic, yet strangely poetic, in his denunciation of the religious implications of Hegel's philosophy.

> Religion is the sigh of the oppressed creature, the sentiment of a heartless world, and the soul of soulless conditions. It is the opium of the people. The abolition of religion as the illusory happiness of men, is a demand for their real happiness. The call to abandon their illusions about their conditions is a call to abandon a condition which requires illusions. The criticism of religion is, therefore, the embryonic criticism of this vale of tears of which religion is the halo.[25]

Marx believed one of the main functions of religion is to blind people so they cannot realistically evaluate their true situation and interests. Religion does this by emphasizing that compensation for misery and exploitation on earth will come in the next world.

Marx's fourth criticism of Hegel is that idealism is politically conservative rather than revolutionary. It creates the illusion of a community of people rather than the reality of a society riddled with opposing interests. This illusion results in part from Hegel's assertion that the state, a practical and physical entity, emerges out of the Spirit, or thought. In this way Hegel imbued the state with a sacred quality. As Marx noted, Hegel "does not say 'with the will of the monarch lies the final decision' but 'the final decision of the will is—the monarch.' "[26] When the state is sacred, then history can be seen as part of an overall divine plan that is not only reasonable but necessary. For this reason Marx interpreted Hegel's philosophy as politically conservative.

Marx's Acceptance of Hegel's Dialectical Method

Despite his complete rejection of idealism, Marx saw a significant tool in Hegel's use of the dialectic. But in Hegel's hands, the entire analysis is couched in terms of a mystical theology. Thus, as Marx noted in *Capital*, Hegel's dialectic "is standing on its head. It must be turned right side up again, if you would discover the rational kernal within the mystical shell."[27] As we will show in Chapter 5, the process

---

[25]Marx, "Contribution to the Critique of Hegel's *Philosophy of Right*," p. 54.

[26]Quoted in Sidney Hook, *From Hegel to Marx* (Ann Arbor: University of Michigan Press, 1962), p. 23.

[27]Marx, *Capital*, p. 20.

by which Marx turned the dialectic right side up involved its application to the finite world where people make history by producing their sustenance from the environment. Rather than being concerned with the existence of God, Marx emphasized that the focus must be on concrete societies (seen as social systems) and with actual people who have conflicting interests.

The significance of turning Hegel "right side up" is that, for Marx, no product of human thought or action can be final; there can be no absolute truth that, when discovered, needs only be memorized. From this point of view, science can only increase knowledge, it cannot discover absolute knowledge. Moreover, there can be no end to human history, at least in the sense of attaining an unchanging utopia, a perfect society. Such social structures can only exist in the imagination. Rather every society is only a transitory state in an endless course of human development. This development occurs as conflict is systematically generated out of people's opposing interests. While each stage of history is necessary, and hence justified in terms of the conditions in which it originated, progress occurs as the old society inevitably loses its reason for being. In Marx's work, the dialectical method means that nothing can be final or absolute or sacred: Everything is transitory, and conflict is everywhere.

LUDWIG FEUERBACH AND KARL MARX

As emphasized earlier, Marx's sociology was also affected by the Young Hegelians. The most important influence among them was unquestionably Ludwig Feuerbach. In this section we outline some of the Young Hegelians' ideas and suggest how Feuerbach's ideas altered the direction of Marx's thought.

The Young Hegelians and Marx's Thought

Like Hegel, the Young Hegelians tried to understand the nature of reality and the relationship between religious beliefs and reality. However, since religion legitimated oppressive political conditions, the Young Hegelians rejected the political conservatism that seemed inherent to Hegel's thought. They reacted in this way partly because of the social conditions in which they lived, since during most of the nineteenth century Prussia was an extremely repressive nation. And in Prussia religion served as one of the chief pillars of the state. The Young Hegelians believed the church's emphasis on the sanctity of tradition, authority, and the renunciation of wordly pleasures helped to prop up an oppressive governmental apparatus. But since political agitation was not possible (without being arrested or expatriated), the

Young Hegelians sought to criticize the state indirectly by investigating the sacred texts, doctrines, and practices of Christianity.

For example, in 1835 David Strauss published *The Life of Jesus Critically Examined*, in which he tried to show that the Gospels are not accurate historical narratives.[28] This book prompted great controversy, since if the life of Jesus as portrayed in the Gospels is not to be believed, then the authority of the church is seemingly undermined. Shortly thereafter, Bruno Bauer published a series of articles in which he denied the historical existence of Jesus altogether and tried to explain the Gospels as works of pure fiction.[29] By debunking the nature and logic of Christian tenets (and hence the church) in this way, the Young Hegelians hoped also to impugn the authority of the state. However, the Prussian government recognized the seditious implications of these works, and as a result the Young Hegelians suffered varying degrees of surveillance, political harassment, and dismissal from their university posts.

Nonetheless, despite their political stance, all these men were still Hegelian in orientation, and this fact eventually led to Marx's split with them. For example, in *The Ego and His Own: The Case of the Individual Against Authority* (1844), Max Stirner argued that nothing is objective outside the individual.[30] According to Stirner, social institutions, such as the church, are oppressive to the individual's spirit. Like a true Hegelian, Stirner then asserted that reality is not based on people's sense perceptions. As for Hegel, reality is created by the imagination and will of each person and, as a corollary, there is no objective reality apart from the ego. Thus, according to Stirner, individuals should avoid participating in the society as much as possible, and in this way they can avoid being oppressed by authority. With this argument, Stirner anticipated the development of anarchist thought some years later. Marx, however, believed Stirner's position was politically futile, since social institutions must be controlled rather than ignored.

As will be seen in our discussion of *The German Ideology* in Chapter 5, Marx believed the Young Hegelians were intellectual mountebanks, and he wrote hundreds of pages of vituperation against them. For example, he and Engels made fun of Stirner, Bauer, and others by calling them "The Holy Family" and referring to them as "Saint Max" and "Saint Bruno." More generally, Marx developed four main criticisms of

---

[28]David Strauss, *The Life of Jesus Critically Examined* (London: Swan Sonneschein, 1902).

[29]On Bauer, see Hook, *From Hegel to Marx*.

[30]Max Stirner, *The Ego and His Own: The Case of the Individual against Authority* (New York: Libertarian Book Club, 1963).

progression of ideas never proceeds apart from human practices

the Young Hegelians, all of which can be seen as variations on his criticisms of Hegel. First, their writings treated the development of theology independently of the actual activities of the church and other social institutions that were pervaded by theological ideas. Such an emphasis ignored the fact that the development of ideas never proceeds apart from human practices. Second, the Young Hegelians were essentially idealists in that the origin of religious as well as other kinds of thought was to be found in the Spirit. But for Marx, religion and all other ideas emerge from people's actual social relationships and in their need to survive. Third, the Young Hegelians' writings were fatalistic in that the historical process was seen as automatic and inexorable, either because it was directed by the Spirit or because it was directed by individuals (such as the Prussian king) who were somehow connected with the Spirit. For Marx, while history has direction and continuity, it can also be shaped by human action. Fourth, and most fundamental, the Young Hegelians foolishly believed that by changing ideas they could change human behavior. Therefore they fought a war against the state, using words as the primary weapons. Wars must be fought with guns, Marx believed, and those who do not recognize this elementary fact are very unrealistic. There is one exception to his indictment of the Young Hegelians, however. The only member of the group whom Marx did not vilify, even though the two men disagreed, was Ludwig Feuerbach.

human action can shape history

Feuerbach and Marx's Thought

Like the other Young Hegelians, Feuerbach was also interested in the religious implications of Hegel's philosophy; but unlike the others, Feuerbach fundamentally altered the direction of Marx's thought. This occurred in terms of Marx's critique of Hegel and in the development of Marx's peculiar but highly effective version of social theory.

In his book *The Essence of Christianity* (1841), Feuerbach undercut both Hegel's and the Young Hegelians' writings by arguing that religious beliefs arise out of people's unconscious deification of themselves.[31] According to Feuerbach, human beings have taken all that they believe is good in themselves and simply projected these characteristics onto God. He showed how the "mysteries" of Christianity— the mysteries of the Creation, the suffering God, the Holy Trinity, the Immaculate Conception, the Resurrection, and the like—all represent human ideals. Thus Feuerbach argued that theology is simply a

---

[31]Ludwig Feuerbach, *The Essence of Christianity* (New York: Harper & Row, 1957).

mythical vision of human aspirations and that "what man praises
and approves, that is God to him; what he blames [and] condemns is
the nondivine."[32] The true essence of religion, Feuerbach believed,
was to be found in anthropology, not theology, for "religion is man's
earliest . . . form of self-knowledge."[33]

This analysis revealed Feuerbach to be the most original of the
Young Hegelians. While most of them were content to analyze and
critique Christian theology, Feuerbach decisively rejected any analysis
that treated theology as existing independently of empirical activities.
Moreover, while many Young Hegelians still accepted the idea that
God necessarily directed human affairs, Feuerbach argued that an abstract and amorphous Spirit cannot be the guiding force in history,
since people are simply worshipping projections of their own characteristics and desires. Finally, while the other Young Hegelians continued to be mired in idealism, Feuerbach was a materialist in the sense
that he believed people's consciousness of the world is the product of
their brains and hence of physical matter. To Marx and others, this
position seemed clearsighted after the obfuscations and puerile logic
of Hegel, Strauss, Bauer, and Stirner.

Feuerbach's argument had yet another consequence for Marx. In
Feuerbach's work, Marx found the key to criticizing Hegel and, ultimately, to developing a social theory designed to promote revolutionary action. Marx realized that Feuerbach's analysis of religion as an
expression of human desires could be generalized to people's relationships to other social institutions (especially the state) and, in fact, to
any situation in which human beings are ruled by their own creations.
Thus, following Feuerbach, Marx reversed Hegel's argument, which asserted that the state emerges from the spirit, by arguing that the modern state emerged out of capitalist social relationships (which he called
"civil society"). This argument has important implications, for if the
state is the product of human action, then it can be changed by human
action. Marx's mature social theory follows from this fundamental
insight.

ADAM SMITH AND KARL MARX

By the late eighteenth century, England had already become a relatively industrialized and commercial nation. As such, it constituted
the first fully capitalist society, with the result that scholars attempted
to account for the origins of capitalism, its nature, and its future devel-

---

[32]Quoted in Hook, *From Hegel to Marx*, p. 246.
[33]Feuerbach, *Essence of Christianity*, p. 13.

opment. Such men as Adam Smith, David Ricardo, and many others developed a new mode of analysis, called political economy, and sought to understand the characteristics of industrial capitalism. After being introduced to the study of political economy by Friedrich Engels and others, Marx began to deal with the topics characteristic of the new discipline. For example, in *The Economic and Philosophical Manuscripts* he analyzed (among other things) the origin of the value of commodities, the origin of profit, the role of land in a capitalist economy, and the accumulation of capital. However, his most detailed analyses and criticisms did not occur until the 1850s in his notebooks (subsequently published as the *Grundrisse*) and *A Contribution to a Critique of Political Economy.* From these efforts Marx's great work, *Capital,* eventually emerged.

Political Economy and Marx's Thought

Marx's detailed analyses of various political economists are less important today than his more general criticisms of their works. In his opinion, the literature in political economy displayed two fundamental defects. First, capitalist social relations were assumed to reflect "irrefutable natural laws of society." As a result of this emphasis, basic types of social relations, such as exchange, exploitation, and alienation, were all assumed (at least by implication) to be historically immutable. Second, the political economists analyzed each part of society separately, as if it had no connection with anything else.[34] For example, even such strictly economic categories as production, exchange, distribution, and consumption were generally treated as if they were separate and unconnected phenomena. But Marx had learned from Hegel and Feuerbach that history has a dialectical pattern to it. As a result, Marx saw capitalism as a historically unique pattern of social relationships that would inevitably be supplanted in the future. Thus he set himself the task of developing a scientific analysis of capitalist society that could account for both its pattern of development and its eventual demise.

While Marx regarded most political economists as simply bourgeois ideologues, he believed Adam Smith and David Ricardo were the two most objective and insightful observers of the economics of capitalism. In the course of analyzing their work, many of Marx's fundamental insights into the dynamics of capitalism emerged. For illustrative purposes, we focus here on Smith's work.

---

[34]Marx, "Introduction," in *Contribution to the Critique of Political Economy,* pp. 188–217.

Adam Smith and Marx's Thought

Adam Smith was a moral philosopher as well as a political economist. In his first book, *The Theory of Moral Sentiments,* originally published in 1759, Smith argued that there is a natural order to the world, including both its physical and social aspects, that was created by God and carefully balanced so as to benefit all species.[35] Hence Smith emphasized the beneficent qualities of the natural order and the general inadequacy of human institutions that tried to change or alter this order. His subsequent book, *An Inquiry into the Nature and Causes of the Wealth of Nations,* published in 1776, represented Smith's attempt at applying the principles of naturalism to the problems of political economy.[36]

The Wealth of Nations focuses on three main issues. First, Smith wanted to discover the "laws of the market" holding society together. In dealing with this issue, he hoped to show both the way in which commodities acquired value and why this value included profit for the capitalist. Second, Smith wanted to understand the laws of evolution characteristic of capitalist society. Third, like most work in political economy (at least according to Marx), *The Wealth of Nations* is a thoroughgoing defense of capitalist society, a defense Marx was to find inadequate. Each of these facets of Smith's work is briefly analyzed below.

Laws of the Market.   Smith's attempt at showing how the economic laws of the market hold society together begins with the assertion that people act out of self-interest when they produce commodities for other members of the society to purchase. For "it is not from the benevolence of the butcher, brewer, or the baker, that we expect our dinner but from their regard to their own interest. We address ourselves, not to their humanity, but to their self-love, and never talk to them of our own necessities but of their advantages."[37] And the advantage accrued to the butchers, bakers, and other capitalists is profit. Indeed, in Smith's view, the exchange of commodities for profit becomes a fundamental characteristic of human society whenever the division of labor and private property develop beyond a certain point. However, Marx believed Smith was guilty of trying to make patterns of interaction that were characteristic of capitalist social relationships valid for all times and places. As an alternative, Marx envisioned a modern so-

---

[35]Adam Smith, *The Theory of Moral Sentiments* (Oxford: Clarendon Press, 1976).
[36]Adam Smith, *An Inquiry into the Nature and Causes of the Wealth of Nations* (Oxford: Clarendon Press, 1976).
[37]Ibid., pp. 26–27.

ciety without exchange relationships, since he felt they are inherently exploitive. Nonetheless, for Smith the origin of value and profit resided in the process of commodity exchange, and by distinguishing between the "use value" and the "exchange value" of commodities, Smith achieved an insight that was later to guide Marx's thought.

Smith went on to formulate a version of the labor theory of value in which the amount of labor time going into a product is the source of its value—a thesis Marx would take over some ninety years later. But if labor is the source of value, then Smith could not account for the origin of profit, since those who profit generally contribute very little labor to the creation of the product. They merely invest money and reap a return on it. Thus, while *The Wealth of Nations* displays much vacillation and confusion, Smith ultimately dropped the labor theory of value and simply argued that profit was added onto the costs of production by the capitalists. As we shall see in the next chapter, Marx was able to adopt the labor theory of value and still account for the origin of profit by distinguishing between the workers' labor and their labor power (or capacity to work).

By arguing that profit is merely part of the cost of production, Smith created a potential problem: The "natural price" of a commodity is difficult to determine since nothing prevents capitalists from constantly and arbitrarily raising prices. His solution was to argue that competition operates to prevent avaricious persons from pushing prices too high, for those capitalists who try to raise prices unduly (and Smith was very aware that they constantly try to do just that) will inevitably find other enterprising persons underselling them, thereby forcing prices back down. Similarly, those capitalists who attempt to keep wages too low will find that they have no workers because others offer them higher wages. In this way, then, both profits and wages are more or less automatically regulated—as if by an "invisible hand." And, paradoxically, people's selfish motives promote social harmony through the natural operation of the market, even though that goal is not their objective. In Smith's words, "by directing that industry in such a manner as its produce may be of the greatest value, he intends only his own gain . . . he is in this, as in many other cases, led by an invisible hand to promote an end which was no part of his intention."[38]

The final step in Smith's analysis is to argue that these laws of the market also ensure the proper quantities of products are produced. For example, if the public prefers to own coats rather than tables, then a greater number of the former will be produced, since the profit involved in making tables will fall as a result, capitalists (and workers)

---

[38]Ibid., p. 73.

will turn to the manufacture of coats. Thus natural mechanisms inherent to the market govern the allocation of resources in the society and hence the production of goods. And once again, this process occurs as a result of people acting in terms of their own self-interest.

Laws of Evolution. During the latter portion of the eighteenth century and well into the nineteenth, many political economists speculated that as capitalism advanced, the rate of profit on investment would fall. However, Smith had a rather optimistic view of the process of history, and he did not believe this calamity would occur. To Smith, in addition to being self-regulating, society seemed to be improving because of the operation of two relatively simple laws of evolution. The first can be called the "law of capital accumulation." Smith saw that capitalists continuously try to accumulate their savings or profits, invest them, accumulate even more savings or profits, and invest them again. The latent consequence of this activity is that it increases both production and employment. Thus, from Smith's point of view, selfish motives can be seen once again to redound to the public good, since the expansion of production and employment benefits everyone in some way. (Smith did not worry about whether savings would be invested; that was to become a problem for later economists.)

It was argued, however, that if accumulation is to continue and production expand, more and more workers are required. And when the supply of workers is exhausted, then profits will fall, and hence the rate of accumulation will also fall—just as many feared. Smith dealt with this problem by formulating a "law of population," his second law of evolution. Basically, this hypothesis asserts that when wages are high, the number of workers will increase; and when wages are low, the number of workers will decrease. He meant this statement literally, in terms of people living and dying, not their periodic ventures into or out of the labor market. Mortality rates, especially among children, were extraordinarily high in those days; it was not uncommon for a woman to have a dozen or more children and have only one or two survive. Yet it was still possible for a higher standard of living to affect decisively people's ability to feed, clothe, and protect their children. As a result, Smith argued, higher wages would allow for greater numbers of children to survive and become workers themselves. Lower wages, of course, would have the reverse effect. Thus Smith believed the advance of capitalism would be accompanied by an increase in population and this increase would, in turn, allow capital accumulation to continue. Therefore, according to Smith, the rate of profit will not fall and a capitalist society will constantly improve itself, all because of the natural forces, unencumbered by rules and regulations established by the state. While he recognized that an expanding population would always act to deflate wages, as long as capital accumulation continued, wages had to remain above the level of subsistence. Of course, Smith's argument in Marx's view assumes that capitalist social relations are somehow irrefutable "natural laws" of the social universe.

The Defense of Capitalism.   As enunciated by Adam Smith, the logical implication of *The Wealth of Nations* is fairly simple: Leave the market alone. From Smith's point of view, this stricture meant that the natural regulation of the market would occur as consumers' purchasing practices forced business to cater to their needs. Such a process could only occur, Smith believed, if business was not protected by the government and did not form monopolies. Hence he opposed all efforts to protect business advantage. However, Smith's analysis quickly became an ideological justification for preventing government regulation in some important areas. Moreover, since any act of government could be seen as interfering with the natural operation of the market, *The Wealth of Nations* was used to oppose humanitarian legislation designed to protect workers from the many abuses already apparent in Smith's time.

For Marx, this result showed the inherent weakness in classical political economy, for there is nothing natural about the operation of the market or any other social relationship. The market could not be left alone without the use of governmental power, which was impossible because the capitalists, like all ruling classes, controlled the government. Hence Marx argued that theory must take into account the interconnections among the parts of society, with special attention to the way in which political power is used to justify and enforce exploitive social relationships. The capitalists, again like all ruling classes, also controlled the dissemination of ideas, which suggested to Marx why they were able to use *The Wealth of Nations* for their own ideological purposes. Hence, the development of his own theory, Marx emphasized the importance (and the difficulty) of stimulating an awareness in the working classes of their true interests.

FRIEDRICH ENGELS AND KARL MARX

Friedrich Engels and Karl Marx were friends and collaborators for more than forty years. When possible, they saw each other every day; at other times they corresponded about every other day. Despite Marx's sometimes churlish temperament, the two men never broke off their relationship. Most commentators see Engels's role in the development of Marx's theory as secondary; and with regard to their joint works, especially *The German Ideology* and *The Communist Manifesto*, this appears to be an accurate assessment. Yet two of Engels's own writings, "Outlines of a Critique of Political Economy" (1844) and his much-neglected classic, *The Condition of the Working Class in England (1845)*, fundamentally influenced the development of Marx's thought at a time when he was still searching for a way of understanding and changing the world.

Engels's Critique of Political Economy and Marx's Thought

Engels's short and angry essay, "Outlines of a Critique of Political Economy," appeared in the same journal as did Marx's critique of Hegel's philosophy. In this essay, which is characterized by the excessively acerbic prose of a young man, Engels indicted both the science of political economy and the existence of private property. He began by noting caustically that political economy ought to be called "private economy," since it existed only to defend the private control of the means of production. He continued (although in a quite disorganized way) by stridently attacking the institution of private property. According to Engels, a modern industrial society based on the private ownership of property is inevitably inhumane, inefficient, and alienating. In the process of his attack, Engels also suggested (albeit vaguely) that, despite these faults, capitalism is historically necessary in order for a communist society to emerge in the future.

From Engels's point of view, capitalism is inhumane for two reasons. First, people do not and cannot trust each other. When private property exists in an industrial context, Engels wrote, trade and competition are the center of life. And since everyone seeks to buy cheap and sell dear, people must distrust and try to exploit each other. In Engels's words, "trade is legalized fraud."[39] The second reason capitalism is inhumane is that competition generates an increased division of labor, one of the major manifestations of which is the factory system. As we shall see below, Engels regarded factory work and the urban lifestyle accompanying it as one of the most inhumane and exploitive forms of social organization in history. Yet the factory system was becoming more pervasive in the 1840s and, as a result, capitalist society was being divided into two groups: those who owned the means of production and those who did not.

Engels argued that capitalism is inefficient because those who dominate it can neither understand nor control the recurrent and steadily worsening economic crises that afflict every nation. Capitalist

[39]Engels, "Outlines of a Critique of Political Economy," p. 202.

society is, therefore, beset by a curious paradox: while its productive power is incredibly great, overproduction periodically results in misery and starvation for the masses. "The economist has never been able to explain this mad situation," Engels wrote.[40] Moreover, he believed people living under capitalism are inevitably alienated because they have no sense of community with one another. In the competitive environment characteristic of capitalism, each person's interests are always opposed to every other person's. As a result, "private property isolates everyone in his own crude solitariness," with the consequence that people's lives have little meaning and carry no intrinsic rewards.[41] Underlying this entire argument, however, is Engels's belief that the rise of capitalism is historically necessary in order to make a communist society possible, for only now are people "placed in a position from which we can go beyond the economics of private property" and end the "unnatural" separation of individuals from each other and from their work.[42]

Prior to 1843 the still youthful Marx was relatively unfamiliar with political economy. It was Engels's essay that, as much as any other event, introduced Marx to the topic and made him recognize its importance in developing a theory of society. Thus, after reading the essay, Marx began an intensive study of political economy that was to last for more than twenty years. Ultimately, Marx indicted the science of political economy for essentially the same reason as had Engels: It defended capitalist society. In addition, all the main ideas noted above subsequently appeared in a more sophisticated fashion in Marx's theory.

Engels's Analysis of the Working Class and Marx's Thought

In order to continue his business training at the textile mills in which his father was part owner, Engels left his native Germany for Manchester, England, in 1842. At that time Manchester was the greatest industrial city in the most industrialized nation in the world; to many observers it was the epitome of the new kind of society forming as a result of the industrial revolution. Engels spent two years in Manchester, leading something of a double life since he not only learned the textile business but also gathered the materials for his book. During this period nearly all his leisure time was spent walking through Manchester and the surrounding towns, talking to and

---

[40]Ibid., p. 217.
[41]Ibid., p. 213.
[42]Ibid., pp. 199, 212.

drinking with working-class people, and reading the many governmental reports and other descriptions of living conditions in Manchester. The result was the first urban ethnography—and a damning
indictment of the English ruling class.

Engels's analysis of *The Condition of the Working Class in England* can
be divided into three parts. First, he sketched an idyllic rural society
that existed prior to industrialization and briefly suggested the factors
that had destroyed that society. Second, he described the conditions of
working-class life in Manchester. And third, he indicted the attitudes
of the bourgeoisie toward the proletariat and concluded that a violent
revolution is inevitable.

Peasant Life prior to Industrialization.   Like many other observers, Engels saw that the Industrial Revolution had utterly transformed
Western society. And also like other observers, he believed feudal society had been better for people in many ways. As a result he described
the feudal past in a very idyllic manner. While he has been justifiably
criticized for idealizing the past, it is not altogether clear how (in the
middle of the nineteenth century) he could have obtained a sound or
accurate portrayal of feudal society. Thus *The Condition of The Working
Class* begins with a description of simple, God-fearing peasants who
lived in a stable and patriarchal society where "children grew up in
idyllic simplicity and in happy intimacy with their playmates." Engels
saw feudal life as "comfortable and peaceful" and believed most peasants generally had a higher standard of living in the past than did
factory workers in 1844.

> They were not forced to work excessive hours; they themselves fixed the
> length of their working day and still earned enough for their needs.
> They had time for healthy work in their gardens or smallholdings and
> such labor was in itself a recreation. They could also join their neighbors
> in various sports such as bowls and football and this too kept them in
> good physical condition. Most of them were strong, well-built people,
> whose physique was virtually equal to that of neighboring agricultural
> workers. Children grew up in the open air of the countryside, and if
> they were old enough to help their parents work, this was only an oc-
> casional employment and there was no question of an eight- or twelve-
> hour day.[43]

At the same time, Engels argued, these peasants were "spiritually
dead" because they were ignorant, concerned only with their "petty
private interests," and contented with their "plantlike existence."[44]

---

[43]Engels, *Condition of the Working Class*, p. 10.
[44]Ibid., pp. 11–12.

While this depiction of life prior to industrialization is clearly not accurate, it does identify some of the themes that Engels used in his indictment of capitalist society: People are forced to work excessive hours; they are in chronic ill health; and child labor is pervasive. In addition, this sketch of feudal life also implied the historical inevitability of a communist revolution; for according to Engels, industrialization not only shattered forever this idyllic lifestyle, it also forced people to become aware of their subordination, exploitation, and alienation. As we shall see, Marx and Engels believed this recognition is the first necessary step to a communist revolution. Thus Engels's portrayal of the atrocities characteristic of urban life in the 1840s should be seen in light of his optimistic vision of the historical development of a revolutionary proletariat capable of seizing the world for itself. All of Marx's subsequent work was imbued with this vision, which he and Engels shared and tried to actualize in the political arena.

Having described peasant life prior to industrialization, Engels noted the four interrelated factors that went into making the modern working class that he observed in Manchester. First, the use of water-and-steam power in the productive process meant that, for the first time in human history, muscle power was not the primary motive force in producing goods. Second, the massive introduction of modern machinery into the productive process signaled not only that machines rather than people set the pace of work but also that more goods were being produced than ever before. Third, the intensification of the division of labor meant that the number of tasks in the productive process increased while the requirements for each task were simplified. And fourth, the tendency in modern society for concentration of both work and ownership caused not only the rise of the factory system but also a division of society into owners and producers. According to Engels, and he was not alone, these factors were the "great levers" of the Industrial Revolution that have been used to "heave the world out of joint."[45] In *Capital*, Marx was to take these same ideas and place them in a theoretical context that, in his mind, allowed him to demonstrate why a proletarian revolution was inevitable.

Working-Class Life in Manchester.   The world Engels saw was indeed out of joint. His description began with a portrayal of the neighborhoods in which working-class people were forced to live. Manchester was a city that had grown from a town of 24,000 people in 1773 to a metropolitan area of more than 400,000 persons in 1840. Yet throughout this period, it had no effective city government, little

---

[45]Ibid., pp. 27–29.

police protection, and no sewage system. Engels observed that middle-class people and the owners of the factories and mills lived apart and provided themselves with city services, police protection, and sewage disposal. In contrast, the working classes were forced to live with pigs in the slums available to them. When Engels said that human beings lived with pigs (and, unavoidably, like pigs) he meant it literally.

Since there were no modern sewage facilities in Manchester, people had to use public privies. In some parts of the city, over two hundred people were served by a single receptical. In a city without government, there were few provisions for cleaning the streets or removing debris. Engels described the result in some detail; for example, in one courtyard, "right at the entrance where the covered passage ends, is a privy without a door. This privy is so dirty that the inhabitants can only enter or leave the court by wading through puddles of stale urine and excrement."[46] Thus, in *The Condition of the Working Class*, Engels portrayed a situation in which thousands of men, women, and children were living amid their own bodily wastes. And if it can be imagined, the situation was even worse for those thousands of people living in cellars, below the waterline. As Steven Marcus has observed, "that substance [their bodily waste] was also a virtual objectification of their social condition, their place in society: that was what they were."[47]

Engels continued by describing the neighborhoods where pigs and people lived together:

Heaps of refuse, offal and sickening filth are everywhere interspread with pools of stagnant liquid. The atmosphere is polluted by the stench and is darkened by the thick smoke of a dozen factory chimneys. A horde of ragged women and children swarm about the streets and they are just as dirty as the pigs which wallow happily on the heaps of garbage and in the pools of filth. In short, the horrid little slum affords as hateful and repulsive a spectacle as the worst courts to be found on the banks of the Irk [river]. The inhabitants live in dilapidated cottages, the windows of which are broken and patched with oilskin. The doors and the door posts are broken and rotten. The creatures who inhabit these dwellings and even their dark, wet cellars, and who live confined amidst all this filth and foul air—which cannot be dissipated because of the surrounding lofty buildings—must surely have sunk to the lowest level of humanity.[48]

---

[46]Ibid., p. 58.

[47]Steven Marcus, *Engels, Manchester, and the Working Class* (New York: Vintage Books, 1975), pp. 184–85.

[48]Engels, *Condition of the Working Class*, p. 71.

It is not hard to conclude, as many did, that a society in which people have gone back to living like animals has something terribly, deeply wrong with it. And yet, as noted above, for many observers Manchester epitomized a new and better kind of world, an industrial world.

The Bourgeoisie, the Proletariat, and Revolution. Engels concluded *The Condition of the Working Class* by describing the attitudes of the bourgeoisie toward the proletariat. In Engles's prose they are portrayed as debased persons who know nothing except greed and see all human ties as having a "cash nexus." He used the following vignette to illustrate these traits.

> One day I walked with one of these middle-class gentlemen into Manchester. I spoke to him about the disgraceful unhealthy slums and drew his attention to the disgusting condition of that part of the town in which the factory workers lived. I declared I had never seen so badly built a town in my life. He listened patiently and at the corner of the street at which we parted company he remarked: "And yet there is a great deal of money made here. Good morning, Sir."[49]

Yet the proletarians were not incapable of responding to their condition in life. While much self-destructive behavior always occurs among oppressed people (as with the use of drugs, alcohol, and the like), Engels noted that Manchester was "the mainspring of all working-class movements" in England.[50] And he described the long history of working-class efforts at organizing themselves in opposition to the factory owners, for only by acting together rather than competing with one another could they effectively oppose the capitalists. More generally, however, Engels argued that the proletarians' true interest was in establishing a noncompetitive society, which meant the abolition of the private ownership of the means of production (although this last point was not made explicitly).

> Every day it becomes clearer to the workers how they are affected by competition. They appreciate even more clearly than the middle classes that it is competition among the capitalists that leads to those commercial crises which cause such dire suffering among the workers. Trade unionists realize that commercial crises must be abolished, and they will soon discover *how* to do it.[51]

---

[49]Ibid., p. 312.
[50]Ibid., p. 50.
[51]Ibid., p. 249 (emphasis in original).

The Condition of the Working Class ends with Engels's prophecy of a violent proletarian revolution. While this "revolution must come," Engels believed, he had not shown why, since his work accounts for neither how capitalist society functions nor why it would inevitably be destroyed. He had not, in short, developed a theory to explain what he had observed. But at a time when Marx was searching for the underlying dynamics of society, Engels had demonstrated the significance of the proletariat. Furthermore, Engels had recognized (although the point is not made very clearly) that the evils of capitalism were a necessary prelude to a communist revolution. Yet it was Marx, rather than Engels, who developed a set of theoretical concepts and propositions that would purport to show why a revolution would occur in capitalist societies. And it is in developing these theoretical arguments that Marx contributed to the emergence of sociological theory.

CHAPTER 5

The Sociology of Karl Marx

The nineteenth century was filled with revolutionaries and revolutions, mainly because industrialization heaved the feudal world out of joint, destroying patterns of social relationships that had existed for a millenium. Karl Marx believed these relationships produced a paradoxical result. While industrialization meant sustenance and amenities could be available for everyone, only a few people actually benefited—the very rich who owned capital (income-producing assets). The capitalists exploited the masses, who lived in great misery and depravity. In order to remedy this situation, Marx tried to stimulate people to reorganize social arrangements so that everyone's needs could be met. He argued that such a change was inevitable, the only question being when it would occur. Throughout his life he served as a participant, organizer, and leader of revolutionary groups dedicated to ending the exploitation of the masses.

Of all the great classical sociologists, Karl Marx was unique in that he acted as both revolutionary and social scientist, a combination that constitutes the greatest weakness in his sociology. Marx's orientation can be summarized in the following way. As a revolutionary, he sought to overthrow the existing order and substitute collective control of society by the people so that, in a cooperative context, they could be free to develop their potential as human beings. As a social scientist, he tried to show that such collective control is historically inevitable. According to Marx, history has a direction that can be observed. This direction, Marx and Engels wrote in *The Communist Manifesto*, would lead inevitably to a communist society in which "the free development of each is the condition for the free development of all."[1] In such a context, Marx believed, the few would no longer exploit the many.

Before proceeding to an explication of Marx's writings, it is important to recognize that his works are often difficult to understand, partly because of their revolutionary intent and partly because his theoretical methodology is unclear.

As a literary genre, revolutionary writings are polemical and argumentative since they are designed to stimulate action. They also

---

[1] Karl Marx and Friedrich Engels, "The Communist Manifesto," in *The Birth of the Communist Manifesto*, ed. Dirk Struik (New York: International, 1971), p. 112.

tend to deal with historical events in a jargon-laden manner. These characteristics mean that readers who are unfamiliar with the historical situation in which the revolutionaries lived, with the disagreements separating various political factions, and with the names of the various protagonists, frequently find the arguments obscure. For example, portions of the long third section of *The Communist Manifesto,* titled "Socialist and Communist Literature," are difficult for those persons unfamiliar with the disagreements between Marx and such figures as Pierre-Joseph Proudhon, Henri Saint-Simon, and the Young Hegelians. Most of the people Marx fought with go unread today. Hence many of the references in his writings are difficult to comprehend.

More important, Marx's writings are hard to understand because his theoretical methodology is unclear and he never really explained it. Marx had no predecessors, for he belonged to the first generation of social scientists. As a whole their works mark the end of social philosophy and the beginning of a true science of society. This fact means, however, Marx had to make his own way in establishing a social science where none existed. So he developed an interpretation of the nature of capitalist society and, more than the other classical theorists dealt with in this book, left it to subsequent scholars to explain his methodology. But this strategy leads to major problems of explanation. For example, as noted in the last chapter, in the opening pages of *Capital* Marx asserted that Hegel had been standing on his head and that he, Marx, stood him right side up. Unfortunately, what this phrase means is not at all obvious to those unfamiliar with Hegel's philosophy and the arguments surrounding it. Similarly, in *The German Ideology* and other places, Marx said production is simultaneously consumption and that the proletariat, or working class, is identical to the bourgeoisie, or capitalist class. Again, what these phrases mean is unclear. How can one thing be "identical" to or "simultaneously" another? Marx used such language often, especially in his early works. His use of words in this way reflects a specific (and unique) theoretical methodology.

In this chapter we explain the major themes in Marx's writings and his theoretical methodology by examining his three most important works: *The German Ideology, The Communist Manifesto,* and *Capital.*

THE GERMAN IDEOLOGY

The German Ideology was completed in 1846, when Marx was twenty-eight years old and Engels twenty-six. Much of the rather lengthy book is given over to heavy-handed and satirical polemics against various Young Hegelians. The publisher declined to accept the manuscript at the time, perhaps for political reasons since Marx was already well known as a radical and had been expelled from both Germany and France, or perhaps because of the arcane writing style. In any case, Marx later recalled, the manuscript was "abandoned to the gnawing criticism of the mice . . . since we had achieved our main purpose—self-clarification."[2]

The Attack on the Young Hegelians

Marx opened *The German Ideology* with a bitter attack on the Young Hegelians, whom he described at one point as engaging in "theoretical bubble blowing."[3] For the Young Hegelians, Marx observed, great conflicts, struggles, and revolutions take place only in the realm of thought, since no buildings are destroyed and no one is injured or dies. Thus, despite their excessive verbiage, Marx believed the Young Hegelians had merely criticized the essentially religious nature of Hegel's work and substituted their own negative religious canons. "It is an interesting event we are dealing with," he said caustically, "the putrescence of the absolute spirit."[4]

Marx's rejection of German philosophy as it was then practiced was total. Like all idealists, the Young Hegelians saw people's relationships, their opportunities, and their limitations as merely products of the mind and consciousness, and the Young Hegelians' solution to the problems of the world was merely to demand a change in people's consciousness. Yet this demand only amounts to asserting that human beings should interpret reality in another way, which is to say they should accept their lot in life by means of another interpretation. For this reason Marx called them the "staunchest conservatives," since they supported the status quo and would change nothing in this world, only the phrases used to describe it.

---

[2]Karl Marx, "Preface," *A Contribution to the Critique of Political Economy* (New York: International, 1970), p. 22.

[3]Karl Marx and Friedrich Engels, *The German Ideology* (New York: International, 1947), p. 3. Only part 1 of the text is translated, and it is generally assumed that Engels's contribution to this portion of the book was minimal. This is mainly because the text appears to be an elaboration of Marx's "Theses on Feuerbach," which he outlined for himself in 1845; see pp. 43–45 in *The Marx-Engels Reader,* ed. Robert C. Tucker (New York: W. W. Norton, 1978). In addition, Engels stated repeatedly that Marx had already developed his conception of history prior to the beginning of their collaboration. Therefore in what follows we shall generally refer only to Marx.

[4]Marx, *German Ideology.*

The Nature of Social Theory

As an alternative to the "idealistic humbug" of the Young Hegelians, Marx argued that theoretical analyses should be empirically based. Social theory, he said, should be grounded in the "existence of living human individuals" who must survive, often in a relatively hostile environment.[5] This orientation is necessary because human beings are unlike other animals in that they manipulate the environment in order to obtain need satisfaction. They "begin to produce their means of subsistence, a step which is conditioned by their physical [i.e., social] organization."[6] This idea implies that people are "conscious"—that is, they are self-reflective. Thus human beings are also unlike other animals in that they can look at themselves and their environment and then act rationally in terms of their own interests. This fact means consciousness arises out of experience, an argument directly opposed to Hegel's idealism, in which notions of morality, religion, and all other forms of awareness are considered to exist independently of human beings. Put in modern language, Marx was asserting that people produce their ideas about the world in light of the social structures in which they are born, raised, and live. Further, as social structures change the content of people's ideas (their consciousness) changes as well. In breaking with the idealists in this way, however, Marx did not imply a simple-minded materialist orientation. For Marx, the human mind is not a passive receptacle; rather it is active, both responding to and changing the material world.

According to Marx, then, the focus of a social scientific explanation should be on how people influence and are influenced by their material conditions: for example, their degree of hunger, degree of protection from the environment, opportunity to enjoy the amenities of life, and ability to realize their creative potential. This emphasis constitutes a fundamental epistemological break with idealism. In effect Marx stood Hegel "right side up" by transforming philosophy into an empirical social science.

The Real Process of Production

Based on this premise, Marx emphasized that analyses should be oriented to what he called "the real process of production"—that is, the most essential characteristics that all societies have in common. These characteristics (Marx called them *moments*) do not refer to evolutionary stages of development but rather to social conditions that

---

[5]Ibid., p. 7.
[6]Ibid., p. 8

have "existed simultaneously since the dawn of history and the first men, and they still assert themselves in history today."[7] Marx's language is significant. He used a phrase that appears to have narrow, economic connotations—"the real process of production"—to refer to more general sociological issues. This sort of phrasing occurs frequently in Marx's writings.

The first characteristic of all societies is that human beings, unlike other animal species, produce sustenance from the environment in order to live and thereby "make history." Marx noted that human "life involves before anything else eating and drinking, a habitation, clothing, and many other [material] things."[8] Such needs are satisfied by employing technology to manipulate the environment in some socially organized manner. For Marx, this fact clearly implied that social theory had to deal with more than just ideas. It had to be grounded in "the existence of living human individuals," who have material needs that must be satisfied through production. From this angle of vision, the task of social theory is to explain how people "produce their means of subsistence."

material needs

The second characteristic of all societies is that people create new needs over time. Need creation occurs because production (or work) always involves the use of tools or instruments of various sorts, and these tools are periodically improved, yielding more and better consumer goods. Thus Marx said the processes of production and consumption always feed back on one another in a cumulative fashion such that as one set of needs is satisfied, new ones emerge.[9]

new needs

This close connection between production and consumption is why he asserted the two are "identical" to or "simultaneously" one another, since it is not possible to consider one apart from the other. For Marx, the process of need creation, as indicated by the changing modes of production and consumption, implies that social theory must deal with historical change, its direction, and its source. As will become clear, he believed human history displays an evolutionary pattern from less complex to more complex social structures, and the origin of change is internal to each society.

It is important to understand here that the process of need creation involves not only the desire for improved food, clothing, and shelter but also for the various amenities of life. Marx observed that in the production and consumption of goods beyond the minimum necessary for survival, what are called amenities, people become "civilized" in

---

[7]Ibid., p. 18.
[8]Ibid., p. 16.
[9]Marx, "Introduction," *Contribution to the Critique of Political Economy*, pp. 188–217.

the sense that they distinguish their uniquely human characteristics from those of other species. Thus people's work—which is the act of production—serves a dual purpose: (1) to satisfy physical needs and (2) to express their uniquely human creativity. According to Marx this duality is why other animals work only to satisfy an "immediate physical need, whilst man produces even when he is free from physical need and only truly produces in freedom therefrom." Unfortunately, he believed, most people are prevented from expressing their human potential through work because the exploitation and alienation inherent in the division of labor prevent it.

The third characteristic of all societies is that production is based on a division of labor, which in Marx's writings always implies a hierarchical stratification structure, with its attendant exploitation and alienation. The division of labor means the tasks that must be done in every society—placating the gods, deciding priorities, producing goods, raising children, and so forth—are divided up. But Marx observed that in all societies the basis for this division is private ownership of land or capital, which he called the *means of production*. Private ownership of the means of production produces a stratification structure comprised of the dominant group, the owners, and the remaining classes arrayed below them in varying degrees of exploitation and alienation. Nonowners are exploited and alienated because, since they do not own the means of production, they cannot control either the work they do or the products produced. For example, capitalists, not employees, organize a production line to produce consumer goods; and capitalists, not employees, own the finished products. But because employees, whom Marx called *proletarians*, need these products to survive, they are forced to return their wages to the capitalists, who use the money to make more consumer goods and enrich themselves further. In this context alienation takes the form of a fantastic reversal in which people only feel themselves to be truly free in their animallike functions—such as eating, drinking, and fornicating—while in their peculiarly human tasks, such as work, they do not feel human because they control neither the process nor the result. On this basis, Marx concluded, in capitalism "what is animal becomes human and what is human becomes animal."[10] Thus, paradoxically, the division of labor means proletarians continually recreate that which enslaves them: capital.

In some form or another, Marx argues, exploitation and alienation occur in all societies characterized by private ownership of the means

---

[10]Karl Marx, *The Economic and Philosophical Manuscripts* (New York: International, 1964), p. 111.

of production. That is, in all societies a stratification structure exists in which the members of the subordinate classes are forced to continuously exchange their labor power for sustenance and amenities so they can keep on producing goods to benefit the members of the dominant class. For Marx, this situation implied that social theory had to focus on who benefits from existing social arrangements by systematically describing the structure of stratification that accompanies private ownership of the means of production. In addition this situation also implied that only collective ownership could eliminate these problems.

The fourth characteristic of all societies is that ideas and values emerge from the division of labor. Put differently, ideas and values result from people's practical efforts at obtaining sustenance, creating needs, and working together. As a result, ideologies usually justify the status quo. Ideologies are systematic views of the way the world ought to be, as embodied in religious doctrines and political values. Thus, Marx argued, religious and political beliefs in capitalist societies state that individuals have a right to own land or capital; they have a right to use the means of production for their own rather than the collectivity's benefit. It is perverse, he noted, for everyone to accept these values even though only a few people can exercise this right, such as landowners and capitalists.

Marx believed the values (or *ideologies,* to use his word) characteristic of a society are the tools of the dominant class because they mislead the populace about their true interests. This is why he described religion as "the opium of the masses."[11] He reasoned that religious belief functions to blind people so they cannot recognize their exploitation and their real political interests. Religion does this by emphasizing that salvation, compensation for misery and alienation on earth, will come in the next world. In effect religious beliefs justify social inequality. For Marx, the fact that ideas and values emerge from the division of labor implies that social theory must focus on both the structural sources of dominant ideas and the extent to which such beliefs influence people.

Marx contended that while societies differ in many ways, all display these four characteristics, and his subsequent works built on this insight. Interestingly, this orientation does not make Marx unique today. Virtually all modern social theories recognize that societies have such characteristics, although the ideas are usually phrased rather differently. What makes Marx unique is the theoretical methodology that emerged from these premises.

---

[11]Karl Marx, "A Contribution to the Critique of Hegel's Philosophy of Right," in Tucker, ed., *Marx-Engels Reader,* pp. 16–26, 53–66.

The Stages of History

Based on the analysis above, Marx sketched the "real basis of ideology" in terms of the stages of history since the Middle Ages. He argued that two great divisions in society arose about that time. The first division was between town and country. Marx believed, and he was wrong on this point, that towns arose anew in the Middle Ages as freed serfs fled the domination of the nobility. These people had little property at first—skills and the tools of their trade, perhaps. But the development of towns signifies the separation of capital from landed property. The second great division occurred within the towns themselves—the formation of guilds. Marx insisted, and he appears to have been correct, that guilds were designed to curb competition as well as to regulate and control labor—that is, they protected property in its new urban form. The "serfs, persecuted by their lords in the country, came separately into the towns, where they found an organized community, against which they were powerless, in which they had to subject themselves to the station assigned to them by the demand for their labour and the interest of their organized competitors."[12] These workers remained an unorganized rabble, forced to compete with one another for jobs in an urban context where they could not provide for their own needs without employment by guild members or nascent capitalists.

According to Marx, "the next extension of the division of labor was the separation of production and commerce" such that a special class of merchants was formed.[13] As a consequence, communication and contact among towns assumed greater importance as buying and selling increased in volume. Towns began to interact with each other; began to specialize in producing particular products; and gradually, the traditional barriers to trade were broken down. Over time, with the gradual ascendence of capital as the dominant form of property, the bourgeois class arose.

The bourgeoisie was formed as individual merchants and producers in the different towns recognized their common interests and began to act in concert. Concomitantly, the process of transforming landed property into industrial or commercial capital continued, although not without a great deal of conflict. The process by which serfs were transformed into proletarians was neither smooth nor easy. In Marx's view the nascent capitalists' productive forces (both the tools used and the social organization of production) existed very precar-

---

[12]*German Ideology*, p. 45.
[13]Ibid., p. 47.

iously in most places. Only the extension of trade and communication assured the permanence of the newly acquired productive forces. As this occurred, individuals found their conditions of existence predestined such that their position in the division of labor and their personal destiny was assigned to them by their class membership.[14]

Manufacturing, the next stage in the transformation of Western society, arose as one consequence of the division of labor between towns and the development of commerce. The concentration of population in urban areas, the availability of mobile capital in the form of cash, and the existence of advanced machines combined to allow manufacturing to develop. Textiles were the first major manufacturing industry, Marx claimed, and there is some basis for this judgment. The employment of unskilled workers in textiles and other new manufacturing entities "became a refuge of the peasants from the guilds." As a result the thousands of vagabonds created by the demise of the feudal system were gradually absorbed by these emerging industries.[15] The rise of manufacturing had great political significance as well, Marx believed, because trade had to be protected and labor regulated so people could acquire the newly available amenities and profit could be made. The guilds could perform neither of these tasks, and hence they declined in all areas where manufacturing took hold.

Inevitably, "big industry" arose and completed the transformation of society. According to Marx, big industry was based on the existence of a completely dependent proletarian class, a world market, worldwide communication, mobile capital that circulates freely and rapidly, and the modern state, which operates to protect private property. In this context Marx dwelt again on the importance of the state under capitalism, asserting that in an environment where "pure private property" exists—that is, where there are no communal ties among people because landed property has been converted into cash and other forms of capital—the state has been purchased by the owners of property in order to protect their investment. He meant this literally, claiming that the existence of the state "has become wholly dependent on the commercial credit which the owners of property, the bourgeois, extend to it."[16]

In Marx's analysis, industrialization has two interrelated consequences. The first is the exploitation and alienation of labor, since with industrialization all "natural relationships" with other people, based

---

[14]Ibid., p. 49.
[15]Ibid., p. 51.
[16]Ibid., p. 59.

on personal and patriarchal ties, are transformed into "money relation-ships."[17] This process occurs as industry makes use of the "automatic system," by which machines are linked with new forms of power, such as steam. As a result, human beings become dependent on the machines at which they toil and must adjust their needs (both biological and social) to those of the machines. In addition, the necessity for a large and concentrated labor pool means that people are forced to live in the miasmatic atmosphere of large cities, of which Manchester was only one example. Thus modern life is paradoxical, for in an environment characterized by the greatest productive forces in history, labor only sustains people's lives by stunting them, by preventing them from recognizing and developing their peculiarly human abilities. Work is no longer an expression of human creativity or impulse because people are now just like animals: They work constantly in an environment they cannot control in order to barely subsist.

The second consequence of industrialization follows from the first and is interrelated with it. A revolutionary class is created—the proletariat—"which in all nations has the same interest and with which nationality is already dead; a class which is really rid of all the old world and at the same time stands pitted against it."[18] In *The German Ideology*, however, Marx did not suggest the conditions under which the proletarians might be able to unite, as that analysis first appeared in the *Manifesto*, written two years later. Nonetheless, he believed life in capitalist society was so intolerable and incapable of amelioration that "individuals must appropriate the existing totality of productive forces, not only to achieve self-activity, but also, merely to safeguard their very existence."[19]

Thus Marx's description of the transition from feudalism to capitalism emphasized the dialectic between the new and the old. And as is also evident, the emergence of capitalism created new pressures for social transformation. Eventually, Marx hoped, capitalism would be displaced by communism. Yet at this stage in his thinking, Marx believed it would be unwise to predict the nature of the society to come after a communist revolution. We can, nevertheless, offer a few obser-

---

[17]Marx used the term *natural* in several different ways. Sometimes he meant that which occurs in nature without interference by humans. Sometimes he meant relationships determined by "natural predispositions" (ibid., p. 20), such as physical strength. Sometimes he meant relationships reflecting human dependence on the physical environment, such as landed property (ibid., p. 63). And sometimes he meant capitalist social relationships. "Civilized" (or cooperative) relationships, however, are never described as "natural" by Marx.

[18]Ibid., p. 57.

[19]Ibid., p. 66.

vations based on hints found in the final section of *The German Ideology*. In Marx's eyes communism represents a systematic effort by people to transform collectively their relations with one another so that they can act cooperatively rather than individualistically. In addition, the communist revolution will bring with it both the abolition of private property and the end of alienation. Up until the present, people have been alienated because their work and all other aspects of their lives were determined by external forces over which they had no control. But under communism, the community or proletarians "puts the conditions of the free development and movement of individuals under their control—conditions which were previously abandoned to chance and had won an independent existence over against the separate individuals."[20]

Marx's Theoretical Methodology

The exposition in *The German Ideology* is an early example of Marx's dialectical materialism. Although he did not use this phrase, it expresses discontinuity and continuity between Hegel and Marx. As we explained previously, Marx rejected Hegel by grounding social theory in the real world where people must satisfy their physical and psychological needs. The term *materialism* denotes this fact. Having rejected the substance of Hegel's idealism, however, Marx continued to use the Hegelian method of analysis. The term *dialectical* denotes this fact. In Marx's hands dialectical materialism transforms the historical analysis described above into what can be called a "scientific political doctrine."

Dialectical materialism has four characteristics. First, society is a social structure or *system*. This is a modern term, one that Marx did not use. It means societies can be seen as having interrelated parts, such as classes, social institutions, cultural values, and so forth. These parts form an integrated whole. Thus the angle of the observer is very important when viewing a society. For example, in tracing the connections among the parts of the stratification structure it can be seen that from one angle a specific label can be applied (for example, bourgeoisie), while from another angle an opposing label can be applied (for example, proletariat). But there is an inherent connection between the two classes, which is why Marx noted in *The Communist Manifesto* that it is tautologous to speak of wage-labor and capital, for one cannot exist without the other. Similarly, as observed previously, this is why he described production and consumption as "identical" or as occurring "simultaneously." He meant they are parts of a coherent structure or

---

[20]Ibid., p. 75.

Dialectical materialism
① society is a social system → parts integrated into a whole
② social change inherent as people make history by satisfying their needs
③ social change evolves in a recognizable direction
④ people shape the direction of history in light of opposition

system, and there is an inherent connection between them. Furthermore, the process of production and consumption (which today would be called the economy) is connected to stratification. More generally, class relations are reflected in all arenas of social behavior: the economy, kinship, illness and health care, crime, religion, education, and government. Although Marx emphasized the primacy of economic factors, especially ownership of the means of production, his work is not narrowly economic; it is, rather, an analysis of how social structures function and change.

Second, social change is inherent in all societies as people make history by satisfying their ever-increasing needs. This orientation is an endogenous (or internal) theory of social change. Thus it asserts that the most fundamental source of change comes from within societies rather than from outside of them. According to Marx, not only are all the parts of society connected, they also contain their own inherent "contradictions," which will cause their opposites to develop. For example, as described in the last section, Marx argued that feudalism contained within itself the social relations that eventually became capitalism. Similarly, in the *Manifesto,* Marx claimed capitalism contained within itself the social relations that would inevitably engender a new form of society: communism.

Third, social change evolves in a recognizable direction. For example, just as a flower is inherent in the nature of a seed, so the historical development of a more complex social structure, such as capitalism, is inherent in the nature of a less complex one, such as feudalism. The direction of history is from less complex to more complex social structures, which is suggested by the pattern of need creation depicted earlier. As Robert Nisbet comments, Marx was a child of the Enlightenment, and he believed in the inevitability of human progress.[21] He had a vision of evolutionary development toward a utopian endpoint. For Marx, this endpoint was a communist society.

Fourth, freely acting people decisively shape the direction of history in light of the predictable patterns of opposition and class conflict that develop in every society. As with all of Marx's concepts, his use of the term *class* is sometimes confusing.[22] The key to understanding this concept lies in the idea of opposition, for Marx always saw classes as opposed to one another. It should be remembered, however, that this opposition occurs within a stratification structure; classes are opposed but connected.

---

[21]Robert A. Nisbet, *Social Change and History* (New York: Oxford University Press, 1968).

[22]Bertell Ollman, "Marx's Use of 'Class,'" *American Journal of Sociology* 73, March 1968, pp. 573–80.

Thus, regardless of their number or composition, the members of different classes are enemies because they have opposing interests. This is not a result of choice, but of location within the stratification structure. For example, if the position of an aggregate of people makes obtaining food and shelter a constant problem and if these people cannot control their own activities or express their human potential, then they are clearly in a subordinate position in relationship to others. In their alienation they have an interest in changing the status quo, whether they are aware of it or not. On the other hand, if the position of an aggregate of people is such that their basic needs are satiated, they can control their daily activities, and they can devote themselves to realizing their human potential, then such persons have an interest in preserving the status quo. Marx believed these opposing interests cannot be reconciled.

Hence, given a knowledge of the division of labor in capitalism, the differing interests and opportunities of the proletarians and capitalists are predictable, as is the generation of class conflict. The latter, however, is a matter of choice. History does not act, people do. From this point of view, Marx's theoretical task was to identify the social conditions under which people will recognize their class interests, unite, and produce a communist revolution. As will become clear later on, Marx believed he had achieved this goal. The important point to remember here is that his theoretical methodology combines determinism, or direction, with human freedom: A communist revolution is a predictable historical event ushered in by freely acting people who recognize and act in their own interests.

Dialectical materialism can be summarized in the following way. Within any society a way of producing things exists, both in terms of what is produced and the social organization of production. Marx called this aspect of society the "productive forces."[23] In all societies the productive forces are established and maintained in terms of a division of labor. Those few who own the means of production comprise the dominant class, which benefits from the status quo. The masses make up the subordinate class (or classes). They are exploited and alienated because they have little control over their lives, and hence they

---

[23]Sometimes Marx uses the phrase *forces of production* narrowly, so that it only refers to the instruments used in the productive process. Sometimes, however, he uses the phrase such that it refers to both the instruments used in production and the social organization that accompanies their use. By *social organization* is meant not only the organization of work (as in factories) but also family life, law, politics, and all other institutions. This tactic occurs with many of Marx's key concepts. See Bertell Ollman, *Alienation: Marx's Conception of Man in Capitalist Society* (New York: Oxford University Press, 1976).

have an interest in change. Over time new ways of producing things are devised, whether based on advances in technology, changes in the way production is organized, or both. Such new forces of production better satisfy old needs and also stimulate new ones. They are in the hands of a new class, and they exist in opposition to current property relationships and forms of interaction. Over the long run the tension between these opposing classes erupts into revolutionary conflict, and a new dominant class emerges.

Marx's methodology is unique because it is a logically closed theoretical system that cannot be refuted. This fact separates Marxist and non-Marxist social scientists today. Among non-Marxists, theories are evaluated in light of observations, which means they can be disproved. The goal is to develop abstract statements that summarize patterns of social organization. From this point of view the social sciences resemble the natural sciences in orientation.

Among Marxists, however, theories are evaluated in light of what they lead people to do (or not do), which means they cannot be disproved. Because the goal is to assess where a society is along an evolutionary continuum, theories are constantly adjusted in light of changing political conditions.[24] As we noted at the beginning of the chapter, the endpoint of this continuum is a communist society, a communal social organization in which there is collective control of the means of production (in today's societies, this is capital) so people, acting cooperatively, can be free. In such a social context, Marx argued, exploitation and alienation will not exist because the division of labor will not be based on private ownership of property. Thus, from this point of view, the social sciences are radically different from the natural sciences. This orientation is why we described Marx's work as a scientific political doctrine. We will show later on, however, that Marx's perspective has serious flaws, and that the phrase *scientific political doctrine* is a contradiction in terms.

The German Ideology constitutes the first presentation of Marx's theory. It is, however, incomplete. It does not, for example, raise one of the most crucial issues: How are the oppressed proletarians to become aware of their true interests and seize control of the society for the benefit of all? This and other problems of revolutionary action are dealt with in *The Communist Manifesto*.

---

[24]See Richard Appelbaum, "Marx's Theory of the Falling Rate of Profit: Towards a Dialectical Analysis of Structural Change," *American Sociological Review* 43, February 1978, pp. 73–92.

THE COMMUNIST MANIFESTO

In 1847 Marx and Engels joined the Communist League, which they soon dominated. Under their influence its goal became the overthrow of bourgeois society and the establishment of a new social order without classes and private property. As described in Chapter 4, Marx and Engels decided to compose a manifesto that would publicly state the Communist League's doctrines. The result constitutes one of the greatest political pamphlets ever written.

The *Manifesto* opens with a menacing phrase that immediately reveals its revolutionary intent: "A spector is haunting Europe—the spector of Communism. All the Powers of old Europe have entered into a holy alliance to exorcise this spector." In a political context where opposition parties of all political orientations were called communist, Marx wrote, it was time for the communists themselves to "meet this nursery tale of the spector of Communism with a Manifesto of the party itself."[25] The remainder of the *Manifesto* is organized into four sections, which are summarized below.

Bourgeois and Proletarians

Marx presents his theoretical and political position in the very first line of the text: "The history of all hitherto existing society is the history of class struggles." He continues by observing that in every era "oppressor and oppressed stood in constant opposition to one another [and] carried on an uninterrupted, now hidden, now open fight, a fight that each time ended either in a revolutionary reconstitution of society at large or in the common ruin of the contending classes."[26] Put differently, Marx believed in every social order those who own the means of production always oppress those who do not. Thus, in his view, bourgeois society has merely substituted a new form of oppression, and hence struggle, in place of the old feudal form. Marx argued, however, that bourgeois society is distinctive in that it has simplified class antagonisms, since the "society as a whole is splitting up more and more into two great hostile camps, into two great classes directly facing each other: Bourgeoisie and Proletariat."[27] Because one class owns the means of production and the other does not, the two have absolutely opposing interests: the bourgeoisie in maintaining the status

---

[25]*Communist Manifesto*, p. 87.
[26]Ibid., p. 88.
[27]Ibid., p. 89.

quo and the proletariat in a complete reorganization of society so that production can benefit the collectivity as a whole. This situation reflected a long historical process. As in *The German Ideology,* the analysis in the *Manifesto* is an example of Marx's dialectical materialism.

Historically, Marx argued, capitalism emerged inexorably from feudalism. "From the serfs of the Middle Ages sprang the chartered burghers of the earliest towns. From these burgesses the first elements of the bourgeoisie [capitalists] were developed." Such changes were not historical accidents, Marx said, but the inevitable result of people acting in terms of their own interests. The rise of trade and exchange, stimulated by the European discovery of the Americas, constituted new and powerful production forces, which faced a feudal nobility that had exhausted itself by constant warfare. Further, as they were increasingly exposed to other cultures, the members of the nobility wanted new amenities, and so they enclosed the land in order to raise cash crops using new methods of production. It should be recalled here that production and consumption reciprocally affect one another, and they are tied to the nature of the class structure. As this historical process occurred, the serfs were forced off the land and into the cities, where they had to find work.

During this same period a merchant class arose. At first the nascent capitalists existed to serve the needs of the nobility by facilitating trade and exchange. But over time money, or capital, became the dominant productive force. This process occurred as new sources of energy (such as steam) were discovered, as machines were invented and speeded up the production process, and as the former serfs were pressed into service in new industries as wage laborers. The result, Marx noted, was that in place of feudal retainers and patriarchal ties, there was "left no other nexus between man and man than naked self-interest, than callous 'cash payment.' "

The *Manifesto* summarizes the situation in the following way:

> The feudal system of industry, under which industrial production was monopolized by closed guilds, now no longer sufficed for the growing wants of the new markets. The manufacturing system took its place; the guild masters were pushed on one side by the manufacturing middle class; division of labor between the different corporate guilds vanished in the face of division of labor in each single workshop.
>
> Meantime, the markets kept ever growing, the demand ever rising. Even manufacture no longer sufficed. Thereupon steam and machinery revolutionized industrial production. The place of manufacture was taken by the giant, modern industry, the place of the industrial middle class by industrial millionaires, the leaders of whole industrial armies, the modern bourgeois. . . .

We see then: the means of production and of exchange, on whose foundation the bourgeoisie built itself up, were generated in feudal society. At a certain stage in the development of these means of production and of exchange, the conditions under which feudal society produced and exchanged, the feudal organization of agriculture and manufacturing industry, in one word, feudal relations of property, became no longer compatible with the already developed productive forces; they became so many fetters. They had to be burst asunder, they were burst asunder.[28]

Thus the rise of capitalism means the forces of production changed, and therefore so did the class structure. Marx said that while these developments were the result of freely acting people pursuing their self-interest, they were also predictable—indeed, inevitable—historical events. Furthermore, as a result of the rise of capitalism, the class structure became simplified. Now there existed a new oppressed class, the proletarians, who had to sell their labor in order to survive. Because these people could no longer produce goods at home for their own consumption, they constituted a vast exploited and alienated work force that was constantly increasing in size. Opposed to the proletarians was a new oppressor class, the bourgeoisie (or capitalists), as a few former artisans and petty burghers became entrepreneurs and eventually wealthy. These people owned the new productive forces on which the proletarians depended.

Marx then described the truly revolutionary nature of the capitalist mode of production. As a result of the Industrial Revolution, the bourgeoisie "has accomplished wonders far surpassing Egyptian pyramids, Roman aqueducts, and gothic cathedrals; it has conducted expeditions that put into the shade all former Exoduses of nations and crusades."[29] However, in order for the bourgeoisie to exist, Marx predicted, they must constantly revolutionize the instruments of production and thereby create new needs that can be filled by manufactured products. As this process occurs the bourgeoisie also seizes political power in each country, so that "the executive of the modern state is but a committee for managing the common affairs of the whole bourgeoisie."[30]

Having described the great historical changes accompanying the rise of capitalism, Marx then made two of his most famous predictions concerning the ultimate demise of the capitalist system. The first prediction is that capitalism is inherently unstable because of its recur-

---

[28]Ibid., pp. 90, 94.
[29]Ibid., p. 92.
[30]Ibid., p. 91.

1st prediction: capitalism unstable because of fluctuations, cycles

rent industrial cycles, and its downfall is inevitable as a result. Capital-ism, Marx wrote, is characterized by "an absurdity—the epidemic of overproduction." According to Marx, the essential problem of nine-teenth-century capitalism was that its industrial cycles, epitomized by recurrent commercial crises, were weathered only by the destruction of products, more thorough exploitation of old markets, and the contin-ued conquest of new markets. But such tactics clearly could not suc-ceed over the long run because capitalists continually undercut each other. Thus, Marx argued, as industrialization advances, the produc-tive forces become no longer capable of operating efficiently in a com-petitive context where people try to maximize profits by pursuing their individual self-interest.

Marx's second prediction was that "the modern working class, the proletarians" would become increasingly impoverished and alienated under capitalism. Because they could no longer be self-supporting, the proletarians had become "a class of laborers who live only so long as they find work, and who find work only so long as their labor increases capital."[31] Thus, in an industrial context characterized by the extensive use of machinery owned and controlled by others, proletarians have no control over their daily lives or the products of their activities. Each person becomes, in effect, a necessary but low-priced appendage to a machine. In this situation, Marx said, even women and children are thrown into the maelstrom. Thus, under capitalism, human beings are simply instruments of labor whose only worth is the cost of keeping them minimally fed, clothed, and housed. Confronted with their own misery, Marx predicted, the proletarians would ultimately become class conscious and overthrow the entire system.

class consciousness

The rise of the proletariat as a class for itself proceeds with great difficulty, however, primarily because individual proletarians are forced to compete among themselves. For example, some are allowed to work in the capitalists' factories, while others are not. Within the factories a few are allowed to work at somewhat better-paying or easier jobs, while most labor at lower-paying and more difficult tasks. After work proletarians with too little money still compete with each other for the inadequate food, clothing, and shelter that is available. Under these competitive conditions it is difficult to create class consciousness among people. Nonetheless, individuals and aggregates of workers have periodically rebelled since the beginnings of capitalism, although they often directed their attacks against the instruments of production rather than the capitalists. When they did organize, the proletarians

proletarians would become class-conscious and overthrow the system

[31]Ibid., p. 96.

were often co-opted into serving the interests of the bourgeoisie.[32] However, with the development of large-scale industry, the proletariat constantly increases in size. Like many other observers of nineteenth-century society, Marx predicted the number of working-class people would continually increase as elements of the lower-middle class—artisans, shopkeepers, and peasants—were gradually absorbed into it. Furthermore, Marx believed even those persons in professions such as medicine, law, science, and art would increasingly become mere wage laborers. He thought all the skills of the past are being swept aside by modern industry, which creates but two great classes.

The revolutionary development of the proletariat would, Marx argued, be aided by the fact that it was increasingly urban, and hence its members were better able to communicate with one another. Further, they were becoming better educated and politically sophisticated, partly because the bourgeoisie constantly dragged them into the political arena. And although the proletarians' efforts at organizing against the bourgeoisie were often hindered, Marx believed they were destined to destroy capitalism because the factors mentioned here would stimulate the development of class consciousness among the proletariat.

Proletarians and Communists → abolition of private property

As Marx expressed it, the major goal of the communists could be simply stated: the abolition of private property. After all, he noted, under capitalism nine-tenths of the population has no property anyway. As might be imagined, the bourgeois were especially critical of this position. But Marx felt that just as the French Revolution abolished feudal forms of private property in favor of bourgeois forms, so the communist revolution would abolish bourgeois control over capital—without substituting a new form of private ownership. Marx emphasized, however, that the abolition of the personal property of the petty artisan or the small peasant was not at issue. Rather the communists wished to abolish bourgeois "capital, i.e., that kind of property which exploits wage labor and which cannot increase except upon condition of begetting a new supply of wage labor for fresh exploitation."[33]

In order to change this situation, the proletarians periodically organized and rebelled during the nineteenth century. As noted in

---

[32]See Karl Marx, "The Civil War in France," in Karl Marx and Friedrich Engels, *Selected Works* (Moscow: Progress Publishers, 1969), pp. 178–244. Marx shows here how the proletarians actively participated in subjecting other classes to the rule of the bourgeoisie.
[33]*Communist Manifesto,* p. 104.

Chapter 4, shortly after publication of the *Manifesto*, revolts occurred throughout Europe. Even though such efforts were always smashed, Marx believed the proletariat was destined to rise again, "stronger, firmer, mightier," ready for the final battle.

It is important to understand that he viewed this process as an inevitable evolutionary development. In the *Manifesto* Marx emphasized that "the theoretical conclusions of the Communists . . . express, in general terms, actual relations springing from an existing class struggle, from an historical movement going on under our very eyes."[34] According to Marx, just like the feudal nobility before it, "the Bourgeoisie [has] forged the weapons that bring death to itself." This process occurred because the productive forces of capitalism make it possible for everyone to satisfy their needs and realize their human potential. But for such a change to actually happen, productive forces must be freed from private ownership and allowed to operate for the common good. Furthermore, the bourgeoisie has also "called into existence the men who are to wield those weapons—the modern working class—the proletarians." Marx believed the working classes in all societies would, in their exploitation and alienation, eventually bring about a worldwide communist revolution.

Although Marx did not say much about the future, he knew the transition to communism would be difficult, probably violent. This is because the communists aimed at destroying the core of the capitalist system: private ownership of the means of production. In order to achieve this goal, Marx believed the means of production had to be "a collective product" controlled by the "united action of all members of the society." Such cooperative arrangements are not possible in bourgeois society, with its emphasis on "free" competition and its apotheosis of private property. Collective control of the society, Marx thought, is only possible under communism, where "accumulated labor [or capital] is but a means to widen, to enrich, to promote the existence of the laborer." This drastic change required a revolution.

The first step in a working-class revolution, Marx argued, would be for the proletariat to seize control of the state. Once attaining political supremacy, the working class will then wrest "all capital from the bourgeoisie," "centralize all instruments of production in the hands of the state," and "increase the total of productive forces as rapidly as possible."[35] Furthermore, the following measures would also be taken in most countries:

1. Abolition of private ownership of land.

---

[34]Ibid., pp. 103–4.
[35]Ibid., p. 111.

means of production not bad —> private ownership of m.o.p. is bad

2. A heavy progressive income tax.
3. Abolition of all rights of inheritance.
4. Confiscation of the property of emigrants and rebels.
5. Centralization of credit and banking in the hands of the state.
6. Centralization of communication and transportation in the hands of the state.
7. State ownership of factories and all other instruments of production.
8. Equal liability of all to labor.
9. Combination of agricultural and manufacturing industries so as to abolish the distinction between town and country.
10. Free public education for all children and the abolition of child labor.

Marx understood perfectly that these measures could only be implemented arbitrarily, and he forecast a period of temporary communist despotism in which the Communist party acted in the interests of the proletariat as a whole. In an essay written many years after the *Manifesto,* Marx labeled this transition period the "revolutionary dictatorship of the proletariat."[36] Ultimately, however, Marx's apocalyptic vision of the transition to communism was one in which people would become free, self-governing, and cooperative instead of alienated and competitive. They would no longer be mutilated by a division of labor over which they had no control. "The public power will lose its political character," Marx wrote. "In place of the old bourgeois society with its classes and class antagonisms, we shall have an association in which the free development of each is the condition for the free development of all."[37] It is a splendid vision; unfortunately, it is not that of the sorcerer, but of the sorcerer's apprentice.

Socialist and Communist Literature

In the third section of the *Manifesto,* Marx attacked the political literature of the day. He recognized that in all periods of turmoil and change there is inevitably a desire by some to return to times past or to invent fantastic utopias as the way to solve humankind's ills. Marx believed such dreams are, at best, a waste of time and, at worst, a vicious plot on the part of reactionaries. Thus this section of the

[36]Karl Marx, "Critique of the Gotha Program," in Marx and Engels, *Selected Works,* pp. 9–11.
[37]*Communist Manifesto,* p. 112.

Manifesto is a brief critique of socialist literature as it then existed. He classified this literature as (1) reactionary socialism (including here feudal socialism, petty-bourgeois socialism, and German "true" socialism), (2) conservative or bourgeois socialism, and (3) critical-utopian socialism. Each of these is discussed briefly below.

Reactionary Socialism.   Because the bourgeoisie supplanted the feudal nobility as the ruling class in society, the remaining representatives of the aristocracy attempted revenge by trying to persuade the proletarians that life had been better under their rule. Marx characterized this pernicious literature as "half lamentation, half lampoon; half echo of the past, half menace of the future" and said their efforts are misbegotten primarily because the mode of exploitation is different in an industrial context and a return to the past is not possible.

Petty-bourgeois socialism is also ahistorical and reactionary. While its adherents have dissected capitalist society with great acuity, they also have little to offer but a ridiculous return to the past: a situation in which corporate guilds exist in manufacturing and patriarchal relations dominate agriculture. Because they manage to be both reactionary and utopian, which is difficult, this form of socialism always ends "in a miserable fit of the blues." Marx had previously criticized German or "true" socialism in *The German Ideology*. In the *Manifesto* he merely emphasized once again (with typically acerbic prose) that the Germans wrote "philosophical nonsense" about the "interest of human nature, of Man in General, who belongs to no class, has no reality, who exists only in the misty realm of philosophical fantasy."[38]

Conservative or Bourgeois Socialism.   In Marx's estimation bourgeois socialists, such as Proudhon, wanted to ameliorate the miserable conditions characteristic of proletarian life without abolishing the system itself. Today he might call such persons liberals. In any case, Marx believed this goal was impossible to achieve, for what Proudhon and others did not understand was that the bourgeoisie cannot exist without the proletariat and all the abuses inflicted on it.

Critical-Utopian Socialism.   Utopian socialism is represented by the early communist systems devised by Saint-Simon, Fourier, Owen, and others. While these writers had many critical insights into the nature of society, Marx believed their efforts were historically premature because the full development of the proletariat had not yet occurred, and hence they were unable to see the material conditions necessary

---

[38]Ibid., p. 117.

for its emancipation. As a result they tried to construct a new society independent of the flux of history. For the utopian socialists, the proletarians were merely the most suffering section of society rather than a revolutionary class destined to abolish the existence of all classes.

Communist and Other Opposition Parties

In the final section of the *Manifesto* Marx described the relationship between the Communist party, representing the most advanced segment of the working class, and other opposition parties of the time. Basically, in every nation the communists are supportive of all efforts to oppose the existing order of things, for Marx believed the process of opposition would eventually "instill into the working class the clearest possible recognition of the hostile antagonism between the bourgeoisie and the proletariat."[39] In this regard communists would always emphasize the practical and theoretical importance of private property as the means of exploitation in capitalist society.

Marx, the revolutionary, concludes the *Manifesto* with a final thundering assault on the bourgeoisie:

> The communists disdain to conceal their views and aims. They openly declare that their ends can be attained only by the forcible overthrow of all existing social conditions. Let the ruling classes tremble at a Communist revolution. The proletarians have nothing to lose but their chains. They have a world to win. WORKING MEN OF ALL COUNTRIES, UNITE![40]

As Isaiah Berlin has commented, the power of the *Manifesto*'s opening and closing statements has never been equaled anywhere.[41] If Marx had written nothing else, this document would have ensured his lasting fame.

Marx's Model of Stratification and Class Conflict

Modern readers often have two contrasting reactions when studying *The Communist Manifesto*, neither of which are very clearly articulated. On the one hand, it is easy to see how aspects of his analysis can be applied to societies today. After all, exploitation does occur, and people in different classes do have opposing interests. On the other hand, Marx's political orientation seems both naive and threatening. It

---

[39]Ibid., p. 125.

[40]Ibid.

[41]Isaiah Berlin, *Karl Marx: His Life and Environment* (New York: Oxford University Press, 1963), p.167.

appears naive because a truly cooperative industrial society is hard to imagine. It appears threatening because subsequent history shows that a totalitarian government (like that in the Soviet Union) seems to follow from any application of his ideas. Both reactions reflect Marx's peculiar combination of revolution and theory, which, as stated earlier, constitute the greatest weakness in his writings. Nonetheless, it is possible to extrapolate a useful model of social stratification and class conflict from *The Communist Manifesto.*

Before doing so, however, we must recognize that any discussion of Marx's legacy demands a political confession: We are not Marxists. Thus, in what follows, the analysis implies nothing about the inevitability of a communist revolution or the transformation of society, but rather, it implies a concern with those ideas in Marx's writings that can still serve sociological theory.

Figure 5–1 displays a model of stratification and class conflict taken from the *Manifesto.* It illustrates some of the key variables to look for in studying social stratification and conflict, and it implies a modern sociological orientation. As described earlier, Marx asserted that in a stable social structure goods are produced to satisfy the material needs of people, a process necessitating a division of labor and justified in terms of dominant values. This situation is depicted in the first box in Figure 5–1.

Many past observers have construed Marx's emphasis on productive activity to be a form of economic determinism. But this is too narrow a reading. Marx's point is not that economic activity determines behavior in other areas but rather that all social action is conditioned by, and reciprocally related to, the type of productive activity that exists. For example, family life is likely to be different in a hunting-and-gathering society than in an industrial one, as are the form of government, education, religious beliefs, law, cultural values, and so on. These variations occur, in part, because the way people obtain food, clothing, and shelter differs. Alternatively, however, in two societies at the same level of economic development, the organization of economic

FIGURE 5–1   Marx's Model of the Generation of Stratification, Class Conflict, and Change

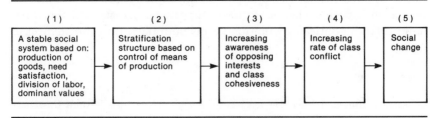

activity is likely to vary, in part, because of differences in religious beliefs, law, family life, and so on.[42]

The recognition of such variation implies an essential sociological orientation: The range of options available to people is shaped by the nature of the society, its way of producing goods, its division of labor, and its cultural values. This orientation is fundamental to sociology today. Some writers like to begin with economic issues, others focus on some aspect of the division of labor (such as the family or criminal justice), still others start by looking at how values circumscribe behavior. In every case, however, sociologists emphasize that society is a social system with interrelated parts and that social facts circumscribe behavior.

Marx argued, and he is probably correct, that a structure of stratification emerges in all societies based, at least in part, on control over the means of production. This fact, which is depicted in the second box in Figure 5–1, means the upper class also has the capacity to influence the distribution of resources because it dominates the state. Thus those persons who benefit because they control the means of production have an interest in maintaining the status quo, in maintaining the current distribution of resources, and this interest is pervasive across all institutional arenas. For example, classes in the United States today have different sources of income, they have different political resources, and they are treated differently in the criminal justice system, they provide for their children differently, they worship at different churches, and so forth.[43]

In assessing what modern sociologists can learn from Marx, the use of the word *control* rather than *ownership* in box 2 in Figure 5–1 is an important change, since control over the means of production can occur in ways that he did not realize. For example, in capitalist societies the basis of social stratification is private ownership of property, while in communist societies the basis of social stratification is Communist party control of property. In effect the Communist party is a new kind of dominant class ushered in by the revolution.[44] In both cases the group controlling the means of production exploits those who do not, while acting to justify its benefits by dominating the state and promulgating among the masses values that legitimize its exploitation.

---

[42]All of these factors constitute what Marx called the forces of production. See footnote 23.

[43]See Leonard Beeghley, *The Structure of Stratification in the United States* (Boston: Allyn & Bacon, 1988).

[44]See Milovan Djilas, *The New Class* (New York: Praeger Publishers, 1965), and *Rise and Fall* (New York: Harcourt Brace Jovanovich, 1985). See also Michael Voslensky, Nomenklatura: The Soviet Ruling Class (Garden City, N.Y.: Doubleday, 1986).

When he looked at social arrangements, Marx always asked a simple question, one that modern sociologists also ask: Who benefits? For example, the long empirical sections of *Capital* (to be reviewed subsequently) are designed to show how attempts at lengthening the working day and increasing productivity also increased the exploitation of the working class in order to benefit the capitalists. Marx, however, also applied this question to nonobvious relationships. For example, his analysis of the "fetishism of commodities" in the early part of *Capital* shows how people's social relationships are altered by the reification (or worship) of machines and products that commonly occurs in capitalist societies, again to the benefit of capitalists. In effect Marx teaches modern observers that an emphasis on who is benefiting from social arrangements and public policies can always improve an analysis. For example, macroeconomic decisions that emphasize keeping inflation low and unemployment high benefit the very rich in American society at the expense of working people. In every arena—at home, at work, in court, at church, in the doctor's office, and so forth—it is useful to ascertain who is benefiting from current social arrangements.

The second box in Figure 5–1 is important in another way as well. As emphasized in the *Manifesto,* Marx divided modern capitalist societies into two great classes: bourgeoisie and proletarians. While he recognized that this basic distinction was too simplistic for detailed analyses, his purpose was to highlight the most fundamental division within these nations. Whenever he chose, Marx would depict the opposed interests and experiences of various segments of society, such as bankers, the "lower middle classes," or the *lumpenproletariat* (the very poor). But he did this on an ad hoc basis. Max Weber, whose work is considered in the next two chapters, outlined a more complete, and therefore more useful, map of the stratification structure. In so doing, he built on Marx's insights.

Boxes 3, 4, and 5 in Figure 5–1 outline the process of class conflict and social change. Under certain conditions members of subordinate classes may become aware that their interests oppose those of the dominant class. In such a context, Marx taught, class conflict ensues and social change occurs.

In Marx's work, of course, this process is linked to assumptions about the direction of history and the inevitability of a communist revolution. But this need not be the case. Members of a class can become aware of their true interests and be willing to act politically without seeking a revolutionary transformation of society. This process occurs because, while classes may be opposed to one another in any ongoing social structure, they are also tied to one another in a variety of ways. As Reinhard Bendix argues, citizenship, nationalism, religion, ethnicity, language, and many other factors bind aggregates of people together despite class divisions.[45] Furthermore, to the extent that a subordinate class participates effectively in a political system, as when it obtains some class-related goals, it then acquires an interest in maintaining that system and its place within it. In the United States, at least, most mass movements composed of politically disenfranchised persons have sought to get into the system rather than overthrow it. The labor movement, various ethnic movements, and the feminist movement are all examples of this tendency. Thus while there is little doubt that the very rich dominate the political process in American society, subordinate classes do have political power and do influence public policy. This fact militates against a revolutionary transformation of U.S. society along communist lines.

Marx: a structural approach

The emphasis on class conflict that pervades Marx's writings implies what sociologists today call a *structural* approach—that is, a focus on how rates of behavior among aggregates of people are influenced by their location in the society. Their differing locations dictate that classes have opposing interests. Moreover, Marx usually avoided looking at individual action since it is influenced by different variables. Rather he wanted to know how the opportunity set (or range of options) people had influenced rates of behavior. For example, his analysis of the conditions under which proletarians transform themselves into a revolutionary class does not deal with the decision-making processes or cost-benefit calculations of individuals; rather it shows that urbanity, education, political sophistication, and other factors are the social conditions that will produce class consciousness among the proletarians. Sociology at its best deals with structural variables. Although his work is misbegotten in many ways, Marx was a pioneer in this regard.

CAPITAL → *capital accumulation through exploitation of labor*

In *The German Ideology* Marx attacked the Young Hegelians because they avoided an empirical examination of social life. In *Capital* he demonstrated the intent of this criticism by engaging in his own analysis of the workings of capitalist society. Using England (and copious amounts of British government data) as his primary example, Marx sought to show that the most important characteristic of the capitalist mode of production is the constant drive to accumulate capital through the use of exploited and alienated labor. As a result of the need to accumulate capital, Marx argued, the processes of production are

---

[45]Reinhard Bendix, "Inequality and Social Structure: A Comparison of Marx and Weber," *American Sociological Review* 39, April 1974, 149–61.

incessantly revolutionized, and over the long run the instability and degradation of people characteristic of capitalist society will lead to its complete transformation. Thus, in contrast to the *Manifesto,* which is a call to arms, *Capital* is a scholarly attempt to show why such a transformation of capitalist society will inevitably occur. As such, *Capital* is much more than a narrow work of economics; it is an analysis of capitalist social structure and its inevitable transformation.

This explication of *Capital* is divided into five sections. First, Marx began by sketching the labor theory of value. All the analyses that follow are based on this initial idea. The second section comprises Marx's description of the process of exchange and the development of capital. The third section contains his analysis of surplus value and shows why it is the source of capitalist social relations. The fourth section sketches Marx's explanation of capital accumulation and its consequences for the eventual downfall of capitalism. And the final section explicates Marx's analysis of the origins of capitalism, which he called *primitive accumulation.*

The Labor Theory of Value

The labor theory of value is sketched in the opening chapter of *Capital.* While Marx approached this issue from what appears to be a strictly economic vantage point—the nature and value of commodities—his discussion turns out to have considerably broader implications. A commodity is "an object outside of us, a thing that by its properties satisfies human wants of some sort or another."[46] For purposes of his analysis, both the origin of people's wants and the manner in which commodities satisfy them are irrelevant. Rather the more important question is: What makes a commodity valuable? In the answer to this question lies the key to Marx's analysis of capitalist society.

Two analytically different sources of value are inherent in all commodities, each of which can be treated independently. One source of value resides in the "use value" of commodities—that is, in the fact that they are produced in order to be consumed. For example, people use paper to write on, autos for transportation, and so forth. Clearly some things that have value, such as air and water, are not produced but are there for the taking (at least they were in the nineteenth century). In referring to use values in capitalist society, Marx was primarily interested in those items manufactured by people. Commodities having use value are qualitatively different from one another; for ex-

---

[46]Karl Marx, *Capital: A Critical Analysis of Capitalist Production,* vol. 1 (New York: International, 1967). The original spelling is retained in all quotations.

ample, a coat cannot be compared to a table. As a result, when thinking of use values the amount of labor that has gone into appropriating
them is irrelevant.

Another source of value can be found in the "exchange value" of
commodities. As we shall see, Marx believed an emphasis on the exchange value of commodities is peculiar to capitalist social relations
and it comprises capitalism's greatest strength and weakness. Because
the exchange of commodities occurs independently of their use, Marx
argued that exchange value must exist independently of use value. Yet
commodities had to have some basis for comparison in order for exchange to take place. Thus Marx decided the only way they could be
compared to one another was in terms of the labor time required to
produce them. Essentially, then, the labor theory of value states that
the value of commodities is determined by the labor time necessary to
produce them. Marx phrased the labor theory of value in the following
way:

> That which determines the magnitude of the value of any article is the
> amount of labour socially necessary, or the labour-time socially neces-
> sary for its production. Each individual commodity, in this connexion,
> is to be considered, as an average sample of its class. Commodities,
> therefore, in which equal quantities of labour are embodied, or which
> can be produced in the same time, have the same value. The value of
> one commodity is to the value of any other, as the labour-time necessary
> for the production of the one is to that necessary for the production of
> the other. As values, all commodities are only definite masses of con-
> gealed labor-time.[47]

Marx supplemented the labor theory of value in five ways. First,
different kinds of "useful labour" are not comparable. For example, the
tasks involved in producing a coat are qualitatively different than those
involved in producing linen. All that is comparable is the expenditure
of human labour power in the form of brains, nerves, and muscles.
Thus the magnitude of exchange value is determined by the quantity
of labor as indicated by its duration in terms of hours, days, or weeks.
Marx called this quantity "simple average labour."

Second, although different skills exist among workers, Marx recognized that "skilled labour counts only as simple labour intensified,
or rather, as multiplied simple labour."[48] Thus, in order to simplify the
analysis, he assumed that all labor is unskilled. In practice, he asserted, people make a similar assumption in their everyday lives.

[47]Ibid., pp. 39–40.
[48]Ibid., p. 44.

Third, the value of a commodity differs according to the technology available. With mechanization, the labor time necessary to produce a piece of cloth is greatly reduced (and so, by the way, is the value of the cloth—at least according to Marx). During the initial stages of his analysis, Marx wished to hold technology constant. Thus he asserted that the value of a commodity is determined by the labor time socially necessary to produce an article under the normal conditions of production existing at the time.

Fourth, and this point will become very important later on, under capitalism labor itself is a commodity with exchange value. The production of commodities requires expenditure of energy—brains, nerves, muscles, and so on—that must be replenished. Because other people must work to provide each person with sufficient food, clothing, shelter, and the various amenities of life that are deemed necessary in any society, labor is a commodity just like linen and coats. Thus "the value of labor power is determined as in the case of every other commodity, by the labor time necessary for the production, and consequently, the reproduction, of this special article."[49]

Fifth, an important implication of the labor theory of value is the development of what Marx called the "fetishism of commodities." The fetishism of commodities occurs when people come to believe the products they produce have human attributes that make them capable of interacting with and exploiting people. Marx thought such beliefs are only possible when commodities are produced by alienated labor for purposes of exchange. In capitalist society the fetishism of commodities manifests itself in two different ways. (1) Machines (as a reified form of capital) are seen as exploiting workers, which is something only other people can do. Thus products that were designed and built by people, and can be used or discarded at will, not only come to be seen as having human attributes but even as independent participants in human social relationships. (2) When machines are seen to exploit workers, the social ties among people are hidden such that their ability to understand or alter the way they live is impaired. In this context, Marx wrote, "there is a definite social relation between men, that assumes, in their eyes, the fantastic form of a relation between things."[50]

In later chapters of *Capital* Marx illustrated what he meant by the fetishism of commodities by showing that machines rather than laborers set the pace and style of work and by showing that machines "need" the night work of laborers so they may be in continuous oper-

---

[49]Ibid., p. 170.
[50]Ibid., p. 72.

ation. Of course, as we shall see, hidden behind the machines stand capitalists, who are the real villains.

Marx concluded his chapter on the labor theory of value by briefly alluding to an alternative form of society that would not be characterized by the fetishism of commodities. In passages reminiscent of *The German Ideology* and *The Communist Manifesto,* he described a "community of free individuals, carrying on their work with the means of production in common, in which the labour-power of all the different individuals is consciously applied as the combined labour-power of the community."[51] Such a communist society would be cooperative rather than competitive and, as a result, would be characterized by the production of commodities as use values rather than as exchange values. From the point of view of people oriented to the production of use values, commodities are "social" in the sense that they belong to everyone. However, in a cooperative community where neither exchange nor alienation exists, some principle for distributing the means of subsistence must be found, and Marx said the basis for distributing goods in a communist society is "from each according to his ability, to each according to his needs."[52]

The Process of Exchange and the Development of Capital

Historically, commodities with differing use values were exchanged directly by bartering, but over time some commodities began to be produced specifically to be bartered, and the volume of trade increased so that exchange became a normal act. In such a context a universal measure of value and price was necessary, with the result that money, either in the form of gold or backed by it, became that measure. Money became, in effect, a symbol of the human labor embodied in commodities.

According to Marx, the process of exchange initially involves the metamorphosis of commodities into money and back again into commodities, which he represented by the following formula:

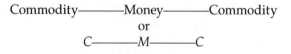

Commodity————Money————Commodity
or
C————M————C

In the process of commodity circulation shown above, money lubricates the exchange. However, Marx was more interested in the devel-

[51]Ibid., p. 78.

[52]Ibid., pp. 78–79. The quotation is from Marx, "Critique of the Gotha Program," p. 9.

opment of capital, since in modern society it is the possession of capital (whether in the form of money or machines) that allows some persons to exploit others. The basic formula for capital is precisely the reverse of that presented above. Rather than C————M————C, it is M————C————M. In the latter case one's object is to use money to purchase a commodity and then sell it for money. As Marx noted, the formula for capital "commences with money and ends with money. Its leading motive, and the goal that attracts it, is therefore mere exchange value." But this process is ludicrous, Marx observed, since one ends up with the same amount of money at the end as at the beginning, and there is no point to the exchange. Thus the capitalist transaction is really M————C————M', where M' is larger than M. In other words, one "buys cheap and sells dear." Marx called the increment that results "surplus value" (or profit).

The significance of surplus value in capitalism can be suggested with the following example. A tailor has $1,000 and purchases linen from a weaver. The tailor then employs other tailors to make suits out of the linen. The suits sell for a total of $2,000. After deducting the amount paid to employees, say, $500, the tailor makes $500. This $500 is profit, or surplus value. What differentiates this type of transaction from others is that capitalists have no intention of consuming the products they purchase, since use values are of little interest to them. Marx writes that "the restless never-ending process of profit-making alone is what [the capitalist] aims at."[53] In this way capitalists continually throw their money into circulation in a constant effort to increase its supply.

Surplus Value

The Source of Surplus Value.   In discovering the origin of surplus value, Marx had to resolve a key problem. We should recall here his assertion that labor is the source of value—whether of linen, suits, or any other commodity. How then does capital increase, as indicated by the appearance of surplus value? Marx considered several alternatives: among them, buying commodities above or below their value and speculation. However, he quickly dismissed these arguments. Since Marx believed the source of all value is labor, he had to show how labor creates surplus value for the capitalists. He finally decided that paying people in the form of wages hides the true exchange taking place, since wages make all labor appear to be paid labor. For example,

---

[53]Marx, *Capital,* p. 149.

a person is paid three shillings for twelve hours' work, and thus, from a superficial point of view, it appears reasonable to refer to the "value of labour" as three shillings. But this formulation is misleading because the source of surplus value is not evident. For example, if a worker takes leather worth six shillings and makes one pair of boots each day, then (adding three shillings in wages) the value of the boots is nine shillings and there is no profit for the capitalist. But since capitalists clearly do make a profit, Marx had to account for its origin.

Marx believed he could show where surplus value came from by distinguishing between "labor" and "labor power." Labor is the work people actually do when they are employed by capitalists, whereas labor power is the capacity to work that the capitalist purchases from the worker. As Marx puts it, "by labour-power or capacity for labour is to be understood the aggregate of those mental and physical capabilities existing in a human being, which he exercises whenever he produces a use-value of any description."[54] Labor power is a commodity just like any other, and in fact it is all the workers have to sell. Marx noted that the laborer, "instead of being in the position to sell commodities in which his labour is incorporated, [is] obliged to offer for sale as a commodity that very labour-power, which exists only in his living self."[55] Furthermore, in a capitalist society the proletarians can only sell their labor power to capitalists, who own the means of production. The two meet, presumably on an equal basis, one to sell labor power and the other to buy it.

The value, or selling price, of labor power is "determined, as in the case of any other commodity, by the labour-time necessary for the production, and consequently also the reproduction, of this special article."[56] Thus labor power is, at least for the capitalist, a mass of congealed labor time—as represented by the cost of food, clothing, shelter, and all the other things necessary to keep the workers returning to the marketplace with their peculiar commodity. Since workers must also reproduce new generations of workers, the cost of maintaining wives and children must be included—although, as will be seen below, capitalists have use for them also.

The key to the production of surplus value, then, resides in the fact that proletarians are forced to work longer than is necessary to obtain subsistence, and the capitalists keep for themselves the excess value created by the laborers. This is possible, Marx believed, precisely because the capitalists have purchased labor power rather than labor.

---

[54]Ibid., p. 167.
[55]Ibid., p. 168–69.
[56]Ibid., p. 170.

For example, Marx speculated, it cost three shillings, on the average, to support workers and their families. Without at least that amount of money, the workers' labor power, or their capacity to work, would deteriorate (through sickness and death), and they would be unable to return to the marketplace. So the capitalists purchase labor power for three shillings. Marx further speculated that it took, on the average, six hours of labor to produce commodities valued at three shillings. So the capitalists, having purchased the workers' labor power rather than their labor, simply make them work for twelve hours. In that time the workers produce commodities worth six shillings. The capitalists, who have not worked, pay the agreed three shillings to the proletarians and keep the other three for themselves. This situation seemed unfair to Marx, and he found this inequity to be the key to capitalist exploitation, class conflict, and eventually communism.

Having discovered the source of surplus value in labor power, Marx wished to be able to calculate its rate. In order to do so, and to understand the examples that follow, two definitions are necessary. First, Marx defined "constant capital" as "that part of capital which is represented by the means of production, by the raw material, auxiliary material, the instruments of labor, and does not undergo any quantitative alteration of value" in the production process.[57] For example, in the textile industry constant capital (or means of production) would include the cost of raw cotton, spindles and looms, buildings, and all other materials necessary to turn cotton into linen. In the productive process the value of all these items is transformed into the finished product—in this case, linen. Second, "variable capital" is that portion of the means of production "represented by labour power, [that] does, in the process of production, undergo an alteration of value. It both reproduces the equivalent of its own value, and also produces an excess, a surplus value."[58] In calculating surplus value, constant capital is ignored since, as noted above, its value is simply transferred in altered form to the product. The rate of surplus value, then, is simply a ratio of surplus value over variable capital, or:

$$\frac{s}{v}$$

Marx thus provided a very precise definition of exploitation, since "the rate of surplus value is therefore an exact expression for the degree of exploitation of labour-power by capital, or of the labourer by the capitalist."[59] More broadly, in *Capital* exploitation is not simply a

---

[57]Ibid., p. 209.
[58]Ibid.
[59]Ibid., p. 218.

form of economic injustice, although it originates from a view of the economy based on the labor theory of value. The social classes that result from the acquisition of surplus value by one segment of society are also precisely defined. Those classes accruing surplus value, administering the government, passing laws, and regulating morals are the capitalists (or bourgeoisie), while those classes being exploited are the workers (or proletarians).

In order to obtain the greatest imaginable benefits for themselves, capitalists attempt to exploit workers as much as possible. Their efforts can be conceptualized and measured in terms of the rate of surplus value, as denoted by the ratio given above. For example, we can recall that Marx speculated it took three shillings per day to support workers and their families, and by making people work twelve hours per day, the capitalists were able to pocket three shillings per day for themselves, for each worker in their employ. In this case the rate of surplus value was calculated by Marx as follows:

$$\frac{s}{v} = \frac{3}{3} = 1.0$$

However, this rate can be changed in favor of the capitalists by increasing the numerator and decreasing the denominator. By increasing s, which Marx now called "absolute surplus value," the capitalists benefit. They do this by lengthening the working day. By decreasing v, which Marx now called "relative surplus value," the capitalists also benefit. They do this by making labor more productive. Each of these concepts is explained below.

Absolute Surplus Value.   As noted above, the essential idea in the capitalists' continuing efforts at increasing surplus value is to keep laborers working longer than is necessary to sustain them and to pay them no more than is necessary to keep them returning to the labor market. Absolute surplus value is increased by lengthening the working day. Marx used an example dealing with the production of cotton to show how the capitalists obtain absolute surplus value from laborers.

	Hypothetical Costs per Worker
Constant capital (spindles, machines, etc.)	12 shillings/day
Constant capital (raw cotton)	12 " "
Variable capital (labor power)	3 " "
Total daily costs to capitalists	27 shillings/day
Value of finished cotton produced by each worker in twelve hours	30 shillings/day
Minus costs	27 " "
Surplus value created by each worker	3 shillings/day

Because the length of the working day was an important source of surplus value for the capitalists, it was also an arena of conflict throughout the nineteenth century. Thus Marx spent a considerable amount of space documenting the manner in which the early capitalists forced laborers to work as many hours as possible.[60] However, the significance of these remarkable pages of *Capital* is that they are probably the first systematic use of historical and governmental data in social scientific research. Further, despite their anecdotal quality (by today's standards), Marx's data are clearly correct: They show the extent to which capitalists sought to extend the working day and keep the proletarians in an utterly depraved condition. In general Marx believed the drive to extend the working day so as to obtain as much absolute surplus value as possible is characteristic of capitalism, and the proletariat is helpless to resist.

Relative Surplus Value.   Marx called the surplus value that is produced by lengthening the working day absolute surplus value. The surplus value produced by curtailing necessary labor time, and hence increasing the productiveness of labor, was called relative surplus value.

The productiveness of labor can be increased in two interrelated ways. The first is by altering the organization of the productive process, and the second is by the application of advanced forms of technology to the productive process. In either case, by increasing the workers' productivity (so that more is produced in the same or less time), the capitalists can cheapen the prices of their commodities and yet still increase their profit—at least temporarily. From the capitalists' point of view, the fact that the degree of exploitation of the proletarians has increased is irrelevant. Similarly, the possible long-term consequences of this practice are ignored because of the capitalists' all-consuming need for increased profit.

Marx illustrated how relative surplus value is increased with the following hypothetical example. At one level of technology, one pair of boots can be produced by each worker per day.

	Shillings
Constant capital	6
Variable capital	3
Total costs	9
Value of finished boots	11
Minus cost	9
Surplus value	2

---

[60]Ibid., pp. 231–312.

With increasing technology, two pairs of boots can be produced by each worker per day.

	Shillings
Constant capital	12
Variable capital	3
Total costs	15
Value of each pair of boots	10
Value of two pair of boots	20
Minus costs	15
Surplus value	5

Thus, with the implementation of advanced forms of technology, capitalists can produce more boots or any other item, undersell their competitors, and still realize greater profit (that is, surplus value). In this example Marx assumed capitalists actually compete with one another, a viable assumption in the nineteenth century.

By discovering the advantages of increasing productivity, Marx thought he had uncovered the hidden dynamic of capitalism that would lead inexorably to increasing exploitation, increasing industrial crises, and ultimately to the overthrow of the capitalist system itself. His rationale was that the capitalist's increased profits are short-lived, since others immediately copy any innovation, and thus the extra surplus value generated by increasing productivity disappears "so soon as the new method of productivity has become general, and has consequently caused the difference between the individual value of the cheapened commodity and its social value to vanish."[61] In terms of the example cited above, other capitalists soon learn to produce two boots per day and change their system of production accordingly, with the result that the innovator's advantage is obviated. However, over time someone else figures out how to produce three boots per day and begins to do so, realizing greater relative surplus value for a time. Soon, however, other capitalists copy the new system of production and again eliminate the innovator's initial advantage. This process continues inexorably, as capitalists are constantly motivated to increase productivity. The ultimate result, Marx predicted, would be the sort of chaos originally depicted in *The Communist Manifesto*.

Since the reorganization of the productive process and the introduction of machines into the workplace were important sources of surplus value for the capitalists, they were also the locus of much conflict

---

[61]Ibid., p. 319.

during the nineteenth century. For such changes meant the proletarians had to either work harder or in a more dehumanizing environment. As in his analysis of absolute surplus value, Marx spent much time empirically documenting the capitalists' efforts at increasing relative surplus value.[62] By using historical and governmental data, Marx was again able to show how productivity had steadily increased through greater exploitation of the proletarians.

The Accumulation of Capital

Marx's discussion of surplus value was a systematic attempt at showing the dynamics of capitalist exploitation. His description of the process of capital accumulation expands on this analysis by dealing with two interrelated issues stemming from the nature of surplus value. The first, which he called *simple reproduction,* focuses on the way capitalist social relations are continuously recreated by wage laborers. The second issue, which Marx called the "conversion of surplus value into capital," focuses on the way in which surplus value is used to accumulate capital. As we shall see, the result of capital accumulation is a contradiction in capitalist society so great that its transformation to "a higher form of society" ultimately becomes inevitable.

Simple Reproduction.   Simple reproduction occurs as workers continuously produce products that become translated into surplus value for capitalists and wages for themselves. Proletarians use their wages in two ways, both of which contribute to the stability of the capitalist system. First, because capitalists own the means of production and the commodities produced with them, as proletarians purchase the necessities of life they must give their wages back to the capitalists. The capitalists, of course, use that money all over again to make still more money for themselves. Second, after minimally satisfying their needs, workers return to the marketplace ready to sell their labor power and prepared once again to augment capital by creating surplus value. Over time, then, capitalist society is continuously renewed, since proletarians produce not only commodities, not only their own wages, and not only surplus value, but also capitalist social relations: with exploited and alienated workers on one side and capitalists on the other.

The Conversion of Surplus Value into Capital.   Capitalists consume at least part of the surplus value they obtain from proletarians.

---

[62]Ibid., pp. 336–507.

The remainder is reinvested in such a way that the reproduction of capital occurs on a progressively increasing scale, with the result, as Marx observed, that "the circle in which simple reproduction moves, alters its form and . . . changes into a spiral."[63]

Marx predicted that the conversion of surplus value into capital, which he called *capital accumulation,* would have three interrelated consequences for the future of capitalism. His first prediction was that proletarians will be separated from owning or controlling private property, even their own labor. This situation occurs because capitalists consume first their own capital and then the unpaid labor of others. Yet, paradoxically, the laborers have not been defrauded—at least according to capitalist rules of the game—for as we saw above, the capitalists merely pay laborers for the value of their commodity, labor power. And since proletarians have only labor power to sell, they have little choice but to participate according to the capitalists' rules.

Marx's second prediction regarding the consequences of the conversion of surplus value into capital is that proletarians will become increasingly impoverished and an industrial reserve army of poor people would be created. He labeled this process the "general law of capital accumulation," and he believed it would occur as capitalists increasingly used machines in the factories in order to make labor more productive and hence lower the price of goods. As laborers become more productive, fewer of them are needed and their labor power can be purchased at a lower price. Thus Marx predicted not only that proletarians will continuously reproduce their relations with the capitalists, but also that they will produce the means by which they are rendered into a superfluous population forced to work anywhere, anytime, for any available wages. However, Marx believed that under these extreme conditions proletarians will become increasingly class conscious.

Marx's third prediction about the consequences of capital accumulation is that the rate of profit will inevitably fall, bring on industrial crises of even greater severity, and eventually produce an impoverished proletariat that will overthrow a chaotic capitalist system in favor of a more humane and cooperative one. The logic of Marx's analysis can be understood when it is recalled that labor power is the source of surplus value. As the proportion of surplus value invested in machines (constant capital) goes up in comparison to the amount invested in labor power (variable capital), profits fall.[64] In those areas where profits become unacceptably low, even though large quantities of goods are

---

[63]Ibid., p. 581.
[64]See Appelbaum, "Marx's Theory of the Falling Rate of Profit."

being produced, production has to slow down or cease altogether, throwing more people out of work. Marx argued that as industrial cycles repeatedly occur, they will become ever more serious, and he predicted that the logic of capitalist development will produce the conditions necessary for its overthrow: an industrial base along with an impoverished and class-conscious proletariat. Ultimately, these dispossessed people will usher in a classless society in which production occurs for the common good.

The Origins of Capitalism

Marx's analysis of capitalism presupposes that it is an ongoing social system. Thus in the final pages of *Capital* he once again sketched the origins of capitalism, which he now called the process of *primitive accumulation*. We should recall that capitalist social relations only occur under quite specific circumstances—that is, the owners of money (the means of production) who desire to increase their holdings confront free laborers who have no way of obtaining sustenance other than by selling their labor power. Thus, in order to understand the origins of capitalist social relations, Marx had to account for the rise of both the proletariat and the bourgeoisie. Typically, Marx opted for a structural explanation.

According to Marx, the modern proletariat arose because self-supporting peasants were driven from the land (and from the guilds) and transformed into rootless and dependent urban dwellers. This process began in England during the fifteenth and sixteenth centuries and then spread throughout Western Europe. Using England as his example, Marx argued that this process began with the clearing of the old estates by breaking up feudal retainers, robbing peasants of the use of common lands, and abolishing their rights of land tenure under circumstances he described as "reckless terrorism." In addition, Marx argued, one of the major effects of the Protestant Reformation was "the spoilation of the church's property" by its conversion into private property—illegally, of course. Finally, the widespread theft of state land and its conversion into privately owned property ensured that nowhere in England could peasants continue to live as they had during medieval times. In all these cases (although this analysis is clearly too simplistic) the methods used were far from idyllic, but they were effective, and they resulted in the rise of capitalist agriculture capable of supplying the needs of a "free" proletariat. Further, given that they had nowhere to go, thousands of displaced peasants became beggars, robbers, and vagabonds. Hence throughout Western Europe beginning in the sixteenth century there was "bloody legislation against vagabondage" with severe sanctions against those who would not work for the nascent capitalists who were then emerging.

For Marx, the emergence of the capitalist farmer and the industrial capitalist occurred concomitantly with the rise of the modern proletariat. Beginning in the fifteenth century, those who owned or controlled land typically had guarantees of long tenure, could employ newly "freed" workers at very low wages, and benefited from a rise in the price of farm products of all sorts. In addition, they were able to increase farm production, despite the smaller number of people working the land, through the use of improved methods and equipment, which increased cooperation among workers in the farming process and concentrated land ownership in fewer hands. Thus primitive accumulation of capital could occur.

Marx felt industrial capitalism developed as the result of a variety of interrelated events. First, he emphasized, usury and commerce had existed throughout antiquity—despite laws against such activity—and laid a basis for the primitive accumulation of capital to occur. Second, the exploration and exploitation of the New World brought great wealth into the hands of just a few people. In this regard Marx pointed especially to the discovery of gold and silver, along with the existence of native populations that could be exploited. Finally, Marx noted the emergence of a system of public credit and its expansion into an international credit system. On this basis, he claimed, capitalism emerged in Western Europe.

In *Capital* Marx believed he had described the nature and destiny of capitalist societies. Although he was wrong, *Capital* remains a book of creative genius unequaled in the history of the social sciences. Nonetheless, it is misbegotten both theoretically and politically. We conclude our analysis by describing these two problems in Marx's sociology.

THEORETICAL PROBLEMS IN MARX'S SOCIOLOGY

Marx's sociology was described earlier as a scientific political doctrine. He believed that he had discovered the pattern of history and that a communist revolution and the destruction of capitalism are inevitable historical events. He thus linked science and politics. These elements of his thought make it absolutely unique in comparison to the other founders of sociology. They also make his work fundamentally flawed because it is not possible to predict the future in scientific terms. Put differently, no predictor—whether a human being making economic forecasts, a computer, or an astrologer—can foresee its future results scientifically.

Now Marxists often argue that dialectical materialism is not designed to make predictions at all, that it is merely a useful guide to reality.[65] They further point to Marx's and Engels's many assertions about the importance of studying actual historical events. Nonetheless, the attempt at showing the inherently contradictory character of capitalist society leads inexorably to an interpretation of the pattern of history and to predictions about the future. Such analyses are based on a leap of faith: that a communist revolution and the destruction of capitalism are inevitable. These tenets constitute the core of Marxist thought.

The results, however, are very peculiar. As Karl Popper observes, such orientation can explain anything.[66] This fact means, of course, that it explains nothing because the theory cannot be disproved. Contrary evidence is simply disregarded. For example, if a communist revolution has not yet occurred in a capitalist society, such as the United States, Marxists commonly argue that all the inherent contradictions have not yet worked themselves out. After all, they can demonstrate that most workers are exploited and alienated, since they have little control over their work. Thus Marxists continue to maintain that working people in America will eventually become aware of their true interests and act politically to overthrow the entire social order. Similarly, if the state becomes oppressive after a communist revolution and if a new dominant class emerges, as in the Soviet Union, Marxists commonly argue that the post-revolutionary society remains in a period of transition that might last for centuries.[67]

After a while, they assert, the state will in fact "wither away" and a true communist society will evolve, one in which "the free development of each is a condition for the free development of all." In both cases Marx's theoretical methodology allows uncomfortable observations to be explained away by positing the need for further political action that will verify the "scientific" prediction.

Although brilliantly conceived, Marx's orientation is not scientific because, as Popper argues, theories must ultimately be subjected to a critical test. That is, a situation must be devised that is capable of refuting the theory. Dialectical materialism cannot be tested in this way and therefore cannot be scientific. Thus a "scientific political doctrine" is a contradiction in terms, for political action can only be justified in

[65]Ollman, *Alienation*.

[66]Karl Popper, *Conjectures and Refutations* (New York: Harper & Row, 1968), pp. 33–37.

[67]Harry Braverman, *Labor and Monopoly Capital* (New York: Monthly Review Press, 1974).

terms of values, not science. Marx constructed a political doctrine that proved to be of enormous historical significance.

POLITICAL IMPLICATIONS OF MARX'S SOCIOLOGY

Marx had a utopian vision of a classless society within which people acted cooperatively for the common good and, in the process, realized their human potential. Paradoxically, he believed this goal could be achieved through the centralization of political power in the hands of the state. This belief is why we described him previously as a sorcerer's apprentice. The image is that of a leader without wisdom who inadvertently releases the power of the nether world on the earth. Put bluntly, Marx's vision of the transition from capitalism to communism invites the establishment of a regime in which the individual is subordinate to the state and there is strict control over all aspects of life; it invites, in other words, modern totalitarianism.

To understand why Marx proceeded in this way, one needs to appreciate the dilemma he faced. As a revolutionary, he sought to overthrow a brutal and exploitive society in favor of a humane and just community. It is worth remembering that Engels's description of the living condition of the working class was horribly accurate, and many nineteenth-century observers saw the situation as becoming steadily worse. Thus, as he saw it, the problem was to get from a competitive society to a communal one, which would free individuals to realize their potential as human beings.

So he made a series of proposals that are worth restating: the abolition of private ownership of land, confiscation of the property of emigrants and rebels, centralization of credit by the state, centralization of communication and transportation by the state, ownership of factories by the state, and several others. These measures imply a belief that unrestrained political power can be redemptive, that the way to freedom is through totalitarian control. As Marx put it, the transition to communism would require a temporary "dictatorship of the proletariat." But experience has shown that this strategy can only mean total rule by the Communist party, which justifies its exploitation of the masses by invoking the common good. Now the political issue here is not whether the ends justify the means. It is, rather, whether the means can produce the ends—that is, can power, unfettered by accountability, produce freedom for individuals? The answer is no. There is no evidence that totalitarianism can produce freedom. Despite its grandiose vision, Marx's writings have had perverse political consequences.

THE ENDURING LEGACY

Despite the theoretical and political implications of Marx's work, it is nonetheless possible to extrapolate from his writings, mainly *The Communist Manifesto,* a set of abstract theoretical statements specifying some of the conditions under which oppressed people will organize themselves and class conflict will ensue. These propositions constitute an enduring legacy to subsequent sociologists.[68]

1. The greater the level of productivity in a society, the greater the division of labor, and vice versa.
2. The greater the division of labor in a society, the greater the inequality.
3. The greater the level of productivity, the greater the solidarity among subordinates.
4. The greater the class solidarity among subordinates, the greater the rate of conflict between dominant and subordinate classes.
   a. The greater the communication among subordinates, the greater their class solidarity.
       i. The more educational opportunities among subordinates, the greater their communication.
      ii. The more urbanized subordinates are, the greater their communication.
     iii. The more subordinates have common life experiences, the greater their communication.
   b. The more subordinates become aware of their common interests, the greater their class solidarity.
       i. The more widespread are feelings of alienation among subordinates, the more they are aware of their common interests.
      ii. The greater the inequality in a society, the more subordinates are aware of their common interests.
     iii. The more actions by dominant classes disrupt stable relationships among subordinates, the more the latter are aware of their common interests.
      iv. The more skills and wages are equalized at a very low level, the more subordinates are aware of their common interests.
       v. The greater the rate of downward mobility in a society, the more subordinates are aware of their common interests.
   c. The more subordinates develop a unifying ideology, the greater their class solidarity.

---

[68]See Jonathan H. Turner, *Societal Stratification* (New York: Columbia University Press, 1984).

    i. The more subordinates recruit or generate ideological leaders, the greater their ideological unity.

    ii. The less that dominant classes are able to regulate socialization among subordinates, the greater the ideological unity among the latter.

    iii. The less that dominant classes are able to regulate communication networks among subordinates, the greater the ideological unity among the latter.

5. The more dominants and subordinates become polarized, the greater the rate of conflict between them and the more likely it is to be violent.

    a. The greater the class solidarity among subordinates, the more polarized are dominants and subordinates.

    b. The greater the class solidarity among dominants, the more polarized are dominants and subordinates.

CHAPTER 6

The Origin and Context of Max Weber's Thought

BIOGRAPHICAL INFLUENCES ON WEBER'S THOUGHT

Max Weber, the first of seven children, was born to Max and Helene Weber on April 21, 1864, in the city of Erfurt in Thuringia. Thuringia was located in Prussia, the most powerful of the German states at that time. Today, however, it is part of Eastern Germany and is largely forgotten by Westerners. Weber was descended from Protestants on both sides of his family. His father's ancestors were Lutheran refugees from Austria, while his mother's forebears were Huguenot emigrants from France. As we shall see, Weber's Protestantism weighed heavily on him, serving as a source of torment and eventually as motivation for one of the greatest sociological analyses ever written: *The Protestant Ethic and the Spirit of Capitalism.*[1]

The Early Years

Max Weber senior, a lawyer and judge in Erfurt, became a politician in Berlin, where the family moved in 1869. In Berlin the elder Weber began his political career as a city councillor and subsequently served as a member of the Landtag (Regional Assembly) and the Reichstag (Imperial Parliament). In this context the Weber family entertained a wide assortment of distinguished people. For example, the historians Theodor Mommsen and Wilhelm Dilthey lived nearby and frequently visited the Weber household.[2] This background allowed the young Max Weber to meet the leading politicians and scholars of the day, listen to and participate in their discussions, and become aware of the issues facing the nation.

---

[1] Max Weber, *The Protestant Ethic and the Spirit of Capitalism* (New York: Charles Scribner's Sons, 1958). The original appeared in two parts in 1904 and 1905.

[2] Marianne Weber, *Max Weber: A Biography* (New York: John Wiley & Sons, 1975), p. 39. The original was published in 1926. Unless otherwise noted, all biographical material comes from this source.

By all accounts Weber's father enjoyed the freewheeling lifestyle of a German politician, with its emphasis on material success, its lack of religiosity, and its rough–and–tumble world of gossip, deals, and accommodation. He was a hedonist, a man who enjoyed bourgeois living to the fullest. Within the family, however, the senior Weber ruled absolutely. He did not tolerate young people holding opinions different than his own and felt compelled, as a patriarch, to control his wife's behavior in myriad ways. The elder Weber was nonetheless devoted to his children, active in supervising their education and frequently taking them on outings in the German countryside. During his youth the young Max Weber was close to his father, an orientation that would change later on.

Weber's mother was altogether different than her husband. Helene Weber, a shy and sensitive woman, was religiously devout. When she was sixteen, an older friend of the family sexually attacked her, and one result of this episode was that she came to hate sexuality. Marianne Weber reports that "the physical aspect of marriage was to her not a source of joy but a heavy sacrifice and also a sin that was justified only by the procreation of children. Because of this, in her youthful happiness she often longed for old age to free her from that 'duty.' " A loving and affectionate mother, Helene Weber nonetheless adhered to strict Calvinist standards of hard work, ascetic behavior, and personal morality, which she tried to instill in her children. "She was never satisfied with herself and always felt inadequate before God," with the result that her life was marked by great inward struggle.[3] Moreover, because they were so mismatched, Weber's parents became permanently estranged very early in their marriage, a conflict that affected Weber throughout his life. Marianne Weber claims plausibly that Max not only believed he had to choose between his parents but that this choice could be decisive for his own personality development. It is as if the "choice" became an issue of personal morality rather than an emotional dilemma.[4] Weber lived with this agony throughout his life.

Max Weber was a sickly child. He contracted a serious disease, possibly meningitis, at age two, and the experience left him smaller and less physically capable than other children. Nonetheless, he was intellectually precocious. His youthful letters, many of which survive, are filled with reflections on the classical Greek and Roman writers as well as the philosophers Johann Goethe, Bennedetto Spinoza, and Immanual Kant. His conversations at home also ensured that Weber became politically sophisticated at a very young age, a characteristic that

---

[3]Ibid., pp. 21–30.
[4]Ibid., p. 84.

apparently made him a discipline problem in school, where he thought the level of instruction too low and the ignorance of his classmates appalling. More generally, the twin problem of authority's nature and use preoccupied Weber throughout his life, both personally and intellectually.

In 1882 Weber graduated from the gymnasium (high school) and enrolled at the University of Heidelberg. Like his father, he chose the law as a field of study and professional training. In addition, however, he also studied economics, history, philosophy, and theology. Sociology was not offered at that time. Weber became active in his father's fraternity, joining in the ritual dueling and drinking bouts characteristic of German university life in those days. The large amount of beer consumed and the hedonistic lifestyle transformed the frail youth into a rather heavy-set young man, complete with fencing scars on his face.

In 1883 Weber served an obligatory year of military service and came under the influence of his aunt Ida Baumgarten (his mother's sister) and his uncle, the historian Herman Baumgarten. It proved to be a turning point in Weber's life. Stronger and more forceful than her sister, Ida Baumgarten led a simple and ascetic religious life. In so doing she helped Weber understand and appreciate his mother's Christian piety. As a result, although this way of phrasing the issue is somewhat crude, he began to identify with his mother rather than with his father.

Before the Breakdown

Weber returned to Berlin in the following year, where he enrolled at the University of Berlin and lived at home. He remained there for the next seven years, financially dependent on a father he increasingly disliked and condemned, while completing his apprenticeship in law. Like Marx, Weber was a polymath (a person with encyclopedic learning). While working for several years as a full-time unpaid legal apprentice, he also completed a Ph.D. dissertation titled "The History of Trading Companies in the Middle Ages" and a post-doctoral thesis titled "Roman Agrarian History," which qualified him to teach at the university level.[5] Weber also joined the Evangelical Social Union, a Protestant political group reacting against the excesses of industrialization in Germany, and the Social Political Union, an academic organization committed to doing research on social problems confronting Germany. Under the aegis of the latter, Weber investigated the conditions of rural peasants. The result, a nine-hundred page book titled

---

[5]Neither of these works has been translated into English.

The Situation of Farm Workers in Germany East of the Elbe River, established Weber's reputation as a young scholar.[6] In order to produce three books while working full time as a junior barrister, Weber "repressed everything," living an ascetic life strictly regulated by the clock.[7] These characteristics of his own life assumed intellectual significance in his subsequent work, *The Protestant Ethic and the Spirit of Capitalism.*

Although convinced he was not a "true scholar," Weber nonetheless decided to pursue a combined academic and legal career. Thus in 1892 he accepted an instructor's position at the University of Berlin. During this same period he courted and married his cousin, Marianne Schnitger, whose loving biography of her husband remains the standard source about his life.

Weber had a passion for work. "Hardly was one [task] complete when his restless intellect took hold of a new one." Thus his chronic overwork and unhealthy lifestyle became a cause of concern for both his mother and wife, who urged him to slow down. Their remonstrations, however, had little effect. In 1894 the couple moved to Freiburg, where Max took a position as professor of political economy. According to Marianne Weber, the workload there "surpassed everything up to then."[8] Over the next several years Weber maintained a punishing academic, legal, and political schedule. He was apparently regarded as an outstanding professor, a promising lawyer, and a man with a future in public service. In addition the Webers (who were by all accounts, not just Marianne's, happily married) maintained an unconventional lifestyle for the period. Over time Marianne became a student under Heinrich Rickert, a social worker, and a supporter of women's rights. As a result Weber soon became "more of a feminist than she was."[9]

Against this background Weber's long-simmering anger toward his father erupted in 1897, with disastrous consequences for all. Each year Helene Weber usually spent several weeks visiting her children and their families. The elder Weber, however, always made these trips difficult, believing he should control his wife's every activity. During the summer father and son clashed violently over this issue and parted without reconciliation. Shortly thereafter the old man died. And soon after that, Weber, at age thirty-three and now a professor of political economy at the University of Heidelberg, suffered a complete nervous breakdown, which incapacitated him for more than five years.

---

[6]Untranslated, this work is summarized in Reinhard Bendix, *Max Weber: An Intellectual Portrait* (Garden City, N.Y.: Doubleday, 1962), pp. 14–30.

[7]Marianne Weber, *Max Weber,* p. 145.

[8]Ibid., pp. 195–201.

[9]Ibid., p. 229.

It is intriguing, of course, to speculate about the causes of Weber's psychic break.[10] While there exists little doubt that the fight with, and subsequent death of, his father constituted the precipitating incident, the more general issues contributing to Weber's psychological trauma were unresolved difficulties of identification with his parents and inner conflicts over the contradictory values of his mother and father. Further, it makes sense to assert that chronic overwork along with his sexual impotence (the marriage to Marianne was probably never consummated) served as both symptoms of his underlying stress and additional causes of the breakdown. In any case, and it should be recognized that the above remarks are very superficial, Weber spent the following years unable to work. During a period prior to the availability of psychotherapy, the only "cure" for those afflicted with any form of mental fatigue was rest and relaxation.

Weber did little work for nearly six years. Sustained by an inheritance, he traveled widely, periodically recovering for short periods, only to collapse again and again. In 1900 Weber was retired by the University of Heidelberg. He did not teach again for nearly two decades.

The Transition to Sociology

Beginning in 1903 Weber found himself able to write again. He first produced a rather laborious work criticizing the German historical economists, Wilhelm Roscher and Karl Knies.[11] Shortly afterward he wrote an important methodological essay, " 'Objectivity' in Social Science and Public Policy," in which he first analyzed the place of values in the emerging social scientific disciplines.[12] This piece was followed in 1904 and 1905 with the seminal work for which Weber is primarily remembered, *The Protestant Ethic and the Spirit of Capitalism*, in which he outlined the historical significance of Protestantism for the development of capitalist cultural values. These last two items mark the beginning of Weber's self-conscious identification as a sociologist.

The transition to sociology is important since Weber's writings prior to his breakdown were composed from the point of view of historical economics. Thus, as a professor of political economy, he infused

---

[10]See Arthur Mitzman, *The Iron Cage: A Historical Interpretation of Max Weber* (New York: Alfred A. Knopf, 1970).

[11]Max Weber, *Roscher and Knies: The Logical Problems of Historical Economics* (New York: Free Press, 1975).

[12]Max Weber, " 'Objectivity' in Social Science and Social Policy," *The Methodology of the Social Sciences* (New York: Free Press, 1949), pp. 50–112, The original appeared in 1904.

his empirical analyses with a definite value standard. For example, in his study of farm workers he argued that agrarian policy in Germany must be determined by the interests of the state, an angle of vision that disapproved of Polish workers being brought into the eastern portions of the nation because their presence undermined the German claim of sovereignty over the area. However, as he began to recover the ability to work, Weber studied Rickert, Dilthey, and others and saw more clearly the necessity for separating social science and values. His subsequent writings emphasize that the two spheres—social science and values—must be kept as separate as possible. Thus, while social scientific knowledge can inform political decisions, such actions can only be justified in terms of values.

separation of science & values [margin annotation]

In the years between 1906 and 1914, Weber continued research and writing, now confining himself to the role of private scholar. He studied religion, the origin of cities, and social scientific methodology, producing a series of books and essays. Among them are the methodological *Critique of Stammler* (1907), *The Sociology of Religion* (1912), *The Religion of China* (1913), *The Religion of India* (which appeared in 1916–17), and *Ancient Judaism* (which appeared in 1917).[13]

In addition to scholarly work, Weber also participated in the social life of German intellectuals.[14] Max and Marianne's home served as a meeting place for distinguished persons in many fields. Sociologists Georg Simmel and Robert Michels, historian Heinrich Rickert, and philosopher Karl Jaspers were among the many scholars who regularly took part in wide-ranging discussions of politics and social science. In 1910 Weber helped found the German Sociological Association, serving as its secretary for several years. In this context he continued to press his views on the nature of sociology, especially the importance of objectivity in social research.

With the outbreak of World War I, Weber, a passionate German nationalist, became a hospital administrator in the Heidelberg area. Over time, however, he began to oppose the German conduct of the war, advocating limited aims and prophesying defeat if unrestricted submarine warfare brought the United States into the conflict. Few people paid any attention.

In 1918 Weber accepted an academic position at the University of Vienna and offered a course for the first time in twenty years. In the

---

[13]Max Weber, *Critique of Stammler* (New York: Free Press, 1977); *The Religion of China* (New York: Free Press, 1951); *The Religion of India* (New York: Free Press, 1958); *The Sociology of Religion* (Boston: Beacon Press, 1963); *Ancient Judaism* (New York: Free Press, 1952).

[14]For the next three paragraphs we are indebted to Lewis A. Coser, *Masters of Sociological Thought* (New York: Harcourt Brace Jovanovich, 1977), p. 241.

following year he taught at the University of Munich, giving two of his most famous addresses: "Science as a Vocation" and "Politics as a Vocation."[15] During this period he began reworking the material from the prewar years, writing what became part 1 of his *Economy and Society*.[16] He also gave a series of lectures that were posthumously published under the title *General Economic History*.[17]

In the twilight of his life, Weber evidently found some release from the traumas of the past. Although he had little time for relaxation, Marianne Weber says his capacity for work became steadier and his sleep more regular. During the summer of 1920 Max Weber developed pneumonia. He died on June 14.

While Max Weber stands as one of the greatest classical sociologists, the exact lines of his theoretical contributions are sometimes difficult to ascertain. Part of the reason for this lack of precision is the breadth of Weber's work. Indeed some have argued that no sociologist before or since has displayed Weber's intellectual range or sophistication. He analyzed the historical significance of the Protestant Reformation, the characteristics of Indian and Chinese social structure and religion, the genesis of modern legal systems, the nature of modern bureaucracies, the types of political domination, the origin of the city in the West, and many other topics. As a result of this breadth of concern with a variety of substantive topics, his influence on the development of modern sociological theory remains unclear. For the scope of Weber's empirical concerns suggests that he was not primarily interested in development of abstract laws of human behavior and organization. Nonetheless, we will show that while his theoretical goals were limited, Weber's works have contributed enormously to sociological theory.

The origins of Weber's sociology lie in his reaction to intellectual trends in Germany at the turn of the century. The remainder of this chapter focuses on four of the most important influences on his thought. First, and perhaps most significantly, Weber rejected both Marx and Marxism as too simplistic and inherently nonscientific. Second, Weber rejected as nonproductive the long-standing debate over the nature of the social sciences that dominated late nineteenth-century German thought. This debate, called the *methodenstreit* (or methodological controversy), involved two competing schools of thought whose attitudes toward the practice of social science were quite at odds with one another: the classical or theoretical economists and the historical

---

[15]These essays are reprinted in Hans Gerth and C. Wright Mills, *From Max Weber* (New York: Oxford University Press, 1946), pp. 77–158.

[16]Max Weber, *Economy and Society* (New York: Bedminster Press, 1968).

[17]Max Weber, *General Economic History* (New York: Collier Books, 1961).

economists. The third major influence on Weber's thought was Wilhelm Dilthey, who emphasized the importance of understanding the subjective meanings people attach to their behavior. In a somewhat altered form, this idea became one of the cornerstones of Weber's thought. Fourth, Weber took many of the methodological precepts developed by Heinrich Rickert for use in the study of history and altered them in such a way as to facilitate his own brand of sociology. As will be seen in Chapter 7, the result of these four influences was an original form of sociological analysis.

KARL MARX AND MAX WEBER

Despite the fact that Marx is rarely cited in Weber's works, he carried on a "silent dialogue" with the dead revolutionary. Hans Gerth and C. Wright Mills, in fact, have carried this idea so far as to argue that Weber's writings should be seen as an effort at "rounding out," or supplementing, Marx's interpretation of the rise and fall of capitalist society.[18] While this point of view ignores the fundamental differences between Marx and Weber, many modern scholars have agreed with Gerth and Mills. Hence it is worth noting some of the points of similarity between the two men prior to emphasizing their essential differences.

First, in *The Protestant Ethic and the Spirit of Capitalism*, Weber showed the relationship between the cultural values associated with the Protestant Reformation and the rise of the culture of capitalism in the West, but he explicitly did not deny the importance of the material factors that Marx had previously identified. In fact, apart from the transformative impact of Puritanism, Marx and Weber generally agreed on the structural factors involved in the rise of modern society. Second, both Marx and Weber can be seen as "systems theorists" in the sense that their conceptual schemes represent an attempt at mapping the connections among the situational and environmental contexts in which people act. Third, both scholars recognized the extent to which individuals' freedom of action is limited in modern societies, although each did so in a somewhat different way: In Marx's work people are alienated because they do not control the means of production, while in Weber's work individuals often find themselves in an "iron cage" constructed by increasingly omnipresent and powerful bureaucracies. Fourth, despite the constraints just noted, both Marx and Weber observed the importance of human decision making in shaping history. For Marx, who was always a hopeful utopian and revolutionary, action

---

[18]Gerth and Mills, "Introduction," in *From Max Weber*, pp. 3–76.

will usher in a new era of freedom for all people; for Weber, who was less hopeful about the future, individuals have a wider range of choices in modern societies than was possible in the traditional communities of the past. Finally, as will be seen in Chapter 7, there is some complementarity in the theoretical principles that can be extrapolated from Marx's and Weber's work.

Nonetheless, despite these areas of similarity, Weber's work was different than Marx's in origin, purpose, and style. Marx combined revolution and theory in order to explain what he saw as the pattern of history. Weber helped to establish an academically based sociology committed to the objective observation and understanding of historical processes, which he regarded as inherently unpredictable. These differences in orientation cannot be reconciled without obliterating the distinctiveness of each man's work. Hence, rather than "rounding out" Marx, it is clear that Weber had an overriding interest in refuting Marxist thought as it existed at the turn of the twentieth century. For example, in the *Protestant Ethic,* Weber went out of his way to note that his findings flatly contradicted those postulated by "historical materialism," and he wondered at the naiveté of those Marxists who espoused such doctrines.[19] More generally, Weber disagreed with Marx and the Marxists (the two are not the same) on three interrelated and fundamental topics: (1) the nature of science, (2) the inevitability of history, and (3) economic determinism.

The Nature of Science

As seen in Chapter 5, Marx combined science and revolution in such a way that theories are verified by action, by what they lead people to do (or not do) based on their material interests. Weber, on the other hand, saw science as the search for truth and argued that knowledge is verified by observation. In making observations he said research must be "value free" in the sense that concepts are clearly defined, agreed upon rules of evidence are followed, and logical inferences are made. Only in this way could there be an objective science of sociology.[20]

While recognizing that Marxists are often motivated by moral outrage at the conditions under which most people are forced to live, Weber asserted that ethical positions are not scientifically demonstrable, no matter how laudable they might be. Further, by combining science and revolution in order to justify their view of the future, Weber as-

---

[19]Weber, *Protestant Ethic,* pp. 55, 75, 90–92, 266, 277.
[20]Weber, "Science as a Vocation."

serted that Marxists inevitably confuse "what is" and "what ought to be," with the result that their ethical motives are undermined.[21] Such confusion should be eliminated as much as possible, Weber insisted, by making social science objective through an exclusive emphasis on "what is." Nonetheless, Weber recognized that social scientists' values inevitably intrude into social inquiry, since they influence the topics considered important for research. But this fact, Weber argued, does not preclude the possibility that the process of research can and should be objective. Thus while Weber believed science cannot tell people how to live or how to organize themselves, it can provide them with the sort of information necessary to make such decisions. On this basis Weber sought to understand the origin and characteristics of modern societies by developing a set of concepts that could be used in understanding social action.

The Inevitability of History

Marx posited the existence of historical laws of development, with the result that he saw feudalism as leading inevitably to capitalism and the latter leading inexorably to a more humane communist society. Against this position, Weber argued that there are no laws of historical development and that capitalism arose in the West as a result of a series of historical accidents.

As will be shown in Chapter 7, Weber's sociology is oriented to understanding how modern Western societies could have arisen when and where they did. Essentially he argued that a number of historical processes occurred together and resulted in the rise of modern capitalism in the West. Among these processes were the following: industrialization, the rise of a free labor force, the development of logical accounting methods, the rise of free markets, the development of modern forms of law, the increasing use of paper instruments of ownership (such as stock certificates), and the rise of what Weber called the *spirit of capitalism.*[22] As will be seen, he believed the last factor to be the most significant. Further, Weber argued that none of these phenomena could have been predicted in advance; rather they were all dependent on chance. Thus from his point of view, societies are always perpetually balanced between the opposing forces of determinism and chance, for the course of history is often altered by unforeseen political struggles, wars, ecological calamities, or the charisma of single individuals.

---

[21]Guenther Roth, "[Weber's] Historical Relationship to Marxism," in *Scholarship and Partisanship: Essays on Max Weber,* ed. Reinhard Bendix and Guenther Roth (Berkeley: University of California Press, 1971), pp. 227–52.

[22]Weber, *General Economic History,* pp. 207–76.

Economic Determinism

By the beginning of the twentieth century, many Marxists were arguing that certain economic arrangements, especially the private ownership of the means of production, inevitably caused specific political forms as well as other social structures to develop. While this crude form of economic determinism distorts Marx's analysis and eliminates its subtlety, it had the advantage of allowing for quick and easy (not to mention nasty) assessments of modern capitalist societies. Weber attempted to refute this rather congealed form of Marx's analysis in two somewhat different ways. First, in the *Protestant Ethic* he showed the importance of religious ideas in shaping the behavior of the Puritans and, by extrapolation, all Western people. Second, in *Economy and Society*, he outlined the extent to which systems of domination are maintained because they are viewed as legitimate by citizens—a commitment that generally overwhelms the socio-economic divisions that always exist. In Weber's words "it is one of the delusions rooted in the modern overestimation of the 'economic factor' . . . to believe that national solidarity cannot survive the tensions of antagonistic economic interests, or even to assume that political solidarity is *merely* a reflection of the economic substructure."[23]

THE *METHODENSTREIT* AND MAX WEBER

The methodological controversy that dominated German academic life in the latter half of the nineteenth century can only be understood in light of two interrelated factors. First, in Germany there tended to be a rather rigid division between the natural sciences and the cultural disciplines such that only natural phenomena—such as those studied in physics, chemistry, biology, and the like—were seen as amenable to theoretical (that is, scientific) analysis. Based on the philosophy of Immanuel Kant (and Hegel, but to a much lesser extent), it was believed that the social and cultural realms, the world of the "spirit," could not be analyzed in scientific terms. Hence studies of natural and social phenomena developed in much different directions in Germany.[24]

Second, after the early work of Adam Smith and David Ricardo, non-Marxist economic theory became stagnant, with the result that economists had great difficulty in trying to explain the workings of

---

[23]Weber, quoted in Roth, "[Weber's] Historical Relationship to Marxism," p. 234 (emphasis in original).
[24]See Talcott Parsons, *The Structure of Social Action* (New York: Free Press, 1948), pp. 473–86.

actual industrial economies as they existed in the nineteenth century. Now there were two main ways of dealing with the problem. One was to develop better theory, while another was to eschew science altogether and to concentrate on depicting the historical development of particular economic systems. The members of the historical school of economics chose the latter course, a position that fit comfortably with the dominant German intellectual tradition. Nonetheless, there remained a number of scholars (although they were a very small minority in German academic circles) who chose to develop non-Marxist economic theory. For the most part these theoretical economists were non-Germans who came from a positivistic background roughly similar to Durkheim's.

The major figures in the German historical school were individuals who are generally not remembered today, largely because their writings have not proven to be of enduring significance. Wilhelm Roscher, Bruno Hildebrand, and Karl Knies, all contemporaries of Marx, are generally credited with founding the movement during the middle portion of the nineteenth century. Later such men as Lujo Brentano and Gustav Schmoller added to and modified this perspective. While there were inevitably some differences in the way each of these scholars approached the study of economics and, by extrapolation, social science in general, they shared a number of basic criticisms of theoretical economics as well as a relatively common methodological approach to their subject matter.

On the other side of the conflict were the members of the theoretical school, many of whom remain well-known figures in the history of economic thought, largely because their writings furthered the development of the discipline as a science. Among these scholars are Leon Walras, W. S. Jevons, Eugen Böhm-Bawark, and Karl Menger. However, Menger is by far the most important because he discovered the theory of marginal utility, an idea that went a long way toward solving the theoretical dilemmas that had plagued economics throughout the latter half of the nineteenth century. Since the *methodenstreit* is primarily remembered in terms of the acimonious and often vicious debate between Menger and Schmoller that occurred during the 1870s, we shall refer to them as the representative of each school of thought.

Methodological Issues Dividing Historical and Theoretical Economics

There were four fundamental issues over which the historical school and the theoretical school disagreed, all of them stemming from the divergence between economic theory and economic reality noted previously.[25] The first involved the importance of deduction versus induction. Schmoller and the historical economists charged that the theoreticians' use of deductive methods was faulty, chiefly because their theories could not explain reality. Hence the historical economists emphasized as an alternative the importance of observing and describing people's concrete patterns of action (often down to the smallest details), and they spent many years compiling such data. Unlike some of the other historians, for whom description quickly became an end in itself, Schmoller asserted that the long-run result of this descriptive work would be the discovery of economic laws through the use of inductive methods. He believed the resulting propositions would better describe reality because they would take the complexity of people's actual behavior into account. Alternatively, Menger and the theoretical economists charged (correctly, as it turned out) that the historians were so immersed in data that no laws would ever result. Further, Menger said the more realistic response to the inadequacies of economic theory is to develop better theories, which was precisely what he and others were doing at that time.

The second issue dividing the two schools had to do with the universality versus relativity of findings. Schmoller and the historical economists asserted that the theoreticians' emphasis on the universal applicability of economic laws was absurd. Rather, from the historians' point of view, their empirical research had shown that economic development occurs in evolutionary stages unique to each society, which implies that it is possible to understand a society's present stage of economic advancement only by ascertaining previous stages. Menger and the theoreticians responded by observing that theory, whether in the social sciences or the natural sciences, is oriented toward that which is common rather than that which is unique. Hence economic theories can (at least in principle) explain certain aspects of human behavior that are common to all societies, but, admittedly, not every element of social action can be explained theoretically. On this basis Menger argued that there is a place for both theory and history in economics and the other social sciences.

The third issue of debate in the *methodenstreit* had to do with the degree of rationality versus nonrationality in human behavior. Schmoller and the historical economists believed the theoretical economists' view of economic man as rational and motivated only by nar-

---

[25]The following paragraphs have benefited from Thomas Burger, *Max Weber's Theory of Concept Formation: History, Laws, and Ideal Types* (Durham, N.C.: Duke University Press, 1976), pp. 140–50; Joseph Schumpeter, *Economic Doctrine and Method* (New York: Oxford University Press, 1954), pp. 152–201; and Charles Gide and Charles Rist, *A History of Economic Doctrine* (Lexington, Mass.: D.C. Heath, 1948), pp. 383–409.

row self-interest was unrealistic. They went on to assert that there is a unity to all of social life in the sense that people act out of a multiplicity of motives, which are not always rational. Thus, in order to obtain a comprehensive view of social reality, historical research often went far beyond the narrow confines of economic action, dealing with the interrelationships among economic, political, legal, religious, and other social phenomena. While Schmoller was right here, Menger simply replied that economic theory deals with only one side of human behavior (that is, people's attempts at material need satisfaction), and the other social sciences must focus on other aspects of social action. Over the long run, Menger believed, the result would be a comprehensive understanding of human behavior.

Finally, the fourth issue separating the two schools had to do with economics as an ethical discipline versus economics as a science. Schmoller and other members of the historical school unquestionably saw economics an an ethical discipline that could help solve many of the problems facing German society, with the result that their scholarly writings often had an avowedly political intent. This attitude was partly a consequence of the long-standing German division between the natural sciences and the cultural disciplines and partly a consequence of the fact that Schmoller and many of the others held important university and governmental positions. In opposition, Menger charged that Schmoller's political value judgments were hopelessly confused with his scholarly analyses, to the detriment of both. In science, Menger said, the two must be kept separate.

Weber's Response to the *Methodenstreit*

In economics the *methodenstreit* eventually dissipated, although more by the force of theoretical developments than the rhetoric of the participants. However, on several occasions Weber appears to have used the arguments raised in the controversy as a baseline from which to develop his own methodological orientation.[26]

In regard to the first issue, the importance of inductive versus deductive methods, Weber tried to bridge the gap between the two schools so as to create a historically based social science. With the historical economists Weber argued that if the social sciences imitated the natural sciences by seeking to discover general laws of social behavior,

---

[26]For Weber's views on Menger and the theoretical economists, see his " 'Objectivity' in Social Science and Social Policy," in *The Methodology of the Social Sciences*; and "Marginal Utility Theory and the So-Called Fundamental Law of Psychophysics," *Social Science Quarterly* 56, June 1975; pp. 48–159. For Weber's views on the historical economists, see his *Roscher and Knies*.

unique phenomena are most historically significant

then not very much useful knowledge would be produced. His reasoning was that any social science oriented toward the development of timelessly valid laws would, of necessity, emphasize those patterns of action that are common from one society to another, with the result that idiographic events would inevitably be omitted from consideration. Yet it is often the case that unique phenomena, such as the Protestant Reformation, are the most significant factors influencing the development of a culture. Hence a science seeking to understand the structure of social action in any society must necessarily focus on precisely those factors not amenable to lawlike formulations. Put differently, Weber argued that the social sciences had to make use of historical materials. Nonetheless, with the theoretical economists Weber asserted that the development of abstract concepts was absolutely necessary in order to guide empirical research. As will be seen in the next chapter, Weber's goal was an objective (that is, scientific) comprehension of modern Western society, and for that reason he needed to develop a set of clear and precise concepts, which he called *ideal types* that could be used in understanding historical processes.

relativity

Weber's response to the second issue dividing the two schools follows from the first—that is, a historically based social science cannot be universally applicable; rather findings are always relative to a particular culture and society. One implication of this point of view is that while Weber tried to understand the origins of modern Western society, his findings may not have any relevance for the process of modernization in the Third World today because those societies are operating in a rather different historical context. However it should be emphasized here that Weber strongly disagreed with the historical economists' evolutionary interpretations. Rather he believed economic development does not occur in evolutionary stages since unpredictable events, such as wars, ecological changes, charismatic leaders, and myriads of other phenomena, alter the course of history.

The third issue in the *methodenstreit* was to become essential to Weber's sociology, for the protagonists inadvertently identified one of the fundamental characteristics of modern Western society: the tension between rational and nonrational action. Thus Menger's argument that rational economic behavior needs to be conceptually distinguished from other modes of action seemed reasonable to Weber because he had observed that action in the marketplace is characterized by an emphasis on logic and knowledge, which is often absent in other arenas. Yet at the same time, Schmoller's emphasis on the unity of social life and people's multiplicity of motives, some of which are based on values other than logic, also seemed reasonable. Hence Weber tried to conceptually summarize the "types of social action" so as to systematically distinguish modern Western societies from the traditional ones that had preceded them and to show the wider range of behavioral choices available to occidental people.[27]

Weber's reaction to the fourth issue in the methodological controversy was similar to his response to Marx and the Marxists—that is, Weber asserted that Menger was absolutely correct: The social sciences must be value free. While Schmoller and the other historical economists were generally political liberals with whom Weber was in sympathy, he believed there can be no scientific justification for any ethical or political point of view. However Weber argued that objective scientific analyses can provide people with the knowledge necessary to make intelligent ethical decisions based on their values.

WILHELM DILTHEY AND MAX WEBER

The origin of Weber's response to the *methodenstreit* can be found in the works of Wilhelm Dilthey and Heinrich Rickert. Essentially, Weber built his sociology with the methodological tools they provided, although he went beyond each of them in a number of fundamental ways. Neither Rickert or Dilthey is very well known in the English-speaking world, primarily because the problems they addressed are peculiar to the German intellectual scene during the late nineteenth century. Given the traditional idealist separation of the worlds of nature and human activity, the establishment of the social sciences as sciences was an extremely vexing problem.

Dilthey's Methodology of the Social Sciences

Essentially, Dilthey argued that while both the sphere of human behavior and the sphere of nature can be studied scientifically, it must be recognized that the subject matter of each and the kind of knowledge that each produces are different. He then went on to explore some of the implications of this argument.[28]

The logic of Dilthey's analysis can be seen in three steps. First, and most obvious, the two sciences have different subject matters. The

---

[27]Weber, *Economy and Society*, pp. 24–26.

[28]See Wilhelm Dilthey, *Meaning and History: W. Dilthey's Thoughts on History and Society* (Winchester, Mass.: Allen & Unwin, 1961); and Wilhelm Dilthey, *Selected Writings* (New York: Cambridge University Press, 1976). Among secondary sources, see H. P. Rickman, *Wilhelm Dilthey: Pioneer of the Human Studies* (New York: Cambridge University Press, 1979); and H. Stuart Hughes, *Consciousness and Society: The Reorientation of German Social Thought, 1890–1930* (New York: Vintage, 1958). Our sketch of Dilthey's ideas is adapted mainly from Hughes's discussion.

natural sciences are oriented toward the explanation of physical or natural events, while the social sciences are oriented toward the explanation of human action. Second, and as a result of the first, researchers in each field obtain quite different forms of knowledge. In the natural sciences knowledge is external in the sense that physical phenomena are affected by one another in ways that can be seen and explained in terms of timelessly valid laws. In the social sciences, however, knowledge is of necessity internal in the sense that each person has an "inner nature" that must be comprehended in some way in order to explain events. Third, as a result researchers in the two spheres must have altogether different orientations to their subject matter. In the natural sciences it is enough to observe events and relationships. For example, an object falling through space can be explained in terms of the force of gravity, and this explanation is true regardless of the cultural background of different researchers who may concern themselves with this topic. In the social sciences, however, scholars must go beyond mere observation and seek some sort of intuitive understanding (*verstehen*) of each person's inner nature in order to adequately explain events and relationships. Further, the explanations offered may well vary depending on the cultural background of the different researchers.

For Dilthey, then, the means by which observers obtain an understanding of each person's inner nature is the key to the scientific knowledge of human action. In this light he tried to classify the various fields devoted to the study of social behavior in terms of their typical mode of analysis. The first type of analysis consists of descriptions of reality, of events that have occurred, and this is the field of history. Unlike Rickert, Dilthey does not appear to have been very concerned with whether historical descriptions are accurate or objective. The second way of discussing human action consists of value judgments made in light of historical events, and this is the field of ethics or politics. The third way of dealing with social behavior consists of formulating abstractions from history, and this is the field of the social sciences. This last mode of analysis is the most important for understanding action, Dilthey asserted, because abstractions provide the conceptual tools without which it would be impossible to comprehend behavior. However, he was unable to face the implications of this insight, for Dilthey went on to argue that the systematic development of abstract concepts would not be of much long-term use in understanding people's inner states, and he opted instead for the necessity of relying on intuition (what he called the "fantasy of the artist") in comprehending social action. Such intuitive understanding occurs when, in some unexplainable and imperfect way, observers reexperience in their own consciousness the experiences of others. The result of this emphasis on the manner in which one mind becomes aware of another was that Dilthey's point of view led ultimately to a dead end. In the long run, as Weber realized, an excessive reliance on the researcher's subjective impressions cannot lead to an objective social science.

Weber's Response to Dilthey's Work

From Weber's point of view Dilthey's methodological orientation was useful in three ways.[29] First, Dilthey was correct in noting that the social sciences can obtain a quite different form of knowledge than the natural sciences. Second, social scientific statements are different from and, Weber added, must be kept separate from value judgments of any sort. And third, the key to social scientific knowledge is understanding (*verstehen*) the subjective meanings people attach to their actions.

However, Weber believed the major problem in Dilthey's work lies in his emphasis on understanding each person's inner nature, as if an objective social science could be founded on some sort of mystical and intuitive reexperiencing of others' desires and thoughts. Hence Weber developed a rather different way of emphasizing the importance of *verstehen*, one that proved to be a great deal more successful than Dilthey's. Essentially, Weber argued, while social action can only be understood when "it is placed in an intelligible and more inclusive context of meaning," the key to such understanding resides in the development of a set of abstract concepts (ideal types) that classify the dimensions of social action and reflect the norms appropriate in different spheres. By focusing his work in this way, Weber emphasized the importance of understanding individual behavior while, at the same time, he was able to assess the significance of historical events (such as the Reformation) in an objective manner.

HEINRICH RICKERT AND MAX WEBER

Like Dilthey, Rickert was concerned with the problems created by the disjunction between the world of nature and the world of human activity that had been created by idealist philosophy. However, the two men had somewhat different solutions in mind. As seen above, Dilthey's work addressed the problem of the dissimilar subject matter

---

[29]While Weber never wrote a formal commentary on Dilthey's work, his writings suggest an easy familiarity with Dilthey's teachings. See Hughes, *Consciousness and Society*, p. 309. For Weber's analysis of *verstehen* and its relationship to ideal types, see Weber, *Economy and Society*, pp. 8–20.

characterizing the natural and social sciences, emphasizing that the different forms of knowledge in each sphere require distinct methodological orientations on the part of researchers. Rickert, however, had a more narrow interest; he tried to show that history could be an objective scientific discipline because the knowledge it produced was based on a valid principle of concept selection. Like Dilthey, Rickert was not entirely successful in his task, largely because he misperceived the nature of science and drifted into metaphysical speculation.[30] Nonetheless, Rickert's writings constituted an important influence on Max Weber's work, for Weber, who was much more practical than Rickert, adapted some of Rickert's methodological principles for his own more general purposes.

Rickert on the Objectivity of History

Rickert began his attempt at demonstrating that history can be an objective science by dealing with a number of relatively noncontroversial epistemological issues. He argued that empirical reality is infinite in space and time, which for him meant that reality can, in principle, be divided into an infinite number of objects for study, and these objects can in turn be dissected into an unlimited number of parts. An important implication of this fact is that reality can never be completely known because there will always be some other way of looking at it. The practical problem, then, becomes how people can know anything at all about the world around them, and Rickert's answer was that by formulating concepts human beings select out those aspects of reality that are important to them. Thus concepts are the means by which we know the world, for without them people could not distinguish among its significant parts. In light of this necessity, Rickert came to the peculiar conclusion that the essence of science centered around the problem of concept formation. From this point of view a discipline can be regarded as a science if it uses a principle of concept selection that everyone agrees produces objective knowledge. Not surprisingly, Rickert said there are two valid principles of concept selection—those used in the natural sciences and history—and in this way he tried to show that history is a scientific discipline.

In the natural sciences, Rickert noted, concepts are designed to identify the common traits of the empirical objects to which they refer.

---

[30]Heinrich Rickert's works remain untranslated. This account draws on H. H. Bruun, *Science, Values, and Politics in Max Weber's Methodology* (Copenhagen: Muunksgaard, 1972), pp. 84–99; Burger, *Weber's Theory of Concept Formation*, pp. 3–56; and Hughes, *Consciousness and Society*, pp. 190–91.

This tactic allows concepts to become more and more abstract and hence fit into a theory that summarizes empirical regularities (for example, the movements of the planets and their effects on one another through the force of gravity). The result is a set of general concepts that can, at least in principle, be used in a single all-embracing law of nature. On this basis Rickert concluded the principle of concept selection used in the natural sciences is valid because it succeeds in identifying regular and recurrent features of the physical environment.

In history, however, Rickert argued that scholars' interests are altogether different, which means the principle of concept selection must be different as well. In order to chronicle the events of the past and their significance for the present, historians must focus on their uniqueness. With this purpose in mind, historical concepts are formulated so as to identify those aspects of the past that make them distinctive and different from one another (for example, traditional society or the spirit of capitalism). Thus historians produce concepts, which Rickert called "historical individuals," that summarize a complex set of events in terms of their historical significance (that is, their uniqueness). On this basis Rickert concluded the principle of concept selection used in history is valid because it allows observers to understand how particular societies developed their specific characteristics. This result would be impossible if the historians imitated the natural sciences and conceptualized only those aspects of the past that were common to all societies. Hence despite these differences in concept formation, according to Rickert, history is a science.

Rickert next confronted the problem of how scholars select topics for study, and at this point his emphasis on concept formation as the essence of science trapped him in a nonproductive philosophical argument. Essentially, Rickert asserted, the researchers' choice of topics is made in terms of "value-relevance." That is, some events are seen as worth conceptualizing based on the scientists' interpretation of what the members of a society value. However, this emphasis on value-relevance implies a subjective rather than objective conception of knowledge, since scientists are inevitably forced to rely on their own values in determining what topics are worth knowing about, or conceptualizing. Now Rickert tried to avoid this implication by postulating that a kind of "normal consciousness" characterizes all human beings. On this basis, he argued, there are areas of concern shared by all members of every society, for example, religion, law, the state, customs, the physical world, language, literature, art, and the economy. But this postulate is inherently metaphysical (and typically idealist) since it assumes values have an existence independent of human beings.

Ultimately, as with Dilthey, Rickert's analysis led to a dead end, for he failed to recognize that concept formation is only one essential aspect of science and, partly as a result, found himself entangled in idealism. Nonetheless, Rickert's work provided a fundamental baseline from which Weber could establish sociology as a science.

Weber's Response to Rickert

Weber was intimately familiar with Rickert's writings, as is indicated by acknowledgments of Rickert in his early methodological essays.[31] However, these citations do not indicate the extent to which Weber adapted some of Rickert's ideas for his own rather different purposes. While it cannot be known for sure, it is probable that Weber's preoccupation with refuting Marxism and solving the dilemma created by the *methodenstreit* allowed him to recognize what Rickert failed to see: The essence of science involves not only a coherent conceptual scheme but also, and just as important, the use of logical and systematic procedures in the interpretation of observations. Hence even though the social sciences have different goals because they must deal with quite different data than the natural sciences (Dilthey's "inner nature" of human beings), what unites the two as sciences is their procedural similarity. This insight pervades all of Weber's writings and constitutes the basis for his response to Rickert. The manner in which Weber adapted portions of Rickert's work can be sketched in the following way.

First, there is little doubt that Weber simply accepted Rickert's argument that reality is infinite and human beings can have knowledge only in terms of the concepts used to select out significant aspects of the world for examination.[32] Second, unlike Rickert, Weber recognized that it did not matter why a scholar chooses one topic over another for study, since the only practical basis for such choice can be one's ultimate values. What matters, Weber argued, is that the research process is objective, and this goal is achieved only when the data are clearly conceptualized and systematically analyzed.[33] Third, Weber adapted Rickert's notion of "historical individuals" for his more general purposes. That is, Weber sought to understand the origin of modern Western society, and in order to do this he needed to develop a set of concepts that captured the distinctiveness of historical processes. However, rather than historical individuals, Weber called his concepts *ideal types*, a phrase that seemed to convey more clearly what he meant: con-

---

[31]See Weber, "Objectivity," p. 50; and *Roscher and Knies,* pp. 211–18.

[32]Weber, "Objectivity," pp. 78–79.

[33]Weber, "Science as a Vocation"; Weber, "Critical Studies in the Logic of the Cultural Sciences," in *Methodology of the Social Sciences,* pp. 113–88.

cepts that are logically perfect in the sense that they summarize a "conceptually pure type of rational action."[34] With these and other methodological tools, Weber was able to study modern societies in what he felt was an objective and scientific manner.

MAX WEBER'S THEORETICAL SYNTHESIS

In adapting some of the conceptual tools provided by Dilthey and Rickert, Weber was able to forge a response to Marx and the *methodenstreit* that constitutes a continuing legacy to sociology. As we shall see in the next chapter, Weber's methodology of the social sciences began with a consideration of the overriding importance of objective sociology. No scientific analysis can include ethical values within it and be regarded as objective. The second methodological problem Weber confronted was that of how to treat social and historical data, which he resolved by emphasizing the importance of understanding social action in terms of ideal types. Because these concepts are formulated as rational models, they allow actual historical processes to be dealt with in an objective manner. The way in which Weber went about this task can be seen in his substantive works. Since he did not have modern means of gathering or analyzing data available to him, Weber was forced to construct "logical experiments" designed to show that sociological analyses could be done using scientific procedures. Thus the next chapter depicts Weber's demonstration of the manner in which cultural values circumscribe and direct social action in the *Protestant Ethic*. Similarly, in *Economy and Society* Weber provided subsequent researchers with a system of concepts that has proven to be of enormous use in understanding the nature of modern societies. Chapter 7 illustrates these aspects of Weber's work by focusing on his analysis of stratification and domination in Western societies.

---

[34]Weber, *Economy and Society*, pp. 18–20; "Objectivity," pp. 87–112. Rickert's term, *historical individuals*, appears in Weber's essay on *Roscher and Knies* and (once) in the *Protestant Ethic*, p. 47. Weber appears to have adopted the term *ideal type* from George Jellinek; see Bendix and Roth, *Scholarship and Partisanship*, pp. 160–64.

CHAPTER 7

The Sociology of Max Weber

In one of his last works Max Weber defined the fledgling discipline of sociology in the following way:

> Sociology . . . is a science concerning itself with the interpretive understanding of social action and thereby with a causal explanation of its course and consequences. We shall speak of "action" insofar as the acting individual attaches a subjective meaning to his behavior—be it overt or covert, omission or acquiescense. Action is "social" insofar as its subjective meaning takes account of the behavior of others and is thereby oriented in its course.[1]

Weber believed this definition would allow him to achieve two interrelated goals that, taken together, signify an altogether original approach to the study of social organization. First, he wished to obtain a scientific understanding of the origin and unique characteristics of modern Western civilization. Second, he wanted to construct a system of abstract concepts that would be useful in describing and hence understanding modern Western societies. Without a set of clear and precise concepts, Weber argued, systematic social scientific research would be impossible. The result was an "analytical ordering of reality," or a series of conceptual models of the modern world.

Weber's work can be divided into two periods. In the ten years prior to 1898, he wrote from the point of view of historical economics, dealing with such topics as the history of trading companies in the Middle Ages, the relationship between Roman agrarian history and the development of law, and the characteristics of rural peasants in Eastern Germany. While the works of this first period reveal traces of Weber's mature thought, they are less interesting sociologically and as a result have not been translated. As described in the last chapter, Weber suffered a complete mental breakdown from 1898 until 1903 and did not write. In the years following his recovery, however, Weber produced a massive volume of work that constitutes a decisive turning point in the development of sociological thought. His writings during this period

---

[1]Max Weber, *Economy and Society*, trans. and ed. Guenther Roth and Claus Wittich (New York: Bedminster Press, 1968).

can be divided into three areas, which correspond to the divisions in this chapter. The first section explains Weber's methodological point of view, for it is impossible to appreciate his substantive writings without understanding his overall theoretical strategy. The second section explicates Weber's sociology of religion. And the third section describes his analysis of social stratification in modern societies.

WEBER'S METHODOLOGY OF THE SOCIAL SCIENCES

In 1904 Max Weber posed a fundamental question: "In what sense are there 'objectively valid truths' in those disciplines concerned with social and cultural phenomena?"[2] All of his subsequent writings can be seen as an answer to this simple query. Indeed Weber's goal was to show that objective research is possible in those academic disciplines dealing with subjectively meaningful phenomena. The way he pursued this goal is presented here in two parts. First, Weber's depiction of the problem of values in sociological research is shown. This was the central issue for Weber; if sociology were to be a true science of society he thought it had to be objective. Second, Weber thought every science requires a conceptual map, an inventory of the key concepts describing the phenomenon being studied, and he began to develop such a system of concepts, labeling them "ideal types."

The Problem of Values

During Weber's time many observers did not believe an objective social science was plausible because it seemed impossible to separate values from the research process. So most scholars attempting to describe human behavior infused their analyses with political, religious, and other values. Marx's writings constitute an extreme example of this tactic. Weber confronted the problem of values by observing that sociological inquiry should be objective or, to use his term, *value free*. Having said that, however, he then suggested how values and economic interests are connected to social scientific analyses.

Value-Free Sociology.   Weber's use of the term *value free* is unfortunate because it implies that social scientists should have no values at all, plainly an impossibility. What he meant, however, is that researchers' personal values and economic interests should not affect the

---

[2]Max Weber, " 'Objectivity' in Social Science and Social Policy," in *The Methodology of the Social Sciences*, trans. Edward A. Shils and Henry A. Finch (New York: Free Press, 1949), p. 51.

process of social scientific analysis. He believed if such factors influence the research process, then the structure of social action cannot be depicted objectively. This fundamental concern with attaining objective and verifiable knowledge links all the sciences, natural and social. Objective analyses are only possible, Weber argued, if sociologists use a "rational method" in which the research process is systematic—that is, (1) empirical data must be categorized in terms of clearly formulated concepts, (2) proper rules of evidence must be employed, and (3) only logical inferences must be made.[3]

This methodological orientation carries with it an important implication: It means that sociology cannot be a moral science. Thus, unlike Marx, Spencer, Durkheim, and others, Weber asserted it is not possible to state scientifically which norms, values, or patterns of action are correct or best; rather it is only possible to describe them objectively. And, in fact, Weber believed such descriptions would represent a considerable achievement. After all, they did not then exist. Thus, unlike many others, Weber explicitly distinguished between "what ought to be," the sphere of values, and "what is," the sphere of science, arguing that the social sciences can only focus on the latter. With the exception of Marxists, sociology has followed Weber's lead in making this distinction.

Another implication of Weber's argument for a value-free sociology is that as a science of society, the new discipline contributes to an ongoing process in which magic and other irrational beliefs used to explain events in traditional societies become less and less acceptable to people. Weber referred to this development as the process of "rationalization," and it is a dominant theme in all his work. He believed social life is becoming increasingly "rationalized" in the sense that people tend to lead relatively methodical lives. Sociology participates in the process of rationalization to the extent that it produces objective knowledge about social phenomena, with the result that sociology helps people make decisions by providing them with accurate information.

The Connection between Values and Science.   Weber believed values and science should be kept as separate as possible. Although this separation is very difficult to maintain in practice, it emphasizes an orientation basic to the social sciences: While facts can provide information, only values can guide action. And this is true for both social scientists and policymakers.

Social scientists are faced with a very practical problem: how to choose topics on which to do research. Is there, for example, a scien-

---

[3]Ibid., p. 143.

tific way of deciding whether poverty or premarital sex is a more interesting or important topic to study? Weber's answer was a simple one: No. In considering this response, the phrasing in the previous section should be recalled: The research process must be objective. The choice of topics comes before the research takes place. The only basis for making such a decision is scientists' religious beliefs, economic interests, and other values, which lead some of them to each topic. Once having chosen a topic for study, however, Weber's dictum was that the research process must be objective.

The situation is more complex when dealing with public policy issues. Is there, for example, a scientific way for policymakers to decide about funding for public assistance or national defense? Again, Weber's answer is a simple one: No. Public policy decisions occur either before or after the research process takes place. This response, however, does not mean the social sciences are irrelevant to public policy. As noted above, what sociology can do, and it is quite a lot, is describe the facts. For example, given a specific political goal, Weber said sociologists can determine (1) the alternative strategies for achieving it, (2) the consequences of using different strategies, and (3) the consequences of attaining the goal.[4] He believed they can perform these tasks objectively by categorizing the data in terms of clearly formulated concepts, following proper rules of evidence, and making logical deductions. Once that is done, however, there is no scientific way of choosing public policies. The selection of one goal rather than another and one strategy rather than another ultimately depends on people's political values, their economic interests, and so forth.

Having said that the research process must be objective and that the sphere of values and the sphere of science must be kept separate, Weber drew a unique conclusion. Unlike nearly all the other classical sociologists (except Marx, whose orientation is altogether different), Weber rejected the search for general laws in favor of historical theories that provide an "interpretive understanding of social action and . . . a causal explanation of its course and consequences." Weber took this position not for scientific reasons but for evaluative ones. He perceived that any system of abstract and timeless laws must focus on events that are typical and recurrent, as in the natural sciences. A search for universal laws necessarily excludes from consideration important and unique historical events. Weber summarized his position in the following way:

> For the knowledge of historical phenomena in their concreteness, the most general laws, because they are most devoid of content are also the least valuable. The more comprehensive the validity,—or scope—of a

---

[4]Ibid., p. 53.

term, the more it leads us away from the richness of reality since in order to include the common elements of the largest possible number of phenomena, it must necessarily be as abstract as possible and hence devoid of content. In the [social] sciences, the knowledge of the universal or general is never valuable in itself.[5]

In effect, then, Weber was most interested in focusing on the "big empirical questions," such as why capitalism originated in the West rather than somewhere else, and he knew that an emphasis on the development of general theories would not allow for an examination of such issues.

Ideal Types

All science requires a conceptual map that identifies the parts of the phenomena under investigation. For example, biologists give names not only to each bone and tissue in the body but also to the processes through which information, food, and other elements are transported around. Astrophysicists, chemists, and all other scientists do the same thing with regard to their objects of study. Yet a conceptual map of society did not exist during Weber's time, mainly because human beings seemed so unpredictable. But this unpredictability resulted, in part, from not having a set of concepts that summarize patterns of social action. So Weber set about developing one.

In pursuing this goal, however, Weber had to confront a fundamental problem: Sociology is inherently different than the natural sciences because its essential task is "the interpretive understanding of social action and thereby . . . a causal explanation of its course and consequences." "Understanding" is the usual translation of the German word *verstehen*, and there has been considerable controversy over the years as to the theoretical and methodological implications of this term.[6] Weber's argument, however, can be presented in a reasonably straightforward manner, for he believed only the use of ideal types could lead to an "interpretive understanding of social action" and hence to a "causal explanation" of historical events.

Weber argued that social action exists only "insofar as the acting individual attaches a subjective meaning to his behavior." Sociological

---

[5]Ibid., p. 80.

[6]See Theodore Abel, "The Operation Called *Verstehen*," *American Journal of Sociology* 54, November 1948, pp. 211–18; Peter A. Munch, "Empirical Science and Max Weber's *Verstehende Soziologie*," *American Sociological Review* 22, February 1957, pp. 26–32; Murray L. Wax, "On Misunderstanding *Verstehen*: A Reply to Abel," *Sociology and Social Research* 51, April 1967, pp. 322–33; and Theodore Abel, "A Reply to Professor Wax," *Sociology and Social Research* 51, April 1967, pp. 334–36.

analysis, therefore, must ultimately refer to individual action rather than to collective social phenomena because such entities as a "state" do not think or act; only people act. Yet, as he emphasized, it is generally the case that concepts referring to structural or collective phenomena are necessary in order to understand individual social action. However, he argued that such concepts "must be treated as *solely* the resultants and modes of organization of the particular acts of individual persons, since these alone can be treated as agents in a course of subjectively understandable action."[7] Weber's emphasis on the need for conceptualizing individual action led him to reject functional analysis, as epitomized in his time by "the method of the so-called 'organic' school of sociology." He argued that in functional analysis concepts tend to be reified such that the "needs" of the social system become the focus of attention rather than individual action. Moreover, Weber felt functional analysis is inevitably oriented toward the development of general theories similar to those in the natural sciences, an emphasis that can never result in an understanding of the subjective meaning individuals attach to behavior. This concern with subjective meaning, or *verstehen*, forced Weber to rely on ideal types as a mode of sociological analysis.

As shown in Chapter 6, Wilhelm Dilthey first proposed the concept of *verstehen* as central to the social scientific task. However, in Weber's hands the concept became considerably less mystical and intuitive and more oriented to the necessity of systematic sociological research. Weber's comments on the importance of *verstehen* in sociology are quite brief, focusing on two kinds of understanding. First, there is "direct observational understanding of the subjective meaning of a given act."[8] Such observational understanding implies that extensive knowledge of the broader social context within which an individual's action takes place is not necessary. For example, Weber noted that observations of certain facial expressions or verbal exclamations are immediately understood as representing anger. Thus intrinsic to observational understanding is a certain intuitive knowledge of, or empathetic identification with, other people. However, Weber's definition of sociology as a science focusing on the "interpretive understanding of social action" clearly suggests he intended this kind of understanding as a limiting case; in a science "interpretive" must mean evidence other than intuition is necessary.

Hence Weber also referred to a second kind of *verstehen*: "explanatory understanding," that is, "rational understanding of motivation,

---

[7]Weber, *Economy and Society,* pp. 13–14. Phrases are similarly highlighted in Weber's original.
[8]Ibid., pp. 8, 58.

which consists in placing the act in an intelligible and more inclusive context of meaning."[9] For example, Weber noted that an outbreak of anger can be understood more clearly when it is known that an insult preceded it. Nonetheless, even in this example, understanding seems to involve some intuitive knowledge of how people normally respond in certain situations. But Weber emphasized that while one's intuitive insight may well be right, its correctness must be shown logically and then verified by comparison with concrete events. Thus Weber argued that any attempt at explanatory understanding in the social sciences is at first "only a peculiarly plausible hypothesis," or hunch. In science the verification of such a hunch presupposes that the concepts used to refer to concrete events are precisely defined, that clear rules of evidence are followed in regard to data analysis, and that inferences based on the evidence are logical. Only in this way is it possible to achieve "rational understanding of [people's] motivation."

During Weber's time, however, accurate verification of social scientific hypotheses was only possible in a few cases, such as in controlled psychological experiments. Although he participated in several early survey research projects, modern statistical procedures were not available to describe "mass phenomena," with the result that hypotheses were not seen as verifiable using such techniques. Thus a new way of doing research had to be invented, which, for Weber, turned out to be ideal types.[10]

While there has been some confusion because of his use of the word *ideal*, Weber explicitly stated he did not intend for these concepts to have a normative connotation. Rather they were designed "to be perfect on logical grounds," most of the time by summarizing a "conceptually pure type of rational action." Weber used ideal types in different ways and for somewhat different purposes, and, unfortunately, he did not make any clear or explicit distinction among them, with the result that scholars have often complained about the inconsistent way in which he used his conceptual tools.[11] Yet despite some areas of inconsistency, we can distinguish two kinds of ideal types in Weber's

---

[9]Ibid., pp. 8–10.

[10]Weber's approval of and participation in research projects designed to obtain quantitative data show clearly that he was amenable to the use of such information as one means of "explanatory understanding." See Paul F. Lazarsfeld and Anthony R. Oberschall, "Max Weber and Empirical Social Research," *American Sociological Review* 30, April 1965, pp. 185–99.

[11]See Thomas Burger, *Max Weber's Theory of Concept Formation: History, Laws, and Ideal Types* (Durham, N. C.: Duke University Press, 1976), pp. 130–34.

work. The first can be called the *historical ideal type,* and the second can be termed the *classificatory ideal type.* While Weber did not use these labels, they provide a convenient way of organizing the discussion below.

Historical Ideal Types.   These are reconstructions of past events, or ideas, in which some aspects are accentuated such that they are logically (or *rationally* to use Weber's word) integrated and complete. By conceptualizing historical events in this way, it is possible to systematically compare them to the ideal type and, by observing deviations from the rational model, arrive at causal judgments. This strategy enabled Weber to place historical processes, such as the Protestant Reformation, in "an intelligible and more inclusive context of meaning" and thereby understand their significance for the development of the modern world.

In 1904 Weber noted that the historical ideal type "has the significance of a purely ideal *limiting* concept with which the real situation or action is *compared* and surveyed for the explication of certain of its significant components."[12] On this particular point there was great continuity in Weber's thought, for in part 1 of *Economy and Society* (written around 1919) he made a similar observation:

> The construction of a purely rational course of action . . . serves the sociologist as a type (ideal type) which has the merit of clear understandability and lack of ambiguity. By comparison with this it is possible to understand the ways in which actual action is influenced by irrational factors of all sorts, such as affects and errors, in that they account for the deviation from the line of conduct which would be expected on the hypothesis that the action [is] purely rational.[13]

Classificatory Ideal Types.   During the years between 1904 and 1920, however, Weber apparently became increasingly aware of the need for an inventory of concepts that would serve as a means for more precisely describing the fundamental social processes occurring in all societies. As a result of this awareness, part 1 of *Economy and Society* is spent simply enumerating a system of abstract concepts that could be used in understanding the process of social action. We have labeled these concepts *classificatory ideal types,* and they constitute the

---

[12]Weber, "Objectivity," p. 93.
[13]Weber, *Economy and Society,* p. 6.

conceptual core of the discipline of sociology as Weber ultimately perceived it. While Weber's death prevented completion of his system of concepts, his intent can be illustrated by examining his conceptualization of the types of social action.[14]

According to Weber people's actions may be classified in four analytically distinct ways.[15] The first type of action is *instrumentally rational*, which occurs as a person systematically takes into account the actual and potential behavior of others and uses this knowledge as a set of " 'conditions' or 'means' for the attainment of the actor's own rationally pursued or calculated ends." Thus instrumentally rational action exists when means and ends are systematically related to each other based on knowledge. While the archetypal example of instrumentally rational action is the scientific experiment, the term generally refers to an action based on a logical evaluation of means and ends.

The second type of action is *value rational*, which is behavior undertaken for its own sake, in light of one's basic values and independently of logic or the chance for success. Weber emphasized that "value rational action always involves 'commands' or 'demands' which, in the actors opinion are binding." The archetypal example of value rational action is religious belief, which requires a leap of faith. More generally, people sometimes act contrary to their economic interests because of their values, and Weber wanted to take this fact into account explicitly.

These first two types, instrumentally rational and value rational action, are characteristic of people in modern, industrialized nations, which Weber called *rational-legal* societies. Persons living in such countries tend to move back and forth between the two types of action, depending on the social context. For example, when raising children people will often act in terms that Weber would describe as value rational, even if it costs money and involves severe economic hardship. Caring for sick children, putting braces on their teeth, and sending them to college do not bring any economic benefits to parents. They

---

[14]As an aside, it should be recognized that *Economy and Society* was left in a highly disorganized state at Weber's death in 1920, and what he intended to do with the fragments that were eventually placed together under that title is not altogether clear. Part 1 is actually the last section he wrote, apparently between 1918 and 1920, while part 2 appears to have been written several years earlier, between 1910 and 1914. Titled simply "Conceptual Exposition," part 1 is essentially an unfinished catalog of the meaning Weber attached to each of his key concepts. As such, it is quite different in style and tone from the earlier, more lengthy, and more historically oriented part 2. There is some indication that Weber intended to rewrite the earlier material in terms of the system of concepts he had recently developed.

[15]Weber, *Economy and Society*, pp. 24–26.

perform these tasks because the obligations of childrearing are a fundamental value taught to all people, and this value supersedes economic considerations. In other social contexts, however, people act rather differently, in terms Weber would describe as instrumentally rational. For example, when shopping for groceries, purchasing a house, or buying stock, people try to calculate their potential savings and profits. In this context means-ends considerations dominate, and the end sought is economic success. Once again, this value is pervasive in modern Western societies. The sociological task, which Weber left incomplete, is to specify the contexts in which instrumentally rational and value rational action occur.

The third type of action is *traditional,* which is behavior "determined by ingrained habituation." Weber's point here was that in a social context where beliefs and values are second nature and patterns of action have been stable and repetitive for many years, people generally do not have a wide set of choices. Rather they usually respond out of habit to those situations that have become familiar to them over the centuries. In a sense they govern themselves by customs handed down from generation to generation. In such societies people are very resistant to altering long-established ways of living, which are often sanctified in religious terms. As a result they often continue in the old ways even when some aspect of the situation has changed.

This third type, traditional action, is characteristic of people in pre-industrial social systems, which Weber called traditional societies. He believed the distinction between instrumentally rational and value rational behavior is unnecessary for understanding patterns of action in traditional societies, partly because their division of labor is not very great and partly because custom guides behavior in nearly all spheres. For example, the household is usually both a productive and consumptive unit in such societies, which means caring for children and obtaining food and housing are not separate arenas of action. In addition people living in such societies usually believe they ought to make both familial and economic decisions in light of custom, which almost never includes the calculating, logical evaluation of means and ends typical of instrumentally rational action.

The fourth type of social action is *affectual,* which is behavior determined by a person's emotions in a given situation. This last mode of social action is clearly a residual category that Weber acknowledged but did not explore in any detail.

These types of action classify behavior by visualizing its four "pure forms." While Weber knew actual empirical situations would not correspond perfectly with these types, by conceptualizing the "ideal types" of action he had a common reference point for comparing actual empirical cases. With the common reference point, different empirical cases could be compared since there was a common point of reference—the ideal type. This strategy is represented in Figure 7-1. Ideal types thus represent for Weber a quasi-experimental method. The "ideal" serves as the functional equivalent of the control group in an experiment. Variations or deviations from the ideal are seen as the result of causal forces (or a stimulus in a real laboratory experiment), and effort is then undertaken to find these causes. In this sense Weber could achieve two goals: (1) to analytically and logically accentuate the elements of social action and (2) to discover the causes of unique variations in specific empirical cases. For example, by noting the extent to which actual empirical cases compare to instrumental rational action, the causes of conformity to, or deviation from, this ideal can be as-

FIGURE 7-1   The Ideal Type Methodology

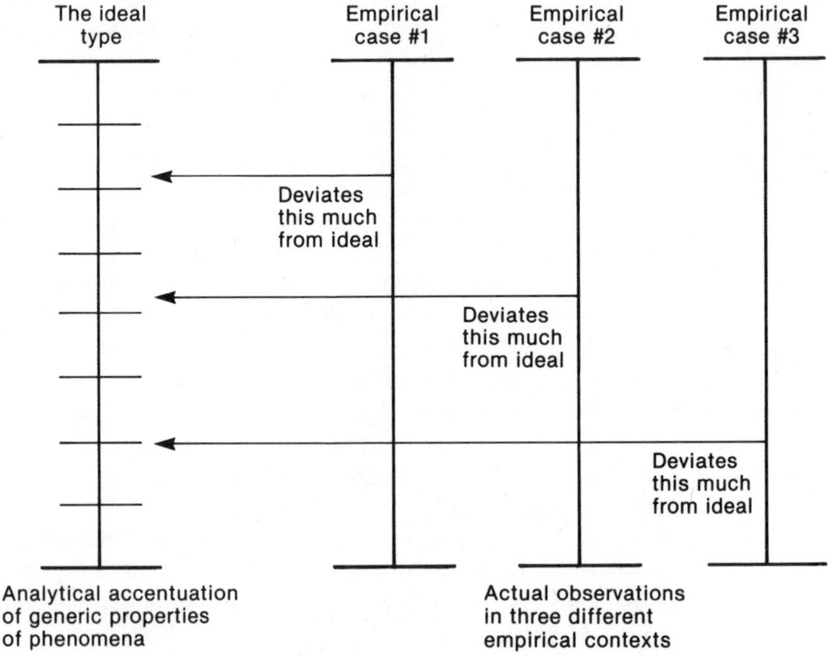

By recording actual deviations from each empirical case from the ideal, the cases are compared to each other using a common reference point. Then, by asking what causes the deviations, or differences among the three cases, the causes of empirical events in each case can be isolated and compared.

sessed. In this way the unique aspects of empirical cases can be emphasized and yet systematically and logically analyzed.

WEBER'S STUDY OF RELIGION

The Protestant Ethic and the Spirit of Capitalism is Weber's most famous and in some ways his most important study.[16] Published in two parts in 1905 and 1906, it was one of his first works to be translated into English, and even more significant, it was the first application of his mature methodological orientation. As a result the Protestant Ethic is neither a historical analysis nor a politically committed interpretation of history. Rather it is part of an exercise in historical hypothesis testing in which Weber constructed a logical experiment using ideal types as conceptual tools.

In retrospect it can be seen that Weber had three interrelated purposes in writing the Protestant Ethic. First, he wanted to refute those forms of Marxist analysis prevalent at the turn of the century. Second, he wished to understand why the culture of capitalism emerged in the West. As such, Weber's work is not only an explanation of how the modern world, dominated by instrumental rationality, came into being but also a demonstration that an objective sociology can deal with historical topics. Third, Weber also wanted to demonstrate that cultural values and other ideas or beliefs circumscribe social action, primarily by directing people's interests in certain directions.

While the Protestant Ethic is by far the most important of Weber's studies in the sociology of religion, it is nonetheless only a small portion of a much larger intellectual enterprise that he pursued intermittently for about fifteen years. In this grandiose "imaginary experiment," Weber tried to account not only for the confluence of events that were associated with the rise of capitalism in the West, but also to explain, logically, why capitalism was not likely to have developed in any other section of the world—that is, "why did not the scientific, the artistic, the political, and the economic development [of China, India, and other areas] enter upon that path of rationalization which is peculiar to the occident?"[17] Thus the Protestant Ethic is the first

---

[16]Max Weber, The Protestant Ethic and the Spirit of Capitalism, trans, Talcott Parsons (New York: Charles Scribner's Sons, 1958).

[17]Max Weber, "Author's Introduction," in Protestant Ethic, p. 25. It is important to recognize that Weber wrote this introduction in 1920 for the German edition of his Collected Essays in the Sociology of Religion. Thus it is an overall view of Weber's work in the sociology of religion rather than an introduction to the Protestant Ethic. Scribner's more recent 1976 edition of the book does not make this fact clear.

portion of a two-stage experiment. The second element in Weber's experiment is contained in a series of book-length studies on *The Religion of China* (1913), *The Religion of India* (1916–17), and *Ancient Judaism* (1917).[18]

Before reviewing either the *Protestant Ethic* or Weber's other work on religion, we should make explicit the implicit research design of these works. In so doing we will see another sense in which Weber constructed "quasi-experimental designs" for understanding the causes of historical events. Weber's basis question is: Why did industrialization initially occur in the West and not in other parts of the world? Such a question directs attention to the "cause" of industrialization. To isolate this cause, Weber constructed the "quasi-experimental design" diagramed in Figure 7-2.

In Figure 7-2, steps 1 through 5 approximate the stages of a laboratory situation as it must be adapted to historical analysis. The West represents the experimental group in that something stimulated industrialization, whereas China and India represent the control groups since they did not industrialize, even though they were as advanced as the West in terms of technologies and other social forms. The stimulus that caused industrialization in the West was the religious beliefs associated with Protestantism (see step 3 of Figure 7-2), and for this reason Weber wrote *The Protestant Ethic and the Spirit of Capitalism*.

The Protestant Ethic and the Spirit of Capitalism

Weber opened the *Protestant Ethic* with what was a commonplace observation at the end of the nineteenth century: Occupational statistics in those nations of mixed religious composition invariably show that those in higher socio-economic positions are overwhelmingly Protestant. This relationship is especially true, Weber wrote, "wherever capitalism . . . has had a free hand."[19] Many observers in economics, literature, and history had commented on this phenomenon before Weber, and he cited a number of them.[20] Hence in the *Protestant Ethic*

---

[18]Max Weber, *The Religion of China*, trans. Hans Gerth (New York: Free Press, 1951); Max Weber, *The Religion of India*, trans. Hans Gerth and Don Martindale (New York: Free Press, 1958); Max Weber, *Ancient Judaism*, trans. Hans Gerth and Don Martindale (New York: Free Press, 1952). In addition, part 2 of *Economy and Society* contains a book-length study, "Religious Groups (The Sociology of Religion)," that is also available in paperback under the title *The Sociology of Religion*, trans. Ephraim Fishoff (Boston: Beacon Press, 1963).

[19]Weber, *Protestant Ethic*, p. 25.

[20]Ibid., pp. 43–45, 191 (note 23). See also Reinhard Bendix, "*The Protestant Ethic*—Revisited," in *Scholarship and Partisanship: Essays on Max Weber*, ed. Reinhard Bendix and Guenther Roth (Berkeley: University of California Press, 1971), pp. 299–310.

FIGURE 7-2 Weber's Quasi-Experimental Design in the Study of Religion

Group	Step 1 Find two "matched" societies in terms of their minimal conditions	Step 2 Do historical research on their properties before stimulus introduced.	Step 3 Examine the impact of the key stimulus, religious beliefs.	Step 4 Use historical evidence to assess the properties of other stimulus.	Step 5 Differences between Europe and China are viewed as caused by religion beliefs.
Quasi-experimental group	Western Europe	Descriptions of Europe (using historical ideal types)	Experiences stimulus with emergence of Protestantism	Industrial revolution	Western Europe is changed
Quasi-control group	China	Descriptions of China (using historical ideal types)	Experiences no stimulus	No industrial revolution	China is much the same as before
Quasi-control group	India	Descriptions of India (using historical ideal types)	Experiences no stimulus	No industrial revolution	India is much the same as before

Weber was not trying to prove that a relationship between Protestant-ism and economic success in capitalist societies existed, since he took its existence as given. In his words, "it is not new that the existence of this relationship is maintained. . . . Our task here is to explain the relation."[21]

In order to show that Protestantism was related to the origin of the "spirit of capitalism" in the West, Weber began with a sketch of what he meant by the latter term. Like many of Weber's key concepts, the notion of the spirit of capitalism is a historical ideal type in that it is a conceptual accentuation of certain aspects of the real world that he used as a tool for understanding actual historical processes.[22] Although he did not state what he meant very clearly, an omission that helped contribute to the tremendous controversy over the *Protestant Ethic's* the-sis, Weber's concept of the spirit of capitalism appears to have the fol-lowing components.[23]

First, work is valued as an end in itself. Weber was fascinated by the fact that a person's "duty in a calling [or occupation] is what is most characteristic of the social ethic of capitalistic culture, and is in a sense the fundamental basis of it."

Second, in capitalist society, acquisitiveness, trade and profit are taken not only as evidence of occupational success but also as indica-tors of personal virtue. In Weber's words, "the earning of money within the modern economic order is, so long as it is done legally, [seen as] the result and the expression of virtue and proficiency in a calling."

Third, a methodically organized life governed by reason is valued not only as a means to a long-term goal, economic success, but also as an inherently proper and even righteous state of being.

Fourth, embodied in the righteous pursuit of economic success is a belief that immediate happiness and pleasure should be forgone in favor of future satisfaction. As Weber noted, "the *summum bonum* of this ethic, the earning of more and more money, combined with the strict avoidance of all spontaneous enjoyment of life, is above all com-pletely devoid of an eudaemonistic, not to say hedonistic, admixture." In sum, then, these values—the goodness of work, success as personal rectitude, the use of reason to guide one's life, and delayed gratifica-tion—reflect some of the most important cultural values in the West,

---

[21]Weber, *Protestant Ethic*, p. 191.

[22]Weber hints at his ideal type strategy but does not bother to explain it in the initial paragraphs of chapter 2 of the *Protestant Ethic*, p. 47. He refers to the need to develop a "historical individual"; that is, "a complex of elements associated in historical real-ity which we unite into a conceptual whole from the standpoint of their cultural sig-nificance." This phrasing reveals the influence of Heinrich Rickert, as discussed in Chapter 6 of this book.

[23]Weber, *Protestant Ethic*, pp. 53–54.

since they constitute perceptions of appropriate behavior that are shared by all.

Weber emphasized, however, that the widespread application of such values to everyday life is historically unique and of relatively recent origin. Hence he distinguished the modern culture of capitalism from both its premodern form, which he called *adventurer capitalism*, and from the traditional values characteristic of the late Middle Ages. By adventurer capitalism Weber referred to those acquisitive individuals throughout history who have sought to make money ruthlessly and saw themselves "bound to no ethical norms whatever. . . . Capitalistic acquisition as an adventure has been at home in all types of economic society which have known trade with the use of money."[24] However, the activities of adventurer capitalists have rarely received social approval and never embodied dominant conceptions of appropriate behavior. More often, their avariciousness, especially when directed toward outsiders, has been merely tolerated because it was deemed necessary to the community. Weber believed the effect of adventurer capitalists on the development of the modern culture of capitalism was minimal, even though such persons clearly flourished as the new ethos became more and more widespread.

According to Weber the greatest barrier to the rise of the culture of capitalism in the West was the inertial force of traditional values. To varying degrees, European societies prior to the seventeenth century were dominated by what Weber later called "traditional modes of action." For example, religion rather than science was used as the primary means of verifying knowledge (as in Galileo's forced recantment of his findings regarding the movement of the planets). Bureaucracies composed of technical experts were unknown. Patterns of commerce and most other forms of daily life were dominated by status rather than class considerations—that is, people acted in terms of their membership in religious and ethnic groups rather than in light of simple market factors. Finally, legal adjudication did not involve the equal application to all individuals of clear legal codes. In short, the choice between instrumentally rational action and value rational action did not exist.

But over time the power of tradition was broken, and capitalism emerged in Western Europe. In his *General Economic History* written some years later, Weber identified the major historical factors that he believed, taken together, caused the development of capitalism in

---

[24]Ibid., pp. 57–58. See also Max Weber, "Anticritical Last Word on the Spirit of Capitalism," trans. Wallace A. Davis, *American Journal of Sociology* 83, March 1978, p. 1127.

Western Europe rather than elsewhere: (1) the process of industriali-zation through which muscle power was supplanted by new forms of energy, (2) the rise of a free labor force whose members had to work in commerical enterprises or starve, (3) the increasing use of rational ac-counting methods in industrial undertakings, (4) the rise of a free mar-ket unencumbered by irrational restrictions, (5) the gradual imposition and legitimation of a system of calculable law, (6) the increasing com-mercialization of economic life through the use of stock certificates and other paper instruments, and (7) the rise of the spirit of capitalism. While all these developments were to varying degrees unique to the West, in the *General Economic History* Weber still regarded the last factor as the most decisive one.[25] Thus, in attempting to understand the ori-gin of the economic differences between Protestants and Catholics, We-ber's point was not to deny the fundamental significance of these historical factors but merely to show the nature of significance of the culture of capitalism and its logical relationship to the Protestant ethic.

To Weber, the cultural values of traditional society were destroyed by Puritanism and the other Protestant sects, although this was not the intent of those who adopted the Reformed faiths and could not have been predicted in advance. In the *Protestant Ethic* Weber focused mainly on Calvinism, with much shorter discussions of Pietism, Meth-odism, and Baptism appended to the main analysis. His strategy was to describe Calvinist doctrines by quoting extensively from the writ-ings of various theologians, then to impute the psychological conse-quences those doctrines had on people who accepted them, and, finally, to show how they resulted in specific (and historically new) ways of living. In Weber's words, he was interested in ascertaining "those psychological sanctions which, originating in religious belief and the practice of religion, gave a direction to practical conduct and held the individual to it."[26] In this way he believed he could give a powerful example of the manner in which cultural phenomena influ-ence social action and, at the same time, rebut the vulgar Marxists who thought economic factors were the sole causal agents in historical change.

Based on an analysis of Calvinist writings, such as the *Westminster Confession of 1647*, which he quoted extensively, Weber interpreted Cal-vinist doctrine as having four consequences for those who accepted its tenets.

---

[25]Max Weber, *General Economic History*, trans. Frank Knight (New York: Collier Books, 1961), pp. 207–70. In the *Protestant Ethic*, p. 61, Weber does mention the fun-damental importance of free workers who are compelled to sell their labor on the market without restriction.

[26]Weber, *Protestant Ethic*, p. 97.

First, because the Calvinist doctrine of Predestination led people to believe that God, for incomprehensible reasons, had divided the human population into two groups, the saved and the damned, a key problem for all individuals was to determine the group to which they belonged. Second, because people could not know with certainty whether they were saved and because salvation could not be guaranteed either by magical sacraments administered by a priest (as in Catholicism) or by a mystical union with God (as in Lutheranism), they inevitably felt a great inner loneliness and isolation. Third, while a change in one's relative state of grace was seen as impossible, people inevitably began to look for signs they were among the elect. In general, Calvinists believed two clues could be used as evidence: (1) faith, for everyone had an absolute duty to consider themselves chosen and to combat all doubts as temptations of the devil, and (2) intense worldly activity, for in this way the self-confidence necessary to alleviate religious doubts could be generated. Fourth, all believers were expected to lead methodical and ascetic lives such that they were unencumbered by irrational emotions, superstitions, or desires of the flesh. As Weber put it, the good Calvinist was expected to "methodically supervise his own state of grace in his own conduct, and thus to penetrate it with asceticism," with the result that each person engaged in "a rational planning of the whole of one's life in accordance with God's will."[27] The significance of this last doctrine is that in Calvinist communities worldly asceticism was not restricted to monks and other "religious virtuosi" (to use Weber's phrase) but required of everyone as they conducted their everyday lives in their mundane occupations, or callings.

In order to show the relationship between the worldly asceticism fostered by the Protestant sects and the rise of the spirit of capitalism, Weber chose to focus on the Puritan ministers' guidelines for everyday behavior, as contained in their pastoral writings. The clergy's teachings, which were set forth in such books as Richard Baxter's *Christian Directory*, tend to reflect the major pastoral problems they encountered. As such, their writings provide an idealized vision of everyday life in the Puritan communities. While it must be recognized that social action does not always conform to cultural ideals, such values do provide a general direction for people's actions. Most people try, even if imperfectly, to adhere to those standards of appropriate behavior dominant in their community, and the Puritans were no exceptions. Further, the use of this sort of data suggests the broad way in which Weber interpreted the idea of "explanatory understanding" (*verstehen*): Since peo-

---

[27]Ibid., p. 153.

ple's own explanations of their actions often involve contradictory motives that are difficult to reconcile, he was perfectly willing to use an indirect means of ascertaining the subjective meaning of social action among the Puritans.

Based on Weber's analysis, it appears that the Puritan communities were dominated by three interrelated dictums, which, while a direct outgrowth of Puritan theology, eventuated over the long run in a rather utilitarian (and relatively nonreligious) culture of capitalism.

The first of these pronouncements is that God demands rational labor in a calling. As Weber noted, Puritan pastoral literature is characterized "by the continually repeated, often almost passionate preaching of hard, continuous bodily or mental labour."[28] From this point of view there can be no relaxation, no relief from toil, for labor is an exercise in ascetic virtue, and rational, methodical behavior in a calling is taken as a sign of grace. Hence from the Puritan's standpoint, "waste of time is . . . the first and in principle the deadliest of sins," since "every hour lost is lost to labour for the glory of God." As Weber observed, this dictum not only provides an ethical justification for the modern division of labor (in which occupational tasks are divided up rationally) but reserves its highest accolades for those sober, middle-class individuals who best exemplify the methodical nature of worldly asceticism. As an aside, it should be noted that members of this stratum became the primary carriers of Puritan religious beliefs precisely because they garnered immense economic, social, and political power as a result. In general, Weber emphasized that those who are able to define and sanctify standards of appropriate behavior also benefit materially.[29]

The second directive dominating the Puritan believers also follows from Puritan theology and states that the enjoyment of those aspects of social life that do not have clear religious value is forbidden. Thus from the point of view of the Puritan ministers, secular literature, the theatre, and nearly all other forms of leisure-time activity were at best irrelevant and at worst superstitious. As a result, they tried to inculcate in their parishioners an extraordinarily serious approach to life, for people should direct their attention toward the practical problems dominating everyday life and subject them to rational solutions.

The third guideline that permeated the daily lives of the Puritans specifies that people have a duty to use their possessions for socially beneficial purposes that redound to the glory of God. Thus the pursuit of wealth for its own sake was regarded as sinful, for it could lead to

---

[28]Ibid., p. 158.
[29]Weber, *Economy and Society*, pp. 439–517.

enjoyment, idleness, and "temptations of the flesh." From this point of view those who acquire wealth through God's grace and hard work are mere trustees who have an obligation to use it responsibly.

Even allowing for the usual amount of human imperfection, Weber argued that the accumulation of capital and the rise of the modern bourgeoisie were the inevitable results of whole communities sharing values dictating hard work, limited enjoyment and consumption, and the practical use of money. Hence, capitalism emerged. Weber's causal argument is diagramed in Figure 7-3. Over time, of course, Puritan ideals gave way under the secularizing influence of wealth because people began to enjoy their material possessions. Thus while the religious roots of the spirit of capitalism inevitably died out, Puritanism bequeathed to modern people "an amazingly good, we may even say a pharisaically good, conscience in the acquisition of money." The predominance of such a value throughout an entire epoch is absolutely historically unique.

But in the concluding paragraphs of the essay, Weber allowed himself some personal and rather pessimistic observations. He argued that one of the most significant legacies of the Protestant Reformation is that in modern society "the idea of duty in one's calling prowls about in our lives life the ghost of dead religious beliefs," with the result that while "the Puritan wanted to work in a calling; we are forced to do so." Further, because modern people are inexorably tied to the technical and economic conditions of industrial production, our culture has become "an iron cage" from which there appears to be no escape and for which there is no longer a religious justification. This recognition leads to Weber's last, sad lament: "specialists without spirit, sensualists without heart; this nullity imagines that it has attained a level of civilization never before achieved."[30]

Weber's Comparative Studies of Religion and Capitalism

During the years following the publication of the *Protestant Ethic*, considerable controversy and misunderstanding developed over Weber's thesis, and he participated in the debate over it by making several attempts at refuting his critics.[31] In addition, he apparently

---

[30]Weber, *Protestant Ethic*, pp. 180–83.

[31]See Weber, "Anticritical Last Word," as well as the many explanatory footnotes in the *Protestant Ethic*. Most of these footnotes were added around 1920. The controversy over the Protestant ethic thesis has continued up to the present. See Robert L. Green, ed., *Protestantism and Capitalism: The Weber Thesis and Its Critics* (Lexington, Mass.: D. C. Heath, 1959); S. N. Eisenstadt, ed., *The Protestant Ethic and Modernization* (New York: Basic Books, 1968).

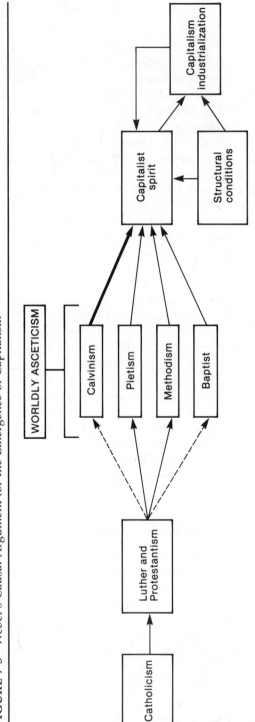

FIGURE 7-3 Weber's Causal Argument for the Emergence of Capitalism

began to see the need for some further studies of the relationship between religious belief and social structure in order to show why it was not very likely that capitalism as an economic system could have emerged anywhere else in the world. Weber's most important works in this regard are *The Religion of China* (1913) and *The Religion of India* (1917), which represent a continuation of the logical experiment begun some years earlier.

Both of these extended essays are similar in format in that Weber began by assessing those characteristics of Chinese and Indian social structure that either inhibited or, under the right circumstances, could have contributed to the development of capitalism in that part of the world (see Figure 7-2 for Weber's implicit experimental design). For purposes of illustration, all the examples used here come from *The Religion of China.* Thus in China during the period when capitalism arose in the West, a number of positive factors existed that could have led to a similar development in the Orient. First, there was a great deal of internal commerce and trade with other nations. Second, due to the establishment and maintenance (for more than 1,200 years) of nation-wide competitive examinations, there was an unusual degree of equality of opportunity in the process of status attainment. Third, the society was generally stable and peaceful, although Weber was clearly too accepting of the myth of the "unchanging China." Fourth, China had many large urban centers, and geographical mobility was a relatively common occurrence. Fifth, there were relatively few formal restrictions on economic activity. Finally, there were a number of technological developments in China that were more advanced than those in Europe at the same time (the use of gunpowder, knowledge of astronomy, book printing, and so forth). As Weber noted, all of these factors could have aided in the development of a Chinese version of modern capitalism.

However, he emphasized that Chinese society also displayed a number of characteristics that clearly inhibited the widespread development of any form of capitalism in that part of the world. First, while possessing an abundance of precious metals, especially silver, an adequate monetary system had never developed. Second, because of the early unification and centralization of the Chinese empire, cities never became autonomous political units. As a result, the development of local capitalistic enterprises was inhibited. Third, Chinese society was characterized by the use of "substantive ethical law" rather than rational and calculable legal procedure. As a result, legal judgments were made in terms of the particular characteristics of the participants and sacred tradition rather than in terms of the equal imposition of common standards. Finally, the Chinese bureaucracy was made up of classically learned persons rather than trained experts. Thus the examinations regulating status attainment "tested whether the candidate's mind was thoroughly steeped in literature and whether or not he possessed the ways of thought suitable to a cultural man."[32] Hence the idea of the trained expert was foreign to the Chinese experience.

In sum, according to Weber, all of these characteristics of Chinese social structure inhibited the development of an oriental form of modern capitalism. Nonetheless, the positive examples noted above do suggest that such a development was not impossible. And yet Weber argued that the rise of capitalism as an economic system was quite unlikely in either China or India, for he found no evidence of patterns of religious beliefs that could be compatible with any facsimile of the spirit of capitalism in either society. And he believed without the transformative power of religion, the rise of a new cultural ethos was not very likely. In China prior to this century the religion of the dominant classes, the bureaucrats, was Confucianism. Weber characterized Confucianism by the fact that it had no concept of sin, but only faults resulting from deficient education. Further, Confucianism had no metaphysic, with the result that there was no concern with the origin of the world or with the possibility of an afterlife and hence no tension between sacred and secular law. According to Weber Confucianism was a rational religion concerned with events in this world, but with a peculiarly individualistic emphasis. Good Confucians were less interested in the state of society than with their own propriety, as indicated by their development as educated persons and by their pious relations with others (especially their parents). In Weber's words the educated Chinese person "controls all his activities, physical gestures, and movements as well, with politeness and with grace in accordance with the status mores and the commands of 'propriety.' "[33] Rather than salvation in the next world, the Confucian accepted this world as given and merely desired to behave prudently.

On this basis Weber asserted that Confucianism was not very likely to result in the development of an oriental form of the culture of capitalism. He came to the same conclusion four years later in his study, *The Religion of India.* Thus by means of these comparative studies, Weber showed not only why Protestantism was associated with the rise of the culture of capitalism in the West but also why no other religion could have stimulated a similar development in any other part of the world.

In conclusion, then, beginning from a relatively simple empirical fact—income differences between Protestants and Catholics in nine-

---

[32]Weber, *Religion of China*, p. 121.
[33]Ibid., p. 156.

teenth-century Europe—Weber asserted that even after taking into account the unique occurrence of a number of important phenomena (free labor, rational law, political independence of cities, early industrialization, and so on), the most important factor accounting for the rise of capitalism as an economic system was the spread of a new cultural ethos, which he called the spirit of capitalism. This ethos was the inadvertent consequence of Puritan religious beliefs, which over the long run produced behavior (among both believers and nonbelievers) that was uniquely compatible with other historical developments occurring during that period. Over time, of course, the religious origin of modern values and action disappeared from view, leaving a secular legacy of beliefs in the innate goodness of work, acquisitiveness, the methodical organization of one's life, and delayed gratification. However, Weber believed that without the canalizing influence of Puritan religious beliefs, modern society would be fundamentally different than it is today. In his words, "it was the power of religious influence, not alone, but more than anything else, which created the differences of which we are conscious today."[34]

Weber's Outline of the Social System

In all of Weber's work he employed, at least implicitly, a vision of society as a social system that consists of three analytically separable dimensions: (1) culture, (2) patterns of social action, and (3) psychological orientations (see Figure 7-4). Cultural values and beliefs, patterned ways of acting in the world, and psychological states are all reciprocally related.[35] *The Protestant Ethic and the Spirit of Capitalism* is perhaps the best illustration of this model. It will be recalled that the components of the spirit of capitalism include an emphasis on work as an end in itself, an emphasis on the legitimacy of acquisition and profit, an emphasis on living a methodical lifestyle in order to obtain economic success, and a belief that immediate happiness and pleasure should be forgone in expectation of greater satisfaction in the future. Stripped of their religious connection, all of these phenomena have become fundamental Western cultural values—that is, they embody shared beliefs about right and wrong, appropriate and inappropriate behavior. The *Protestant Ethic* is, therefore, a book about culture and seeks the origin of the values dominating modern life. And Weber's answer, of course, is that these values are the secular result of certain peculiar religious movements that began in the sixteenth century.

---

[34]Weber, *Protestant Ethic*, p. 89.

[35]This implicit vision of society as a social system influenced Talcott Parsons' sociology; see his *The Social System* (New York: Free Press, 1951).

FIGURE 7-4   Weber's Model of the Social System

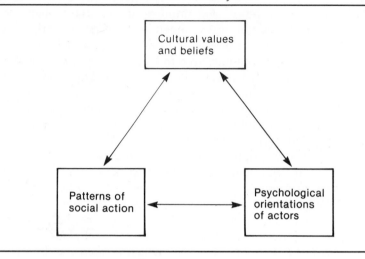

But the book is about much more than cultural phenomena. Indeed Weber was no more an idealist than Marx. Since the Puritans' religious beliefs plainly did not become dominant cultural values by themselves, Weber had to take into account the extent to which both patterns of social action and people's psychological orientations are reciprocally related to the cultural values he was analyzing. Thus he argued that the religious beliefs characteristic of the Reformed faiths fundamentally influenced patterns of social action among people—not only among the Puritans but also among those who came into contact with the underlying beliefs of these faiths. Given the rise of industrialization along with a number of other vitally important historical events, none of which Weber bothered to state explicitly in the *Protestant Ethic* but of which he was clearly aware, Puritan values spread in part because people found them to be congenial to their own secular ambitions as they developed during a time of great change. Hence as people adopted new beliefs and values they altered their daily lives; conversely, as individuals began living in new ways (often because they were forced to) they changed their fundamental beliefs and values. Thus historically new patterns of social action reinforced the new values that had arisen.

Weber, however, concentrated on the Puritans themselves, describing the psychological consequences their beliefs must have had for their daily lives. Because of their uncertainty and isolation, people looked for signs and found them in the ability to work hard and maintain their faith. Hence the Puritans' psychological needs led them to historically new and unique patterns of social action characterized not only by hard work (for medieval peasants certainly worked as hard) but also by a methodical pursuit of worldly goods. The inevitable result was the secularization of Puritan religious values and their transformation into what has come to be called the spirit of capitalism. Hence it is possible to extrapolate from Weber's analysis a set of generic factors—culture, patterns of social action, and psychological orientations—that are taken today as the fundamental features of social organization in social scientific analyses.

Weber's model of the most general components of social organization has proven to be of tremendous significance in the development of sociology. For example, virtually all introductory sociology textbooks (which we will use here as a rough indicator of the state of the field) now contain a series of chapters, usually located at the beginning, titled something like "culture," "social structure" or "society," and "personality and socialization." The reason for this practice is that these topics provide an essential conceptual orientation to the discipline of sociology. Weber's model, then, serves as a heuristic device rather than a dynamic analysis of the process of interaction. It can, however, lead to such an analysis—which is all Weber intended. Thus the model is an essential first step in the construction of a set of concepts that would be useful in describing and hence understanding modern societies.

SOCIAL STRATIFICATION IN MODERN SOCIETY

It will be recalled that Max Weber's sociology can be seen as having two interrelated goals. First, he wished to provide a scientific account of the origin and characteristics of modern Western society. In this chapter the *Protestant Ethic* has been used to illustrate one way Weber achieved this goal: by suggesting how the Puritans' beliefs were transformed into more general cultural values that continue to dominate the structure of social action in the West, he was able to show the religious origins of modern life. Weber's second goal was the development of a system of concepts, what we have called classificatory ideal types, that could be used for understanding social processes in industrial societies. While Weber's attempt at an "analytical ordering of reality" is flawed in some respects, his work in this area has endured because much of his writing is characterized by unusual theoretical insight and prescience. One of the best examples of Weber's conceptual inventory is his analysis of social stratification, especially when seen as an aspect of his more general political sociology (or "sociology of domination," as it is also called).

While *Economy and Society* contains two somewhat overlapping sections on social stratification, the full title of the more well-known essay, "The Distribution of Power within the Political Community: Class, Status, and Party," is suggestive of his overall intent: to show how the structure of inequality in modern societies is interrelated with the nature of domination in such nations.[36] Following Weber's lead, this section begins by examining the theoretical perspective underlying his analysis of social stratification and then focuses on his description of the structure of classes and status groups in modern societies. On that basis we extrapolate Weber's models of the class structure and social change.

Social Stratification and Systems of Domination

Every structure of stratification exists within a specific sociological context, which Weber called a system of domination or authority. The two English terms, *domination* and *authority*, are used because the original German word, *herrschaft*, connotes both.[37] In Weber's scheme, systems of domination are defined by two interrelated elements. The first element characterizing every system of domination comprises beliefs about the legitimacy of authority—that is, the use of power is legitimate when leaders assert their right to command and citizens believe they have a duty to obey.[38] Those who exercise power always attempt to establish a belief in the rightness of their domination, Weber said, because such a commitment obviates the need for using force and therefore leads to long-term stability. Those subjected to authority choose to accept its legitimacy because they are economically or politically dependent on those who hold power, or because its acceptance reflects their values, or both.

The second element intrinsic to any system of domination comprises an administrative apparatus—that is, societywide authority relationships require a staff that can enforce commands and in other ways serve as a link between the leader and the masses.[39] Weber identified three types of domination, each of which has a different basis of legitimacy and a different kind of administrative apparatus. It should be noted, however, that the forms of domination are ideal types that

---

[36]Weber, *Economy and Society*, pp. 284–306, 901–38.

[37]Considerable controversy exists over the proper translation of the German *herrschaft*. See Guenther Roth's long explanatory footnote in Weber, *Economy and Society*, pp. 61–62.

[38]Weber, *Economy and Society*, p. 946.

[39]Ibid., pp. 956–58.

permit classification of a society in terms of its resemblance to one of them. In actuality, every society will display aspects of all three.

Charismatic Domination.   The first type of domination is called charismatic. The term _charisma_ has a religious origin and means literally "gift of grace," implying that a person is endowed with divine powers.[40] However, in practice Weber did not restrict his use of charisma to manifestations of divinity but employed the concept to refer to those extraordinary individuals who somehow identify themselves with the central facts or problems of people's lives and who, by the force of their personality, communicate their inspiration to others and lead them in new directions. Thus persons in other than religious roles can sometimes be considered charismatic: for example, politicians, soldiers, or artists.[41]

In Weber's view charismatic leadership emerges during times of crisis, when traditional ways of doing things seem inappropriate, outmoded, or inadequate to the problems confronting people. The essence of charismatic domination, then, involves people's renunciation of the past in favor of a new direction based on the master's inspiration. As Weber put it, every charismatic leader implicitly or explicitly argues that "it is written . . . but I say unto you. . . . " Thus charismatic domination is usually a vehicle for social change in both traditional and rational-legal contexts, which are the other two types of domination.

The basis for the legitimacy of charismatic domination lies both in the leader's demonstration of extraordinary insight and accomplishment and in the followers' acceptance of the master. It is irrelevant, from Weber's point of view, whether a charismatic leader turns out to be a charlatan or a hero; both Hitler and Gandhi were charismatic leaders. Rather what is important is that the masses are inspired to freely follow the master. Weber believed charisma constitutes an unstable form of authority over extended periods because its legitimacy remains dependent on the leader's claim to special insight and accomplishment. Thus if success eludes the leader for long and crises are not resolved satisfactorily, then it becomes likely the masses will reject the charismatic figure, and his or her authority will disappear.

In charismatic domination the leader's administrative apparatus usually consists only of a band of faithful disciples who serve the mas-

---

[40]Ibid., pp. 241.

[41]See Reinhard Bendix, "Charismatic Leadership," in _Scholarship and Partisanship,_ pp. 170–87; and Edward A. Shils, "Charisma, Order, and Status," _American Sociological Review_ 30, April 1965, pp. 199–213.

ter's immediate personal and political needs. Over the long run, however, every regime led by a charismatic leader faces the "problem of routinization," which involves both finding a successor to the leader and handling the day-to-day decisions that must be made.

Weber noted that the problem of succession can be resolved in a variety of ways: for example, by the masses searching for a new charismatic leader, by the leader's designation of a successor, or by the disciples' designation of a successor. But all of these methods involve political instability. For this reason either customs or legal procedures allowing for the orderly transfer of power usually develop over time.

The problem of making day-to-day decisions (that is, of governing) is usually resolved by either the development of a full-fledged administrative staff or the takeover of an already existing organization. However, in both cases the usual result is the transformation of the relationship between charismatic leader and followers from one based on beliefs in the master's extraordinary qualities to one based on custom or law. These new bases of legitimation represent the other two types of domination, as is explored below.

Traditional Domination.   The second type of domination is based on tradition. In Weber's words, "authority will be called traditional if legitimacy is claimed for it and believed in by virtue of the sanctity of age-old rules and powers."[42]

The basis for legitimacy in traditional systems of domination is custom; leaders usually obtain their positions and justify their power in light of long-established practice. For example, over time it has become customary for the firstborn child of a British monarch to be the legitimate successor to the throne, and this pattern carries religious sanction.[43] In such a context the subordinate classes obey edicts in recognition of the ruler's rightful place, out of personal loyalty, and, of course, because of their economic and political dependence. Thus Weber's analysis of traditional authority suggests how traditional types of social action are generalized into a system of domination. The stratification hierarchy in such societies is usually fairly rigid since people's positions in the social system are dictated at birth by custom.

Weber distinguished between two forms of traditional authority, only one of which has an administrative apparatus. *Patriarchalism* is a type of traditional domination occurring in households and other small

---

[42]Weber, *Economy and Society*, p. 226.

[43]It is important to be realistic about this issue. Patterns of social action do not become customary and are not maintained without conflict. In the case of the British monarchy, for example, many struggles over the right of succession occurred, such as the War of the Roses.

groups where the use of an organizational staff to enforce commands is not necessary. *Patrimonialism* is a form of traditional domination occurring in larger social structures that require an administrative apparatus to execute edicts.

In the patrimonialism form of traditional domination, the administrative apparatus comprises a set of personal retainers exclusively loyal to the ruler. Weber observed that in addition to its grounding in custom, the officials' loyalty is based either on their dependence on the ruler for their positions and remuneration, or on their pledge of fealty to the leader, or both. In either case the essence of patrimonialism (traditional authority coupled with an administrative staff) is expressed by the following characteristics.

1. Officials attain positions based on custom and loyalty to the leader.
2. Obedience is owed only to the person issuing commands rather than to enacted rules.
3. There is no separation of one's office and private affairs because the members of the staff either appropriate the means of production themselves or are granted them by the ruler.[44]

These elements of traditional authority typically reflect cultural values and patterns of social action that have been stable for many years. As such, they distinguish those societies in which custom guides action from those in which instrumentally rational and value rational orientations guide action. Thus it should not be surprising that in *Economy and Society* Weber described traditional modes of domination as inhibiting the development of capitalism, primarily because rules are not logically established, officials have too wide a range for personal arbitrariness, and they are not technically trained.[45] Capitalism and, to some extent, industrialization require an emphasis on logic, procedure, and knowledge. Furthermore, as will be shown, modern class structures are not possible in social systems in which statuses and roles are circumscribed by tradition.

Rational-Legal Domination.   The third type of domination is that based on law, what Weber called rational-legal authority. As he phrased it, "legal domination [exists] by virtue of statute. . . . The basic conception is that any legal norm can be created or changed by a procedurally correct enactment."[46]

---

[44]Weber, *Economy and Society*, pp. 226–36.
[45]Ibid., pp. 237–41.
[46]Quoted in Reinhard Bendix, *Max Weber: An Intellectual Portrait* (Garden City, N. Y.: Doubleday, 1962), pp. 418–19.

Thus the basis for legitimacy in a system of rational-legal domination lies in procedure. Laws are seen as legitimate by the people when they are created and enforced in what is defined as the proper way. Similarly, leaders are seen as having the right to act when they obtain their positions in what is seen as the procedurally correct way, for example, through election or appointment.

Weber called the administrative apparatus in a rational-legal system a *bureaucracy* and observed that it is oriented to the creation and enforcement of rules in the public interest. Essentially, he argued, dominant Western cultural values emphasizing hard work, success, and a methodical (or, to use his word, *rational*) lifestyle reflect the system of authority characteristic of modern political communities—a fact that can be seen in the nature of the state, its administrative apparatus, and its political processes.

Weber called modern nation-states political communities. Historically, they have a number of peculiar characteristics:

1. The state regulates social action in a contiguous territory.

2. The use of the army and other means of force to regulate social action is the exclusive property of the government.

3. Citizens share a common cultural background, what Weber called a "community of memories," epitomized by the elements of the culture of capitalism.

4. Legitimacy is based on the creation of a centralized administrative apparatus, a bureaucracy.

In this context, then, Weber defined the modern state as based on the monopoly of physical coercion, a monopoly made legitimate by a system of laws binding on both the rulers and the ruled. Furthermore, in this setting the bureaucracy, as the archetypal example of instrumentally rational action, is the primary means of governmental administration and the focus of conflict as the members of various strata vie to control it.

Although many people condemn bureaucracies as inefficient, rigid, and incompetent, Weber argued that this mode of administration is the only means of attaining efficient, flexible, and competent regulation under a rule of law in industrial societies. In its logically pure form (that is, as an ideal type) a bureaucratic apparatus has a set of unique characteristics that set it apart from the form of administration typical of a traditional society:

1. Employment and promotion are based on technical training and experience, with the result that administration is based on knowledge rather than custom.

2. The rights and duties of officials are explicitly described in written regulations that have been properly enacted, with the result that staff members owe their primary loyalty to the system of rules governing their action rather than to superiors.

3. Officials receive fixed salaries and do not own either their positions or the means of production, with the result that administrative duties are separated from private affairs.[47]

According to Weber bureaucratic administration in a rational-legal system is realized to the extent that staff members "succeed in eliminating from official business love, hatred, and all purely personal, irrational, and emotional elements."[48] While Weber recognized that no actual bureaucracy operates in this way, his ideal type reflects a fundamental value characteristic of modern societies: Political administration should be impersonal, objective, and based on knowledge; for only in this way can the rule of law be realized. Further, he emphasized that while these characteristics and values seem commonplace today, they are historically new. They arose only in the West and have come to be the dominant form of authority only in the last few hundred years. Finally, Weber's definition of bureaucracy points toward a fundamental arena of conflict in modern societies: Who is to make laws, and who is to administer them through their control of the bureaucracy?

Within the context of a rational-legal system of authority, political parties are the forms in which social strata struggle for power. As Weber put it, "a political party . . . exists for the purpose of fighting for domination" in order to advance the economic interests or values of the group it represents, but it does so under the aegis of statutory regulation.[49] In general the point of the struggle is to direct the bureaucracy via the creation of law, for in this way the goals of the various social strata are achieved. For example, the very rich who own income-producing property in the United States act to make sure their economic interests are codified into law. Similarly, people in all social strata act to protect their interests and values, and the needs of those who do not participate are ignored.[50] The political process in Western societies, then, reflects those basic cultural values whose origin Weber discovered in *The Protestant Ethic and the Spirit of Capitalism:* Economic and social success are highly valued; they are achieved through competition under the rule of law; and the process is rational in the sense of

---

[47]Weber, *Economy and Society,* pp. 217–20.
[48]Ibid., p. 975.
[49]Ibid., p. 951.
[50]See Leonard Beeghley, *The Structure of Stratification* (Boston: Allyn & Bacon, 1988).

being pursued in a methodical manner. Weber's distinction between classes and status groups shows in a different way how the structure of stratification in modern societies also mirrors these values.

Social Strata: Class and Status

In his analysis of the structure of stratification, Weber tried to provide observers with a conceptual map outlining the parts of the stratification system. As noted earlier, he believed such an inventory of concepts would allow for an objective description of stratification processes in modern capitalist societies. As a result his description does not apply to either traditional social systems or modern communist societies. At the core of his scheme are two ideal types: social class and social status.

Unfortunately, Weber's discussion of these two concepts is somewhat confusing. Class-oriented behavior is concerned with economic issues, especially the amount and source of income. As such, it is an example of instrumentally rational action. Status-oriented behavior is concerned with values, mainly the honor or prestige attached to one's lifestyle. People's values are reflected in their choice of housing, friends, marriage partners, leisure-time activities, and other aspects of their lifestyle. As such, status-oriented behavior is an example of value rational action. Class and status are interrelated in that lifestyle is made possible by income, and income is made possible by lifestyle. Thus, and this fact is often misunderstood, status groups do not compete with classes. Rather status and class are different bases for action displayed by people in each stratum, who act to protect their economic interests and values. We should note that Weber did not use the term *strata*, which refers to a set of ranked positions. The title of this section, "Social Strata: Class and Status," is designed to emphasize our view that classes and status groups are coterminous, as shown in Figure 7-5.

Social Class.   According to Weber a class consists of those persons who have a similar ability to obtain positions in society, procure goods and services for themselves, and enjoy them via an appropriate lifestyle.[51] It should be recognized immediately that a class is defined, in part, in terms of status considerations: the lifestyle of the stratum to which one belongs. But in Weber's terminology, classes are statistical aggregates rather than groups. Behavior is class oriented to the extent that the process by which people obtain positions, purchase goods and

---

[51]Weber, *Economy and Society,* pp. 302, 927.

FIGURE 7-5   Class and Status in Max Weber's Work

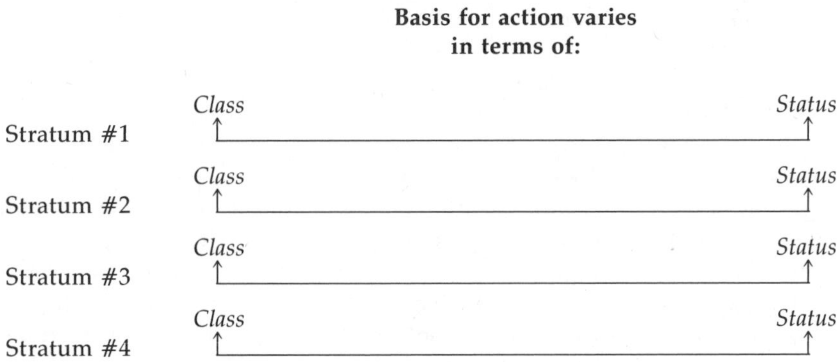

**Basis for action varies
in terms of:**

	Class		Status
Stratum #1	⌐_____⌐		

Class   *Status*
Stratum #1

Class   *Status*
Stratum #2

Class   *Status*
Stratum #3

Class   *Status*
Stratum #4

Class-oriented action: concerned with economic interests, mainly the source and amount of income.

Status-oriented action: concerned with values, as indicated by housing, friends, marriage partners, leisure-time activities, and other elements of lifestyle.

services, and enjoy them is characterized by an individualistic rather than group perspective. For example, even though investors trying to make money on the stock market may have some common interests, share certain kinds of information with one another, and even join together to prevent outsiders from participating, they each act individually in seeking profits or in experiencing losses. Further, in the process of seeking profits their behavior is typically characterized by an instrumentally rational orientation—that is, action reflects a systematic calculation of means and ends based on knowledge (even if such knowledge is imperfect).

In Weber's analysis, classes are essentially economic phenomena that can only exist in a legally regulated money market where income and profit are the desired goals. In such a context people's membership in a class can be determined very objectively, based on their power to dispose of goods or services. For this reason Weber believed one's "class situation is, in this sense, ultimately [a] market situation."[52] Two of the most important characteristics of a money market are that, in its logically pure form, it is impersonal and objective. For example, all that matters (or should matter) in the purchase of stock, groceries, housing, or any other commodity are such objective factors as one's cash and

---

[52]Ibid., p. 928.

credit rating. Similarly, a person's class situation is also objectively determined, with the result that people can be ranked in terms of their common economic characteristics and life chances.

A key problem, of course, involves the basis on which people possessing similar amounts of economic power are placed together in classes. Anthony Giddens argues that the Weberian analysis is not very useful because it allows for the possibility of an infinite number of classes.[53] He bases this argument on the idea that since no two people will have exactly the same positions, goods, and lifestyles, they cannot have the same economic interests or power—ergo, the number of possible classes is infinite. But this interpretation is incorrect, for Weber stated explicitly that while people are never exactly alike, it is still possible to conceptually delineate "the class structure of the advanced societies" in a way that is both helpful to observers and subjectively meaningful to the participants, and he provided sociologists with a conceptual map that remains useful today.

Like Marx, Weber began by distinguishing between those who have property and those who do not. As he put it, " 'property' and 'lack of property' are . . . the basic categories of all class situations." This is because the possession or nonpossession of income-producing property (or capital) allows for fundamentally different styles of life—and, as noted earlier, differences in lifestyle are the key to status distinctions in modern societies.

Considering first those who own income-producing property, Weber argued that they are differentiated according to the use to which their possessions are put. "The propertied, for instance, may belong to the class of rentiers or to the class of entrepreneurs."[54]

In Weber's terminology *rentiers* comprise those persons who live primarily off fixed incomes from investments or trust funds. For example, the German *junkers* (or landowners) of his time were rentiers since these families had controlled much of the land for several generations and received their incomes from the peasants or tenant farmers who actually worked it. As a result of their possession of capital and values that they had acquired over time, the *junkers* chose to lead a less overtly acquisitive lifestyle. Weber called them rentiers because they did not work to increase their assets but simply lived off them, using their time for purposes other than earning a living. For example, they might hold public office or lead lives of idleness.

---

[53]Anthony Giddens, *The Class Structure of the Advanced Societies* (New York: Harper & Row, 1973), p. 78.
[54]Weber, *Economy and Society*, pp. 303, 928.

According to Weber entrepreneurs comprise those persons, such as merchants, shipowners, and bankers, who own and operate businesses. Weber called them a commercial or entrepreneurial class because they actually work their property for the economic gain it produces, with the result that in absolute terms the members of the entrepreneurial class often have more economic power, but less social honor (or prestige), than rentiers.

This distinction between the uses to which income-producing property is put allowed Weber to differentiate between those who work as an avocation and those who work because they want to increase their assets—that is, it reflects fundamental differences in values. In most societies there exist privileged status groups, such as rentiers, the members of which "consider almost any kind of overt participation in economic acquisition as absolutely stigmatizing" despite its potential economic advantages.[55] These are usually families that have possessed wealth for a long time, over several generations. Thus, Weber argued, even though economic- (or class-)oriented action is individualistic and dominated by instrumentally rational action, values of noneconomic origin always impinge themselves on behavior. This point characterizes of all of Weber's work.

Nonetheless, even though the two classes can be distinguished, Weber asserted that the possession of capital by both rentiers and entrepreneurs provides them with great economic and political power and sharply distinguishes them from those who do not own such property.[56] Both rentiers and entrepreneurs are able to monopolize the purchase of expensive consumer items. Both can and do pursue monopolistic sales and pricing policies, whether legally or not. To some extent both can and do control opportunities for others to acquire wealth and property. And finally, both rentiers and entrepreneurs monopolize costly status privileges, such as education, that provide young people with future contacts and skills. In these terms, then, rentiers and entrepreneurs can be seen to have (roughly) similar levels of power and, in part because they are always a very small proportion of the population, they are often able to act together to protect their lifestyles. Even though they live rather differently, their source of income (ownership of capital) sets them apart from the other social classes. The distribution of property, in short, tends to prevent nonowners from competing for highly valued goods and perpetuates the structure of stratification from one generation to another. This fact does not

---

[55]Ibid., p. 937.
[56]Ibid., pp. 303, 927.

mean mobility in either direction is not possible, for such movement often occurs; it does, however, mean mobility is difficult.

In constructing his conceptual map of the class structure, Weber next considered those who do not own income-producing property. Despite the fact that they do not possess the means of production, such persons are not without economically and politically important resources in modern societies, and they can be meaningfully differentiated into a number of classes. The main criteria Weber used in making class distinctions among those without property are the worth of their services and the level of their skills, since both factors are important indicators of people's ability to obtain positions, purchase goods, and enjoy them. In Weber's classificatory scheme the "middle classes" comprise those individuals who today would be called white-collar workers because the skills they sell do not involve manual labor: public officials, such as politicians and administrators; managers of businesses; members of the professions, such as doctors and lawyers; teachers and intellectuals; and specialists of various sorts, such as technicians, low-level white-collar employees, and civil servants.[57]

Because their skills are in relatively high demand in industrial societies, these persons generally have more economic and political power than those who work with their hands.

According to Weber the less-privileged propertyless classes comprise people who today would be called blue-collar workers because their skills primarily involve manual labor. Without explanation, Weber said such persons can be divided into three levels: skilled, semiskilled, and unskilled workers. He did not elaborate much on the lifestyles of those without property.

By means of these ideal types, Weber described the parts of a modern, complex class structure in which the key factors distinguishing one class from another are the uses to which property is put by those who own it and the worth of the skills and services offered by those who do not own property. These factors combine in the marketplace to produce identifiable aggregates, or classes, the members of which have a similar ability to obtain positions, purchase goods, and enjoy them via an appropriate lifestyle.

The final topic of importance in Weber's analysis of social class is the possibility of group formation and unified political action on the part of the propertyless classes. Like Marx, Weber said this phenomenon is relatively rare in history because those who do not own property generally fail to recognize their common interests. As a result, action based on a similar class situation is often restricted to inchoate

---

[57]Ibid., p. 304.

and relatively brief mass reactions. Nonetheless, throughout history perceived differences in life chances have periodically led to class struggles, although in most cases the point of the conflict focused on rather narrow economic issues, such as wages or prices, rather than on the nature of the political system that perpetuates their class situation.[58]

While Weber only briefly alluded to the conditions under which the members of the propertyless classes might challenge the existing political order, he identified some of the same variables that Marx had:

1. Large numbers of persons must perceive themselves to be in the same class situation.

2. They must be ecologically concentrated, as in urban areas.

3. Clearly understood goals must be articulated by an intelligentsia. Here Weber suggested people must be shown that the causes and consequences of their class situation result from the structure of the political system itself.

4. The opponents must be clearly identified.

When these conditions are satisfied, Weber indicated, an organized class results. We turn now to the other basis for action displayed by people in each stratum: social status.

Social Status.   In Weber's work *social status* refers to the evaluations people make of one another, and a status group comprises those individuals who share "a specific, positive or negative, social estimation of honor."[59] As described earlier, Weber used the concepts of "status" and "status group" to distinguish the sphere of prestige evaluation, expressed by people's lifestyles, from that of monetary calculation, expressed by their economic behavior. Although the two are highly interrelated, the analytical distinction is designed to emphasize the fact that people's actions cannot be understood in economic terms alone. Rather their values often play an important role in channeling action in specific directions.

The decisive difference between class and status can be summarized in the following way. On the one hand, because the income from a person's job provides the ability to purchase goods and enjoy them, class membership is objectively determined based on a simple monetary calculation. On the other hand, because status and honor are based on the personal evaluations people make of one another, a person's membership in a status group is always subjectively determined.

---

[58]Ibid., pp. 305, 930–31.
[59]Ibid., pp. 305–6, 932.

Hence status-oriented behavior is illustrative of value rational action—that is, action based on some value or values held for their own sake. Thus, rather than behaving in terms of their economic interests, status-oriented action involves people acting as members of a group with whom they share a specific style of life and level of social honor. In Weber's words, "in contrast to classes, *stande* (status groups) are normally groups. They are, however, of an amorphous kind."[60] That is, they are not tightly organized. For example, corporate executives dining together during the lunch hour rather than with their blue-collar subordinates are engaged in value rational action, since they are acting in terms of their values, or ideas of honor, and they are expressing their common lifestyle. In principle prestige or honor can be attributed on the basis of virtually any quality that is both valued and shared by an aggregate of people.

It is important to remember that, from Weber's point of view, the status groups in any modern society are generally coterminous to the social classes identified previously. Thus skilled blue-collar people (say, unionized construction workers) are as much a status group as corporate executives, and the differences between the two, expressed by a lack of commensality (an unwillingness to eat with one another), suggest both the defining quality of status groups and the link between class and status: Prestige or honor results from a specific style of life expected of all those who would belong to the group. Thus despite the fact that the two concepts refer to analytically distinct phenomena, in practice classes and status groups coalesce such that social strata are formed. This fact was depicted previously in Figure 7-5 on page 221.

With some prescience, Weber noted that individuals develop styles of living in light of their parental background and upbringing, formal education, and occupational experiences, factors subsequently shown as fundamental to the process of status attainment.[61] On these bases people at all levels tend to associate with others whom they perceive as having similar lifestyles, and they frequently try to prevent the entry of outsiders, those seen as having different values of lifestyles, into the group. For despite their amorphous qualities, the members of status groups are both aware of their situation and active in maintaining it. The mechanism by which this is accomplished is inherently based on a subjective judgment, but it is consciously used and powerful in its consequences: social discrimination. Reinhard Bendix describes the significance Weber sees in this mechanism. Although he

---

[60]Ibid., p. 932.
[61]Ibid., p. 306.

expresses himself in what is now considered sexist language, Bendix intended to refer to both genders:

> Status groups are rooted in family experience. Before the individual reaches maturity, he has participated in his family's claim to social prestige, its occupational subculture and educational level. Even in the absence of concerted action, families share a style of life and similar attitudes. Classes without organization achieve nothing. But families in the same status situation need not communicate and organize in order to discriminate against those people they consider inferior.[62]

Essentially, Weber argued, status "always rests on distance and exclusiveness" in the sense that members of a status group actively express and protect their lifestyles in a number of specific ways: (1) People extend hospitality only to social equals. Thus they tend to invite into their homes, become friends with, eat with, and socialize with others who are like themselves in that they share similar lifestyles. (2) People restrict potential marriage partners to social equals (this practice is called connubium). Thus they tend to live in areas and send their children to school with the children of others who are like themselves, with the result that their offspring generally marry others with similar values and ways of living. (3) People practice unique social conventions and activities. Thus they tend to join organizations, such as churches and clubs, and spend their leisure time with others who share similar beliefs and lifestyles. And (4) people try to monopolize "privileged modes of acquisition," such as their property or occupations.[63]

This last tactic is important, for those in common status positions act politically in order to close off social and economic opportunities to outsiders in order to protect their capital or occupational investments. For example, because particular skills (say, in doctoring or carpentry) acquired over time necessarily limit the possibility for acquiring other skills, competing individuals "become interested in curbing competition" and preventing the free operation of the market. So they join together and, in spite of continued competition among themselves, attempt to close off opportunities for outsiders by influencing the creation and administration of law. Such attempts at occupational closure are ever recurring at all stratum levels, and they are "the source of property in land as well as of all guild [or union] monopolies."[64]

---

[62]Reinhard Bendix, "Inequality and Social Structure: A Comparison of Marx and Weber," *American Sociological Review* 39, April 1974, pp. 149–61.

[63]Weber, *Economy and Society*, pp. 306, 935.

[64]Ibid., pp. 342–43.

The results are that "privileged modes of acquisition" are retained, people's lifestyles are protected, and the system of stratification is maintained. It should be noted once again how status and class considerations coalesce.

As a final point in the analysis of status, Weber argued that the attempt by members of status groups to discriminate against others in order to protect their style of life can have extreme consequences, for segregation based on status considerations can develop into castes, rather than strata, in which positions are closed by legal and religious sanctions. However, he believed caste distinctions usually develop only when based on underlying ethnic or racial differences, as occurred in the United States. But Weber emphasized that patterns of ethnic segregation do not inevitably, or even normally, produce caste relations. The latter are always dependent on unique historical events.[65]

Weber's Model of the Class Structure

As described in Chapter 5, Marx posited that modern societies display a basic division between capitalists, those who own income-producing property, and proletarians, those who are forced to sell their labor power to survive. In his words, "society as a whole is splitting up more and more into two great hostile camps, into two great classes facing each other: Bourgeoisie and Proletarian."[66]

Marx knew this assertion was an exaggeration. He meant historical evolution placed these two groups at the center of a class struggle, which would inevitably produce a communist society. But when examining actual historical events, Marx would often look at specific segments of society, such as bankers or the "lower middle class" or the *lumpenproletariat* (the very poor), analyzing their different experiences and interests with great insight.[67] He did this, however, on an ad hoc basis. He did not develop a more systematic, abstract model (or map) of the class structure. Weber did. Marx's and Weber's models are compared in Figure 7-6. It should be noted that we are now using the terms *class* and *stratum* as synonyms, which has become standard in sociology over the years. While Weber's argument that people's behavior at each class or stratum level is based sometimes on their economic inter-

[65]Ibid., p. 933.

[66]Karl Marx and Friedrich Engels, *The Birth of the Communist Manifesto* (New York: International, 1975), p. 90.

[67]Karl Marx, *The Eighteenth Brumaire of Louis Bonaparte* (New York: International, 1963); "Critique of the Gotha Program," in *Selected Works*, vol. 3, ed. Karl Marx and Friedrich Engels (New York: International, 1969), pp. 9–30.

FIGURE 7-6   Marx's and Weber's Models of the Class Structure

Marx's Model	Weber's Model
1. Capitalists	1. Propertied:
– – – – – – – – – – – – – – –	*a.* Rentiers
2. Proletarians	*b.* Entrepreneurs
	– – – – – – – – – – – – – – – – –
	2. Nonpropertied:
	a. Middle classes
	b. Skilled workers
	c. Semiskilled workers
	d. Unskilled workers

ests and sometimes on their values is exactly right, his terminology has not been adopted.

Figure 7-6 shows that both Marx and Weber regarded the differences between those who own capital and those who do not as fundamental divisions in the class structure. The dashed line separating the different sections of each model is designed to suggest that a semipermeable boundary exists that is very difficult to cross. Nonetheless, as indicated in the last section, mobility across this boundary line does occur.

But the figure also shows that Weber's map of the class structure is much more detailed than Marx's. Both those who own property and those who do not can be separated into classes (or strata) in a way that is useful to observers and subjectively meaningful to ordinary people. Thus those capitalists who do not lead acquisitive lives are rentiers, while those who do are entrepreneurs. Sometimes the members of these two strata act together to preserve and protect their source of income, their property; but sometimes they do not, mainly because they have different values. Weber's distinction alerts observers to the need for specifying the conditions under which each occurs.

Similarly, middle-class people see themselves as different than those who are skilled workers. As a result they tend to live in different neighborhoods, make different friends, attend different schools, and participate in different leisure-time activities. Current research reveals that a semi-permeable boundary separates middle-class people (white-collar workers) from working-class people (blue-collar workers) at all skill levels.[68]

---

[68]See Beeghley, *Structure of Stratification.*

Although Weber could not prove this fact since the necessary research had not yet been done, his model alerts observers to be sensitive to the different lifestyles displayed by members of those social strata who do not own property.

Weber's Model of Social Change

Weber's analysis of systems of domination, especially his distinction among the three types of authority, implies a model of social change. Like Marx, Weber saw the source of change as endogenous (or internal) to the society. In effect he posited—implicitly, to be sure—that integrative problems typically associated with disjunction among cultural values, patterns of action, and psychological orientations (see Figure 7-4) produce processes of social change in every society. Figure 7-7 depicts Weber's vision of the internal system dynamics that occur as societies try to resolve the dilemmas they face.

Weber argued that the struggle for power is a continuous process in every society. For example, in traditional societies rulers attempt to enlarge their areas of discretion and power at the expense of administrative officials and notables. They do so by various methods: for example, the use of military force, economic coercion, co-optation, and political alliances. In all cases they justify their action in terms of customs handed down over generations. Conversely, officials and notables attempt to increase their power at the expense of the rulers, and they use many of the same tactics. While this pattern can remain stable for

FIGURE 7-7   Weber's Model of Social Change

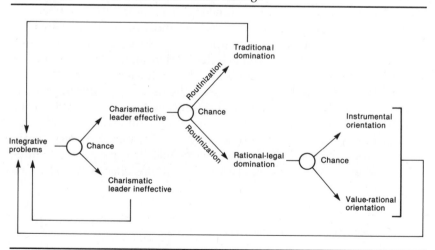

many years, the gradual development of structural disjunctions—as signified by incongruity among values and beliefs, patterns of action, and psychological orientations—is common. As indicated in Figure 7-7, it is during the crises emerging from such malintegration that charismatic leaders are most likely to emerge and attempt to change the course of history. If such leaders are ineffective, the crises may continue and even escalate, with the result that leaders will eventually lose their following as the population turns to some other charismatic figure for solutions. But if the charismatic leaders are effective in resolving crises, then the process of routinization occurs as their authority is implemented over time. The inevitable result is the transformation of charismatic authority into either a traditional or rational-legal form of domination. In this context, Weber argued, the development of rational-legal authority makes a recurrence of traditional domination less likely. More likely is that social systems characterized by rational-legal forms of authority will resolve integrative crises in such a way that patterns of social action reflect either instrumental or value rational orientations. However, the choice between these two alternatives is not inevitable, since Weber emphasized the importance of chance in human history. Hence Figure 7-7 builds in the possibility (even if unlikely) that a society can resolve integrative problems by returning to a form of traditional authority.

THE ENDURING LEGACY

Ordinarily, a theorist's enduring legacy consists of the number and power of abstract laws that emanate from his or her writings. From this point of view Weber's contribution to the emergence of sociological theory is rather limited. Nonetheless, Weber remains a significant influence on modern theorists.

Alone among his contemporaries, Weber saw that a true science of society had to be "value free" or objective, and he constructed methodological rules to produce such results. In addition Weber's use of ideal types in "logical experiments" anticipates developments in sociology, economics, and other disciplines in which computer simulations are used to analyze phenomena that cannot be directly measured. Further, Weber's account of the origin of modern societies remains the most plausible analysis of this unique event. Finally, his outline of the class structure in modern societies constitutes one of the most prescient analyses of social stratification ever written.

It also remains true, however, that Weber's rejection of general theory in sociology was very shortsighted. He greatly underestimated the nature and usefulness of social scientific theory. This fact means that only a small number of theoretical principles can be extracted from his work. These propositions are summarized below. As is evident, most of them concern questions of inequality and conflict—making Weber very much a "conflict sociologist."

1. The lower the level of integration in a social system, the more likely are incumbents in that system to articulate their grievances, and the more likely are they to be receptive to the influence of a charismatic leader.
2. The less effective a charismatic leader in resolving the grievances of incumbents in a system, the more likely are integrative problems to escalate, and hence the more likely is a leader's authority to decrease; conversely, the more effective a charismatic leader in resolving the grievances of incumbents in a system, the more likely are integrative problems to decrease, and hence the more likely is a charismatic leader's authority to endure.
3. The more effective a charismatic leader in resolving system incumbents' grievances, the more likely is that leader to change the existing social structure as well as the cultural values and psychological orientations of system incumbents.
4. The longer the duration of charismatic authority, the more likely are decision-making tasks to be transferred to an administrative staff, and hence the more likely is the relationship between the leader and system incumbents to be transformed from one based on charisma into one based on law or tradition.
5. The more status differences are based on ascriptive criteria and the more salient such criteria are, the greater the range of discrimination against those with different lifestyles.
6. The lower the rate of technological change in a system, the more stable the stratification structure and the higher the level of integration; conversely, the higher the rate of technological change in the system, the less stable the stratification structure and the lower the level of integration.
7. The continuity in patterns of social organization is a positive function of the degree of legitimacy given to political authority, and the degree of legitimacy of political authority is a negative function of the following:
   7a. The degree of correlation of class and status, with the degree of correlation being a negative function of rationality in and complexity of patterns of social organization.
   7b. The degree of discontinuity in social hierarchies, with the degree of discontinuity being a negative function of rationality in and complexity of patterns of social organization.

    7c. The degree to which upward mobility for lower-ranking units is blocked, with the degree of blockage being a negative function of rationality in and complexity of patterns of social organization.

8. The degree of change in patterns of social organization is a positive function of conflict, and the degree of conflict is a positive function of the following:

    8a. The degree of polarization of class and status, with the degree of polarization being a positive function of 7a, 7b, and 7c.

    8b. The availability of charismatic leaders who oppose the existing distribution of power.

CHAPTER 8

The Origin and Context of Georg Simmel's Thought

BIOGRAPHICAL INFLUENCES ON SIMMEL'S THOUGHT

Simmel's Marginality

Georg Simmel was born in 1858 at the very center of Berlin.[1] His father, a successful Jewish businessman, had converted to Christianity; however, Simmel's Jewish background was to haunt him throughout his career. Simmel's father died when Simmel was young, and a friend of the family was appointed his guardian. Simmel appears to have had an emotionally distant relationship to his mother, and so it is reasonable to conclude that he never had any strong ties to his family.

Lewis Coser[2] has stressed that Simmel's work was greatly influenced by this marginality to not only his family but also to the academic establishment in Germany. This marginality, as we will see in the next chapter, helps account for the brilliance of Simmel's analysis of the individual in differentiated and cross-cutting social relationships, for there can be little doubt that Simmel was on the edge of various intellectual worlds. It is difficult to know how embittered Simmel was by this borderline existence. Indeed, in contrast to others of this period who tended to see modern and differentiated social structures as harmful to the individual, Simmel stressed the liberating effects of marginality. For Simmel, the differentiation of structure, the elaboration of markets, and the detached involvement of people in ra-

---

[1] This sketch of Georg Simmel's biography draws heavily from Lewis A. Coser's *Masters of Sociological Thought* (New York: Harcourt Brace Jovanovich, 1971), pp. 177–217. See also Lewis A. Coser, ed., *Georg Simmel* (Englewood Cliffs, N.J.: Prentice-Hall, 1965); Kurt H. Wolff, "Introduction," in *The Sociology of Georg Simmel* (New York: Free Press, 1950); Kurt H. Wolff, ed., *George Simmel, 1858–1918* (Columbus: Ohio State University Press, 1959); and Nicholas Spykman, *The Social Theory of Georg Simmel* (Chicago: University of Chicago Press, 1925).

[2] Coser, *Masters of Sociological Thought.*

tional bureaucratic structures gave them options, choices, and opportunities not available in traditional societies. Whether or not Simmel was justifying his own position in this line of argument can never be known, but one point is clear: Simmel did not conceptualize modern society in the severe pathological terms as Marx (who stressed oppression and alienation), as Durkheim (who worried over anomie and egoism), and as Weber (who warned of the entrapment of individuals in the "iron cage" of bureaucracy).

Yet there is a tragic quality to Simmel's career, despite its many points of success and accomplishment. Let us now turn to this dual character in Simmel's career.

Simmel's Intellectual Career

After graduating from the gymnasium, Simmel studied philosophy at the University of Berlin, and in 1881 he received his doctorate. His Ph.D. thesis was on Immanuel Kant,[3] who, as we will see shortly, exerted enormous influence on Simmel's approach to sociological analysis. At the time of Simmel's graduation, Germany in general, and Berlin in particular, were undergoing a remarkable transition. The nation as a whole was industrializing in record time, and within Simmel's adult lifetime Germany was to surpass both England and France in productivity, lagging only behind the United States. Yet this rapid industrialization revealed a critical disjuncture: Though the bourgeoisie brought about the rapid economic growth, it failed to advance its claims to power, which remained in the hands of the old feudal system.[4] This tension between the old and the new produced the disastrous policies that led to World War I and its aftermath, which ultimately created the conditions for the rise of Hitler and Nazism.

Within this broader and foreboding national context, however, intellectual life flourished, especially in Berlin, which in five decades grew from a city of 500,000 to four million on the eve of World War I. Yet even in this prospering intellectual milieu, there was a duality between freedom and authoritarian constraint. In the lively counterculture and intellectual life around the university and in the city itself, there was a vibrant mix of activity. But within the university system, which in the earlier decades of the nineteenth century had served as the model for the building of research-oriented American universities,

---

[3]The title of his dissertation was "The Nature of Matter according to Kant's Physical Monadology," and in this early confrontation with Kant's ideas can be seen the seeds of his "formal sociology."

[4]Ralf Dahrendorf, "The New Germanies—Restoration, Revolution, and Reconstruction," *Encounter* 23, April 1964, p. 50.

there was a conservative and at times authoritarian undercurrent. The university system was prosperous and, as a result, caught in the dilemma between encouraging academic freedom and open expression, on one side, and maintaining its comfortable position in a social and political climate charged with the tension between the capitalist bourgeoisie and the semi-feudal political system, on the other side.

Many scholars did great work within this system—Max Weber being the best example in sociology. But others, especially Jews, were denied complete access to the academic system or, as was the case with many, were pushed to the provincial universities outside the main urban centers. Not just Jews, but others who revealed more radical political sympathies that might disrupt the status quo suffered this fate—as was the case for Werner Sombart, who was relegated to a marginal university, and Robert Michels, who was denied any academic appointment at all.

Simmel was caught in this conflicting current, and early in his career he decided to stay in Berlin and hope for the best. The result was that he became a *Privat Dozent*, or unpaid lecturer who lived off student fees. The more typical pattern of this time was for academics to move from one university to another, slowly working their way into major university positions.

Perhaps Simmel saw that, as a Jew, the cards were stacked against him, but the results of his decision in 1885 to assume a marginal position and remain in Berlin were profound. On the one hand, he became a popular lecturer who attracted a large lay and academic following. As a lecturer he offered a broad range of courses—from sociology and social psychology to logic, philosophy, and ethics. But on the other hand, this popular success appears to have antagonized the academic establishment. His popularity made many jealous, while his breadth and brilliance threatened narrow specialists. The end result was, in addition to the undercurrent of anti-Semitism, a sense of threat, jealousy, and envy as well as an intolerance of cross-disciplinary scholarship worked against Simmel. Moreover, Simmel's style affronted the academic establishment in many specific ways. For example, Simmel never documented his works in detail, with footnotes and scholarly quotations; he would jump from topic to topic, never pursuing in great depth a subject (except perhaps his brilliant work on *The Philosophy of Money*). He would also write essays for popular magazines and newspapers, a tactic that always antagonizes, even to this day, traditional academics. Indeed Simmel appears to have gone out of his way to annoy the academic establishment.

Yet in addition to his popularity among the broader intellectual and artistic community, Simmel did enjoy much academic success. With Max Weber and Ferdinand Tönnies, he was a co-founder of the

German Society for Sociology, and his works were widely read, cited, and respected by the first generation of sociologists. And despite his marginal academic status, he did not suffer financially since his guardian left him a considerable fortune. Moreover, in 1890 he married his wife, Gertrud, who was an established philosopher in her own right (publishing under the pseudonym of Marie-Luise Enckendorf) and with whom he lived a comfortable upper-middle-class life. Coupled with his fame as a lecturer and his active association with artists, critics, commentators, journalists, and writers, Simmel enjoyed a stimulating and full life.

Yet there was still the stigma and frustration of being a well-known scholar and intellectual figure without a real academic position. For fifteen years Simmel remained a private lecturer, despite the efforts of friends like Max Weber to secure a full-time position for him. In 1901 he was given the status of honorary adjunct professor at the University of Berlin, which confirmed his position as an outsider who was neither paid nor entitled to take part in the administrative affairs of the university. Such an appointment was, in reality, an insult for Simmel, who was now a scholar of world fame, having authored six books and dozens of articles that had been translated into English, French, Italian, Polish, and Russian.

When Simmel finally received a regular academic appointment in 1914, it was at a provincial university in Strasbourg on the border between France and Germany. Moreover, he was now fifty-six years old, well over a decade past the normative time for promotion to full professor. And to top off the frustrations in his career, he arrived at Strasbourg just at the outbreak of World War I. Border university life was suspended during the war, thereby denying Simmel the opportunity to lecture. Simmel's last efforts to secure a chair at a major university failed in 1915 at the University of Heidelberg; and shortly before the end of the war in 1918, Simmel died of cancer.

This futility and marginality in the face of world fame must surely have contributed to Simmel's style of scholarship: He maintained a foot in both philosophy and sociology while sustaining a commitment to both formal analytical analysis and social commentary on events and typical questions.[5] The result is a lack of in-depth scholarship on sociological topics; instead, Simmel analyzes specific sociological topics with flashes of insight and sophistication, only to move on to yet

---

[5]We have not mentioned Simmel's sudden burst of patriotism during the war, since it is so embarrassing: Gone is the cool and analytical Simmel, and in his place is the passionate patriot. In fact, as Coser emphasizes, the latter part of Simmel's career is marked by a romantic emotionalism somewhat similar to Auguste Comte, who, near the end, suffered much the same fate as Simmel (see Chapter 1 of this book).

another, often disconnected topic. And his most in-depth works, particularly *The Philosophy of Money*, are so heavily imbued with philosophical commentary that the sociological theory in them can easily go unnoticed.

Yet despite this topical character to his work, there are two important themes in Simmel's sociology. First, he was concerned, as were all social theorists of this early period in sociology, with the process of differentiation and its effects on the individual. Second, a methodological unity in Simmel's work seeks to extract the underlying essence and form of the particular empirical topics; and so, while Simmel often shifted the substantive content of his analysis, he always sought to discover the underlying forms of social interaction and organization that linked diverse substantive areas. These themes emerged out of personal and intellectual contact with a number of particular thinkers—particularly Max Weber, Herbert Spencer, Immanuel Kant, and Karl Marx.

INTELLECTUAL INFLUENCES ON SIMMEL'S THOUGHT

A Note on Simmel and Weber

Georg Simmel's sociological writings span the same three decades, 1890 to 1920, as those of his German colleague and friend, Max Weber. Yet despite the fact that both men worked in a similar social and cultural environment, their respective orientations to sociology were rather dissimilar, in part because each man was trained differently and thus responded to somewhat different influences.

Weber was trained in the law and in economics, with the result that he was forced to react to the *methodenstreit* (the German methodological controversy, as discussed in Chapter 6). As we have seen, Weber used the works of Dilthey and Rickert to fashion a unique sociology that eschewed the development of abstract laws, because he believed such theoretical statements could not get at the significance of those historical phenomena in which he was most interested. In contrast, Simmel was a philosopher as well as a sociologist; his published works include books and articles on such diverse figures as philosophers Arthur Schopenhauer, Friedrich Nietzsche, and Immanuel Kant; writer Johann Goethe; and painter Rembrandt. In addition, Simmel also considered morals, ethics, aesthetics, and many other topics from a philosophical vantage point. As might be expected, his brand of sociology is unique and quite different than Weber's. After an early dalliance with Herbert Spencer and some elements of Social Darwinism, Simmel's mature works reflect his adaptation of some of Kant's philosophical doctrines to the study of human society. Essentially, Simmel contended that the social processes in which human beings engage constitute organized and stable structures, that these patterns of social organization affect action in systematic ways, and that their consequences can be both observed and predicted independently of the specific objectives of the actors involved. Thus, unlike Max Weber, Simmel held that sociology should be oriented to the development of "timelessly valid laws" of social organization, a point of view that followed from his Kantian orientation.

However, Simmel and Weber were alike in at least one respect, for both felt compelled to react to the ideological and theoretical challenge posed by Marxism as it existed at the turn of the century. While this interest is more central to Weber's sociology than to Simmel's, the latter's analysis is a sociologically sophisticated rejection of Marx and Marxism.

Herbert Spencer, Social Darwinism, and Simmel's Thought

Like most of the classical social theorists, Simmel wished to understand the nature of modern industrial societies. And the title of his first sociological treatise, *Social Differentiation*, published in 1890, suggests immediately the fundamental change that he saw: modern societies are much more differentiated than those of the past.[6] Like Herbert Spencer (see Chapter 3), Simmel saw this change in evolutionary terms and as an indication of human progress. Indeed he labeled it an "upward development." Further, just as Spencer often used organismic analogies to illustrate his argument, so did Simmel. For example, in *Social Differentiation* he argued that just as a more complex organism can save energy in relation to the environment and use that energy to perform more difficult and complex tasks, so can a more highly differentiated society.[7] Like Spencer, Simmel never confused biological analogies with social facts, partly because his arguments are also illustrated with many other kinds of analogies and examples. While some of Simmel's later works did not reveal much systematic concern with either the problem of evolution or the historical transition to industrialization, they display a lasting interest in understanding the

---

[6]Georg Simmel, *Ueber Sociale Differenzierung* (Leipzig: Duncker and Humbolt, 1890). While most of this book remains untranslated, two chapters, "Differentiation and the Principle of Saving Energy" and "The Intersection of Social Spheres," do appear in *Georg Simmel: Sociologist and European*, trans. Peter Laurence (New York: Barnes & Noble, 1976).

[7]Simmel, "Differentiation and the Principle of Energy Saving."

structure of modern, differentiated societies and in showing how people's participation in complex social systems affects their behavior.

The evolutionary discussion in *Social Differentiation* also shows a less attractive side to the young Simmel, since he embraced some of the more questionable aspects of Social Darwinism that were current during the late nineteenth century. For example, he insisted "on the hereditary character of the criminal inclination" and even protested "against the preservation of the weak, who will transmit their inferiority to future generations."[8] However, Simmel's mature writings betray no trace of such views. In fact, while he generally did not comment on political events in a partisan manner, his analyses of the poor, of women, and of working people all suggest a sympathetic understanding of their plight.[9] In all these cases Simmel's discussion reflects his more general attempt at focusing on the consequences of social differentiation in modern societies. His emphasis on demonstrating the manner in which social structures influence interaction among human beings independently of their specific purposes is one result of his neo-Kantian orientation.

Immanuel Kant and Simmel's Thought

Immanual Kant did not finish his most significant work until the age of fifty-one. But that book, *The Critique of Pure Reason*, published in 1781, stimulated a revolution in philosophy.[10] Among other results, it led eventually to Hegel's denial that material phenomena are real (see Chapter 4). However, Hegel is hardly read today, except by Marxists, while Kant's influence has endured. In this section we will begin by sketching Kant's basic ideas and then briefly discuss the way in which Simmel adapted them for use in sociology.

---

[8]Paul Honigsheim, "The Time and Thought of the Young Simmel," in *Essays on Sociology, Philosophy and Aesthetics by Georg Simmel et al.*, ed. Kurt Wolff (New York: Harper & Row, 1965), p. 170.

[9]See Georg Simmel, "The Poor," in *Georg Simmel on Individuality and Social Forms* (Chicago: University of Chicago Press, 1971), pp. 150–78. On working people and women, see Georg Simmel, *Conflict and the Web of Group Affiliations* (New York: Free Press, 1955); also Lewis A. Coser, "Georg Simmel's Neglected Contributions to the Sociology of Women," *Signs* 2, Summer 1977, pp. 869–76.

[10]Immanuel Kant, *The Critique of Pure Reason* (New York: Macmillan, 1929). Like Hegel, Kant is extraordinarily difficult to read and understand. For purposes of this brief discussion of his work we are following the interpretation offered in Will Durant, *The Story of Philosophy* (New York: Simon & Schuster, 1926). For a more complete analysis, see T. E. Wilkerson, *Kant's Critique of Pure Reason: A Commentary for Students* (New York: Oxford University Press, 1976).

Kant's Basic Ideas.   In a short discourse on the nature of philosophy, Simmel remarked that individual philosophers often raise what appears to be a general problem, but they state the issue so that its solution conforms to their preconceptions.[11] Simmel undoubtedly had Kant in mind when stating this little aphorism, for Kant's *Critique of Pure Reason* is an investigation of the knowledge potential of "pure reason" that exists apart from the mundane and disorganized sense impressions that human beings experience. In phrasing the problem in this way, Kant's definition of *pure reason* is crucial. By this term he meant knowledge that exists independently of, or prior to, sense experience, which implies that pure reason is knowledge inherent to the structure of the mind. After defining the issue in this way, Kant was able to conclude that all human conceptions of the external world are products of the activity of the mind, which shapes the unformed and chaotic succession of sense impressions into a conceptual unity that can be understood in terms of scientific laws.[12]

While previous philosophers, such as John Locke and David Hume, had assumed that material phenomena are inherently organized and that human beings' sensations of objects and events in the world merely reflect that organization, Kant held that neither supposition is true. Rather he asserted that the sensations people have are intrinsically chaotic, reflecting nothing more than the endless succession of sights, smells, sounds, odors, and other stimuli that, in and of themselves, are disorganized and meaningless. Kant claimed the mind transforms this chaos of sense impressions into meaningful perceptions through a process he called the *transcendental aesthetic*. Simmel summarized this part of Kant's philosophy by observing that human sensations are "given forms and connections which are not inherent in them but which are imposed on them by the knowing mind as such."[13] This transformation of disorganized sensations into organized perceptions is accomplished by two fundamental "categories," or forms— space and time—that are inherent parts of the mind. In Kant's view space and time are not things perceived but modes of perceiving that exist prior to, or independently of, our knowledge of the world; they are elements of pure reason. Only by using these categories are human beings able to transform the chaotic sensations that they receive from the external world into systematic perceptions. The laws of mathematics are the best examples of both the a priori nature of space and time

---

[11]Georg Simmel, "The Nature of Philosophy," in *Essays by Georg Simmel,* pp. 282–310.

[12]Ibid.

[13]Ibid., pp. 290–99.

and the way in which the mind changes disorder into order. Thus it has always been and always will be true that the shortest distance between two points is a straight line. Mathematical laws such as this are absolute and necessary to human perception of events and objects in the external world, for they allow people to orient themselves to the material phenomena making up the world.

Yet merely being able to perceive objects and events is not enough, for people's perceptions are not spontaneously organized either. Rather, like sensations, perceptions are experienced as confused sequences of observations. Thus Kant emphasized that pure reason aims at the establishment of higher forms of knowledge: general truths that are independent of experience. These are the laws of science, truths that are abstract and absolute. Hence, in a process Kant called *transcendental logic*, the mind transforms perceptual knowledge into conceptual knowledge—for example, the transformation of the observation of a falling apple into the law of gravity or (on a different level) the transformation of observations of action during conflict into laws stating the consequences of social conflict for human behavior. Kant claimed the mind uses a set of a priori "categories," or forms, by which to arrange perceptions. For example, the ideas of cause, unity, reciprocal relations, necessity, and contingency are modes of conceptualizing empirical processes that are inherent to the mind; like space and time, they are elements of pure reason. In Simmel's words, it is only through the activity of the mind that human perceptions "become what we call nature: a meaningful, intelligible coherence in which the diversity of things appears as a principled unity, knitted together by laws."[14] In this regard Kant also insisted that the manner in which observations are conceptualized always depends on the purposes of the mind. For example, consider a system of thought, such as Darwin's theory of evolution or Marx's theory of revolution. Kant said these means of conceptualizing empirical data (perceptions) reveal the purposeful activity of the mind, for in neither case are the objects or events in the world prearranged in the manner conceptualized by the theory. Thus, over the long run, scientific knowledge is one result of the existence of pure reason as an intrinsic characteristic of human beings.

In this context it is important to remember that, unlike Hegel, Kant never denied the existence of the material world; he merely averred that human knowledge of external phenomena occurs through the forms imposed on it by the active mind. Put differently, the empirical world is an orderly place because the categories of thought organize our sensations, organize our perceptions, and organize our con-

---

[14]Ibid.

ceptions to produce systematic scientific knowledge. Nonetheless, while Kant contended that such knowledge is absolute, he also indicated that it is limited to the field of actual experience. Therefore he believed it is impossible to know what objects and events are "ultimately like" apart from the receptivity of human senses. One of the most important implications of this point of view is that attempts at discovering the nature of ultimate reality, either through religion or science, are impossible. In Kant's phrase, "understanding can never go beyond the limits of sensibility."[15]

Simmel's Adaptation of Kant's Ideas.   The link between Kant and Simmel is most clearly explained in the latter's essay "How Is Society Possible?," which was originally appended to the first chapter of his *Sociology: Studies in the Forms of Sociation.*[16] According to Simmel, the basic question in Kant's philosophy is "How is nature possible?" That is, how is human knowledge of nature (the external world) possible? As we have seen, Kant answered this query by positing the existence of certain a priori categories that observers use to shape the chaotic sensations they receive into conceptual knowledge. This point of view means that when the elements of nature are conceptualized in some manner, their unity is entirely dependent on the purposes of the observer.

In contrast, the unity of society is both experienced by the participants and observed by sociologists. In Simmel's words, "the unity of society needs no observer. It is directly realized by its own elements [human beings] because these elements are themselves conscious and synthesizing units."[17] Thus as people conduct their daily lives, they are absorbed in innumerable specific relationships with one another—economic, political, social, and familial, for example—and these connections give them an amorphous sense of their unity, a feeling that they are part of an ongoing and stable social structure. To Max Weber, the fact that people experience and attribute meaning to the social structures in which they participate indicates that neither the methods nor the goals of the natural sciences are appropriate for the social sciences. So he formulated a version of sociology oriented toward the scientific understanding of historical processes.

Simmel, however, took a different view—one that has had lasting consequences for the emergence of sociological theory. Based on his study of Kant, Simmel argued that social structures (which he called

---

[15]Quoted in Durant, *Story of Philosophy,* p. 298.
[16]Georg Simmel, "How Is Society Possible?" in *Essays by Georg Simmel,* pp. 337–56.
[17]Ibid., p. 338.

forms of interaction) systematically influence people's behavior prior to and independently of an actor's specific purposes. And Simmel used this argument to show that theoretical principles of social action can be adduced, despite the complications inherent in the fact that human beings' own experiences are the objects of study. As he put it, the entire contents of *Sociology: Studies in the Forms of Sociation* constitute an inquiry "into the processes—those which, ultimately, reside in individuals—that condition the existence of individuals in society."[18] More generally, as we will show in the next chapter, Simmel's sociology is oriented toward identifying those basic social forms—conflict, group affiliation, exchange, size, inequality, and space—that influence social action regardless of the intentions of the participants. Because these forms constitute the structure (or, as Kant would say, the "categories") within which people seek to realize their goals, knowledge of the manner in which they affect social behavior can lead to theory. In this sense, then Simmelian sociology is thoroughly Kantian in orientation. It is perhaps this philosophical underpinning that allowed Simmel to see some of the major pitfalls in Marx's work.

Karl Marx and Simmel's Thought

Although the extent to which Simmel was familiar with Marx's writings is unknown, it must have been considerable. For Simmel's sociology constitutes a complete repudiation of the substance of Marx's major work, *Capital,* as well as a rejection of his basic revolutionary goal: the establishment of a cooperative society where people would be free to develop their human potential.[19] It will be recalled from Chapter 5 that *Capital* is an attempt at demonstrating that the value of commodities (including human beings) results from the labor power necessary to produce them; Marx called this the labor theory of value. In *The Philosophy of Money* (1907), Simmel rejected the labor theory of value by arguing more generally that people in all societies place value on items in light of their relative desirability and scarcity.[20] By following Kant rather than Hegel, Simmel believed he could better account for the value that individuals attribute to commodities in different societies (capitalist as well as socialist) by showing how cultural and structural phenomena systematically influence what is both scarce and desired. In this way, then, he undercut the theoretical basis for Marx's analysis. However, it should be remembered that Marx had a rather

[18]Ibid., p. 340.
[19]Karl Marx, *Capital* (New York: International, 1967).
[20]Georg Simmel, *The Philosophy of Money* (Boston: Routledge & Kegan Paul, 1978).

different definition of science and theory than did Simmel—or any other classical social theorist.

Simmel rejected Marx's argument in a second way as well, by focusing on the importance of money as a medium of exchange. In *Capital* Marx tried to show that one of the necessary consequences of capitalism is people's alienation from one another and from the commodities that they produce. In this regard he emphasized the fact that actors have no control over those activities that distinguish them, as human beings, from other animals. Simmel approached the problem of alienation by simply recognizing that in any highly differentiated society people are inevitably going to be alienated. Indeed Simmel saw the decline in personal and emotional contact among humans as more fundamental than the lack of control by people of their own activities. Apparently he believed that in most societies, most individuals lack control over their daily lives. However, having recognized the inevitability of alienation, Simmel went on to argue that the dominance of money as a medium of exchange in modern social systems helps to lower alienation, a fact that Marx, writing some forty years earlier, had failed to see. While some of the positive consequences of money are identified here, a much fuller analysis of *The Philosophy of Money* is presented in the next chapter of this book. In opposition to Marx, Simmel argued that the widespread use of money allows exchanges between people who are spatially separated from one another, thereby creating multiple social ties and lowering the level of alienation. In addition, he suggested that the generalized acceptance of money in exchanges increases social solidarity because it signifies a relatively high degree of trust in the stability and future of the society. Finally, Simmel concluded that the dominance of money allows individuals to pursue a wider diversity of activities than is possible in barter or mixed economies, and hence it gives them vastly increased options for self-expression. The result of this last factor, of course, is that people have greater control over their daily lives in money economies. As an aside, Simmel's explanation of the consequences of money in modern societies is a good example of the way in which social processes "condition the existence of individuals in society" independently of their specific purposes. In this case the specific ways money is used are less important, sociologically, than its effects on the general nature and form of human relationships in systems where money is the modal medium of social exchange.

Finally, Simmel also discussed Marx's formulation of the problem of alienation in his essay on the functions of social conflict. In this context he reasoned that individuals probably have the best chance of developing their full human capacities in a competitive rather than a cooperative society:

Once the narrow and naive solidarity of primitive social conditions yielded to decentralization (which was bound to have been the immediate result of the quantitative enlargement of the group), man's effort toward man, his adaptation to the other, seems possible only at the price of competition, that is, of the simultaneous fight *against* a fellowman *for* a third one—*against* whom, for that matter, he may well compete in some other relationship *for* the former. Given the breadth and individualization of society, many kinds of interest, which eventually hold the group together throughout its members, seem to come alive and stay alive only when the urgency and requirements of the competitive struggle force them upon the individual.[21]

Simmel did not deny, of course, that competition can have "poisonous, divisive, destructive effects"; rather he simply noted that these liabilities must be evaluated in light of the positive consequences of competition. Like money, Simmel claimed competition gives people more freedom to satisfy their needs, and in this sense citizens of a society that is competitively organized are probably less alienated. In addition, as indicated in the quotation, Simmel believed competition is a form of conflict that promotes social solidarity in differentiated social systems because people establish ties with one another that involve a relatively constant "concentration on the will and feeling of fellowmen"—an argument that also implies a lessening of alienation. Finally, Simmel indicated that competition is an important means of creating values in society, a process that occurs as human beings produce objective values (commodities, for example) for purposes of exchange; in this way they attain satisfaction of their own subjective needs and desires. This argument not only suggests that competitive societies display less alienation than do noncompetitive ones, it also implies that Marx's revolutionary goal—a cooperative society—is impractical in modern, industrialized, highly differentiated social systems. On this basis Simmel rejected socialist and communist experiments inspired by Marxist thought. He believed that they are attempts at institutionalizing, indeed enforcing, cooperative relationships among people in order to prevent the waste of energy and inequalities that inevitably occur in a competitive environment. However, Simmel insisted that even though such results seem positive, they can only be "brought about through a central [political] directive which from the start organizes all [people] for their mutual interpenetration and supplementation."[22] And Simmel implied that an end to alienation will not and cannot occur in such an authoritarian social context. Thus, while Simmel's

---

[21]Simmel, *Conflict.*
[22]Ibid., pp. 72–73.

works do not represent a long-term debate "with the ghost of Marx," as was the case for Weber, Simmel addressed the same issues as Marx and other early theorists—issues such as the properties of social differentiation, inequality, power, conflict, cooperation, and the procedures for understanding the nature of the social world.

Conclusion

In many ways Simmel's work still remains an enigma in modern sociology. Bits and pieces have exerted enormous influence on modern sociological theory, and yet it is difficult to view Simmel as inspiring a "school" of thought, as has been the case for Marx, Weber, Durkheim, and Mead. Perhaps his outsider role in the German academic establishment kept him from developing cohorts of students who could carry on his "formal sociology." The result is that Simmel's sociology is not, even in this day when the early masters are the subject of much commentary, fully appreciated for its breadth and brilliance. Hopefully, we can help correct this situation in the next chapter by reviewing Simmel's work.

CHAPTER 9

The Sociology of Georg Simmel

Simmel's marginal position between the lay and academic intellectual worlds prevented him from developing a coherent theoretical system.[1] Instead what emerges are flashes of insight into the basic dynamics of a wide variety of phenomena. Moreover, Simmel had a tendency to deal with the same topics repeatedly, each time revising and updating his thinking. If much of his work appears to be a series of lectures, that is just what they often were: lectures that prod and stimulate, often without long-term, detailed, and scholarly annotation. For this reason the corpus of Simmel's work is often frustrating to read; it cries out for synthesis into a more articulated theoretical scheme. But we must live with this limitation in Simmel's work and appreciate it for its points of insight and genius.

In order to illustrate Simmel's contribution to the development of sociological theory, this chapter considers four of his most significant studies. First, Simmel's methodological approach to the analysis of society is explained. Then his sketch of the significance of people's "web of group affiliations" in modern societies is described.[2] Next Simmel's explanation of the functions of social conflict is explicated.[3] And finally, his investigation into the importance of social exchange is reviewed.[4]

---

[1]Georg Simmel, *Sociology: Studies in the Forms of Sociation,* 1908. This book, Simmel's major sociological work, still has not been completely translated, and what has been done appears in many different places. See note 21.

[2]Georg Simmel, "The Web of Group Affiliations," *Conflict and the Web of Group Affiliations,* trans. Reinhard Bendix (New York: Free Press, 1955) pp. 125–95. The original title of this essay was "The Intersection of Social Circles."

[3]Georg Simmel, "Conflict," in *Conflict and the Web of Group Affiliations,* trans. Kurt Wolff, pp. 14–124. There is a long literature on this essay; see Lewis A. Coser, *The Functions of Social Conflict* (New York: Free Press, 1956); and Jonathan H. Turner, *The Structure of Sociological Theory,* rev. ed. (Chicago: Dorsey Press, 1978), pp. 121–42.

[4]Georg Simmel, *The Philosophy of Money,* trans. Tom Bottomore and David Frisby (Boston: Routledge & Kegan Paul, 1978).

SIMMEL'S METHODOLOGICAL APPROACH TO THE STUDY OF SOCIETY

In an essay titled "The Problem of Sociology" Simmel concluded as early as 1894 that an exploration of the basic and generic forms of interaction offered the only viable subject matter for the nascent discipline of sociology.[5] In chapter 1 of *Sociology: Studies in the Forms of Sociation*, written in 1908, he reformulated and reaffirmed his thoughts on this issue.[6] In 1918 he revised his thinking again in one of his last works, *Fundamental Problems of Sociology*.[7] In what follows we rely most on this final brief sketch, since it represents his most mature statement.

Simmel began the *Fundamental Problems of Sociology* by lamenting the fact that "the first difficulty which arises if one wants to make a tenable statement about the science of sociology is that its claim to be a science is not undisputed." In Germany after the turn of the century many scholars still denied that sociology constituted a legitimate science, and in order to retain their power within the university system, they wanted to prevent its establishment as an academic field. Partly for these reasons, it was proposed that sociology should be merely a label to refer to all the social sciences dealing with specific content areas—such as economics, political science, and linguistics. This tactic was a ruse, of course, for Simmel (and many others) recognized that the existing disciplines had already divided up the study of human life and nothing would be "gained by throwing their sum total into a pot and sticking a new label on it: 'sociology.' "[8] In order to combat this strategy and to justify sociology as an academic field of study, Simmel argued that it was necessary for the new discipline to develop a unique and "unambiguous content [or subject matter], dominated by one, methodologically certain, problem idea."[9] However, we shall see that while he succeeded splendidly in identifying a conceptually significant subject for sociology, there is nonetheless an important area of

---

[5]The translation appeared the following year. See Georg Simmel, "The Problem of Sociology," *Annals of the American Academy of Political and Social Science* 6, 1895, pp. 412–23.

[6]Georg Simmel, "The Problem of Sociology," in *Essays on Sociology, Philosophy and Aesthetics by Georg Simmel et al.*, ed. and trans. Kurt Wolff (New York: Harper & Row, 1959), pp. 310–36. This is chapter 1 of Simmel's *Sociology: Studies in the Forms of Sociation*.

[7]Simmel, *Fundamental Problems of Sociology*, appears as part 1 of *The Sociology of Georg Simmel*, trans. Kurt Wolff (New York: Free Press, 1950), pp. 3–86.

[8]Ibid., p. 4.

[9]This remark is from the preface to *Sociology: Studies in the Forms of Sociation*; it is quoted in Kurt Wolff's introduction to *The Sociology of Georg Simmel*, p. xxvi.

weakness inherent in his analysis. Simmel's discussion is organized around three questions: What is society? How should sociology study society? What are the problem areas of sociology?

What Is Society?

Simmel's answer to this question is very simple: "Society" exists when "interaction among human beings" occurs with enough frequency and intensity so that people mutually affect one another and organize themselves into groups or other social units. Thus Simmel used the term *society* rather loosely to refer to any pattern of social organization in which he was interested. As he put it, society refers to relatively "permanent interactions only. More specifically, the interactions we have in mind when we talk about 'society' are crystallized as definable, consistent structures such as the state and the family, the guild and the church, social classes and organizations based on common interests."[10]

The significance of defining society in this way lies in the recognition that patterns of social organization are constructed from basic processes of interaction. Hence interaction, per se, becomes a significant area of study. Sociology, in his words, is founded on "the recognition that man in his whole nature and in all his manifestations is determined by the circumstances of living in interaction with other men."[11] Thus as an academic discipline, "sociology asks what happens to men and by what rules do they behave, not insofar as they unfold their understandable individual existences in their totalities, but insofar as they form groups and are determined by their group existence because of interaction."[12] With this statement Simmel gave sociology a unique and unambiguous subject matter: the basic forms of social interaction.

How Should Sociology Study Society?

Simmel's answer to this question is again very simple: Sociologists should begin their study of society by distinguishing between form and content. Simmel's use of these particular terms has often been misunderstood by subsequent scholars, mainly because their Kantian origin has been ignored.[13] What must be remembered in order to

---

[10]Simmel, *Fundamental Problems*, p. 9.

[11]Ibid., p. 12.

[12]Ibid., p. 11.

[13]The most well-known criticism of Simmel's presumably excessive "formalism" are by Theodore Abel, *Systematic Sociology in Germany* (New York: Octagon Press, 1965);

understand these terms is that Simmel's writings are pervaded by analogies, with the distinction between form and content being drawn from an analogy to geometry. Geometry investigates the spatial forms of material objects; while these spatial forms clearly have material contents of various sorts, the process of abstraction in geometry involves ignoring their specific contents in favor of an emphasis on the common features, or forms, of the objects under examination. Simmel simply applied this geometric distinction between form and content to the study of society in order to suggest how sociology can investigate social processes independently of their content. The distinction between the forms and contents of interaction offers the only "possibility for a special science of society" because it is a means of focusing on the basic processes by which people establish social relations and social structures, while ignoring for analytical purposes the contents (goals and purposes) of social relations.

Thus forms of interaction refer to the modes "of interaction among individuals through which, or in the shape of which, that content attains social reality."[14] Simmel claimed that attention to social forms leads sociology to goals that are fundamentally different than those of the other social scientific disciplines, especially in the Germany of his time. For example, sociology tries to discover the laws influencing small group interaction rather than describing particular families or marriages; it attempts to uncover the principles of formal and impersonal interaction rather than examining specific bureaucratic organizations; it seeks to understand the nature and consequences of class struggle rather than portraying a particular strike or some specific conflict. By focusing on the properties of interaction rather than its purposes, Simmel believed sociology can discover the underlying processes of social reality.[15] For while social structures may reveal diverse contents, they may have similar forms:

> Social groups, which are the most diverse imaginable in purpose and general significance, may nevertheless show identical forms of behavior toward one another on the part of individual members. We find superiority and subordination, competition, division of labor, formation of parties, representation, inner solidarity coupled with exclusiveness toward the outside, and innumerable similar features in the state, in a religious community, in a band of conspirators, in an economic association, in an art school, in the family. However diverse the interests are

and Pitirim Sorokin, *Contemporary Sociological Theories* (New York: Harper & Row, 1928). The best defense of Simmel against this spurious charge is that by F. H. Tenbruck, "Formal Sociology," *Essays by Georg Simmel et al.*, pp. 61–69.

[14]Simmel, "Problem of Sociology," p. 315.

[15]Simmel, *Fundamental Problems*, p. 18.

that give rise to these sociations, the *forms* in which the interests are realized may yet be identical.[16]

On this basis, then, Simmel believed it is possible to develop "timelessly valid laws" about social interaction. For example, the process of competition or other forms of conflict can be examined in many different social contexts at different points in time: within and among political parties, within and among different religious groups, within and among businesses, among artists, and even among family members. The result can be some theoretical insight into how the process of competition (as a form of conflict) affects the participants apart from their specific purposes or goals. Thus even though the terminology has changed over the years, Simmel's distinction between form and content constitutes one of his most important contributions to the emergence of sociological theory. However, the next task Simmel faced was the identification of the most basic forms of interaction; in his words, sociology must delineate its specific problem areas. Sadly, Simmel's inability to complete this task represents the most significant flaw in his methodological work.

What Are the Problem Areas of Sociology?

Unlike his responses to the questions posed above, Simmel's answer to this query has not proven to be of enduring significance for the development of sociological theory. In his initial attempts at conceptualizing the basic social forms with which sociology ought to be concerned, Simmel referred to "a difficulty in methodology." For the present, he felt, the sociological viewpoint can only be conveyed by means of examples, since only later would it be possible "to grasp it by methods that are fully conceptualized and are sure guides to research."[17]

Both the title and the organization of Simmel's *Fundamental Problems of Sociology* (1918) suggest that the major impetus for writing this last little book was his recognition that the "difficulty in methodology" remained unresolved. Unfortunately, this final effort at developing systematic procedures for identifying the generic properties of the social world studied by sociology was not very successful either. In this book Simmel identified three areas that he said constitute the fundamental problems of sociology. First, there is the sociological study of historical life and development, which he called *general sociology.* Second, there is the sociological study of the forms of interaction independently of

---

[16]Ibid., p. 22 (emphasis in original).
[17]Simmel, "Problem of Sociology," pp. 323–24.

history, which he called *pure,* or *formal, sociology.* And third, there is the sociological study of the epistemological and metaphysical aspects of society, which he called *philosophical sociology.* In *Fundamental Problems,* which has only four chapters, Simmel devoted a separate chapter to each of these problem areas.

General Sociology. Simmel began by noting that "general sociology" is concerned with the study "of the whole of historical life insofar as it is formed societally"—that is, through interaction. However, the process of historical development can be interpreted in a number of different ways, and Simmel believed it is necessary to distinguish the sociological from the nonsociological approach. For example, he indicated that Durkheim saw historical development "as a process proceeding from organic commonness to mechanical simultaneousness," while Comte saw it as occurring through three distinct stages: theological, metaphysical, and positive.[18] While both claims are reasonable, Simmel remarked, neither constitutes a justification for the existence of sociology. Rather the historical development of those observable social structures studied by the existing disciplines (politics, economics, religion, law, language, and others) must be subjected to a sociological analysis by distinguishing between social forms and social contents. For example, when the history of religious communities and labor unions is studied, it is possible to show that the members of both are characterized by patterns of self-sacrifice and devotion to ideals. These similarities can, in principle, be summarized by abstract laws.

What Simmel was apparently arguing, although this is not entirely clear, is that studies of the contents of interaction can yield valid theoretical insights only when attention is paid to the more generic properties of the social structures in which people participate. However, Simmel's chapter on general sociology, which deals with the problem of the development of individuality in society, proceeds in ways that are, at best, very confusing.[19] Thus the overall result is that readers are left wondering just what the subject matter of general sociology is and how it relates to the other problem areas.

Pure, or Formal, Sociology. For Simmel, "pure, or formal, sociology" consists of the investigation of "the societal forms themselves." Thus when "society is conceived as interaction among individuals, the description of this interaction is the task of the science of society in its

---

[18]Simmel, *Fundamental Problems,* pp. 19–20. In general, Simmel does not cite his sources. On these two pages, however, his references are relatively clear, even though neither Durkheim nor Comte is mentioned by name.

[19]Ibid., pp. 26–39.

strictest and most essential sense."[20] Simmel's problem was thus to isolate and identify fundamental forms of interaction. In his earlier work he had attempted to do this by focusing on a number of less observable but highly significant social forms, which can be divided (roughly) into two general categories, although Simmel did not use these labels: (1) generic social processes, such as differentiation, conflict, and exchange, and (2) structural role relationships, such as the role of the stranger in society. Nearly all of Simmel's substantive work consists of studies of these less observable social forms. For example, a partial listing of the table of contents of *Sociology: Studies in the Forms of Sociation* reveals that the following topics are considered.

1. The quantitative determinateness of the group.
2. Superordination and subordination.
3. Conflict.
4. The secret and the secret society.
5. Note on adornment.
6. The intersection of social circles (the web of group affiliations).
7. The poor.
8. The self-preservation of the group.
9. Note on faithfulness and gratitude.
10. Note on the stranger.
11. The enlargement of the group and the development of the individual.
12. Note on nobility.[21]

Yet Simmel's description of pure, or formal, sociology suffers from a fundamental defect:[22] It does not remedy the "methodological difficulty" referred to above. For in *Fundamental Problems,* Simmel failed to develop a precise method for either identifying the most basic forms of interaction or analyzing their systematic variation.

---

[20]Ibid., p. 22.

[21]Items 1, 2, 4, 5, and 9 are available in *The Sociology of Georg Simmel.* Items 3 and 6 are in *Conflict and the Web of Group Affiliations.* Item 10 is in *Essays by Georg Simmel.* Item 8 is in the *American Journal of Sociology* 3, March 1900, pp. 577–603. Items 7, 11, and 12 are in *Georg Simmel on Individuality and Social Forms,* trans. Donald Levine (Chicago: University of Chicago Press, 1971). The remaining chapters, about one-fourth of the book, are still untranslated. They deal with such topics as social psychology, hereditary office holding, the spatial organization of society, and the relationship between psychological and sociological phenomena.

[22]Simmel, *Fundamental Problems,* pp. 40–57.

Philosophical Sociology. Simmel's "philosophical sociology" is an attempt to recognize the importance of philosophical issues in the development of sociology as an academic discipline. As he put it, the modern scientific attitude toward the nature of empirical facts suggests a "complex of questions concerning the fact 'society.' " These questions are philosophical, and they center on epistemology and metaphysics. The epistemological problem has to do with one of the main cognitive presuppositions underlying sociological research: Is society the purpose of human existence, or is it merely a means for individual ends?[23] Simmel's explanatory chapter on philosophical sociology deals with this question by studying the relationship between the individual and society in the eighteenth and nineteenth centuries.[24] However, as with the other chapters in *Fundamental Problems*, this material is so confusing as to be of little use. Apparently, Simmel wanted to argue that questions about the purpose of society or the reasons for individual existence cannot be answered in scientific terms, but even this reasonable conclusion is uncertain.[25] Ultimately, then, Simmel's vision of philosophical sociology has simply been ignored, mainly because his analysis is both superficial and unclear.

In the end Simmel had to confess that he had failed to lay a complete methodological foundation for the new discipline. This failure stems from Simmel's uncertainty about his ability to isolate truly basic or generic structures and processes. Thus both *Sociology* and *Fundamental Problems* contain disclaimers suggesting that his analysis of specific topics—such as the significance of group affiliations, the functions of social conflict, and the process of social exchange—can only demonstrate the potential utility of an analysis of social forms.[26] We turn now to an examination of Simmel's three most important studies in formal and pure sociology.

"THE WEB OF GROUP AFFILIATIONS"

"The Web of Group Affiliations" is essentially a sociological analysis of the way in which patterns of group participation are altered with social differentiation and the consequences of such alterations for people's everyday behavior. Simmel first dealt with this topic in his

---

[23]This same issue was dealt with ten years earlier in Georg Simmel, "Note on the Problem: How Is Society Possible?" in *Essays by Georg Simmel et al.*, pp. 337–56.

[24]Simmel, *Fundamental Problems*, pp. 58–86.

[25]Ibid., p. 25.

[26]Ibid., p. 18.

Social Differentiation (1890).[27] However, this early version is not very useful, and the text explicated here is taken from *Sociology: Studies in the Forms of Sociation.* Like all the classical sociologists, Simmel saw a general historical tendency toward increasing social differentiation in modern industrialized societies. But rather than tracing this development either chronologically or in terms of increased functional specialization, he focused on the nature and significance of group memberships. In this way he was able to identify a unique social form.

The Web of Group Affiliations as a Social Form

It will be recalled that social forms refer to the modes of interaction through which people attain their purposes or goals. In "The Web of Group Affiliations" Simmel was interested in the extent to which changes in the network of social structures making up society affect people. Indeed, in Simmel's eye the number of groups a person belongs to and the basis on which they are formed influence interaction apart from the interests that the groups are intended to satisfy.

One of the most important variables influencing the number of groups to which people belong, as well as the basis of their attachment to groups, is the degree of social differentiation; in an undifferentiated society, people are simply unable to come into contact with others who have unique attributes and experiences, since the accident of birth forces people to interact and establish ties within a homogeneous group. But in a more differentiated society, humans are able to choose among a variety of groups and interact with others in terms of "similarity of talents, inclinations, activities," and other factors over which they have some control.[28] The remainder of "The Web of Group Affiliations" is an attempt at showing how structural changes that have occurred with increasing social differentiation have resulted in the increasing potential for role conflict as people express their individuality and freedom through their choice of group affiliations. In this way Simmel demonstrated how a sociological analysis can reveal what happens to people "insofar as they form groups and are determined by their group existence because of interaction."

---

[27]See Georg Simmel, "The Intersection of Social Spheres," in *Georg Simmel: Sociologist and European,* trans. Peter Laurence (New York: Barnes & Noble, 1976), pp. 95–110.

[28]Simmel, "Web of Group Affiliations," pp. 127–28.

Structural Changes Accompanying Social Differentiation

Simmel observed that the process of social differentiation has produced two fundamental changes in the way people interact with one
another in society. The first is that group formation based on what he
called *organic* criteria has been replaced by group formation based on
rational criteria. That is, when group affiliation has an organic basis,
external phenomena over which individuals have no control are the
grounds for participating in a group. Examples of such factors, which
are generally determined by birth, are people's family, place of residence (city), ethnicity, and sometimes age and sex. Alternatively, when
affiliation is rational, groups are formed on the basis of conscious reflection and planning, with the result that individual choice is the primary grounds for joining them. For example, Simmel noted that
English trade unions originally "tended toward local exclusiveness"
and were closed to workers who came from other cities or regions.[29]
But over time workers ended their dependence on local relationships,
and the unions became nationally organized in terms of workers'
trades. Simmel summarized the change he saw in the basis of group
formation in the following way:

> Criteria derived from knowledge came to serve as the basis of social
> differentiation and group formation. Up to the Renaissance, social dif-
> ferentiation and group-formation had been based either on criteria of
> self-interest . . . or emotion (religious), or a mixture of both (familial).
> Now, intellectual and rational interests came to form groups, whose
> members were gathered from many other social groups. This is a strik-
> ing example of the general trend, that the formation of groups, which
> has occurred more recently, often bears a rational character, and that
> the substantive purpose of these groups is the result of conscious reflec-
> tion and intelligent planning. Thus, secondary groups, because of their
> rational formation, give the appearance of being determined by a pur-
> pose, since their affairs revolve around intellectually articulated
> interests.[30]

The second structural change accompanying social differentiation
is that there has been a very large increase in the number of groups
with which people can affiliate. Thus when group participation is
based on organic criteria, people generally belong only to a small number of primary groups, such as their family, church, and city. From
Simmel's point of view, the most important sociological characteristics

---

[29]Ibid., p. 129.
[30]Ibid., p. 137.

of these groups are that individuals have no choice in participation, that everyone belongs to the same groups, and that in most respects people are seen as members of a group rather than as unique persons. This means that in many important ways, every individual is like every other.

However, when group affiliation is based on rational criteria, individuals can belong to a multiplicity of groups. For example, Simmel observed that modern people are affiliated with their family of origin, family of procreation, and their spouse's family. Each of these groups can be quite different in terms of socio-economic status, ethnicity, or place of residence. In addition, everyone may also belong to other kinds of groups, such as occupational groups of various sorts, purely social groups, and a virtually unlimited number of special-interest groups. Further, they may also identify themselves as members of a social class and a military reserve unit. Finally, they may see themselves as citizens of cities, states, regions, and nations. Not surprisingly, Simmel concludes:

> This is a great variety of groups. Some of these groups are integrated. Others are, however, so arranged that one group appears as the original focus of an individual's affiliation, from which he then turns toward affiliation with other, quite different groups on the basis of his special qualities, which distinguish him from other members of his primary group.[31]

Put differently, group affiliations in differentiated societies are characterized by a superstructure of secondary groups that develops over and above primary group membership. From Simmel's point of view, the most important sociological characteristics of these secondary groups are that individuals choose to affiliate, that everyone belongs to different groups, and that people are often treated as individuals having unique attributes and experiences. This means that in many important respects, every person is different from every other.

The Consequences of Social Differentiation

Simmel believed the expansion of people's web of group affiliations, coupled with the fundamental change in the basis of group formation, has important consequences for those who live in modern societies. The most obvious result is that there is a greatly increased potential for role conflict: "As the individual leaves his established position within *one* primary group, he comes to stand at a point at which

---

[30]Ibid., p. 137.

many groups 'intersect.' " The result is that "external and internal conflicts arise through the multiplicity of group affiliations, which
threaten the individual with psychological tensions or even a schizo-
phrenic break."[32] However, Simmel insisted that while role conflict can
have adverse psychological consequences, such need not be the case,
since most people are able to balance their obligations to competing
groups by keeping their activities spatially and temporally separated.

In addition, Simmel argued that in modern and highly differentiated societies each person develops a specific personality (what he
called "a core of inner unity") comprising those attributes and experiences that make each human being a unique individual who is not
irrevocably tied to a primary group. Two indicators of this process are:
(1) people in modern societies do not have the same pattern of group
affiliations and (2) individuals can occupy positions of different ranks
in the various groups to which they belong. Neither phenomenon
would have been observed in, for example, the Middle Ages, where
the group absorbed the whole person. Thus "the mere fact of multiple
group affiliations [has] enabled the person to achieve for himself an
individualized situation in which the groups [have] to be oriented
towards the individual."[33] In this way, then, people become aware of
their own uniqueness. Such awareness is a real step toward increasing
personal freedom, a phenomenon that also appears with an expansion
of the web of group affiliations. As he noted, "the narrowly circumscribed and strict custom of earlier conditions was one in which the
social group as a whole . . . regulated the conduct of the individual in
the most varied ways."[34] Such regulation is not possible in differentiated societies, Simmel observed, because people step out of their primary groups by joining or forming many different secondary groups.

Figure 9–1 summarizes the basic contours of Simmel's argument.
As the model in Figure 9–1 outlines, social differentiation increases the
use of nonascriptive or rational criteria for establishing social relations.
In turn, along with social differentiation per se, the use of such criteria
encourages the proliferation of groups, especially secondary groups.
Both nonascriptive criteria for determining group affiliations and
group proliferation stimulate multiplicity of group affiliations for each
individual, who, as a result, becomes more unique and individualistic.
Yet too much individualism, coupled with too many affiliations, creates role conflict. The feedback arrows in the figure (those moving
from right to left) are an important part, if only implicitly, of Simmel's

---

[32]Ibid., p. 141 (emphasis in original).
[33]Ibid., p. 151; see also pp. 139, 149.
[34]Ibid., p. 165.

FIGURE 9–1   Simmel's Model of Social Differentiation and Patterns of
Group Affiliation

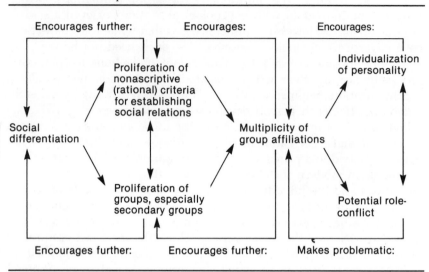

argument. As people become individualized, they desire and seek
unique patterns of multiple group affiliation; as a consequence, they
demand the use of nonascriptive criteria of group membership. In turn
the proliferation of criteria encourages social differentiation and the
proliferation of secondary groups using these "rational" criteria. Role
conflict can create emotional problems not only for the individual but
also for the multiplication of groups, since at some point people exceed
their capacity to cope with group affiliations—thereby setting a limit
to the proliferation of groups and social differentiation.

CONFLICT

Simmel's essay on conflict is a demonstration of its positive functions within and between groups. While his initial adumbration of
"The Sociology of Conflict" appeared in 1903, the basis for our commentary is a much revised version that was included as a chapter in
Sociology: Studies in the Forms of Sociation.[35] Simmel began the latter essay
by remarking that while the social "significance of conflict has in prin-

---

[35]Georg Simmel, "The Sociology of Conflict," *American Journal of Sociology* 9, 1903–
4, pp. 490–525, 672–89, 798–811.

ciple never been disputed," it is most commonly seen as a purely destructive factor in people's relationships, one that should be prevented from occurring if possible. He believed this orientation toward the negative effects of social conflict stems from an emphasis on exploring the contents of interaction; people observe the destructive consequences of conflict on other individuals (both physically and psychologically) and assume it must have a similar effect on collectivities. But in Simmel's view, this emphasis is shortsighted because it fails to recognize that conflict often serves as a means of maintaining or increasing integration within groups. In his words, "it is a way of achieving some kind of unity." For example, people's ability to express their hostilities toward one another can give them a sense of control over their destiny and thereby serve to increase social solidarity within a group.

Conflict as a Social Form

Human beings, Simmel observed, have an *"a priori* fighting instinct"—that is, they have an easily aroused sense of hostility toward others. While this fighting instinct is probably the ultimate cause of social conflict, Simmel emphasized that humans are distinguished from other species by the fact that, in general, conflicts are means to goals rather than merely instinctual reactions to external stimuli. This fact, which is a fundamental principle in Simmel's discussion, means that conflict is a vehicle by which individuals achieve their purposes in innumerable social contexts, such as marriage, work, play, politics, and religion. As such, conflict reveals certain common properties in all contexts, and hence it can be viewed as a basic social form.

Moreover, conflict is nearly always combined with cooperation: People agree on norms that regulate when, where, and how to fight with one another, and this is true in marriage, business, games, war, and theological disputes. As Simmel wrote, "there probably exists no social unit in which convergent and divergent currents among its members are not inseparably interwoven. An absolutely centripetal and harmonious group . . . not only is empirically unreal, it could show no real life process."[36] The importance of this fusion of conflict and cooperation can be seen most clearly in those instances where a cooperative element appears to be lacking, for example, interaction between muggers and their victims or when conflict is engendered exclusively by the lust to fight. However, Simmel believed these examples are clearly limiting cases, for if "there is any consideration, any limit to violence,

---

[36]Simmel, "Conflict," in *Conflict and the Web of Group Affiliations*, p. 15.

there already exists a socializing factor, even though only as the qualification of violence."[37] This is why he emphasized the fact that social conflict is usually a means to a goal; its "superior purpose" implies that people can change or modify their tactics depending on the situation.

In his essay on conflict, then, Simmel sketched some of the alternative forms of conflict, the way in which they are combined with regulatory norms, and the significance this form of interaction has for the groups to which people belong. In order to carry out this task, he first examined how conflict within groups affects the reciprocal relations of the parties involved, and then he turned to the consequences that conflict with an outgroup has for social relations within a group. The following sections deal with each of these topics.

Conflict within Groups

Simmel's investigation of the sociological significance of conflict within groups revolves around three forms: (1) conflicts in which the opposing parties possess common personal qualities, (2) conflicts in which the opposing parties perceive each other as a threat to the existence of the group, and (3) conflicts in which the opposing parties recognize and accept each other as legitimate opponents.

Common Personal Qualities and Conflict.[38]   Simmel noted here that "people who have many common features often do one another worse or 'wronger' wrong than complete strangers do," mainly because they have so few differences that even the slightest conflict is magnified in its significance. As examples, he referred to conflict in "intimate relations," such as marriages, and to the relationship between renegades and their former colleagues. In both cases the solidarity of the group is based on the parties' possessing many common (or complementary) characteristics. As a result, people are involved with one another as whole persons and even small antagonisms between them can be highly inflammatory, regardless of the content of the disagreements. Thus when conflict does occur, the resulting battle is sometimes so intense that previous areas of agreement are forgotten. Most of the time, Simmel observed, opponents develop implicit or explicit norms that serve to keep conflicts within manageable bounds. However, when emotions run high or when the participants see the conflict as transcending their individual interests, then the fight may become violent. At that point, he suggested, the very existence of those who differ may be taken as a threat to the group.

---

[37]Ibid., p. 26.
[38]Ibid., pp. 43–48.

Conflict as a Threat to the Group.[39]   In this case conflict occurs among opponents who have common membership in a group. Simmel argued that this type of conflict should be treated as a distinct form because when a group is divided into conflicting elements, the antagonistic parties "hate each other not only on the concrete ground which produced the conflict but also on the sociological ground of hatred for the enemy of the group itself." Such antagonism is especially intense and can easily become violent, Simmel argued, since each party identifies itself as representing the group and sees the other as a mortal enemy of the collective.

Conflicts among Recognized and Accepted Opponents.   Simmel distinguished two forms of conflicts where the opposing parties are recognized and accepted. When conflict is "direct," the opposing parties act squarely against one another in order to obtain their goals.[40] When conflict is "indirect," the opponents only interact with a third party in order to obtain their goals. Simmel referred to this latter form of conflict as *competition*.[41] Yet both of these forms share certain distinguishing characteristics that differentiate them from the forms of conflict noted above: Opponents are seen to have a right to strive for the same goal; conflict is pursued mercilessly and yet in a nonviolent manner; personal antagonisms and feelings of hostility are often excluded from the conflict; and the opponents either develop agreements among themselves or accept the imposition of overriding norms that regulate the conflict.

The purest examples of direct conflict are antagonistic games and conflicts over causes. In the playing of games "one *unites* [precisely] in order to fight, and one fights under the mutually recognized control of norms and rules."[42] Similarly, in the case of conflicts over causes, such as legal battles, the opponents' essential unity is again the underlying basis for interaction, since in order to fight in court, agreed-upon normative procedures must always be followed. Thus even as parties confront one another, they affirm their agreement on larger principles. The analysis of direct conflict within groups was, however, of less interest to Simmel, with the result that he did not devote much space to it. Rather he emphasized the sociological importance of competition, since this form of fighting most clearly illustrates how conflict can have positive social consequences. By proceeding indirectly, competition functions as a vital source of social solidarity within a group.

---

[39]Ibid., pp. 48–50.
[40]Ibid., pp. 34–43.
[41]Ibid., pp. 57–86.
[42]Ibid., p. 35 (emphasis in original).

While recognizing the destructive and even shameful aspects of competition that Marx and other observers had pointed to, Simmel argued that even after all its negative aspects are taken into account, competition has positive consequences for the group because it forces people to establish ties with one another, thereby increasing social solidarity within the group. Because competition between parties proceeds by the opponents trying to win over a third party, each of them is implicated in a web of affiliations that functions to connect them with one another.[43]

With some exceptions, Simmel noted that the process of competition is restricted because unregulated conflict can too easily become violent and lead to the destruction of the group itself.[44] Hence all collectivities that allow competition usually regulate it in some fashion, either through inter-individual restrictions, in which regulatory norms are simply agreed upon by the participants, or through super-individual restrictions, in which laws and other normative principles are imposed on the competitors.[45] Indeed the existence of competition often stimulates normative regulation, thereby providing a basis of social integration.

Finally, it will be recalled from the previous chapter that Simmel recognized instances where groups or societies try to eliminate competition in the name of a higher principle. For instance, in socialist or communist societies, competition is suspended in favor of an emphasis on organizing individual efforts in such a way as to (a) eliminate the wasted energy that accompanies conflict and (b) provide for the common good. Nonetheless, Simmel appears to have regarded a competitive environment as more useful than a noncompetitive one in modern, highly differentiated societies, not only in economic terms but also in most other arenas of social life. He believed such an environment provides an outlet for people's "fighting instincts" that redounds to the common good as well as a stimulus for regulatory agreements that also contribute to the common good.

Conflict between Groups

In the final section of his essay, Simmel examined the consequences that conflict between groups has "for the inner structure of each party itself."[46] Put differently, he was concerned with understand-

---

[43]Ibid., p. 62.
[44]Ibid., pp. 68–70. Simmel recognized that within families and to some extent within religious groups, the interests of the groups often dictate that members refrain from competing with one another.
[45]Ibid., p. 76.
[46]Ibid., p. 87.

ing the effect that conflict has on social relationships within each re-spective party to the conflict. In order to make his point, Simmel identified the following consequences of conflict between groups: (1) it increases the degree of centralization of authority within each group, (2) it increases the degree of social solidarity within each group and, at the same time, decreases the level of tolerance for deviance and dis-sent, and (3) it increases likelihood of coalitions among groups having similar opponents. Each of these consequences is examined below.

Conflict and Centralization.[47]   Just as fighters must psychologi-cally "pull themselves together," Simmel observed, so must a group when it is engaged in conflict with another group. There is a "need for centralization, for the tight pulling together of all elements, which alone guarantees their use, without loss of energy and time, for what-ever the requirements of the moment may be." This necessity is great-est during war, which "needs a centralistic intensification of the group form." In addition, Simmel noted, the development and maintenance of a centralized group is often "guaranteed best by despotism," and he argued that a centralized and despotic regime is more likely to wage war precisely because people's accumulated energies (or "hostile im-pulses") need some means of expression. Finally, Simmel remarked that centralized groups generally prefer to engage in conflict with groups that are also centralized. For despite the conflict-producing consequences of fighting a tightly organized opponent, conflict with such an oppponent can be more easily resolved, not only because the boundaries separating each side are clearly demarcated but also be-cause each party "can supply a representative with whom one can ne-gotiate with full certainty." For example, in conflicts between workers and employers or between nations, Simmel argued, it is often "better" if each side is organized so that conflict resolution can proceed in a systematic manner.

Conflict, Solidarity, and Intolerance.[48]   Simmel argued that con-flict often increases social solidarity within each of the opposing groups. As he phrased it, a "tightening of the relations among [the party's] members and the intensification of its unity, in consciousness and in action, occur." This is especially true, Simmel claimed, during wars or other types of violent conflicts. Moreover, increasing intoler-ance also accompanies rising solidarity, for while antagonistic members can often coexist during peacetime without harm to the group, this luxury is not possible during war. As a result, "groups in any sort of

[47]Ibid., pp. 88–91.
[48]Ibid., pp. 91–98, 17–19.

war situation are not tolerant" of deviance and dissent, since they often see themselves as fighting for the existence of the group itself and demand total loyalty from members. Thus, in general, conflict between groups means that members must become solidary with one another, and those who cannot are often either expelled or punished. As a result of their intolerance toward deviance and dissent, Simmel remarked, groups in conflict often become smaller, as those who would compromise are silenced or cast out. This tendency can make an ongoing conflict more difficult to resolve, since "groups, and especially minorities, which live in conflict and persecution, often reject approaches or tolerance from the other side." The acceptance of such overtures would mean that "the closed nature of their opposition without which they cannot fight on would be blurred." Finally, Simmel suggested that the internal solidarity of many groups is dependent on their continued conflict with other parties and that their complete victory over an opponent can result in a lessening of internal social solidarity.

Conflict, Coalitions, and Group Formation.[49]   Under certain conditions, Simmel wrote, conflict between groups can lead to the formation of coalitions and ultimately to new, solidaristic groups where none had existed before. In his words, "each element in a plurality may have its own opponent, but because this opponent is the same for all elements, they all unite—and in this case, they may, prior to that, not have had anything to do with each other." Sometimes such combinations are only for a single purpose, and the allies' solidarity declines immediately at the conclusion of the conflict. However, Simmel argued, when coalitions are engaged in wars or other types of violent conflicts and when their members become highly interdependent on one another over a long period, then more cohesive social relations are likely to ensue. This phenomenon is even more pronounced when a coalition is subjected to an ongoing or relatively permanent threat. As Simmel wrote, "the synthetic strength of a common opposition may be determined, not [only] by the number of shared points of interest, but [also] by the duration and intensity of the unification. In this case, it is especially favorable to the unification if instead of an actual fight with an enemy, there is a permanent *threat* by him."

Like so much of Simmel's work, his analysis of conflict does not present a conceptually unified perspective. Rather we get a series of provocative insights. Yet if we ignore some of the conceptual tributaries in Simmel's analysis, an underlying model like that portrayed in Figure 9–2 emerges. As societies differentiate, the number of organized units

---

[49]Ibid., pp. 98–107.

FIGURE 9–2 Simmel's Implicit Model of Social Differentiation, Conflict, and Integration

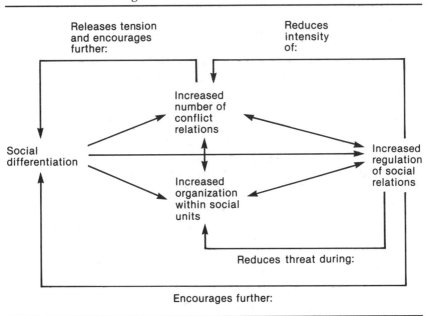

and their potential for conflict increases. Increased numbers of differentiated units, per se, create pressures for regulation of social relations by such mechanisms as centralization of power, laws, courts, mediating agencies, and coalitions among varying social units. But conflict escalates these pressures while, at the same time, unifying or consolidating social units structurally (centralization of authority, normative clarity, increased sanctioning) and ideologically (increased salience of beliefs and values). If conflicts are sufficiently frequent, low in intensity, and regulated, then they release tensions, thereby encouraging further differentiation and elaboration of regulative structures. Such structures also encourage further differentiation by providing the capacity to coordinate increased numbers of units, manage tensions among them, and reduce their respective sense of threat when in potential conflict.

THE PHILOSOPHY OF MONEY

Simmel's *The Philosophy of Money* is a study of the social consequences of exchange relationships among human beings, with special emphasis on those forms of exchange in which money is used as an abstract measure of value. Like all his work, *The Philosophy of Money* is an attempt at exposing how the forms of interaction affect the basic nature of social relations independently of their specific content. While Simmel had first considered this issue as early as 1889 in an untranslated article titled "The Psychology of Money," the final formulation of his ideas did not appear until the second edition of *The Philosophy of Money* was published in 1907.[50] Unlike the works reviewed above, *The Philosophy of Money* is both a sociological and philosophical treatise, and as such it presents problems of analysis. For sociologists, the philosophical portions are generally useful to the extent they provide a set of assumptions from which theoretical propositions are derived. Conversely, the sociological portions are interesting to philosophers to the degree that they illustrate a deeper ontology. This "middle ground" between philosophy and sociology makes *The Philosophy of Money* both more ambiguous and more ambitious than most of Simmel's other writings.[51] In our explication of this book, we will initially place Simmel's ideas into a specifically sociological context by showing how social exchange constitutes a form of interaction and then describe how he translated certain philosophical assumptions into a number of interesting theoretical insights.

Exchange as a Social Form

The Philosophy of Money represents Simmel's effort to isolate another basic social form. Not all interaction is exchange, but exchange is still a universal form of interaction.[52] In analyzing social exchange Simmel concentrated on "economic exchange" in general and on money exchanges in particular. While not all economic exchanges involve the use of money, historically money has come into increasing use as a medium of exchange. This historical trend, Simmel emphasized, reflects the impact of such evolutionary processes as social differentiation, growth, and rationalization. But it does much more: Money is also a major cause and force behind these evolutionary processes. Thus the sociological portions of *The Philosophy of Money* are devoted to analyzing the transforming effects on social life of the ever-increasing use of money in social relations.

---

[50]Georg Simmel, "Psychologie des Geldes," *Jahrbücher für Gesetzgebung, Verwaltung und Volkswirtschaft* 23, 1889, pp. 1251–64. *The Philosophy of Money* was originally published in 1901.

[51]It is often forgotten that Simmel was a philosopher as well as a sociologist. As noted in Chapter 8, he wrote books and articles on the works of Kant, Goethe, Schopenhauer, and Nietzsche and considered more general philosophical issues and problems as well.

[52]Simmel, *Philosophy of Money*, p. 82.

In seeking to analyze social evolution in terms of an exchange perspective, Simmel was able to develop a number of philosophical assumptions and link these to a sociological analysis of the modern world. For, much like his friend and intellectual defender, Max Weber, Simmel was interested in understanding not just the forms of modern life but also their historical origins.[53] But unlike Weber, Simmel did not engage in detailed historical analyses, nor was he interested in constructing elaborate taxonomies. Rather his works always sought to link certain philosophical views about humans and the social universe to understanding the properties of a particular social form. Thus, before explicating Simmel's specific analysis of money and exchange, it is necessary to place his analysis in philosophical context.

Simmel's Assumptions about Human Nature

In *The Philosophy of Money* Simmel presented a vision of human nature that is implicit but less visible in his sociological works. He began by asserting that people are teleological beings—that is, they act on the environment in the pursuit of anticipated goals. In the essay on conflict Simmel emphasized that this fact makes human conflict different than that occurring among other animals. In *The Philosophy of Money* Simmel took the more general position that while people's goals will vary, depending on their biological impulses and social needs, all action reflects the human ability to manipulate the environment in an attempt to realize their goals. In so doing, individuals use a variety of "tools," but not just in the obvious material sense. Rather people use more subtle, symbolic tools, such as language and money, to achieve their goals. In general, Simmel argued that the more tools people possess, the greater their capacity to manipulate the environment and the more the actor can causally influence the flow of events. Moreover, the use of tools allows for the connecting of many events, as is the case when money is used to buy a good (the money, in turn, pays the salary of the seller, becomes profit for the manufacturer, and is transformed into wages for the worker, and so on). Thus for Simmel all action reveals the properties presented in Figure 9–3. (As an interesting aside, compare Simmel's model with George Herbert Mead's analysis of the phases of "the act," reviewed in Chapter 15.)

Money, Simmel asserted, is the ultimate social tool because it is generalized—that is, people can use it in so many ways to manipulate

---

[53]Simmel was excluded from senior academic positions for much of his career, and his work was often attacked. Weber was one of his most consistent defenders and apparently helped Simmel maintain at least a marginal intellectual standing in Germany.

FIGURE 9–3 Simmel's Model of the Dynamics of Human Action

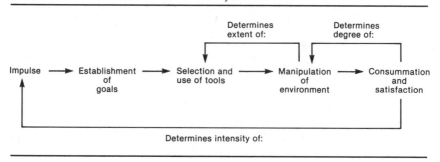

the environment in order to obtain their goals. This fact means money can potentially connect many events and persons who would not otherwise be related. In an indirect way, then, the use of money allows a vast increase in the number of groups to which individuals may belong, and it is thus a prime force behind social differentiation.

A related assumption is that humans have the capacity to divide their world into an (1) internal, subjective state and (2) an external, objective state. This division only occurs when impulses are not immediately satisfied—that is, when the environment presents barriers and obstacles. When such barriers exist, humans separate their subjective experiences from the objects of the environment that are the source of need or impulse satisfaction. For as Simmel emphasized:

> We desire objects only if they are not immediately given to us for our use and enjoyment; that is, to the extent that they resist our desire. The content of our desire becomes an object as soon as it is opposed to us, not only in the sense of being impervious to us, but also in terms of its distance as something not enjoyed.[54]

It is from this subject-object division that "value" inheres. In contrast to Marx, Simmel stressed that the value of an object does not exist in the "labor power" required to produce it, but in the extent to which it is both desired and unattainable—that is, value resides in the process of seeking objects that are scarce and distant. Value is thus tied to humans' basic capacity to distinguish a subjective from objective world and in the relative difficulty in securing objects. Patterns of social organization, Simmel emphasized, perform much of this subject-object separation: They present barriers and obstacles, they create demands for some objects, and they determine how objects will circulate. And

---

[54]Simmel, *Philosophy of Money*, p. 66.

the economic production of goods and their sale in a market is only a special case of the more general process of subject-object division among humans. For long before there were money, markets, and productive corporations, there were humans who desired objects that were not easily obtainable. Thus, whether in the economic marketplace or the more general arena of life, value is a positive function of the extent in which an object of desire is difficult to obtain.[55]

Money, as Simmel was to show, greatly increases the creation and acceleration of value, because it provides a common yardstick for a quick calculation of values (that is, "how much" is this or that commodity or service "worth"). Moreover, as a "tool" it greatly facilitates the acquisition of objects; and as money circulates and is used at each juncture to calculate values, all objects in the environment become assessed in terms of their monetary value. Unlike Marx, Simmel did not see this as a perverse process, but as a natural reflection of humans' innate capacity and need to create values in the objects of their environment.

Yet another assumption about human nature is to be found in Simmel's discussion of "world view."[56] People naturally seek stability and order in their world, he argued. They seek to know the place of objects and of their relationship to these objects. For example, Simmel observed that humans develop totems and religious rituals to regularize their relations to the supernatural; similarly, the development of money as a standardized measurement of value is but another manifestation of this tendency for humans to seek order and stability in their view of the world. By developing money, objects can be readily compared in terms of their respective value, and humans can therefore develop a "sense of order" about their environment.

In sum, then, the development of money is for Simmel an expression and extension of basic human nature. Money is a kind of tool in teleological acts; it is a way to express the value inherent in humans' capacity for subject-object division; and it is a means for attaining stability and order in people's world view. All of these innate tendencies are the driving force behind much human action, and it is for this reason that exchange is such a basic form of social interaction. For exchange is nothing more than the sacrificing of one object of value for the attainment of another. Money greatly facilitates this process because it provides a common reference point for calculating the values of objects that are exchanged.

---

[55]Ibid., pp. 80–98.
[56]Ibid., pp. 102–10.

Money in Social Exchange

For Simmel, social exchange involves the following elements:

1. The desire for a valued object that one does not have.
2. The possession of the valued object by an identifiable other.
3. The offer of an object of value to secure from another the desired object.
4. The acceptance of this offer by the possessor of the valued object.[57]

Contained in this portrayal of social exchange are several additional points that Simmel emphasized. First, value is idiosyncratic and is ultimately tied to an individual's impulses and needs. Of course, what is defined as valuable is typically circumscribed by cultural and social patterns, but how valuable an object is will be a positive function of (a) the intensity of a person's needs and (b) the scarcity of the object. Second, much exchange involves efforts to manipulate situations so that the intensity of needs for an object are concealed and the availability of an object is made to seem less than what it actually is. Inherent in exchange, therefore, is a basic tension that can often erupt into other social forms, such as conflict. Third, to possess an object is to lessen its value and to increase the value of objects that one does not possess. Fourth, exchanges will only occur if both parties perceive that the object given is less valuable than the one received.[58] Fifth, collective units as well as individuals participate in exchange relations and hence are also subject to the four processes listed above. Sixth, the more liquid the resources of an actor in an exchange—that is, the more resources can be used in many types of exchanges—the greater will be that actor's options and power. For if an actor is not bound to exchange with any other, and can readily withdraw resources and exchange them with another, then that actor has considerable power to manipulate any exchange.

Economic exchange involving money is only a special case of this more general social form. But it is a very special case. For when money becomes the predominate means for establishing value in social relationships, the properties and dynamics of social relations are trans-

---

[57]Ibid., pp. 85–88.

[58]Surprisingly, Simmel did not explore in any great detail the consequences of unbalanced exchanges, where people are forced to give up a more valuable object for a less valuable one. Simmel simply assumed that at the time of exchange, one party felt an increase in value had occurred. Retrospectively, a redefinition may occur, but the exchange would not occur if at the moment people did not perceive that they had received more value than they had given up.

formed. This process of displacing other criteria of value, such as logic, ethics, and aesthetics, with a monetary criterion is precisely the long-term evolutionary trend in societies. This trend is, as we mentioned earlier, both a cause and an effect of money as the medium of exchange. Money emerged to facilitate exchanges and to realize even more completely humans' basic needs. But once established, the use of money has the power to transform the structure of social relations in society. It is in seeking to understand how money has this power to alter social relations that Simmel's *The Philosophy of Money* becomes distinctly sociological.

Money and Its Consequences for Social Relations

In much of Simmel's work, there is an implicit functionalism. Simmel often asked: What are the consequences, or functions, of a social form for the larger social whole? As we saw earlier, this functionalism is most evident in Simmel's analysis of conflict, but it is also found in Simmel's analysis of money. For Simmel asked two related questions in tracing the consequences of money for social patterns: (1) What are the consequences of money for the structure of society as a whole? (2) What are the consequences of money for individuals?

In answering these two questions, Simmel added to his lifelong preoccupation with several issues that pervade his work. We should mention these in order to place into context his specific analysis of the consequences of money for society and the individual. One prominent theme in all of Simmel's work is the dialectic between individual attachments to, and freedom from, groups. On the one hand, Simmel praised social relations that allow individuals freedom to choose their options, while on the other hand he was dismayed somewhat over the alienation from, and lack of personal integration of, individuals into the collective fibre of society (although not to the extent of other theorists during his time). This theme is tied to another prominent concern in Simmel's work: the growing rationalization of society or, as he phrased the matter, the "objectification" of social life. As social relations lose their traditional and religious content, they become mediated by impersonal standards—law, intellect, logic, and money. The application of these standards increases individual freedom and social justice, but it also makes life less emotional and involving. It reduces relations to rational calculations, devoid of the emotional bonds that come with attachments to religious symbols and long-standing traditions. It is in the context of these two themes that Simmel's analysis of the "functions" of money for individuals and the social whole must be viewed.

Money and the Social Whole.   Much like Weber, but in a less systematic way, Simmel was concerned with the historical trend toward rationalization, or objectification, of social relations. In general, humans tend to symbolize their relations with both each other and the natural environment. In the past this was done with religious totems and then with laws. More recently, Simmel believed, people have come to express their relationships to physical items and to each other in monetary terms, with the result that they have lost intimate and direct contact with others as well as with the objects in their environment. Thus money represents the ultimate objective symbolization of social relations because, unlike material items, it has no intrinsic value. It merely represents values, and it is used to express the value of one object in relation to another. While initial forms of money, such as coins of valuable metals and stones that could be converted into jewelry, possessed intrinsic value, the evolutionary trend is toward the use of paper money and credit, which merely express values in exchanges. As paper money and credit come to dominate, social relations in society are profoundly altered, in at least the following ways.

1. The use of money enables actors to make quick calculations of respective values.[59] People do not have to bargain and haggle over the standards to be used in establishing the respective values of objects—whether commodities or labor. As a result, the "velocity" of exchanges dramatically increases. People move through social relations more quickly and at a faster pace.

2. Since money increases the rate of social interaction and exchange, it also increases values. As was mentioned earlier, Simmel felt people do not engage in exchanges unless they perceive that they will get more than they give up. Hence the greater the rate of exchange, the greater will be people's accumulation of value—that is, the more they will perceive that their needs and desires can be realized.[60]

3. The use of money as a liquid and nonspecific resource allows for much greater continuity in social relations. It prevents gaps from developing in social relations, as is often the case when people only have hard goods, such as food products or jewelry, to exchange in social relations. Money gives people options to exchange almost anything, since respective values can be readily calculated. As a result, there is greater continuity in social relations

---

[59]Simmel, *Philosophy of Money*, pp. 143, 488–512.
[60]Ibid., p. 292.

since all individuals can potentially engage in exchanges with each other.[61]

4. In a related vein, money also allows for the creation of multiple social ties. With money, people join groups other than those established at birth and thereby establish relations with many more others than is possible with a more restrictive medium of exchange.[62]

5. Money also allows for greatly protracted exchanges among human beings located at great distances. As long as interaction involves exchange of concrete objects, there are limits to how distant people can be from each other and how many actors can participate in a sequence of exchanges. But with money, these limitations are removed. Nations can engage in exchanges; individuals who never see each other—such as a factory worker and consumers of goods produced in the factory—can be indirectly connected in an exchange sequence (since some of the payment for a good or commodity will ultimately be translated into wages for the worker). Thus money greatly extends the scope of social organization; it allows for organization beyond face-to-face contact or beyond the simple barter of goods. With money, more and more people can become connected through direct and indirect linkages.[63]

6. Money also promotes social solidarity in the sense that it represents a "trust"—that is, if people take money for goods or services, they believe it can be used at a future date to buy other goods or services. This implicit trust in the capacity of money to meet future needs reinforces people's faith in and commitment to society.[64]

7. In a related line of argument, money increases the power of central authority, for the use of money requires that there be social stability and that a central authority guarantee the worth of money.[65] As exchange relations come to rely on government to maintain the stability of money, government acquires power. Moreover, with money, it becomes much easier for central government to tax people.[66] As long as only property could be taxed,

---

[61]Ibid., p. 124.
[62]Ibid., p. 307.
[63]Ibid., pp. 180–86.
[64]Ibid., pp. 177–78.
[65]Ibid., pp. 171–84.
[66]Ibid., p. 317.

there were limitations on the effectiveness of taxation by a remote central government, since knowledge of property held would be incomplete and since extracting property, such as land, is not easily converted into values that can be used to increase the power of central government (how can, for example, property effectively buy labor services in the army or administrative staff of government?). As a liquid resource, however, tax money can be used to buy those services and goods necessary for effective central authority.

8. The creation of a tax on money also promotes a new basis of social solidarity. Since all social strata and other collectivities are subject to a monetary taxation system, they have at least one common interest: control and regulation of taxes imposed by central government. This common interest laces diverse interests together vis-à-vis the taxing powers of government.

9. The use of money often extends into virtually all spheres of interaction. As an efficient means for comparing values, it replaces other, less efficient ways to calculate value. Yet as money begins to penetrate all social relations, resistance to its influence in areas of personal value increases. Efforts to maintain the "personal element" in transactions escalate, and norms about when it is inappropriate to use money become established. For example, traditions of paying a bride price vanish; using money to buy influence is considered much more offensive than personal persuasion; paying a price as punishment for certain crimes decreases; and so on.[67]

10. At the same time as these efforts to create spheres where the use of money declines, there is a general "quantification" and "objectification" of social relations.[68] Interactions become quantified as their value is expressed in terms of money. As a result, moral constraints on what is possible decrease, since anything is possible if one just has the money. Money thus increases *anomie*, to borrow Durkheim's term. It releases people from the constraints of tradition and moral authority; it creates a system in which it is difficult to restrain individual aspirations and desires. Deviance and "pathology" are, therefore, more likely in systems where money becomes the prevalent medium of interaction.[69]

---

[67]Ibid., pp. 369–87.
[68]Ibid., p. 393.
[69]Ibid., p. 404.

Money and the Individual. For Simmel, the extensive use of money in social interaction has a number of consequences for individuals. Most of these reflect the inherent tension between individual freedom from constraint, on the one hand, and alienation and detachment from social groups, on the other hand. For money gives people new choices and options, but it also depersonalizes their social milieu. In this light Simmel isolated the following consequences of money for individuals:

1. As a "tool," money is nonspecific and thus gives people an opportunity to pursue many diverse and varied activities. For unlike less liquid forms of expressing value, money does not determine how it can be used. Hence, individuals in a society that uses money as its principal medium of exchange enjoy considerably more freedom of choice than is possible in a society that does not use money.[70]

2. In a similar vein, money gives people many options for self-expression. For to the degree that individuals seek to express themselves in terms of the objects of their possession, money allows unlimited means for self-expression. As a result, the use of money for self-expression leads to, and indeed encourages, diversity in a population that is no longer constrained in the pursuit of their needs (except, of course, by the amount of money they have).[71]

3. Yet at the same time, money creates a distance between one's sense of self and the objects of self-expression. With money, objects are easily acquired and discarded, and hence long-term attachments to objects do not develop.[72]

4. As noted earlier, money allows a person to enter many different types of social relations. One can, for example, buy such relationships by paying membership dues in organizations or by spending money on various activities that assure contacts with particular types of people. Hence money encourages a multiplicity of social relations and group memberships. At the same time, however, money discourages intimate attachments. It increases the multiplicity of involvements, but it atomizes and compartmentalizes individuals' activities and often keeps them from emotional involvement in each of their segregated activities. This trend is,

---

[70]Ibid., p. 307.
[71]Ibid., pp. 326–27.
[72]Ibid., p. 297.

Simmel felt, best personified by the division of labor that is made possible by money wages but that also compartmentalizes individuals, often alienating them from others and their work.[73]

5. Money also makes it less often necessary to know people personally, since their money "speaks" for them. In systems without money, social relations are mediated by intimate knowledge of others, and adjustments among people are made in terms of the particular characteristics of each individual. But as money begins to mediate interaction, the need to know another personally is correspondingly reduced.

Thus in Simmel's analysis of consequences, money is a mixed blessing for both the individual and society. It allows for greater freedom and provides new and multiple ways for connecting individuals. But it also isolates, atomizes, and even alienates individuals from the persons and objects in their social milieu. Money thus alters the nature of social relations among individuals in society, and therefore an analysis of its consequences is decidedly a sociological topic. And the consequences of money as the medium of exchange allowed Simmel to address more philosophical issues on the nature of humans and their patterns of social organization.

In this descriptive analysis of the consequences of money is a more general model of exchange, differentiation, and individualization of the person. Some of the key elements of this model are delineated in Figure 9–4. Social differentiation increases the volume, rate, velocity, and potential scope of social relations among individuals and groups; such is the case because there are more different kinds of units and hence more opportunities of multiple and varied social contacts. Increases in the number of social relations create pressures for the use of objective or rational symbolic media, such as money, to facilitate exchange transactions; reciprocally, the use of money allows for an ever-increasing volume of social ties since money makes it easy to determine the value of each actor's resources and to conduct social transactions. Increases in social exchanges mediated by money feed back on differentiation, encouraging further differentiation, which in turn increases the volume, rate, velocity, and scope of social ties mediated by money. Such processes cause ever more individualization of the person—that is, detachment of their total personality in groups, increased multiple group affiliations, and potential alienation from society. Yet as the feedback arrows in the model in Figure 9–4 underscore, these trends toward individualization are important contributors to the increased

---

[73]Ibid., p. 454.

FIGURE 9-4   Simmel's Model of Social Differentiation and the Dynamics
              of Exchange

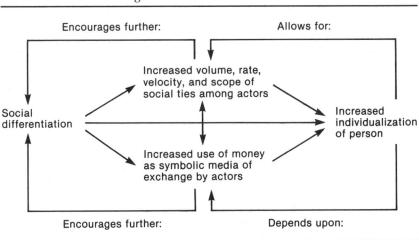

volume and rates of interaction, as well as the escalated use of money,
on which social differentiation depends. Whether these interdependent dynamics, as outlined in Figure 9-4, are good or bad is perhaps
less important than Simmel's recognition of their inevitability in modern societies.

THE ENDURING LEGACY

Looking at Georg Simmel's work as a whole, his major theoretical
contribution to sociology resides in his concern with the basic forms of
interaction. By seeking to look behind differences in the "contents" of
diverse social relations and by attempting to uncover their more generic forms, he was able to show that seemingly different situations
reveal basic similarities. Such similarities, he implicitly argued, can be
expressed as abstract models and/or laws.

Thus while Simmel did not employ the vocabulary of abstract theory, his many essays on different topics reveal a commitment to formulating abstract statements about basic forms of human relationships.
However, a superficial reading of Simmel might initially lead us to the
opposite conclusion, for his works tend to focus on a wide variety of
empirical topics; and even when he explored a particular type of social
relation, such as conflict and exchange, he tended to argue by example. He would, for instance, talk about conflicts among individuals
and wars among nation-states in virtually the same passage. Such

tendencies give his work an inductive and descriptive flair, but a more careful reading indicates that he clearly held a "covering law" or deductive view of theory in sociology.[74] For example, if conflict between such diverse entities as two individuals and two nations reveals certain common forms, then diverse empirical situations can be understood in terms of the same abstract law or principle.

Simmel's work is often difficult to read and understand since he jumps from topic to topic, from the micro to the macro, and from the historical past to what were contemporary situations in his time. Yet if we keep in mind that this seeming lack of focus represents an effort to use abstract models and principles to explain many diverse empirical cases, then much of the confusion surrounding Simmel's work recedes. His goal is similar to that of all theorists: to explain many empirical events with a few highly abstract models and principles. Indeed, unlike others who were influenced by the German tradition, such as Karl Marx and Max Weber, his explanations are committed to transcending historical epochs and specific empirical events.

In Simmel's view sociology could be a unique discipline, primarily because it sought to abstract above the contents of social life. Therefore we should close this analysis of Simmel by making more explicit the theoretical principles that guide his sociological efforts. To realize this goal, we will concentrate on several related areas of inquiry in Simmel's work:

1. Like most theorists of the nineteenth and early twentieth centuries, Simmel was preoccupied with the process of social differentiation. But unlike Weber, or even Durkheim, he was not so much interested in the historical causes of differentiation as in understanding the reciprocal relationship between the process of social differentiation and the changing nature of social interaction.

2. One such change in the nature of interaction revolves around the reciprocal relationship between social differentiation, on the one hand, and the changing criteria by which humans form social relations, on the other. In particular, he was concerned with the relationship among (a) the reliance on rationality and calculation, (b) the decline of ascription, (c) the use of money, and (d) the way in which a, b, and c are connected to social differentiation.

3. In particular, Simmel focused on the changing nature of exchange; and in so doing, he mounted a powerful critique of Marx's theory of value while delineating the basic laws of an exchange theory of human organization.

---

[74]That is, explanation occurs by deduction to empirical cases from abstract laws, which are universal and context free.

4. A related issue in Simmel's theoretical efforts is understanding the reciprocal relationship between social differentiation and alterations in the number, volume, rate, and scope of interpersonal ties as well as patterns of group membership, especially as these are altered by exchange transactions using money.

5. Yet another issue is individuality. Throughout Simmel's work is found a pervasive concern for *individuality* or *individualization* of people. By these terms we mean Simmel was concerned with the growth of personal freedom and autonomy in differentiated societies. At the same time, however, he was also alarmed over the isolation and detachment of individuals from collective involvement in modern society.

6. In all of these concerns is an implicit emphasis on patterns of social integration. For in all of Simmel's major works, such questions as how individuals are attached to each other and to groups or how individuals and collective units develop regulatory agreements prevail.

This theme in Simmel's work is best underscored by the analysis of how conflict promotes social integration.

In developing these six areas of inquiry, or themes, Simmel articulated, at least implicitly, a number of important sociological principles. They are listed below and mark, we believe, Georg Simmel's enduring theoretical legacy.

Principles of Social Exchange

1. The more actors perceive as valuable each other's respective resources, the more likely is an exchange relationship to develop among these actors.

2. The greater the intensity of an actor's needs for a resource of a given type, and the less available that resource, the greater the value of that resource to the actor.

3. The more an actor perceives as valuable the resources of another actor, the greater the power of the latter over the former.

4. The more liquid are an actor's resources, the greater will be the exchange options and alternatives, and hence the greater will be the power of that actor in social exchanges.

5. The more actors in a social exchange manipulate the situation in an effort to misrepresent their needs for a resource and/or conceal the availability of resources, the greater the level of tension in that exchange and the greater the potential for conflict.

6. The greater the degree of differentiation in a social system, the greater will be the use of generalized and symbolic media of social exchange, and vice versa.

7. The greater the use of generalized and symbolic media of exchange in a social system, the greater will be:

   7a. The volume of exchange relations.

   7b. The rate of social exchange.

   7c. The scope of social exchange.

   7d. The accumulation of value in social exchange.

   7e. The continuity of interaction and exchange.

   7f. The multiplicity of social ties and exchanges.

   7g. The differentiation of power to regulate social relations and exchanges.

8. The greater the use of generalized and symbolic media of exchange in a social system, the greater will be:

   8a. The options of individuals.

   8b. The diversity of individuals.

   and the less will be:

   8c. The attachment of individuals to objects, others, and groups.

Principles of Social Conflict

9. The greater the degree of emotional involvement of parties to a conflict, the more likely is the conflict to be violent.

   9a. The greater the respective solidarity among members of conflicting parties, the greater the degree of their emotional involvement.

   9b. The greater the previous harmony between members of conflicting parties, the greater the degree of their emotional involvement.

10. The more a conflict is perceived by members of conflict groups to transcend individual aims and interests, the more likely is the conflict to be violent.

11. The more conflict is perceived as a means to an end, the less likely is the conflict to be violent.

12. The less violent and more frequent is the conflict among social units in a differentiated social system, the more likely is the conflict to:

    12a. Allow units to release hostilities before they accumulate to extremely high levels.

    12b. Encourage the creation of norms to regulate the conflict.

    12c. Encourage the development of authority and judiciary systems to regulate the conflict.

13. The more violent are intergroup hostilities and the more frequent is conflict among groups, the less likely are group boundaries to disappear.

14. The more violent is the conflict, the more likely is centralization of power in the conflict groups.

15. The more violent is the conflict, the greater will be the internal solidarity of conflict groups, especially if:

   15*a*. The conflict group is small.

   15*b*. The conflict group represents a minority position.

   15*c*. The conflict group is engaged in self-defense.

16. The more violent and the more prolonged the conflict between groups, the more likely is the formation of coalitions among previously unrelated groups in a system.

17. The more prolonged is the threat of violent conflict between groups, the more enduring are the coalitions of each of the conflict parties.

Principles of Group Affiliation

"The Web of Group Affiliations" presents a number of interesting propositions on the consequences of social differentiation for social relations and individuals. Yet despite the number of examples in this essay, the argument boils down to relatively few propositions when stated more abstractly. The most important of these abstract principles are listed below:

18. The greater is the degree of social differentiation, the less likely are group affiliations to be concentric (imbedded within homogeneous group structures), and the more likely they are to be multiple and across diverse groups.

19. The more group affiliations cut across diverse groups, the greater is:

   19*a*. The distinctiveness of individual personality.

   19*b*. The freedom of individuals.

   19*c*. The potential for role conflict.

CHAPTER 10

The Origin and Context of Émile Durkheim's Thought

BIOGRAPHICAL INFLUENCES ON ÉMILE DURKHEIM'S THOUGHT[1]

Émile Durkheim was born in Epinal, France, in 1858. Because his Jewish family was deeply religious, the young Durkheim studied Hebrew, the Old Testament, and the Talmud, apparently intending to follow in his father's footsteps and become a rabbi. Durkheim began to move away from religion in his early teens, however, and he eventually abandoned personal religious involvement and proclaimed himself an agnostic. Yet, as will become evident in the next chapter, Durkheim never lost interest in religion as a topic of intellectual inquiry; and perhaps equally importantly, his passion for creating a new "civil morality" in France was fueled by the high sense of morality instilled by his family and early religious training.

Durkheim was an excellent student, and in 1879 he was admitted to the École Normale Supérieure—the traditional training ground for the intellectual elite of France in the nineteenth century. Yet in the new environment, Durkheim became more indifferent, apparently finding the literary, esthetic, and rhetorical thrust of the instruction unappealing. Instead Durkheim preferred the disciplined logic of philosophical arguments and, at the same time, the hard facts and findings of the sciences. Several teachers at the École did exert influence on Durkheim, however. The great French historian Fustel de Coulanges provided Durkheim with a firm appreciation for careful assessment of historical causes, while philosopher Émile Boutroux instilled in Durkheim an understanding of how reality consists of discontinuous levels that reveal emergent properties that distinguish them from one another. As

---

[1]In this section we have drawn heavily on Lewis A. Coser's *Masters of Sociological Thought* (New York: Harcourt Brace Jovanovich, 1977); Steven Lukes's *Émile Durkheim: His Life and Work* (London: Allen Lane, 1973); and Robert Alun Jones's *Émile Durkheim* (Beverly Hills, Calif.: Sage Publications, 1986).

we will see, these concerns for historical cause and emergent realities were to become central to Durkheim's sociology; and for this reason Durkheim acknowledged his debt by later dedicating his two doctoral theses to these teachers at the *École*.

Between 1882 and 1887 Durkheim taught in various schools around Paris, except for a year in Germany, where he studied German academic life and wrote a series of reports on German sociology and philosophy. These reports were to give Durkheim some visibility in academic circles and to promote contacts with important officials in the educational establishment in France. More significantly, during this period Durkheim's sociological orientation was to take on a more coherent form. This orientation represented a mixture of moral commitment to creating an integrated and cohesive society, on the one hand, and the application of rigorous analysis of social processes, on the other. For much like Auguste Comte before him, Durkheim believed the observations of facts and the development of theories to explain these facts would lead to a body of knowledge that could be used to create a "better society." To achieve this goal Durkheim had to recreate sociology in an era when Comte's ideas were not highly regarded and the traditional academic structure was hostile to any "science of society." Thus it is to Durkheim's credit that he could use his powers of persuasion as well as his personal contacts to secure a position at the University of Bordeaux in the Department of Philosophy, where he was allowed to teach a social science course—heretofore an unacceptable subject in French universities.

During this period at Bordeaux, Durkheim wrote the three works that were to make him famous and to place him in a position to change the structure and content of the French educational system—from primary schools to the universities themselves. Indeed, at no other time in the history of sociology has a sociologist exerted this degree of influence in a society.

At Bordeaux Durkheim wrote *The Division of Labor, The Rules of the Sociological Method,* and *Suicide.* These three books[2] established the power of sociological analysis, generating enormous controversy and begrudging respect for Durkheim as a scholar. Perhaps more significant for Durkheim's ultimate influence on French intellectual thinking was his creation of *L'Année Sociologique* in 1898. This journal soon became the centerpiece of an intellectual movement revolving around

---

[2]Émile Durkheim, *The Division of Labor in Society* (New York: Free Press, 1947; originally published in 1893); *The Rules of the Sociological Method* (New York: Free Press, 1938; originally published in 1895); and *Suicide* (New York: Free Press, 1951; originally published in 1897).

Durkheim's approach to sociology. Each annual issue contained contributions by Durkheim and a diverse group of young and creative scholars who, though from varying disciplines, were committed to defending Durkheim's basic position.

In 1902 Durkheim's stature allowed him to move to the Sorbonne in Paris, and in 1906 he became a professor of science and education. Later, by a special ministerial decree, the name of Durkheim's chair was changed in 1913 to Science of Education *and Sociology*. As Lewis Coser notes of this event,[3] "after more than three-quarters of a century, Comte's brainchild had finally gained entry at the University of Paris." In Paris Durkheim continued to edit *L'Année* and inspire a new generation of gifted scholars. Moreover, Durkheim was able to help reform the French educational system: At the time Durkheim rose to prominence, the French government had embarked on a difficult process of secularizing the schools and creating a state system of public education that rivaled and then surpassed the Catholic school system which, until the early decades of this century, dominated the education of children. Through his contacts in high-level government positions, this unique situation allowed Durkheim to create a new kind of curriculum in the public schools and a revolutionary program of teacher education. Emphasis was on secular topics, with the schools serving as a functional substitute for the church. In essence the school was to teach reverence for "society," and the teacher was to be the "priest" who guided this worship of civil society. Durkheim's desire was to create a "civil morality" where students became committed to the institutions of society and, at the same time, developed the secular skills and knowledge to analyze and change society for the better. While Durkheim was very cautious in dictating the precise nature of the school curriculum and in proposing the desirable direction of society, no social scientist has ever exerted more influence on the general profile of such a major institutional structure in a society.

This concern with a civil morality was, of course, inherited from Comte, who in turn had merely carried forth the banner of earlier French philosophers—Montesquieu and Rousseau being the most prominent. For Durkheim, the central question of all sociological analysis is: What forces integrate society, especially as it undergoes rapid change and differentiation? In Durkheim's view, integration will always involve a "morality" or set of values, beliefs, and norms that guide the cognitive orientations and behaviors of individuals. Durkheim approached the analysis of moral integration in many different ways, but the need for a common morality permeates his work—from his first great work on *The Division of Labor* to his last major book,

---

[3]Coser, *Masters of Sociological Thought*, p. 147.

The Elementary Forms of Religious Life.[4] Thus the young boy who was to be a rabbi developed into the secular academic who was to preach for societal integration.

World War I disrupted the "Année School," as it had come to be known. Indeed it killed off many of its most promising members, including Durkheim's son, André, who would have had a distinguished career as a sociological linguist. Durkheim never recovered emotionally from this blow, for he had seen his son as carrying on his work in the social sciences. In 1917, two years after his son's death, Durkheim died at the age of fifty-nine. Emotionally drained and physically declining, Durkheim simply did not care to live any longer.

Émile Durkheim thus died at the height of his intellectual and political prominence. And as we will see in the next chapter on his basic works, he left an intellectual legacy that is as influential on sociological theorizing today as it was at the turn of the century. Durkheim's work represents the culmination of the French intellectual tradition that began with the Enlightenment (see Chapter 1). At the same time, Durkheim's sociology is a response to both the perceived strengths and weaknesses of German and English sociology. The result is an approach that is true to its French pedigree—Montesquieu, Turgot, Rousseau, Saint-Simon, Comte, and Tocqueville. Yet the pedigree is conditioned by Durkheim's reaction against Herbert Spencer and, to a lesser extent, Karl Marx. Let us now turn to this list of influential thinkers and observe how they influenced Durkheim's thinking. In this way we can place into broader intellectual and historical context the works to be examined in the next chapter.

CHARLES MONTESQUIEU'S INFLUENCE ON DURKHEIM'S THOUGHT

As we saw in our analysis of Comte's work, Montesquieu marks the beginning of a French intellectual line that comes to a climax with Durkheim. To appreciate many of Durkheim's concepts, points of emphasis, and his methodological approach, we must return to Montesquieu—one of the giant intellects of the eighteenth century.

Montesquieu as the First Social Scientist

Montesquieu introduced an entirely new approach to the study of society. If we look at any number of scholars whose thought was prominent in Montesquieu's time, we can immediately observe dramatic

---

[4]Émile Durkheim, *The Elementary Forms of Religious Life* (New York: Free Press, 1947; originally published in 1912).

differences between their approach to the study of society and Montesquieu's. Many scholars of the eighteenth century were philosophers who were primarily concerned with the question: What is the ultimate origin of society? Their answer to this question was more philosophical than sociological and tended to be given in two parts. First, humans once existed in a "natural state" before the first society was created. Theory about society thus began with speculations about "the state of nature"—whether this state be warlike (Hobbes), peaceful (Locke), or idyllic (Rousseau). Second, in this state of nature humans formed a "social contract" and thereby created "society." People agreed to subordinate themselves to government, law, values, beliefs, and contracts.

In contrast to these philosophical doctrines, Montesquieu emphasized that humans have never existed without society. In Montesquieu's view humans are the product of society, and thus speculation about their primordial state does not represent an analysis of the facts of human life. Montesquieu was an empiricist; he was concerned with actual data rather than speculation about the essence of humans and the ultimate origins of their society. In many ways he was attracted to the procedures employed by Newton in physics: observe the facts of the universe, and from these make statements about their basic properties and the lawlike relations. While it was left to Comte in the following century to trumpet the new science of "social physics," Montesquieu was the first to see that a science of society, molded after the physical sciences, was possible.

Durkheim saw Montesquieu as positing that society is a "thing" or "fact" in the same sense that physical matter constitutes a thing or fact. Montesquieu was the first to recognize, Durkheim believed, that "morals, manners, customs" and the "spirit of a nation" are subject to scientific investigation. From this initial insight it is a short step to recognizing, as Comte was to do, that a discipline called sociology can study society. Durkheim gave explicit credit to Montesquieu for recognizing that a

> discipline may be called a science only if it has a definite field to explore. Science is concerned with things, realities. . . . Before social science could begin to exist, it had to be assigned a subject matter.[5]

Montesquieu never completely carried through on his view that society could be studied in the same manner as phenomena in the other sciences; but his classic book, *The Spirit of Laws*, represents one

handwritten margin note: Mont: humans never existed w/o society

---

[5]Émile Durkheim, *Montesquieu and Rousseau* (Ann Arbor: University of Michigan Press, 1960), p. 3.

of the first sociological works with a distinctly scientific tone. While Montesquieu had become initially famous for other works, *The Spirit* had the most direct influence on Durkheim.[6] Indeed Durkheim's Latin doctoral thesis was on *The Spirit of Laws* and was published a year before his famous French thesis, *The Division of Labor in Society*.[7] From *The Spirit* Durkheim was to take both methodological and substantive ideas, as is emphasized in the following review of Montesquieu's work and its influence on Durkheim.

Montesquieu's View of "Laws"

The opening lines of *The Spirit of Laws* reads:

> Laws, in their most general signification, are the necessary relations arising from the nature of things. In this sense all beings have their laws: the Deity His laws, the material world its laws, the intelligences superior to man their laws, the beasts their laws, man his laws.[8]

There is an ambiguity in this passage that is never clarified, for Montesquieu used the term *law* in two distinct senses: (1) law as a commandment or rule created by humans to regulate their conduct and (2) law as a scientific statement of the relations among properties of the universe in its physical, biological, and social manifestations. The first is a substantive conception of law—that of the jurist and political scientist. The second is a conception of scientific laws that explains the regularities among properties of the natural world. Durkheim was to incorporate implicitly this distinction in his own work. On the one hand, his first great work on *The Division of Labor in Society*[9] is about law, for variations in laws and the penalties for their violation were used by Durkheim as concrete indicators of integration in the broader society. On the other hand, *The Division of Labor* also involved a search for the scientific laws that explain the nature of social integration in human societies.

Montesquieu also revealed an implicit "hierarchy of laws"—an idea that may have suggested to Comte the hierarchy of the sciences

---

[6]Montesquieu's major works include *The Persian Letters* (New York: Meridian Books, 1901; originally published in 1721); and *Considerations on the Grandeur and Decadence of the Romans* (New York: Free Press, 1965; originally published in 1734). In many ways these two early books represented a data source for the more systematic analysis in *The Spirit of Laws*, 2 vols. (London: Colonial Press, 1900; originally published in 1748).

[7]In academic circles of Durkheim's time, two doctoral dissertations were required—one in French and another in Latin. The Latin thesis on Montesquieu was published in 1892, and the French thesis on the division of labor was published in 1893.

[8]Montesquieu, *Spirit of Laws*, p. 1.

[9]Durkheim, *Division of Labor*.

(see Chapter 1). For Montesquieu, "lower-order" phenomena, such as physical matter, cannot deviate from the scientific laws that govern their operation, but higher-order beings with intelligence can violate and transgress laws, giving the scientific laws of society a probabilistic rather than absolute character. This idea of probabilistic relations among social phenomena was also adopted by Durkheim, who was to view statistical rates as social facts in many of his works.

Montesquieu's Typology of Governments

To search for the scientific laws of the social world, Montesquieu argued that classification and typology are necessary. The enormous diversity of social patterns can easily obscure the common properties of phenomena unless the underlying type is exposed. The first thirteen books of *The Spirit* are thus devoted to Montesquieu's famous typology of governmental forms: (1) republic, (2) monarchy, and (3) despotism. Both methodological and substantive facets of Montesquieu's typology were to influence Durkheim. On the methodological side, Durkheim saw as significant the way in which Montesquieu went about constructing his typology. Durkheim stressed the more strictly methodological technique of using "number, arrangement, and cohesion of their component parts" for classifying social structures. In many ways Durkheim was reading into Montesquieu on this matter, since Montesquieu was never very explicit. Yet Durkheim's lifelong advocacy of typology and his use of the number, arrangement, and cohesion of parts as the basis for constructing typologies were apparently inspired by Montesquieu's classification of governmental forms.

Another methodological technique that Durkheim appeared to borrow from Montesquieu is the notion that laws enacted by governments will reflect not only the "nature" (structural form) of government but also its "principle" (underlying values and beliefs). Moreover, laws will reflect the other institutions that the nature and principle of government influence. Law is thus a good indicator of the culture and structure of society. This premise was to become the central methodological tenet of Durkheim's first major work on the division of labor.

On the substantive side, Montesquieu's view of government as composed of two inseparable elements, nature and principle, probably influenced Durkheim more than he acknowledged. For Montesquieu, each government's nature or structure is a reflection of (*a*) who holds power and (*b*) how power is exercised. Each government also reveals a principle, leading to the classification of governments in terms of structural units and cultural beliefs. For a republic, the underlying principle is "virtue" in which people have respect for law and for the welfare of the group; for a monarchy, the guiding principle is respect for rank, authority, and hierarchy; and for despotism, the principle is fear. The specifics of Montesquieu's political sociology are less important than the general insight they illustrate: Social structures are held together by a corresponding system of values and beliefs that individuals have internalized. Moreover, as Montesquieu emphasized, when a government's nature and principle are not in harmony—or, more generally, when social structures and cultural beliefs are in contradiction—social change is inevitable. These are theoretical issues with which Durkheim was to wrestle for his entire intellectual career. Yet one finds scarce notice in Durkheim's thesis of Montesquieu's profound insight into this aspect of social reality.

Another substantive issue, for which Montesquieu is most famous, is the "balance of powers" thesis. The basic argument is that a separation or division of powers among elements of government is essential to a stable government. Power must be its own corrective, for only counterpower can limit the abuse of power. Thus Montesquieu saw the two branches of the legislature (one for the nobility, the other for commoners) as they interact with each other and with the monarch as providing checks and balances on each other.[10] The judiciary, the third element of government, was not considered by Montesquieu to be an independent source of power—as it became in the American governmental system. Several points of emphasis in this analysis no doubt influenced Durkheim. First, Montesquieu's distrust of mass democracy in which the general population directly influences political decisions was to be retained in Durkheim's analysis of industrial societies. In Durkheim's eye representation is always to be mediated in order to avoid instability in political decisions. Second, Durkheim shared Montesquieu's distrust of a single center of power. Montesquieu feared despotism, while Durkheim distrusted the monolithic and bureaucratized state; but both recognized that in order to avoid the danger of highly centralized power, counterpower must be created.

The Causes and Functions of Governments

In addition to the notion of social types and scientific laws, the most conspicuous portions of Durkheim's Latin thesis are those on the "causes" and "functions" of government—a distinction that became central to Durkheimian sociology.

---

[10]If one computes these balances, they consistently work out in favor of the nobility and against the common person. The nobility and commoners unite to check the monarch, while the nobility and monarch check the commoners. But the monarch cannot, as an elevated figure, unite with the commoners. Monetesquieu's aristocratic bias is clearly evident.

Montesquieu's *The Spirit* is often a confused work; and his analysis of causes has frequently been misunderstood by commentators. After the typology of governments in the first thirteen books of *The Spirit*, Montesquieu suddenly launched into a causal analysis that could appear to undermine his emphasis on the importance of "the principle" in shaping the "nature," or structure, of government. For suddenly, in books 14 through 25, a variety of physical and moral causes of governmental forms are enumerated. Climates, soil fertility, manners, morals, commerce, money, population size, and religion are introduced one after another as causes of governmental and social forms.

The confusion often registered in this abrupt discussion of causes can be mitigated by the recognition of Montesquieu's underlying assumptions. First, these causes do not work directly on governmental forms. Each affects people's behavior, temperament, and disposition in ways that create a "general spirit of the nation"—an idea that was not far from Durkheim's conceptualization of the "collective conscience" and "collective representations" or Comte's similar notions. Thus "physical causes," such as climate, soil, and population size, as well as "moral causes," such as commerce, morals, manners, and customs, all operate to constrain how people act, behave, and think. Out of the collective life constrained and shaped by these causes comes the "spirit of a nation," which is a set of implicit ideas that bind people to one another and give them a sense of their common purpose.[11]

Once it is recognized that these causes do not operate directly on the nature, or structure, of government, a second point of clarification is possible. The underlying principle of government is linked to the general spirit that emerges from the actions and thoughts of people as they are constrained by the list of causes. Montesquieu was not clear of ambiguity on this issue, but this interpretation is the most consistent with how Durkheim probably viewed Montesquieu's argument. Yet curiously, despite the similarity of their views on the importance of collective ideas or "spirits" on social relations, Durkheim did not give Montesquieu much credit for this aspect of his sociology.

Durkheim did give Montesquieu explicit credit, however, for recognizing that a society must assume a "definite form" as a result of its "particular situation" and that this form stems from "efficient causes." In particular, he indicated that Montesquieu's view of ecological and population variables was to stimulate his concern with "material density" and how it influences "moral density." Durkheim recognized that to view social structures and ideas as the result of identifiable causes marks a dramatic breakthrough in social thought,

---

[11]This line of argument is derived from Louis Althuser, *Politics and History* (Paris: Universities of Paris, 1959).

especially since many social thinkers of the time were often locked into discussions of human nature and the "origins" of the first social contract.

Durkheim was, however, highly critical of Montesquieu's causal analysis in one respect: He saw Montesquieu as arguing in terms of "final causes." That is, the ends served by a structure such as law cause it to emerge and persist. As Durkheim stressed:

> Anyone who limits his inquiry to the final cause of social phenomena loses sight of their origins and is untrue to science. This is what would happen to sociology if we followed Montesquieu's method.[12]

Durkheim recognized that Montesquieu was one of the first scholars to argue for what is now termed *cultural relativism*. Social structures must be assessed, not in relation to some absolute, ethnocentric, or moralistic standard, but in their own terms and in view of the particular context in which they are found. For example, Montesquieu could view slavery not so much as a moral evil but as a viable institution in certain types of societies in particular historical periods. Implicit in this kind of argument is the notion of "function": A structure must be assessed in terms of its functions for the social whole; if a social pattern, even one like slavery, promotes the persistence and integration of a society, then it cannot be said, a priori, to be an evil or good pattern. Durkheim felt Montesquieu too easily saw the consequence of structures—that is, integration—as their cause, with the result that Montesquieu's functional and causal analyses frequently became confused. Yet Montesquieu may have suggested to Durkheim a critical distinction between causal and functional analysis.

In sum, Durkheim gave Montesquieu credit for many insights that became a part of his sociology. The social world can be studied as a "thing"; it is best to develop typologies; it is necessary to examine the number, arrangement, and relations among parts in developing these typologies; it is important to view law as an indicator of broader social and cultural forces; and it is wise to employ both causal and functional analyses.

Yet despite Durkheim's praise of Montesquieu, it is interesting to note what he did not acknowledge in Montesquieu's work: the view that laws, like those of physics, can be formulated for the social realm (Durkheim in the thesis gave Comte credit for this insight);[13]

---

[12]Durkheim, *Montesquieu and Rousseau*, p. 44.

[13]As Durkheim noted: "No further progress could be made until it was recognized that the laws of societies are no different from those governing the rest of nature and that the method by which they are discovered is identical with that of the other sciences. This was Auguste Comte's contribution." (Ibid., pp. 63–64).

the recognition that social morphology and cultural symbols are interconnected; the position that causes of morphological structures are mediated through, and mitigated by, cultural ideas; the notion that causes, and the laws that express relations among events, are probabilistic in nature; and the view that power in social relations must be checked by counterpower. Yet there can be little doubt that these ideas became a integral part of Durkheim's thinking, and thus much of Montesquieu's theoretical legacy was to live in Durkheimian sociology.[14]

JEAN-JACQUES ROUSSEAU

Writing his major works in the decade following the 1748 publication of Montesquieu's *The Spirit of Laws,* Jean-Jacques Rousseau produced a philosophical doctrine that contains none of Montesquieu's sense for social science but much of his sense for the nature of social order.[15] While not greatly admired in his time, Rousseau's ideas were, by the beginning of the nineteenth century, viewed in a highly favorable light. Indeed, in retrospect Rousseau was be be considered the leading figure of the Enlightenment, surpassing Hobbes, Locke, Voltaire, and certainly Montesquieu. It is not surprising, therefore, that Durkheim read with interest Rousseau's philosophical doctrine and extracted many ideas.

Rousseau's Doctrine

Rousseau's doctrine was a unique combination of Christian notions of the Fall that came with Original Sin and Voltaire's belief in the progress of humans.[16] Rousseau first postulated a presocietal "state of nature" in which individuals were dependent on nature and had only simple physical needs, for "man's"[17] desires "do not go beyond his

---

[14]For further commentary on Montesquieu's work, see Althuser, *Politics and History,* pp. 13–108; Raymond Aron, *Main Currents in Sociological Thought,* vol. I (Garden City, N.Y.: Doubleday, 1968), pp. 13–72; W. Stark, *Montesquieu: Pioneer of the Sociology of Knowledge* (Toronto: University of Toronto Press, 1961); and Thomas L. Pangle, *Montesquieu's Philosophy of Liberalism: A Commentary on "The Spirit of Laws"* (Chicago: University of Chicago Press, 1973).

[15]Jean-Jacques Rousseau, *The Social Contract and Discourses,* trans. G. D. H. Cole (New York: E. P. Dutton, 1950). This book is a compilation of Rousseau's various *Discourses* and *The Social Contract*—his most important works—which were written separately between 1750 and 1762. Durkheim was to analyze *The Social Contract,* and it appears, along with his Latin thesis on Montesquieu, in Durkheim, *Montesquieu and Rousseau,* pp. 65–138.

[16]J. H. Broome, *Rousseau: A Study of His Thought* (New York: Barnes & Noble, 1963), p. 14.

[17]Rousseau's phraseology uses the term *the natural state of man,* which is here retained.

state of nature → physical needs, little interhuman contact or dependence

physical needs; in all the universe the only desirable things he knows are food, a female, and rest." In the "state of nature" humans had little contact with or dependence on each other; and they had only crude "sensations" that reflected their direct experiences with the physical environment.

It was from this natural state that the great "fall" came. The discovery of agriculture, the development of metallurgy, and other events created a new and distinct entity: society. People formed social relations; they discovered private property; they appropriated property; they competed; those with property exploited others; they began to feel emotions of jealousy and envy; they began to fight and make war; and in other ways they created the modern world. Rousseau felt this world not only deviates from humans' natural state, but it makes their return to this state impossible.

As an emergent reality that destroys the natural state, modern society poses a series of problems that make life agonizing misery. In particular, humans feel no limit to their desires and passions; self-interest dominates; and one human exploits another. For Rousseau, society is corrupt and evil, destroying not only the natural controls on passions and self-interest but also the liberty from exploitation by one's fellows that typified the natural state.

Rousseau's solution to this evil was as original as it was naive, and yet it was to exert considerable influence on Durkheim. His solution was to eliminate self-interest and inequality by creating a situation in which human beings have the same relation to society as they once had to nature. That is, people should be free from each other and yet equally subject to society. In Rousseau's view only the political state could assure individual freedom and liberty, and only when individuals totally subordinate their interest to what he termed the *general will* could inequality, exploitation, and self-interest be eliminated. For if all individuals must subjugate themselves equally to the general will and the state, then they are equal. And if the state can assure individual freedom and maintain equal dependence of individuals on the general will, then the basic elements of nature are re-created: freedom, liberty, and equal dependence on an external force (society instead of nature).

general will

What is the general will? And how is it to be created? Rousseau was never terribly clear on just what constitutes the general will, but it appears to have referred to an emergent set of values and beliefs embodying "individual wills." The general will can be created and maintained, Rousseau asserted, only by several means: (1) the elimination of other-world religions, such as Christianity, and their replacement by a "civil religion" with the general will as the supreme being; (2) the elimination of family socialization and its replacement by common socialization of all the young into the general will (presumably through schools); and (3) the creation of a powerful state that embodies

① elimination of other-world religions
② elimination of family socialization → common socialization
③ creation of powerful state

the general will and the corresponding elimination of groups, organizations, and other "minor associations" that deflect the power of general will and generate pockets of self-interest and potential dissensus among people.[18]

Rousseau and Durkheim

Society as an Emergent Reality.   In Durkheim's courses he gave Rousseau credit for the insight that society constitutes a moral reality, *sui generis*, that can be distinguished from individual morality.[19] While Montesquieu had achieved a similar recognition, Rousseau phrased the matter in a way Durkheim was to emulate on frequent occasions. For Rousseau as well as Durkheim, society is "a moral entity having specific qualities [separate] from those of the individual beings who compose it, somewhat as chemical compounds have properties that they owe to none of their elements."[20]

Thus Durkheim took from Rousseau the view of society as an emergent and moral entity, much like emergent physical phenomena. And like Rousseau, Durkheim also abhorred a society in which competition and exchange dominate over a common morality. Indeed, for Durkheim, society was not possible without a moral component guiding exchanges among individuals.

Social Pathology.   Durkheim viewed Rousseau's discussion of the natural state as a "methodological device" that could be used to highlight the pathologies of contemporary society and to provide guidelines for the remaking of society. While many others in the eighteenth and nineteenth centuries had also emphasized the ills of the social world, Durkheim appeared to be drawn to three central conditions emphasized by Rousseau. Durkheim was to term these (1) *egoism,* (2) *anomie,* and (3) *the forced division of labor,* but his debt to Rousseau is clear. For Durkheim, egoism is a situation where self-interest and self-concern take precedence over commitment to the larger collectivity. Anomie is

---

[18]For more detailed analyses of Rousseau's doctrines, see Broome, *Rousseau;* Ernst Cassirer, *The Question of Jean-Jacques Rousseau* (Bloomington: Indiana University Press, 1963); Ronald Grimsley, *The Philosophy of Rousseau* (New York: Oxford University Press, 1973); John Charuet, *The Social Problem in the Philosophy of Rousseau* (Cambridge University Press, 1974); and David Cameron, *The Social Thought of Rousseau and Burke: A Comparative Study* (Toronto: University of Toronto Press, 1973).

[19]Durkheim's essay on Rousseau in *Montesquieu and Rousseau* was drafted from a course he taught at Bordeaux. It was published posthumously in 1918.

[20] Durkheim, *Montesquieu and Rousseau,* p. 82. Durkheim took this quote from Rousseau.

a state of deregulation such that the collective no longer controls people's desires and passions. The forced division of labor is a condition where one class can use its privilege to exploit another and to force people into certain roles. Indeed the inheritance of privilege and the use of privilege by one class to exploit another was repugnant to Durkheim. Like Rousseau, Durkheim felt that inequalities should be based on "natural" differences that spring from "a difference of age, health, physical strength, and mental and spiritual qualities."[21]

Thus Durkheim was highly sympathetic to Rousseau's conception of what ailed society: People force others to do their bidding; they are deregulated; and they are unattached to a larger purpose. Hence the social order must be structured in ways that mitigate these pathologies.

The Problem of Order.   Durkheim accepted the dilemma of modern society as Rousseau saw it. How is it possible to maintain individual freedom and liberty, without also releasing people's desires and encouraging rampant self-interest while, at the same time, creating a strong and cohesive social order that does not aggravate inequality and oppression?

For Rousseau, this question could be answered with a strong political state that assured individual freedom and a general will that emulated nature. Like Rousseau, Durkheim believed the state was the only force that would guarantee individual freedom and liberty, but he altered Rousseau's notion of society as the equivalent of the physical environment in the state of nature. For Durkheim, society and the constraints it imposes must be viewed as natural, with the result that people must be taught to accept the constraints and barriers of society in the same way they accept the limitations of their biological makeup and the physical environment. Only in this way could both egoism and anomie be held in check. For Durkheim, constraint by the moral force of society is in the natural order of things.

Like Rousseau, Durkheim was also to argue for a view of society as "sacred" and for the transfer of the same sentiments toward civil and secular society that people traditionally had maintained toward the gods (which, Durkheim would come to emphasize, are only symbolizations of society).[22] Moreover, like Rousseau, Durkheim was to stress the need for a moral education outside of the family in which

---

[21]Ibid., p. 86.

[22]Many of the specifics of Durkheim's ideas about religion as the symbolization of society were borrowed from Roberton Smith. See Lukes, *Émile Durkheim*, p. 450. For a further documentation of the influences on Durkheim's sociology of religion, see Robert Alun Jones and Mariah Evans, "The Criticial Moment in Durkheim's Sociology of Religion," paper read at the American Sociological Association, September 1978.

children could be taught in schools to understand and accept the importance of commitment to the morality of the collective.

Such a commitment could be achieved, Durkheim was to argue, through a unified "collective conscience" or set of "collective representations" that could regulate people's desires and passions. Such a view represented a reworking of Rousseau's view of absolute commitment to the general will. Yet in sharp contrast to Rousseau, Durkheim came to believe that only through attachment to cohesive subgroups, or what Rousseau had called "minor associations," could egoism be mitigated. Such groups, Durkheim felt, could attach individuals to the remote collective conscience and give them an immediate community of others. Morever, like Montesquieu, Durkheim distrusted an all-powerful state, and hence he came to view these subgroups as a political counterbalance to the powers of the state.

Thus Durkheim borrowed many ideas from Rousseau. Some of his most central concepts about social pathologies—anomie, egoism, and the forced division of labor—owed much to Rousseau's work. His vision of society as integrated by a strong state and by a set of common values and beliefs also reflected Rousseau's vision of how to eliminate these pathologies. His desire to use schools to provide moral education for the young and to rekindle the spirit of commitment to secular society that people once had toward the sacred was also inspired by Rousseau.

Yet Durkheim could never accept Rousseau's trust of the state. For Durkheim, the state could not be too powerful; its power must be checked and balanced. And people must be free to associate and to join groupings that encourage diversity based on common experiences and that create centers of counterpower to mitigate the state's power. Durkheim thus internalized Rousseau's vision of an integrated society in which individual freedom and liberty prevail. And he accepted the challenge of proposing ways to achieve that society. But he could never abide by Rousseau's vision of an all-powerful state and almost oppressive general will.[23]

Rousseau's impact on Durkheim was, no doubt, profound, but the extremes of Rousseau's philosophy are mitigated in Durkheim's work. Montesquieu's emphasis on the balancing of power with counterpower, and his emphasis on empirical facts rather than moral precepts, represented one tempering influence on Durkheim. Still another motivating influence came from Auguste Comte, whose work consolidated many intellectual trends into a clear program for a science of society that could be used to create the "good society."

---

[23]For a discussion of Durkheim's differences with Rousseau, see Lukes, *Émile Durkheim*, chap. 14.

AUGUSTE COMTE

It is difficult to know how much of the French intellectual tradition of the eighteenth century came to Durkheim through Auguste Comte, since Durkheim did not always acknowledge his debt to the titular founder of sociology. This difficulty is compounded by the fact that, like Durkheim's work, Comte's intellectual scheme represents a synthesis of ideas from Montesquieu, Rousseau, Turgot, Condorcet, Saint-Simon,[24] and others in the French lineage. Yet clearly many of the specific features of Durkheimian sociology owed much to Comte's grand vision for the science of society. Since we have reviewed Comte's thought in Chapter 1, we will only focus on the specific aspects of Comte's intellectual scheme that appear to have exerted the most influence on Durkheim.

The Science of Positivism

Comte must have reinforced for Durkheim Montesquieu's insistence that "facts" and "data," rather than philosophical speculation, should guide the science of society. Borrowing Comte's vision of a science of "social facts," Durkheim agreed with Comte in the latter's view that the laws of human organization could be discovered. These laws, as Montesquieu had stressed, will not be as "rigid" or "deterministic" as in sciences lower in the hierarchy of sciences, but they will be the equivalent of those laws in physics, chemistry, and biology in that they will allow for the understanding of phenomena. Thus Comte cemented in Durkheim's mind the dictum that the search for sociological laws must be guided by empirical facts, and conversely, the gathering of facts must be directed by theoretical principles.

The Methodological Tenets of Positivism

To collect facts requires a methodology, and Comte was the first to make explicit the variety of methodological approaches that could guide the new science of society. As he indicated, four procedures are acceptable: (1) "observation" of the social world by the use of human senses (best done, he emphasized, when guided by theory); (2) "experimentation," especially as allowed by social pathologies; (3) "historical" observation in which regular patterns of change in the nature of society—especially in the nature of its ideas—can be seen; and (4) "comparison" in which (a) human and animal societies, (b) coexisting

---

[24]Many have noted how much Comte took from his teacher, Saint-Simon. Yet we can argue that Saint-Simon's more scientific concerns reached Durkheim via Comte's reinterpretation. Saint-Simon's utopian socialism was rejected by Durkheim.

human societies, and (c) different elements of the same society are compared with an eye toward isolating the effects of specific variables. Durkheim was to employ all of these methods in his sociology, and hence there can be little doubt that Comte's methodological approach influenced Durkheim's methodology.

Another methodological aspect of Comte's thought revolved around the organic analogy. Comte, as we saw in Chapter 1, often viewed society as like a biological organism, with the result that a part, such as the family or the state, could be understood in terms of what it did for or contributed to the "body social." Montesquieu had made a similar point, although Comte first drew the clear analogy between the social and biological organisms. The functional method developed by Durkheim thus owed much to Comte's biological analogy. Indeed, as Durkheim was to emphasize, complete understanding of social facts is not possible without assessing their functions for maintaining the integration of the social whole.[25]

Much less prominent in Comte's than Montesquieu's scheme was the emphasis on typology. Yet Comte recognized that the construction of somewhat "idealized" types of social phenomena could help in sociological analysis. While many intermediate cases would not conform to these extreme types, their deviations from the types could allow for their comparison against a common yardstick—that is, the idealized type.[26] In his early work Durkheim was to develop typologies of societies, and thus we can assume that Montesquieu's emphasis on types, as reinforced by Comte's emphasis on the use of types as an analytical device for comparison, must have shaped Durkheim's approach. Throughout his career Durkheim was to insist that classification of phenomena in terms of their "morphology" or structure must precede either causal or functional analysis.

Social Statics and Dynamics

Durkheim was also influenced by the substance of Comte's scheme. As can be recalled from Chapter 1, Comte divided sociology into "statics" and "dynamics"—a distinction that Durkheim was to implicitly maintain. Moreover, the specific concepts Comte used to understand statics and dynamics were adopted by Durkheim.

---

[25]For a more complete analysis of Comte's organicism and its impact on Durkheim's functionalism, see Jonathan H. Turner and Alexandra Maryanski, *Functionalism* (Menlo Park, Calif.: Benjamin/Cummings, 1979).

[26]This approach obviously anticipated by a half-century Max Weber's ideal type method.

With regard to social statics, Durkheim shared Comte's concern with social solidarity and with the impact of the division of labor on this solidarity. In particular, Durkheim was to ask the same question as Comte: How can *consensus universalis,* or what Durkheim was to term the *collective conscience,* be a basis for social integration with growing specialization of functions in society? How can consensus over ideas, beliefs, and values be maintained at the same time people are differentiated and pulled apart by their occupational specialization? *The Division of Labor,* Durkheim's first major work, addressed these questions; and while Rousseau in the eighteenth century and a host of others in the nineteenth century had also tried to answer these same issues, Durkheim's approach owed more to Comte than to any other thinker.[27]

With respect to social dynamics, Comte held an evolutionary vision of human progress. Societies, especially their ideas, are moving in a direction—from theological, through metaphysical, to positivistic modes of thought. Durkheim was to adopt this specific view of the evolution of ideas from a religious to a positivistic basis late in his career in his work on religion. But more fundamentally, he retained the evolutionary approach to studying social change held by Comte and a host of other thinkers. Societies were seen by Durkheim as moving from simple to complex patterns of social structure and, correspondingly, from religious to secular systems of ideas. Almost everything Durkheim examined was couched in these evolutionary terms, which, to a very great extent, were adopted from Comte.

Science and Social Progress

Like his teacher and collaborator, Saint-Simon, Comte saw the development of sociology as a means to creating a better society. Although Durkheim's sense of pathology about the modern world probably owes more to Rousseau than to either Saint-Simon or Comte, Durkheim accepted their hope for a society based on the application of sociological laws. Durkheim was much less extreme than either Saint-Simon or Comte, who tended to make a religion out of science and to advocate unattainable utopias, but he retained Comte's view that a science of society could be used to facilitate social progress. Indeed Durkheim never abandoned his dream that a just and integrated social order could be created by applying the laws of sociology.

In sum, then, Durkheim's debt to Rousseau was mitigated by his exposure to Comte. Durkheim's view of science as reliant on data and as generating laws of human organization came as much from Comte

---

[27]Durkheim, *Division of Labor.*

as from any other thinker, as did his adoption of explicit methodological techniques. Durkheim's substantive view of society similarly reflected Comte's emphasis: a concern for social integration of differentiated units and for determining how ideas (values, beliefs, and norms) are involved in such integration. And Comte's insistence that science be used to promote the betterment of the human condition translated Rousseau's passionate and moralistic assessment of social ills into a more rational concern with constructing an integrated society employing sociological principles.

ALEXIS DE TOCQUEVILLE

In 1835 Alexis de Tocqueville, a young member of an elite family, published the first two volumes of a book based on his observations of American society. *Democracy in America* was an almost immediate success, propelling Tocqueville into a lifelong position of intellectual and political prominence in France. The third and fourth volumes of *Democracy in America* appeared in 1840,[28] and after a short political career culminating in his abbreviated appointment as foreign minister for France, Tocqueville retired to write what he defined as his major work, *The Old Regime and the French Revolution*, which appeared in 1857.[29] His death in 1859 cut short the completion of *The Old Regime*, but the completed volumes of *Democracy in America* and the first part of *The Old Regime* established Tocqueville as the leading political thinker in France, one who carried the tradition of Montesquieu into the nineteenth century and one whom Durkheim read carefully.

Tocqueville probably never read Comte, but his effort to emulate Montesquieu's method of analysis must have had considerable influence on Durkheim. Indeed from Tocqueville's analysis of democracy in America Durkheim was to get many of the ideas that were to mitigate the extremes of Rousseau's political solutions to social pathologies.

Tocqueville's *Democracy in America*

Tocqueville saw the long-term trend toward democracy as the key to understanding the modern world. In *Democracy in America* the young Tocqueville attempted to discover why individual freedom and liberty were being preserved in the United States, and implicitly, why French

---

[28]Alexis de Tocqueville, *Democracy in America* (New York: Alfred A. Knopf, 1945; originally published in 1835 and 1840).

[29]Alexis de Tocqueville, *The Old Regime and the French Revolution* (Garden City, N.Y.: Doubleday, 1955; originally published in 1857).

efforts toward democracy had experienced trouble (a theme more ex-plicitly developed in *The Old Regime and the French Revolution*). In this effort Tocqueville isolated two trends that typified democracies:

1. *The trend toward a leveling of social status.* While economic and politi-cal ranks are preserved, democratic societies bestow equal social status on their members—creating, in Tocqueville's eye, an increas-ingly homogeneous mass.

2. *The trend toward centralization of power.* Democratic governments tend to create large and centralized administrative bureaucracies and to concentrate power increasingly in the hands of legislative bodies.

Tocqueville saw a number of potential dangers in these two trends. First, as differences among people are leveled, the only avenue for social recognition becomes ceaseless material acquisition motivated by blind ambition. Tocqueville felt traditional status and honor distinc-tions had kept ambition and status striving in check; but as these are released and as the old hereditary basis bestowing honor is destroyed, the individual is atomized and freed of constraint—a condition remi-niscent of Rousseau's analysis and was, no doubt, to stimulate Durkheim's conceptualization of egoism and anomie.

Second, the centralization of administrative power can become so great as to result in despotism, which then undermines individual freedom and liberty. Moreover, centralized governments tend to rely on external war and to suppress internal dissent in an effort to pro-mote further consolidation of power.

Third, the centralization of decision making in the legislative branch can make government too responsive to the immediate, short-lived, and unreasoned sentiments of the social mass. Under these con-ditions government becomes unstable as it is pulled one way, and then another, by public sentiment.

Montesquieu's influence is clearly evident in these concerns. But unlike Montesquieu, Tocqueville saw another side of democracy, a side where individual liberty and freedom could be preserved even with the centralization of power, and where people's ambitions and atomi-zation could be held in check even as the old system of honor and prestige recedes. The democratic pattern in America, Tocqueville be-lieved, provided an illustration of conditions that could promote this other side of democracy.

As a student of Montesquieu, it is not surprising that Tocqueville's analysis of democracy in America made references to historical causes, placing emphasis on geography, unique historical circumstances, the system of laws (in particular the Constitution), and most important, the "customs, manners, and beliefs" of the American people. Out of these causes, Tocqueville delineated several conditions that mitigate the concentration of political power and the overatomization of individuals:

1. The system of checks and balances in government, with power in the federal government divided into three branches.

2. The federalist system in which state and local governments, with their own divisions of powers, check each other's power as well as that of the federal government.

3. A free and independent press.

4. A strong commitment of the people to use and rely on local institutions.

5. The freedom to form and use political and civil associations to achieve individual and collective goals.

6. A powerful system of values and beliefs stressing individual freedom and liberty.

The power and subtlety of Tocqueville's description of America cannot be captured with a short list like that above. Yet this list probably best communicates what Durkheim was to pull out of Tocqueville's work. Rousseau and Tocqueville had both highlighted the ills of the modern world—unregulated passions and rampant self-interest—but Rousseau's solution to these problems was too extreme for the liberal Durkheim, whereas Tocqueville's analysis of America provided a view of a modern and differentiated social structure where freedom, liberty, and individualism could be maintained without severe pathologies or without recourse to a dictatorial state.

Durkheim and Tocqueville

Durkheim was to view modern social structure as integrated when (*a*) differentiated functions are well coordinated, (*b*) individuals are attached to collective organizations, (*c*) individual freedom is preserved by a central state, (*d*) this central state sets broad collective goals and personifies common values, and (*e*) the state's broad powers are checked and balanced by countersources of power.

It is not hard to find these themes in Tocqueville's work. In particular, Durkheim was to find appealing the idea of "civil and political" associations. These associations can provide people with a basis for attachment and identification, and they can also serve as a mechanism for mediating between their members and the state. Durkheim was to term these associations *occupational* or *corporate* groups, and there can be little doubt that he took much from Tocqueville's analysis of voluntary civil and political associations. Moreover, in adopting Montesquieu's emphasis on customs, manners, and beliefs that promote strong commitments to freedom and liberty, without also promoting atomization, Durkheim recognized in Tocqueville's work the importance of general values and beliefs (Rousseau's general will and Comte's consensus universalis and general spirit) for promoting integration among the diversified groupings of modern societies. For even if these values and beliefs emphasize individual freedom and liberty, they can be used to unite people by stressing a collective respect for the rights of the individual.

Thus Tocqueville gave to Durkheim a sense for some of the general conditions that could mitigate the pathologies of modern societies. These conditions were to become a part of Durkheim's practical program as well as his more strictly theoretical analysis.

HERBERT SPENCER'S INFLUENCE

Montesquieu, Rousseau, Comte, and Tocqueville represent the French intellectual heritage from which Durkheim took many of his more important concepts.[30] His criticism of these thinkers is not severe, and we can sense that Durkheim never reacted against their thought. He took what was useful and ignored obvious weaknesses. Such is not the case with Herbert Spencer, for throughout Durkheim's career Spencer was singled out for very special criticism.

Durkheim and Spencerian Utilitarianism

Durkheim was to react vehemently against any view of social order that ignored the importance of collective values and beliefs. Utilitarian doctrines stress the importance of competition and exchange in creating a social order held together by contracts among actors pursuing their own self-interests. Durkheim was not to ignore the importance of competition, exchange, and contract, but he was to see blind self-interest as a social pathology. A society could not be held together by self-interest and legal contracts alone; there must also be a "moral" component or an underlying system of collective values and beliefs guiding people's interactions in the pursuit of "collective" goals or interests.

Durkheim was thus highly critical of Spencer, who, as we saw in Chapters 2 and 3, coined such phrases as "survival of the fittest" and

---

[30]This is not to deny the influence of specific teachers and less well-known scholars. But we think the degree to which Durkheim took from the giants of French thought has been underemphasized in commentaries. There is too much similarity in the combined legacy of Montesquieu, Rousseau, Comte, and Tocqueville, on the one hand, and Durkheim's thought, on the other, for the impact of these prominent social thinkers to be ignored.

emphasized that modern society is laced together by contracts negoti-
ated out of the competition and exchange of self-interested actors. In
fact Durkheim's works are so filled with references to the inadequacies
of Spencerian sociology that we might view Durkheimian sociology as
a lifelong overreaction to the imputed ills in Spencerian sociology.[31]

Durkheim and Spencerian Organicism

As we noted in Chapter 3, Spencer wore two intellectual hats: (1)
the moralist, who was a staunch individualist and utilitarian and (2)
the scientist, who sought to develop laws of both organic and super-
organic forms. Moreover, in attempting to realize the latter, Spencer
took Comte's organic analogy and converted it into an explicit functionalism: System parts function to meet explicit needs of the "body
social." Durkheim clearly drew considerable inspiration from this
mode of analysis, since one of his major methodological tenets is to
stress the importance of assessing the functions of social phenomena.
We might even go so far as to speculate that had Spencer not formulated functionalism, it is unlikely that Durkheim would have adopted
this mode of sociological analysis.

Durkheim and Spencerian Evolutionism

As we also observed in Chapter 3, Spencer had an evolutionary
view of societies as moving from a simple to a treble-compound state.
While perhaps deficient in some respects, Spencer's description was far
more attuned than Comte's to the structural and cultural aspects of
social evolution. Comte's evolutionism had been vague, with references
to the movement of systems of thought and the view of the social organicism as embracing all of humanity. In contrast Spencer's analysis
was far more sociological and emphasized explicit variables that could
distinguish types of societies from one another and that could provide

---

[31]For a more detailed analysis of Durkheim and Spencer, see Turner and Maryanski,
Functionalism, chap. 1. Indeed if Durkheim's and Spencer's actual theories of social
differentiation are compared, side by side, they are virtually identical. This can be
seen by examining the closing portions of Chapter 3 and the next chapter of this
book. For further analysis and commentary, see Jonathan H. Turner, *Herbert Spencer:
Toward a Renewed Appreciation* (Beverly Hills, Calif.: Sage Publications, 1985);
"Durkheim's and Spencer's Principles of Social Organization: A Theoretical Note,"
Sociological Perspectives 27, January 1984, pp. 21–32; and "The Forgotten Giant: Herbert
Spencer's Theoretical Models and Principles," *Revue Europeene Des Sciences Sociales* 29,
no. 59 (1981), pp. 79–98.

a view of the dimensions along which evolutionary change could be described. Thus it is difficult to imagine that Durkheim was unimpressed with Spencer's analysis of the broad contours of social evolution.[32] Indeed Durkheim's first major work was to explore social evolution from simple to complex societies—a task that had initially occupied Spencer in volume 1 of his *Principles of Sociology*.

KARL MARX'S INFLUENCE

Durkheim analyzed social and communist doctrines in his courses, especially in a course on the history of social thought. He was often critical, as can be seen in posthumously published essays taken from course lectures.[33] Yet there is some evidence that Durkheim wanted to devote a full course to Karl Marx's thought, but apparently he never found the time. Durkheim was thus aware of Marx but was generally dismayed by socialism's "working-class bias" and by the emphasis on revolution and conflict. Durkheim felt the problems of alienation, exploitation, and class antagonism are issues relevant to all sectors of society, and revolution causes more pathology than it resolves. Yet in his first work Durkheim discussed the forced division of labor, the value theory of labor, and the problems of exploitation—points of emphasis highly reminiscent of Marx's conceptualization.

On balance, however, Marx's influence was negative. Durkheim reacted against Marx's insistence that integration in capitalist societies could not be achieved because of its "internal contradictions." What for Marx were the "normal" conflict-generating forms of capitalism were for Durkheim "abnormal forms," which could be eliminated without internal revolution. Indeed French sociology in the aftermath of the French Revolution and the lesser revolution of 1848 was decidedly conservative and did not consider revolutionary conflict as a productive and constructive way to bring about desired change. Thus while Marx's influence on Durkheim is evident, it is not profound. Unlike Weber, for whom the "ghost of Marx" was ever present, Durkheim considered Marx's thought, reacted against Marx's ideas in his first works, and eventually rejected and ignored Marx in later works.

---

[32]Recent commentaries, surprisingly those by British scholars, have tended to underemphasize Spencer's impact on Durkheim. While all commentaries note the positive reaction of Durkheim to the German organicist Albert Schaffle, they fail to note that Schaffle was simply adopting Spencer's ideas. We suspect Durkheim knew he was restating Spencer's ideas.

[33]See, for example, Émile Durkheim, *Socialism and Saint-Simon* (Yellow Springs, Ohio: Antioch Press, 1959; originally published in 1928).

ANTICIPATING DURKHEIMIAN SOCIOLOGY

A scholar's ideas are the product of multiple influences, some obvious and others more subtle. We have mentioned some biographical influences on Durkheim's thought, but our emphasis has been on those scholars from whom he took concepts and methodologies. Surprisingly, much less has been said about these more obvious sources of Durkheim's ideas than about the subtle influence of his biography. Our view is that by simply looking at the key elements of Durkheim's thought, and then examining the major figures of Durkheim's intellectual milieu, the sources of his basic concepts and concerns become startlingly clear.

The influence of various scholars on Durkheim's sociology is evident at different points in his career, a fact that will become clear in the next chapter. By way of anticipating this discussion, we close this chapter with a brief listing of the elements of Durkheim's sociology. All of these elements derive from the scholars discussed in this chapter, but Durkheim's unique biography led him to combine them in ingenious ways, creating a distinctive sociological perspective. Durkheimian sociology can be seen as (*a*) a series of methodological tenets, (*b*) a theory-building strategy, (*c*) a set of substantive topics, and (*d*) a host of practical concerns. Each is briefly summarized in an effort to anticipate the detailed analysis of the next chapter.

Methodological Tenets

From Montesquieu and Comte, Durkheim came to view a science of society as possible only if social and moral phenomena are considered as a distinct reality. Moreover, a science of the social world must be like that of the physical and biological worlds; it must be based on data or facts. Montesquieu had initially emphasized this point, but Comte provided the articulation of methods to be employed by the science of society. Historical, comparative, experimental, and observational techniques must all be used to discover the social facts that can build a theory of society.

Theoretical Strategy

Again, it was from Montesquieu and Comte that Durkheim received the vision that sociological laws can be discovered. In particular, it was from Montesquieu that causal analysis came to be an integral part of Durkheim's approach. Theory should seek the general causes of phenomena, for only in this way can the abstract laws of social organization be uncovered. Yet without a corresponding, but nonetheless separate, analysis of the functions served by social phenomena, these laws will remain hidden—a point of emphasis implicit in Montesquieu's and Comte's work that became explicit in Herbert Spencer's sociology. Thus for Durkheim, the laws of sociology will come from the causal and functional analysis of social facts.

Substantive Interests *what holds society together*

For Durkheim, the basic theoretical question was: What forces hold society together? At a substantive level, this question involved the examination of (*a*) social structures, (*b*) symbolic components, such as values, beliefs, and norms, and (*c*) the complex relations between *a* and *b*. From Montesquieu, Tocqueville, and Spencer, Durkheim acquired a sense for social structure; and from Montesquieu's spirit of a nation, Rousseau's general will, and Comte's consensus universalis, he came to understand the significance of cultural symbols for integrating social structures. The specific topics of most concern to Durkheim—religion, education, government, the division of labor, intermediate groups, and collective representations—come from all the scholars discussed in this chapter and from specific intellectual and academic concerns of Durkheim's time. But the emphasis on symbolic and structural integration connected Durkheim's examination of specific topics—a fact that will become increasingly clear in the next chapter.

Practical Concerns

Like Rousseau and Comte, Durkheim wanted to create a well-integrated society. Such a goal could only be achieved by recognizing the pathologies of the social order, which were first articulated with a moral passion in Rousseau's work and then reinforced in Tocqueville's more dispassionate analysis of American democracy. As Durkheim came to view the matter, the solution to these pathologies involved the creation of a system of constraining ideas (Comte, Rousseau, and Montesquieu), integration in intermediate subgroups (Tocqueville), coordination of differentiated functions through exchange and contract (Comte and Spencer), and the creation of a central state that provides overall coordination while maintaining individual freedom (Rousseau, Tocqueville, and Comte).

In sum, then, these methodological, theoretical, substantive, and practical concerns mark the critical elements of Durkheim's sociology. It is now our task to explore the specific works that can yield further insight into Durkheim's thought.

CHAPTER 11

The Sociology of Émile Durkheim

While all commentators agree Durkheim was concerned with social order—indeed many think he was overconcerned—there is considerable disagreement as to whether his theoretical perspective changed between the publication of his first and last major works. Some scholars, such as Anthony Giddens, argue that all of the basic questions and elements of Durkheim's approach are clearly evident in his first important work, *The Division of Labor in Society* (published in 1893), and that subsequent writings represent merely extensions and elaborations.[1] Others, such as Talcott Parsons, stress that during the course of his career Durkheim increasingly came to recognize the importance of idea systems, and their internalization by individuals, as the basic process underlying social order.[2] Our analysis of Durkheim's major works will lend support to both positions. Giddens is certainly correct in noting that Durkheim's collective work represents an elaboration of ideas first presented in *The Division of Labor.* But Parsons is also correct, at least to some degree, in his view that Durkheim became increasingly interested in social-psychological issues, especially with how social structures and idea systems influence the cognitive structure of individuals.[3]

Our goal in this chapter, therefore, is to communicate both the continuity and the shifting areas of inquiry found in Durkheim's work. We will not examine all of Durkheim's written work—a task that is

---

[1]Anthony Giddens, *Capitalism and Modern Theory: An Analysis of the Writings of Marx, Durkheim, and Max Weber* (Cambridge: Cambridge University Press, 1971); and Anthony Giddens, ed. and trans., *Émile Durkheim: Selected Writings* (Cambridge: Cambridge University Press, 1972).

[2]Talcott Parsons, *The Structure of Social Action* (New York: McGraw-Hill, 1937).

[3]Steven Lukes, *Émile Durkheim, His Life and Work: A Historical and Critical Study* (London: Allen Lane, 1973), p. 66. See also Jonathan H. Turner, *A Theory of Social Interaction* (Stanford, Calif.: Stanford University Press, 1988); and Robert Alun Jones, *Émile Durkheim* (Beverly Hills, Calif.: Sage Publications, 1985).

beyond our reach.[4] Rather we will examine in detail Durkheim's four major works: *The Division of Labor in Society* (1893), *The Rules of the Sociological Method* (1895), *Suicide* (1897), and *The Elementary Forms of Religious Life* (1913). While these four works can offer a fairly comprehensive overview of Durkheim's intellectual concerns, we will supplement our discussion with references to a variety of other written works and posthumously published lectures.

THE DIVISION OF LABOR IN SOCIETY

Durkheim's first major work was the published version of his French doctoral thesis, *The Division of Labor in Society*.[5] The original subtitle of this thesis was *A Study of the Organization of Advanced Societies*.[6] On the surface the book is about the causes, profile, and functions of the division of labor in modern societies, but, as we will explore, the book presents a more general theory of social organization—one that can still inform sociological theorists.[7] In our review of this classic work, we will pursue a number of issues Durkheim stressed: (1) social solidarity, (2) the collective conscience, (3) social morphology, (4) mechanical and organic solidarity, (5) social deviation, (6) social functions, (7) the causes of change, and (8) social pathology.

Social Solidarity

The Division of Labor is about the shifting basis of social solidarity as societies evolve from an undifferentiated and simple[8] to a complex and differentiated profile.[9] Today this topic would be termed *social*

---

[4]For the most complete bibliography of Durkheim's published works, see Lukes, *Émile Durkheim*, pp. 561–90. See also Robert A. Nisbet, *The Sociology of Émile Durkheim* (New York: Oxford University Press, 1974), pp. 30–41, for an annotated bibliography of the most important works forming the core of Durkheim's theoretical system.

[5]Émile Durkheim, *The Division of Labor in Society* (New York: Free Press, 1947; originally published in 1893).

[6]See Lukes, *Émile Durkheim*, chap. 7, for a detailed discussion.

[7]Our view of Durkheim's *The Division of Labor in Society* underemphasizes the social evolutionism contained in this work, since we think too much concern is placed on the model of social change and not enough on the implicit theory of social organization.

[8]Durkheim described such simple societies as based on mechanical solidarity. *Mechanical* was a term intended to connote an image of society as a body where cohesion is imposed on like elements: "the social molecules . . . could operate in harmony in so far as they do not operate independently."

[9]Such societies were seen as based on organic solidarity. *Organic* was intended to be an analogy to an organism in which "society becomes more capable of operating in harmony, in so far as each of its elements operates more independently."

integration, since concern is with how units of a social system are co-ordinated. For Durkheim, the question of social solidarity or integration turns on several related issues: (1) How are individuals made to feel part of a larger social collective? (2) How are their desires and wants constrained in ways that allow them to participate in the collective? (3) How are individuals' and other social units' activities coordinated and adjusted to each other? These questions, we should emphasize, not only dominated *The Division of Labor,* but they guided all of Durkheim's subsequent substantive works.

As is evident, these questions take us into the basic problem of how patterns of social organization are created, maintained, and changed. It is little wonder, therefore, that Durkheim's analysis of social solidarity contains a more general theory of social organization, and so we should explore those concepts that Durkheim developed to explain social organization in general. One of the most important of these concepts is "the collective conscience."

The Collective Conscience

Throughout his career Durkheim was vitally concerned with "morality" or "moral facts." While he was often somewhat vague on what constituted a moral fact, we can interpret the concept of morality to embody what sociologists now call *culture.* That is, Durkheim was concerned with the systems of symbols—particularly the norms, values, and beliefs—that humans create and use to organize their activities.

It should be remembered that Durkheim had to assert the legitimacy of the scientific study of moral phenomenon since other academic disciplines, such as law, ethics, religion, philosophy, and psychology, all laid claim to symbols as their subject matter. Thus Durkheim was to insist:

> Moral facts are phenomena like others; they consist of rules of action recognizable by certain distinctive characteristics. It must, then, be possible to observe them, describe them, classify them, and look for laws explaining them.[10]

We should emphasize, however, that Durkheim in his early work often used the concept of moral facts to denote structural patterns

---

[10]Durkheim, *Division of Labor,* p. 32. This idea owes its inspiration to Comte. As Durkheim noted in his Latin thesis on Montesquieu: "No further progress could be made until it was recognized that the laws of societies are no different from those governing the rest of nature. . . . This was Auguste Comte's contribution." Émile Durkheim, *Montesquieu and Rousseau* (Ann Arbor: University of Michigan Press, 1960; originally published in 1892), pp. 63–64.

(groups, organizations, and so on) as well as systems of symbols (values, beliefs, laws, norms). Yet, in *The Division of Labor*, we can find clear indications that he wanted to separate analytically the purely structural from the symbolic aspects of social reality. This isolation of cultural or symbolic phenomena can best be seen in Durkheim's formulation of another, somewhat ambiguous concept that suffers in translation: the "collective conscience." Durkheim was later to drop extensive use of this term in favor of "collective representations," which, unfortunately, adds little clarification. But we can begin to understand Durkheim's meaning with the formal definition provided in *The Division of Labor:*

> The totality of beliefs and sentiments common to average citizens of the same society forms a determinate system which has its own life; one may call it the *collective* or *common conscience*.[11]

Durkheim went on to indicate that while the terms *collective* and *common* are "not without ambiguity," they suggest that societies reveal a reality independent of "the particular conditions in which individuals are placed." Moreover, people are born into the collective conscience, and it comes to regulate their perceptions and behaviors. What Durkheim was denoting with the concept of collective conscience, then, is the fact that social systems evidence systems of ideas, such as values, beliefs, and norms, that constrain the thoughts and actions of individuals.

In the course of his analysis of the collective conscience, he conceptualized its varying states in terms of four variables: (1) volume, (2) intensity, (3) determinateness, and (4) religious versus secular content.[12] *Volume* denotes the degree to which the values, beliefs, and rules of the collective conscience are shared by the members of a society; *intensity* indicates the extent to which the collective conscience has power to guide a person's thoughts and actions; *determinateness* denotes the degree of clarity in the components of the collective conscience; and *content* pertains to the ratio of religious to purely secular symbolism in the collective conscience.

Social Morphology

Borrowing from Montesquieu, Durkheim saw social structure (or as he termed it, *morphology*) as involving an assessment of the "nature," "number," "arrangement," and "interrelations" among parts, whether

---

[11]Durkheim, *Division of Labor,* pp. 79–80 (emphasis in original).

[12]Ibid., p. 152 for 1, 2, 3, and throughout book for 4. For interesting secondary discussions, see Lukes, Émile Durkheim, and Giddens, *Selected Writings.*

these parts be individuals or corporate units, such as groups and organizations. Their nature is usually assessed in terms of such variables as size and functions (economic, political, familial, and so on). Arrangement concerns the distribution of parts in relationship to each other; interrelations deals with the modes of communication, movement, and mutual obligations among parts.

Although Durkheim's entire intellectual career involved an effort to demonstrate the impact of social structures on the collective conscience as well as on individual cognitions and behavior, he never made explicit use of these variables—that is, nature, number, arrangement, and interrelations—for analyzing social structures. In his more methodological statements he argued for the appropriateness of viewing social morphology in terms of nature, size, number, arrangement, and interrelations of specific parts. Yet his actual analysis of social structures in his major substantive works left these more formal properties of structure implicit.[13]

Mechanical and Organic Solidarity

Following the methodology borrowed from Montesquieu, Durkheim developed a typology of societies in terms of their basis of solidarity. One type is termed *mechanical* and the other *organic*.[14] As will be shown below, each of these types rests on different principles of social integration, involving different morphologies, different systems of symbols, and different relations between social and symbol structures. Durkheim's distinction between mechanical and organic is both a descriptive typology of traditional and modern societies and a theoretical statement about the changing forms of social integration that emerge with increasing differentiation of social structure.

At a descriptive level, mechanical solidarity is based on a strong collective conscience regulating the thought and actions of individuals located within structural units that are all alike. In terms of the four variables by which Durkheim conceptualized the collective conscience, the cultural system is high in volume, intensity, determinateness, and

---

[13]The concern for "social morphology" was, no doubt, an adaptation of Comte's idea of social statics, as these were influenced by German organicist Albert Schaffle, with whom Durkheim had been highly impressed. See Lukes, *Émile Durkheim*, pp. 86–95.

[14]Such typologizing was typical in the nineteenth century. As we saw in Chapter 3, Spencer had distinguished societal types, but more influential was Tönnies's distinction between *Gemeinschaft* and *Gesselleschaft*. Durkheim spent a year in Germany as a student in 1885–86, and while Tönnies's famous work was not yet published, his typology was well known and influenced Durkheim's conceptualization of mechanical and organic solidarity.

religious content. Legal codes, which in Durkheim's view are the best empirical indicator of solidarity, are repressive and sanctions are punitive. The reason for such repressiveness is that deviation from the dictates of the collective conscience is viewed as a crime against all members of the society and the gods. The morphology or structure of mechanical societies reveals independent kinship units that organize relatively small numbers of people who share strong commitments to their particular collective conscience. The interrelations among kin units are minimal, with each kin unit being like the others and autonomously meeting the needs of its members. Not surprisingly, then, individual freedom, choice, and autonomy are low in mechanical societies. People are dominated by the collective conscience, and their actions are constrained by its dictates and by the constraints of cohesive kin units.

In contrast, organically structured societies are typified by large populations, distributed in specialized roles in many diverse structural units. Organic societies reveal high degrees of interdependence among individuals and corporate units, with exchange, legal contracts, and norms regulating these interrelations. The collective conscience becomes "enfeebled" and "more abstract," providing highly general and secular value premises for the exchanges, contracts, and norms regulating the interdependencies among specialized social units. This alteration is reflected in legal codes that become less punitive and more "restitutive," specifying nonpunitive ways to redress violations of normative arrangements and to reintegrate violators back into the network of interdependencies that typify organic societies. In such societies individual freedom is great, and in fact, the secular and highly abstract collective conscience becomes dominated by values stressing respect for the personal dignity of the individual.

This descriptive contrast between mechanical and organic societies is summarized in Table 11–1.[15]

At the more theoretical level, Durkheim's distinction between mechanical and organic solidarity posits a fundamental relationship in the social world among "structural differentiation," "value-generalization," and "normative specification." Let's explore this relationship in more detail. As societies differentiate structurally, values become more abstract.[16] The collective conscience

> changes its nature as societies become more voluminous. Because these societies are spread over a vaster surface, the common conscience is

---

[15]This table is similar to one developed by Lukes, *Émile Durkheim*, p. 151, but it differs in many important respects.

[16]Durkheim, *Division of Labor*, p. 171.

TABLE 11–1   Descriptive Summary of Mechanical and Organic Solidarity

Morphological Features	*Mechanical Solidarity*	*Organic Solidarity*
1. Size	Small	Large
2. Number of parts	Few	Many
3. Nature of parts	Kinship based	Diverse: dominated by economic and governmental content
4. Arrangement	Independent, autonomous	Interrelated, mutually interdependent
5. Nature of interrelations	Bound to common conscience and punitive law	Bound together by exchange, contract, norms, and restitutive law
Collective conscience		
1. Volume	High	Low
2. Intensity	High	Low
3. Determinateness	High	Low
4. Content	Religious, stressing commitment and conformity to dictates of sacred powers	Secular, emphasizing individuality

itself obliged to rise above all local diversities, to dominate more space, and consequently to become more abstract. For not many general things can be common to all these diverse environments.[17]

Yet as basic values lose their capacity to regulate the specific actions of large numbers of differentiated units, then normative regulations arise to compensate for the inability of general values to specify what people should do and how individuals as well as corporate units should interact.

> If society no longer imposes upon everybody certain uniform practices, it takes greater care to define and regulate the special relations between different social functions and this activity is not smaller because it is different.[18]

---

[17]Ibid., p. 287.
[18]Ibid., p. 205.

> It is certain that organized societies are not possible without a devel-
> oped system of rules which predetermine the functions of each organ.
> In so far as labor is divided, there arises a multitude of occupational
> moralities and laws.[19]

Thus in his seemingly static comparison of mechanical and organic societies, Durkheim was actually proposing lawlike relationships among
structural and symbolic elements of social systems.

Social Change

Durkheim's view of social change revolves around an analysis of
the causes and consequences of increases in the division of labor:

> The division of labor varies in direct ratio with the volume and density
> of societies, and, if it progresses in a continuous manner in the course
> of social development, it is because societies become regularly denser
> and generally more voluminous.[20]

Some translation of terms is necessary if this "proposition," as
Durkheim called it, is to be understood. *Volume* refers to population
size and concentration; *density* pertains to the increased interaction
arising out of escalated volume. Thus the division of labor arises out of
increases in the concentration of populations whose members increasingly come into contact. Durkheim also termed the increased rates of
interaction among those thrust into contact *dynamic* and *moral* density.
Durkheim then analyzed those factors that increase the volume and
density of a population. Ecological boundaries (rivers, mountains, and
so on), migration, urbanization, and population growth all operate directly to increase volume and thus indirectly to increase the likelihood
of dynamic density (increased contact and interaction). Technological
innovations, such as new modes of communication and transportation,
directly increase rates of contact and interaction among individuals.
But all of these direct and indirect influences are merely lists of empirical conditions influencing the primary explanatory variable, dynamic
or moral density.

How, then, does dynamic density cause the division of labor? Dynamic density increases competition among individuals who, if they
are to survive the "struggle," must assume specialized roles and then
establish exchange relations with each other. The division of labor is
thus the mechanism by which competition is mitigated.

> Thus, Darwin says that in a small area, opened to immigration, and
> where, consequently, the conflict of individuals must be acute, there is

---

[19]Ibid., p. 302.
[20]Ibid., p. 262.

always to be seen a very great diversity in the species inhabiting it. . . . Men submit to the same law. In the same city, different occupations can co-exist without being obliged mutually to destroy one another, for they pursue different objects.[21]

Figure 11–1 delineates these causal connections. To recapitulate, Durkheim saw migration, population growth, and ecological concentration as causing increased "material density," which in turn caused increased moral or dynamic density—that is, escalated social contact and interaction. Such interaction could be further heightened by varied means of communication and transportation, as is illustrated in the model in Figure 11–1. The increased rates of interaction characteristic of a larger population within a confined ecological space cause increased competition or "struggle" among individuals. Such competition allows those who have the most resources and talents to maintain their present positions and assume high-rank positions, while the "less fit" seek alternative specialties so as to mitigate the competition. Out of this competition and differentiation comes the division of labor, which, when "normal," results in organic solidarity.

The major problem with the model is the implicit argument by "final causes." The function of the division of labor is to promote social solidarity; and Durkheim implied that the need for social solidarity causes the struggle to be resolved by the division of labor, and yet Durkheim never specified precisely how the needs met by the division of labor (that is, social solidarity) cause it to emerge. Without clear specification of this causal connection, the model becomes an illegitimate teleology in which the end-state (social solidarity) causes the very thing (the division of labor) that brings about this end-state. As is denoted by the feedback arrow moving from right to left in the model, Durkheim implies that the model is also circular or tautological in that cause and effect become difficult to separate: The division of labor causes social solidarity, while the need for social solidarity causes the division of labor. In such an argument, just what causes what becomes unclear.

The model in Figure 11–1 thus contains some suggestive ideas, particularly the notion that material density causes moral density, that moral density causes competition, that competition causes differentiation, and that differentiation causes new mechanisms of integration. But on the other hand, without specifying the conditions under which (a) moral density causes competition, (b) competition causes differentiation, and (c) differentiation causes new integrative processes, the model is vague. Yet as our concluding remarks in this chapter will

---

[21]Ibid., pp. 266–67.

FIGURE 11-1 Durkheim's Causal Model of the Division of Labor

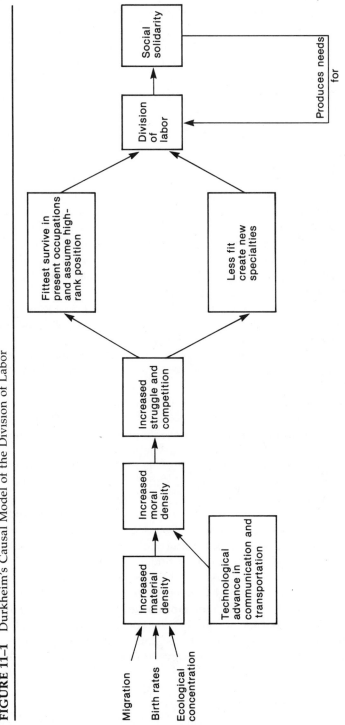

illustrate, there is still great power in these causal statements. In our view they do constitute one of the lawlike properties of the social universe. The problems emerge as Durkheim sought to perform functional analysis. Let us explore, then, why Durkheim was led to embrace functionalism.

Social Functions

As we observed in the discussion of Spencer's sociology in Chapter 3, Spencer clearly formulated the notions of structure and function, with functions assessed in terms of the needs of the social organism being met by a structure. Durkheim appears to have borrowed these ideas and, indeed, opened *The Division of Labor* with an assessment of its functions.[22] The function of the division of labor is to promote social solidarity, or societal integration. Such functional analysis, Durkheim argued, must be kept separate from causal analysis. It will be recalled from the previous chapter that Durkheim was highly critical of Montesquieu's analysis in terms of "final causes" or functions. And thus, in his first major work, Durkheim attempted to keep his functional and causal analyses separated. But, as the model in Figure 11–1 illustrates, Durkheim was less than successful in maintaining such separation.

We might now ask a more fundamental question: Why did Durkheim engage in functional analysis at all? That is, why did he feel it necessary to determine the consequences for society of the division of labor? In his Latin thesis, Durkheim had been highly critical of Montesquieu for not separating his scientific observations from his personal feelings about what society should be. However, Durkheim was more sympathetic to Comte, who explicitly argued that the science of society could be used to create a better society. It was thus in the French tradition—Montesquieu, Rousseau, Saint-Simon, and Comte— to seek a better society. Beginning with Comte and culminating with Durkheim, then, scholars felt an understanding of the laws of society could be used to create a new and better society.

Yet Durkheim wanted to keep the science of sociology separated from such disciplines as moral philosophy and ethics. He had utter contempt for what he saw as the idle speculation and moral imperialism of these and related disciplines. Rather he had a vision of sociology as like the applied side of biology—that is, sociologists could be the "physicians of society."

---

[22]For a more detailed analysis of Durkheim's debt to Spencer and of his contribution to functionalism, see Jonathan H. Turner and Alexandra Maryanski, *Functionalism* (Menlo Park, Calif.: Benjamin/Cummings, 1979).

The concept of function was central to this vision, especially in conjunction with the related notions of societal types. By assessing what a structure "does for" a society of a particular type or at a specific stage of evolution, one is in a position to determine what is "normal" and "abnormal" for that society—a point that Comte had first made in his advocacy of the experimental method as it could be used in sociology. The concept of function allowed Durkheim to judge whether a structure, such as the division of labor, is functioning normally for a particular type of society. And hence, to the degree that the division of labor fails to promote societal integration or social solidarity in a society, Durkheim viewed that society as in a "pathological" state and in need of alterations to restore "normality" to the "body social." These considerations led Durkheim to analyze "abnormal forms" of the division of labor at the close of this first major work, since abnormality of structures can only be determined in reference to their "normal functions."

Pathology and Abnormal Forms

Durkheim opened his discussion of abnormal forms with the following statement:

> Up to now, we have studied the division of labor only as a normal phenomenon, but, like all social facts, and, more generally, all biological facts, it presents pathological forms which must be analyzed. Though normally the division of labor produces social solidarity, it sometimes happens that it has different, and even contrary results.[23]

Durkheim isolated three abnormal forms: (1) the anomic division of labor, (2) the forced division of labor, and (3) the inadequately coordinated division of labor. In discussing these abnormal forms, he drew considerable inspiration from his French predecessors, particularly Rousseau and Tocqueville, while carrying on a silent dialogue with Marx and other socialists. Thus Durkheim's analysis of abnormal forms represents his effort to address issues that had been discussed and debated for several previous generations of intellectuals. Indeed individuals' isolation, their detachment from society, their sense of alienation, their exploitation by the powerful, and related issues had been hotly debated in both intellectual and lay circles. Yet while Durkheim's selection of topics is not unique, his conclusions and their theoretical implications are highly original.

The Anomic Division of Labor. The concept of anomie (or anomy) was not well developed in *The Division of Labor*. Only later, in the

---

[23]Durkheim, *Division of Labor*, p. 353.

1897 work *Suicide*, did this concept become theoretically significant. Durkheim's discussion in *The Division of Labor* is explicitly directed at Comte, who had noted the essence of the basic dilemma confronting organic social systems. As Comte had stated:

> From the moral point of view, while each individual is thus made closely dependent on the mass, he is naturally drawn away from it by the nature of his special activity, constantly reminding him of his private interests, which he only very dimly perceives to be related to the public.[24]

For Durkheim, this dilemma was expressed in terms of maintaining individuals' commitment to a common set of values and beliefs, while at the same time allowing them to pursue their specialized interests. At this stage in Durkheim's thinking, anomie represented insufficient normative regulation of individuals' activities, with the result that they do not feel attached to the collectivity.

Anomie is inevitable when the transformation of societies from a mechanical to an organic basis of social solidarity is rapid and causes the "generalization" or "enfeeblement" of values. With value-generalization, individuals' attachment to, and regulation by, these values is lessened. The results of this anomic situation are diverse. One result is that individuals feel alienated since their only attachment is to the monotony and crushing schedule dictated by the machines of the industrial age. Another is the escalated frustrations and the sense of deprivation, manifested by increased incidence of revolt, that come in a state of underregulation.

Unlike Marx, however, Durkheim did not consider these consequences inevitable. He rejected the notion that there are inherent contradictions in capitalism, for "if, in certain cases, organic solidarity is not all it should be . . . [it is] because all the conditions for the existence of organic solidarity have not been realized."[25] Nor would he accept Comte's or Rousseau's solution to anomie: the establishment of a strong and somewhat dictatorial central organ, the state.

Yet in the first edition of *The Division of Labor*, Durkheim's own solution is vague, since the solution to anomie involves reintegration of individuals into the collective life by virtue of their interdependence with other specialists and the common goals that all members of a society ultimately pursue.[26] In many ways this line of argument substitutes for Adam Smith's invisible hand of order the "invisible power of the collective" without specifying how this integration into the collective is to occur.

24Quoted in Lukes, *Émile Durkheim*, p.141.
25Durkheim, *Division of Labor*, pp. 364–65.
26Ibid., pp. 372–73.

Durkheim recognized the inadequacy of this solution to the problem of anomie. Moreover, his more detailed analysis of anomie in *Suicide* (1897) must have further underscored the limitations of his analysis in *The Division of Labor.* Thus the second edition of *The Division of Labor,* published in 1902, contained a long preface that sought to specify the mechanism by which anomie is to be curbed. This mechanism is the "occupational" or "corporate" group.[27]

Durkheim recognized that industrialism, urbanization, occupational specialization, and the growth of the bureaucratized state all operate to lessen the functions of family, religion, region, and neighborhood as mechanisms promoting the integration of individuals into the societal collectivity. And with the generalization and enfeeblement of the collective conscience, coupled with the potential isolation of individuals in an occupational specialty, Durkheim saw that new structures would have to evolve in order to avoid anomie. These structures promote social solidarity in several ways: (1) they organize occupational specialties into a collective; (2) they bridge the widening gap between the remote state and the specific needs and desires of the individual; and (3) they provide a functional alternative to the old loyalties generated by religion, regionalism, and kinship. These new intermediate structures are not only occupational but also political and moral groupings that lace together specialized occupations, counterbalance the power of the state, and provide specific interpretations for the more abstract values and beliefs of the collective conscience.

As is evident, Durkheim had taken the idea of "occupational groups" from Tocqueville's analysis of intermediate organizations in America (see Chapter 10). But he extended the concept considerably, and in so doing, he posited a conception of how a society should be economically, politically, and morally organized.[28] Economically, occupational groups would bring together related occupational specialties into an organization that could set working hours and wage levels and that could bargain with management of corporations and government.

Politically, the occupational group would become a kind of political party whose representatives would participate in government. Like most French scholars in the post-revolutionary era, Durkheim distrusted mass democracy, since short-term individual passions and moods can render the state helpless in setting and reaching long-range goals. He also distrusted an all-powerful and bureaucratized state, because its remote structure is too insensitive and cumbersome to deal

---

[27]Ibid., pp. 1–31.

[28]We are supplementing Durkheim's discussion of occupational groups with additional works; see Émile Durkheim, *Professional Ethics and Civil Morals* (Boston: Routledge & Kegan Paul, 1957), and his *Socialism and Saint-Simon* (Yellow Springs, Ohio: Antioch Press, 1958).

with the specific needs and problems of diverse individuals. Moreover, Durkheim saw that unchecked state power inevitably leads to abuses—an emphasis that comes close to Montesquieu's idea of a balance of powers in government. Thus the power of the state must be checked by intermediate groups, which channel public sentiment to the state and administer the policies of the state for a particular constituency.[29]

Morally, occupational groups are to provide many of the recreational, educational, and social functions formerly performed by family, neighborhood, and church. By bringing together people who, because they belong to related occupations, are likely to have common experiences, occupational groups can provide a place where people feel integrated into the society and where the psychological tensions and monotony of their specialized jobs can be mitigated. Moreover, these groups can make the generalized values and beliefs of the entire society relevant to the life experiences of each individual. Through the vehicle of occupational groups, then, an entire society of specialists can be reattached to the collective conscience.[30]

Inequality and the Forced Division of Labor.   Borrowing heavily from Rousseau, Saint-Simon, and Comte, but reacting to Marx, Durkheim saw inequalities based on ascription and inheritance of privilege as "abnormal." He advocated an inheritance tax that would eliminate the passing of wealth, and indeed he felt that in the normal course of things, this would come about. But unlike Marx, he had no distaste for the accumulation of capital and privilege, as long as it was earned and not inherited.

What Durkheim desired was for the division of labor and inequalities in privilege to correspond to differences in people's ability. For Durkheim, it was abnormal in organic societies for wealth to be inherited and for this inherited privilege to be used by one class to oppress and exploit another. Such a situation represents a "forced division of labor," and in the context of analyzing this abnormality Durkheim examined explicitly Marxian ideas: (1) the value theory of labor and exploitation and (2) the domination of one class by another. Each of these is briefly examined below.

1. Durkheim felt the price one pays for a good or service should be proportional to the "useful labor which it contains."[31] To

---

[29]"Preface to the Second Edition," in Durkheim, *Division of Labor,* p. 28.

[30]Durkheim rarely addressed Marx directly. Though he wanted to devote a special course to Marx's ideas in addition to his course on Saint-Simon and socialism, he never got around to doing this. Yet, much as with Weber, one suspects Durkheim's discussion of "abnormal forms" represented a silent dialogue with Marx.

[31]Durkheim, *Division of Labor,* p. 382.

the degree that this is not so, he argued, an abnormal condition prevails. What is necessary, and inevitable in the long run, is for buyers and sellers to be "placed in conditions externally equal"[32] in which the price charged for a good or service corresponds to the "socially useful labor" in it and where no seller or buyer enjoys an advantage or monopoly that would allow prices to exceed socially useful labor.

2. Durkheim recognized that as long as there is inherited privilege, especially wealth, one class can exploit and dominate another. Durkheim felt that the elimination of inheritance was inevitable, since people could no longer be duped by a strong collective conscience into accepting privilege and exploitation (a position that parallels Marx's notion of false consciousness). For as religious and family bonds decrease in salience, and as individuals are liberated from mechanical solidarity, people can liberate themselves from the beliefs that have often been used to legitimate exploitation.

Durkheim was certainly naive in his assumption that these aspects of the forced division of labor would, like Marx's state, "wither away." What Durkheim saw as normal was a situation that sounds reminiscent of Adam Smith's utilitarian vision.[33]

Lack of Coordination.   Durkheim termed the lack of coordination *another abnormal form* and did not devote much space to its analysis.[34] At times, Durkheim noted, specialization of tasks is not accompanied by sufficient coordination, creating a situation where energy is wasted and individuals feel poorly integrated into the collective flow of life. In Durkheim's view specialization must be "continuous," where functions are highly coordinated and where individuals are laced together through their mutual interdependence. Such a state, Durkheim argued, would be achieved as the natural and normal processes creating organic solidarity become dominant in modern society.

On this note, *The Division of Labor* ends. Durkheim's next major work, published two years after *The Division of Labor,* sought to make assumptions and methodological guidelines implicit in *The Division of Labor* more explicit. *The Rules of the Sociological Method* (1895), as we will come to see, represents a methodological interlude in Durkheim's efforts to understand how and why patterns of social organization are created, maintained, and changed.

---

[32]Ibid., p. 383.
[33]Ibid., p. 377.
[34]Ibid., pp. 389–95.

THE RULES OF THE SOCIOLOGICAL METHOD

The Rules of the Sociological Method is both a philosophical treatise and set of guidelines for conducting sociological inquiry.[35] Durkheim appears to have written the book for at least three reasons.[36] First, he sought intellectual justification for his approach to studying the social world, especially as evidenced in *The Division of Labor*. Second, he wanted to persuade a hostile academic community as to the legitimacy of sociology as a distinctive science. And third, because he wanted to found a school of scholars, he needed a manifesto to attract and guide potential converts to the science of sociology. The chapter titles of *The Rules* best communicate Durkheim's intent: (1) "What Is a Social Fact?" (2) "Rules for the Observation of Social Facts," (3) "Rules for Distinguishing between the Normal and the Pathological," (4) "Rules for the Classification of Social Types," (5) "Rules for the Explanation of Social Facts," and (6) "Rules Relative to Establishing Sociological Proofs." Each of these is examined below.

What Is a Social Fact?

As we have already observed, Durkheim was engaged in a battle to establish the legitimacy of sociology. In *The Division of Labor* he had proclaimed "moral facts" to be sociology's subject matter, but in *The Rules* he changed his terminology to that employed earlier by Comte and argued that "social facts" are the distinctive subject matter of sociology. For Durkheim, a social fact "consists of ways of acting, thinking, and feeling, external to the individual, and endowed with power of coercion, by which they control him."[37]

In this definition Durkheim lumped behaviors, thoughts, and emotions together as the subject matter of sociology. The morphological and symbolic structures in which individuals participate are thus to be the focus of sociology, but social facts are, by virtue of transcending any single individual, "external" and "constraining." They are external in two senses:

1. Individuals are born into an established set of structures and an existing system of values, beliefs, and norms. Hence these structural and symbolic "facts" are initially external to individuals; and as people learn to play roles in social structures, to abide by norms,

---

[35]Émile Durkheim, *The Rules of Sociological Method* (New York: Free Press, 1938; originally published in 1895).

[36]Lukes, *Émile Durkheim*, chap. 10.

[37]Durkheim, *The Rules*, p. 3.

and to accept basic values, they feel and sense "something" outside of them.

2. Even when humans actively and collaboratively create social structures, values, beliefs, and norms, their "nature is not different," for once created they become an emergent reality that is external to any single individual.

This externality is accompanied by a sense of constraint and coercion. The structures, norms, values, and beliefs of the social world compel certain actions, thoughts, and dispositions. They impose limits, and when deviations occur, sanctions are applied to the deviants. Moreover, social facts are "internalized" in that people want and desire to be a part of social structures and to accept the norms, values, and beliefs of the collective. In the 1895 edition of *The Rules*, this point had been underemphasized, and thus in the second edition Durkheim noted that:

> Institutions may impose themselves upon us, but we cling to them; they compel us, and we love them.[38]

> [Social facts] dominate us and impose beliefs and practices upon us. But they rule us from within, for they are in every case an integral part of ourself.[39]

Durkheim thus asserted that when individuals come into collaboration, a new reality consisting of social and symbolic structures emerges. This emergent reality cannot be reduced to individual psychology, because it is external to, and constraining on, any single individual. And yet, like all social facts, it is registered on the individual and often "rules the individual from within." Having established that sociology has a distinct subject matter—social facts—the rest of the book is devoted to explicating rules for studying and explaining social facts.

Rules for Observing Social Facts

Durkheim offered several guidelines for observing social facts: (1) Personal biases and preconceptions must be eliminated. (2) The phenomena under study must be clearly defined. (3) An empirical indicator of the phenomenon under study must be found, as was the case for "law" in *The Division of Labor*. (4) And in a manner reminiscent of Montesquieu, social facts must be considered as "things." Social facts

---

[38]Ibid., footnote 5.
[39]Ibid., "Preface to Second Edition," p. 7.

are things in two different, although related, ways. First, when a phenomenon is viewed as a thing, it is possible to assume "a particular mental attitude" toward it. We can search for the properties and characteristics of a thing and we can draw verifiable conclusions about its nature. Such a position was highly controversial in Durkheim's time, since moral phenomena—values, ideas, morals—were often not considered as proper topics of scientific inquiry, and when they were, they were seen as a subarea in the study of individual psychology. Second, Durkheim said phenomena such as morality, values, beliefs, and dogmas constitute a distinctive metaphysical reality, not reducible to individual psychology. And hence they can be approached with the same scientific methods as any material phenomenon in the universe.[40]

Rules for Distinguishing between the Normal and the Pathological

Throughout his career, Durkheim never wavered from Comte's position that science is to be used to serve human ends:

> Why strive for knowledge of reality if this knowledge cannot serve us in life? To this we can make reply that, by revealing the causes of phenomena, science furnishes the means of producing them.[41]

To use scientific knowledge to implement social conditions requires a knowledge of what is normal and pathological. Otherwise, one would not know what social facts to create and implement, or one might actually create a pathological condition. To determine normality, the best procedure, Durkheim argued, is to discover what is most frequent and typical of societies of a given type, or at a given stage of evolution. That which deviates significantly from this average is pathological.

Such a position allowed Durkheim to make some startling conclusions for his time. In regard to deviance, for example, a particular rate of crime and some other form of deviance could be normal for certain types of societies. Abnormality is present only when rates of deviance exceed what is typical of a certain societal type.

Rules for the Classification of Social Types

Durkheim's evolutionary perspective, coupled with his strategy for diagnosing normality and pathology in social systems, made inevitable a concern with social classification. While specific systems reveal

---

[40]Many commentators, such as Giddens, *Capitalism and Modern Theory,* and Lukes, *Émile Durkheim,* emphasize that Durkheim was not making a metaphysical statement. We think he was making both a metaphysical and methodological statement.

[41]Durkheim, *The Rules,* p. 48.

considerable variability, it is possible to group them into general types on the basis of (*a*) the "nature" and "number" of their parts and (*b*) the "mode of combination" of parts.

In this way, Durkheim believed, societies that reveal superficial differences can be seen as belonging to a particular class or type. Moreover, by ignoring the distracting complexities of a society's "content" and "uniqueness," it is possible to establish the stage of evolutionary development of a society.

Rules for the Explanation of Social Facts

Durkheim emphasized again a point he made in *The Division of Labor:*

> When the explanation of social phenomena is undertaken, we must seek separately the efficient cause which produces it and the function it fulfills.[42]

Causal analysis involves searching for antecedent conditions that produce a given effect. Functional analysis is concerned with determining the consequences of a social fact (regardless of its cause) for the social whole or larger context in which it is located. Complete sociological explanation involves both causal and functional explanations, as Durkheim had sought to illustrate in *The Division of Labor* (see Figure 11–1).

Rules for Establishing Sociological Proofs

Durkheim advocated two basic procedures for establishing "sociological proofs"—proofs being documentation that causal and, by implication, functional explanations are correct. One procedure involves comparing two or more societies of a given type (as determined by the rules for classification) in order to see if one fact, present in one but not the other(s), leads to differences in these otherwise similar societies.

The second procedure is the method of concomitant variation. If two social facts are correlated and one is assumed to cause the other, and if all alternative facts that might also be considered causative cannot eliminate the correlation, then it can be asserted that a causal explanation has been "proven." But if an established correlation, and presumed causal relation, can be explained away by the operation of another social fact, then the established explanation has been disproven and the new social fact can, until similarly disproven, be considered "proven." The essence of Durkheim's method of concomitant

---

[42]Ibid., p. 95.

variation, then, was similar in intent to modern multivariate analyses: to assert a relation among variables, controlling for the impact of other variables.[43]

The Rules marks a turning point in Durkheim's intellectual career. It was written after his thesis on the division of labor and while he was pondering the question of suicide in his lectures. Yet it was written before his first public course on religion.[44] Durkheim had clearly established his guiding theoretical interests: the nature of social organization and its relationship to values, beliefs, and other symbolic systems. He had developed a clear methodology: asking causal and functional questions within a broad comparative, historical, and evolutionary framework. He had begun to win respect in intellectual and academic circles for the fact that social organization represents an emergent reality, sui generis, and that it is the proper subject matter for a discipline called sociology.

His next work appears to have been an effort to demonstrate the utility of his methodological and ontological advocacy. For he sought to understand sociologically a phenomenon that, at the time, was considered uniquely psychological: suicide. In this work Durkheim attempted to demonstrate the power of sociological investigation of seemingly psychological phenomena, employing social facts as explanatory variables. But far more important than the specifics of suicide, we believe, is the fact that Durkheim extended concepts introduced in *The Division of Labor,* and in so doing he presented additional theoretical principles on why patterns of social organization are created, maintained, and changed.

SUICIDE

In *Suicide* Durkheim self-consciously appeared to follow the "rules" of his sociological method.[45] He was interested in studying only a social fact, and hence he did not study individual suicides but rather the general pervasiveness of suicide in a population—that is, a society's aggregate tendency toward suicide. In this way suicide could be considered as a social rather than individual fact, and it could be approached as a "thing." Suicide is clearly defined as "all causes of death resulting directly or indirectly from a positive or negative act of the

---

[43]Durkheim made other assertions: A social fact can only have one cause, and this cause must be another social fact (as opposed to an individual or psychological fact).

[44]Lukes, *Émile Durkheim,* p. 227.

[45]Émile Durkheim, *Suicide: A Study in Sociology* (New York: Free Press, 1951; originally published in 1897).

victim himself which he knows will produce this result."[46] The statistical rate of suicide is then used as the indicator of this social fact.[47] Suicide is classified into four types: egoistic, altruistic, anomic, and fatalistic. The cause of these types is specified in terms of the degree and nature of individual integration into the social collective. And a variant of modern correlational techniques is employed to demonstrate or "prove" that other hypothesized causes of suicide are spurious and that integration into social and symbolic structures is the key explanatory variable.

The statistical manipulations in *Suicide* are important because they represent the first systematic effort to apply correlational and contingency techniques to causal explanation. Our concern, however, is with the theoretical implications of this work, and hence the following summary will focus on theoretical rather than statistical issues.

Types of Suicide

Durkheim isolated four types of suicide in terms of varying causes. We should emphasize that despite Durkheim's statistical footwork, isolating types in terms of causes, and then explaining these types in terms of the causes used to classify them, is a suspicious, if not spurious, way to go about understanding the social world. But these flaws aside, Durkheim's analysis clarified notions of social integration that are somewhat vague in *The Division of Labor*. Basically, Durkheim argued that suicides can be classified in terms of the nature of an individual's integration into the social fabric. There are, in Durkheim's eye, two types of integration:

1. *Attachment* to social groups and their goals. Such attachment involves the maintenance of interpersonal ties and the perception that one is a part of a larger collectivity.

2. *Regulation* by the collective conscience (values, beliefs, and general norms) of social groupings. Such regulation limits individual aspirations and needs, keeping them in check.

In distinguishing these two bases of integration, Durkheim was explicitly recognizing the different "functions" of the morphological and symbolic elements of the social world. Interpersonal ties that bind individuals to the collective operate to keep them from becoming too

---

[46]Ibid., p. 44.

[47]Ibid., p. 48. It should be emphasized that suicide had been subject to extensive statistical analysis during Durkheim's time, and thus Durkheim was able to borrow the data compiled by others.

"egoistic"—a concept borrowed from Tocqueville and widely discussed in Durkheim's time. Unless individuals can be attached to a larger collective and its goals, they become egoistic or self-centered in ways that are highly destructive to their psychological well-being. In contrast, the regulation of individuals' aspirations, which are potentially infinite, operates to prevent anomie (or anomy). Without symbolic constraints, individual aspirations, as Rousseau[48] and Tocqueville had emphasized, escalate and create perpetual misery for individuals who pursue goals that constantly recede as they are approached. These two varying bases of individual integration into society, then, form the basis for Durkheim's classification of four types of suicide—egoistic, altruistic, anomic, and fatalistic. Each is briefly discussed below.

Egoistic Suicide.   When a person's ties to groups and collectivities are weakened, then there is the potential for excessive individualism and hence egoistic suicide. Durkheim stated this relation as a clear proposition: "Suicide varies inversely with the degree of integration of social groups of which the individual forms a part."[49] And as a result:

> The more weakened the groups to which he belongs, the less he depends on them, the more he consequently depends only on himself and recognizes no other rules of conduct than what are founded on private interest. If we agree to call this state egoism, in which the individual ego asserts itself to excess in the face of the social ego and at its expense, we may call egoistic the special type of suicide springing from excessive individualism.[50]

Altruistic Suicide.   If the degree of individual integration into the group is visualized as a variable continuum, ranging from egoism on the one pole to a complete fusion of the individual with the collective at the other pole, then the essence of Durkheim's next form of suicide can be captured. Altruistic suicide is the result of individuals being so attached to the group that, for the good of the group, they commit suicide. In such a situation individuals count for little; the group is paramount, with individuals subordinating their interests to those of the group. Durkheim distinguished three types of altruistic suicide:

1. *Obligatory altruistic suicide*—where individuals are obliged, under certain circumstances, to commit suicide.

---

[48]As Rousseau noted: "The more one has, the more one wants." This view of humans, we should note, is very similar to that of Marx.

[49]Durkheim, *Suicide*, p. 209.

[50]Ibid.

2. *Optional altruistic suicide*—where individuals are not obligated to commit suicide, but where it is the custom for them to do so under certain conditions.

3. *Acute altruistic suicide*—where the individual "kills himself purely for the joy of sacrifice, because, even with no particular reason, renunciation in itself is considered praiseworthy."[51]

In sum, then, egoistic and altruistic suicides result from either overintegration or underintegration into the collective. Altruistic suicide tends to occur in traditional systems—what Durkheim termed *mechanical* in *The Division of Labor*—and egoistic suicide is more frequent in modern, organic systems that reveal high degrees of individual autonomy. But at the more abstract level, Durkheim is positing a critical dimension of individual and societal integration: the maintenance of interpersonal bonds within coherent group structures.

Anomic Suicide. In *The Division of Labor* Durkheim's conceptualization of anomie was somewhat vague. In many ways he incorporated both anomie (deregulation by symbols) and egoism (detachment from structural relations in groups) into the original definition of anomie. But in *Suicide* Durkheim clarified this ambiguity in that anomic suicide came to be viewed narrowly as the result of deregulation of individuals' desires and passions. Although both egoistic and anomic suicide "spring from society's insufficient presence in individuals,"[52] the nature of the disjuncture or deficiency between the individual and society differs.

> In egoistic suicide it is deficient in truly collective activity, thus depriving the latter of object and meaning. In anomic suicide, society's influence is lacking in the basically individual passions, thus leaving them without a check-rein.[53]

Fatalistic Suicide. Durkheim discussed this form of suicide in a short footnote. Just as altruism is the polar opposite of egoism, so fatalism is the opposite of anomie. Fatalistic suicide is the result of "excessive regulation, that of persons with futures pitilessly blocked and passions violently choked by oppressive discipline."[54] Thus when individuals are overregulated by norms, beliefs, and values in their

---

[51]Ibid., p. 223.
[52]Ibid., p. 258.
[53]Ibid.
[54]Ibid., p. 276, in footnote.

social relations, and when they have no individual freedom, discretion, or autonomy in their social relations, then they are potential victims of fatalistic suicide.

Suicide and Social Integration

These types of suicide reveal a great deal about Durkheim's conception of humans and the social order. With respect to human nature, the study of suicide allows us a glimpse at how Durkheim conceived of humans. Reading between the lines in *Suicide,* the following features of human nature are posited:

1. Humans can potentially reveal unlimited desires and passions, which must be regulated and held in check.
2. Yet total regulation of passions and desires creates a situation where life loses all meaning.
3. Humans need interpersonal attachments and a sense that these attachments connect them to collective purposes.
4. Yet excessive attachment can undermine personal autonomy to the point where life loses meaning for the individual.[55]

These implicit notions of human nature, it should be emphasized, involve a vision of the "normal" way in which individuals are integrated into the morphological and symbolic structures of society. Indeed Durkheim was unable to even address the question of human nature without also talking about the social order. For Durkheim, the social order is maintained only to the degree that individuals are attached to, and regulated by, patterns of collective organization. This fact was to lead Durkheim in his later career to explore in more detail an essentially social-psychological question: In what ways do individuals become attached to society and willing to be regulated by its symbolic elements?

Suicide and Deviance

Durkheim made an effort to see if other forms of deviance, such as homicide and crime, are related to suicide rates, but the details of his correlations are not as important as the implications of his analysis for a general theory of deviance. As he had in *The Division of Labor,* Durkheim recognized that a society of a certain type will reveal a "typical" or "average" level of deviance, whether suicide or some other form. However, when rates of suicide, or deviance in general, exceed

---

[55]See also Lukes, *Émile Durkheim,* chap. 9, for a similar but different discussion.

certain average levels for a societal type, then a "pathological" condition prevails.

Durkheim's great contribution was to recognize that deviance is caused by the same forces that maintain conformity in social systems. Moreover, he specified the key variables in understanding both conformity and deviance: (1) the degree of group attachment and (2) the degree of value and normative regulation. Thus excessive or insufficient attachment and regulation will cause varying forms of deviance in a social system. Moreover, the more a system reveals moderate degrees of regulation and attachment, the less likely are pathological rates of deviance and the greater is the social integration of individuals into the system.

Thus Durkheim's analysis in *Suicide* is much more than a statistical analysis of a narrowly defined topic. It is also a venture into understanding how social organization is possible. This fact becomes particularly evident near the end of the book, where Durkheim proposes his solution to the high rates of suicide and other forms of deviance that typify modern or "organically" structured societies.

Suicide and the Social Organization of Organic Societies[56]

At the end of *Suicide* Durkheim abandoned his cross-sectional statistical analysis and returned to the evolutionary perspective contained in *The Division of Labor.* During social change, as societies move from one basis of social solidarity, deregulation (anomie) and detachment (egoism) of the individual from society can occur, especially if this transition is rapid. Deregulation and detachment create not only high rates of deviance but also problems in maintaining the social order. If these problems are to be avoided and if social "normality" is to be restored, new structures that provide attachment and regulation of individuals to society must be created.

In a series of enlightening pages, Durkheim analyzed the inability of traditional social structures to provide this new basis of social integration. The family is an insufficiently encompassing social structure; religious structures are similarly too limited in their scope and too oriented to the sacred; and government is too bureaucratized and hence remote from the individual. For Durkheim, the implications of these facts are that modern social structures require intermediate groups to replace the declining influence of family and religion, to mediate between the individual and state, and to check the growing power of the

---

[56]Durkheim dropped the term *organic societies,* but we have retained the term here to emphasize the continuity between *Suicide* and *The Division of Labor.*

state. The occupational group was seen by Durkheim as the only potential structural unit that could regulate and attach individuals to society.

Thus, in *Suicide*, the ideas that were later to be placed in the 1902 preface to the second edition of *The Division of Labor* find their first forceful expression. And while suicide is, on the surface, a social-psychological study,[57] the issue of how social order is possible remains the central focus of the book. The analysis of suicide allowed Durkheim to explore further the concept of social integration, and for this reason *Suicide* represents both an application of the method advocated in *The Rules* and a clarification of substantive ideas contained in *The Division of Labor.*

THE ELEMENTARY FORMS OF RELIGIOUS LIFE

Although Durkheim turned to the study of religion in his last major work, it had been an important interest for a long time. Indeed his family background assured that religion would be a central concern; and from 1895 on, he had taught courses on religion.[58] Regardless of any biographical reasons for his interest, we suspect Durkheim pursued the study of religion over most of his career because it allowed him to gain insight into the basic theoretical problem that guided all of his work: the nature of symbols and the reciprocal effects with social organization. In *The Division of Labor* he had argued that in mechanical societies the collective conscience is religious in content and that it integrates the individual into the collective. But he had recognized that in organic systems, the collective conscience becomes "enfeebled," and religion as a pervasive influence recedes. The potential pathologies that can occur with the transition from mechanical to organic solidarity— particularly anomie—became increasingly evident to Durkheim. Indeed the naive optimism that these pathologies would "spontaneously" wither away became increasingly untenable, and as is evident in *Suicide*, Durkheim began to ponder how to create a social system in which individuals are both regulated by a general set of values and attached to concrete groups. As Durkheim came to view the matter, these concerns revolved around the more general problem of "morality."

Durkheim never wrote what was to be the culmination of his life's work: a book on morality. But in many ways, his study of religion rep-

---

[57]Durkheim would, of course, not admit to this label.

[58]Émile Durkheim, *The Elementary Forms of Religious Life* (New York: Free Press, 1947; originally published in 1912).

resents the beginning of his formal work on morality. While he had lectured on morality in his courses on education[59] and had written several articles on morality,[60] he saw in religion a chance to study how interaction among individuals leads to the creation of symbolic systems that (a) lace together individual actions into collective units, (b) regulate and control individual desires, and (c) attach individuals to both the symbolic and structural (morphological) facets of the social world. In the face of anomie and egoism, Durkheim thought an understanding of religious morality in primitive social systems would throw light on how such morality could be created in modern, differentiated systems. Thus we could retitle *The Elementary Forms of Religious Life* "the fundamental forms of moral integration" and be close to Durkheim's major purpose in examining religion in primitive societies, particularly the Arunta aborigines of Australia.[61]

In the course of writing what was his longest work, however, Durkheim introduced many other intellectual issues that had come to occupy his attention over the years. Thus *Elementary Forms* is more than a study of social integration; it is also an excursion into human evolution, the sociology of knowledge, functional and causal analyses, the origin and basis of thought and mental categories, the process of internalization of beliefs and values, and many other issues. Between the long descriptive passages on tribal life among the Australian tribes, a myriad of ideas burst forth and give evidence of the wide-ranging concerns of Durkheim's intellect.

Elementary Forms is thus a long, complex, and, unlike his earlier works, less coherently organized book. This fact requires that the analysis be divided into a number of separate topics. After a brief overview of the argument in *Elementary Forms,* we will examine in more detail some of its implications.

---

[59]The work on "moral education" will be examined later in this chapter in a discussion of Durkheim's more general concern with "morality."

[60]See, for example, Émile Durkheim, "The Determination of Moral Facts," *Sociology and Philosophy,* trans. D. F. Poccock (New York: Free Press, 1974). This article was originally published in 1906.

[61]Baldwin Spencer and F. J. Gillian, *The Native Tribes of Central Australia* (New York: Macmillan, 1899), presented the first collection of "accounts" of these primitive peoples, which was in itself fascinating to urbane Europeans. Sigmund Freud, in *Totem and Taboo* (New York: Penguin Books, 1938; originally published in 1913); and anthropologists, Bronislaw Malinowski, in *The Family among the Australian Aborigines* (New York: Schocken, 1963; originally published in 1913); and A. R. Radcliffe-Brown, in "Three Tribes of Western Australia," *Journal of Royal Anthropological Institute of Great Britain and Ireland* 43, 1913, were all preparing works on the aborigines of Australia at the same time Durkheim was writing *The Elementary Forms of Religious Life.*

The Elementary Forms of Religious Life: **An Overview**

By studying the elementary forms of religion among the most primitive[62] peoples, it should be possible, Durkheim felt, to understand the essence of religious phenomena, without the distracting complexities and socio-cultural overlays of modern social systems.[63] As dictated in *The Rules,* a clear definition of the phenomenon under study was first necessary. Thus Durkheim defined religion as:

> A unified system of beliefs and practices relative to sacred things, that is to say, things set apart and forbidden—beliefs and practices which unite into one single moral community called a Church, all those who adhere to them.[64]

Durkheim believed religiosity first emerged among humans when they would occasionally assemble in a larger mass. Out of the mutual stimulation and "effervescence" that comes from animated interaction, people came to perceive a force, or "mana," that seemed superior to them. The mutual stimulation of primitive peoples thus made them "feel" an "external" and "constraining" force above and beyond them.[65] This force seemed to be embued with special significance and with a sense that it was not part of this world. It was, then, the first notion of a "sacred" realm distinct from the routine or "secular" world of daily activities. The distinction between sacred and secular was thus one of the first sets of mental categories possessed by humans in their evolutionary development.

As humans came to form more permanent groupings or clans, the force that emerges out of their interaction needed to be more concretely represented.[66] Such representation came with "totems," which are an-

---

[62]Obviously Durkheim was wrong on this account, but this was one of his assumptions.

[63]It should be noted that this strategy was the exact opposite of that employed by Max Weber, who examined the most complex systems of religion with his ideal-type methodology.

[64]Durkheim, *Elementary Forms,* p. 47. Durkheim's earlier definition of religious phenomena emphasized the sacred—beliefs and ritual—but did not stress the morphological units of community and church. For example, an early definition read: "Religious phenomena consist of obligatory beliefs united with divine practices which relate to the objects given in the beliefs." (Quoted in Lukes, *Émile Durkheim,* p. 241.) His exposure to the compilation in Spencer and Gillian, *Native Tribes,* apparently alerted him to these morphological features.

[65]Durkheim clearly borrowed the ideas of crowd behavior developed by Gustave LeBon and Gabriel Tarde, even though the latter was his lifelong intellectual enemy.

[66]Durkheim, in both *The Division of Labor* and *The Rules,* had stressed that the segmental clan was the most elementary society. The presocietal "mass" out of which the clan emerges was termed *the horde* by Durkheim.

imals and plants that symbolize the force of mana. In this way the sacred forces could be given concrete representation, and groups of people organized into "cults" could develop "ritual" activities directed toward the totem and indirectly toward the sacred force that they collectively sensed.

Thus the basic elements of religion are (1) the emergence of beliefs in the sacred, (2) the organization of people into cults, and (3) the emission of rituals or rites toward totems that represent the forces of the sacred realm. What the primitives did not recognize, Durkheim argued, is that in worshiping totems, they are worshiping society. Totemic cults are nothing but the material symbolization of a force created by their interaction and collective organization into clans.

As people first became organized into clans and associated totemic cults, and as they perceived a sacred realm that influenced events in the secular world, their first categories of thought were also formed. Notions of causality could emerge only after people perceived that sacred forces determine events in the secular world. And notions of time and space could only exist after the organization of clans and their totemic cults. According to Durkheim, the basic categories of human thought—cause, time, space, and so on—first emerged after people developed religion. And thus in an ultimate sense, science and all forms of thought have emerged from religion—a line of argument, we might note, reminiscent of Comte's law of the three stages. Prior to religion, humans experienced only physical sensations[67] from their physical environment; but with religion, their mental life became structured by categories. In Durkheim's view mental categories are the cornerstone of all thought, including scientific thought and reasoning. In looking back on *Elementary Forms* a year after its publication, Durkheim was still moved to conclude:

> The most essential notions of the human mind, notions of time, of space, of genus and species, of force and causality, of personality, those in a word, which the philosophers have labeled categories and which dominate the whole logical thought, have been elaborated in the very womb of religion. It is from religion that science has taken them.[68]

For Durkheim the cause of religion was the interaction among people created by their organization into the simplest form of society, the clan. The functions of religion are (*a*) to regulate human needs and

---

[67]As can be recalled, Durkheim takes this idea from Rousseau and his description of the "natural state of man."

[68]Quoted in Lukes, *Émile Durkheim* p. 445 (taken from *L'Année Sociologique,* 1913). This line of thought is simply Comte's idea of the movement of thought from the theological through metaphysical to positivistic.

actions through beliefs about the sacred and (b) to attach people, through ritual activities (rites) in cults, to the collective. Because they are internalized, religious beliefs generate needs for people to belong to cults and participate in rituals. And as people participate in rituals, they reaffirm these internalized beliefs and hence reinforce their regulation by, and attachment to, the dictates of the clan. Moreover, the molding of such basic mental categories as cause, time, and space by religious beliefs and cults functions to give people a common view of the world, thus facilitating their interaction and organization.

This line of argument is represented in Figure 11–2, where Durkheim's model on the origins of functions of religion is delineated. With respect to origins, Durkheim had an image of primitive peoples periodically migrating and concentrating themselves in temporary gatherings. Once gathered, increased interaction escalates collective emotions, which produce a sense that there is something external and constraining to each individual. This sense of constraint is given more articulate expression as a sacred force, or mana. This causal sequence occurs, Durkheim maintained, each time primitives gather in their periodic festivals. But once they come to form more permanent groupings, called clans, the force of mana is given more concrete expression as a sacred totem. The creation of, beliefs about, and rituals toward the totem function to promote clan solidarity.

This model is substantively inaccurate, as are all of Durkheim's intellectual expeditions into the origins of society. For example, clans were not the first kinship structure, and many primitives do not worship totems. These errors can be attributed to Durkheim's reliance on Australian aborigine kinship and religious organization, which, in many ways, deviate from modal patterns among hunting-and-gathering peoples. Aside from these factual errors, the same problems evident in the model of the division of labor resurface. First, the conditions under which any causal connection holds true are not specified. Second, the functions of religious totems (for social solidarity) are also what appear to promote their very creation. And in addition, a psychological need—the "primitive need" to make concrete and symbolize "mana"—is invoked to explain why totems emerge.

In light of these problems, it must be concluded that the model does not present any useful information in its causal format. But as a statement of relationships among rates of interaction, structural arrangements, emotional arousal, and symbolic representation, Durkheim's statements are suggestive and emphasize: (1) highly concentrated interactions increase collective sentiments, which mobilize actors' actions, (2) small social structures tend to develop symbols to represent their collective sentiments, and (3) these structures will evidence high rates of ritual activity to reinforce their members' commitment.

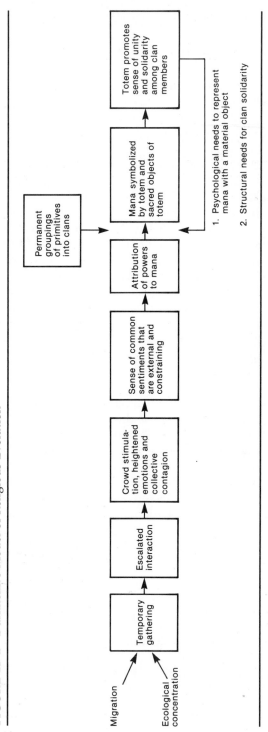

FIGURE 11–2 Durkheim's Model of Religious Evolution

341

Some Further Implications of *Elementary Forms*

Practical Concerns.   Durkheim's analysis of pathologies in *Suicide* had, along with other essays, forced the recognition that a more active program for avoiding egoism and anomie might be necessary to create a normal "organic" society. Religion, he thought, offered a key to understanding how this could be done. But early in his career, he had rejected the idea that religion could ever again assume major integrative functions. The modern world was too secular and individualistic for the subordination of individuals to gods. He had also rejected, to a much lesser degree, Saint-Simon's and Comte's wish to create a secular religion of humanity based on science and reason. While the functions of religion and the basic elements of religion needed to be maintained, Durkheim had difficulty accepting Comte's ideal of positivism, which, as Robert Nisbet notes, was "Catholicism minus Christianity." For Comte, the Grand Being was society, and the church was the hierarchy of the sciences, and the rites were the sacred canons of the positive method.[69] And yet neither could Durkheim accept Max Weber's pessimistic view of a secular, rational world filled with disenchantment and lacking in commitments to a higher purpose.

The "solution" implied in *Elementary Forms* and advocated elsewhere in various essays is for the re-creation in secular form of the basic elements of religion: the feeling of the sacred, beliefs and values about the sacred, common rituals directed toward the sacred, and cult structures in which these rituals and beliefs are reaffirmed. Since society is the source and object of religious activity anyway, the goal must be to make explicit this need to "worship" society. Occupational groups and the state would become the church and cults; nationalistic beliefs would become quasi sacred and would provide underlying symbols; and activities in occupational groups, when seen as furthering the collective goals of the nation, would assume the functions of religious ritual in (*a*) mobilization of individual commitment, (*b*) reaffirming beliefs and values, and (*c*) integrating individuals into the collective.

Theoretical Concerns.   Contained in these practical concerns are a number of important theoretical issues. First, integration of social structures presupposes a system of values and beliefs that reflects and symbolizes the structure of the collective. Second, these values and beliefs require rituals directed at reaffirming them as well as those social structures they represent or symbolize. Third, large collectivi-

---

[69]Nisbet, *Émile Durkheim*, p. 159.

ties, such as a nation, require subgroups in which values and beliefs can be affirmed by ritual activities among a more immediate community of individuals. And fourth, to the degree that values and beliefs do not correspond to actual structural arrangements and to the extent that substructures for the performance of actions that reaffirm these values and beliefs are not present, then a societal social system will experience integrative problems.

It can be seen, then, that Durkheim's practical concerns follow from certain theoretical principles he had tentatively put forth in *The Division of Labor*. The study of religion seemingly provided Durkheim with a new source of data to affirm the utility of his first insights into the social order. There are, however, some noticeable shifts in emphasis, the most important of which is the recognition that the "conscience collective" cannot be totally "enfeebled"; it must be general but also strong and relevant to the specific organization of a social system. Yet despite these refinements, *Elementary Forms* affirms the conclusion contained in the preface to the second edition of *The Division of Labor*.

The most interesting aspect of the analysis is perhaps the social psychological emphasis of *Elementary Forms*. While Durkheim, in courses and essays, had begun to feel comfortable with inquiry into the social psychological dynamics of social and symbolic structures, these concerns are brought together in this last major book.

Social Psychological Concerns. *Elementary Forms* contains the explicit recognition that morality—that is, values, beliefs, and norms—can only operate to integrate the social order if they become part of an individual's psychological structure. Statements in *Elementary Forms* mitigate the rather hard line taken in the first edition of *The Rules*, where social facts are seen as external and constraining things. With the second edition of *The Rules*, Durkheim felt more secure in verbalizing the obvious fact of internalization of values, beliefs, and other symbolic components of society into the human psyche. And in *Elementary Forms* he revealed even fewer reservations:

> For the collective force is not entirely outside of us; it does not act upon us wholly from without; but rather, since society cannot exist except in and through individual consciousnesses, this force must also penetrate us and organize itself within us, it thus becomes an integral part of our being.[70]

Durkheim hastened to add in a footnote, however, that although society is an "integral part of our being," it cannot ever be seen as reducible to individuals.

---

[70]Durkheim, *Elementary Forms*, p. 209.

Another social psychological concern in *Elementary Forms* is the issue of human thought processes. For Durkheim, thought occurs in terms of categories that structure experience for individuals.

> At the roots of all our judgments there are a certain number of essential ideas which dominate all our intellectual life; they are what philosophers since Aristotle have called the categories of the understanding: ideas of space, class, number, cause, substance, personality, etc. They correspond to the most universal properties of things. They are like the solid frame which encloses all thought.[71]

Durkheim had sought in *Elementary Forms* to reject the philosophical positions of David Hume and Immanuel Kant. Hume, the staunch empiricist, had argued that thought is simply the transfer of experiences to the mind and that categories of thought are merely the codification of repetitive experiences. In contrast to Hume, Kant had argued that categories and mind are inseparable—the essence of mind is categorization. Categories are innate and not structured from experience. Durkheim rejected both of these positions; in their place he wanted to insert the notion that categories of thought—indeed, all thinking and reflective mental activity—are imposed on individuals by the structure and morality of society. Indeed this imposition of society becomes a critical condition not just for the creation of mind and thought but also for the preservation of society.[72] Thus Durkheim believed the basic categories of thought, such as cause, time, and space, are social products in that the structure of society determines them in the same way that values and beliefs also structure human "will" or motivations. For example, the idea of a sacred force, or mana, beyond individuals became, in the course of human evolution, related to ideas of causality as rituals and beliefs came to concern the effects of sacred acts in the secular world. Similarly, the idea of time emerged among humans as they developed calendrical rituals and tied them to solar and lunar rhythms. And the conception of space was shaped by the structure of villages, so that if the aboriginal village is organized in a circle, the world will be seen as circular and concentric in nature. These provocative insights were at times taken to excessive extremes in other essays, especially in the essay written with his nephew and student, Marcel Mauss, on "primitive classification."[73] Here mental categories are seen to be exact representations of social structural divisions and arrangements. Moreover, Durkheim and Mauss appeared

---

[71]Ibid., p. 9.

[72]Ibid., pp. 17–18.

[73]Émile Durkheim and Marcel Mauss, *Primitive Classification*, trans. Rodney Needham (Chicago: University of Chicago Press, 1963; originally published in 1903).

FIGURE 11–3 Durkheim's Structuralism

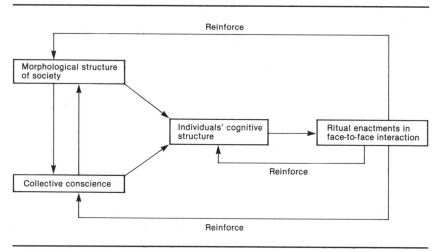

to have selectively reported data from primitive societies to support their excessive claims.[74]

Durkheim is often viewed as the "father of structuralism"—a school of thought in the twentieth century that embraced social science, linguistics, and literature. In Durkheim's *Elementary Forms* and other works of this period can be found an implicit model that appears to have inspired this structuralist reasoning. Figure 11–3 outlines the contours of this model. In Durkheim's view, the morphology of a society or the number, nature, size, and arrangement of parts (see Table 11–1) determines the structure of the collective conscience or the volume, density, intensity, and content of values, beliefs, and norms. Reciprocally, the collective conscience reinforces social morphology. Both morphology and collective conscience circumscribe each individual's cognitive structure by determining the nature of basic categories of thought with respect to time, space, and causality. In turn, these categories mediate between morphology and the collective conscience, on the one hand, and the nature of rituals that individuals emit in face-to-face interaction, on the other. The feedback loops in the model are crucial to Durkheim's argument: The emission of rituals reinforces not only cognitive categories but also the structure and idea systems of society. In this way the macrostructural features of society—morphology and idea systems—are conceptually tied to the microstructural

---

[74]See introduction to translation for documentation of this fact.

dimensions of reality—that is, the internal psychological structure of thought and the face-to-face interactions among individuals in concrete settings.

A SCIENCE OF "MORALITY"

As early as *The Division of Labor*, Durkheim defined sociology as the science of "moral facts," and he always wanted to write a book on morality. In light of this unfulfilled goal, perhaps we should close our analysis of Durkheim by extracting from his various works what would have been the core ideas of this uncompleted work.[75]

What Is Morality?

In only two places did Durkheim provide a detailed discussion of morality.[76] For Durkheim, morality consisted of (1) rules, (2) attachment to groups, and (3) voluntary constraint. Each is examined briefly below.

Rules. Morality is ultimately a system of rules for guiding the actions of people. Yet for rules to be moral they must reveal two additional elements:

1. *Authority.* Moral rules are invested with authority—that is, people feel they ought to obey them, and they want to abide by them. Moral rules are a "system of commandments."
2. *Desirability.* Moral rules also specify the "desirable" ends toward which a collectivity of people should direct their energies. They are more than rules of convenience; they carry conceptions of the good and desirable and must therefore be distinguished from strictly utilitarian norms.

Attachment to Groups. Moral rules attach people to groups. Moral rules are the product of interactions in groups, and as they emerge, they bind people to groups and make them feel a part of a network of relations that transcends their individual being.

Durkheim termed these two facets of morality *the spirit of discipline*. Morality provides a spirit of self-control and a commitment to the col-

---

[75]See, in particular, Émile Durkheim, *Moral Education: A Study in the Theory and Application of the Sociology of Education*, trans. E. K. Wilson and H. Schnurer (New York: Free Press, 1961; originally published in 1922). This is a compilation of lectures given in 1902–3. The course was repeated in 1906–7.

[76]One is in Durkheim, *Moral Education*; the other is an article, published in 1906, on "The Determination of Moral Facts." Reprinted in Émile Durkheim, *Sociology and Philosophy* (New York: Free Press, 1974), from papers originally collected and translated in 1924.

lective. In terms of the concepts developed in *Suicide,* morality eliminates anomie and egoism because it regulates desires and attaches
people to the collective. But true morality in a modern society must do
something else: It must allow people to recognize that the constraints
and restraints it imposes on them are in the "natural order of things."

Voluntary Constraint. Modern morality must allow people to
recognize that unlimited desires (anomie) and excessive individualism
(egoism) are pathological states. These states violate the nature of human society and can only be corrected by morality. In simple societies
morality seems to operate automatically, but "the more societies become complex, the more difficult [it becomes] for morality to operate
as a purely automatic mechanism."[77] And thus morality must be constantly implemented and altered to changing conditions. But individuals must also come to see that such alteration is necessary and
essential, since to fail in establishing a morality and to allow people to
feel free of its power is to invite the agonies of anomie and egoism.

Durkheim then resumed an argument first made by Rousseau: Morality must be seen as a natural constraint in the same way the physical
world constrains individuals' options and actions. So it is with morality; humans can no more rid themselves of its constraint than they can
eliminate the physical and biological world on which their lives de-
pend. In light of this situation, then, the only recourse is to use a science of morality, just as we use the physical and biological sciences, to
understand how morality works.[78]

Thus Durkheim never abandoned his original notion, first given
forceful expression in *The Division of Labor,* that sociology is the science
of moral facts. But Durkheim's conception of morality had become considerably more refined, in several senses:

1. Morality is a certain type of rule that must be distinguished from
   (*a*) the morphological aspects of society and (*b*) other, nonmoral,
   types of normative rules.
2. Morality is therefore a system of rules that reflects certain underlying value premises about the desirable.
3. Morality is not only external and constraining; it is also internal. It
   calls people to obey from within. For while morality "surpasses us
   it is within us, since it can only exist by and through us."[79]

By the end of Durkheim's career, the study of morality involved
a clear separation among types of norms and rules: those vested
with value premises and those that simply mediate and regularize

---

[77]Durkheim, *Moral Education,* p. 52.
[78]Ibid., pp. 119–20.
[79]Durkheim, "Determination of Moral Facts," p. 55.

interactions. Moreover, an understanding of these types of rules could only come by visualizing their relationship to the morphological aspects of society—nature, size, number, and relations of parts—and to the process by which internalization of symbols occurs. Durkheim had thus begun to develop a clear conception of the complex relations among normative systems, social structures, and personality processes of individuals.

What would Durkheim have said in his last work—the book on morality—if he had lived to write it? Durkheim's *Moral Education*, when viewed in the context of his other published books, can perhaps provide some hints about the direction of his thought. For *Moral Education* offers a view of how a new secular morality can be instilled.

For a new secular morality to be effective, the source of all morality must be recognized: society. This means moral rules must be linked to the goals of the broader society. But they must be made specific to individuals through their participation in occupational groups. And the commitment to the common morality must be learned in schools, where the teacher operates as the functional equivalent of the priest. As such the teacher gives young students an understanding of, as well as reverence for, the nature of the society and the need to have a morality that regulates passions and provides attachments to groupings organized to pursue societal goals. Such educational socialization must assure that the common morality is a part of students' motivational needs (their "will," in Durkheim's language), their cognitive orientations ("categories of mind"), and their self-control processes ("self-mastery").

A modern society that cannot meet these general conditions, Durkheim would have argued in this unwritten work, is a society that will be rife with pathologies revolving around (1) the failure to limit individual passions, desires, and aspirations and (2) the failure to attach individuals to groups with higher purposes and common goals.

Durkheim must have felt that the implicit theory of social organization contained in this line of argument had allowed him to realize Comte's dream of a science of society that could create "the good society." Although Durkheim was cautious in implementing his proposals, they were often simplistic, if not somewhat reactionary. But at the same time there is the germ of a theory of human organization. This theory, we believe, marks Durkheim's enduring legacy.

THE ENDURING LEGACY

Émile Durkheim's work continues to inform and inspire sociological theory because, we believe, it contains a number of abstract laws of human organization. Thus, in reviewing Durkheim's legacy, it is best to present his ideas in propositional form so that these laws are highlighted. In particular, we feel Durkheim provided sociology with insight into the basic dynamics of (1) social system differentiation, (2) social system integration, (3) deviance in social systems, and (4) malintegration in social systems. Durkheim's implicit propositions on these four processes are listed below.

Principles of System Differentiation

1. The greater is the level of concentration among the members of a population, the greater is the degree of social contact among these members, and hence the greater is the rate of interaction among members of that population.
   1a. The greater the size of a population, the more likely it is to be concentrated.
   1b. The more pronounced the ecological barriers confronting a population, the more likely it is to be concentrated.
2. The greater is the rate of interaction among members of a concentrated population, the greater is their level of competition over scarce resources.
   2a. The greater is the number and diversity of communication channels available to members of a population, the more likely are these members to interact and hence compete.
   2b. The more available and the greater the variety of transportation facilities in a system, the more likely are members of this system to interact and hence compete.
3. The greater is the level of competition for resources among members of a population in a social system, the more likely are they to become socially differentiated.
   3a. The more bounded a population, the more likely competition over scarce resources will result in social differentiation.
      3a(1). The more pronounced are geographical or ecological boundaries, the more bounded a population.
      3a(2). The more politically organized a system, the more bounded its population.
   3b. The more symbolically unified a population, the more likely competition over scarce resources will result in social differentiation.

Principles of System Integration

4. The greater is the degree of differentiation in a social system, the more generalized are the values, beliefs, and other evaluational symbols in that system.

5. The greater is the degree of differentiation and value-generalization in a social system, the more likely is normative specification of evaluational premises for relations within and between social units in that system.
6. The greater is the degree of differentiation and value-generalization in a social system, the more likely are subgroups to form around similar or related role activities in that system.
    6a. The more members of subgroups emit rituals in their interpersonal behavior, the greater their sense of attachment to groups and, as a result, the more clearly differentiated their respective subgroups.
    6b. The more members of subgroups emit rituals in their interpersonal behavior, the more likely will the generalized values and structural parameters within which the subgroups function be reinforced.
7. The greater is the degree of differentiation and value-generalization in a social system, the more likely will coordination of activity be politically centralized in that system.
8. The greater is the degree of centralized authority in a differentiated social system revealing subgroups, the more likely will subgroups become centers of counterauthority, mitigating the centralized authority of that system.
9. The greater is the degree of differentiation and value-generalization in a social system, the more likely will the distribution of scarce resources correspond to the unequal distribution of talents among members of that system.
10. The greater is the degree of differentiation and value-generalization in a social system, the more likely will sanctions against deviance be restitutive rather than punitive in that system.

Principles of Deviance

11. The greater is the degree of structural differentiation and value-generalization without a corresponding degree of normative specification in a social system, the greater is the level of anomie, and hence the greater is the rate of deviance in that group.
12. The greater is the degree of structural differentiation and value-generalization without a corresponding degree of subgroup formation in a social system, the greater is the level of egoism, and hence the greater is the rate of deviance in that system.

Principles of System Malintegration

13. The greater is the degree of differentiation and value-generalization in a social system, and the less the degree of normative spec-

ification, then the greater is the level of anomie, and hence the more likely will individuals be poorly integrated into that system.

14. The greater is the degree of differentiation and value-generalization in a social system, and the less the formation of subgroups and the emission of rituals, then the greater is the level of egoism, and hence the more likely will individuals be poorly integrated into that system.

15. The greater is the degree of differentiation and value-generalization in a social system, and the less the degree of normative specification of relations among social units, then the less is the coordination of units, and hence the less integrated is that system.

16. The greater is the degree of differentiation and generalization of values in a social system, and the less the centralization of authority, then the less is the degree of coordination among units, and hence the less integrated is that system.

17. The greater is the degree of differentiation, value-generalization, and centralization of authority in a social system, and the less the level of countervailing power emanating from subgroups, then the greater is the degree of tension between those with and without power, and hence the less integrated is that system.

18. The greater is the degree of differentiation and value-generalization in a social system, and the lower the correlation between the distribution of scarce resources and talents, then the greater is the level of tension between those with and without resources, and hence the less integrated is that system.

CHAPTER 12

The Origin and Context of Vilfredo Pareto's Thought

BIOGRAPHICAL INFLUENCES ON PARETO'S THOUGHT

In this chapter we will present a personal profile of Vilfredo Pareto. Biographical influences are always interesting to explore. And they are especially important in Pareto's case, because his substantive concerns and theoretical style so directly reflect his early experiences and training.[1]

Family Background

Vilfredo Pareto's ancestors came from the vicinity of Genoa, Italy. They were prominent merchants and citizens of good standing. In fact, Pareto's great-great-great-grandfather was enobled as a marquis in 1729. This rank, which Vilfredo Pareto was himself to inherit, is just below that of a duke.

Americans automatically expect the nobility to favor autocratic government. But Genoa was basically a small city-state run on quasi-

---

[1]This chapter borrows heavily from Charles Powers, "The Life and Times of Vilfredo Pareto," in Vilfredo Pareto, *The Transformation of Democracy*, ed. Charles Powers and trans. Renata Girola (New Brunswick, N.J.: Transaction, 1984), pp. 1–23; and from Charles Powers, *Vilfredo Pareto* (Beverly Hills, Calif.: Sage Publications, 1987). Biographical insights have been collected from a number of sources including: (1) Norberto Bobbio, *On Mosca and Pareto* (Geneva: Librairie Droz, 1972). (2) Placido Bucolo, *The Other Pareto* (New York: St. Martin's Press, 1980). (3) Giovanni Busino, ed., *Correspondence 1890–1923*, two volumes (Geneva: Librairie Droz, 1975). (4) S. E. Finer, "Pareto and Pluto-Democracy: The Retreat to Galapagos," *American Political Science Review* 62 (1968), pp. 440–50. (5) Arthur Livingston, "Vilfredo Pareto: A Biographical Portrait," *Saturday Review*, May 25, 1935. (6) Maffeo Pantaleoni, "Vilfredo Pareto," *Economic Journal* 33, September 1923, pp. 582–90. (7) Joseph Schumpeter, "Vilfredo Pareto, 1848–1923," *The Quarterly Journal of Economics* 63, May 1949, pp. 147–73. (8) Vincent Tarascio, *Pareto's Methodological Approach to Economics* (Chapel Hill: University of North Carolina Press, 1966).

republican principles by a commercial elite, and it was fiercely antagonistic to expansionist monarchies, such as Austria. Ardent republicans, Pareto's grandfather and grand-uncle occupied important government positions during the Napoleonic period.

After Napoleon's defeat the Republic of Genoa was given as a war prize to the hereditary rulers of Piedmont, and local interests suffered a setback. But republicanism did not wane among members of the Pareto family. In fact, when Giuseppe Mazzini mobilized republican resistance against the monarchy in the 1830s, Pareto's future father (Marquis Raffaele Pareto) was forced to flee to France. Several other members of the family were imprisoned or otherwise punished.

Raffaele Pareto was a well-known hydrological engineer and was able to support himself in France. He eventually married a French Calvinist by the name of Marie Mattenier, and they had two daughters and one son. Vilfredo Frederico Damaso Pareto was born on July 15, 1848, at rue Guy, La Brosse, Number 10, Paris.

For as long as Vilfredo Pareto lived, he never really escaped his republican activist roots, for his later writings were always critical of the ruling class.[2] A lifelong opponent of autocratic regimes, he made his major social scientific contributions by identifying the ways in which self-aggrandizing regimes first gain and then lose political power. This latent republicanism was to have great influence on the substance of Pareto's sociological theories.[3]

Early Life Experiences

Pareto enjoyed a reasonably affluent upper-middle-class French upbringing for the first ten years of his life. By the late 1850s his father was able to return to Italy, and the family settled in Turin. Vilfredo completed his undergraduate degree in engineering at the Polytechnic Institute of Turin in 1869.

At the Polytechnic Institute Pareto became enthralled with the concept of equilibrium, which would mark so much of his later work.

---

[2] One does not have to look very hard at Pareto's work to realize that despite his conservatism, he was from the start a champion of the underdog. See, for example, Vilfredo Pareto, "The Parliamentary Regime in Italy," *Political Science Quarterly,* 1893, pp. 677–721.

[3] Pareto taught his first sociology course—the first in Switzerland—in 1898. His first sociology publication, "An Application of Sociological Theory," deals explicitly with the demise of corrupt government and lays out the sociological agenda Pareto would spend the rest of his life following. See Vilfredo Pareto, *The Rise and Fall of the Elites,* intro. Hans Zetterberg (Totowa, N.J.: Bedminster Press, 1968; originally published in 1901).

Basically, Pareto's senior thesis examines the ways in which expansion and contraction operate as countervailing forces to determine the volume of solid substances.[4]

Many students of sociological theory overlook Pareto's thesis because it deals purely with engineering and has nothing whatsoever to say about society. But this undergraduate thesis may be more important than any other single work if we are to understand Pareto's later sociological theory, for the engineering thesis lays Pareto's scientific epistemology open to view. Many of his writings take on new meaning when one understands how Pareto conceived of complex phenomena, how he sought to conduct scientific inquiry, and what he viewed as the role of theory in science.

Years later Pareto would apply the same equilibrium strategy to the study of sociology, examining the ways in which countervailing forces of economic expansion and contraction, political centralization and decentralization, and liberalization versus conservatism in public sentiment interact to affect changes in the overall character of the society.[5] If Pareto had not had his engineering training, or if he had not utilized an equilibrium model in his senior thesis in 1869, it is unlikely he would ever have produced the kind of sociological theory he eventually became famous for. Pareto's training as an engineer had more influence than anything else on the *form* of explanation he would employ as a sociologist.

Experiences in the Corporate World

After graduation from college Pareto occupied a number of engineering positions. He worked, first in Rome and then in Florence, as a civil engineer with the Italian railway. In 1874 he left the railroad for a management position with Societá Ferriere Italiana, which operated mining and industrial concerns in this region of Italy. While with this firm Pareto had a number of occasions to travel to England and Scotland on business, where he became enchanted with laissez-faire economic doctrine and the apparent success of British government policies promoting free trade.

---

[4]Vilfredo Pareto, "Principi fondamentali della teoria della elasticité de' corpi solidi e ricerche sulla intergrazione delle equazioni differenziali che ne definiscono l'equilibrio," (1869). Reprinted in Vilfredo Pareto, *Scritti teorici* (Milan: Malfasi, 1952), pp. 593–639.

[5]This approach receives its fullest development in Vilfredo Pareto, *Treatise on General Sociology* (first translated into English as *The Mind and Society*), ed. Arthur Livingston and trans. A. Bongiorno and A. Livingston with J. Rogers (New York: Harcourt Brace Jovanovich, 1935; reprinted under the original title by Dover in 1963 and AMS in 1983). Pareto presents a much more brief and somewhat refined analysis in *Transformation of Democracy*.

His preoccupation with European trade issues marked another important development in Pareto's thinking, for he began to focus on the latent effects government policy can have on volume of trade. This subject was tailormade for the kind of theorizing Pareto enjoyed: specifying the nature of interdependence among elements in complex systems. At this point Pareto stopped thinking like a technician and began to think like a social scientist.

Indeed Pareto may have been the first real administrative scientist. Approaching managerial problems sociologically led him to make a number of discoveries that have had lasting impact on the corporate world. For example, his 80/20 rule suggests 20 percent of the items in an inventory account for 80 percent of sales volume, and most of the supply problems a corporation faces are associated with that (80 percent) portion of the inventory that is rarely used. For people often misplace seldom-used items or fail to restock such items as they run out. Under Pareto's management the introduction of fixed slots for stock items, along with other methods of inventory control, marked a significant organizational advance.[6]

Yet another of our intellectual debts to Pareto stems from his realization that management style is crucial to organizational success. This theme has been prominent in the administrative science literature since Chester Barnard, borrowing from Pareto, demonstrated the pivotal role of management in maintaining a cooperative environment in which people try to work together as part of a team.[7]

Sixty-five years after his death, Pareto's contributions to the field of business administration continue to be of some importance. But in his early management work we see only a glimmer of his greatness, for Pareto's managerial concerns were very narrowly focused and highly concrete. There is no sign here of the ambitiousness that would eventually characterize his overarching sociological theory. Nonetheless, Pareto's management experience allowed him to apply systems analysis to a reasonably complex form of social organization: the industrial corporation.

Experiences as a Social and Political Commentator

As a member of the managerial elite, Pareto made influential friends of many people in artistic, commercial, and intellectual circles, and he participated in a number of social clubs and discussion groups in Florence, such as the Adam Smith Society and the Academy of

---

[6]See, for example, *Encyclopedia of Professional Management* (New York: McGraw-Hill, 1978).

[7]Chester Barnard, *The Functions of the Executive* (Cambridge, Mass.: Harvard University Press, 1938).

Geography. Pareto taught himself to read Greek and, by studying the classics, began to see patterns of emergence and decline in Western civilization. These studies provided much of the data he was to use for serious sociological research and theorizing decades later.

Fired by his analysis of political economy, Pareto ran for Parliament in 1881. His loss convinced him that voters hear only what they want to hear and ignore obvious truths. This realization had tremendous impact on his later sociological work, convincing him that whatever people may say to the contrary, they are certainly not governed by logic. This failed candidacy left Pareto with the conviction that sociological theory should be predicated on the analysis of human sentiment. And indeed, as we shall see in Chapter 13, a theory of sentiment is the cornerstone of his sociology.

Vilfredo Pareto retreated somewhat after the death of his father in 1882. He did not even marry until after the death of his mother in 1889. By the time of this first marriage (to Dina Bakunin, a Russian woman who ran off with another man around 1901) Pareto was actively engaged in writing political commentary for newspapers and magazines.[8] Most of this work was polemic. He argued in favor of free trade and attacked the government for establishing protective tariffs, granting monopolies, and other interventionist policies. As a mark of his effectiveness, Pareto was harrassed by the police. But Pareto was more than a polemicist. By 1891 he was putting his engineering skills to use by translating the discursive economic theories of his day into mathematical formulas. European economists took immediate note, and Pareto was appointed professor of political economy at the University of Lausanne, filling a vacancy created by the retirement of Leon Walras.

Experience as an Academic

In the years that followed, Pareto produced a number of important books, including two classics in economics: *Course in Political Economy* (1896-97) and *Manual of Political Economy* (first edition published in 1906, revised edition in 1909).[9] Pareto's combined contributions were so important and so distinctive that he came to be known as "the father of mathematical economics." While the specific content of these

---

[8]In order to get the flavor of Pareto's commentary, see Vilfredo Pareto, *La liberté Economique et les Événements d'Italie* (New York: Burt Franklin, 1968; originally compiled in 1898 as a collection of previously published newspaper and magazine articles).

[9]Vilfredo Pareto, *Cours d'Economie Politique* (Geneva: Librairie Droz, 1964; originally published 1896-7); and Vilfredo Pareto, *Manual of Political Economy*, 2nd ed., Ann Schwier and Alfred Page and trans. Ann Schwier (New York: August M. Kelley, 1971; translated from the revised edition, originally published in 1909).

economic works played little part in his later sociology, this time spent as an economist was nevertheless an essential part of Pareto's development as a sociologist. For in his capacity as professor of political economy, Pareto began his rigorous study of society as a holistic system. The economy gave Pareto some tangible reference points to begin applying equilibrium models to aggregate patterns of change in the society at large. Thus the stage was set for him to make a lasting contribution to sociology.

Pareto was just breaking into his stride as an academic economist when he inherited a small fortune from a rich uncle in 1898. Purchasing a quiet country villa in Céligny, a small village located west of Lausanne on Lake Geneva, he was able to give full concentration to his work. After being abandoned by his wife in 1901, Pareto was joined by Jane Régis (born in 1877), who remained his true love and trusted companion until his death. (Pareto and Régis were married early in 1923, when Pareto was finally able to procure a divorce from his first wife.) Céligny must truly be one of the most beautiful and tranquil spots on the face of the earth. Interestingly, most of what we remember Pareto for was written here, where he could work in quiet contemplation.

By this time Pareto's stature as an economist was unsurpassed. Yet he was deeply troubled by the course being charted within that discipline, for Pareto was convinced that economic events could only be adequately understood within the broader socio-political context. Pareto was rebuffed for expressing these views, drifted somewhat from the mainstream of opinion among economists, and entered partial retirement. This gave him the time he needed to work on sociological manuscripts, including his massive one-million-word tome, *Treatise on General Sociology* (1916).[10] The final years of Pareto's life were spent in ill health. But he continued writing and produced *The Transformation of Democracy* (1921), which adds some final touches to his overall theory of society.[11] Vilfredo Frederico Damaso Pareto died on August 19, 1923.

Psychological Profile

It is impossible to know with certainty what kind of person Pareto was. However, it is difficult to resist the temptation to try. First among his qualities was confidence in his own intellectual ability. What kind of person thinks they can unlock the secrets of the social universe? The kind of person whose idea of entertainment is teaching himself to read Greek, and whose idea of a ten-year intellectual project is to formalize

---

[10]Pareto, *Treatise on General Sociology.*
[11]Pareto, *Transformation of Democracy.*

and mathematize most of the extant literature in the entire field of economics. Pareto was completely confident in his own intellectual ability. So confident, in fact, that he could be curt and intolerant of people holding opinions differing from his own. So in Pareto we find a person who, like many great human beings, was at times capable of being rather egotistical.

One of Pareto's other prominent qualities was love of freedom. He was a steadfast advocate of freedom of speech and an unwavering opponent of autocratic government as well as foreign imperialism. Although he was conservative in his own tastes and inclinations, Pareto was also a kind of libertarian who saw nothing wrong with people exercising high levels of personal autonomy. As is the case with many libertarians, Pareto loathed taking orders from others, particularly people he did not respect.

Pareto was clever and witty. However, he was deeply disillusioned with humanity. One would have to say Pareto was a cynic who readily found fault with the world, which is one reason he had few admirers and many detractors. Pareto was confident he had unlocked some of the secrets of the social universe, but he was also certain his contemporaries would fail to recognize the enormity of his contribution.

One might also want to keep in mind that Pareto had a compelling sense of obligation. He remained true to his principles even when doing so carried great personal cost. Last but not least, Pareto was an insomniac, which is one reason he was able to accomplish so much. With limitless time and without distractions of the modern era, he stayed up late into the night reading, analyzing, speculating, researching, and writing.

NINETEENTH-CENTURY INTELLECTUAL CURRENTS AND PARETO'S THOUGHT

Pareto was an intellectual maverick and trailblazer. This description was most accurate during the period he worked on his sociological manuscripts in the relative tranquility and isolation of Céligny. Yet while Pareto worked alone in his last years, he was very much the product of powerful intellectual currents of the nineteenth century. This must be recognized if his work is to be properly understood.

In seeking to unravel the intellectual milieu in which Pareto's economic, political, and sociological analysis developed, we begin with the recognition that Pareto was a child of the Newtonian revolution and its view of science. At the same time, he was greatly influenced by three dominant schools of thought—utilitarianism, positivism, and historicism—as well as by the Italian intellectual tradition.[12] The influence on Pareto of each intellectual current is briefly examined below.

Pareto and the Newtonian Revolution

Pareto was formally trained as a mathematician and civil engineer, and as a result, he was greatly influenced by the promise of Newtonian physics: Through observation of the empirical world, the basic and fundamental properties of this world can be isolated and their law-like relations discovered. Throughout his varied intellectual career, whether as an engineer, social polemicist, academic economist, or sociologist, Pareto never waivered from the position that his "sole interest is the quest for social uniformities, social laws."[13]

From Pareto's view, then, the ultimate goal of all reflection on the social world is the development of universal laws. And thus metatheoretical speculation, philosophical schemes, and concrete empirical observations are useful only to the extent that they help to develop abstract laws of the social universe. Unbridled philosophical speculation, Pareto maintained, can remove discourse from the actual properties of the world, while the mindless accumulation of empirical facts can impede the process of abstraction that is so essential to the development of universal laws. Hence social theory will emerge when facts and philosophy are harnessed to the goals of all science: the discovery of uniformities and the articulation of laws that make these uniformities understandable.[14]

Positivism and Pareto's Thought

As we observed in Chapter 2 on Auguste Comte, the Newtonian vision fostered the development of positivism in the social sciences. Yet while Pareto read and admired Comte's work, he rejected many of the points of emphasis contained in positivist doctrines: that analogies to the biological realm are useful, that social systems reveal stages of progress and evolution, that structures can be analyzed in terms of

---

[12]A brief but interesting review of the intellectual milieu in which Pareto was raised is provided in chap. 1 of Tarascio, *Pareto's Methodological Approach to Economics*. Comments interspersed throughout Pareto's work indicate the comparative importance of a variety of intellectual influences.

[13]Pareto, *Treatise*, p. 86.

[14]Pareto, *Manual*, pp. 47–50; *Treatise*, pp. 2, 102, 144.

their functions, and that the laws of sociology could be used to recon-struct society.[15]

Rather he accepted only aspects of the Newtonian vision as they had been reformulated by Comte and other positivists. That is, the general principles of the social realm can be discovered through the direct observation of social facts, through experimentation, through comparisons of different types of societies, and through the analysis of historical records. Thus Pareto absorbed from positivism the view that diverse methods of empirical inquiry can be used to uncover the laws governing the operation of empirical regularities in the social world.

Utilitarianism and Pareto's Thought

As we observed in our discussion of Herbert Spencer, utilitarian thinkers of the last century, inspired by Adam Smith, tended toward an atomistic view of humans and an evolutionary view of society in which order and progress ensue from people's pursuit of individual self-interest. Out of such pursuits, individuals find their place or niche in society, with the character of society being determined by the qual-ities of its members. From this perspective, a science of society must be based on the study of individuals. As such, rationality and pursuit of happiness are thought by utilitarians to be the major forces moti-vating human behavior, and like the principle of attraction in astron-omy, they are seen to occupy a place of central theoretical importance.

In his early works Pareto accepted the utilitarian position that un-impaired free market conditions lead to the optimum collective good; but by the middle of his career, he became aware that government in-tervention, corporate monopolies, and labor unions all violate precepts of classical economics and make policy decisions based on the assump-tion of free market operations invalid. After spending years trying to justify laissez-faire and free trade policies as the best possible economic system, Pareto eventually came to realize that those who try to "dis-cover" what form of society is "best" simply disguise their own senti-ments in the cloak to pseudo "scientific" investigation.[16]

In reacting to what he perceived to be the failings of utilitarian-ism, Pareto brought into clearer focus properties essential to under-standing patterns of social organization: power, interest, and ideological rationalization. Yet while Pareto was rejecting much of the substance of utilitarian doctrines, he retained elements of the utilitar-ian mode of analysis. In particular, notions of cycles, supply and de-

---

[15]Pareto, *Treatise*, pp. 217, 287–88, 827–28.
[16]Pareto, *Manual*, pp. 268–69.

mand, and equilibrium were to become a prominent part of Pareto's sociological system.

Historicism and Pareto's Thought

Historicists of the nineteenth century tended to view a given society as the product of unique events rather than as a manifestation of certain lawlike relations among properties of the social world. Even more analytical historicists, such as Hegel and Marx, tended to confine their notions of "social laws" to specific historical epochs, rejecting the idea of universal laws applicable to all times and places. In discussing this tradition, Pareto saw as unfortunate the unwillingness of historicists to broaden their vision and to adopt the Newtonian premise.[17]

Yet at the same time, Pareto's positivism led him to view historical events as a major source of data, especially since he was most interested in the rhythmic and cyclic dynamics of social systems over time. Thus Pareto remained sympathetic to historical inquiry—indeed his work is filled with historical illustrations—but he rejected what he saw as the atheoretical bias of most historicists.

A Note on the Italian Tradition and Pareto's Thought

The established schools of thought that influenced Pareto were, to a very great extent, tied to a particular country: positivism to France, utilitarianism to England and Scotland, and historicism to Germany. In contrast to predominant modes of thinking in these nations, social thought in Italy was more eclectic, drawing inspiration from many diverse sources.

Yet Italy did reveal some unique intellectual traditions, most notably the concern with social power and its use. While German scholars, such as Max Weber, were also concerned with power, the work of Niccolò Machiavelli set the tone of much Italian scholarship. Indeed Pareto felt criticisms of Machiavelli's *The Prince* had been unjust, for Machiavelli had described not so much his personal ideas as a paramount reality of the social world: the use of power to create more power.[18] Another trend of thought in Italian intellectual circles concerned the way values and beliefs are used to control and manipulate populations. For example, the work of Giambattista Vico on the

---

[17]Vilfredo Pareto, "Introduction to Marx," in *Marxisme et Economie Pure* (Geneva: Librairie Droz, 1966; originally published in 1893). Also see *Treatise,* p. 1790.

[18]Niccoló Machiavelli, *The Prince* (New York: Heritage Press, 1954; originally published in 1532).

importance of cycles in belief systems exerted considerable influence on Pareto.

Thus, to the extent it was distinctive, the Italian intellectual tradition focused on two related issues: the use of power and the impact of cyclical changes of beliefs on social arrangements. Both issues were to become prominent in Pareto's sociology.

SPECIFIC LINES OF INFLUENCE ON PARETO'S THOUGHT

Working within the broad intellectual traditions of Pareto's time were a number of scholars from whom Pareto borrowed key assumptions and concepts. In order to fully appreciate the genesis of Pareto's social theories, then, it is critical to review the influences of several immediate intellectual predecessors as well as some of his contemporaries.

Auguste Comte and Pareto

While rejecting Comte's organismic analogy, his concern for normalcy and social planning, and his moralistic pronouncements, Pareto accepted—indeed he embraced—Comte's concern with "social facts" and his proposed methodology. Moreover, he adopted Comte's definition of social facts as widespread patterns of observable behavior and the patterns of beliefs guiding such behavior.

Adam Smith and Pareto

Although Pareto was eventually to reject Smith's advocacy of free and open competition, Pareto did embrace Smith's insights on the laws of supply and demand. And in fact, Pareto was to advance the science of economics significantly in his formulation of structural equations to describe the dynamics of supply, demand, and other economic forces. Moreover, the equilibrium processes implied in Smith's economic analysis were to be adopted and altered in a way that would allow for the analysis of socio-political phenomena. In particular, Pareto took from Smith's *The Wealth of Nations* the notion that the social world can be viewed as a system of interdependent properties, tending toward equilibrium points but also subject to change with alterations in the value of any one property.[19]

---

[19]Adam Smith, *An Inquiry into the Nature and Causes of the Wealth of Nations* (New York: Random House, 1937; originally published in 1776–84).

Maffeo Pantaleoni, Leon Walras, and Pareto

Even after publication of *The Wealth of Nations,* economics remained a largely discursive and inexact discipline. The role Maffeo Pantaleoni played in creating a science of economics is seldom recognized, but in his *Pure Economics* Pantaleoni attempted to formalize verbal propositions on the relationships among such major economic concepts as cost, supply, demand, interest, wages, rent, profit, utility, and value.[20] Pareto read Pantaleoni's book in 1891 and was charged with excitement by the prospects it offered for the development of scientific economics. Within a short time, Pareto established correspondence with Pantaleoni and directed his effort away from political commentary to the development of mathematical equations corresponding to Pantaleoni's propositions.

Pantaleoni suggested Pareto reread the works of Leon Walras, who had articulated a theory of marginal utility and developed a general theory of equilibrium that characterized economic activity as the result of understandable competitive market adjustments and responses to events occurring within a unified socio-economic system. Walras had sought to develop his equilibrium model into a general framework for the scientific study of economics, complete with equations specifying relationships among aspects of the economic system. When Walras retired from his professorial chair in political economy at the University of Lausanne, he followed Pantaleoni's recommendation and requested that Pareto replace him. In his new position Pareto was to spend several years clarifying and formalizing Walras's economic equilibrium theory and, from his efforts, founding mathematical economics.

Equally important, as Pareto worked with the idea of equilibrium, he soon came to realize the limitations of the concept when it included purely economic variables. Thus Pareto's exposure to economics gave him a profound appreciation for the analytical power of formal equilibrium models, but at the same time, he came to recognize their limitations. This recognition led Pareto to examine more carefully the sociological works of Herbert Spencer, the dominant utilitarian social thinker of the nineteenth century.

Herbert Spencer and Pareto

Following publication of several of his works in economics, Pareto attracted considerable attention, and yet he became increasingly disillusioned with two shortcomings of economic analysis: (1) many im-

---

[20]Maffeo Pantaleoni, *Pure Economics* (New York: Macmillan, 1898; originally published in 1889).

portant factors that are known to vary are assumed constant in economic models and (2) the analysis of human motivation in economic models tends to be simplistic. Spencer's early treatment of these two subjects encouraged Pareto to broaden his equilibrium theory, changing it fundamentally in the process.[21]

First, Pareto found Spencer's essays on the interdependent nature of social systems appealing, and thus he concluded that sociological and economic phenomena that are part of the same system must be studied by the same methods of analysis and treated within a common theoretical framework. Indeed Pareto came to emphasize that studying social and economic phenomena separately merely serves to obscure the most fascinating theoretical questions about the nature of their interdependence. Second, Spencer's early work was credited by Pareto for the critical insight that much human behavior is nonlogical and therefore not subject to economic models assuming the rationality of behavior.

Karl Marx and Pareto

There was a natural affinity between Marx's and Pareto's analyses of social systems. Both Marx and Pareto recognized the importance of economic interests, both saw the connection between economic and political processes, both realized the significance of cultural symbols in legitimating social conditions, and both saw inequality in the distribution of resources as a driving force behind social change. Indeed Pareto gave much credit to Marx for demonstrating the connections among economic interests, political power, cultural beliefs, and patterns of inequality.

Yet Pareto disagreed with the specifics of Marx's analysis of capitalism. He regarded Marx's belief in the intrinsic value of labor as a vestige of outmoded economic theory. The importance of surplus value in Marx's analysis led Pareto to the conclusion that Marx built a misguided theoretical edifice on false assumptions. Moreover, Pareto regarded Marx's analysis of the expansion and collapse of capitalism as flawed. In Pareto's eye, Marx maintained that consumption is the driving force behind capitalist expansion (money begets money through the circulation of commodities). In contrast, Pareto argued that high levels of consumption are associated with capital depletion and economic

---

[21]Pareto was particularly impressed with Herbert Spencer's *The Classification of the Sciences* (New York: Appleton-Century-Crofts, 1864). Pareto was less impressed with Spencer's other works, although he seems to have read them with interest.

downturn. But even more fundamental is Pareto's criticism of Marx's tendency to infuse his theory with ideology and to make his doctrine a religious faith—a criticism similar to that leveled against Comte's "religion of humanity." But despite these sources of disagreement, Pareto reinforced Marx's critical insight that societies constitute systems and that the key properties of such systems are economic interests, power, inequality, and cultural symbols.[22]

Georges Sorel and Pareto

As a Marxist who became increasingly disillusioned with the Communist party, Georges Sorel provided some of the most penetrating attacks on the self-serving tendencies of elites who seek to use power to create additional power, and hence, to increase their capacity to exploit others. For whatever their ideological position, Sorel argued, the leaders of political parties are driven by the paramount interest to preserve their privileged position. Sorel's analysis supported Pareto's insights on the "circulation of elites" and encouraged Pareto to continue refining the theory for which he is best known.[23] Coupled with his observation that history is the "graveyard of elites," and his reinterpretation of Marx, Pareto came to recognize that elites come into power, exploit others, create conditions for their own downfall, and are then replaced by others who initiate the cycle again.

RECURRENT THEMES IN PARETO'S WORK

Family background, personal experience, intellectual training, personal disposition, and the intellectual climate of the time all subtly direct a person's work. Keeping these things in mind, we can see why certain themes reappear throughout Pareto's career. These themes are like the woof and warp of a tapestry. They constituted the basic fabric of Pareto's worldview and gave shape to his sociological endeavors.

To begin with, Pareto had an elitist orientation. This should come as no surprise when we recall his aristocratic background, academic achievements, and professional mastery. He held studied expertise in

---

[22]Pareto, "Introduction to Marx."

[23]Many people credit the theory of circulating elites to Gaetano Mosca, who published on the subject before Pareto. However, similarities between their theories seem to have been the result of independent invention. To the extent that Pareto's theory was influenced by others, the intellectual debt is probably to Sorel. See, for example, *From Georges Sorel: Essays in Socialism and Philosophy*, ed. and intro. John Stanley, trans. John Stanley and Charlotte Stanley (New York: Oxford University Press, 1976).

high regard and showed great disdain for ignorance and lack of culti-
vation, especially in members of the privileged elite, who enjoyed society's advantages.

It may sound paradoxical, but Pareto was an elitist and also an
egalitarian. He understood that members of the privileged classes are
innately no more capable than members of the laboring classes, and,
in fact, the former are often slovenly. Unfortunately, elites tend to block
upward mobility of the most capable and energetic members of subordinate groups while at the same time exercising the power at their
disposal for personal benefit rather than collective good. Pareto was an
early advocate of meritocracy.[24]

Intellectually, Pareto was a positivist. In his estimation Sir Isaac
Newton was the greatest human being who ever lived. Newtonian inspiration was visible as early as 1869, when Pareto tried to formalize
the laws of expansion and contraction influencing the volume of solids.
And the quest to isolate fundamental laws governing the social universe become increasingly apparent after 1900, when he wrote his sociological works. Pareto summed it up nicely at the celebration of his
Jubilee at Lausanne: "The principle end of my studies has been to apply to the social sciences, of which economics is only a part, the experimental method which has given such brilliant results in the natural
sciences."[25] Unfortunately, Pareto was never able to capture in any clear
terms the principles of sociology he so strenuously searched for. But
he did provide all the ingredients (in a somewhat chaotic way) in his
Treatise on General Sociology. At least one version of his theory has been
articulated in a set of succinct interrelated propositions and translated
into simultaneous equations as we imagine Pareto would have appreciated.[26]

In his search for sociological laws, Pareto focused on interdependence and mutual determination among the structural components of
social systems. Harking back to his engineering training, Pareto came
to understand that every event has potential for reinforcing or undermining the status quo. Any occurrence can trigger a chain of events
either returning a system to some semblance of its previous state or

---

[24]For example, Pareto did not like people referring to him by his hereditary title of
marquis. However, he was comfortable when people referred to him by the achieved
title of professor.

[25]Bernard DeVoto, "Sentiments and the Social Order," *Harper's Monthly Magazine*
167, October 1933, pp. 569–81.

[26]Charles Powers, "Pareto's Theory of Society," *Cahiers Vilfredo Pareto* 19 (1981), pp.
99–119; and Charles Powers and Robert Hanneman, "Pareto's Theory of Social and
Economic Cycles: A Formal Model and Simulation," ed. Randall Collins, *Sociological
Theory* 1 (1983), pp. 59–89.

propelling the system to an entirely different structural configuration. Thus Pareto used the concept of equilibrium expressly for the purpose of studying change. He never implied the world is static. As a sociologist he consistently used this analytical strategy, examining the complex interplay of socio-economic and political forces in order to understand how and why societies change the way they do over long periods of time.

As a final note, it would be hard to understand Pareto without recognizing him as a disaffected liberal. He came to believe powerful people manipulate the government to serve their own selfish interests and then use rhetoric to disguise their own greed under the cloak of national interest. And what Pareto found most disconcerting is that common people are reluctant to recognize the deceptiveness of their leaders. They hear only what they want to hear, ignoring the truth unless it happens to be in harmony with their short-term interests.

CHAPTER 13

The Sociology of
Vilfredo Pareto

Pareto's works reflect his long and varied career. During the course of his life, he was a practicing engineer who wrote a baccalaural dissertation on molecular mechanics, a political and social commentator who published nearly two hundred articles, an academic who made major breakthroughs in economics and political science, and finally, a retired academic who wrote a major treatise on sociology. Thus in approaching Pareto's work we are faced with the immediate problem of selecting the most sociologically important pieces. This task of selection is particularly difficult in light of the fact that each varied stage in Pareto's career provided him with certain key concepts that were to become an integral part of his culminating work in sociology.

Thus we should initially approach Pareto's sociology by analyzing how various nonsociological works set the conceptual stage for his purely sociological efforts. We will therefore discuss Pareto's work as the product of five distinct stages: (1) engineering, (2) management, (3) commentary, (4) academic, and (5) sociological.[1]

PARETO AS AN ENGINEER

Pareto's dissertation for the School of Applied Engineering in Turin, Italy, examines a theoretical topic, the "Fundamental Principles of the Theory of Elasticity in Solid Bodies and Research Concerning the Integration of the Differential Equations Defining Their Equilibrium."[2] The details of his analysis are not particularly important. But the approach to scientific inquiry Pareto employed in his engineering thesis is highly important, because he was to transfer the same metatheoretical assumptions and epistemology to the study of sociological phenomena.

---

[1]This chapter draws heavily from Charles H. Powers, *Vilfredo Pareto* (Beverly HIlls, Calif.: Sage Publications, 1987).

[2]Vilfredo Pareto, "Principi fondamentali della teoria della elasticité de' corpi solidi e ricerche sulla integrazione della equazione differenziali che ne definiscono l'equilibrio," *Scritti teorici* (Milan: Malfasi, 1952; originally published in 1869), pp. 593–639.

Pareto's thesis presents an integrated set of equations defining elasticity in solids. Since every system is composed of interdependent parts, any event affecting some elements has repercussions for the system as a whole. Pareto tried to identify principles governing the ways in which change reverberates through a system. These were the "equilibrium dynamics" that became his trademark. In the case of his engineering thesis, the volume of a solid is determined by countervailing forces of expansion and contraction. A relatively stable balance or equilibrium may be reached when a system is undisturbed by outside shocks. However, when the external environment changes, the precarious balance among countervailing forces is altered, and the system changes.

This kind of analysis has a number of interesting features. First of all, a clear distinction is made between the dynamic processes internal to a system and shocks from the external environment, which trigger those internal processes. Second, no effort is made to explain why external shocks occur. They are simply taken as given. The important question is, what happens *inside* a system when it confronts a changing environment? The only way to answer this question is to understand the dynamics of balance among components internal to the system. Third, depending on specific empirical conditions, countervailing forces can either amplify or retard change. Hence the same theoretical framework can be used to study both stability or change. And fourth, by understanding the nature of interdependence among system elements, it is possible to predict how the system will be transformed when it confronts changes in its environment.

The equilibrium model employed by Pareto is inherently dynamic. It implies neither that the world is static nor that the status quo is good. All "equilibria" undergo change because no system exists in a vacuum. Hence the internal configuration of system elements is modified whenever some of the interdependent components of the system are influenced by external events. Since change is constant, the goal of science should be to reveal the general dynamics of balance among countervailing forces and the way changes in that balance produce internal structural alterations when a system is confronted with changing exigencies. Later stages in Pareto's work can be viewed as a slow process of clarifying concepts and discovering principles that would allow him to apply equilibrium analysis to the study of social systems.

After graduating from college in 1869, Pareto went to work as a civil engineer with the government-owned Italian railroad. In 1874 he entered the private sector and occupied a variety of posts allowing him to apply his engineering training and skills. And as time went by, he assumed greater managerial responsibilities.

PARETO AS A MANAGER

In 1874 Pareto left government service and assumed a post with Societá Ferriere Italiana. This position involved complex managerial responsibilities, dealing with issues as diverse as movement of freight, shifting foreign exchange rates and customs duties, labor problems, inventory control, maintenance of equipment, and technical problems in the manufacturing process. Involved as he was in industrial management, Pareto saw the broad picture of a corporate system in which events transpiring in one location influenced the overall production process. This marked a significant milestone in his life, for he had the perfect opportunity for examining the inner workings of a fairly complex form of social organization: an industrial corporation.[3]

Pareto's first "social scientific" efforts yielded concrete results. For instance, having a fixed slot for items of inventory and supply significantly reduces the number of work stoppages by making it simpler to locate essential parts and easier to recognize when those parts need to be restocked. During the late nineteenth century developments of this kind constituted major innovations in administrative science, and they contributed significantly to organizational productivity and to the control of operating costs.[4]

Perhaps even more important were Pareto's discoveries about the decision-making process. Contrary to common opinion, there is rarely a single optimal solution to any given business problem. Technical constraints limit what is feasible, but one usually finds a range or frontier of possible alternatives involving roughly similar cost/benefit ratios for the actor. It is important to note that this makes it possible to select options having the least fallout for others, and Pareto strategies can be used to make decisions as important as where to locate power plants and how to select among possible responses to air and water pollution.[5] The implication for decision science is that managers have a certain number of options and should consider factors like morale, which

---

[3]Many of the lessons Pareto learned as a manager are alluded to in various passages of Vilfredo Pareto, *Cours d'economie politique* (Geneva: Librairie Droz, 1965; originally published in 1896–97).

[4]The 80/20 rule is an outstanding example. The insight that 80 percent of your business revolves around 20 percent of the items in your inventory enables firms to make such mundane but important decisions as where to place things in order to maximize the overall accessibility of merchandise and equipment. This is an incredibly important consideration from the standpoint of maximizing productivity and controlling costs. For example, see *Encyclopedia of Professional Management* (New York: McGraw-Hill, 1978).

[5]See, for example, Jacques Gros, *A Paretian Environmental Approach to Power Plant Siting in New England* (New York: Garland Press, 1979).

may not always be tangible but are nonetheless critically important, when making decisions.[6]

PARETO AS A POLITICAL COMMENTATOR

Pareto's life changed completely in 1889. His mother died (Marie Mattenier, 1816–1889); he married his first wife (Dina Bakunin); and he gave up regular employment for work as a private consultant. This freed him to spend much of his time writing political commentary for newspapers and magazines. Working at a fever pitch, approximately 160 of his articles were published over the next few years.[7]

Pareto understood what the methods and goals of science should be, but the social sciences were as yet undeveloped. So the articles Pareto wrote during this period were more like insightful journalism than sophisticated social science. And yet this stage was critical to Pareto's development as a sociologist, for without a well-developed body of social scientific literature from which to draw, he had to identify for himself the most important features of the social world. The basic ingredients for his later sociological works—economic interests, political power, social mobility, inequality, and sentiment—all began to appear in his journalistic commentary.

Most of Pareto's work at this time was highly polemic. He was an outspoken advocate of free trade and a critic of government intervention in the economy. He argued that forms of government involvement, such as protective tariffs, government-granted monopoly rights, and the use of subsidies and loans to protect corporations, all serve to promote the interests of the rich while undermining general prosperity by supporting inefficient enterprise and discouraging modernization. One of his most damning observations was that governments tend to give special assistance to big corporations, which can hardly claim to be foundling industries. Pareto was also a constant opponent of militarization and colonial expansion.[8]

Gradually, Pareto began to isolate certain social structural dynamics essential to understanding society. This new focus to his thought

---

[6]Chester Barnard, *The Functions of the Executive* (Cambridge, Mass.: Harvard University Press, 1938).

[7]For an excellent selection of articles from Pareto's commentary stage, see Vilfredo Pareto, *La liberté Economique et les Événements d'Italie* (New York: Burt Franklin, 1968; originally printed in 1898 as a compilation of previously published newspaper and magazine articles).

[8]The ardent nature of Pareto's commentary is perhaps most apparent to English-speaking audiences in Vilfredo Pareto, "The Parlimentary Regime in Italy," *Political Science Quarterly* 3, 1893, pp. 677–721.

would remain incomplete for many years, but by the early 1890s Pareto had come to recognize the importance of a number of processes:

1. Powerful economic lobbies operate to consolidate their position by exerting influence on political elites to intervene on behalf of the rich.
2. Political elites seek to consolidate their support by transferring wealth from the nonelite classes to the elite classes.
3. Economic and political elites create ideologies to legitimize their activities while attempting to provide the masses with some benefits in order to maintain their allegiance.
4. At some point, elites lose their vitality and capacity to control nonelites, setting into motion processes that lead to radical change.

Just as Pareto had adopted an approach to scientific inquiry while an engineer and had begun to focus on the interdependent aspects of social systems while engaged in industrial management, the substantive ingredients for a theory of society emerged from his political commentary. But the task of integrating these insights into a sophisticated theory of social systems remained unfinished.

PARETO'S ACADEMIC WORKS

After reading Matteo Pantaleoni's *Pure Economics,* Pareto became convinced that social science was possible and that economics would be its cutting edge.[9] Drawing on the view of equilibrium developed in this engineering phase, as it became reinforced by Leon Walras's equilibrium theory (see Chapter 12), Pareto set out to formalize economics. But as he did so, he apparently had a broader vision that involved applying the same analytical approach to political phenomena.

Pareto's early economic work attracted Walras's attention, with the result that on Walras's retirement, Pareto replaced him in the professorial chair of political economy at the University of Lausanne, Switzerland. And thus began Pareto's academic phase. During this stage in his career, Pareto wrote two great works in economics: *Course in Political Economy* (1896–97)[10] and *Manual of Political Economy* (1906–9).[11] In the decade between publication of these works, Pareto began to extend his

---

[9]Maffeo Pantaleoni, *Pure Economics* (New York: Macmillan, 1898; originally published in 1889).

[10]Pareto, *Cours.*

[11]Vilfredo Pareto, *Manual of Political Economy,* 2nd ed., ed. Ann Schwier and Alfred Page, trans. Ann Schwier (New York: August M. Kelley, 1971; originally published in 1909).

analysis to noneconomic phenomena. The result was his *The Rise and Fall of the Elites* (1901),[12] which contains the ideas for which Pareto is perhaps best known, and his *Les Systèmes Socialistes* (1902–3).[13] Written between the first and last revisions of his purely economic work, these books sensitized Pareto to the complex interconnections among social, economic, political, and ideological phenomena. And by his retirement from academia in 1907, Pareto had become convinced that:

> Human society is the subject of many researches. Some of them constitute specialized disciplines: law, political economy, political history, the history of religions, and the like. Others have not yet been distinguished by special names. To the synthesis of them all, which aims at studying society in general, we may give the name of *sociology*.[14]

To appreciate how Pareto came to this conclusion and why he chose to analyze social systems in his own distinctive way, we need to summarize the substance, style, and strategy evident in Pareto's academic stage. Hence, we will first analyze the two great economic works and then those dealing with political phenomena, for out of these works Pareto's sociology was to emerge after his retirement from academia.

Course in Political Economy and Manual of Political Economy

Course in Political Economy is, in many ways, a defense of classical economics, and ideological biases are evident. The basic contribution of *Course* is its application of the equilibrium concept to major economic functions—production, capital formation and movement, and economic cycles. In particular, Pareto demonstrated considerable methodological sophistication in *Course*, employing formal equations as well as occasionally using longitudinal and cross-cultural data.

Besides the formalization of equilibrium analysis as it applies to the economy, *Course* also contains the initial statement of Pareto's "law of income distribution."[15] Pareto argued that the distribution of wealth tends to be relatively stable in any given society and that efforts to

---

[12]Vilfredo Pareto, *The Rise and Fall of the Elites*, intro. Hans Zetterberg (Totowa, N. J.: Bedminster Press, 1968; originally published in 1901).

[13]Vilfredo Pareto, *Les Systèmes Socialistes* (Geneva: Librairie Droz, 1965; originally published in 1902–3).

[14]Vilfredo Pareto, *Treatise on General Sociology* (first translated into English as *The Mind and Society*), ed. Arthur Livingston, trans. A. Bongiorno and A. Livingston with J. Rogers (New York: Harcourt Brace Jovanovich, 1935; reprinted under the original title by Dover in 1963 and AMS in 1983), sect. 1.

[15]Pareto, *Cours*, sect. 965.

substantially alter the distribution of wealth, making it either more equitable or less equitable, stimulate powerful countervailing forces, resulting in a return to the norm for that society.[16] No matter what politicians may find it convenient to say, drastic reductions in inequality are unlikely because those in power usually find ways of protecting their own interests. This has an important policy implication: If relative shares of the "economic pie" remain essentially constant, the best way to relieve poverty and help the poor is by "baking a bigger pie."

More important than *Course in Political Economy* is *Manual of Political Economy*, in which Pareto rejected his past polemics and sought to sharpen his analytical edge. The result is a classic in economics in which a theory of maximum efficiency is developed, indifference curves are introduced, and a refined statement on the equilibrium dynamics of supply and demand is presented. Drawing renewed inspiration from his early engineering works, Pareto reasserted that theory must seek general principles by isolating generic properties of systems from the mass of empirical data at our disposal and, then, attempt to specify the conditions under which these principles hold true. The concept of equilibrium is also expanded to admit political, social, and cultural variables.[17]

Pareto's equilibrium model takes on special clarity in *Manual*. He treated economic decisions as choices reflecting a balance between countervailing *tastes* (desires people want to satisfy) and *obstacles* (factors standing in the way of satisfaction of desires). Tastes are not at all logical. However, once a given nonlogical taste develops, the individual rationally calculates how to maximize the satisfaction of that taste in light of known obstacles.

Pareto did not argue, as some have maintained, that all existing structural features are the products of equilibrium. For example, conditions of exchange are often set by government regulation (e.g., price controls). Nor did Pareto maintain that the status quo, even if conceived as a product of equilibrium, is necessarily the best of all possible states.

Further refinements in the concept of equilibrium took on importance in *Manual*, as Pareto outlined two kinds of equilibrium movements. *Stable equilibrium* occurs when a change in one component of a system stimulates modifications within the system that tend to minimize or reverse the original change. For example, an increase in con-

---

[16]See, for example, Vilfredo Pareto, *Escruits sur la Courbe de la Repartition de la Richesse* (Geneva: Librairie Droz, 1965). Pareto's ground-breaking ideas sparked a significant body of research on welfare economics. See Warren Samuels, *Pareto on Policy* (New York: Elsevier, 1974).

[17]Pareto, *Manual*, especially chaps. 1 and 3.

sumer demand can lead to price increases that dampen demand. *Unstable equilibrium* occurs when change in one compartment results in modifications that further add to the initial change. For instance, increasing demand can lead to an increase in the number of competing suppliers, changes in economy of scale, or technological innovations, each of which can result in lower prices and stimulate still greater demand. The hand calculator industry serves as a good illustration, since one had to be affluent to purchase a hand calculator prior to 1965, whereas by 1980 everybody could afford to own one.

It is important to recognize that stable and unstable states are both types of equilibria and are understandable in terms of balances among those social, cultural, and political variables that influence the economy. To mistake Pareto's discussions of stable periods (which he generally refers to simply as *equilibria*) for his entire equilibrium perspective is an error that should be avoided.

Thus Pareto thought the economic system can be analyzed in much the same way he had once studied molecular structure. Mutual interdependence of parts creates a situation where change in one direction can produce pressures in the opposite direction, with the result that equilibrium phenomena frequently reveal cyclical patterns of change. Thus in contradiction to the evolutionary theories of his time, Pareto saw economic and social systems as moving equilibria revealing cyclical patterns of change. This metaphor was to be the hallmark of Pareto's sociological theory.

The Rise and Fall of the Elites and Les Systèmes Socialistes

The original title of *The Rise and Fall of the Elites* was "An Application of Sociological Theory"—a clear indication of the direction in Pareto's thinking. In this work Pareto sought to identify the major features of society that fluctuate cyclically, to describe the movement of these cycles in equilibrium terms, and to indicate ways in which the structural features and general form of society emerge from operations of the equilibria being described. *The Rise and Fall of the Elites* is an initial statement of Pareto's theory of circulation of elites, for which he was to become well known. But frequently forgotten in commentaries on this work is that Pareto intended the theory of circulation of elites to be but a single aspect of his more general sociological theory of society and to serve only as a provisional statement and model that could be used in specifying other aspects of his sociological theory.[18]

---

[18]Pareto, *Rise and Fall of the Elites,* for instance, pp. 30–31, 36, 40–41, 59–60, and 68–71.

The basic argument in *The Rise and Fall of the Elites* can be stated as follows:

1. Cyclical changes occur in the *sentiments*—that is, values, beliefs, and world view—of economic and political elites as well as nonelites.

2. At any point in time, political processes are dominated by elites, who, in terms of their underlying sentiments, are either *lions* or *foxes*. Lions are strong willed, direct, and conservative. They favor adherence to tradition and show little reluctance to use force. On the other hand, foxes are cunning and devious. Their bravado can be toothless posturing and false imagery. They view government as the art of deceit, misinformation, and secret deals, all cloaked behind a veil of propaganda.

3. At any given time, economic processes are dominated by elites, who, in terms of their underlying sentiments, are either *rentiers* or *speculators*. Rentiers tend to be conservative, are interested in long-term investments, and tend to favor enterprises that produce tangible goods and/or provide necessary services. Speculators, as the name suggests, accept risk, are interested in short-term profitability, and tend to engage in enterprises that provide middleman services—making money by transferring things from one set of hands to another without incurring production costs.

4. Since elites tend to recruit others like themselves, excluding those who violate their sentiments, political and economic elites tend to become homogeneous over time.

5. Homogeneous elites destroy economic and political vitality and are vulnerable to overthrow by their opposites. Therefore, a country dominated by one kind of elite loses strength and stature. Lions and rentiers are eventually replaced by foxes and speculators, and vice versa.

6. The rate at which change occurs is a dual function of (*a*) how exploitive elites become and (*b*) the skill with which elites use force, co-optation, and propaganda to maintain their position.

7. As nonelites become alienated by exploitive activities, their alienation eventually creates pressures that exceed the capacity of elites to use force, thereby resulting in the replacement of one type of elite by another type.

8. The cycles of elites are positively correlated with each other and with economic conditions, with the result that lions and rentiers tend to ascend to elite positions together during times of economic contraction, whereas foxes and speculators tend to ascend the elite positions during times of economic growth and prosperity.

9. Accompanying, and roughly corresponding to, these political and economic cycles are cycles in ideological beliefs between conservative and liberal tenets.

In these arguments we can see Pareto's more sociological imagination beginning to assert itself, even though he was still primarily concerned with formal economic models. The concepts of equilibrium and cyclical change have now been extended to embrace sociological variables: elites, mobility, underlying values or sentiments, and more clearly articulated ideologies. While Pareto had recognized the importance of these variables in his commentaries, they are now part of a more formal equilibrium model of human organization—a model that only matured after Pareto's excursion into formal economics.

By the time Pareto wrote *Les Systèmes Socialistes* he was completely convinced that people were motivated by nonlogical sentiments disguised in a veneer of ex post facto logic. Thus to truly understand the dynamics of history, it is necessary to develop a theory of sentiment in order to explain why people in a given society and a particular time period make the kinds of choices they do.

In *Les Systèmes Socialistes* high priority is given to cultural beliefs and ideology as basic properties of social systems, and Pareto's insights on this subject are an important feature of the *Treatise*. Pareto saw people reacting to events as they are filtered through the prism of their beliefs. Moreover, he saw beliefs as cycling between two poles, one revolving around "faith" and the other around "skepticism." The term *faith* denotes the fact that during some periods beliefs emphasize adherence to tradition and the status quo, whereas during other periods beliefs stress an attempt to assess events logically, even though such "logical assessments" are always an illusion.

One cannot, Pareto argued, understand the nature of a social system unless an assessment of beliefs is made. Of particular importance is determining not only the direction of beliefs, whether toward faith or skepticism, but also their location in the cycle between these two poles.[19] Moreover, in *Treatise* Pareto specifies an inherent dialectic in belief systems, with the dominance of beliefs based on faith setting into motion changes toward those based on skepticism, and vice versa. Thus as blind conformity to tradition creates tensions between people's beliefs and their actual experiences, they become disillusioned with these beliefs and seek those that "rationally fit" their

---

[19]Pareto, *Systèmes Socialistes*, chaps. 1, 5, and 6. A number of interesting issues relating to sentiment are raised in Brigitte Berger, "Vilfredo Pareto's Sociology as a Contribution to the Sociology of Knowledge," unpublished Ph.D. dissertation, New School for Social Research, 1964.

actual circumstances. But as beliefs become dominated by pseudo logic, several tensions may be generated. When beliefs are constantly altered to meet changing circumstances people begin to seek certainty and fixity in their beliefs, thereby setting into motion pressures for beliefs based on faith. Moreover, pseudo-logical beliefs sometimes have less social utility than beliefs based on faith, and hence there may be pressure to return to old ways.[20]

Thus by the end of *Les Systèmes Socialistes* beliefs are as prominent as economic and political variables in Pareto's emerging analytical system. And like the circulation of economic and political elites, beliefs reveal a cyclical pattern that is, to some extent, connected to economic and political cycles. With Pareto's retirement from academia in 1907, the stage was set for his most ambitious work, a theory of human social organization.

PARETO'S SOCIOLOGICAL STAGE

During his career Pareto had come to view economic and political events as only parts of more general social processes. And thus after semiretiring from Lausanne in 1907 (Pareto continued to teach a sociology course until 1916), "the lone thinker of Céligny" began to work on a purely sociological analysis of social phenomena. This work was to be the climax of his career, building on all of his previous work. The avowed purpose of his *Treatise on General Sociology* is to "discover the form that society assumes in virtue [sic] of the forces acting upon it."[21]

The *Treatise* is divided into four volumes, each with its own distinctive emphasis. Volumes 1, 2, and 3 are, in many ways, preliminary and lay the groundwork for sociology. Volume 1 is devoted to establishing the nonrational basis of human behavior and organization. Volume 2 develops his famous concepts of "sentiments" and "residues." And volume 3 posits a theory of "derivations." Much of the confusion over Pareto's work revolves around these rather unconventional terms, but as we will see, volume 4 on the "general form of society" employs these concepts in a way that renders their meaning less ambiguous. In our discussion of the *Treatise*, then, we will briefly examine volumes 1, 2, and 3, and then devote most of our attention to volume 4, where Pareto finally, at the age of sixty-five, pulled together some of the diverse strands of his theoretical perspective.[22]

---

[20]Pareto, *Treatise*, sects. 1678–1683.
[21]Ibid., footnote to sect. 1687.
[22]Most of volume 4 appears to have been written during 1913.

Treatise on General Sociology: Volume 1

The basic argument of volume 1 can be summarized as follows: Most human action is nonrational and is guided by "sentiments" rather than by logic. Pareto had frequently employed the term *sentiments* in his previous work but had never given the concept rigorous definition. Unfortunately, even in this great tome Pareto failed to employ a formal and consistent definition. But from the context of his works, we can sense the phenomena that Pareto sought to denote with this term. He wished to stress that humans hold, often unconsciously, basic values and beliefs that serve to guide conduct. We acquire basic standards of evaluation, and they shape our thoughts, mold our perceptions, and guide our actions.[23]

The two most important types of sentiments are values emphasizing the importance of (1) *group persistence* and (2) *combinations*. With these terms Pareto sought to communicate that people's basic value standards cohere around two issues: adherence to tradition (which he alternately phrased "group persistence" or "persistence of aggregates") and desire for change, including the propensity to innovate (which he phrased "combination").

These two basic value standards are somewhat contradictory, and Pareto emphasized that one sentiment or the other tends to dominate at any given point. Over time the aggregate pattern of social sentiments oscillates back and forth from one pole to the other, from insistence on conformity to the compulsion to try new things, and the character of the society changes accordingly.[24]

Treatise on General Sociology: Volume 2

Pareto recognized that many of the forces influencing human behavior, such as instincts and value standards, cannot be directly measured. Thus to discover the operation of these forces, it is necessary to monitor a residual by-product of sentiment—behavior. In this way Pareto introduced the concept of "residues," by which he meant observable conduct that serves as empirical indicators of the underlying human sentiments guiding behavior.

It is of the utmost importance to understand Pareto's use of the terms *sentiment* and *residue*. Sentiments are underlying value orientations, while residues are the behaviors that actors emit in accordance

---

[23]Pareto, *Treatise*, sect. 888 ff.
[24]Ibid., sects. 304, 1806–1847, and 2048–2050.

with their orientations. Pareto's meaning has been the subject of some misunderstanding because he often refers to sentiments as residues.

> Returning to the matter of our modes of expression, we must further note that since sentiments are manifest by residues we shall often, for the sale of brevity, use the word "residues" as including the sentiments that they manifest. So we shall say, simply, that residues are among the elements which determine social equilibrium.[25]

What Pareto did, then, was to use behaviors as empirical indicators of value orientations. This is not unlike the approaches employed by other sociologists. However, Pareto regarded the distinction between sentiments and residues as important. Therefore *sentiment* will be used whenever sentiments were the object of Pareto's intent, even if they are referred to as residues in the Paretian passages under consideration.

In Pareto's view all human behavior represents one of six instinctive drives. However, societies differ in the extent to which collective sentiments impede, legitimize, or give rise to behavioral expression of instincts. Thus behavioral expressions, or residues, reflect underlying patterns of sentiment and influence the form of society. Pareto's delineation of six basic types, or "classes," of residues reveals the following form.[26]

Combinations	Inventive cunning, guile, and creative imagination
Persistence of aggregates	Stubborn adherence to established ways and vehement defense of tradition
Activity	The need to act and express feelings
Sociality	The desire for affiliation and acceptance
Integrity	Material self-interest and desire for status and self-identity
Sex	The urge for carnal gratification

Since Pareto assumed instincts are a constant while sentiments vary enormously, variations in behavior will reflect differences in value standards. For values will determine the degree to which instincts are allowed to find expression. Thus Pareto's list of sentiment-residue types accomplished several analytical tasks: (1) It allowed him to view human action as directed along six major axes and thus gave him an

---

[25]Ibid., sect. 1690.
[26]Ibid., sects. 885–899 and 992.

exhaustive system of categories for classifying behaviors. (2) It allowed him to classify different populations in terms of varying configurations among the six types of value standards. In this way, then, Pareto felt he had captured both the constancy and variability of human action and organization.

In examining Pareto's actual use of these categories, several themes are evident. First, the distribution of sentiments varies from population to population. Second, an individual's personality or character can be assessed in terms of enduring patterns of sentiments as they shape and guide basic instincts. Third, the residues of combinations and group persistence are the most important because many of the dynamics of social systems must be viewed as a result of shifts in the ratio between these sentiments in the population at large. Sex is only of interest as an empirical indicator of combinations and group persistences, for Pareto hypothesized that literary and other forms of sexual expression are more likely to be tolerated in times when sentiments of combinations are strong.

When we cut through Pareto's awkward terminology and his effort to simultaneously classify instincts, sentiments, and overt behavior with a typology of six classes of residues, we see that a rather simple analytical and empirical point is being emphasized: Human behavior is motivated in basic directions; each line of potential action is circumscribed by corresponding value standards; overt behavior will thus reflect the way in which values have channeled instinctual drives; some classes of residues—behavior shaped by the ratio of values for combinations and group persistence—are more important than others for understanding social system dynamics.

Treatise on General Sociology: **Volume 3**

In his commentary phase Pareto had come to recognize that humans seek to rationalize and justify their conduct. The products of these efforts are what Pareto termed *derivations*, by which he meant the rationalizations constructed to legitimize a particular line of conduct. As such, derivations rarely reflect actual intentions or the real situation, but rather they represent efforts to throw into an acceptable light narrow and often destructive interests. Furthermore, if one derivation is discovered to be false, others can easily be created to justify the same behavior. For example, when colonial powers felt, at the turn of the century, "civilizing" local inhabitants was no longer an appropriate justification for pillaging China, they then contented themselves with pillaging in order to protect "vital interests."

Since derivations are reconstituted at will, without any necessary change in sentiments or interests, they must be analyzed cautiously.

As long as their content is not taken literally, derivations can provide clues as to which interests in a society are most active and hence most involved in justifying their conduct. Moreover, they can provide an indicator as to which sentiments prevail at a given time in a particular society. Again, as long as the accuracy of derivations is not assumed, the general profile of derivations—that is, their emphasis and the nature of their appeal—can provide a rough indicator of underlying value standards, since people and groups are likely to attempt to legitimize their actions by appealing to basic and underlying value premises.

Pareto also saw derivations as critical to understanding social system dynamics. The cyclical fluctuations in sentiment that are so important in Pareto's model result, in part, from an inherent contradiction between the usefulness of derivations and their correspondence with reality. People want derivations that allow them to do things that might otherwise be questionable, but they also want derivations that seem consistent with the real world. For example, shifts in beliefs from those based on faith to those on skepticism occur as people search for beliefs that are both useful and in apparent correspondence with their perceptions of reality. But there is an inherent dialectic in people's efforts to justify their actions: The more they seek rational accounts, the greater likelihood they will see contradictions and hence be driven to rely on faith and tradition. Conversely, the more people rely on blind faith, the more it contradicts actual conditions, and thus the more they will seek to rationalize their accounts of their actions:

> Hence those perpetually recurrent swings of the pendulum, which have been observable for so many centuries, between skepticism and faith, materialism and idealism, logico-experimental science and metaphysics. And so it is, considering for the moment only one or two of such oscillations, that in a little more than a hundred years, and, specifically, from the close of the eighteenth to the beginning of the twentieth century, one witnesses a wave of Voltairean skepticism, and then Rousseau's humanitarianism as a sequel to it; then a religion of Revolution, and then a return to Christianity; then skepticism once more— Positivism; and finally, in our time, the first stages of a new fluctuation in a mystico-nationalist direction.[27]

By the end of volume 3, Pareto had performed the preliminary work for his general treatise, but he had not developed, to any great degree, his general analysis of social systems. He had, nevertheless, confirmed in his mind that most human behavior is nonlogical, that people construct symbolic edifices or derivations to justify their conduct, that human action is ultimately guided by value standards or

---

[27]Ibid., sects. 1680–1681.

sentiments that are reflected in their behavior or residues, and that politics, economics, and value standards reveal both cyclical and equilibrium tendencies. With these initial insights, Pareto then began volume 4 of his *Treatise*.

The Transformation of Democracy and Volume 4 of *Treatise on General Sociology*

One can sense Pareto's frustration over the time he devoted to volumes 1, 2, and 3, which in his mind were only preliminary works. As an aging scholar, Pareto appeared to recognize that he had spent too much time on the early volumes and that only a little time would be left to realize the goal of this last volume on the "general form of society." Perhaps, because he was hurried, impatient, and frustrated, this volume lacks complete clarity, and yet it is sociologically the most important.

Unfortunately, *Treatise* is so long and convoluted that few people bothered to read it, and even fewer have been able to understand it. Readers were overwhelmed by the case studies Pareto introduced. As a consequence, the sociological theory he tried to advance ended up getting lost in a sea of historical detail. Reviewers seem to have regarded *Treatise on General Sociology* as little more than a compendium of awkward terms, without recognizing that Pareto identified dynamics giving rise to cyclical change in the economy, in politics, and in popular mood.

When the book was finally published Pareto was sixty-eight years old and in declining health. He did not have the energy to fight many more battles. But at the same time, events in Italy and elsewhere were lending credence to his theories. Pareto made one last effort to clarify his ideas for readers and to introduce a few key modifications. The most important of these modifications was to move beyond the crude psychologism of his earlier work by surpassing his analysis of circulation of elites with a penetrating structural analysis of centralization and decentralization of power. This final effort to clarify and extend his theory is found in a series of articles, which appeared in 1920 and were then published together as *The Transformation of Democracy* in 1921.

Any serious effort to understand Pareto's sociological theory must focus foremost on these two works: *The Transformation of Democracy* and volume 4 of *Treatise on General Sociology*. With volume 4 of the *Treatise* Pareto finally confronted the task of articulating his theory of society. And in *The Transformation of Democracy* Pareto tried to refine and correct that theory by introducing certain pivotal modifications as well as by clarifying his presentation somewhat, in order to reduce the number of misinterpretations by readers. For these reasons we will treat the two works together. In our opinion no serious examination of Pareto can neglect either one, nor should it really separate the two.

Given Pareto's career development, one should not be surprised that his general sociology is predicated on the assumption that societies are really *systems* composed of interdependent parts. Hence any event affecting part of the system is expected to have consequences for the whole. The economy influences public sentiment, which in turn influences politics, and so on. Pareto sought to explain how these patterns of interdependence affect the overall form and character of a society and give rise to predictable patterns of social change. The implication for the social sciences is that the study of economy, politics, and sentiment should be integrated in some way. His general sociology was intended to provide that integration.

If one accepts Pareto's reasoning about systems, anything can affect anything else. Seen in this light, standard causal modeling is rather ridiculous. Instead of selecting a particular event and tracing its causes, Pareto sought to identify the nature of interdependence among societal elements and to make generalizations about long-term patterns of societal change. In his opinion history's most striking lesson is that things oscillate. Bad times follow good times, and good times follow bad; and Pareto's sociology should be seen as a search for the cyclical dynamics that give rise to such patterns of change.

Pareto began with the rather startling observation that society moves along *three* different cycles simultaneously. One is the business cycle. Another is a cycle between what we might loosely term *liberalism* and *conservatism* in public mood. And the third is a cycle between centralization and decentralization of power. See Figure 13–1. It is sometimes difficult to see three separate cycles because each individual cycle influences and tends to synchronize the other two, with the effect that all three tend to move in the same direction at more or less the same time, although Pareto noted that sentiments tend to lag somewhat behind changes in the other two cycles. Economies expand, governments decentralize control, and social constraint is relaxed, all at about the same time. That synchronization results from feedback mechanisms that Pareto hoped to identify.

Until this point Pareto's sociological work had been essentially empirical. He had been trying to figure out what persistent regularities needed to be explained. Now the interesting theoretical work was to begin. What are the cyclical dynamics that give rise to undulatory change in social sentiment, economic productivity, and political organization? And if each cycle is linked to the others, how do those linkages operate? Thus Pareto's general sociology took form as he attempted to define six separate sets of operating dynamics: dynamics intrinsic to each of the three cycles and dynamics linking each pair of cycles.

FIGURE 13–1   The General Form of Society

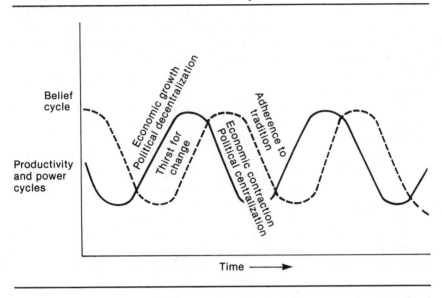

For Pareto, discussion of cycles immediately invoked the image of equilibria: Prolonged movement in one direction tends to generate countervailing pressures, which at first halt and then reverse the direction of change. The same thing happens again later in the cycle, as change in the opposite direction gains momentum until such time as resistance builds to counteract further movement, eventually spawning a reaction in the opposite direction.[28] At this point Pareto's greatness really shows. Most social scientists are content if they can made projections for the near future based on current indicators, but Pareto was far more ambitious and sought to understand what causes the turning points when trends change direction. Let us now explore in detail the theoretical ideas in volume 4 of *Treatise on General Sociology* and *The Transformation of Democracy*.

PARETO'S ELEMENTARY THEORIES

In Pareto's view, history displays cyclical patterns of change precisely because the economy, politics, and public sentiment each change rhythmically over time. Each cycle is in certain respects autonomous. That is, strictly economic factors account for a considerable portion of business cycle activity, strictly political factors account for much of the

---

[28]Charles Feinstein calls this the "overshoot" problem.

oscillation between periods of centralization and decentralization of power, and strictly sociological factors account for a good deal of the swing between periods of liberalism and conservatism in public mood. Pareto's writings suggest three separate sets of equilibria govern the separate and independent aspects of movement on these three cycles. We term these three equilibria his *elementary* theories of sentiment, the economy, and politics.

But as we emphasized earlier in the chapter, Pareto was convinced that sentiment, economy, and politics are in many ways interdependent. Pareto therefore sought to understand the ways in which movement on one cycle affects movement on the other two cycles. This led him to identify three additional sets of equilibrium dynamics, which govern the interdependence of sentiment with economy, sentiment with politics, and economy with politics.

These linkages (between sentiment and economy, sentiment and politics, and economy and politics) will be dealt with later in the chapter. They are important because they unify the various topics of interest to Pareto within a single theoretical framework. This overarching theory is what he called his *general sociology*. We will proceed by describing each of Pareto's elementary theories and will later examine components linking his elementary theories into a general sociology.

An Elementary Theory of Sentiment

Sociology deals with topics that overlap with a number of other fields, such as political science, economics, anthropology, psychology, and religious studies. Public sentiment is important because it is perhaps the one domain of inquiry both absolutely central to sociology and largely unclaimed by any other discipline. Social sentiment nonetheless received surprisingly little attention. And yet, as Pareto made so clear, it is impossible to make sense of history without understanding the dynamics that give rise to changes in social sentiment. The study of sentiment was at the very heart of Pareto's general sociology.

Sentiments, or underlying value orientations, are never directly observable. What we can do is record the things people say (which Pareto called "derivations") and the things people do (which Pareto called "residues").[29] It is then possible to triangulate, if you will, in order to determine social sentiment, and we can take fairly accurate readings of aggregate patterns of change taking place over a period of time across a society at large. This kind of shift in popular sentiment

---

[29]Pareto, *Treatise*, sect. 1690.

is, after all, what people mean when they talk about the social climate becoming more liberal or more conservative.

> Even a very superficial view of present society reveals streams of opinion that manifest underlying patterns of sentiment and interests. These underlying sentiments and interests [rather than opinions about specific issues] are the forces at work determining the character of social equilibrium. We must therefore avoid becoming overly preoccupied with exactly what people say, at the expense of our interest in the underlying sentiments which those indicators reflect. And because we are interested in aggregate patterns of sentiment, we should avoid preoccupation with highly unusual cases.[30]

Pareto's first crucial observation about sentiment is that societies alternate between periods when change is valued and periods when conformity is demanded. Although each society has a different midpoint on the continuum, no society ever remains stationary. All societies move back and forth between times of relative tolerance and relative intolerance of nonnormative behavior, and a clear pattern of oscillation emerges.[31]

Pareto's second observation is that cohort experiences help to mold public opinion. Periods of inflation, prosperity, depression, social unrest, or war can leave social sentiments permanently marked. In Pareto's day Italy was one of the last countries to embark on colonial adventures, in part because so many Italians could remember the Austrian domination of Northern Italy and could therefore sympathize with the plight of colonized peoples. But as 1900 approached and the older generation died off, it was easier for the Italian government to mobilize support for imperial adventure in Africa and the Adriatic Sea.[32]

Pareto's third observation is that changes in sentiment alter the course of history. Every society moves through periods of ascendence and decay, propelled in part by changes in sentiment that encourage or retard innovation, stimulate or impede economic growth, legitimize or defuse political dissent. As sentiments go, so goes the social order as a whole. A mix of different kinds of people having a variety of talents and dispositions is a necessary precondition for continued prosperity. Bad times are in the offing when, on aggregate, a society becomes either so "liberal" and decadent that all people can think about is personal gratification or so "conservative" and intransigent that any behavior out of the ordinary is punished.

---

[30]Pareto, *Transformation of Democracy*, p. 63.
[31]Pareto, *Treatise*, sect. 1681.
[32]Ibid., sect. 1839.

Social sentiments undulate because people want things that are fundamentally incompatible. For example, most people want to live in a world where rules about appropriate behavior are clear and unambiguous. But individuals also want to view norms as flexible guidelines rather than rigid constraints. This presents a dilemma. No society can maximize freedom and at the same time maximize constraint; and every society reacts against excesses of the past by moving in the opposite direction on the freedom/conformity continuum. Discontent builds when a society moves too far in either direction. Such discontent forges itself into a consensus that there is either too much or too little freedom.[33] This consensus does not have to be verbalized. It permeates people's attitudes, affects perceptions, and influences responses. An undulatory pattern of change emerges as a result. "Keeping to surfaces one may say that in history a period of faith will be followed by a period of skepticism, which will in turn be followed by another period of faith, this by another period of skepticism, and so on . . . ."[34]

What, then, is Pareto's elementary theory of sentiment? There are times when traditional norms and values seem to be out of date. Speaking in general terms, it is possible to say that a populus sometimes comes to feel, in general, that rules are too restrictive and that the social climate needs to be relaxed. Traditions lose their grip, questioning of authority becomes legitimate, and all kinds of previously punishable behaviors are suddenly tolerated. The society can move in this direction for a long time, with liberalization becoming more and more pronounced, until a collective sense is reached that too much has been lost. On aggregate, people can reach the conclusion that the society tolerates far more unrestricted ("irresponsible") behavior than it should. At this point a conservative backlash sets in. Presumption is then on the side of people who want to erect more restrictive rules rather than on the side of the purveyors of unregulated freedom, and the entire climate of the society changes. See Figure 13–2.

Pareto was certainly not the only scholar to note that history is marked by cyclical change. But Pareto did more than repeat old adages and mirror well-worn generalizations. He suggested a theoretical explanation for changes in sentiment. The important point is that most people do not want to live in either of the worlds that extremes in social sentiment compel us to create. A world devoid of freedom and creativity is sterile and responsive. But a world devoid of rules is a

---

[33]Ibid., sects. 1256–1383.
[34]Ibid., sect. 2341.

FIGURE 13–2   An Elementary Theory of Sentiment

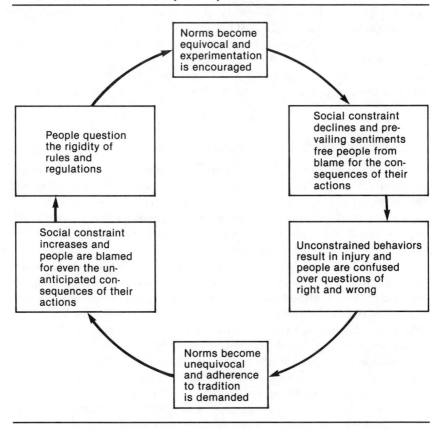

world in which people have little protection against the excesses of others. So society oscillates. Pareto's theory reminds us that sentiments compel people to seek relief from one unhappy state of existence by replacing the old regimen with its equally distasteful antithesis.

Pareto emphasized that art, science, philosophy and commerce tend to flourish during periods of liberalization, whereas religion and nationalism tend to do well in conservative periods.[35] For research purposes, he used pornography as an indicator of social change, arguing that pornographic expression is tolerated by a wider audience during periods of liberalization than during periods of conservative backlash,

---

[35]Ibid., sect. 2513.

when smut is likely to be viewed as a symbol of moral decay. Consequently, changes in the availability of pornographic materials can provide a concrete indicator of shifts in popular sentiment.[36]

The theory of sentiment is the core of Pareto's general sociology. In the next two sections we will examine Pareto's elementary theories of economy and politics. We will then go on to explore the linkages unifying his three elementary theories into a general theory of society.

An Elementary Theory of the Economy

As for most economists of his day, the business cycle was a major preoccupation for Pareto. And as with other things, Pareto confronted the problem directly. If the economy does cycle between periods of prosperity and depression, it must mean that depressions create the preconditions for economic expansion, whereas prosperity erodes the conditions necessary for sustained growth.

Pareto began his business cycle analysis by focusing on economic fluctuation as a purely economic, rather than sociological, problem. In particular, he identified the availability of capital as the critical economic ingredient in the business cycle. And herein lies a dilemma. It takes the investment of a great deal of capital to spur periods of economic growth, but, Pareto argued, massive investment over prolonged periods tends to deplete the reservoir of savings available for future use. When money becomes scarce interest rates rise, investment declines, and the economy slows down.

Pareto's analysis of the economy is similar in important respects to contemporary treatments of accelerator and multiplier effects. The higher the level of net investment, which is defined as investment in excess of depreciation and replacement costs, then the greater the number of people who are put to work building and operating new facilities (the accelerator effect). Those new employees spend money in local shops and further stimulate the economy (the multiplier effect). So investment is the engine that keeps the machine running. Lower investment means fewer people building new plants, which translates into lower sales, with the consequence that wholesale orders decline, and so on. The more scarce capital becomes, the more expensive it is to raise investment funds necessary to fuel increased economic growth, and the more likely it becomes that net investment will decline.

Risk factors also come into play. Entrepreneurs are reluctant to invest in an economy that seems on the decline, especially if the econ-

---

[36]Ibid., sect. 2521.

omy is perceived to have nowhere to go but down. A mood of this kind in the business community can seriously aggravate an economic downturn. In contrast, entrepreneurs are eager to invest in an economy that seems on the rise, especially if it is perceived to have nowhere to go but up.

Pareto added to this rather conventional treatment a sophisticated analysis of investment patterns. During depressed periods many consumer-oriented firms go out of business, with the consequence that the economic infrastructure becomes oriented toward the capital-producing sector. When an economy does expand, people want to satisfy pent-up desires for consumer goods and services. Investment patterns shift as entrepreneurs respond to opportunities for profit in the consumer sector, and over time the economic infrastructure is transformed. The capital-producing sector begins to shrink in size relative to the rest of the economy. In the long run, Pareto maintained, this shrinkage of the capital-producing sector compounds the difficulty of replacing worn-out equipment and outmoded facilities in a bloated, consumer-oriented economy characterized by high rates of depreciation.[37]

An elementary theory of the economy emerges from this analysis. Investment creates jobs and generates economic activity. The higher the level of net investment (total investment minus depreciation), the greater the level of economic expansion. But in the long run, expansion can be a factor inhibiting further increases in net investment for three reasons. First of all, initial investment can erode the pool of available savings, placing upward pressure on interest rates and making future investments more costly. Second, the bigger the economy becomes, the greater the number of investment dollars needed to offset depreciation each year. So gross investment must increase substantially in order for net investment to remain at the same level. This also puts upward pressure on interest rates. And finally, after long periods of prosperity an economic infrastructure tends to be transformed by growth of consumer-oriented businesses. Pareto thought this would aggravate the sheer physical availability of capital goods and equipment needed by a large and expanding economy.

The more an economy grows, the greater the probability that capital available for investment will fall short of investment needs. At that point the economy enters a downturn, which can be aggravated and prolonged if there is lack of confidence among potential investors. But shrinkage in the economy also means lower levels of annual depreciation, so that relatively low levels of gross investment translate into

---

[37]Pareto, *Manual*.

FIGURE 13–3 An Elementary Theory of the Economy

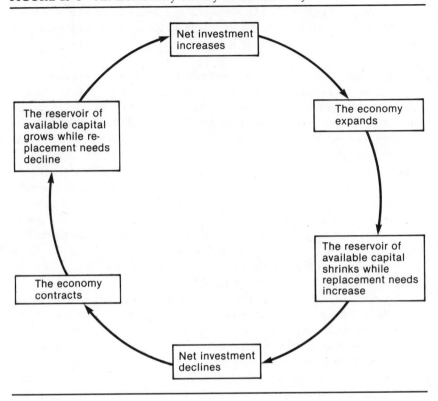

comparatively high levels of net investment, thus enhancing the prospects for economic recovery.[38] See Figure 13–3.

Below the surface of this elementary theory of the economy, Pareto alludes to sociological dynamics involving sentiment. Pareto entered the domain of sentiment when, for example, he tried to understand consumer spending and when he referred to the level of faith entrepreneurs have in the economy. At this point his general sociology comes into play. For Pareto recognized that long-term change in society could only be understood by looking at the interdependence of social and economic, social and political, and economic and political phenomena. But before we delve into Pareto's general sociology, we will finish our review of his elementary theories by examining equilibrium dynamics intrinsic to politics.

---

[38]Charles Powers, "Sociopolitical Determinants of Economic Cycles: Vilfredo Pareto's Final Statement," *Social Science Quarterly* 65, no. 4 (December 1984), pp. 988–1001.

An Elementary Theory of Politics

Pareto had a lifelong interest in the kind of radical political change in which one regime replaces another. It seemed clear to him that the longer a regime stays in power, the more decadent it becomes. As elites become more decadent, they exploit their fellow citizens more and more; and as a result, discontent grows. As this trend continues, Pareto felt it is only a matter of time before a revolutionary cadre leads the masses in a successful uprising in the name of equality and other lofty-sounding ideals.

For much of his life Pareto was an idealist who believed revolutionaries were actually driven by a desire to ease the plight of the masses. By the turn of the century, however, he had seen enough to conclude that rhetoric and commitment are essentially uncorrelated. For he felt politicians who spout populist slogans generally do so in order to enhance their own power rather than out of any compulsion to redress injustice. Over a period of a few generations, energetic new elites develop many of the characteristics of decadent old elites, and the cycle starts over again.

This line of argument is Pareto's famous theory of the circulation of elites.[39] Most sociologists remember him for this theory more than anything else. But Pareto had other things in mind. Without ever actually rejecting the theory of circulating elites, Pareto subsumed it within a structural analysis of politics in *The Transformation of Democracy*, his final monograph. His mature theory examines a cycle between consolidation and erosion of central power, characterized by changes in political structure.

The structural theory developed in *The Transformation of Democracy* moves away from crude psychologism involving the personalities of leaders and focuses instead on the way systems of political organization change over time. In essence Pareto argued that political control can either be centralized or decentralized, with each organizational strategy having its strengths and weaknesses. When erosion of government power reaches dangerous levels, organizational strategies are changed in an effort to consolidate more power.[40]

One holdover from Pareto's theory of circulating elites is his preoccupation with force and co-optation as methods of social control. Pareto began (in *The Rise and Fall of the Elites*) with the observation that some leaders (lions) are adept at the use of force, while others (foxes) are proficient in gaining compliance through the use of co-optation. But by the 1920s Pareto had abandoned psychologism in favor of a

---

[39]Pareto, *Rise and Fall of the Elites.*
[40]Pareto, *Transformation of Democracy.*

structural analysis of politics, and he came to see force as the primary social control mechanism of centralized regimes, while decentralized regimes characteristically use patronage in order to try to co-opt people.

Relying almost exclusively on either force or co-optation can be very dangerous, Pareto believed. Regimes are more likely to success-fully maintain their own power when they can use both a carrot and a stick, co-optation and force, to ensure compliance. Even though force can be used to crush opposition for a time, its use also spawns hatred for those in power.

A regime cannot last long when it relies exclusively on force to retain its power.[41] Just as surely, no regime can stay in power by relying exclusively on co-optation. Governments can try a wide range of pro-grams designed to co-opt important sectors of the population—for ex-ample, minimum wage laws, social welfare safety nets, free public schools and parks, government contracts and subsidies, protective tar-iffs, and certification for professionals. But patronage and co-optation are inefficient and expensive.[42]

The Transformation of Democracy is really a case study on the erosion of power that occurs when a government relies too fully on decentral-ized political organization and the use of patronage to gain compli-ance. The book is intended as an examination of one-half of the complete cycle between political centralization and decentralization: a cycle propelled by shifts in the balance countervailing forces of consol-idation and erosion of power.

Authority is relatively consolidated when a regime has the capac-ity and the will to adjudicate grievances and dispense justice through-out its realm. This capacity is most often present in systems of political organization resting somewhere in between extremes of centralization and decentralization. In contrast, authority erodes when governments lose the capacity for effective and independent action. Erosion of power tends to occur in decentralized systems when a regime loses its ability to solve problems because it is busy pandering to special inter-ests, or because it parcels out its sovereignty by abandoning responsi-bility for activities occurring within its geographic borders. In contrast, erosion of power tends to occur in centralized systems when rulers forbid independent initiative by an uncontrolled private sector, stifle public sector initiative by failing to delegate working authority to func-

---

[41]Melvin Gurtov and Ray Maghroori, *Roots of Failure: United States Foreign Policy in the Third World* (Westport, Conn.: Greenwood Press, 1984).

[42]S. E. Finer, "Pareto and Pluto-Democracy: The Retreat to Galapagos," *American Political Science Review* 62 (1968), pp. 440–50. Also see Suzanne Vromen, "Pareto on the Inevitability of Revolutions," *American Behavioral Scientist* 20 (1974), pp. 521–28.

FIGURE 13-4   An Elementary Theory of Politics

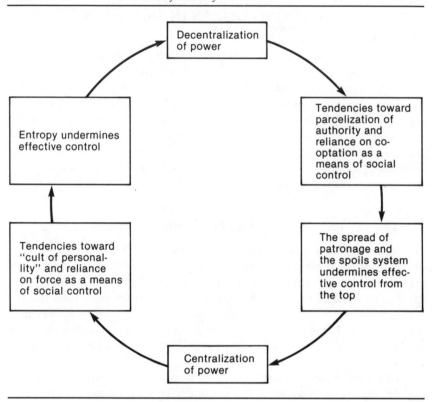

tionaries, or use force so capriciously that common people come to hate the regime. See Figure 13–4. Readers will note the striking similarity between Pareto's theory and Herbert Spencer's analysis of shifts between militant and industrial organization.[43]

The point is that the government power and authority tend to erode whenever centralized or decentralized organizational strategies are carried to an extreme. So the history of any society involves a repetitive cycle of centralization and decentralization of political power. In this sense we can speak of an elementary theory of politics, in the same way we identified an elementary theory of sentiment and economy.[44]

---

[43]See, for example, Jonathan Turner, *Herbert Spencer* (Beverly Hills, Calif.: Sage Publications, 1985).

[44]Having moved away from the image of circulating elites to a theory of structural change at such a late date (1920), Pareto can be excused if he left us with theoretical

PARETO'S GENERAL SOCIOLOGY: DYNAMIC INTERACTION AMONG CYCLES IN SENTIMENT, POWER, AND THE ECONOMY

There is a clear sense of both mission and progression in Pareto's sociology. He sought to significantly advance our understanding of societal phenomena by recognizing the complexities posed by interdependence among people and events.[45] Most people pay lip service to multiple causality, but Pareto was one of the few to actually identify principles of interdependence linking social, economic, and political realms. These principles of interdependence unify Pareto's analysis of economy, polity, and community within a single theoretical framework, which, when taken together, constitutes his general sociology.

The Interaction of Social and Economic Phenomena

It is important to remember that Pareto turned to sociology in order to address fundamental questions he was unable to answer as an economist. He regarded the studies of economics and sociology as inextricably linked because changes in social sentiment dictate the future course of the economy by altering savings and consumption patterns, just as changes in the economy dictate the future course of social sentiment by alternately inbuing people with optimism and fear about the future.

In terms of the economy, changes in social sentiment are tremendously important because of the impact they have on saving and consumption. Consumer saving and consumption are highly elastic, especially in regard to credit buying of durable goods, such as cars and refrigerators. At some points in time, social values tend to legitimize hedonism and encourage the pursuit of personal gratification. If people see no end to prosperity in sight, it makes "sense" (in terms of prevailing sentiments) to go out and borrow money in order to buy

---

rough edges to work out for ourselves. One of the conceptual problems with his scheme is that some societies seem to combine the worst characteristics of centralized and decentralized government. For example, it is possible to have decision making concentrated at the center, leaving functionaries without the discretionary power they need to operate government agencies in an effective manner, and at the same time to rely on the high levels of co-optation and patronage Pareto believed to be associated with decentralized systems. It may be that we should divorce ourselves from the notion that patronage is more widespread in decentralized systems than it is in centralized systems.

[45]Jean-Martin Rabot, "Le Concept d'Équilibre et le Philosophie de Vilfredo Pareto," *Cahiers Vilfredo Pareto* 22, no. 67 (1984), pp. 117–26.

consumer goods. Although Pareto did not use the term, he was clearly referring to a *consumer-led boom.*

A consumer-led boom is fueled by two sources: depletion of savings and utilization of credit. Aggregate shifts in sentiment are of critical importance because they influence the relative propensities to augment or deplete savings and to extend or retire debt. The gross national product balloons when people busy themselves depleting savings and utilizing credit. But what happens when there are no savings left to deplete and all one's credit has been utilized? The answer is that spending declines, sending shock waves throughout the economy.

Yet from Pareto's vantage point, there was some good news even in a dire economic prognosis. Depressions turn people into frugal pessimists who work hard, save their money, and avoid debt. These meager spenders with their careful ways and growing savings accounts provide the backbone for a *business-led* economic recovery. That backbone consists of huge savings reserves that can be borrowed at relatively low rates of interest.[46]

Pareto's great contribution to economics was to provide a sociological explanation for many factors economists tended to treat as givens. People save less and buy more during periods when self-centered pursuit of gratification is deemed legitimate. Conversely, people save more during conservative times when a higher premium is placed on the value of self-denial. See Figure 13–5.

For Pareto, then, there is a clear linkage between experiences, social sentiment, and economic behavior. Economic expansion creates new opportunities, including opportunities for self-indulgence, all of which put a strain on old norms. As emphasized earlier, people lose their inhibitions during periods of normative relaxation. What was once regarded as hedonistic overindulgence comes to be thought of as normal, and the pursuit of self-gratification comes to be viewed as completely acceptable, even desirable.

The business cycle is inherently tied to cycles in social sentiment. Values that encourage saving also create the conditions for business-led economic growth. Prosperity transforms social values, thus making people more hedonistic and fueling a consumer-led economic boom. But an economic downturn begins when debts rise so high that people can no longer maintain their spending habits. Under these conditions economic contraction is usually accompanied by a conservative reaction, consumer spending declines, the rate of savings increases, and the conditions for a business-led recovery are created anew.

---

[46]Powers, "Sociopolitical Determinants," 1984.

FIGURE 13–5   The Interaction of Social and Economic Phenomena

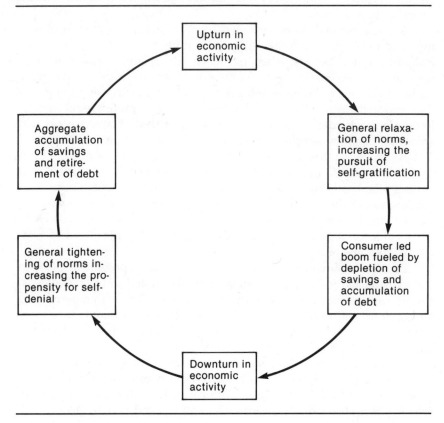

The Interdependence of Social and Political Phenomena

People are implicitly aware of the control strategies employed by a regime, Pareto felt. Each strategy encourages a particular worldview while, at the same time, discouraging certain values and outlooks. For example, the use of co-optation encourages people to view success in terms of who one knows rather than what one accomplishes. And widespread corruption fosters hedonistic attitudes at the expense of the work ethic. Thus politics can have important consequences for the tenor of public sentiment.

Ultimately, people who view the government as a center of bribery and largesse wish to share in the benefits of patronage. But as Karl Marx noted, human desires are infinitely elastic. The more people get, the more they think they deserve. And the more people see others get, the more likely they are to feel cheated. Thus governments that practice patronage confront a steady increase in demands for special treat-

FIGURE 13–6   The Interaction of Social and Political Phenomena

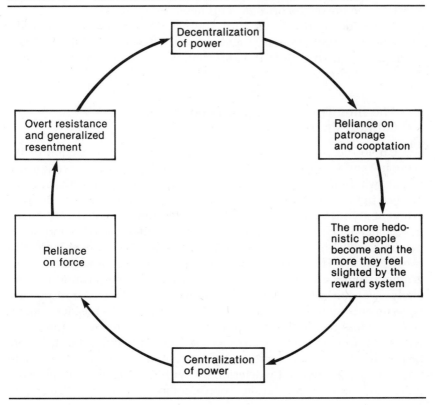

ment. This is simply more than most regimes can afford, and discontent rises.

The Transformation of Democracy provides a case in point. By 1920 the decentralized Italian government was facing a crisis. According to Pareto, it was unable to resist the demands made by unions or corporations. As a result, the government was unable to act decisively. It could not even get railroad workers to uniformly adopt schedules based on daylight savings time, which was one of the many reasons the trains had trouble running on time. The government had simply lost power.[47]

Overreliance on force has the opposite effect. Blind, capricious, rigid enforcement of rules creates resistance, which seriously undermines social control. Resistance stimulates repression, which breeds greater resistance, and government power erodes. See Figure 13–6.

---

[47]Pareto, in *Transformation of Democracy,* reveals these dynamics.

What emerges from this analysis is a close interdependence between Pareto's elementary theories of sentiment and politics.

These ideas provide us with another illustration of the interdependence of social, economic, and political phenomena. And as Pareto pointed out, the nature of this interdependence determines the future direction of change in the overall character of society.

The Interdependence of Economic and Political Phenomena

Pareto did not write very much about the interconnection of the economy and the polity.[48] He seems to suggest that centralized governments (where decisions are made at the top) discourage activities that are not tightly controlled by the regime, with the result that the government stymies entrepreneurship. On the other hand, decentralized governments tolerate all kinds of behavior, allowing corporations to maximize short-term profits without regard to social costs or long-term consequences. This kind of tolerance undermines confidence in government and is economically unhealthy over the long term. More generally, we can couch Pareto's argument as follows: Unresponsive governments tend not to create conditions amenable to business expansion. The less responsive government is, the more likely that pressure will build, forcing a decentralization of decision making. But the more responsive to special interests the government becomes, the more product quality tends to deteriorate, with the result that pressure builds for more centralization, coordination, and control. See Figure 13–7.

Once again, Pareto's approach to understanding the world involves equilibrium dynamics generating cyclical change. Business conditions affect the nature of political organization, and vice versa. Taken together with the other aspects of Pareto's general sociology, we see the form of society being determined by analytically distinct but functionally interdependent cycles in public sentiment, the economy, and political organization.

THE ENDURING LEGACY

Pareto's general sociology is predicated on the assumption that societies are really systems. Hence, anything having an impact on part of the society has effects on the whole. This led Pareto to the inescapable conclusion that changes in popular beliefs, economic trends, or

---

[48]The authors wish to acknowledge a stimulating exchange of views with Jürgen Backhaus, a Paretian scholar deeply interested in the linkages connecting the economy and polity.

FIGURE 13–7   The Interdependence of Economic and Political Phenomena

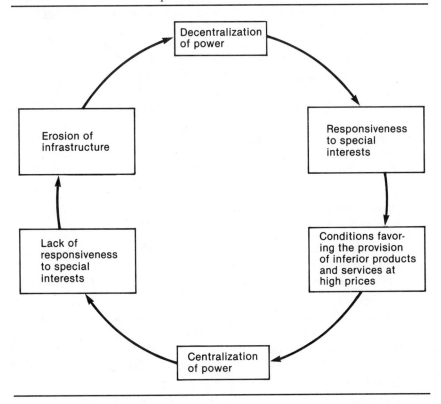

political structure can best be understood within the context of an overarching theoretical framework that examines the connections among these domains.

Perhaps more than any other theorist, Pareto provides us with a coherent and convincing explanation for change in popular attitudes and beliefs. Inexorable system dynamics propel societies along a cycle between periods of liberalism and conservatism. This cycle in public sentiment is at the core of Pareto's theory of society, for shifts in sentiment ultimately determine how much people will save, what they will buy, and what kinds of government they will tolerate. At the same time, through complex feedback loops, economic and political events influence changes in sentiment. Few theoretical perspectives can claim to be as comprehensive or illuminating as Pareto's.[49] Indeed the works

[49]Charles Powers and Robert Hanneman, "Pareto's Theory of Social and Economic Cycles: A Formal Model and Simulation," ed. Randall Collins, *Sociological Theory* 1 (1983), pp. 59–89.

of Vilfredo Pareto stand out for their continued relevance and lasting ability to inform us about the course of social change in contemporary society.[50]

Pareto wanted to isolate universal laws that would enable him to understand differences in the character of societies and make sense of the course of human history. Unfortunately, he fell short of accomplishing this mission in his own life, leaving us with long and convoluted treatises rather than succinctly stated theoretical principles. And yet where Pareto was heading seems clear enough to us.[51] Below we have taken the liberty of distilling his works down to their essential propositional ingredients, for these mark Pareto's enduring contribution to sociological theory.

Principles of Cyclical Change Intrinsic to Social Sentiment

1. The more equivocal are norms (see principle 6 below), the less constrained are people in their behavior and the greater is the level of tolerance for actions of potential but unproven detriment to others.

2. The less constraining norms are and the more tolerant are people of actions of potential but unproven detriment (see principle 1), then the greater is the confusion over definitions of appropriate behavior, and the more likely are people to be injured or offended by the imprudent acts of others.

3. The greater is the confusion over definitions of appropriate behavior and the more injury and offense people sustain as a result of the imprudent acts of others (see principle 2), then the more likely are people to seek clear rules and coherent traditions.

4. The less equivocal are prescriptions (see principle 3), then the more constrained people are, and the more likely are people to fear being blamed for the anticipated and unanticipated consequences of actions.

5. The more constraining are norms and the more inhibited are people out of fear of blame (see principle 4), then the less likely are

---

[50]For an examination of Pareto's influence in the 1930s see Barbara Heyl, "The Harvard 'Pareto Circle'" *Journal of the History of the Behavioral Sciences* 4 (1968), pp. 316–34. For an overall review of Pareto's impact in America, see Joseph Lopreato and Sandra Rusher, "Vilfredo Pareto's Influence on U.S.A. Sociology," *Cahiers Vilfredo Pareto* 69 (1983), pp. 69–122. Pareto's influence in Europe is most keenly felt through Giovanni Busino's editorship of *Revue Européenne des Science Sociales et Cahiers Vilfredo Pareto.*

[51]Charles H. Powers, *Vilfredo Pareto* (Beverly Hills, Calif.: Sage Publications, 1987).

people to help others, and the more likely are they to question the rationality of normative beliefs.

6. The more people question the rationality of beliefs (see principle 5), then the more likely are they to seek relaxed prescriptions and freedom for autonomous action (see principle 1).

Principles of Cyclical Change Intrinsic to the Economy

7. The greater is the availability of capital to invest (see principle 12), then the more probable is economic expansion, and the more prolonged is that expansion likely to be.

8. The more extended is the period of expansion and the greater is the increase in productivity (see principle 7), then the greater are the replacement needs of the economy, and the greater is the probability that the reservoir of savings available for investment will become depleted.

9. The greater are the replacement needs of the economy and the more depleted is the reservoir of savings (see principle 8), then the greater is the probability of capital shortages and high interest rates.

10. The greater is the capital shortfall and the higher are the interest rates (see principle 9), then the more likely will net investments decline, and the more severe and prolonged is the contraction likely to be.

11. The more severe and prolonged is an economic downturn (see principle 10), the more modest capital replacement needs become, and the more likely is the reservoir of savings available for investment to grow.

12. The more modest are replacement needs and the greater is the accumulation of savings available for investment (see principle 11), then the greater is the likelihood of an increase in net investment (see principle 7).

Principles of Cyclical Change Intrinsic to Political Organization

13. The greater is the level of political decentralization (see principle 18), then the more likely is the government to rely on co-optation as an instrument of social control, and the greater is the amount of sovereignty parceled out to powerful interests.

14. The greater is the parceling of authority and the reliance on co-optation as an instrument of social control (see principle 13), then the more likely will a patronage and a spoils system undermine government efficiency.

15. The greater is the level of organizational inefficiency resulting from patronage and spoils (see principle 14), then the more problematic are coordination and control, and the more likely are reorganizational efforts aimed at centralization.

16. The greater is the level of political centralization (see principle 15), then the greater are the tendencies toward a cult of personality, an insistence that all decisions be made at the top, and a reliance on force as an instrument of social control.

17. The less is the delegation of authority that exists and the more punitive is the system of social control (see principle 16), then the fewer are the objectives that government actually attempts to accomplish, and the fewer are the objectives that it will allow independent groups to pursue, thus resulting in significant signs of organizational entropy.

18. The greater is the level of organizational entropy resulting from failure to perform important functions or delegate authority (see principle 17), then the more problematic are coordination and control, and the more likely are reorganizational efforts aimed at political decentralization (see principle 13).

Principles of Mutual Dependence Linking Cycles in Social Sentiment with Cycles in the Economy

19. The greater is the rate of increase in productivity (see principle 24), then the more likely are increasing complexity and opportunity in life to bring traditional beliefs into conflict with actual experiences, resulting in increased pressure for relaxation of social prescriptions.

20. The more relaxed are social prescriptions (see principle 19), then the more legitimate is self-gratification, thus encouraging a consumer-based economic boom and infrastructural transformation to a consumer-oriented economy.

21. The greater are the levels of consumer debt and infrastructural transformation to a consumer-oriented economy (see principle 20), then the more scarce is unutilized capital, and the more likely is the economy to contract.

22. The more severe is an economic downturn (see principle 21), then the greater is the shortfall between economic aspirations and socioeconomic attainment, the more pronounced is the shift toward conservatism, and the more restrictive are social prescriptions.

23. The more constraining are social prescriptions (see principle 22), then the less legitimate is pursuing self-gratification, with the result that consumer spending diminishes, consumer-oriented industries are undermined, and the aggregate level of savings increases.

24. The greater are the levels of consumer savings and infrastructural transformation to a capital-producing economy (see principle 23), then the more plentiful is unutilized capital, and the more likely is the economy to expand (see principle 18).

Principles of Mutual Dependence Linking Cycles in Social Sentiment with Cycles in Political Organization

25. The more fully centralized is a regime (see principle 30), then the less is its responsiveness to diverse interests, the more it relies on force as an instrument of social control, and the more it encourages austerity on the part of the masses.

26. The less responsive is a regime to diverse interests, the more it exclusively relies on force as an instrument of social control, and the more austere is the outlook of the masses (see principle 25), with the result that resistance will increase (in part because people want government to be active on their behalf and in part because the arbitrary use of force generates resentment).

27. The more widespread is resistance (see principle 26), then the greater is the erosion of government power, and the more likely are reorganizational efforts aimed at decentralization of power and authority.

28. The more fully decentralized is a regime (see principle 27), then the greater is its responsiveness to demands from diverse interests, and the more it relies exclusively on co-optation as an instrument of social control, thereby encouraging hedonistic attitudes on the part of the masses.

29. The more responsive is a regime to demands from diverse interests, the more it relies on co-optation as an instrument of social control, with the result that as the attitudes of the masses become more hedonistic (see principle 28), widespread patronage and special treatment will be more visible, thereby increasing the number of people who are likely to feel passed over or slighted by the reward system.

30. The greater is the number of people who feel passed over or slighted by the reward system (see principle 29), then the greater is the erosion of government power and the more likely will reor-

ganizational efforts be aimed at centralization of power and authority (see principle 25).

Principles of Mutual Dependence Linking Cycles in the Economy with Cycles in Political Organization

31. The more fully centralized is a regime (see principle 36), then the less responsive are government leaders to corporate needs, and the slower is the rate of development in the societal infrastructure.

32. The less responsive are government leaders to corporate needs and the slower is the rate of development in the societal infrastructure (see principle 31), then the more difficult are business transactions, and the greater is the pressure for the government to perform a wider array of functions.

33. The greater is the pressure for the government to perform a wider array of functions (see principle 33), then the more likely are reorganizational efforts aimed at decentralization of power and authority.

34. The more fully decentralized is a regime (see principle 33), then the more responsive are government leaders to corporate needs, and the more likely is government to create conditions fostering the sale of inferior products and services at high prices by established firms.

35. The lower is the ratio between product quality and cost (see principle 34), the greater is the pressure for restrictive regulation.

36. The greater is the pressure for restrictive regulation (see principle 35), then the more likely are reorganizational efforts aimed at centralization of power and authority.

CHAPTER 14

The Origin and Context of George Herbert Mead's Thought

In the early decades of this century, sociological theory understood very little about the microprocesses of interaction that connect individuals to the macrostructural dimensions of society. How are society and the individual related? How do individual acts and social structure influence each other? How do societies reproduce themselves through the acts and interactions of individuals? How does society shape people's thoughts and behaviors? These and many related questions remained poorly conceptualized, as can be seen by examining Max Weber's crude categories of action or Émile Durkheim's imprecise attempts to link society, consciousness, ritual, and solidarity (see Chapters 7 and 11, respectively). In America answers to these questions were given their first definitive answer; and a quiet and unassuming philosopher—George Herbert Mead—made the critical conceptual breakthrough.

Mead's breakthrough was not a blazing new insight but rather a synthesis of existing concepts into a new perspective, which unlocked the mysteries of how humans interact and, as a consequence, reproduce social structures. Mead did not consider his synthesizing to be highly original; but as his many students could see and as modern theory now fully appreciates, Mead's work was seminal and changed the course of sociological theorizing. How, then, did such an unpretentious scholar produce such a conceptual breakthrough? The answer resides in Mead's obvious native genius as it was conditioned by his personal biography and by the prominent intellectual figures who introduced Mead to crucial ideas.

BIOGRAPHICAL INFLUENCES ON MEAD[1]

George Herbert Mead was born in South Hadley, Massachusetts, in 1863. His father was a minister in a long line of Puritan farmers and clergymen. His mother, who eventually would become president of

---

[1]As Lewis Coser notes, biographical materials on Mead are rather scarce, and so much of the information in this chapter relies primarily on his excellent review of

Mount Holyoke College, came from a background similar to her husband's, although perhaps with a more intellectual than religious bent. In 1870 the family moved to Ohio, where Mead's father assumed a position at Oberlin College as a chair of homiletics, or the art of preaching. In 1881 Mead's father died, forcing his mother to sell their house and move into rented rooms. In order to make ends meet, Mead's mother taught at the college, while he waited on tables to support himself as a student at Oberlin. In 1883 Mead graduated from Oberlin, and for the next four years he appeared to be at loose ends. He taught school for awhile, but for the most part he tutored students and worked as a surveyor on railroad construction in the Northwest. Yet during this period Mead read voraciously, and as was always evident throughout his career, he was a broadly read intellectual.

In 1887 Mead decided to enroll in Harvard and pursue further study in philosophy. Here he was exposed to a fuller range of ideas than at Oberlin, which at the time was still a religious school, despite its history of involvement in progressive social affairs. Mead's reading of Charles Darwin was the last decisive link in his growing disenchantment with his father's religion and his subsequent abandonment of formal religion; but more important, the substance of Darwin's work was to have considerable impact on Mead's philosophy and social psychology—as we will explore shortly. Moreover, Mead read and studied Adam Smith, whose utilitarian position remained an implicit theme in Mead's theorizing. Perhaps an even more important influence was Mead's direct contact with William James, whose pragmatic philosophy was also to become a prominent theme in his work.

As was often the custom at this time, Mead went abroad in his second year of graduate study to Leipzig, Germany. At Leipzig Mead became familiar with the laboratory work of Wilhelm Wundt, whose psychological experiments and more general theorizing further moved Mead's philosophical interests toward social psychology. Subsequently, Mead went to Berlin in 1889 where, Lewis Coser speculates, he may have listened to lectures by Georg Simmel and come to appreciate more completely the importance of status position and roles in the dynamics of interaction.

In 1891 Mead married and assumed the position of instructor of philosophy at the University of Michigan. Here Mead encountered Charles Horton Cooley and John Dewey, both of whom were to provide Mead with critical concepts in his eventual theoretical synthesis. But Mead did not stay long in Ann Arbor, for in 1894 he followed his friend and colleague, John Dewey, to the new and ambitious University of

---

Mead's biography. See Lewis A. Coser, *Masters of Sociological Thought* (New York: Harcourt Brace Jovanovich, 1977).

Chicago. Mead was to remain at the University of Chicago until his death in 1931.

At Chicago Mead always remained somewhat in the shadow of the charismatic Dewey. More significant, he had great difficulty writing and publishing, and as a result, much of his most important work comes to us as transcriptions of his lectures. These lectures were to exert considerable influence among students at Chicago, and their recognition that something very important and revolutionary was being said led students to take virtually verbatim notes. In his lifetime, however, Mead never perceived that he had achieved a great theoretical synthesis—one that was to become the conceptual base on which all subsequent theorizing about social interaction would be laid. Indeed, while Mead was an active and confident man who was very much involved in local efforts at social reform, he saw himself in very modest terms as an intellectual. Yet as the next chapter will document in detail, Mead's modesty was misplaced because he stands as one of the giants of sociological theory.

Before exploring the details of Mead's theory, however, we should pause and examine further the influences on his work. In particular, we will initially explore the various schools of thought, such as utilitarianism, pragmatism, behaviorism, and Darwinism, that shaped Mead's thinking; and then we will turn to the key individuals in Mead's intellectual biography and examine the specific concepts he drew from such scholars as Wilhelm Wundt, William James, Charles Horton Cooley, and John Dewey.

MEAD'S SYNTHESIS OF SCHOOLS OF THOUGHT

As a philosopher, Mead was attuned to basic philosophical issues and to currents in many diverse intellectual arenas. His broader philosophical scheme reflects this fact; but even more significant, his seminal theoretical synthesis on social psychology also pulls together the general metaphors contained within four dominant intellectual perspectives of his time: (1) utilitarianism, (2) Darwinism, (3) pragmatism, and (4) behaviorism.[2] Just how each of these influenced Mead is examined below.

Utilitarianism

In England during the eighteenth and nineteenth centuries, the economic doctrine that became known as utilitarianism dominated social thought.[3] Mead had clearly read such prominent thinkers as Adam

---

[2]See also, Jonathan H. Turner, *The Structure of Sociological Theory*, 4th ed. (Chicago: Dorsey Press, 1985).

[3]See Chapter 1 of this book.

Smith, David Ricardo, John Stuart Mill, Jeremy Bentham, and, to the extent that he can be classified as a utilitarian, Thomas Malthus. Mead absorbed several key ideas from utilitarian doctrines.

First, utilitarians saw human action as self-interested actors who seek to maximize their "utility" or benefit in free and openly competitive marketplaces. While this idea was expressed somewhat differently by various advocates of utilitarianism, Mead appears to have found useful the emphases on (a) actors as seeking rewards, (b) actors as attempting to adjust to a competitive situation, and (c) actors as goal directed and instrumental in their behaviors. Later versions of utilitarianism stressed "pleasure" and "pain" principles, which captured the essence of the behaviorism that was to emerge in Mead's time and exert considerable influence on his scheme.

Second, utilitarians often tended to emphasize—indeed to over-emphasize—the rationality of self-seeking actors. From a utilitarian perspective, actors are rational in that they gather all relevant information, weigh alternative lines of conduct, and select an alternative that will maximize utilities, benefits, or pleasures. Mead never came to accept this overly rational view of human action, but his view of the human "mind" as a process of reflective thought in which alternatives are covertly designated, weighed, and rehearsed was, no doubt, partially inspired by the utilitarian position.

Thus while utilitarianism was perhaps least influential on Mead, his theoretical scheme was to correspond to several central points of emphasis in utilitarianism. Mead probably borrowed these points both directly and indirectly, since utilitarianism influenced the other schools of thought that more directly shaped Mead's philosophical scheme. For as we will come to see, early behaviorism and pragmatism, while rejecting extreme utilitarianism, nonetheless incorporated some of its basic tenets.

Darwinism

Charles Darwin's formulation of the theory of evolution influenced not only biological theory[4] but also social thought.[5] The view that a species' profile is shaped from the competitive struggle with other species attempting to occupy an environmental niche was highly compatible with utilitarian notions. As a result of this superficial compatibility, utilitarianism was to be carried to absurd extremes in

---

[4]Charles Darwin, *On the Origin of Species* (London: Murry, 1859).

[5]See, for example, William G. Sumner, *What Social Classes Owe Each Other* (New York: Harper & Row, 1883).

the late nineteenth and early twentieth centuries by a group of think-ers who became known as "Social Darwinists."[6] From their viewpoint, social life is a competitive struggle in which the "fittest" will be the best able to "survive" and prosper.[7] Hence those who enjoy privilege in a society deserve these benefits because they are the "most fit," whereas those who have the least wealth are less fit and worthy. Ob-viously, Social Darwinism was a gross distortion of the theory of evo-lution, but its flowering illustrates the extent to which Darwin's theory represented an intellectual bombshell in Europe and America in the nineteenth and early twentieth centuries.

Other social theorists borrowed Darwin's ideas more cautiously. George Herbert Mead was to use the theory of evolution as a broad metaphor for understanding the processes by which the unique capac-ities of humans emerge. For Mead, all animals, including humans, must seek to adapt and adjust to an environment; and hence many attributes that an organism comes to reveal are the product of its ef-forts to adapt to a particular environment. In the distant past, there-fore, the unique capacities of humans for language, for mind, for self, and for normatively regulated social organization emerged as a result of selective pressures on the ancestors of humans for these unique capacities.

But Mead was not so much interested in the origins of humans as a species as in the development of the infant human from an asocial to social creature. For at birth, Mead argued, an infant is not a human. It acquires the unique behavioral capacities of humans only as it seeks to adapt to a social environment. Thus just as the species as a whole acquired its distinctive characteristics through a process of "natural selection," so the infant organism develops its "humanness" through a process of "selection." Because the environment of a person is other people who use language, who possess mind and self, and who live in society, the young must adapt to this environment if they are to sur-vive. And as they adapt and adjust, they acquire the capacity to use language, to reveal a mind, to evidence a sense of self, and to partici-pate in society. Thus Mead borrowed from Darwinian theory the met-aphor of adaptation or adjustment as the key force shaping the nature

---

[6]Richard Hofstadter, *Social Darwinism in American Thought*, 1860–1915 (Philadelphia: University of Pennsylvania Press, 1945).

[7]Spencer first used the phrase "survival of the fittest," which apparently influenced Darwin, as he acknowledges in *On the Origin of Species*. Other early American sociol-ogists, such as William Graham Sumner, took this idea to extremes. As we noted for Spencer, however, his utilitarianism was recessive in his sociological works, and so it is unfair to count Spencer as a Social Darwinist.

of humans.[8] This metaphor was given its most forceful expression in the works of scholars who developed a school of thought known as pragmatism.

Pragmatism

Mead is frequently grouped with pragmatists, such as Charles Pierce, William James, and John Dewey. Yet although Mead was profoundly influenced by James and Dewey, his theoretical scheme is only partially in debt to pragmatism.[9] For as we have emphasized, Mead took his ideas from a variety of sources, and pragmatism is only one of them.

The American scientist and philosopher Charles Pierce first developed the ideas behind pragmatism in an article entitled "How to Make Our Ideas Clear," which appeared in *Popular Science Monthly* in 1878.[10] But it was not until William James delivered a lecture in 1898 entitled "Philosophical Conceptions and Practical Results" that pragmatism became an acknowledged philosophical school.[11] And as John Dewey developed his "instrumentalism," pragmatism became a center of philosophical controversy in America during the early decades of this century. Pragmatism was primarily concerned with the process of thinking and how it influences the action of individuals, and vice versa. While pragmatists were each to carry its banner in different directions, the central thrust of this philosophical school is to view thought as a process that allows humans to adjust, adapt, and achieve goals in their environment.

Thus pragmatists became concerned with symbols, language, and rational thinking as well as with the way action in the world is influenced by humans' mental capacities. Pierce saw pragmatism as con-

---

[8]Mead also reacted to Darwin's later efforts to understand emotions in animals. See Charles Darwin, *The Expression of Emotions in Man and Animals* (London: Murry, 1872). Mead used this analysis as his straw man in developing his own theory of gestures and interaction.

[9]For relevant summaries of pragmatism, see Charles Morris, *The Pragmatic Movement in American Philosophy* (New York: George Braziller, 1970); and Edward C. Moore, *American Pragmatism: Pierce, James, and Dewey* (New York: Columbia University Press, 1961).

[10]For Pierce's general works, see Charles Sanders Pierce, *The Collected Papers of Charles Sanders Pierce*, 8 vols. (Cambridge, Mass.: Harvard University Press, 1931–58). Pierce's "How to Make Our Ideas Clear" is in vol. 5, pp. 248–71.

[11]This lecture was delivered at Berkeley, California. See also, William James, *Pragmatism* (Cambridge, Mass.: Harvard University Press, 1975).

cerned with "self-controlled conduct," which is guided by "adequate deliberation," and hence pragmatism was based on:

> a study of that experience of the phenomena of self-control which is common to all grown men and women; and it seems evident that to some extent, at least, it must always be so based. For it is to conceptions of deliberate conduct that pragmatism would trace the intellectual purpost of symbols; and deliberate conduct is self-controlled conduct.[12]

For Pierce, then, pragmatism stressed the use of symbols and signs in thought and self-control, a point of emphasis that Mead was later to adopt. James and Dewey supplemented Pierce's emphasis by stressing that the process of thinking is intimately connected to the process of adaptation and adjustment. James stressed that "truth" is not absolute and enduring; rather he argued that scientific as well as lay conceptions of truth are only as enduring as their ability to help people adjust and adapt to their circumstances.[13] Truth, in other words, is determined only by its "practical results." Dewey similarly emphasized the significance of thinking for achieving goals and adjusting to the environment. Thought, whether lay or scientific, is an "instrument" that can be used to achieve goals and purposes.[14]

Pragmatism emerged as a reaction to, and an effort to deal with, a number of scientific and philosophical events of the nineteenth century. First, the ascendance of Newtonian mechanics posed the question of whether all aspects of the universe, including human thought and action, could be reduced to invariant and mechanistic laws. To this challenge, pragmatists argued that such laws do not make human action mechanistic and wholly determinative, but rather these laws are instruments to be used by humans in achieving goals.[15] Second, the theory of evolution offered the vision of continuity in life processes. To this idea pragmatists added the notion that humans as a species, and as individuals, are engaged in a process of constant adjustment and adaptation to their environment and that thought represents the principal means of achieving such adjustment. Third, the doctrines of utilitarians presented a calculating, rational, and instrumental view of human action. To this perspective pragmatists were highly receptive,

---

[12]Morris, *Pragmatic Movement*, p. 11.

[13]William James, *The Meaning of Truth: A Sequel to "Pragmatism"* (New York: Longmans, Green, 1909).

[14]John Dewey, *Human Nature and Conduct* (New York: Holt, Rinehart & Winston, 1922).

[15]In particular, see John Dewey, *The Quest for Certainty* (New York: Minton, Balch, 1925); or James, *Meaning of Truth*.

although their concern was with the process of thought and how it is linked to action. Fourth, the ascendance of the scientific method with its emphasis on the verification of conceptual schemes through experienced data presented a consensual view of "proper" modes of investigation. To this point of emphasis the pragmatists responded that all action involves an act of verification as people's thoughts and conceptions are "checked" against their experiences in the world. For the pragmatist, human life is a continuous application of the "scientific method" as people seek to cope with the world around them.[16]

Pragmatism thus represents the first distinctly American philosophical system. Mead was personally tied to several of its advocates while being intellectually involved in the debate surrounding the system and its critics. He clearly was influenced by the pragmatists' concern with the process of thinking and with the importance of symbols in thought. He accepted the metaphor that thought and action involve efforts to adjust and adapt to the environment. And he embraced the notion that such adaptation involves a continuous process of experiential verification of thought and action. In many ways utilitarianism and Darwinism came to Mead through pragmatism, and hence to some extent, Mead must be considered a pragmatist. Yet Mead was also a behaviorist, and if his social psychology is to be given a label, it is more behavioristic than pragmatic.

Behaviorism

As a psychological perspective, behaviorism began from insights derived from observations of an accident. Russian physiologist Ivan Petrovich Pavlov discovered that experimental dogs associated food with the person bringing the food.[17] He observed, for instance, that dogs on whom he was performing secretory experiments would secrete saliva not only when presented food but also when they heard their feeder's footsteps approaching. After considerable delay and personal agonizing,[18] Pavlov undertook a series of experiments on animals to understand such "conditioned responses." From these experiments he developed several principles that later were incorporated into behaviorism. These include:

---

[16]See Morris, *Pragmatic Movement*, pp. 5–11.

[17]See, for relevant articles, lectures, and references, I. P. Pavlov, *Selected Works*, ed. K. S. Kostoyants, trans. S. Belsky (Moscow: Foreign Languages Publishing House, 1955); and *Lectures on Conditioned Reflexes*, 3rd ed., trans. W. H. Gantt (New York: International, 1928).

[18]I. P. Pavlov, "Autobiography," in *Selected Works*, pp. 41–44.

1. A stimulus consistently associated with another stimulus producing a given physiological response will, by itself, elicit that response.

2. Such conditioned responses can be extinguished when gratifications associated with stimuli are no longer forthcoming.

3. Stimuli that are similar to those producing a conditioned response can also elicit the same response as the original stimulus.

4. Stimuli that increasingly differ from those used to condition a particular response will decreasingly be able to elicit this response.

Thus Pavlov's experiments exposed the principles of conditioned responses, extinction, response generalization, and response discrimination. While Pavlov clearly recognized the significance of these findings for human behavior, his insights came to fruition in America under the tutelage of Edward Thorndike and John B. Watson—the founders of behaviorism.[19]

Edward Lee Thorndike conducted the first laboratory experiments on animals in America. In the course of these experiments, he observed that animals would retain response patterns for which they are rewarded.[20] For example, in experiments on kittens placed in a puzzle box, Thorndike found that they would engage in trial-and-error behavior until emitting the response allowing them to escape. And with each placement in the box, the kittens would engage in less trial-and-error behavior, thereby indicating that the gratifications associated with a response allowing the kitten to escape caused the kitten to learn and retain this response. From these and other studies, which were conducted at the same time as Pavlov's, Thorndike formulated three principles or laws: (1) the "law of effect," which holds that acts in a situation producing gratification will be more likely to occur in the future when that situation recurs; (2) the "law of use," which states that the situation-response connection is strengthened with repetitions and practice; and (3) the "law of disuse," which argues that the connection will weaken when practice is discontinued.[21]

These laws overlap with those presented by Pavlov, but there is one important difference. Thorndike's experiments were conducted by animals engaged in free trial-and-error behavior, whereas Pavlov's

---

[19]For an excellent summary of their ideas, see Robert I. Watson, *The Great Psychologists*, 3rd ed. (Philadelphia: J. B. Lippincott, 1971), pp. 417–46.

[20]Edward L. Thorndike, "Animal Intelligence: An Experimental Study of the Associative Processes in Animals," *Psychological Review Monograph*, Supplement 2 (1898).

[21]See Edward L. Thorndike, *The Elements of Psychology* (New York: Seiler, 1905); *The Fundamentals of Learning* (New York: Teachers College Press, 1932); and *The Psychology of Wants, Interests, and Attitudes* (New York: Appleton-Century-Crofts, 1935).

work was on the conditioning of physiological—typically glandular—responses in a tightly controlled laboratory situation. Thorndike's work could thus be seen as more directly relevant to human behavior in natural settings.

John B. Watson was only one of several thinkers to recognize the significance of Pavlov's and Thorndike's work,[22] but he soon became the dominant advocate of what was becoming explicitly known as "behaviorism." Watson's opening shot for the new science of behavior was fired in an article entitled "Psychology as the Behaviorist Views It":

> Psychology as the behaviorist views it is a purely objective experimental branch of natural science. Its theoretical goal is the prediction and control of behavior. Introspection forms no essential part of its methods, nor is the scientific value of its data dependent upon the readiness with which they lend themselves to interpretation in terms of consciousness. The behaviorist, in efforts to get a unitary scheme of animal response, recognizes no dividing line between man and brute.[23]

Watson thus became the advocate of the extreme behaviorism against which Mead so vehemently reacted.[24] For Watson, psychology is the study of stimulus-response relations, and the only admissible evidence is overt behavior. Psychologists are to stay out of the "mystery box" of human consciousness and to study only observable behaviors as they are connected to observable stimuli. Mead rejected this assertion and argued that just because an activity such as thinking is not directly observable does not mean it is not behavior. For as Mead was to argue, covert thinking and the capacity to view oneself in situations are nonetheless behaviors and hence subject to the same laws as overt behaviors.

Mead thus rejected extreme behaviorism but accepted its general principle: Behaviors are learned as a result of gratifications associated with them. In accordance with the views of pragmatists, and consistent

---

[22]The others included Max F. Meyer, *Psychology of the Other-One* (Columbus: Missouri Books, 1921); and Albert P. Weiss, *A Theoretical Basis of Human Behavior* (Columbus: Adams, 1925).

[23]J. B. Watson, "Psychology as the Behaviorist Views It," *Psychological Review* 20 (1913), pp. 158–77. For other basic works by Watson, see *Psychology from the Standpoint of a Behaviorist*, 3rd ed. (Philadelphia: J. B. Lippincott, 1929); *Behavior: An Introduction to Comparative Psychology* (New York: Holt, Rinehart & Winston, 1914).

[24]For example, in his *Mind, Self, and Society* (Chicago: University of Chicago Press, 1934), Mead has eighteen references to Watson's work and was highly critical of the latter's extreme methodological position. But Mead considered himself a behaviorist nonetheless. For further documentation of this conclusion, see Jonathan H. Turner, "A Note on G. H. Mead's Behavioristic Theory of Social Structure," *Journal for the Theory of Social Behavior* 12, July 1982, pp. 213–22; and John D. Baldwin, *George Herbert Mead* (Beverly Hills, Calif.: Sage Publications, 1986).

with Mead's Darwinian metaphor, the gratifications of humans typically involve adjustment to a social environment. And most important, some of the most distinctive behaviors of humans are covert, involving thinking, reflection, and self-awareness. In contrast to Watson's behaviorism, Mead was to postulate what some have called a *social behaviorism*. From this perspective covert and overt behaviors are to be understood in terms of their capacity to produce adjustment to society.

In sum, we can conclude that Mead borrowed the broad assumptions from a number of intellectual perspectives, particularly utilitarianism, Darwinism, pragmatism, and behaviorism. Utilitarians and pragmatists emphasized the process of thinking and rational conduct; utilitarians and Darwinists stressed the importance of competitive struggle and selection of attributes; Darwinists and pragmatists argued for the importance of adaptation and adjustment to an understanding of thought and action; and behaviorists presented a view of learning as the association of behaviors with gratification-producing stimuli. Each of these general ideas became a part of Mead's theoretical scheme, but as Mead synthesized these ideas they took on new meaning.

Mead was not only influenced by these general intellectual perspectives; he also borrowed specific concepts from a variety of scholars, only some of whom worked within these general perspectives. By taking specific concepts, reconciling them with each other, and then incorporating them into the metaphors of these four general perspectives, Mead was able to produce the theoretical breakthrough for which he is deservedly given credit.

WILHELM WUNDT AND G. H. MEAD

Even a casual reading of Mead's written work and posthumously published lectures reveals a large number of citations to German psychologist Wilhelm Wundt.[25] Wundt is often given credit for being the father of psychology, since by the 1860s he was conducting a series of experiments that could be clearly defined as psychological in nature. And in the 1870s he was one of the first, along with American William James, to establish a psychological laboratory.

Mead studied briefly in Germany, although not in Heidelberg, where Wundt had established his laboratory and school of loyal followers. Yet there can be little doubt that Wundt's eminence prompted Mead to read his works carefully.[26] At first glance, it might appear that

---

[25]*Mind, Self, and Society* alone contains over twenty references to Wundt's ideas.

[26]For basic references on Wundt's work, see Wilhelm Wundt, *Principles of Physiological Psychology* (New York: Macmillan, 1904; originally published in 1874); *Lectures on*

Mead, the philosopher, would find little of interest in Wundt's voluminous output. Most of Wundt's laboratory work deals with efforts to understand the structure of consciousness—a point of emphasis not conducive to Mead's insistence on mind as a process. However, Wundt was also a philosopher, social psychologist, and sociologist. Although Wundt would write strictly psychological books like *Physiological Psychology,* he also founded the journal *Philosophical Studies,* in which he published his laboratory studies. Indeed he saw little reason to distinguish psychology from philosophy. He also was to devote many pages in his *Outlines of Psychology* to gestures, language, self-consciousness, mental communities, customs, myths, and child development—all topics likely to interest philosopher and social psychologist George Herbert Mead. Moreover, his *Elements of Folk Psychology* was one of the first distinctly social psychological studies, examining the broad evolutionary development of human thought and culture. Thus Wundt was a scholar of great range and enormous productive energy. Mead would apparently find much in the work of Wundt to stimulate his own thought.

Wundt's View of Gestures

In much of his work Mead devoted considerable space to Wundt's view of "gestures" and "speech."[27] Mead argued that Wundt was the first to recognize that gestures represent signs marking the course of ongoing action and that animals use these signs as ways of adjusting to each other. Human language, Wundt had argued, represents only an extension of this basic process in lower animals, since common and consensual meanings were, over the course of human evolution, given to signs. And as human mental capacities had grown, such gestures could be used for deliberate communication and interaction.

All of these points of emphasis, while greatly distorted by Wundt's poor ethnographic accounts, were to be incorporated in altered form into Mead's scheme.[28] Gestures were to be viewed as the basis for communication and interaction, and language was to be defined as gestures that carry common meanings. And as Wundt had implied,

---

Human and Animal Psychology, 2nd ed. (New York: Macmillan, 1894; originally published in 1892); *Outlines of Psychology,* 7th ed. (Leipzig: Engleman, 1907; originally published in 1896); and *Elements of Folk Psychology: Outlines of a Psychological History of the Development of Mankind* (London: George Allen, 1916).

[27]See, for a more complete discussion, Wilhelm Wundt, *The Language of Gestures* (The Hague: Mouton, 1973).

[28]See, for example, Wundt, *Folk Psychology.*

humans are unique creatures, and society is possible only by virture of language and its use to create customs, myths, and other symbol systems.

Wundt's View of "Mental Communities"

Mead did not give Wundt credit for inspiring more than a sociological vision of gestures and language. Yet sprinkled throughout Wundt's work are ideas that bear considerable resemblance to those developed by Mead. One such idea is what Wundt termed the *mental community*.[29] Wundt saw the development of speech, self-consciousness, and mental activity in children as emerging out of interaction with the social environment. Such interaction, he argued, makes possible identification with a mental community that guides and directs human action and interaction in ways functionally analogous to the regulation of lower animals by instincts. Such mental communities can vary in their nature and extensiveness, producing great variations in human action and patterns of social organization. Just as Durkheim in France had emphasized the significance of the collective conscious, Wundt saw humans as regulated by a variety of mental communities. Mead was, we suspect, to translate this notion of mental community into his vision of "generalized others"or "communities of attitudes" that regulate human action and organization.

In sum, then, Mead appears to have taken from Wundt two critical points. First, interaction is a process of gestural communication, with language being a more developed form of such communication. Second, social organization is more than a process of interaction among people; it is also a process of socialization in which humans acquire the ability to create and use mental communities to regulate their action and interaction. As we will come to see, these two points are at the core of Mead's theory of mind, self, and society.

WILLIAM JAMES AND G. H. MEAD

By 1890 William James was the most prominent psychologist in America, attracting students and worldwide attention. Yet James was also a philosopher who, along with Dewey, became the foremost advocate of pragmatism. Mead borrowed from both James's philosophy and his psychology, incorporating the general thrust of James's philosophy and his specific views on consciousness and self-consciousness.

---

[29]Wundt, *Outlines of Psychology*, pp. 296–98.

James's Pragmatism

In many ways James was the most extreme of the pragmatists, advocating the view that there is no such thing as "absolute truth."[30] Truth is temporary and lasts only as long as it works—that is, only as long as it allows for adjustment and adaptation to the environment. James thus rejected the notion that truth involves a search for isormorphism between theoretical principles and empirical reality and that science represents an effort to increase the degree of isomorphism. For James, theories are merely "instruments" to be used for a time in an effort to facilitate adjustment. Hence objective, permanent, and enduring truth cannot be found.

Mead never completely accepted this extreme position. Indeed much of his work was directed at discovering some of the fundamental principles describing the basic relationship between individuals and society. Mead did, however, accept and embrace the pragmatic notion that human life is a constant process of adjustment and that the faculty for consciousness is the key to understanding the nature of this adjustment.

James's View of Consciousness

James defined psychology as the "science of mental life."[31] As a science, the goal of psychology is to understand the nature of mental processes—that is, the nature of "feelings, desires, cognitions, reasons, decisions, and the like."[32] His classic text, *The Principles of Psychology*, became the most important work in American psychology since it sought to summarize what was then known about mental life. It also contained James's interpretation of mental phenomena, and by far the most important of these interpretations was James's conceptualization of consciousness as a process. For James, consciousness is a "stream" and "flow," not a structure of elements, as Wundt had proposed.[33] Thus, for James, "mind" is simply a process of thinking, and with this simple fact psychological investigation must begin:

> The only thing which psychology has a right to postulate at the outset is the fact of thinking itself, and that must first be taken up and analyzed.[34]

---

[30]James, *Meaning of Truth*.

[31]William James, *The Principles of Psychology* (New York: Holt, Rinehart & Winston, 1890), p. 1.

[32]Ibid.

[33]James had also developed the notion of a "stream of consciousness" in his *The Varieties of Religious Experience* (New York: Longmans, Green, 1902).

[34]James, *Principles of Psychology*, p. 224.

James then went on to list five characteristics of thought: (1) thought is personal and always, to some degree, idiosyncratic to each individual; (2) thought is always changing; (3) thought is continuous; (4) to the individual, it appears to deal with objects in an external world; and (5) it is selective and focuses on some objects to the exclusion of others.[35] Of these characteristics, Mead appears to have been most influenced by 4 and 5. For Mead, mind is to be seen as a process of selectively denoting objects and of responding to these objects. While the details of his conceptualization of thinking reflect Dewey's influence more than that of James, this early discussion by James likely shaped Mead's emphasis on selective perception of objects in the environment.

Far more influential on Mead's thought than James's view of consciousness in general was James's conceptualization of self-consciousness.[36] Here Mead borrowed much and was directly influenced by James's recognition that one of the objects in the flow of consciousness is oneself.

James's View of Self-Consciousness

James's examination of self began with the assertion that people recognize themselves as objects in empirical situations. He called this process the *empirical self* or *me*—the latter term being adopted by Mead in his examination of self-images. But James went on to describe various types of empirical selves that all people evidence: (1) the material self, (2) the social self, and (3) the spiritual self. Moreover, each type or aspect of self was seen by James as involving two dimensions: (1) self-feelings (emotions about oneself) and (2) self-seekings (actions prompted by each self). Not only are there types of selves, revealing variations with respect to self-feelings and self-seeking, but there is a hierarchy among the various selves. Thus James offered an elaborate taxonomy of self-related processes, and although Mead's own conceptualization was sparse by comparison, he selectively borrowed from the entire scheme.

Types of Empirical Selves.   For James, the material self embraces people's conceptions of their body as well as their other possessions, since one's actual body and possessions both evoke similar feelings and actions. The social self is, in reality, a series of selves that people have in different types of situations. Thus one may have somewhat

---

[35]Ibid., pp. 225–90.
[36]Ibid., pp. 291–401.

different self-feelings and action tendencies depending on the type of social situation—whether work, family, club, community, and so on. For Mead, this vision of a social self was to become most important, for people's self-feelings and actions are, Mead was to argue, most influenced by their conception of themselves in social meetings. The spiritual self was not clearly described by James, but it appears to embody those most intimate feelings people have about themselves—that is, their worth, their talents, their strengths, and their failings. In *The Principles of Psychology,* James summarized his conceptualization of empirical selves and their constituent dimensions with a table, which is shown in Table 14–1.[37]

The Hierarchy of Empirical Selves. James felt some aspects of different empirical selves are more important than others. As he noted:

> A tolerably unanimous opinion ranges the different selves of which a man may be "seized and possessed," and the consequent different orders of his self-regard, in an [sic] *hierarchical scale, with the bodily Self at the bottom, the spiritual Self at Top, and the extracorporeal material selves and the various social selves between.*[38]

TABLE 14–1 James's Conceptualization of Empirical Selves

	The Empirical Life of Self is Divided into		
	Material	*Social*	*Spiritual*
Self-seeking	Bodily appetites and instincts Love of adornment, foppery, acquisitiveness, constructiveness Love of home, and so on	Desire to please, be noticed, admired, and so on Sociability, emulation, envy, love, pursuit of honor, ambition, and so on	Intellectual, moral and religious aspiration, conscientiousness
Self-estimation	Personal vanity, modesty, and so on Pride of wealth, fear of poverty	Social and family pride, vainglory, snobbery, humility, shame, and so on	Sense of moral or mental superiority, purity, and so on Sense of inferiority or of guilt

---

[37]Ibid., p. 329.
[38]Ibid., p. 313 (emphasis in original).

Thus some degree of unity among a person's selves is achieved through their hierarchical ordering, with self-feelings and action tendencies being greatest for those selves high in the hierarchy. A further source of unity comes from the nonempirical self, or what James termed the *pure ego*.

The Pure Ego and Personal Identity. Above these empirical selves, James argued, is a unity. People have "a personal identity" or *pure ego* in that they have a sense of continuity and stability about themselves as objects. Like all sensations, humans take their somewhat diverse empirical selves and integrate them, seeing in them continuity and sameness.[39] Mead was, no doubt, greatly influenced by this conception of a stable and unified self-conception. For as Mead was to argue, humans develop over time, from their experiences in the empirical world, a more "unified" or "complete" self—that is, a stable self-conception. This stable self-conception, Mead was to emphasize, gives individuals a sense of personal continuity and their actions in society a degree of stability and predictability.

In sum, then, Mead's view of self as one of the distinctive features of humans was greatly influenced by William James's work. James was not as concerned as Mead was with understanding the emergence of self or its consequences for the social order. But he provided Mead with several critical insights about the nature of self: (1) self is a process of seeing oneself as an object in the stream of conscious awareness; (2) self varies from one empirical situation to another, and yet (3) self also reveals unity and stability across situations. Mead never adopted James's taxonomy, but he took the broad contours of James's outline and demonstrated their significance for understanding the nature of human action, interaction, and organization.

CHARLES HORTON COOLEY AND G. H. MEAD

Mead and Charles Horton Cooley were approximate contemporaries; and as we noted, they were colleagues in their early careers at the University of Michigan. Their direct interaction was, no doubt, significant, but Cooley's influence extended beyond their period of colleagial contact. Indeed it is from Cooley that Mead was to adopt a number of critical insights into the origins and nature of self as well as its significance for social organization.

It must be admitted that Cooley's sociology is often vague, excessively mentalistic, and highly moralistic. Yet we can observe several

---

[39]Ibid., p. 334.

lines of influence on Mead in Cooley's recognition that (1) society is constructed from reciprocal interaction, (2) interaction occurs through the exchange of gestures, (3) self is created from, and allows for the maintenance of, patterns of social organization, and (4) social organization is possible by virtue of people's attachment to groups that link them to the larger institutions of society. We should therefore examine in more detail these lines of influence.

Cooley's View of Social Organization

Cooley held the view that society is an organic whole in which specific social processes work to create, maintain, and change networks of reciprocal activity.[40] Much as Mead was to argue, Cooley saw the "vast tissue" of society as constructed from diverse social forms— from small groups to large-scale social institutions. Yet the cement linking these diverse forms together is the capacity of humans to interact with each other and to share common ideas and conceptions. Such interaction is dependent on the unique capacities of humans to use gestures and language.

Cooley's View of Interaction

Cooley saw that humans have the ability to assign common meanings and interpretations to their gestures—whether words, bodily countenance, facial expressions, or other gestural emissions. In this way humans can communicate, and out of this communication they establish social relations.

> By communication is here meant the mechanism through which human relations exist and develop—all the symbols of the mind, together with the means of conveying them through space and preserving them in time.[41]

Mead was to accept Cooley's view of social organization as constructed gestural communication. But more important, Cooley gave Mead a clue as to how gestural communication leads to interaction and organization. By reading each other's gestures, peole are able to "read each other's mind"—that is, to see and interpret the dispositions of others. Hence

---

[40]Charles Horton Cooley, *Social Process* (New York: Charles Scribner's Sons, 1918), p. 28.

[41]Charles Horton Cooley, *Social Organization: A Study of the Larger Mind* (New York: Charles Scribner's Sons, 1916), p. 61.

Society is an interweaving and interworking of mental selves. I imagine your mind . . . I dress my mind before yours and expect that you will dress yours before mine.[42]

Mead was to take this somewhat vague idea and translate it into an explicit view of interaction and social organization as a process of reading gestures, placing oneself mentally into the position of others, and adjusting conduct so as to cooperate with others. Moreover, Mead was to accept Cooley's recognition that self is the critical link in the creation and maintenance of society from patterns of reciprocal communication and interaction.

Cooley's View of Self

Cooley emphasized that humans have the capacity for self-consciousness. This capacity emerges out of interaction with others in groups, and once it exists, it allows people to organize themselves into society. Mead was to adopt the general thrust of this argument, although he was to make it considerably more explicit and coherent. Mead appears to have taken three distinct lines of argument from Cooley's somewhat vague and rambling discussion: (1) self as constructed from the *looking glass* of other people's gestures, (2) self as emerging out of interaction in groups, and (3) self as a basis for self-control and hence social organization. Each of these is examined below.

The "Looking-Glass Self."   Cooley adopted William James's view of self as the ability to see and recognize oneself as an object. But he added a critical insight: Humans use the gestures of others to see themselves. The images people have of themselves are similar to reflections from a looking glass, or mirror; they are provided by the reactions of others to one's behavior. Thus by reading the gestures of others, humans see themselves as an object:

As we see our face, figure, and dress in the glass, and are interested in them because they are ours, . . . so in imagination we perceive in another's mind some thought of our appearance, manners, aims, deeds, character, friends, and so on, and are variously affected by it.[43]

As people see themselves in the looking glass of other people's gestures, then, they (1) imagine their appearance in the eyes of others,

[42]Charles Horton Cooley, *Life and the Student* (New York: Alfred A. Knopf, 1927), p. 200.

[43]Charles Horton Cooley, *Human Nature and the Social Order* (New York: Charles Scribner's Sons, 1902), p. 184.

(2) sense the judgment of others, and (3) have self-feelings about themselves. Thus during the process of interaction, people develop self-consciousness and self-feelings. While Cooley did not develop the idea in any great detail, he implied that humans develop, over time and through repeated glances in the looking glass, a more stable sense of self.

The Emergence of Self.   Cooley argued that the life history of an individual is evolutionary. Because their ability to read gestures is limited, young infants cannot initially see themselves as objects in the looking glass. But with time, practice, biological maturation, and exposure to varieties of others, children come to see themselves in the looking glass, and they develop feelings about themselves. Such a process, Cooley felt, is inevitable as long as the young must interact with others, since as the young act on their environment, others will react, and this reaction will be perceived.[44] Through this process, as it occurs during infancy, childhood, and adolescence, an individual's "personality" is formed. And as Mead was to argue, the existence of a more stable set of self-feelings gives human action stability and predictability, thereby facilitating cooperation with others.

Self and Social Control.   Cooley saw self as only one aspect of consciousness in general. And thus he divided consciousness into three aspects: (1) "self-consciousness" or self-awareness of, and feelings about, oneself; (2) "social consciousness" or a person's perceptions of, and attitudes toward, other people; and (3) "public consciousness" or an individual's view of others as organized in a "communicative group."[45] Cooley saw all three aspects of consciousness as "phases of a single whole."

Cooley never developed these ideas to any great degree, but Mead apparently saw much potential in these distinctions. For Mead, the capacity to see oneself as an object, to perceive the dispositions of others, and to assume the perspective of a broader "public" or "community" gives people a basis for stable action and cooperative interaction. Because of these capacities, then, society is possible.

Cooley's View of Primary Groups

Cooley argued that the most basic unit of society is the "primary group," which was defined as those associations characterized by "intimate face-to-face association and cooperation."

---

[44]Ibid., pp. 137–211.
[45]Cooley, *Social Organization*, p. 12.

They are primary in several senses but chiefly in that they are fundamental in forming the social nature and ideals of individuals. The result
of intimate association, psychologically, is a certain fusion of individu-
alities in a common whole, so that one's very self, for many purposes at
least, is the common life and purpose of the group.[46]

Thus the looking glass of gestures emitted by those in one's primary group are the most important in the emergence and maintenance
of self-feelings. Moreover, the link between individuals and the
broader institutional structure of society is the primary group. Institutions could not, Cooley stressed, be maintained unless past traditions and public morals are given immediate relevance to individuals
through intimacy of primary groups. Indeed, for Cooley, primary
groups "are the springs of life, not only for the individual but for social
institutions."[47]

Cooley's concept of the primary group appears to have influenced
Mead in two ways. First, Mead retained Cooley's position that self
emerges, in large part, by virture of an individual's participation in
face-to-face, organized activity. Second, Mead implicitly argued that
one of the bridges between the individual and broader institutional
structure of society is the small group, although Cooley's emphasis on
this point was much greater than Mead's.

Thus Mead was enormously influenced by the work of Charles
Horton Cooley. Although much of Cooley's work is excessively moralistic and goes to mentalistic extremes, Mead saw the full implications
of his ideas for understanding the nature of the relationship between
the individual and society. As we will come to appreciate in the next
chapter, Mead borrowed, extended, and integrated into a more coherent theory Cooley's views on gestures, interaction, self and its emergence, and social organization.

JOHN DEWEY AND G. H. MEAD

As we noted earlier, John Dewey and Mead were initially young
colleagues at the University of Michigan, and when Dewey moved to
the then new University of Chicago in 1894, he invited Mead to join
him in the Department of Philosophy and Psychology. Mead and
Dewey were thus colleagues until 1905, when Dewey left for Columbia
University. As colleagues, Dewey and Mead engaged in much dialogue;
therefore it is not surprising that their thoughts reveal many similarities. Yet as we emphasized earlier, Dewey was the intellectual star of
Chicago, and Dewey wrote in many diverse areas and generated much

---

[46]Ibid., p. 23.
[47]Ibid., p. 27.

attention, in and outside the academic world.[48] In contrast, the retiring Mead, who had great difficulty writing, was constantly in Dewey's shadow. But ironically, Mead in the long run made the more important intellectual contribution to sociology.

Mead accepted the broad contours of Dewey's pragmatism, but a more important influence on Mead's thought was Dewey's conceptualization of thought and thinking. Thus as Dewey extended his brilliance into philosophy, morals, education, methodology, the history of science, psychology, and virtually any area of inquiry that caught his interest,[49] Mead selectively borrowed several key ideas from Dewey's wide-ranging inquiries and incorporated them into a vision of what he was to term *mind*.

Dewey's Pragmatism

Dewey's pragmatism attacked the traditional dualisms of philosophy: knower and known, objects and thought of objects, and mind and external world. Dewey thought this dualism is false, the act of knowing and the "things" to be known are interdependent. Objects may exist in a world external to an individual, but their existence and properties are determined by the process of acting toward these objects. For Dewey, the basic process of human life consists of organisms acting on, and making inquiry into, their environment. Indeed the history of human thought has been a quest for greater certainty about the consequences of action. In a scheme that resembles Comte's law of the three stages, Dewey argued that religion represented the primitive way to achieve certainty; the classical world classified experience to achieve certainty; and the modern world now seeks to control nature through

---

[48]Dewey's bibliography is over seventy-five pages long, indicating his incredible productivity.

[49]Dewey's most important works, in addition to those cited earlier, include: *Outlines of a Critical Theory of Ethics* (Ann Arbor, Mich.: Register, 1891); *The Study of Ethics* (Ann Arbor, Mich.: Register, 1894); *The School and Society* (Chicago: University of Chicago Press, 1900); *Studies in Logical Theory* (Chicago: University of Chicago Press, 1903); with James H. Tufts, *Ethics* (New York: Holt, Rinehart & Winston, 1908); *How We Think* (Boston: D. C. Heath, 1910); *The Influence of Darwin on Philosophy* (New York: Holt, Rinehart & Winston, 1910); *Democracy and Education* (New York: Macmillan, 1916); *Essays in Experimental Logic* (Chicago: University of Chicago Press, 1916); *Reconstruction in Philosophy* (New York: Holt, Rinehart & Winston, 1920); *Experience and Nature* (La Salle, Ill.: Open Court, 1925); *Philosophy and Civilization* (New York: Minton, Balch, 1931); *Art as Experience* (New York: Minton, Balch, 1934); *A Common Faith* (New Haven, Conn.: Yale University Press, 1934); *Logic: The Theory of Inquiry* (New York: Holt, Rinehart & Winston, 1938); *Theory of Valuation* (Chicago: University of Chicago Press, 1939); *Problems of Men* (New York: Philosophical Library, 1946); and with A. F. Bentley, *Knowing and the Known* (Boston: Beacon Press, 1949).

the discovery of its laws of operation.[50] With the development of modern science, Dewey argued, a new problem emerges: Moral values can no longer be legitimized by God or by appeals to the natural order.[51]

Such is the philosophical dilemma Dewey proposed and then resolved with his pragmatism. Values, morality, and other evaluational ideas are to be found in the action of people as they seek to cope with their environment. Value is discovered and found as people try to adjust and adapt to a problematic situation. Thus when humans do not know the morality of a situation, they will seek to construct one and use it as an "instrument" to facilitate their adjustment to that situation. Value-oriented action is like all thought and action: It emerges from people's acts in a problematic situation. Mead was never to absorb the details of Dewey's "instrumentalism" or Dewey's almost frantic efforts to create the "good society."[52] But he did adopt the view that thinking and thought arise from the process of dealing with problematic situations.

Dewey's View of Thinking

Dewey's pragmatism led him to a vision of thinking as a process involving: (1) blockage of impulses, (2) selective perception of the environment, (3) rehearsal of alternatives, (4) overt action, (5) assessment of consequences; then if a situation is still problematic, a new sequence of perception, rehearsal, action, and so on until the problematic situation is eliminated.[53]

Mead was to adopt two aspects of this vision. First, he saw thinking as part of a larger process of action. Thinking occurs when an organism's impulses are blocked and when it is in maladjustment with its environment.[54] This line of argument became a part of Mead's theory of motivation and "stages of the act." Second, thinking for Mead involved selective perception of objects, covert and imaginative rehearsal of alternatives, anticipation of the consequences of alternatives, and selection of a line of conduct. These behavioral capacities Mead was to term *mind*, and they were clearly adapted from Dewey's discussion of human nature and conduct.[55]

---

[50]Dewey, *Quest for Certainty.*

[51]Dewey, *Influence of Darwin*, p. 22.

[52]However, it should be emphasized that Mead's ideals paralleled those of Dewey and that he was occasionally drawn into various reform causes.

[53]See, for example, Dewey, *Human Nature and Conduct* and *How We Think.*

[54]Indeed, Mead appeared to borrow Dewey's exact terms in *Human Nature and Conduct.*

[55]Ibid.

MEAD'S SYNTHESIS

We can now appreciate the intellectual world as Mead encountered it. The convergence of utilitarianism, pragmatism, Darwinism, and behaviorism gave Mead a general set of assumptions for understanding human behavior. The specific concepts of Wundt, James, Cooley, and Dewey gave Mead the necessary intellectual tools to understand that humans are unique by virtue of their behavioral capacities for mind and self. Conversely, mind and self emerge out of gestural interaction in society. But once they emerge, mind and self make for a distinctive form of gestural interaction and for an entirely revolutionary creation: symbolically regulated patterns of social organization. In broad strokes, such is the nature of Mead's synthesis. We can now examine the details of this synthesis in the next chapter. But we should remember that Mead, like most great intellects, built his synthesis on "the shoulders of giants."

CHAPTER 15

The Sociology of George Herbert Mead

Because G. H. Mead wrote relatively little in his lifetime, his major works are found in the published lecture notes of his students. As a result, the four posthumous books that constitute the core of Mead's thought are somewhat long and rambling. Moreover, with the exception of *Mind, Self, and Society,* his ideas are distinctly philosophical rather than sociological in tone.[1] Our goal in this chapter, therefore, is to pull from Mead's philosophical works key sociological insights, while devoting most of our analysis to the explicitly social psychological work, *Mind, Self, and Society.* Let us begin by briefly touching on Mead's broader philosophical vision in order to place into context his more sociological approach.

MEAD'S BROADER PHILOSOPHY

Much of Mead's sociology is only a part of a much broader philosophical view. This view was never fully articulated, nor was it well integrated, but two posthumous works, *Movements of Thought in the Nineteenth Century* and *The Philosophy of the Present,* provide a glimpse of Mead's broader vision.

Many fascinating themes are contained in these works, but one of the most persistent is that all human activity represents an adjustment and adaptation to the world. In *Movements of Thought* Mead traced the development of social thought from its early, prescientific phases to the contemporary modern, scientific stage. In a way reminiscent of Comte's

---

[1]The philosophical tone of his posthumously published lectures is revealed in the titles of the four books: *The Philosophy of the Present* (La Salle, Ill.: Open Court, 1959; originally published in 1932); *Mind, Self, and Society* (Chicago: University of Chicago Press, 1934); *Movements of Thought in the Nineteenth Century* (Chicago: University of Chicago Press, 1936); and *The Philosophy of the Act* (Chicago: University of Chicago Press, 1938). *Mind, Self, and Society* contains a bibliography of Mead's published work (pp. 390–92).

law of the three stages, Mead saw the great ideas of history as moving toward an ever more rational or scientific profile, because with the emergence of rational scientific thought, a better level of adaptation and adjustment to the world could be achieved.

The Philosophy of the Present is a somewhat disjointed series of essays that represent a more philosophical treatment of ideas contained in his social psychology, particularly in *Mind, Self, and Society.* Here again Mead emphasized that what is uniquely human is nothing but a series of particular behavioral capacities that have evolved from adaptations to the ongoing life process. Much of the discussion addresses purely philosophical topics about the ontological status of consciousnesses in the past, present, and future; but between the lines Mead stressed that the capacities of humans for thought and self-reflection do not necessitate a dualism between mind and body, because all of the unique mental abilities of humans are behaviors directed toward facilitating their adjustment to the environment as it is encountered in the present.

For sociologists, Mead's general philosophy is not of great importance, except that it led him to develop a conception of the relation between the individual and society. Mead's contribution resides in his capacity to isolate the basic properties of the relation between the individual and society. And so his works embody a theoretical perspective that marks a major contribution to sociological analysis. Most of this perspective is in Mead's posthumously published lectures on mind, self, and society.

MIND, SELF, AND SOCIETY

Mead's "book" on *Mind, Self, and Society* represents verbatim transcripts from his famous course on social psychology at the University of Chicago. While the notes come from the 1927 and 1930 versions of the course, the basic ideas on social interaction, personality, and social organization had been clearly developed a decade earlier.

At the time Mead addressed his students, the behaviorism of J. B. Watson and others simply abandoned serious effort to understand consciousness, personality, and other variables in the "black box" of human cognition. Mead felt such a "solution" to studying psychological processes was unacceptable.[2] Mead also felt the opposite philosophical

---

[2]As he observed with respect to Watson's efforts to deal with subjective experience: "John B. Watson's attitude was that of the Queen in *Alice in Wonderland*—Off with their heads!—there were no such things." Mead, *Mind, Self, and Society*, pp. 2–3.

tendency to view "mind," "spirit," "will," and other psychological states as a kind of spiritual entity was untenable. What is required, he argued, is for mind and self, as the two most distinctive aspects of human personality, and for "society" as maintained by mind and self, to be viewed as part of ongoing social processes.

Mead's View of the "Life Process"

The Darwinian theory of evolution provided Mead with a view of life as a process of adaptation to environmental conditions. The attributes of a species, therefore, are the result of selection for those characteristics allowing for adaptation to the conditions in which a species finds itself. This theory provided Mead with a general metaphor for viewing life in general and thus with a broad perspective for analyzing humans. Pragmatism, as philosophical doctrine, represented one way of translating the Darwinian metaphor into principles for understanding human behavior: Humans are "pragmatic" creatures who use their facilities for achieving "adjustment" to the world; and conversely, out of making adjustments to the world, much of what is unique to any individual arises. Dewey's pragmatism, termed *instrumentalism,* stressed the importance of critical and rational thought in making life adjustments to the world, giving Mead a view of thinking as the basic adjustment by which humans survive. Behaviorism, as a prominent psychological school of thought, converged with this emphasis in pragmatism, since it emphasized that all animals tend to retain those responses to environmental stimuli that are rewarded or reinforced. While the processes of thinking were regarded as too "psychical" by behaviorists like Watson, the stress on the retention of reinforced behaviors was not inconsistent with Darwinian notions of adaptation and survival or with pragmatist ideas of response and adjustment. Even utilitarianism—especially that of such thinkers as Jeremy Bentham, who emphasized the pleasure and pain principles—could be seen by Mead as compatible with the theories of evolution, behaviorism, and pragmatism. The utilitarian emphasis on "utility," "pleasure," and "pain" was certainly compatible with behaviorist notions of reinforcement; the utilitarian concern with rational thought and the weighing of alternatives was compatible with Dewey's instrumentalism and its concept of critical thinking; and the utilitarian view that order emerges out of competition among free individuals seemed to parallel Darwinian notions of struggle as the underlying principle of the biotic order.

Thus the unique attributes of humans, such as their capacity to use language, their ability to talk to each other as well as to themselves, their ability to view themselves as objects, and their capacity to reason, must all be viewed as emerging out of the life processes of adaptation and adjustment. Mind and self cannot be ignored, as behaviorists often sought to do, nor can they be seen as a kind of mystical and spiritual force that elevated humans out of the basic life processes influencing all species. Humans as species evolved like other life forms, and hence their most distinctive attributes—mind, self, and society—must be viewed as emerging out of the basic process of adaptation. Further, each individual member of the human species is like the individuals of other species: What they are is the result of the common biological heritage of their species as well as their adjustment to the particulars of a given environment.

Mead's Social Behaviorism

Mead did not define his work as *social* behaviorism, but subsequent commentators have used this term to distinguish his work from Watsonian behaviorism. In contrast to Watson, who simply denied the distinctiveness of subjective consciousness, Mead felt it is possible to use broad behavioristic principles to understand "subjective behavior":

> Watson apparently assumes that to deny the existence of mind or consciousness as a psychical [sic] stuff, substance, or entity is to deny its existence altogether, and that a naturalistic or behavioristic account of it as such is out of the question. But, on the contrary, we may deny its existence as a psychical entity without denying its existence in some other sense at all; and if we then conceive of it functionally, and as a natural rather than a transcendental phenomenon, it becomes possible to deal with it in behavioristic terms.[3]

If subjective experiences in humans are viewed as behavior, then it is possible to understand them in behavioristic terms. For the unique mental capacities of humans are a model of behavior that arises from reinforcement processes that explain nonsubjective and overt behavior. Of particular importance for understanding the attributes of humans, then, is the reinforcement that comes from adaptation and adjustment to environmental conditions. At some point in the distant past, the unique mental capacities of humans, and the creation of society employing these capacities, emerged out of the process of natural selection under natural environmental conditions. But once the unique patterns of human organization are created, the "environment" for any individual is social—that is, it is an environment of other people to whom an individual must adapt and adjust.

---

[3]Ibid., p. 10.

Thus social behaviorism stresses the processes by which individuals come to acquire a certain behavioral repertoire by virtue of their adjustments to ongoing patterns of social organization. This analysis must begin with the observable fact that organized activity occurs and then attempt to understand the particular actions of individuals in terms of their adjustment to such organized activity:

> We are not, in social psychology, building up the behavior of the social group in terms of the behavior of separate individuals composing it; rather, we are starting out with a given social whole of complex group activity, into which we analyze (as elements) the behavior of each of the separate individuals composing it. We attempt, that is, to explain the conduct of the individual in terms of the organized conduct of the social group, rather than to account for the organized conduct of the social group in terms of the conduct of the separate individuals belonging to it.[4]

The behavior of individuals—not just their observable actions but also their internal behaviors of thinking, assessing, and evaluating—must be analyzed within a social context. For what is distinctively human emerges out of adjustment to ongoing social activity or "society." Thus Mead's social behaviorism must be distinguished from the behavioristic approach of Watson[5] in two ways. First, the existence of inner subjective experiences is not denied or viewed as methodologically irrelevant,[6] but rather these experiences are viewed as behavior. Second, the behaviors of humans—including those distinctly human behaviors of mind and self—arise out of adaptation and adjustment to ongoing and organized social activity. Reinforcement is thus equated with the degree of adjustment and adaptation to society.

Mead's Behavioristic View of Mind

For any given individual, "mind" is a type of behavioral response that emerges out of interaction with others in a social context. Without interaction, mind could not exist:

> We must regard mind, then, arising and developing within the social process, within the empirical matrix of social interactions. We must, that is, get an inner individual experience from the standpoint of social acts which include the experiences of separate individuals in a social context wherein those individuals interact. The processes of experience which the human brain makes possible are made possible only for a

---

[4]Ibid., p. 7.
[5]And, of course, the more recent version of B. F. Skinner and others of this stripe.
[6]That is, since they cannot be directly observed, they cannot be studied.

group of interacting individuals: only for individual organisms which are members of a society; not for the organism in isolation from other individual organisms.[7]

Gestures and Mind.   The social process in which mind emerges is one of communication with gestures. Mead gave German psychologist Wilheim Wundt credit for understanding the central significance of the gesture to communication and interaction. In contrast to Darwin, who had viewed gestures as expressions of emotions, Wundt recognized that a gesture is that part of ongoing behavior of one organism that stimulates behavior of another organism.[8] Mead took this basic idea and extended it in ways that became the basis for not only the emergence of mind and self but also for the creation, maintenance, and change of society.

Mead formulated the concept of the "conversation of gestures" to describe the simplest form of interaction. During action on the part of one organism, gestures are emitted that stimulate a response from a second organism. In turn, the response of the second organism involves emission of gestures that stimulate an "adjusted response" from the first organism. Then, if interaction still continues, the adjusted response of the first organism involves emitting gestures that result in yet another adjustment of behavior by the second organism, and so on, as long as the two organisms continue to interact. Mead frequently termed this conversation of gestures the *triadic matrix*, because it involves three interrelated elements:

1. Gestural emission by one organism as it acts on its environment.

2. A response by another organism in the environment as it reacts to this gestural emission. This response then becomes a gestural stimulus to the acting organism.

3. An adjusted response by the acting organism that takes into account the gestural stimuli of the responding organism.

This triadic matrix constitutes the simplest form of communication and interaction among organisms. This form of interaction, Mead felt, typifies "lower animals" and human infants. For example, if one dog growls, indicating to another dog that it is about to attack, then the other will react, perhaps by running away, requiring the growling dog to adjust its response by chasing the fleeing dog or by turning elsewhere to vent its aggressive impulses. Or, to take another example, a

---

[7]Mead, *Mind, Self, and Society*, p. 133.

[8]As Mead observed: "The term *gesture* may be identified with these beginnings of social acts which are stimuli for the response of other forms." Ibid., p. 43.

hungry infant cries, which in turn arouses a response in its mother (for example, the mother feeds the infant), which in turn results in an adjusted response by the infant.

Much of the significance of Mead's discussion of the triadic matrix is that the mentalistic concept of "meaning" is lodged in the interaction process rather than in "ideas" or other mentalistic notions that might reside outside interaction. If a gesture "indicates to another organism the subsequent behavior of a given organism, then it has meaning."[9] Thus if a dog growls and another dog uses this gesture to predict an attack, then this gesture of growling has meaning. Meaning is thus given a behavioristic definition: It is a kind of behavior—a gesture—of one organism that signals to another subsequent behavior of this organism. Meaning, therefore, need not involve complex cognitive or mental activity. A dog that runs away from another growling dog, Mead would assert, is reacting without "ideas" or "elaborate deliberation"; yet the growl has meaning to the dog, since it uses the growl as an early indicator of what will follow. Thus meaning is

> not to be conceived, fundamentally, as a state of consciousness, or as a set of organized relations existing or subsisting mentally outside the field of experience into which they enter; on the contrary, it should be conceived objectively, as having its existence entirely within this field itself.[10]

The significance of the conversation of gestures for ongoing activity resides in the fact that the triadic matrix, and associated meanings, allow organisms to adjust their responses to each other. Thus as organisms use each other's gestures as a means for adjusting their respective responses, they become increasingly capable of organized and concerted conduct. Yet such gestural conversations limit the capacity of organisms to organize themselves and to cooperate with each other. But among humans, Mead asserted, a qualitatively different form of communication evolved. This is communication involving *significant symbols*. And Mead felt the development of the capacity to use significant symbols distinguishes the human from other species. And it is from the development of the capacity to use significant symbols in a maturing human infant that *mind* arises. In turn, as we will come to see, the existence of mind assures the development of self and the perpetuation and change of society.

Significant Symbols and Mind. The gestures of "lower organisms," Mead felt, do not call out the same response in the organism

---

[9]Ibid., p. 76.
[10]Ibid., p. 78.

emitting a gesture and the one interpreting the gesture. As he observed, the roar of the lion does not mean the same thing to the lion and its potential victim. When organisms become capable of using gestures that evoke the same response in each other, then they are employing what Mead termed *significant* or *conventional* gestures. As Mead illustrated, if a person shouts the word *fire* in a movie theater, this gesture evokes the same response tendency (escape, fleeing, and so on) in the person emitting the gesture and in those receiving it. Such gestures, Mead felt, are unique to humans and make possible their capacities for mind, self, and society.[11]

Significant symbols are, as Mead emphasized, the basis for language. Of particular significance are vocal significant symbols, because sounds can be readily heard by both sender and receiver, thus evoking a similar behavioral tendency. Other nonvocal gestures, however, are also significant in that they can come to mobilize similar tendencies to act. Thus a frown, glare, clenched fist, rigid stance, and the like can all become significant in that they serve as a stimulus to similar responses by senders and receivers. Thus the human capacity for language—that is, communication by significant symbols—makes for the emergence of their unique capacities for mind and self. And not until an infant of the species acquires the rudimentary capacity for language can it have a mind.

In what ways, then, does language make mind possible? Mead borrowed Dewey's vision of "reflective" and "critical" thinking, as well as the utilitarian's vision of "rational choice," in formulating his conceptualization of mind. For Mead, mind involves several behavioral capacities:

1. The capacity to denote objects in the environment with significant symbols.

2. The capacity to use these symbols as a stimulus to one's own response.

3. The capacity to read and interpret the gestures of others and use these as a stimulus for one's response.

4. The capacity to temporarily suspend or inhibit overt behavioral responses to one's own gestural denotations, or those of others.

5. The capacity to "imaginatively rehearse" alternative lines of conduct, visualize their consequences, and select the response that will facilitate adjustment to the environment.

---

[11]However, the evidence is now clear that other higher primates can use such "significant gestures."

Mind is thus a behavior, not a substance or entity. It is behavior that involves using significant symbols to stimulate responses, but at the same time, to inhibit or delay overt behavior so that potential responses can be covertly rehearsed and assessed. Mind is thus an "internal conversation of gestures" using significant symbols, since an individual with mind talks to itself. It uses significant symbols to stimulate a line of response; it visualizes the consequences of this response; and if necessary, it inhibits the response and uses another set of symbols to stimulate alternative responses; and so on, until the organism is satisfied with its response and overtly pursues a given line of conduct.

This capacity for mind, Mead stressed, is not inborn. It depends on a certain level of biological maturation in the central nervous system and cerebral cortex; but most important, it depends on interaction with others and the acquisition of the ability to interpret and use their significant symbols. As Mead noted, feral children who are raised without significant symbols do not seem "human" because they have not had to adjust to an environment mediated by significant symbols and hence have not acquired the behavioral capacities for mind.

Role-Taking and Mind.   Mind emerges in an individual because human infants, if they are to survive, must adjust and adapt to a social environment—that is, to a world of organized activity. At first, an infant is like a "lower animal" in that it responds reflexively to the gestures of others and emits gestures that do not evoke similar responses in it and those in the environment. But such a level of adjustment, Mead implied, is neither efficient nor adaptive. A baby's cry does not indicate what it wants, whether food, water, warmth, or whatever, and by not reading accurately the vocal and other gestures emitted by others in their environment, the young can frequently create adjustment problems for themselves. Thus with a metaphor that is both Darwinian and behavioristic, there is "selective pressure" for acquiring the ability to use and interpret significant gestures, and hence those gestures that bring reinforcement—that is, adjustment to the environment—are likely to be retained in the response repertoire of the infant.

A critical process in using and interpreting significant gestures is what Mead termed "taking the role of the other," or *role-taking*. An ability to use significant symbols means the gestures emitted by others in the environment allow a person to read or interpret the dispositions of these others. For example, an infant who has acquired the rudimentary ability to interpret significant symbols can use its mother's tone of voice, facial expressions, and words to imagine her feelings and potential actions—that is, to "take on" her role or perspective. Role-taking is critical to the emergence of mind, for unless the gestures of others, and

FIGURE 15–1   Mead's Model on the Genesis of Mind

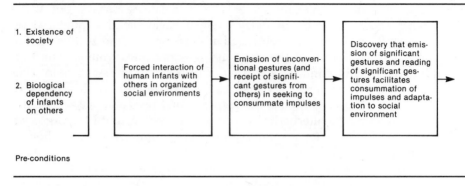

Pre-conditions

the disposition to act that these gestures reveal, can become a part of the stimuli used to covertly rehearse alternative lines of conduct, overt behavior will often produce maladjustment to the environment. For without the ability to assume the perspective of others with whom one must deal, it is difficult to adjust to, and coordinate responses with, these others.

The Genesis of Mind.   Mead saw mind as developing in a sequence of phases, as is represented in Figure 15–1. Because an infant is dependent on others, and in turn these others are dependent for their survival on society, mind develops out of the forced dependency of an infant on society. Since society is held together by actors who use language and who can role-take, the infant must seek to meet its needs in a world mediated by symbols. Through conscious coaching by others, and through simple trial and error, the infant comes to use significant symbols to denote objects relevant to satisfying its needs (such as food, mother, and so on). To consummate other impulses, the infant eventually must acquire greater capacities to use and understand language; once an infant can use language, it can begin to read the gestures of others and call out in itself the dispositions of others. When a young child can role-take, it can soon begin to consciously think, reflect, and rehearse responses. In other words it reveals the rudimentary behavioral abilities Mead termed *mind*.[12]

---

[12]For other published statements by Mead on the nature and operation of mind, see "Image and Sensation," *Journal of Philosophy* 1 (1904), pp. 604–7; "Social Consciousness and the Consciousness of Meaning," *Psychological Bulletin* 7 (1910), pp. 397–405; "The Mechanisms of Social Consciousness," *Journal of Philosophy* 9 (1912), pp. 401–6; "Scientific Method and Individual Thinker," in *Creative Intelligence* (New York: Holt, Rinehart & Winston, 1917), pp. 176–227; "A Behavioristic Account of the Significant Symbols," *Journal of Philosophy* 19 (1922), pp. 157–63.

FIGURE 15–1 *(continued)*

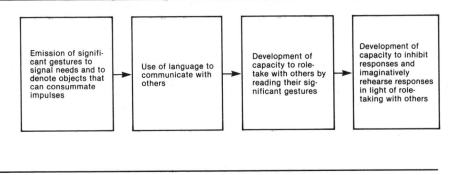

The causal arrows in Figure 15–1 actually represent a series of pre-conditions for the next stage of development. The model is "value added" in that certain conditions must be met before subsequent events can occur. Underlying these conditions is Mead's implicit vision of "social selection," which represents his reconciliation of learning theory principles with pragmatism and Darwinism. The development of abilities for language, role-taking, and mind are selected for as the infant seeks to consummate impulses in society. If the infant is to adjust and adapt to society, it must acquire the ability for minded behavior. And thus as the infant lives in a social environment, it learns those behaviors—first significant symbols, then role-taking, and eventually mind—that facilitate, to ever-increasing degrees, its adjustment to the social environment.

Thus the model presented in Figure 15–1 underscores Mead's view that there is nothing mysterious or mystical about the human mind. It is a behavior acquired like other behavioral tendencies as a human organism attempts to adapt to its surroundings. And it is a behavioral capacity acquired in stages, with each stage setting the conditions for the next. As mind emerges, so does self-awareness. And in many respects the emergence of mind is a precondition for the genesis of self. Yet the rudiments of self begin with an organism's ability to role-take, for it can then derive self-images or see itself as an object.

Mead's Behavioristic View of Self

The Social Nature of Self. As a "social behaviorist," Mead emphasized that the capacity to view oneself as an object in the field of experience is a type of learned behavior. It is learned through interaction with others:

The self is something which has a development; it is not initially there, at birth, but arises in the process of social experience and activity, that is, develops in the given individual as a result of his relations to that process as a whole and to other individuals within that process.[13]

Self emerges out of the capacity to use language and to take the role of the other. Borrowing the essentials of Cooley's "looking-glass self,"[14] Mead viewed the social self as emerging out of a process in which individuals read the gestures of others, or "take their attitudes," and derive an image or picture of themselves as a certain type of object in a situation. This image of oneself then acts as a behavioral stimulus, calling out certain responses in the individual. In turn, these responses of an individual cause further reactions on the part of others, resulting in the emission of gestures that enable role-taking by an individual, who then derives new self-images and new behavioral stimuli. Thus, like mind, self arises out of the triadic matrix of people interacting and adjusting their responses to each other. For the individual does not experience self directly, but only indirectly through reading the gestures of others:

> The individual experiences himself, not directly, but only indirectly, from the particular standpoints of other individual members of the same social group, or from the generalized standpoint of the social group as a whole to which he belongs . . . and he becomes an object to himself only by taking the attitudes of other individuals toward himself within a social environment or context of experience and behavior in which both he and they are involved.[15]

The Structure of Self.   Mead appeared to use the notion of "self" in several different ways. One usage involves viewing self as a "transitory image" of oneself as an object in a particular situation. Thus as people interact with each other, they role-take and derive self-images of themselves in that situation. In contrast to this conceptualization, Mead also viewed self as a structure, or configuration of typical responses that people have toward themselves as objects. For "after a self has arisen, it in a certain sense provides for itself its social experiences."[16]

---

[13]Mead, *Mind, Self, and Society*, p. 135.

[14]Mead did reject many of the specifics in Cooley's argument about "the looking-glass self." See, for example, ibid., p. 173; "Cooley's Contribution to American Social Thought," *American Journal of Sociology* 35 (1929–30), pp. 385–407; and "Smashing the Looking Glass," *Survey* 35 (1915–16), pp. 349–61.

[15]Mead, *Mind, Self, and Society*, p. 138.

[16]Ibid., p. 140.

These views are not, of course, contradictory. The process of deriving self-images leads to the crystallization of a set of attitudes toward oneself as a certain type of object. As such, humans begin to interpret selectively the gestures of others in light of their attitudes toward themselves, and thus their behaviors take on a consistency. For if the view of oneself as a certain type of object is relatively stable, and if we use self as an object like all other environmental objects as a stimulus for behavior, then overt behavior will reveal a degree of consistency across social situations.

Mead sometimes termed this development of stable attitudes toward oneself as an object, the *complete* or *unified* self. Yet he recognized that this complete self is not a rigid structure and that it is not imperiously and inflexibly imposed on diverse interactions. Rather, in different social contexts various aspects of the complete self are more evident. Depending on one's audience, then, different "elementary selves" will be evident:

> The unity and structure of the complete self reflects the unity and structure of the social process as a whole; and each of the elementary selves of which it is composed reflects the unity and structure of one of the various aspects of that process in which the individual is implicated. In other words, the various elementary selves that constitute, or are organized into, a complete self are the various aspects of the structure of that complete self answering to the various aspects of the structure of the social process as a whole; the structure of the complete self is thus a reflection of the complete social process.[17]

In this passage a further insight into the structure of self is evident: While elementary selves are unified by a complete self, people who experience a highly contradictory social environment with *disunity* in the social process will also experience difficulty in developing a complete self, or a relatively stable and consistent set of attitudes toward themselves as a certain type of object. To some extent, then, people present different aspects of their more complete and unified selves to different audiences, but when these audiences demand radically contradictory actions, then the development of a unified self-conception becomes problematic.

In sum, then, Mead's conceptualization is behavioristic in that he viewed seeing oneself as an object as a behavior unique to humans. Moreover, like other objects in one's environment, the self is a stimulus to behavior. And thus as people develop a consistent view of themselves as a type of object—that is, their self reveals a structure—their responses to this stable stimulus take on a consistency. However,

---

[17]Ibid., p. 144.

Mead's conceptualization of the structure of self involved the recognition that the stability of self is, to a very great extent, a consequence of the unity and stability in the social processes from which the self arises.

Phases of the Self.   Mead wanted to avoid connoting that the structure of self limited a person's repertoire of potential responses. While a unified self-conception provides considerable stability in, and predictability to, overt behaviors, there is always an element of spontaneity and unpredictability to action. This fact is inherent in the "phases of self," which were conceptualized by Mead in terms of the *I* and *me.*

The image of a person's behavior is what Mead termed the *me.* As such, the "me" represents the attitudes of others and the broader community as these influence an individual's retrospective interpretation of behavior. For example, if we talk too loudly in a crowd of strangers, we see the startled looks of others and will become cognizant of general norms about voice levels and inflections when among strangers. These are "me" images that are received by reading the gestures of specific others in a situation and by role-taking, or assuming the attitude, of the broader community. In contrast to the "me" is the "I," which is the actual emission of behavior. If a person speaks too loudly, this is "I"; and when this person reacts to his or her loudness, the "me" phase of action is initiated. Mead emphasized that the "I" "can only be known in experience," since we must wait for "me" images to know just what the "I" did. People cannot know until after they have acted ("I") just how the expectations of others ("me") are actually carried out.

Mead's conceptualization of the "I" and "me" allowed him to conceptualize the self as a constant process of behavior and self-image. People act; they view themselves as objects; they assess the consequences of their action; they interpret other's reaction to their action; and they resolve how to act next. Then, they act again, calling forth new self-images of their actions. This conceptualization of the phases of self enabled Mead to accomplish several conceptual tasks. First, he left room for spontaneity in human action; if the "I" can only be known in experience, or through the "me," then one's actions are never completely circumscribed. Second, and as we will explore in more detail later, it gave Mead a way of visualizing the process of self-control. Humans are, in Mead's view, cybernetic organisms who respond, receive feedback and make adjustment, and then respond again. In this way Mead could emphasize that, like mind, self is a process of adaptation; it is a behavior in which an organism successively responds to itself as an object as it adjusts to its environment. And third, the "I" and "me" phases of self gave Mead a way to conceptualize variations in the extent to which the expectations of others and the broader community constrain action. The *relative values* of the "I" and "me," as he phrased the matter,[18] are a positive function of people's status in a particular situation. The more involved in a group, the greater the values of "me" images and the greater the control of "I" impulses. Conversely, the less the involvement of a person in a situation, the less salient "me" images, and hence the greater the variation in that person's overt behavior.

The Genesis of Self.   Mead devoted considerable attention to the emergence of self and self-conceptions in humans. This attention allowed him to emphasize again that the self is a social product and a type of behavior that emerges from the efforts of the human organism to adjust and adapt to its environment. Self arises out of the same processes that lead to the development of "mind," while being dependent on the behavioral capacities of mind.

For self to develop, a human infant must acquire the ability to use significant symbols. For without this ability, it is not possible to role-take with others and thereby develop an image of oneself by interpreting the gestures of others. Self is also dependent on the capacities of mind, since people must be able to designate linguistically themselves as an object in their field of experience and to organize responses toward themselves as an object. Thus the use of significant symbols, the ability to role-take, and the behavioral capacities of mind are all preconditions for the development of self, particularly a more stable self-conception or "unified" self.

Mead visualized self as developing in three stages, each one marked by an increased capacity to role-take with a wider audience of others. The *play* stage is marked by a very limited capacity to role-take. A child can assume the perspective of only one or two others at a time, and play frequently involves little more than discourse and interaction with "imaginary companions" to whom the child talks as it enacts a particular role. Thus a child who plays "mother" may also, at the same time, assume the role of its baby, and in fact, the child may move back and forth between the mother's and infant's roles. The play stage is thus typified by the ability to assume the perspective of only a few others at a time.

With biological maturation and with practice at assuming the perspectives of others, a child eventually acquires the capacity to take the role of multiple others engaged in ongoing and organized activity. The

---

[18]Ibid., p. 199.

game is perhaps the most prototypical form of such role-taking, since in order to be a participant in a game, such as baseball, the child must assume the role of other players, anticipate how they will act, and co-ordinate responses with their likely course of action. Thus the child begins to see itself as an object in an organized field, and it begins to control and regulate its responses to itself and to others in such a way as to facilitate the coordination of activity. During this stage in the development of self, the number and variety of such game situations expands:

> There are all sorts of social organizations, some of which are fairly last-ing, some temporary, into which the child is entering, and he is playing a sort of social game in them. It is a period in which he likes "to be-long," and he gets into organizations which come into existence and pass out of existence. He becomes something which can function in the organized whole, and thus tends to determine himself in his relation-ship with the group to which he belongs.[19]

In both the play and game situations, individuals view themselves in relation to specific others. By role-taking with specific others lodged in particular roles, individuals derive images of themselves from the viewpoint of these others. Yet the self, Mead contended, cannot be complete until a final stage of role-taking is reached: the capacity to assume the perspective of the *generalized other.* Mead saw the general-ized other as a "community of attitudes" among members of an ongo-ing social collective. When an individual can view itself in relation to this community of attitudes and then adjust its conduct in accordance with the expectations of these attitudes, then it is role-taking with the generalized other. For Mead, the play and game represent the initial stages in the development of self, but in the final stage, the individual can generalize the varied attitudes of others and see itself and regulate its actions from a broader perspective.

Without this capacity to view oneself as an object in relation to the generalized other, behavior could only be situation specific. For unless people can see themselves as objects implicated in a broader social process, their actions cannot reveal continuity across situations. More-over, humans could not create larger societies, composed of multiple groupings, without the members of the society viewing themselves, and controlling their responses, in accordance with the expectations of the generalized other.[20]

---

[19]Ibid., p. 160.

[20]The similarity between Durkheim's notion of the collective conscience and Mead's conception of generalized other should be immediately apparent. But in contrast to

Mead recognized that in complex social systems there can be multiple generalized others. There can be a variety of broader perspectives from which an individual views itself and controls its behaviors. Moreover, a generalized other can represent the embodiment of collective attitudes of concrete and functioning groups, or it can be more abstract, pertaining to broad social classes and categories:

> In the most highly developed, organized, and complicated human social communities . . . , [the] various socially functional classes or subgroups of individuals to which any given individual belongs . . . are of two kinds. Some of them are concrete social classes or subgroups, such as political parties, clubs, corporations, which are all actually functional social units, in terms of which their individual members are directly related to one another. The others are abstract social classes or subgroups, such as the class of debtors and the class of creditors, in terms of which their individual members are related to one another only more or less indirectly, and which only more or less indirectly function as social units, but which afford or represent unlimited possibilities for the widening and ramifying and enriching of the social relations among all the individual members of the given society as an organized and unified whole.[21]

The capacity to take the role of multiple and diverse generalized others—from the perspective of a small group to that of a large category—enables diversely located individuals to engage in the processes of self-evaluation, self-criticisms, and self-control in terms of broader criteria than those provided by specific others in concrete groups. Thus by virtue of self-images derived from role-taking with specific others in concrete groups *and* from role-taking with generalized others that personify varying and multiple communities of attitudes, people come to themselves as a particular type of object, with certain strengths, weaknesses, and other attributes, and become capable of regulating their responses in terms of this vision of themselves as a certain type of object. And as people come to see themselves, and consistently respond to themselves, in terms of their particular configuration of specific and generalized attitudes of others, they come to possess what Mead termed a *complete* and *unified* self.

Durkheim, Mead provided the mechanism—role-taking and self-related behaviors—by which individuals become capable of viewing and controlling their actions in terms of the perspective of the collectivity. For more details along this line of argument, see Jonathan H. Turner, "A Note on G. H. Mead's Behavioristic Theory of Social Structure," *Journal for the Theory of Social Behavior* 12, July 1982, pp. 213–22; and *A Theory of Social Interaction* (Stanford, Calif.: Stanford University Press, 1988), chap. 10.

[21]Mead, *Mind, Self, and Society*, p. 157.

FIGURE 15–2 Mead's Model of the Genesis of Self

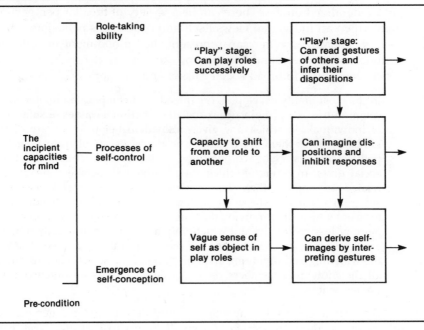

Figure 15–2 attempts to summarize the dynamic processes involved in creating a self. Figure 15–2 is more complex than Figure 15–1 because, as we mentioned above, Mead used the concept of "self" in several interrelated ways. And so, for purposes of interpreting the model portrayed in Figure 15–2, let us recapitulate Mead's various notions about self. First, Mead saw the development of self as a process of role-taking with increasingly varied and generalized "others." This facet of self is represented at the top of Figure 15–2, because increasing acuity at role-taking influences the other aspects of self (this is emphasized by the vertical arrows connecting the boxes at each stage in the emergence of self). Second, Mead visualized self as a process of self-control, as he emphasized in his notion of the "I" and "me" phases of self and in his view of "mind." This facet of self involves the growing ability to read the gestures of others, to inhibit inappropriate responses in relation to these others, and to adjust responses in a way that will facilitate interaction. But in its more advanced stages, self-control also comes to include the capacity to assume the "general" perspective or "community of attitudes" of specific groups, and eventually, of the broader community. The process of self-control thus represents the extensions of the capacities for mind, and for this reason the precondi-

FIGURE 15–2 *(continued)*

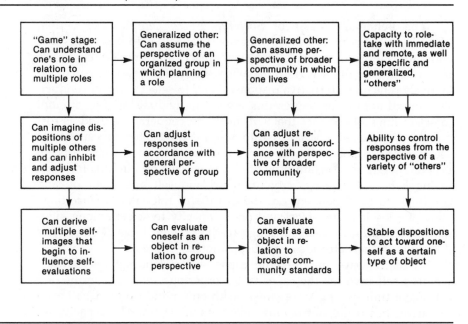

tion for self—that is, the "incipient capacity for mind" at the left of the model—is seen to tie almost directly into the self-control aspect of self. Third, self was also seen by Mead as involving the emergence of a self-conception, or stable disposition to act toward oneself as a certain type of object. Such a stable self-conception evolves out of the accumulation of self-images and self-evaluations with reference to specific, and then increasingly generalized, others.

Thus in reading Mead's model, the arrows that move from left to right denote the development of each aspect of self. The arrows that move down the columns stress Mead's emphasis on the role-taking process and on how developments in the ability to role-take influence the etiology of self-control processes and self-conceptions. Of course, we might also draw arrows back up the columns since, to some extent, self-control processes and self-conceptions influence role-taking abilities. But we feel the arrows, as currently drawn, appear to capture best Mead's vision of causal processes in the initial emergence of those multiple behavioral capacities he subsumed under the label *self*. These capacities are, in turn, vital to the production and reproduction of society, as is explored below.

Mead's Conception of Society

The Behavioral Basis of Society. As we emphasized earlier, Mead labeled as "mind" those behavioral capacities in organisms that allow for the use of symbols to denote objects and to role-take, to use objects as a stimuli for various behaviors, to inhibit responses, to imaginatively rehearse alternative responses, and to select a line of conduct. Thus mind allows for cooperation among individuals as they attempt to select lines of conduct that will facilitate cooperation. And as just noted, *self* is the term Mead used to describe the behavioral capacity to see oneself as an object in the environment and to use a stable conception of oneself as a certain type of object as a major stimulus for organizing behavior. The capacity for mind and self arises out of, and continues to be dependent on, the process of role-taking, since one's view of oneself as an object and one's capacity to select among alternative behaviors is possible through reading the gestures of others and determining their attitudes and dispositions.

In many ways mind is the capacity for denoting alternatives, whereas self involves the capacity for ordering choices in terms of a consistent framework. An organism with only mind could visualize alternatives but could not readily select among them. The capacity for self allows for the selection of behaviors among alternatives. And in so doing, self provides a source of stability and consistency in a person's behavior, while integrating that behavior into the social fabric, or society. Mead appears to have viewed several ways in which self provides for the integration of behavior into society.

First, the capacity to see oneself as an object in a field of objects allows for individuals to see themselves vis-à-vis other individuals. As such, they can see their place in the field of perception and hence adjust their responses (through the capacity for mind) so as to coordinate their activities.

Second, the emergence of a unified and complete self, or stable self-conception, means individuals consistently place into their perceptual field a view of themselves as a certain type of object. This object becomes a stimulus to subsequent behaviors that reveal a consistency of response, since they are responses to the self as a type of object that has certain stable attributes. People's behavior across widely divergent situations thus reveals consistency, because they introject, to some degree, a stable self-conception of themselves as a certain type of object, and this object, as much as any of the objects peculiar to a situation, serves as a stimulus to the organization of behavior in that situation. And the more rigid the self-conception, the more gestures of others are selectively interpreted and used to organize responses consistent with one's self-conception. The consequence for society of these self-related processes is that as people's actions take on consistency from situation to situation or from time to time in the same situation, their behaviors become predictable, thereby making it easier for individuals to adjust to, and cooperate with, each other.

Third, the process of role-taking allows individuals to see themselves not only in relation to specific others in particular situations but also in relation to varieties of generalized others. Thus by evaluating one's actions in terms of a generalized other, behaviors will take on consistency from situation to situation and from time to time. Moreover, to the degree that all participants to an interaction role-take with the same generalized other, they will approach and perceive situations within "common meanings," and they will be prepared to act in terms of the same perspective. By viewing themselves as objects in regard to the same set of expectations, then, people approach situations with common understandings that will facilitate their adjustment to each other.

A fourth—and related—point is that the capacity to role-take with varieties of generalized others allows individuals to elaborate patterns of social organization. Individuals are now liberated from the need for face-to-face interaction as the basis for coordinating their activities, for once they can role-take with varieties of generalized others, some of whom are abstract conceptions, they can come to guide their conduct in terms of a common perspective without directly role-taking with each other. Thus the capacity to view oneself as an object, and to adjust responses, in relation to the perspective of an abstract generalized other greatly extends the potential scope of patterns of social organization.

Fifth, in addition to providing behavioral consistency and individual integration into extended networks of interaction, self also serves as a vehicle of social change. The phases of self—the *I* and *me*, as Mead termed them—assure that individual behaviors will, to some degree, alter the flow of the social process. For even if "me" images reflect perfectly the expectations in a situation, and even if one's view of oneself as a certain type of object is totally congruent with these expectations, actual behavior—that is, the "I"—can deviate from what is anticipated in "me" images. This deviation, however small or great, forces others in the situation to adjust their behaviors, providing new "me" images to guide subsequent behaviors ("I")—and so on, in the course of interaction that moves in and out of "I" and "me" phases. Of course, when expectations are not clear, and when one's self-conception is at odds with the expectations of others, then "I" behaviors are likely to be less predictable, requiring greater adjustments on the part of others. Or, when the capacity to develop "me" images dictates changes in a situation for an individual—and this is often the case among individuals whose self-conception or generalized others are at odds—then even greater behavioral variance and social change can be expected as the "I" phase of action occurs. Thus the inherent phases of self—the "I" and "me"—make inevitable change in patterns of interaction. Sometimes these changes are small and imperceptible, and only after the long accumulation of small adjustments is the fact of change noticeable.[22] At other times the change is great, as when a person in political power initiates a new course of activity. In either case Mead went to great lengths to emphasize that self not only provides a source of continuity and integration for human behavior, it is also a source of change in society.[23]

In his analysis of "society" or patterns of social organization, then, Mead attempted to visualize how society is created, maintained, and changed through the processes of interaction among organisms with minds and selves. In emphasizing this connection between personality and society, Mead provided a valuable supplement to the more macrostructural analyses of European sociology. Yet the result is often a rather vague portrayal of society, since Mead had little interest in developing a coherent or detailed view of social structure. Thus one does not find in Mead the sense of substructures and superstructures evident in Marx's works, nor does one find Weber's passion for constructing ideal types of structural relations. To some extent Mead and Durkheim converge, in that both are vitally concerned with the symbolic bases for social integration; but they diverge in that Durkheim tended to view integration in terms of cultural and social structures, while Mead saw integration in terms of the behavioral capacities of mind and self. Mead and Simmel reveal some affinity, in that both were concerned with interaction, roles, and self; but Simmel's emphasis on the "forms of sociation" and Mead's interest in the mechanisms of symbolic interaction took them in different, but still compatible, directions.

What emerges from Mead's view of society, then, is not a vision of social structure and the emergent properties and forms of these structures. Rather Mead reaffirms that patterns of social organization, whatever their form and profile, are mediated by human behavioral capacities for language, role-taking, mind, and self. Aside from a general view stressed by all thinkers of his time, that societies are becoming more differentiated and complex, Mead offered only a few clues about the properties of social structures in human societies.

---

[22]Ibid., pp. 180, 202, and 216 for the relevant statements.

[23]For Mead's explicitly published works on self, see "The Social Self," *Journal of Philosophy* 10 (1913), pp. 374–80; "The Genesis of the Self and Social Control," *International Journal of Ethics* 35 (1924–25), pp. 251–77; and "Cooley's Contribution."

His analysis of society, therefore, is actually a series of statements on the underlying processes that make coordination among individuals possible. As long as this fact is recognized, we can avoid severe criticism of Mead's fragmentary and superficial discussion of social evolution and morphology. For his real contribution resides in his understanding of the behavioral mechanism—role-taking by language-using organisms with minds and selves—by which humans are able to coordinate their activities and construct elaborate patterns of social organization.

The Process of Society.   For Mead, the term *society* was simply a way of denoting the fact that interactive processes can reveal stability and that humans act within a framework imposed by stabilized social relations. The key to understanding society lies in the use of language and the practice of role-taking by individuals with mind and self. For by means of the capacity to use and read significant gestures, individuals can role-take and use their mind and self to articulate their actions to specific others in a situation and to a variety of generalized others. Since generalized others embody the broader groups—organizations, institutions, and communities—that mark the structure of society, they provide a common frame of reference for individuals to use in adjusting their conduct to each other.

Society is thus maintained by virtue of humans' ability to role-take with each other and to assume the perspective of generalized others. Mead implicitly argued that society as presented to any given individual represents a series of perspectives or "attitudes," which the individual assumes in regulating behavior. Some attitudes are those of others in one's immediate field; other perspectives are those of less immediate groups; still other attitudes come from more remote social collectives; additional perspectives come from the abstract categories used as a frame of reference; and ultimately, the entire population using a common set of symbols and meanings constitutes the most remote generalized other. Thus at any given time, an individual is role-taking with some combination of specific and generalized others. The attitudes embodied by these others are then used in the processes of mind and self to construct lines of conduct.

For Mead, then, the structure and dynamics of society concern those variables that influence the number, salience, scope, and proximity of generalized others. Thus, by implication, Mead argued that to the degree individuals can accurately take the role of each other and assume the perspective of common generalized other(s), patterns of interaction will be stable and cooperative. Conversely, to the degree that role-taking is inaccurate and occurs with respect to divergent generalized other(s), interaction will be disrupted and perhaps conflictual.[24]

From this perspective, the theoretical key to explaining patterns of social organization involves isolating those variables that influence (1) the accuracy of role-taking and (2) the convergence of generalized others. What might some of these variables be? Mead did not discuss these variables in any great detail, since he was not interested in building formal sociological theory. Rather his concerns are more philosophic and hence stress recognizing the general nature of the processes underlying the maintenance of the social order. Yet in a number of places he offered some clues about what variables influence the capacity of actors to role-take with the same generalized order.

One barrier to role-taking with the same generalized other is social differentiation.[25] As people play different roles, they experience different sets of expectations with others connected with these roles. Moreover, to the degree that differentiated roles exist within different structural units, the most immediate generalized others for these roles will be different. This is, of course, a somewhat different way of stating Comte's and Durkheim's concerns about the malintegrative effects of differentiation. Durkheim's conceptualization emphasized the "enfeeblement" of the collective conscience, and the resulting anomie and egoism, whereas Mead's conceptualization stressed the importance of role-taking with divergent generalized others. Mead's view, however, offers the recognition that people role-take with multiple generalized others; and thus while the community of attitudes of two individuals' immediate groups may diverge somewhat, they may at the same time assume the perspective of a more remote, or even abstract, generalized other and use this community of attitudes as a common perspective for guiding their conduct. Unlike Durkheim, who saw structural units like "occupational groups" as necessary mediators between the "collective conscience" and the individual, Mead's formulation of mind and self implicitly argues that through the capacity to role-take with multiple and remote others, diversely located individuals can become integrated into a common social fabric. Thus structural differentiation will tend, Mead appears to have argued, to force role-taking with more remote and abstract generalized others. And in this way the dimensions of a society can be greatly extended, since people's interactions are mediated and regulated by reference to a common community of attitudes rather than by face-to-face interaction.

---

[24]Mead, *Mind, Self, and Society*, pp. 321–22.
[25]Ibid.

Also related to differentiation—indeed, it is a type of differentiation—is stratification.[26] Class barriers increase the likelihood that individuals in different classes will not share the same community of attitudes. And thus to the degree that a system of hierarchical differentiation is to be integrated, role-taking with a more distant generalized other will supplement the community of attitudes peculiar to a particular social class.

Related to differentiation is the size of a plurality of actors.[27] As populations increase in size, it becomes increasingly likely that any two individuals will role-take with somewhat different perspectives in their interaction with specific others in their immediate groups. If a large population is to remain integrated, Mead appears to have argued, individuals will supplement their immediate communities of attitudes by role-taking with more abstract generalized others. Hence as the size of interaction networks increases, it can be expected that these networks are integrated by role-taking with an ever more abstract perspective or community of attitudes.

In sum, then, Mead's view of society is dominated by a concern with social psychological mechanisms by which social structures are integrated. For Mead, *society* is but a term for the processes of role-taking with varieties of specific and generalized others and the consequent coordination of action made possible by the behavioral capacities of mind and self. By emphasizing the processes underlying social structures, Mead presented a highly dynamic view of society. For not only is society created by role-taking, but it can be changed by these same processes. Thus as diverse individuals come into contact, role-take, and adjust their responses, they create a community of attitudes, which they then use to regulate their subsequent actions. And as more actors are implicated, or as their roles become more differentiated, they generate additional perspectives to guide their actions. Similarly, because actors possess unique self-conceptions and because they role-take with potentially diverse perspectives, they often must restructure existing patterns as they come to adjust to each other.

Thus we get little feeling in Mead's work for the majesty of social structure. Mead's conceptualization can perhaps be seen as a demystification of society, since society is nothing more than a process of role-taking by individuals who possess mind and self and who seek to make adjustments to each other. Yet we should note that Mead did offer some partial views of social morphology—that is, of the structural

---

[26]Ibid., p. 327.
[27]Ibid., p. 326.

forms created by role-taking. And we should briefly examine these more morphological conceptualizations of society.

The Morphology of Society.   Mead frequently used terms that carry structural connotations, with notions of *group, community, institution,* and *society* being the most common. To some degree these terms are used interchangeably to denote regularity in patterns of interaction among individuals. Yet at times Mead appears to have had an image of basic structural units that compose a total society.

The term *society* was used by Mead in two senses. On the one hand, society simply refers to ongoing, organized activity. On the other hand, society pertains to geopolitical units, such as nation-states. The former usage, however, is the most frequent, and thus we will retain the view that *society* is the term for ongoing and organized activity among pluralities of actors, whether this activity be that of a small group or of a total society.

Mead's use of the term *community* was ambiguous and often appeared the same as the concept of society. His most general usage appears to have been the following: a plurality of actors who share a common set of significant symbols, who perceive they constitute a distinguishable entity, and who share a common generalized other, or community of attitudes. As such, a community can be quite small or large, depending on whether people perceive they constitute an entity. Yet Mead typically employed the concept of community to denote large pluralities of actors, and thus other structural units were seen to operate within communities.

Within every community there are certain general ways people are supposed to act. These are what Mead defined as *institutions:*

> There are, then, whole series of such common responses in the community in which we live, and such responses are what we term "institutions." The institution represents a common response on the part of all members of the community to a particular situation.[28]

Institutions, Mead argued, are related, and thus when people act in one institutional context, they implicitly invoke responses to others. As Mead emphasized:

> Institutions . . . present in a certain sense the life-habits of the community as such; and when an individual acts toward others in, say, economic terms, he is calling out not simply a single response but a whole group of related responses.[29]

---

[28]Ibid., p. 261.
[29]Ibid., p. 264.

Institutions represent only general lines of response to varying life situations, whether economic, political, familial, religious, or educational. People take the role of the generalized other for each institution, and since institutions are interrelated, they also tend to call out appropriate responses for other institutions. In this way people can move readily from situation to situation within a broader community, calling out appropriate responses and inhibiting inappropriate ones. One moves smoothly, for example, from economic to familial situations, since responses for both are called out in the individual during role-taking with one or the other.

Mead recognized that institutions, and the attendant generalized other, provide only a broad framework guiding people's actions. People belong to a wide variety of smaller units that Mead tended to call *groups*. Economic activity, for example, is conducted by different individuals in varying economic groups. Familial actions occur within family groups, and so on for all institutional activity. Groups reveal their own generalized others, which are both unique and yet consistent within the community of attitudes of social institutions or of the broader community. Groups can vary enormously in terms of size, differentiation, longevity, and restrictiveness, but Mead's general point is that activity of individuals involves simultaneous role-taking with the generalized other in groups, clusters of interrelated institutions, and broad community perspectives.

The Culture of Society. Mead never used the concept of *culture* in the modern sense of the term. Yet his view of social organization as mediated by generalized others is consistent with the view that culture is a system of symbols by which human thought, perception, and action are mobilized and regulated. As with social structure or morphology, however, Mead was not interested in analyzing in detail the varieties of symbol systems humans create and use to organize their affairs. Rather he was primarily concerned with the more general insight that humans use significant symbols, or language, to create communities of attitudes. And, by virtue of the capacity for role-taking, humans regulate their conduct not only in terms of the attitudes of specific others but also in regard to generalized others who embody these communities of attitudes.

The concept of *generalized other* is Mead's term for what would now be seen as those symbol systems of a broader cultural system that regulate perception, thought, and action. Mead's generalized other is thus norms, values, beliefs and other such regulatory systems of symbols. Mead never made careful distinctions, for example, among values, beliefs, and norms, for he was interested only in isolating the basic processes of "society": Individuals with mind and self role-take with varieties of generalized others in order to regulate their conduct and thus coordinate their actions.

Mead's conception of society, therefore, emphasizes the basic nature of the processes underlying ongoing social activity. He was not concerned, to any great degree, with the details of social structure or the components of culture. His great insight was that regardless of the specific structure of society, the processes by which society is created, maintained, and changed are the same. Social organization is the result of behavioral capacities for mind and self as these allow actors to role-take with varieties of others and to thus regulate and coordinate their actions. This insight into the fundamental relationship between the individual and society marks Mead's great contribution in *Mind, Self, and Society.* Before Mead's synthesis, we should emphasize, the nature of this relationship had not been conceptualized, as can best be illustrated by comparing Mead's analysis with those of the theorists examined in previous chapters.[30]

THE PHILOSOPHY OF THE ACT

Mead left numerous unpublished papers, many of which were published posthumously in *The Philosophy of the Act.*[31] Much of this work is not of great interest to sociologists, and yet in the first essay, one on which the editors imposed the unfortunate title "Stages of the Act," Mead offered new insights that cannot be found in his other essays or in his lectures. In this piece Mead presented a theory of human motivation that should be viewed as supplemental to his conceptualization of mind, self, and society.

Mead did not present his argument in terms of the concept of *motivation,* but his intent is to understand why and how human action is initiated and given direction. For Mead, the most basic unit of behavior is "the act," and much of *The Philosophy of the Act* concerns understanding the nature of this fundamental unit. For the behavior of an individual is ultimately nothing more than a series of acts, sometimes enacted singularly but more often emitted simultaneously. Thus if insight into the nature of human behavior is to be achieved, it is necessary to comprehend the constituent components of behavior—that is, "acts."

In his analysis of the act, Mead retained his basic assumptions. Acts are part of a larger life process of organisms adjusting to the environmental conditions in which they find themselves. And human acts are unique because of their capacities for mind and self. Thus

---

[30]See, in particular, Weber's and Durkheim's analyses to appreciate how crudely the interactive basis of social structure had been conceptualized before Mead's synthesis.

[31]Mead, *Philosophy of the Act.*

Mead's theory of motivation revolves around understanding how the behavior of organisms with mind and self and operating within society is initiated and directed. He visualized the act as composed of four "stages," although he emphasized that humans can simultaneously be involved in different stages of different acts. And he also recognized that acts vary in length, degree of overlap, consistency, intensity, and other variable states. But in his analysis of the stages of the act, he was more interested in isolating the basic nature of the act than in developing propositions about its variable properties.

Mead saw acts as consisting of four stages: (1) impulse, (2) perception, (3) manipulation, and (4) consummation.[32] These are not entirely discrete, for they often blend into each other, but they constitute distinctive phases involving somewhat different behavioral capacities. Our discussion will focus on each stage separately, but it should be emphasized that Mead did not view the stages of a given act as separable from each other or as isolated from the stages of other acts.

Impulse

For Mead, an *impulse* represents a state of disequilibrium or tension between an organism and its environment. While Mead was not concerned with varying states of impulses—that is, their direction, type, and intensity—he did offer two implicit propositions: (1) The greater the degree of disequilibrium between an organism and its environment, the stronger its impulse and the more likely is behavior to reflect this fact. (2) The longer an impulse persists, the more it will serve to initiate and guide behavior until it is consummated.

The source of disequilibrium for an organism can vary. Some impulses come from organic needs that are unfulfilled, while others come from interpersonal maladjustments.[33] Still others stem from self-inflicted reflections. And many are a combination of organic, interpersonal, and intrapsychic sources of tension. The key point is that impulses initiate efforts at their consummation, while giving the behavior of an organism a general direction. However, Mead was quick to point out that a state of disequilibrium can be eliminated in many different ways and that the specific direction of behavior will be determined by the conditions of the environment. For Mead, humans are

---

[32]For an excellent secondary discussion of Mead's stages of the act, see Tamotsu Shibutani, "A Cybernetic Approach to Motivation," in *Modern Systems Research for the Behavioral Scientist*, ed. Walter Buckley (Hawthorne, N.Y.: Aldine Publishing, 1968); and Tamotsu Shibutani, *Society and Personality, An Interactionist Approach to Social Psychology* (Englewood Cliffs, N.J.: Prentice-Hall, 1961), pp. 63–93.

[33]For Mead's conceptualization of biologic needs, see the supplementary essays in *Mind, Self, and Society,* particularly essay 2.

not pushed and pulled around by impulses. On the contrary, an impulse is defined in terms of the degree of harmony with the environment, and the precise ways it is consummated are influenced by the manner in which an organism is prepared to adjust to its environment.

For example, even seemingly organic drives such as hunger and thirst are seen as arising from behavioral adaptations to the environment. Hunger is often defined by cultural standards as to when meals are to be eaten, and it arises when the organism has not secured food from the environment. And the way in which this disequilibrium will be eliminated is greatly constrained by the social world of the individual. The types of foods considered edible, the way they are eaten, and when they can be eaten will all be shaped by environmental forces as they impinge on actors with mind and self. Thus, for Mead, an impulse initiates behavior and gives it only a general direction. The next stage of the act—perception—will determine what aspects of the environment are relevant for eliminating the impulse.

Perception

What humans see in their environment, Mead argued, is highly selective. One basis for selective perception is the impulse: People become attuned to those objects in their environment perceived relevant to the elimination of an impulse. But even here, past socialization, self-conceptions, and expectations from specific and generalized others all constrain what objects are seen as relevant to eliminating a given impulse. For example, a hungry person in India will not see a cow as a relevant object of food but rather will become sensitized to other potential food objects.

The process of *perception* thus sensitizes an individual to certain objects in the environment. As objects, they become stimuli for repertoires of behavioral responses. Thus as an individual becomes sensitized to certain objects, he or she is prepared to behave in certain ways toward those objects. For Mead, then, perception is simply the arousal of potential responses to stimuli—that is, as the organism becomes aware of relevant objects, it also is prepared to act in certain ways. Humans thus approach objects with a series of hypotheses or notions about how certain responses toward objects can eliminate their state of disequilibrium.

Manipulation

The testing of these hypotheses—that is, the emission of behaviors toward objects—is termed *manipulation*. Because humans have mind and self, they can engage in covert as well as overt manipulation. A human can often covertly imagine the consequences of action toward objects for eliminating an impulse. Hence humans frequently manipulate their world mentally, and only after imagining the consequences of various lines of action do they emit an overt line of behavior. At other times, humans manipulate their environment without deliberate or delayed thinking; they simply emit a line of behavior perceived as likely to eliminate an impulse.

What determines whether manipulation will be covert before it is overt? The key condition is what Mead saw as *blockage*. For Mead, blockage is a condition where the consummation of an impulse is inhibited or delayed. Blockage produces imagery and initiates the process of thinking. For example, breaking a pencil while writing (creating impulse or disequilibrium with the environment) leads to efforts at manipulation: One actor may immediately perceive a pile of sharpened pencils next to the writing pad, pick up a new pencil, and continue writing without a moment's reflection. Another writer, who did not prepare a stack of pencils, may initially become attuned to the drawer of the desk, open it, search for a pencil, and generally start searching "blindly" for a pencil. At some point, frequently after a person has "wandered around unconsciously" for awhile, the blockage of the impulse begins to generate conscious imagery, and a person's manipulations become covert. Images of where one last left a pencil are now consciously evoked, or the probable location of a pencil sharpener is anticipated. Thus when the impulse, perception, and overt manipulation stages of the act do not lead to consummation, thinking occurs and manipulation becomes covert, utilizing the behavioral capacities of mind and self.

Thinking can also be initiated earlier in the act. For example, if perception does not yield a field of relevant objects, then blockage occurs at this stage, with the result that by virtue of the capacities for mind, an actor immediately begins covert thinking. Thus thinking is a behavioral adaptation of an organism experiencing disequilibrium with its environment and unable to perceive objects or manipulate behaviors in ways leading to consummation of an impulse.

In the process of thinking, then, an actor comes to perceive relevant objects; the actor may even role-take with the object if it is another individual or a group; a self-image may be derived, and one may see self as yet another object; and then various lines of conduct are imaginatively rehearsed until a proper line of conduct is selected and emitted. Of course, if the selected behavior does not eliminate the impulse, the process starts over again and continues until the organism's behavior allows it to achieve a state of equilibrium with its environment.

The stage of manipulation is thus "cybernetic" in that it involves behavior, feedback, readjustment of behavior, feedback, readjustment, and so on until an impulse is eliminated.[34] Mead's vision of thinking as "imaginative rehearsal" and his conceptualization of the "I" and "me" fit into this more general cybernetic view of the act. Thinking involves imagining a line of behavior and then giving oneself the feedback as to the probable consequences of the behavior. The "I" and "me" phases of self involve deriving "me" images (feedback) from behaviors ("I") and then using these images to adjust subsequent behaviors. Thus unlike many views of motivation, Mead saw acts as constructed from a succession of manipulations that yield feedback, which, in turn, is used to make subsequent manipulations. Motivation is thus a process of constant adjustment and readjustment of behaviors to restore equilibrium with the environment.

While Mead did not develop any formal propositions on the manipulatory stage of the act, he implicitly assumed the more often an impulse is blocked, the more it grows in intensity and the more it consumes the process of thinking and the phases of self. Thus individuals who have not eliminated a strong impulse through successful manipulation will have a considerable amount of their thinking and self-reflection consumed by imagery pertaining to objects and behaviors that might eliminate the impulse. For example, people who cannot satiate their hunger or sexual appetites or who cannot achieve the recognition they feel they deserve are likely to devote a considerable, and ever-increasing, amount of their time in covert and overt manipulations in an effort to control their impulses.

Consummation

This stage of the act simply denotes the completion of an act through the elimination of the disequilibrium between an organism and its environment. As a behaviorist, Mead emphasized that successful *consummation* of acts by the emission of behaviors in relation to certain objects leads to the development of stable behavior patterns. Thus general classes or types of impulses will tend to elicit particular lines of responses from an individual if these responses have been successful in the past in restoring equilibrium. Individuals will tend to perceive the same or similar objects as relevant to the elimination of the impulse, and they will tend to use these objects as stimuli for eliciting certain lines of behavior. In this way people develop stable behavioral tendencies to act on their environment.

Figure 15–3 diagrammatically represents Mead's conceptualization of these phases of the act. For any person, of course, there are multiple

---

[34]See Shibutani, "Cybernetic Approach," for a more detailed discussion.

FIGURE 15–3 Mead's Model of the Act

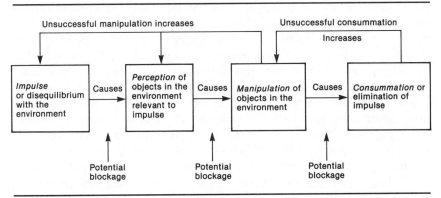

impulses operating, each at various stages of consummation and at potential points of blockage. For humans, perception involves seeing not only physical objects but also oneself, others, and various generalized others as part of their environment. Manipulation for humans with the capacities for mind and self not only involves overt behavior but can also include covert deliberations where individuals weigh alternatives and assess their consequences with reference to their self-conception, the expectations of specific others, and various generalized others. Consummation for humans, who must live and survive in social groups, almost always revolves around adaptation to, and cooperation with, others in ongoing collective enterprises. And, as the feedback arrows denoting blockage emphasize, the point of blockage influences the salience of any phase in the flow of an act. Moreover, this process of blockage determines the strength of the causal arrows connecting stages in the act. Intense impulses are typically those that have been blocked, thereby causing heightened perception. In turn heightened perception generates greater overt and covert manipulation; and if blockage occurs, then perception is further heightened, as are impulses. And if manipulation is unsuccessful, escalated covert manipulation ensues, thereby heightening perception and the impulse (via the feedback arrows at the top of Figure 15–3).

This model of the act allows for an understanding of how individuals can be "driven" to seemingly irrational or excessively emotional behavior, or it can provide insight into the dynamics of compulsive behavior. These behaviors would result from the blockage of powerful impulses that persist and escalate in intensity, thereby distorting an individual's perceptions, covert thinking, and overt behavior. For example, individuals who were rejected by significant others in their early years may have a powerful series of unconsummated impulses that distort their perception and manipulations to abnormal extremes. And given the fact that the unstable or abnormal self-conceptions of such individuals may distort the process of perception, as well as covert and overt manipulation, they may never be able to perceive that they have consummated their impulses in interpersonal relations.

Unlike Freud or other clinicians and psychologists of his time, Mead was not interested in types of abnormal behavior. He was more concerned with constructing a model that would denote the fundamental properties of human action, whether normal or abnormal. Mead's social behaviorism is often portrayed by his critics as overly rational, but this view does not take into account Mead's model of the act. This model contains the elements for emotional as well as rational action, and while Mead was not interested in assessing the consequences of various weights among the arrows in Figure 15–3, the model provides a valuable tool for those who are concerned with how various types of impulses, when coupled with different patterns of impulse blockage, will produce varying forms of covert and overt behavior.

Mead's analysis of the stages of the act thus provides a useful supplement to his discussion of *Mind, Self, and Society.* We now have a better vision of why people initiate action and why behaviors take a certain direction. In many ways Mead's conception of motivation represents a synthesis of diverse schools of thought. The stimulus-response, or reflex-arc, approach of J. B. Watson, and more recently of B. F. Skinner, is retained without the restrictive tendency to avoid the "black box" of human cognition. The Gestalt psychology of Mead's time is evident through the emphasis of behavior as initiated by a desire to maintain harmony within a perceptual field of objects and relations. The psychoanalytic view of behavior as a reconciliation of impulses and ego processes is maintained in the emphasis of bio-social sources of disequilibrium and the stages of perception and covert manipulation by actors with mind and self. Moreover, Mead's emphasis on blockage, and how blockage increases the intensity of impulses, is consistent with the psychoanalytic view of the sources of disruptive emotional states.

In sum, then, Mead's theory of motivation, much like his view of mind, self, and society, represents a synthesis of diverse and often contradictory viewpoints. The biologic individual is not ignored; the internal psychological processes of individuals are highlighted; and the relation of acts to the ongoing processes of society is still prominent. Mead's view of motivation is thus distinctly sociological, emphasizing the relationship of individuals to each other and to the social as well as physical environments. What drives actors and what shapes the course of their behaviors is this relationship of the organism to its environment. And for human actors, who by virtue of mind and self are able to live and participate in society, this environment is decidedly social. Therefore humans initiate and direct their actions in an effort to achieve integration into the ongoing social process.

THE ENDURING LEGACY

As we have emphasized, George Herbert Mead's *social* behaviorism marked a synthesis of utilitarian, pragmatist, behaviorist, and even Darwinian notions. Its basic premise is: Behaviors that facilitate the adjustment and adaptation of organisms to their environment will be retained.

For any individual organism, its environment is society. Thus the young infant must adjust to society, developing the behavioral capacities for language, role-taking, mind, and self. And for the mature individual, the continued use of these fundamental capacities is essential for ongoing adjustment and adaptation to society. The critical insight of Mead's social behaviorism is that the capacities for mind and self are behaviors. Moreover, these capacities assure that among humans much action will be covert and involve role-taking, reflective thinking, self-criticism, and self-assessment.

These behavioral capacities for mind and self make humans distinctive. And only out of interaction by actors with mind and self is society possible. For a species not organized by instincts, as are ants and bees, the ability to role-take becomes crucial in such interactions. Indeed, impulses are both caused and constrained by the capacity to role-take not only with each other but with broader perspectives, values, beliefs, and norms. All of these constraints on impulses allow for the organization of the species into society. This behavioral ability also makes human social organization flexible, thereby facilitating the adjustment and adaptation of the species as a whole to the environment.

Thus the acquisition of mind and self enables the individual to adapt to its social environment, while the flexible interactive abilities of individuals with mind and self facilitate the species' adaptation to the environment through the creation, maintenance, and change of society. It is within this basic framework that Mead's ideas must be viewed. As we saw in Chapter 14, Mead borrowed much from other scholars, but he combined their ideas in new ways into an approach that unraveled the basic nature of the relationships between the individual and society.

In his efforts Mead did not explicitly develop models and theoretical principles. But he continues to inspire sociological theorizing precisely because a number of models and principles can be pulled from his work. To properly assess his theoretical legacy, then, we should close this chapter with a more formal list of the theoretical principles contained in his approach.

Principles of Animal Action

1. The greater is the degree of maladjustment of an organism to its environment, the stronger are its impulses.
2. The greater is the intensity of an organism's impulse, the greater is the organism's perceptual awareness of objects that can potentially consummate the impulse, and the greater is its manipulation of objects in the environment.
   2a. The more maladjustment stems from unconsummated organic needs, the greater the intensity of the impulse.
   2b. The longer an impulse goes unconsummated, the greater the intensity of the impulse.
3. The more impulses have been consummated by the perception and manipulation of certain classes of objects in the environment, the more likely will perceptual and behavioral responses be directed at these and similar objects when similar impulses arise.

Principles of Animal Interaction

4. The more organisms seek to manipulate objects in their environment in an effort to consummate impulses, the greater is the visibility of gestures they emit during the course of their action.
5. The greater is the number and visibility of gestures emitted by acting organisms, the more likely will these organisms respond to each other's gestures and adjust responses to each other.

Principles on the Emergence of the Human Mind

6. The more an infant must adapt to an environment composed of organized collectivities of actors, the more likely will the infant be exposed to significant gestures.
7. The more an infant must seek to consummate its impulses in an organized social collectivity, the more likely will learning how to read and use significant gestures have selective value for consummating the infant's impulses.
8. The more an infant can come to use and read significant gestures, the greater its ability to role-take with others in its environment, and hence the greater is its capacity to communicate its needs and

to anticipate the responses of others on whom it depends for the consummation of impulses.

9. The greater is the capacity of an infant to role-take and use significant gestures, the greater is its capacity to communicate with itself.

10. The greater is the capacity of an infant to communicate with itself, the greater is its ability to covertly designate objects in its environment, inhibit inappropriate responses, and select a response that will consummate its impulses and thereby facilitate its adjustment.

11. The greater is the ability of an infant to reveal such minded behavior, the greater is its ability to control its responses, and hence to cooperate with others in ongoing and organized collectivities.

Principles on the Emergence of Self

12. The more a young actor can engage in minded behavior, the more it can read significant gestures, role-take, and communicate with itself.

13. The more a young actor can read significant gestures, role-take, and communicate with itself, the more it can see itself as an object in any given situation.

14. The more diverse is the specific others with whom a young actor can come to role-take, the more it can increasingly come to see itself as an object in relation to the dispositions of multiple others.

15. The more generalized is the perspective of others with whom a young actor can come to role-take, the more it can increasingly come to see itself as an object in relation to general values, beliefs, and norms of increasingly larger collectivities.

16. The greater is the stability in a young actor's images of itself as an object in relation to both specific others and generalized perspectives, the more reflexive is its role-taking and the more consistent are its behavioral responses.

    16a. The more the first self-images derived from role-taking with others have been consistent and noncontradictory, the greater the stability, over time, of an actor's self-conception.

    16b. The more self-images derived from role-taking with generalized perspectives are consistent and noncontradictory, the greater the stability, over time, of an actor's self-conception.

17. The more a young actor can reveal stability in its responses to itself as an object, and the more it can see itself as an object in relation to specific others as well as generalized perspectives, the greater is its capacity to control its responses, and hence to cooperate with others in ongoing and organized collectivities.

Principles of Human Action and Interaction

18. The greater is the intensity of impulses of humans with mind and self, (a) the more likely will perceptual awareness of objects that can potentially consummate the impulse be selective, (b) the more likely will manipulation be covert, and (c) the more likely will both perception and manipulation be circumscribed by a self-conception, expectations of specific others, and the generalized perspective of organized collectivities.

19. The more humans with mind and self seek to consummate impulses in the presence of others, the more likely are they to emit overt significant gestures, and the more likely are they to read the significant gestures of others, and hence the greater their role-taking activity.

20. The more humans role-take with each other, the more likely will the course of their interaction be guided by specific dispositions of others present in a situation, by images of the self as a certain type of object in the situation, and by generalized perspectives of the organized collectivity in which they are participating.

Principles of Human Social Organization

21. The more actors can role-take with pluralities of others, and use the dispositions of multiple others as a source of self-evaluation and self-control, the greater their capacity to create and maintain patterns of social organization.

22. The more actors can role-take with the generalized perspective of organized collectivities, and use this perspective as a source of self-evaluation and self-control, the greater is their capacity to create and maintain patterns of social organization.

23. The more actors can role-take with a common and generalized perspective, and use this common perspective as a source of self-evaluation and self-control, the greater is their capacity to create and maintain cohesive patterns of social organization.

    23a. The more similar the position of actors, the more likely will they be able to role-take with a common and generalized perspective.

    23b. The smaller the size of a population of actors, the more likely will these actors role-take with a common and generalized perspective.

24. The more actors can role-take with multiple but consistent generalized perspectives, and the more they can use these perspectives as a source of self-evaluation and self-control, the greater is their

capacity to differentiate roles and extend the scope of social organization.

25. The more actors can simultaneously role-take with a common and abstract perspective, and at the same time role-take with a variety of specific perspectives of particular collectivities integrated with the abstract perspective, and the more these integrated perspectives can be a source of self-evaluation and self-control, the greater is their capacity to extend the scope of social organization.

CHAPTER 16

The Emergence of Modern Theoretical Perspectives

"ON THE SHOULDERS OF GIANTS"

In all of the preceding chapters our goal has been to communicate sociology's theoretical legacy. As is evident, this is a rich legacy, filled with insightful models and abstract theoretical principles. On the base laid by the masters examined in the previous chapters has modern sociological theory been built. Indeed to paraphrase Newton and many others who have recognized a debt to their predecessors, "If we have seen farther, it is by standing on the shoulders of giants." Some might contend that modern sociologists have not seen farther; rather we remain in "the shadows of giants." Others would object to such a cynical conclusion. We suspect modern theorists have "seen farther," but not as far as they could. The reason for this "shortsightedness" is, we feel, a lack of complete appreciation for the formal elegance and sophistication of early work in sociology. We hope our efforts in this book have contributed, even if only in a modest way, to communicating the theoretical power of our first masters' works.

In this last chapter we will seek to outline in general terms the various directions in which the masters' works have taken modern sociologists. To do so, we will introduce five theoretical perspectives that currently dominate in sociology: functionalism, conflict theory, exchange theory, interactionism, and structural theorizing.[1]

THE EMERGENCE OF FUNCTIONAL THEORY IN SOCIOLOGY

As we saw in Chapter 1, Auguste Comte first articulated a clear vision of a "science of society." In seeking legitimacy for this new science, Comte saw sociology as growing out of biology, for both sociol-

---

[1]For more detailed accounts of these and other modern perspectives, see Jonathan H. Turner, *The Structure of Sociological Theory* (Chicago: Dorsey Press, 1974, 1978, 1986).

ogy and biology are concerned with "organic bodies." Yet Comte was quick to assert that while "biology has hitherto been the guide and preparation for sociology . . ., sociology will in the future . . . [provide] the ultimate systematization of Biology."[2]

Comte went on to make a number of analogies between social and biological "organisms." He argued that social structures could be "decomposed anatomically" into "elements, tissues, and organs" and that it is possible to treat the "Social Organism" as "definitely composed of the Families which are the true elements or cells, next the classes or castes which are its proper tissues, and lastly of the cities and communes which are its real organs."[3]

This line of analogizing formally initiated what was in the twentieth century to become known as "functionalism" and "structural-functionalism." For if social systems are "like biological organisms," then it is appropriate to ask: What is "the function" of a particular social structure for the survival and operation of the body social? Herbert Spencer began to codify this line of reasoning in the latter half of the last century.

As we outlined in Chapters 2 and 3, Spencer's sociological works owe much to his earlier analysis of biological processes.[4] Indeed, throughout his work, one finds a persistent comparison between the organization of organic and "super-organic" bodies. But he went much further than Comte and argued that sociological analysis of functions must seek to understand the "need" served by a social structure. That is, to determine the "function" of a structure, it is necessary to know the "need" of the social whole it meets. Such needs are the "survival requisites" of the social whole; they are what must be done if the social whole is to remain viable.

While Émile Durkheim was highly critical of both Comte and Spencer, he retained the critical elements of their functionalism. Indeed he contributed to this perspective by distinguishing "causal" from "functional" analysis. For Durkheim stressed that sociological explanations must involve two elements: (1) an understanding of the causes of a particular social form and (2) an assessment of its functions for the integration of the social whole.[5]

---

[2]Auguste Comte, *System of Positive Polity* (London: Burt Franklin, 1875), pp. 239–40.
[3]Ibid., pp. 241–42.
[4]In particular, his monumental *Principles of Biology.* For a more detailed review of the origins and profile of functionalism, see Jonathan H. Turner and Alexandra Maryanski, *Functionalism* (Menlo Park, Calif.: Benjamin/Cummings, 1978).
[5]Émile Durkheim, *The Division of Labor in Society* (New York: Free Press, 1947; originally published in 1893); and *The Rules of the Sociological Method* (New York: Free Press, 1950; originally published in 1895).

Thus by the turn of the century, much sociological and anthropological analysis was "functional" in its approach. This approach embodied the following elements:

1. Social systems are composed of interconnected parts.
2. Social systems confront external and internal problems of survival.
3. Such problems of survival can be visualized as the "needs" or "requisites" of the system.
4. Social systems and their constituent parts can only be understood by assessing how a part contributes to meeting the needs or requisites of the systemic whole.

These are the basic elements of all functional analyses. But they have been taken in many different directions over the last decades. Anthropologists used the elements as a way to interpret data on traditional societies, for by understanding the function of a cultural item, such as a religious ritual or kinship pattern, then that item could be explained.[6] Other anthropologists and sociologists took a more analytical approach and began to construct typologies of "system needs" and to catalog structures in terms of the needs they meet.[7] Still others argued that "needs" varied from one empirical system to another and that only after empirically establishing a system's requisites could an analysis of functions (and dysfunctions) of structures for meeting these needs be undertaken.[8]

For many decades functional analyses dominated sociology and anthropology. But in recent years functional analysis has come under heavy attack. Yet much anthropological and sociological work, both theoretical and empirical efforts, is still decidedly functional. Thus one of the major legacies of the masters was functionalism, which, for all of its acknowledged deficiencies, forced theorists to view the social world as composed of systems of interconnected parts and to construct theories about the basic properties of such systems.

---

[6]For an early illustration of this approach, see A. R. Radcliff-Brown, "Structure and Function in Primitive Society," *American Anthropologist* 37, July-September 1935, pp. 1–25.

[7]See, for example, Talcott Parsons, *The Social System* (New York: Free Press, 1951); and Bronislaw Malinowski, *A Scientific Theory of Culture* (Chapel Hill: University of North Carolina Press, 1944).

[8]See, for example, Robert K. Merton, "Manifest and Latent Functions" in *Social Theory and Social Structure* (New York: Free Press, 1968).

THE EMERGENCE OF CONFLICT THEORY

Conflict was a prominent concern among nineteenth-century scholars. Indeed the tumultuous eruptions that accompanied the Industrial Revolution in Europe gave the analysis of conflict processes an immediate relevance. Even the founders of functionalism with their emphasis on intergrated social systems evidence an implicit concern with conflict, since they all were vitally interested in those conditions that mitigate conflict and promote integration.

Yet despite this pervasive concern with conflict, modern conflict theory owes its primary inspiration to one scholar, Karl Marx, and only to a lesser extent to others, such as Georg Simmel and Max Weber. For in Marx's work we first see the guiding assumptions of conflict sociology. These include:

1. All social systems reveal inequalities in the distribution of scarce and valuable resources.

2. Such inequalities inevitably and inexorably create conflicts of interests among system units.

3. Such conflicts of interest will, over time, generate overt conflict among those who possess, and those who do not possess, valuable resources.

4. These conflicts will result in reorganization of the social system, creating new patterns of inequality that will serve as the next fulcrum for conflict and change.

Most modern conflict theories employ these assumptions and then seek to develop models and principles for specifying the conditions under which inequalities lead to varying forms of conflict and social change. The major variables are not much different than those originally proposed by Marx: Inequality is usually seen as a function of productivity, size, and political centralization. Conflict is viewed as the result of subordinates withdrawing legitimacy from the system. Such withdrawal is related to the degree of inequality, the level of upward social mobility, the availability of grievance channels, and the strength of unifying cultural symbols, such as values and beliefs. In turn, the withdrawal of legitimacy is viewed as escalating subordinates' emotions to a point that they seek to become organized. Such emotional arousal is conceived to be a function of coercive acts by elites, the degree of alienation of key institutional positions, and the escalation of perceived deprivations. This arousal is then typically seen as leading to organization of subordinates to pursue conflict. The degree of violence of the conflict is usually viewed as a positive function of the ecological concentration of subordinates, the availability of targets for violent actions, and the lack of clear leadership, unifying symbols, networks of communication, and articulation of interests.[9]

While this brief cataloging does not capture all of the variables employed by conflict theorists, virtually every conflict analysis embodies most of these variables. But despite this commonality, conflict theory has become quite diverse in recent decades. Some scholars have sought to translate into more abstract and formal terms Marx's,[10] Simmel's,[11] or Weber's[12] ideas; others have focused on specific conflict processes, such as societywide revolutions; still others have extended the conflict view to the level of the "world system"; and another group has begun to apply a conflict perspective to more micro processes in groups and organizations.

Thus conflict theories focus on one of the most pervasive social processes in human systems: conflict. But they also provide indirect insights on another pervasive set of processes: social integration and cooperation. For by understanding the conditions that generate conflict, we have gained insight into what does not generate conflict—that is, the converse of those conditions producing conflict will provide us with many fruitful leads into the conditions that promote integration and cooperation. Hence conflict is not a parochial perspective that focuses on one process; it takes us into the heart of sociological inquiry and allows us to visualize how and why patterns of social organization are created, maintained, and changed.

THE EMERGENCE OF EXCHANGE THEORY

The explicit roots of exchange theory begin with classical economics of the eighteenth century. Working under the banner of "utilitarianism," the social world was conceptualized as a kind of open

---

[9]Here is where Simmel's insights proved more powerful than Marx's, since Marx felt violence is positively related to organization. Simmel showed this was not necessarily the case and, in fact, violence is most likely when the deprived are only incipiently organized, and yet, emotionally aroused.

[10]See, for example, Ralf Dahrendorf, "Toward a Theory of Social Conflict," *Journal of Conflict Resolution* 2, June 1958, pp. 170–83; and Jonathan H. Turner, "Marx and Simmel Revisited," *Social Forces* 53, June 1975, pp. 723–29; and "A Strategy for Reformulating the Dialectical and Functional Theories of Conflict," *Social Forces* 53, March 1975, pp. 433–44.

[11]See, for example, Lewis A. Coser, *The Functions of Social Conflict* (New York: Free Press, 1956); and Turner, *Structure of Sociological Theory*, pp. 127–58.

[12]The best example here is Randall Collins' *Conflict Sociology* (New York: Academic Press, 1975).

marketplace in which rational actors competed with each other and chose the best means to maximize their "utilities" (or gratifications). The basic metaphor of social life as the exchange of valued resources was retained in the explicitly sociological and anthropological thought of the nineteenth century. Herbert Spencer and Émile Durkheim both saw exchange as a critical dimension of social life. And George Herbert Mead adopted the utilitarian perspective and then adapted it to his social behaviorism. And Georg Simmel in his *Philosophy of Money* articulated an exchange perspective. Yet we could not proclaim any of the nineteenth-century founders of sociology to be impetus behind modern exchange theory. Rather exchange theory is a more recent perspective that owes its inspiration to a variety of sources, ranging from economics through sociology and anthropology to behaviorism in psychology.[13] As a result of this diversity, exchange theorists often employ different vocabularies and stress somewhat different variables. But common to all exchange theories are the following assumptions:

1. All actors possess resources that they will expend in order to receive valued resources from other actors.
2. All actors make calculations as to the reward value or utility of resources other actors have to offer and as to the costs they must incur in the loss of their resources and the loss of alternative resources from other actors. Such calculations are made in terms of:
   a. The needs and/or goals of actors.
   b. The availability of resources in the environment.
   c. The level and value of actors' own resources.
3. All actors make calculations in order to receive from other actors resources that exceed in value or utility those resources that must be expended.
4. Social relations involve a constant process of exchange of resources among actors, and both the dynamics and statics of social relations are to be explained by reference to the degree of balance or imbalance in such exchanges of resources among actors.

These assumptions have been translated into a wide variety of abstract principles. Such principles emphasize that exchanges of valued resources create pressures for the differentiation of social systems into ranks and that such rank differentiations create, under conditions similar to those listed by conflict theorists, conflict and change. In fact we

---

[13]See ibid. For a list of references representing the diversity of the sociological perspectives on exchange, see Harry C. Bredemeier, "Exchange Theory," in *A History of Sociological Analysis,* ed. Tom Bottomore and Robert A. Nisbet (New York: Basic Books, 1978), pp. 454–56.

might view conflict theory as a special case of exchange theory—that is, a theory that specifies what is likely to occur in social systems where exchange relations have become dramatically asymmetrical, with some actors hoarding resources at the expense of others.

Yet exchange theorists examine many topics other than conflict. Moreover, one can see applications of exchange principles[14] in many diverse empirical contexts, from the analysis of interaction in dyads and small groups to discussions of national and international politics. Thus exchange theory represents a prominent strategy in contemporary sociology to unify empirical inquiry and conceptual effort under one theoretical perspective.

THE EMERGENCE OF INTERACTIONIST THEORY

With the exception of Georg Simmel's analysis of interaction or "sociation" and examination of the "web of group affiliations" as well as with Max Weber's concern over the "subjective meaning" attached to social action, European sociology of the nineteenth century was decidedly "macro" in emphasis. It focused on large-scale events and processes—evolution, revolution, differentiation, integration, and other processes where the attributes of individuals and specific processes of interaction could be ignored, or at least subordinated to a concern with the structural properties of the world. Only in America were scholars seeking to examine systematically how the attributes of individuals are connected to ongoing social patterns and how specific interactive mechanisms made society a viable entity. As we emphasized in Chapters 15 and 16, this line of inquiry culminated in the work of George Herbert Mead. And out of his synthesis was modern interactionist theorizing born.

For Mead, as for modern-day interactionists, the emphasis is on how the process of interaction mediates between the attributes of the individual and society. On the one hand, ongoing patterns of social organization are seen as constructed from people's capacities to read each other's gestures, to rehearse alternative lines of conduct, to visualize themselves as objects, and to become cognizant of broader cultural expectations. On the other hand, individual capacities for reflective thought, role-playing, and self are viewed as the result of prolonged socialization and other interactive experiences in existing patterns of social organization.

---

[14]See Turner, *Structure of Sociological Theory,* and Jonathan H. Turner and Charles Powers, "Theory and Political Sociology" in *Handbook of Political Sociology,* vol. 3 (New York: Plenum Press, 1981), for summaries of these principles.

Modern interactionists tend to develop theoretical models and principles about specific social processes,[15] such as role-playing, techniques and strategies of interaction, deviant behavior, socialization, social control, and other processes in the social world. Rarely do interactionists study structures, such as community, organizations, societies, and even small groups, per se; rather their emphasis is always on the specific interactive processes that lead to the construction, maintenance, or change of a particular structure. While some interactionists firmly believe macro structures like class, community, bureacracy, and society are only understandable in terms of their constituent processes of interaction, most modern interactionists recognize that their theoretical efforts revolve around the microprocesses that underlie patterns of social organization.[16] As a consequence, interactionism is a theoretical perspective within which a great deal of diverse theoretical effort and empirical work are conducted. There is no coherent interactionist "theory of" the social universe. Instead there are a series of "theories about" specific processes in the social world. Such theories are guided by the general thrust of Mead's synthesis, but each elaborates on Mead's insights in ways allowing for more complete understanding of the specific topics under investigation. Thus all types of interactionist theorizing stress the following assumptions:

1. Macro or large-scale patterns of social organization are all ultimately constructed and sustained by face-to-face interactions among individuals.

2. Such face-to-face interactions revolve around individuals' capacities to use and read gestures, to interpret each others' dispositions, to define situations, to see oneself as an object in a situation, to construct joint lines of conduct, and to reassess, redefine, and reconstruct their joint conduct.

3. Therefore, human organization can only be understood by concepts and propositions that explain how people interact in micro, face-to-face contexts.

These ideas have been supplemented and to some extent challenged by another prominent interactionist approach: phenomenology.

---

[15]For some prominent examples, see Edwin M. Lemert, *Social Pathology* (New York: McGraw-Hill, 1951); Edwin H. Sutherland, *Principles of Criminology* (Philadelphia: J. B. Lippincott, 1939); Ralph H. Turner and Lewis Killian, *Collective Behavior* (Englewood Cliffs, N.J.: Prentice-Hall, 1972); and Erving Goffman, *The Presentation of Self in Everyday Life* (Garden City, N.Y.: Doubleday, 1959).

[16]For an exception to this recognition, see Herbert Blumer, *Symbolic Interactionism: Perspective and Method* (Englewood Cliffs, N.J.: Prentice-Hall, 1969).

In some respects phenomenological theorizing has emerged independently of the early scholars discussed in this book. Weber's concern with action "at the level of meaning" and Mead's emphasis on the process of role-taking have exerted some influence on phenomenological theorizing. But even if we give some credit to early sociological theorists, phenomenology still represents a reaction—indeed an overreaction—against current theoretical perspectives.[17]

The nature of this reaction differs somewhat depending on which variant of phenomenology is being analyzed. But all phenomenological theorizing questions and challenges, with varying degrees of intensity, the underlying assumptions of other theoretical perspectives in sociology. In particular, phenomenology questions the following assumptions:

1. There exists "out there" a reality, sui generis, that exists independently of human consciousness and thought.
2. This external reality can be understood with the methods and tools of science.
3. While scientists' subjective states and biases can influence "what they see out there" in the world, these biases can be overcome.

Phenomenologists question these implicit assumptions of "normal science" by postulating an alternative vision. The subjective world of human actors is the major topic of social science inquiry. What exists "out there" in an "external world" is not known independently of states of consciousness, and hence the logically prior topic of inquiry is understanding the properties and processes of human consciousness. Thus all phenomenological perspectives view the processes of consciousness as the key topic of empirical and conceptual inquiry. Just whether there is a world "out there" existing independently of subjective consciousness is "bracketed" or suspended as a secondary issue. As an alternative, the more sociologically inclined phenomenologists, who work under labels such as "ethnomethodology" and "cognitive sociology,"[18] argue that the real topics of sociological inquiry are:

1. The interpersonal processes by which people come to feel and sense that they participate in a common reality, even if this sense is somewhat illusionary.

---

[17]In particular, Edmund Husserl and Alfred Schutz are the founders of modern phenomenology; see Turner, *Structure of Sociological Theory*, for a summary of their work. Also see Kurt H. Wolff, "Phenomenology and Sociology" in Bottomore and Nisbet, *History of Sociological Analysis*, pp. 499–556.

[18]See ibid. for a review of these sociological phenomenologies.

2. The interpersonal practices by which people come to believe an external reality exists "out there," again, even if this is somewhat illusionary.

In light of these considerations, sociological analysis cannot assume such a "thing" as society exists independently of what people do in concrete interactions as they mutually construct a sense, feeling, and perhaps false presumption that they share and participate in a common world "out there." Such a line of inquiry is often not seen as a variant of, or as an adjunct to, interactionism. Most phenomenologists believe the only reality is the interpersonal techniques used by people to construct a sense of an external and internal/subjective reality. For many there is no reality "out there"; the only reality is the activity of people trying to convince each other that there is an external world "out there." This kind of extreme assertion, however, has been tempered in recent years. Now the emphasis is more on how the conceptualization of interpersonal procedures for constructing a sense of a reality can supplement the more traditional forms of interactionist theorizing inspired by G. H. Mead.

STRUCTURAL THEORIZING

Most sociological theories explore the topic of "social structure," or patterns of social relations among individual and collective actors that endure over time. Herbert Spencer, Karl Marx, Émile Durkheim, Max Weber, George Simmel, and Vilfredo Pareto were all concerned with the processes by which macro social structures—classes, organizations, communities, societies—are organized, especially during industrialization. In very different ways they all addressed a similar set of underlying questions:

1. What forces cause the change of societal social structures from simple to more complex forms?
2. What basic units—cultural ideas, classes, modes of production, organizations, political institutions, or individuals—are most important in determining both causes and consequences of structural change?
3. How can theory best explain these transformations? Can a deductive natural science approach, like that advocated by Auguste Comte, be used? Or is there something different about human organization that makes such an approach less useful than a more descriptive and historical approach?

Structural theorizing has gone in many different directions in the modern era. One direction is functionalism,[19] as we discussed earlier. Another is the revival of historical sociology, where specific events, such as revolutions,[20] are analyzed in detail or where long-term patterns of social change in empires,[21] the world system,[22] and other macro units are explored. These historical approaches are typically less theoretical than a recent series of efforts to synthesize and expand existing theories to understand the basic properties of all social structures and to explain the dynamic processes by which structures are produced and reproduced. This last approach has many labels, but all of the theorists have in common a concern with structure and its underlying dynamics. Theorists working in this more synthetic tradition emphasize:

1. The subject matter of sociological theory revolves around how social structures—that is, patterns of relations among actors—are created, sustained, and changed.
2. The central theoretical task is to develop a series of concepts and models depicting the basic processes underlying all structural patterns.
   a. For some, this task is to be decidedly micro and revolve around conceptualizing the capacities of individual agents to reproduce the macro structural order in their interpersonal behavior.[23]
   b. For others, this task is to be macro and concern the emergent properties of structure, independently of what individuals do at the micro level.[24]
   c. For still others, this task is to be both micro and macro, with micro interpersonal processes seen as creating emergent macro

---

[19]In fact, functionalism has undergone a considerable revival in recent years, primarily as a result of Jeffrey Alexander's advocacy. See his *Neofunctionalism* (Beverly Hills, Calif.: Sage Publications, 1985).

[20]See, for example, Theda Skocpol, *States and Social Revolutions* (Cambridge: Cambridge University Press, 1979).

[21]See, for example, Reinhard Bendix, *Kings or People* (Berkeley: University of California Press, 1978), and *Nation-Building and Citizenship* (New York: John Wiley & Sons, 1964); or Michael Mann, *The Sources of Social Power* (Cambridge: Cambridge University Press, 1986).

[22]Immanuel Wallerstein, *The Modern World-System* (New York: Academic Press, 1974).

[23]For example, Anthony Giddens, *The Constitution of Society* (Berkeley: University of California Press, 1985).

[24]For example, Peter M. Blau, *Inequality and Heterogeneity* (New York: Free Press, 1977).

dynamics that feed back and constrain the actions and interactions of individuals.[25]

These new structural approaches are highly eclectic, drawing concepts from many different sources, especially the theorists examined in this book. But they take sociology back to its most central question: How is the organization of individuals into social structures to be understood? In answering this question, divisions of modern theory along functional, conflict, exchange, and interactionist lines are beginning to break down in favor of a new line of division: Is sociological theory to explain structure in terms of micro or macro processes? In fact, contemporary theorizing is increasingly concerned with this micro–macro issue; and while theorists still disagree over many other issues, the problem of reconciling the micro and macro orders increasingly dominates, primarily because the micro and macro properties and dynamics of structure have increasingly become the central topics of analysis in sociological theory.

CONCLUSION

The nature of modern sociological theory is, of course, another story told in many books.[26] Our goal in this book has been to summarize and analyze in detail the theoretical legacy on which modern theory is now built. Our rationale for presenting this legacy as a series of models and propositions is to invite others to reexamine sociology's first one hundred years in a more positivistic light, or in the terms first expressed by Auguste Comte. That is, we hope others share our belief that the scholars examined in these pages discovered some of the basic properties and dynamics of the social universe. By rereading "the classics," we believe, it is possible to gain considerable insight into the proper subject of sociological theory. We do not, therefore, offer this book as a history of ideas, or as history in any sense, but as a stimulus for sociologists to construct theories, borrowing and adapting the ideas of the early masters.

---

[25]Collins, *Conflict Sociology.*
[26]See, for example, Turner, *Structure of Sociological Theory,* 4th ed.

Name Index

A

Abel, Theodore, 192n, 250n
Alexander, Jeffrey, 480n
Althuser, Louis, 292n, 294n
Annenkov, Paul, 97
Appelbaum, Richard, 134n, 159n
Aron, Raymond, 294n

B

Backhaus, Juergen, 400n
Bakunin, Dina, 356, 371
Bakunin, Michael, 96
Baldwin, John D., 41
Barnard, Chester, 355, 371n
Barnes, Harry Elmer, 1n
Bauer, Bruno, 95–97, 106
Baumharten, Ida and Herman, 168
Baxter, Richard, 205
Becker, Howard, 1n
Beeghley, Leonard, 84n, 145n, 219n
Belski, S., 414n
Bendix, Reinhard, 146, 147n, 169n,
    175n, 187n, 200n, 215n, 217n,
    226–27, 248n, 480n
Bentham, Jeremy, 410, 433
Berger, Brigitte, 377n
Berlin, Isaiah, 94n, 143
Bertalanffy, C., 64n
Blau, Peter, 480n
Blumer, Herbert, 477n
Bobbio, Norberto, 352n
Bohm-Bawark, Eugen, 177
Bonald, Louis de, 24, 35–36
Bongiorno, A., 354n, 373n
Bottomore, Tom, 248n, 475n, 478n
Boutroux, Emile, 284
Braverman, Harry, 162n
Bredemeier, Harry C., 475n
Brentano, Lujo, 177
Broome, J. H., 294n, 296n

Brunn, H. H., 184n
Buckley, Walter, 64n, 459n
Bucolo, Placido, 352n
Burger, Thomas, 178n, 184n, 194n
Busino, Giovanni, 352n, 402n

C

Cameron, David, 296n
Cassirer, Ernst, 1n
Charuet, John, 296n
Cole, G. D. H., 294n
Colletti, Lucio, 102n
Collier, James, 89n
Collins, Randall, 204n, 366n, 474n,
    481n
Comte, Auguste, 1–36
    and Durkheim, 285–87, 293, 299–302,
    314n, 322, 339, 342
    and Pareto, 359, 362
    and Spencer, 46, 50
Condorcet, Jean, 5–7, 12–14
Cooley, Charles Horton, 408, 423–27, 442
Coser, Lewis, 7n, 34n, 38n, 171n, 234n,
    237n, 240n, 248n, 284n, 286, 407n,
    408n, 474n
Coulanges, Fustel de, 284

D

Dahrendorf, Ralf, 235n, 474n
Darwin, Charles, 40, 43, 45, 408, 410–12
Davis, Wallace A., 203n
De Voto, Bernard, 366n
Dewey, John, 408–9, 412–13, 427–29
Diderot, Denis, 6
Dilthey, Wilhelm, 166, 171, 173, 181, 193
Djilas, Milovan, 145n
Duncan, David, 38n, 88n
Du Pont de Nemours, Pierre Simon, 9n,
    11n

i

Subject Index

ABOUT THE AUTHORS

Jonathan H. Turner is Professor of Sociology at the University of California at Riverside. He received his Bachelor of Arts degree from the University of California at Santa Barbara in 1965, his Master of Arts in 1966, and his Ph.D. in 1968 from Cornell University. He is the author of sixteen books and many articles on sociological theory, stratification, ethnic relations, comparative institutions, and American social structure.

Leonard Beeghley is Associate Professor of Sociology at the University of Florida. He received the Bachelor of Arts degree in 1969, the Master of Arts degree in 1971, and the Ph.D. in 1974, all from the University of California at Riverside. He is the author of five books on sociological theory, social stratification, and poverty in the United States.

Charles H. Powers is an Assistant Professor in the Department of Anthropology and Sociology at Santa Clara University. He received his Bachelor of Arts degree from the University of Illinois in 1972 and his Ph.D. from the University of California at Riverside in 1981. Dr. Powers is the author of *Vilfredo Pareto* (1987) and the editor of the English translation of Pareto's final monograph, *The Transformation of Democracy* (1984). His current project, in collaboration with Jerald Hage, focuses on family and work roles in postindustrial society. Professor Powers is also the editor of *Perspectives*, the newsletter of the Theory Section of the American Sociological Association.

A NOTE ON THE TYPE

The text of this book was set in 10/12 Palatino using a film version of the face designed by Hermann Zapf that was first released in 1950 by Germany's Stempel Foundry. The face is named after Giovanni Battista Palatino, a famous penman of the sixteenth century. In its calligraphic quality, Palatino is reminiscent of the Italian Renaissance type designs, yet with its wide, open letters and unique proportions it still retains a modern feel. Palatino is considered one of the most important faces from one of Europe's most influential type designers.

Composed by Weimer Typesetting Co., Inc., Indianapolis, Indiana.

Printed and bound by Arcata Graphics/Kingsport; Kingsport, Tennessee.